Foundations of
Software Testing

Foundations of Software Testing

Fundamental Algorithms and Techniques

An Undergraduate and Graduate Text
A Reference for the Practicing Software Engineer

ADITYA P. MATHUR

Purdue University

PEARSON
Education

Delhi • Chennai • Chandigarh
Upper Saddle River • London • Sydney
Singapore • Hong Kong • Toronto • Tokyo

ISBN 81-317-1660-0

First Impression

Published by Dorling Kindersley (India) Pvt. Ltd., licensees of Pearson Education in South Asia.

Head Office: 482, F.I.E., Patparganj, Delhi 110 092, India.
Registered Office: 14 Local Shopping Centre, Panchsheel Park, New Delhi 110 017, India.

Laser typeset by EON PreMedia Pvt. Ltd

Printed in India at Sanat Printers.

TO
Late Dr Ranjit Singh Chauhan

Contents

PART III: TEST ADEQUACY ASSESSMENT AND ENHANCEMENT 399

6. TEST ADEQUACY: ASSESSMENT USING CONTROL FLOW AND DATA FLOW 401

7. TEST-ADEQUACY ASSESSMENT USING PROGRAM MUTATION 502

PREFACE

Welcome to Foundations of Software Testing! This book intends to offer exactly what its title implies. It is important that students planning a career in information technology take a course in software testing. It is also important that such a course offer students an opportunity to acquire material that will remain useful throughout their careers in a variety of software applications, products, and changing environments. This book is an introduction to exactly such material and hence an appropriate text for a course in software testing. It distills knowledge developed by hundreds of testing researchers and practitioners from all over the world and brings it to its readers in an easy-to-understand form.

Test generation, selection, prioritization, and assessment lie at the foundation of all technical activities involved in software testing. Appropriate deployment of the elements of this strong foundation enables the testing of different types of software applications as well as testing for various properties. Applications include Object Oriented systems, Web services, graphical user interfaces, embedded systems, and others, and properties relate to security, timing, performance, reliability, and others.

The importance of software testing increases as software pervades more and more into our daily lives. Unfortunately, few universities offer full-fledged courses in software testing and those that do often struggle to identify a suitable text. I hope that this book will allow academic institutions to create courses in software testing, and those that already offer such courses will not need to hunt for a textbook or rely solely on research publications.

Conversations with testers and managers in commercial software development environments have led me to believe that though software testing is considered an important activity, software testers often complain of not receiving treatment at par with system designers and developers. I believe that raising the level of sophistication in the material covered in courses in software testing will lead to superior testing practices, high-quality software, and thus translate into positive impact on the career of software testers. I hope that exposure to even one-half of the material in this book will establish a student's respect for software testing as a discipline in its own right and at the same level of maturity as subjects such as compilers, databases, algorithms, and networks.

Target audience: It is natural to ask: What is the target level of this book? My experience, and that of some instructors who have used earlier drafts, indicates that this book is best suited for use at senior undergraduate and early graduate levels. While the presentation in this book is aimed at students in a college or university classroom, I believe that both practitioners and researchers will find it useful. Practitioners, with patience, may find this book as a rich source of techniques they could learn and adapt in their development and test environment. Researchers are likely to find it to be a rich source of reference material.

Nature of material covered: Software testing covers a wide spectrum of activities. At a higher level, such activities appear to be similar whereas at a lower level they might differ significantly. For example, most software development environments engage in test execution. However, test execution for an operating system is carried out quite differently than that for a pacemaker; while one is an open system, the other is embedded and hence the need for different ways to execute tests.

The simultaneous existence of similarities and differences in each software testing activity leads to a dilemma for an author as well as an instructor. Should a book and a course focus on specific software development environments, and how they carry out various testing activities? Or should they focus on specific testing activities without any detailed recourse to specific environments? Either strategy is subject to criticism and leaves the students in a vacuum regarding the applications of testing activities or about their formal foundations.

I have resolved this dilemma through careful selection and organization of the material. Parts I, II, and III of this book focus primarily on the foundations of various testing activities. Part I illustrate through examples the differences in software test processes as applied in various software development organizations. Techniques for generating tests from models of expected program behavior are covered in Part II, while the measurement of the adequacy of the tests so generated, and their enhancement, is considered in Part III.

Organization: This book is organized into three parts. Part I covers terminology and preliminary concepts related to software testing. Chapter 1, the only chapter in this part, introduces a variety of terms and basic concepts that pervade the field of software testing. Some adopters of earlier drafts of this book have covered the introductory material in this chapter during the first two or three weeks of an undergraduate course.

Part II covers various test-generation techniques. Chapter 2 introduces the most basic of all test-generation techniques widely applicable in almost any software application one can imagine. These include equivalence partitioning, boundary-value analysis, cause–effect graphing, and predicate testing. Chapter 3 introduces powerful and fundamental techniques for automatically generating tests from finite state models. Three techniques have been selected for presentation in this chapter: W-, Wp-, and Unique Input-Output methods. Finite state models are used in a variety of applications such as in OO testing, security testing, and GUI testing. Generation of combinatorial designs and tests is the topic of Chapter 4. Regression testing forms an integral part of all software development environments where software evolves into newer versions and thus undergoes extensive maintenance. Chapter 5 introduces some fundamental techniques for test selection, prioritization, and minimization of use during regression testing.

Part III is an extensive coverage of an important and widely applicable topic in software testing: test enhancement through measurement of test adequacy. Chapter 6 introduces a variety of control-flow- and data-flow-based code coverage criteria and explains how these could be used in practice. The most powerful of test adequacy criteria based on program mutation are introduced in Chapter 7. While some form of test adequacy assessment is used in almost every software development organization, material covered in these chapters promises to take adequacy assessment and test enhancement to a new level, thereby making a significant positive impact on software reliability.

Practitioners often complain, and are mostly right, that many white-box adequacy criteria are impractical to use during integration and system testing. I have included a discussion on how some of the most powerful adequacy assessment criteria can be, and should be, used even beyond unit testing. Certainly, my suggestions to do so assume the availability of commercial-strength tools for adequacy assessment.

Each chapter ends with a detailed bibliography. I have tried to be as comprehensive as possible in citing works related to the contents of each chapter. I hope that instructors and students will find the Bibliographic Notes sections rich and helpful in enhancing their knowledge beyond this book. Citations are also a testimony to the rich literature in the field of software testing.

What does this book not cover?: Software testing consists of a large number of related and intertwined activities. Some of these are technical, some administrative, and some merely routine. Technical activities include test case and oracle design at the unit, subsystem, integration, system, and regression levels. Administrative activities include manpower planning, budgeting, and reporting. Planning activities include test planning, quality assessment and control, and manpower allocation. While some planning activities are best classified as administrative, for example manpower allocation, others such as test planning are intertwined with technical activities like test case design.

Several test-related activities are product specific. For example, testing of a device driver often includes tasks such as writing a device simulator. Simulators include heart simulator in testing cardiac pacemakers, a USB port simulator useful in testing I/O drivers, and an airborne drone simulator used in testing control software for airborne drones. While such activities are extremely important for effective testing and test automation, they often require a significant development effort. For example, writing a device simulator and testing it is both a development and a testing activity. Test-generation and assessment techniques described in this book are applicable to each of the product-specific test activity. However, product-specific test activities are illustrated in this book only through examples and not described in any detail. My experience has been that it is best for students to learn about such activities through industry-sponsored term projects.

Suggestions to instructors: There is a wide variation in the coverage of topics in courses in software testing I have tried to cover most, if not all, of the important topics in this area. Tables 1 and 2 provide suggested outline of undergraduate and graduate courses, respectively, that could be based entirely on this book.

Sample undergraduate course in software testing: We assume a semester-long undergraduate course worth 3-credits that meets twice a week, each meeting lasts 50 min and devotes a total of 17 weeks to lectures, examinations, and project presentations. The course has a 2-h per week informal laboratory and requires students to work in small teams of three or four to complete a term project. The term project results in a final report and possibly a prototype testing tool. Once every 2 weeks, students are given one laboratory exercise that takes about 4–6 h to complete.

Table 3 contains a suggested evaluation plan. Carefully designed laboratory exercises form an essential component of this course. Each exercise offers the students an opportunity to use a testing tool to accomplish a task. For example, the objective of a laboratory exercise could be to familiarize the students with JUnit as test runner or JMeter as a tool for the performance

Table 1   A sample undergraduate course in software testing

Week	Topic	Chapter
1	Course objectives and goals, project assignment, testing terminology, and concepts	1
2	Test process and management	1
3	Errors, faults, and failures	1
4	Boundary-value analysis, equivalence partitioning, decision tables	2
5, 6	Test generation from predicates	2
7	Interim project presentations	
	Review, midterm examination	
8	Test adequacy: control flow	6
9	Test adequacy: data flow	6
10, 11	Test adequacy: program mutation	7
12, 13, 14	Special topics, e.g. OO testing and, security testing	Separate volume
15, 16	Review, final project presentations	
17	Final examination	

Table 2   A sample graduate course in software testing

Week	Topic	Chapter
1	Course objectives and goals, testing terminology and concepts	1
2	Test process and management	Separate volume
	Errors, faults, and failures	Separate volume
3	Boundary-value analysis, equivalence partitioning, decision tables	2
4	Test generation from predicates	2
5, 6	Test generation from finite-state models	3
7, 8	Combinatorial designs	4
	Review, midterm examination	
9	Test adequacy: control flow	6
10	Test adequacy: data flow	6
11, 12	Test adequacy: program mutation	7
13, 14	Special topics, e.g. real-time testing and security testing	Separate volume
15, 16	Review, research presentations	
17	Final examination	

Table 3   Suggested evaluation components of the undergraduate and graduate courses in software testing

Level	Component	Weight	Duration
Undergraduate	Midterm examination	15 points	90 min
	Final examination	25 points	120 min
	Quizzes	10 points	Short duration
	Laboratory assignments	10 points	10 assignments
	Term project	40 points	Semester
Graduate	Midterm examination	20 points	90 min
	Final examination	30 points	120 min
	Laboratory assignments	10 points	5 assignments
	Research/Term project	40 points	Semester

Table 4   A sample set of tools to select from for use in undergraduate and graduate courses in software testing

Purpose	Tool	Source
Combinatorial designs	AETG	
Code coverage measurement	TestManager™	JUnit CodeTest Suds
Defect tracking Bugzilla FogBugz	GUI testing WebCoder	JfcUnit Mutation testing muJava
Proteum		
Performance testing	Performance Tester	JMeter Regression testing Eggplant Suds Test management ClearQuest™ TestManager
Telcordia Technologies IBM Rational Freeware Freescale Semiconductor	Telcordia Technologies Freeware Fog Creek Software Crimson Solutions Freeware	Professor Jeff Offut offutt@ise.gmu.edu
Professor Jose Maldonado jcmaldon@icmc.usp.br	IBM Rational™ Apache, for Java Redstone Software Telcordia Technologies	IBM Rational™ BM Rational™

measurement of Web services. Instructors should be able to design laboratory exercises based on topics covered during the previous weeks. A large number of commercial and open-source-testing tools are available for use in a software-testing laboratory.

Sample graduate course in software testing: We assume a semester-long course worth 3-credits. The students entering this course have not had any prior course in software testing, such as the undergraduate course described above. In addition to the examinations, students will be required to read and present recent research material. Students are exposed to testing tools via unscheduled laboratory exercises.

Testing tools: There is a large set of testing tools available in the commercial, freeware, and open-source domains. A small sample of such tools is listed in Table 4.

Evolutionary book: I expect this book to evolve over time. Advances in topics covered in this book, and any new topics that develop, will be included in subsequent editions. Any errors found by me and/or reported by the readers will be corrected. Readers are encouraged to visit the following site for latest information about the book.

www.pearsoned.co.in/adityapmathur

While this book covers significant material in software testing, several advanced topics could not be included to limit its size. I am planning a separate volume of the book to take care of the advanced topics on the subject and can be used by students who would like to know much more about software testing as well as professionals in the industry.

Cash awards: In the past, I have given cash rewards to students who carefully read the material and reported any kind of error. I plan to retain the cash-reward approach as a means for continuous quality improvement.

Aditya P. Mathur

Part I

Preliminaries

Software testing deals with a variety of concepts, some mathematical and others not so mathematical. In the first part of this book, we bring together a set of basic concepts and terminology that pervades software testing.

Chapter 1 in this volume defines and explains basic terms and mathematical concepts that a tester ought to be familiar with.

A chapter in Volume II covers the topic of errors that are the raison d'être of software testing. Some of you might find the treatment of errors unique in that we present, among others, a grammar-based method for the classification of coding errors. While faults in a program can be traced back to any of the several stages of the development life cycle, eventually it is the code that fails with respect to some requirements and reveals the fault. It is therefore important for us to understand how errors made by system analysts, designers, and coders get reflected in the final code that is delivered to the customer.

A chapter in Volume II covers various elements of the software test process and its relation to the encompassing software development and quality assurance processes. A variety of terms used in the industry, such as test case, test plans, test cycle, as well as a test process maturity model, are covered in this chapter.

1

Basics of Software Testing

CONTENT

■ ■

The purpose of this introductory chapter is to familiarize the reader with the basic concepts related to software testing. In this chapter, we set up a framework for the remainder of this book. Specific questions, answered in substantial detail in subsequent chapters, will be raised here. After reading this chapter, you are likely to be able to ask meaningful questions related to software testing and reliability.

1.1 HUMANS, ERRORS, AND TESTING

Errors are a part of our daily life. Humans make errors in their thoughts, in their actions, and in the products that might result from their actions. Errors occur almost everywhere. Humans can make errors in any field, for example in observation, in speech, in medical prescription, in surgery, in driving, in sports, in love, and similarly even in software development. Table 1.1 provides examples of human errors. The consequences of human errors vary significantly. An error might be insignificant in that it leads to a gentle friendly smile, such as when a slip of tongue occurs. Or, an error may lead to a catastrophe, such as when an operator fails to recognize that a relief valve on the pressurizer was stuck open and this resulted in a disastrous radiation leak.

To determine whether there are any errors in our thought, actions, and the products generated, we resort to the process of *testing*. The

Table 1.1 Examples of errors in various fields of human endeavor

Area	Error
Hearing	Spoken: He has a garage for repairing *foreign* cars Heard: He has a garage for repairing *falling* cars
Medicine	Incorrect antibiotic prescribed
Music performance	Incorrect note played
Numerical analysis	Incorrect algorithm for matrix inversion
Observation	Operator fails to recognize that a relief valve is stuck open
Software	Operator used: $\neq$, correct operator: $>$ Identifier used: new_line, correct identifier: next_line Expression used: $a \wedge (b \vee c)$, correct expression: $(a \wedge b) \vee c$ Data conversion from a 64-bit floating point to a 16-bit integer not protected (resulting in a software exception)
Speech	Spoken: *Waple malnut*, intended: *Maple walnut* Spoken: *We need a new refrigerator*, intent: We need *a new washing machine*
Sports	Incorrect call by the referee in a tennis match
Writing	Written: What kind of *pans* did you use? Intent: What kind of *pants* did you use?

primary goal of testing is to determine if the thoughts, actions, and products are as desired, that is they conform to the requirements. Testing of thoughts is usually designed to determine if a concept or method has been understood satisfactorily. Testing of actions is designed to check if a skill that results in the actions has been acquired satisfactorily. Testing of a product is designed to check if the product behaves as desired. Note that both syntax and semantic errors arise during programming. Given that most modern compilers are able to detect syntactic errors, testing focuses on semantic errors, also known as faults, that cause the program under test to behave incorrectly.

> **Example 1.1:** An instructor administers a test to determine how well the students have understood what the instructor wanted to convey. A tennis coach administers a test to determine how well the understudy makes a serve. A software developer tests the program developed to determine if it behaves as desired. In each of these three cases, there is an attempt by a tester to determine if the human thoughts, actions, and products behave as desired. Behavior that deviates from the desirable is possibly because of an error.

> **Example 1.2:** Deviation from the expected may *not* be due to an error for one or more reasons. Suppose that a tester wants to test a program to sort a sequence of integers. The program can sort an input sequence in both descending or ascending orders depending on the request made. Now suppose that the tester wants to check if the program sorts an input sequence in ascending order. To do so, he types in an input sequence and a request to sort the sequence in descending order. Suppose that the program is correct and produces an output which is the input sequence in descending order.

> Upon examination of the output from the program, the tester hypothesizes that the sorting program is incorrect. This is a situation where the tester made a mistake (an error) that led to his incorrect interpretation (perception) of the behavior of the program (the product).

1.1.1 Errors, Faults, and Failures

There is no widely accepted and precise definition of the term *error*. Figure 1.1 illustrates one class of meanings for the terms error, fault, and failure. A programmer writes a program. An *error* occurs in the process of writing a program. A *fault* is the manifestation of one or more errors. A failure occurs when a faulty piece of code is executed leading to an

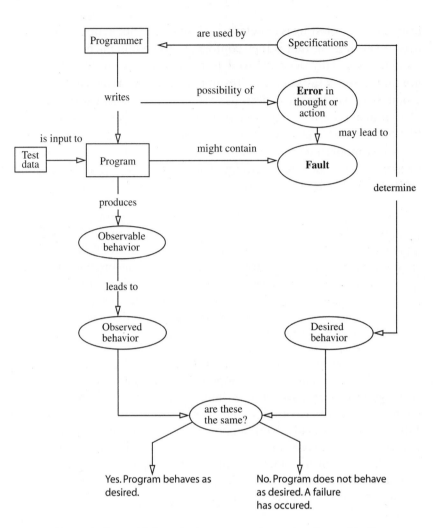

Fig. 1.1   Errors, faults, and failures in the process of programming and testing.

incorrect state that propagates to the program's output. The programmer might misinterpret the requirements and consequently write incorrect code. Upon execution, the program might display behavior that does not match with the expected behavior, implying thereby that a failure has ocurred. A fault in the program is also commonly referred to as a *bug* or a *defect*. The terms error and bug are by far the most common ways of referring to something wrong in the program text that might lead to a failure. In this text we often use the terms *error* and *fault* as synonyms. Faults are sometimes referred to as *defects*.

In Figure 1.1, notice the separation of *observable* from *observed* behavior. This separation is important because it is the observed behavior that might lead one to conclude that a program has failed.

Certainly, as explained earlier, this conclusion might be incorrect due to one or more reasons.

1.1.2 Test Automation

Testing of complex systems, embedded and otherwise, can be a human intensive task. Often one needs to execute thousands of tests to ensure that, for example, a change made to a component of an application does not cause previously correct code to malfunction. Execution of many tests can be tiring as well as error-prone. Hence, there is a tremendous need for automating testing tasks.

Most software development organizations automate test-related tasks such as regression testing, graphical user interface (GUI) testing, and I/O device driver testing. Unfortunately, the process of test automation cannot be generalized. For example, automating regression tests for an embedded device such as a pacemaker is quite different from that for an I/O device driver that connects to the USB port of a PC. Such lack of generalization often leads to specialized test automation tools developed in-house.

Nevertheless, there do exist general-purpose tools for test automation. While such tools might not be applicable in all test environments, they are useful in many of them. Examples of such tools include Eggplant, Marathon, and Pounder for GUI testing; eLoadExpert, DBMonster, JMeter, Dieseltest, WAPT, LoadRunner, and Grinder for performance or load testing; and Echelon, TestTube, WinRunner, and XTest for regression testing. Despite the existence of a large number and variety of test automation tools, large development organizations develop their own test automation tools due primarily to the unique nature of their test requirements.

AETG is an automated test generator that can be used in a variety of applications. It uses combinatorial design techniques discussed in Chapter 4. Random testing is often used for the estimation of reliability of products with respect to specific events. For example, one might test an application using randomly generated tests to determine how frequently does it crash or hang. DART is a tool for automatically extracting an interface of a program and generating random tests. While such tools are useful in some environments, they are again dependent on the programming language used and the nature of the application interface. Therefore, many organizations develop their own tools for random testing.

1.1.3 Developer and Tester as Two Roles

In the context of software engineering, a developer is one who writes code and a tester is one who tests code. We prefer to treat developer and tester as two distinct though complementary roles. Thus, the same individual could be a developer and a tester. It is hard to imagine an individual who assumes the role of a developer but never that of a tester, and vice versa. In fact, it is safe to presume that a developer assumes two roles, that of a *developer* and of a *tester*, though at different times. Similarly, a tester also assumes the same two roles but at different times.

Certainly, within a software development organization, the primary role of an individual might be to test and hence this individual assumes the role of a *tester*. Similarly, the primary role of an individual who designs applications and writes code is that of a developer.

A reference to *tester* in this book refers to the role someone assumes when testing a program. Such an individual could be a developer testing a class she has coded, or a tester who is testing a fully integrated set of components. A *programmer* in this book refers to an individual who engages in software development and often assumes the role of a tester, at least temporarily. This also implies that the contents of this book are valuable not only to those whose primary role is that of a tester, but also to those who work as developers.

1.2 SOFTWARE QUALITY

We all want high-quality software. There exist several definitions of software quality. Also, one quality attribute might be more important to a user than another quality attribute. In any case, software quality is a multidimensional quantity and is measurable. So, let us look at what defines quality of software.

1.2.1 QUALITY ATTRIBUTES

There exist several measures of software quality. These can be divided into static and dynamic quality attributes. Static quality attributes refer to the actual code and related documentation. Dynamic quality attributes relate to the behavior of the application while in use.

Static quality attributes include structured, maintainable, and testable code as well as the availability of correct and complete documentation. You might have come across complaints such as "Product X is excellent, I like the features it offers, but its user manual stinks!" In this case, the user manual brings down the overall product quality. If you are a maintenance engineer and have been assigned the task of doing corrective maintenance on an application code, you will most likely need to understand portions of the code before you make any changes to it. This is where attributes related to items such as code documentation, understandability, and structure come into play. A poorly documented piece of code will be harder to understand and hence difficult to modify. Further, poorly structured code might be harder to modify and difficult to test.

Dynamic quality attributes include software reliability, correctness, completeness, consistency, usability, and performance. Reliability refers to the probability of failure-free operation and is considered in the following section. Correctness refers to the correct operation of an application and is always with reference to some artifact. For a tester, correctness is with respect to the requirements; for a user, it is often with respect to a user manual.

Completeness refers to the availability of all the features listed in the requirements or in the user manual. An incomplete software is one that does not fully implement all features required. Of course, one usually encounters additional functionality with each new version of an application. This does not mean that a given version is incomplete because its next version has few new features. Completeness is defined with respect to a set of features that might themselves be a subset of a larger set of features that are to be implemented in some future version of the application. One can easily argue that every piece of software that is correct is also complete with respect to some feature set.

Consistency refers to adherence to a common set of conventions and assumptions. For example, all buttons in the user interface might follow a common color-coding convention. An example of inconsistency could arise when a database application displays the date of birth of a person in the database. However, the date of birth is displayed in different formats, without regard for the user's preferences, depending on which feature of the database is used.

Usability refers to the ease with which an application can be used. This is an area in itself and there exist techniques for usability testing. Psychology plays an important role in the design of techniques for usability testing. Usability testing also refers to testing of a product by its potential users. The development organization invites a selected set of potential users and asks them to test the product. Users in turn test for ease of use, functionality as expected, performance, safety, and security. Users thus serve as an important source of tests that developers or testers within the organization might not have conceived. Usability testing is sometimes referred to as user-centric testing.

Performance refers to the time the application takes to perform a requested task. Performance is considered as a nonfunctional requirement. It is specified in terms such as "This task must be performed at the rate of X units of activity in one second on a machine running at speed Y, having Z gigabytes of memory." For example, the performance requirement for a compiler might be stated in terms of the minimum average time to compilation of a set of numerical applications.

1.2.2 RELIABILITY

People want software that functions correctly every time it is used. However, this happens rarely, if ever. Most software that is used today contains faults that cause it to fail on some combination of inputs. Thus, the notion of total correctness of a program is an ideal and applies to only the most academic and textbook programs.

Given that most software applications are defective, one would like to know how often a given piece of software might fail. This question can be answered, often with dubious accuracy, with the help of software reliability, hereafter referred to as reliability. There are several definitions of software reliability, a few are examined below.

ANSI/IEEE STD 729-1983: RELIABILITY

Software reliability is the probability of failure-free operation of software over a given time interval and under given conditions.

The probability referred to in this definition depends on the distribution of the inputs to the program. Such input distribution is often referred to as the operational profile. According to this definition, software reliability could vary from one operational profile to another. An implication is that one user might say "this program is lousy" while another might sing praises for the same program. The following is an alternate definition of reliability.

RELIABILITY

Software reliability is the probability of failure-free operation of software in its intended environment.

This definition is independent of "who uses what features of the software and how often". Instead, it depends exclusively on the correctness of its features. As there is no notion of operational profile, the entire input domain is considered as uniformly distributed. The term *environment* refers to the software and hardware elements needed to execute the application. These elements include the operating system (OS), hardware requirements, and any other applications needed for communication.

Both definitions have their pros and cons. The first of the two definitions above requires the knowledge of the profile of its users that might be difficult or impossible to estimate accurately. However, if an operational profile can be estimated for a given class of users, then an accurate estimate of the reliability can be found for this class of users. The second definition is attractive in that one needs only a single number to denote reliability of a software application that is applicable to all its users. However, such estimates are difficult to arrive at.

1.3 REQUIREMENTS, BEHAVIOR, AND CORRECTNESS

Products, software in particular, are designed in response to requirements. Requirements specify the functions that a product is expected to perform. Once the product is ready, it is the requirements that determine the expected behavior. Of course, during the development of the product, the requirements might have changed from what was stated originally. Regardless of any change, the expected behavior of the product is determined by the tester's understanding of the requirements during testing.

> **Example 1.3:** Two requirements are given below, each of which leads to a different program.
>
> Requirement 1:   It is required to write a program that inputs two integers and outputs the maximum of these.
> Requirement 2:   It is required to write a program that inputs a sequence of integers and outputs the sorted version of this sequence.

Suppose that program max is developed to satisfy Requirement 1 above. The expected output of max when the input integers are 13 and 19 can be easily determined to be 19. Suppose now that the tester wants to know if the two integers are to be input to the program on one line followed by a carriage return, or on two separate lines with a carriage return typed in after each number. The requirement as stated above fails to provide an answer to this question. This example illustrates the incompleteness Requirement 1.

The second requirement in the above example is ambiguous. It is not clear from this requirement whether the input sequence is to be sorted in ascending or descending order. The behavior of sort program, written to satisfy this requirement, will depend on the decision taken by the programmer while writing sort.

Testers are often faced with incomplete and/or ambiguous requirements. In such situations a tester may resort to a variety of ways to determine what behavior to expect from the program under test. For example, for program max above, one way to determine how the input should be typed in is to actually examine the program text. Another way is to ask the developer of max as to what decision was taken regarding the sequence in which the inputs are to be typed in. Yet another method is to execute max on different input sequences and determine what is acceptable to max.

Regardless of the nature of the requirements, testing requires the determination of the expected behavior of the program under test. The observed behavior of the program is compared with the expected behavior to determine if the program functions as desired.

1.3.1 INPUT DOMAIN AND PROGRAM CORRECTNESS

A program is considered correct if it behaves as desired on all possible test inputs. Usually, the set of all possible inputs is too large for the program to be executed on each input. For example, suppose that the max program above is to be tested on a computer in which integers range from $-32,768$ to $32,767$. To test max on all possible integers would require it to be executed on all pairs of integers in this range. This will require a total of 2^{32} executions of max. It will take approximately 4.2 s to complete all executions assuming that testing is done on a computer that will take 1 ns ($=10^{-9}$ s) to input a pair of integers, execute max, and check if the output is correct. Testing a program on all possible inputs is known as *exhaustive testing*.

A tester often needs to determine what constitutes all possible inputs. The first step in determining all possible inputs is to examine the requirements. If the requirements are complete and unambiguous, it should be possible to determine the set of all possible inputs. Before we provide an example to illustrate this determination, a definition is in order.

INPUT DOMAIN

The set of all possible inputs to a program P is known as the input domain, *or* input space, *of P.*

Example 1.4: Using Requirement 1 from Example 1.3, we find the input domain of max to be the set of all pairs of integers where each element in the pair integers is in the range from $-32,768$ to $32,767$.

Example 1.5: Using Requirement 2 from Example 1.3, it is not possible to find the input domain for the sort program. Let us, therefore, assume that the requirement was modified to be the following:

Modified Requirement 2: It is required to write a program that inputs a sequence of integers and outputs the integers in this sequence sorted in either ascending or descending order. The order of the output sequence is determined by an input request character which should be "A" when an ascending sequence is desired, and "D" otherwise. While providing input to the program, the request character is entered first followed by the sequence of integers to be sorted; the sequence is terminated with a period.

Based on the above modified requirement, the input domain for sort is a set of pairs. The first element of the pair is a character. The second element of the pair is a sequence of zero or more integers ending with a period. For example, following are three elements in the input domain of sort:

```
< A — 3 15 12 55 . >
< D 23 78 . >
< A . >
```

The first element contains a sequence of four integers to be sorted in ascending order, the second one has a sequence to be sorted in descending order, and the third one has an empty sequence to be sorted in ascending order.

We are now ready to give the definition of program correctness.

CORRECTNESS

A program is considered correct if it behaves as expected on each element of its input domain.

1.3.2 VALID AND INVALID INPUTS

In the examples above, the input domains are derived from the requirements. However, due to the incompleteness of requirements, one might have to think a bit harder to determine the input domain. To illustrate why, consider the modified requirement in Example 1.5. The requirement mentions that the request characters can be "A" or "D", but it fails to answer the question "What if the user types a different character?" When using sort, it is certainly possible for the user to type a character other than "A" or "D". Any character other than "A" or "D" is considered as an invalid input to sort. The requirement for sort does not specify what action it should take when an invalid input is encountered.

Identifying the set of invalid inputs and testing the program against these inputs are important parts of the testing activity. Even when the requirements fail to specify the program behavior on invalid inputs, the programmer does treat these in one way or another. Testing a program against invalid inputs might reveal errors in the program.

> **Example 1.6:** Suppose that we are testing the sort program. We execute it against the following input: < E 7 19 . >. The requirements in Example 1.5 are insufficient to determine the expected behavior of sort on the above input. Now suppose that upon execution on the above input, the sort program enters into an infinite loop and neither asks the user for any input nor responds to anything typed by the user. This observed behavior points to a possible error in sort.

The argument above can be extended to apply to the sequence of integers to be sorted. The requirements for the sort program do not specify how the program should behave if, instead of typing an integer, a user types in a character such as "?". Of course, one would say, the program should inform the user that the input is invalid. But this expected behavior from sort needs to be tested. This suggests that the input domain for sort should be modified.

> **Example 1.7:** Considering that sort may receive valid and invalid inputs, the input domain derived in Example 1.5 needs modification. The modified input domain consists of pairs of values. The first value in the pair is any ASCII character that can be typed by a user as a request character. The second element of the pair is a sequence of integers, interspersed with invalid characters, terminated by a period. Thus, for example, the following are sample elements from the modified input domain:
>
>   < A 7 19 . >
>   < D 7 9F 19 . >

In the example above, we assumed that invalid characters are possible inputs to the sort program. This, however, may not be the case in all situations. For example, it might be possible to guarantee that the inputs to sort will always be correct as determined from the modified requirements in Example 1.5. In such a situation, the input domain need not be augmented to account for invalid inputs if the guarantee is to be believed by the tester.

In cases where the input to a program is not guaranteed to be correct, it is convenient to partition the input domain into two subdomains. One subdomain consists of inputs that are valid and the other consists of inputs that are invalid. A tester can then test the program on selected inputs from each subdomain.

1.4 CORRECTNESS VERSUS RELIABILITY

1.4.1 CORRECTNESS

Though correctness of a program is desirable, it is almost never the objective of testing. To establish correctness via testing would imply testing a program on all elements in the input domain, which is impossible to accomplish in most cases that are encountered in practice. Thus, correctness is established via mathematical proofs of programs. The proof uses the formal specification of requirements and the program text to prove or disprove that the program will behave as intended. While a mathematical proof is precise, it too is subject to human errors. Even when the proof is carried out by a computer, the simplification of requirements specification and errors in tasks that are not fully automated might render the proof incorrect.

While correctness attempts to establish that the program is error-free, testing attempts to find if there are any errors in it. Thus, completeness of testing does not necessarily demonstrate that a program is error free. However, as testing progresses, errors might be revealed. Removal of errors from the program usually improves the chances, or the probability, of the program executing without any failure. Also, testing, debugging, and the error-removal processes together increase our confidence in the correct functioning of the program under test.

Example 1.8: This example illustrates why the probability of program failure might not change upon error removal. Consider the following program that inputs two integers x and y and prints the value of $f(x, y)$ or $g(x, y)$ depending on the condition $x < y$.

```
integer x, y
input x, y
if(x < y)  ← This condition should be x ≤ y.
  { print f(x, y)}
else
  { print g(x, y)}
```

The above program uses two functions f and g, not defined here. Let us suppose that function f produces incorrect result whenever it is invoked with $x = y$ and that $f(x, y) \neq g(x, y)$, $x = y$. In its present form the program fails when tested with equal input values because function g is invoked instead of function f. When the error is removed by changing the condition $x < y$ to $x \leq y$, the program fails again when the input values are the same. The latter failure is due to the error in function f. In this program, when the error in f

is also removed, the program will be correct assuming that all other code is correct.

1.4.2 Reliability

The probability of a program failure is captured more formally in the term *reliability*. Consider the second of the two definitions examined earlier: "The *reliability* of a program P is the probability of its successful execution on a randomly selected element from its input domain."

A comparison of program correctness and reliability reveals that while correctness is a binary metric, reliability is a continuous metric over a scale from 0 to 1. A program can be either correct or incorrect; its reliability can be anywhere between 0 and 1. Intuitively, when an error is removed from a program, the reliability of the program so obtained is expected to be higher than that of the one that contains the error. As illustrated in the example above, this may not be always true. The next example illustrates how to compute program reliability in a simplistic manner.

Example 1.9: Consider a program P which takes a pair of integers as input. The input domain of this program is the set of all pairs of integers. Suppose now that in actual use there are only three pairs that will be input to P. These are as follows:

$$\{< (0, 0) \ (-1, 1) \ (1, -1) >\}$$

The above set of three pairs is a subset of the input domain of P and is derived from a knowledge of the actual use of P, and not solely from its requirements.

Suppose also that each pair in the above set is equally likely to occur in practice. If it is known that P fails on exactly one of the three possible input pairs then the frequency with which P will function correctly is $\frac{2}{3}$. This number is an estimate of the probability of the successful operation of P and hence is the reliability of P.

1.4.3 Program Use and the Operational Profile

As per the definition above, the reliability of a program depends on how it is used. Thus, in Example 1.9, if P is never executed on input pair $(0, 0)$, then the restricted input domain becomes $\{< (-1, 1) \ (1, -1) >\}$ and the reliability of P is 1. This leads us to the definition of *operational profile*.

> OPERATIONAL PROFILE
>
> *An operational profile is a numerical description of how a program is used.*
>
> In accordance with the above definition, a program might have several operational profiles depending on its users.

Example 1.10: Consider a `sort` program which, on any given execution, allows any one of two types of input sequences. One sequence consists of numbers only and the other consists of alphanumeric strings. One operational profile for `sort` is specified as follows:

Operational profile 1

Sequence	Probability
Numbers only	0.9
Alphanumeric strings	0.1

Another operational profile for `sort` is specified as follows:

Operational profile 2

Sequence	Probability
Numbers only	0.1
Alphanumeric strings	0.9

The two operational profiles above suggest significantly different uses of `sort`. In one case it is used mostly for sorting sequences of numbers and in the other case it is used mostly for sorting alphanumeric strings.

1.5 TESTING AND DEBUGGING

Testing is the process of determining if a program behaves as expected. In the process one may discover errors in the program under test. However, when testing reveals an error, the process used to determine the cause of this error and to remove it is known as *debugging*. As illustrated in Figure 1.2, testing and debugging are often used as two related activities in a cyclic manner.

1.5.1 PREPARING A TEST PLAN

A test cycle is often guided by a *test plan*. When relatively small programs are being tested, a test plan is usually informal and in the tester's mind,

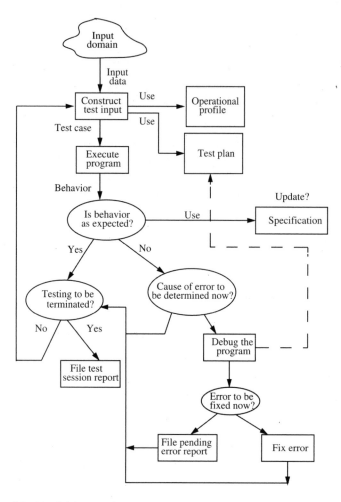

Fig. 1.2   A test and debug cycle.

or there may be no plan at all. A sample test plan for testing the `sort` program is shown in Figure 1.3.

The sample test plan in Figure 1.3 is often augmented by items such as the method used for testing, method for evaluating the adequacy of test cases, and method to determine if a program has failed or not.

1.5.2 Constructing Test Data

A test case is a pair consisting of test data to be input to the program and the expected output. The test data is a set of values, one for each input variable. A test set is a collection of zero or more test cases. The notion

---

Test plan for sort

The sort program is to be tested to meet the requirements given in Example 1.5. Specifically, the following needs to be done:

1. Execute the program on at least two input sequences, one with "A" and the other with "D" as request characters.

2. Execute the program on an empty input sequence.

3. Test the program for robustness against erroneous inputs such as "R" typed in as the request character.

4. All failures of the test program should be recorded in a suitable file using the Company Failure Report Form.

Fig. 1.3   A sample test plan for the sort program.

of *one execution* of a program is rather tricky and is elaborated later in this chapter. Test data is an alternate term for test set.

Program requirements and the test plan help in the construction of test data. Execution of the program on test data might begin after all or a few test cases have been constructed. While testing relatively small programs, testers often generate a few test cases and execute the program against these. Based on the results obtained, the testers decide whether to continue the construction of additional test cases or to enter the debugging phase.

Example 1.11: The following test cases are generated for the sort program using the test plan in Figure 1.3.

Test case 1:
    Test data: `<"A"12 −29 32.>`
    Expected output: `−29 12 32`

Test case 2:
    Test data: `<"D"12 −29 32.>`
    Expected output: `32 12 −29`

Test case 3:
    Test data: `<"A".>`
    Expected output: `No input to be sorted in ascending order.`

Test case 4:
    Test data: `<"D" .>`
    Expected output: `No input to be sorted in ascending order.`

Test case 5:

 Test data: `<"R"3 17.>`

 Expected output: `Invalid request character;`

         Valid characters: "A" and "D".

Test case 6:

 Test data: `<"A"c 17.>`

 Expected output: *Invalid number.*

Test cases 1 and 2 are derived in response to item 1 in the test plan; 3 and 4 are in response to item 2. Note that we have designed two test cases in response to item 2 of the test plan even though the plan calls for only one test case. Note also that the requirements for the sort program as in Example 1.5 do not indicate what should be the output of sort when there is nothing to be sorted. We, therefore, took an arbitrary decision while composing the *Expected output* for an input that has no numbers to be sorted. Test cases 5 and 6 are in response to item 3 in the test plan.

As is evident from the above example, one can select a variety of test sets to satisfy the test plan requirements. Questions such as "Which test set is the best?" and "Is a given test set adequate?" are answered in Part III of this book.

1.5.3 EXECUTING THE PROGRAM

Execution of a program under test is the next significant step in testing. Execution of this step for the sort program is most likely a trivial exercise. However, this may not be so for large and complex programs. For example, to execute a program that controls a digital cross-connect switch used in telephone networks, one may first need to follow an elaborate procedure to load the program into the switch and then yet another procedure to input the test cases to the program. Obviously, the complexity of actual program execution is dependent on the program itself.

Often a tester might be able to construct a test harness to aid in program execution. The harness initializes any global variables, inputs a test case, and executes the program. The output generated by the program may be saved in a file for subsequent examination by a tester. The next example illustrates a simple test harness.

Example 1.12: The test harness in Figure 1.4 reads an input sequence, checks for its correctness, and then calls sort. The sorted array sorted_sequence returned by sort is printed using the print_sequence procedure. Test cases are assumed to be available in the Test pool file shown in the figure. In some cases the tests might be generated from within the harness.

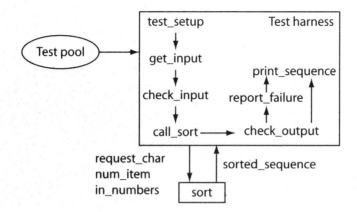

Fig. 1.4 A simple test harness to test the sort program.

In preparing this test harness we assume that (a) sort is coded as a procedure, (b) the get-input procedure reads the request character and the sequence to be sorted into variables request_char, num_items, and in-numbers, and (c) the input is checked prior to calling sort by the check_input procedure.

The test_setup procedure is usually invoked first to set up the test that, in this example, includes identifying and opening the file containing tests. The check_output procedure serves as the oracle that checks if the program under test behaves correctly. The report_failure procedure is invoked in case the output from sort is incorrect. A failure might be simply reported via a message on the screen or saved in a test report file (not shown in Figure 1.4). The print_sequence procedure prints the sequence generated by the sort program. The output generated by print-sequence can also be piped into a file for subsequent examination.

1.5.4 SPECIFYING PROGRAM BEHAVIOR

There are several ways to define and specify program behavior. The simplest way is to specify the behavior in a natural language such as English. However, this is more likely subject to multiple interpretations than a more formally specified behavior. Here we explain how the notion of program *state* can be used to define program behavior and how the *state transition diagram*, or simply *state diagram*, can be used to specify program behavior.

The state of a program is the set of current values of all its variables and an indication of which statement in the program is to be executed next. One way to encode the state is by collecting the current values of program variables into a vector known as the *state vector*. An indication of where the control of execution is at any instant of time can be given by using an identifier associated with the next program statement. In the case of programs in assembly language, the location of control can be specified more precisely by giving the value of the program counter.

Each variable in the program corresponds to one element of this vector. Obviously, for a large program, such as the Unix OS, the state vector might have thousands of elements. Execution of program statements causes the program to move from one state to the next. A sequence of program states is termed as program behavior.

Example 1.13: Consider a program that inputs two integers into variables X and Y, compares these values, sets the value of Z to the larger of the two, displays the value of Z on the screen, and exits. Program P1.1 shows the program skeleton. The state vector for this program consists of four elements. The first element is the statement identifier where control of execution is currently positioned. The next three elements are, respectively, the values of the three variables X, Y, and Z.

Program P1.1

```
1 integer X, Y, Z;
2 input (X, Y);
3 if (X < Y)
4   {Z=Y;}
5 else
6   {Z=X;}
7 endif
8 output (Z);
9 end
```

The letter u as an element of the state vector stands for an *undefined* value. The notation $s_i \rightarrow s_j$ is an abbreviation for "The program moves from state s_i to s_j." The movement from s_i to s_j is caused by the execution of the statement whose identifier is listed as the first element of state s_i. A possible sequence of states that the max program may go through is given below.

$[2 \ u \ u \ u] \rightarrow [3 \ 3 \ 15 \ u] \rightarrow [4 \ 3 \ 15 \ 15] \rightarrow [5 \ 3 \ 15 \ 15] \rightarrow$
$[8 \ 3 \ 15 \ 15] \rightarrow [9 \ 3 \ 15 \ 15]$

Upon the start of its execution, a program is in an *initial state*. A (correct) program terminates in its *final state*. All other program states are termed as *intermediate states*. In Example 1.13, the initial state is [2 u u u], the final state is [9 3 15 15], and there are four intermediate states as indicated.

Program behavior can be modeled as a sequence of states. With every program one can associate one or more states that need to be observed to decide whether the program behaves according to its requirements. In some applications it is only the final state that is of interest to the tester. In other applications a sequence of states might be of interest. More complex patterns might also be needed.

Example 1.14: For the max program (P1.1), the final state is sufficient to decide if the program has successfully determined the maximum of two integers. If the numbers input to max are 3 and 15, then the correct final state is [9 3 15 15]. In fact it is only the last element of the state vector, 15, which may be of interest to the tester.

Example 1.15: Consider a menu-driven application named myapp. Figure 1.5 shows the menu bar for this application. It allows a user to position and click the mouse on any one of a list of menu items displayed in the menu bar on the screen. This results in *pulling down* of the menu and a list of options is displayed on the screen. One of the items on the menu bar is labeled File. When File is pulled down, it displays open as one of several options. When the open option is selected, by moving the cursor over it, it should be highlighted. When the mouse is released, indicating that the selection is complete, a window displaying names of files in the current directory should be displayed.

Figure 1.6 depicts the sequence of states that myapp is expected to enter when the user actions described above are performed. When started, the application enters the initial state wherein it displays the menu bar and waits for the user to select a menu item. This state diagram depicts the expected behavior of myapp in terms of a state

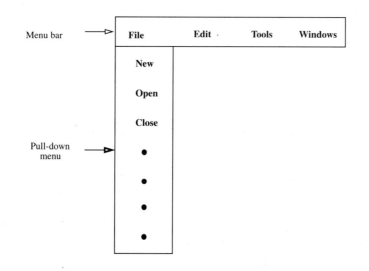

Fig. 1.5 Menu bar displaying four menu items when application myapp is started.

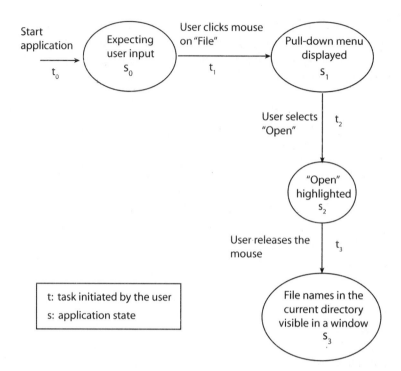

Fig. 1.6 A state sequence for `myapp` showing how the application is expected to behave when the user selects the `open` option under the `File` menu item.

sequence. As shown in Figure 1.6, `myapp` moves from state s_0 to s_3 after the sequence of actions t_0, t_1, t_2, and t_3 has been applied. To test `myapp`, the tester could apply the sequence of actions depicted in this state diagram and observe if the application enters the expected states.

As you might observe from Figure 1.6, a state sequence diagram can be used to specify the *behavioral* requirements of an application. This same specification can then be used during testing to ensure if the application conforms to the requirements.

1.5.5 Assessing the Correctness of Program Behavior

An important step in testing a program is the one wherein the tester determines if the observed behavior of the program under test is correct or not. This step can be further divided into two smaller steps. In the first step, one observes the behavior and in the second, one analyzes the observed behavior to check if it is correct or not. Both these steps can be trivial for small programs, such as for max in Example 1.3, or extremely complex as in the case of a large distributed software system. The entity that performs the task of checking the correctness of the observed

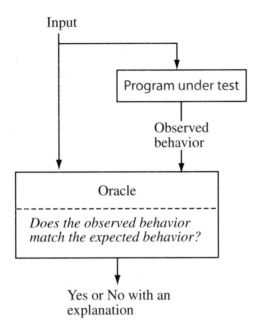

Input

Program under test

Observed
behavior

Oracle

- -

*Does the observed behavior
match the expected behavior?*

Yes or No with an
explanation

Fig. 1.7 Relationship between the program under test and the oracle. The output
from an oracle can be binary such as *Yes* or *No* or more complex such as an
explanation as to why the oracle finds the observed behavior to be same or
different from the expected behavior.

behavior is known as an *oracle*. Figure 1.7 shows the relationship between the program under test and the oracle.

A tester often assumes the role of an oracle and thus serves as a *human oracle*. For example, to verify if the output of a matrix multiplication program is correct or not, a tester might input two 2×2 matrices
and check if the output produced by the program matches the results of
hand calculation. As another example, consider checking the output of
a text-processing program. In this case a human oracle might visually inspect the monitor screen to verify whether the italicize command works
correctly when applied to a block of text.

Checking program behavior by humans has several disadvantages.
First, it is error prone as the human oracle might make error in analysis. Second, it may be slower than the speed with which the program
computed the results. Third, it might result in the checking of only trivial input–output (I/O) behaviors. However, regardless of these disadvantages, a human oracle is often the best available oracle.

Oracles can also be programs designed to check the behavior of other
programs. For example, one might use a matrix multiplication program
to check if a matrix inversion program has produced the correct output.
In this case, the matrix inversion program inverts a given matrix A and

generates B as the output matrix. The multiplication program can check to see if $A \times B = I$, within some bounds, on the elements of the identity matrix I. Another example is an oracle that checks the validity of the output from a sort program. Assuming that the sort program sorts input numbers in ascending order, the oracle needs to check if the output of the sort program is indeed in ascending order.

Using programs as oracles has the advantage of speed, accuracy, and the ease with which complex computations can be checked. Thus, a matrix multiplication program, when used as an oracle for a matrix inversion program, can be faster, accurate, and check very large matrices when compared to the same function performed by a human oracle.

1.5.6 CONSTRUCTION OF ORACLES

Construction of automated oracles, such as the one to check a matrix multiplication program or a sort program, requires the determination of I/O relationship. For matrix inversion, and for sorting, this relation is rather simple and is expressed precisely in terms of a mathematical formula or a simple algorithm as explained above. Also, when tests are generated from models such as finite-state machines (FSMs) or statecharts, both inputs and the corresponding outputs are available. This makes it possible to construct an oracle while generating the tests. However, in general, the construction of automated oracle is a complex undertaking. The next example illustrates one method for constructing an oracle.

Example 1.16: Consider a program named HVideo that allows one to keep track of home videos. The program operates in two modes: data entry and search. In the data entry mode, it displays a screen into which the user types in information about a DVD. This information includes data such as the title, comments, and the date when the video was prepared. Once the information is typed, the user clicks on the Enter button which adds this information to a database. In the search mode, the program displays a screen into which a user can type some attribute of the video being searched for and set up a search criterion. A sample criterion is "Find all videos that contain the name Magan in the title field." In response the program returns all videos in the database that match the search criteria or displays an appropriate message if no match is found.

To test HVideo we need to create an oracle that checks whether the program functions correctly in data entry and search modes. In addition, an input generator needs to be created. As shown in Figure 1.8, the input generator generates inputs for HVideo. To test the data entry operation of HVideo, the input generator generates a data entry request. This request consists of an operation code, Data Entry, and the data to be entered that includes the title, comments,

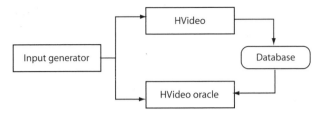

Fig. 1.8   Relationship between an input generator, `HVideo`, and its oracle.

and the date on which the video was prepared. Upon completion of execution of the `Enter` request, `HVideo` returns control to the input generator. The input generator now requests the oracle to test if `HVideo` performed its task correctly on the input given for data entry. The oracle uses the input to check if the information to be entered into the database has been entered correctly or not. The oracle returns a Pass or No Pass to the input generator.

To test if `HVideo` correctly performs the search operation, the input generator formulates a search request with the search data, the same as the one given previously with the `Enter` command. This input is passed on to `HVideo` that performs the search and returns the results of the search to the input generator. The input generator passes these results to the oracle to check for their correctness. There are at least two ways in which the oracle can check for the correctness of the search results. One is for the oracle to actually search the database. If its findings are the same as that of `HVideo` then the search results are assumed to be correct, and incorrect otherwise. Another method is for the oracle to keep track of what data has been entered. Given a search string, the oracle can find the expected output from `HVideo`.

1.6 TEST METRICS

The term *metric* refers to a standard of measurement. In software testing, there exist a variety of metrics. Figure 1.9 shows a classification of various types of metrics briefly discussed in this section. Metrics can

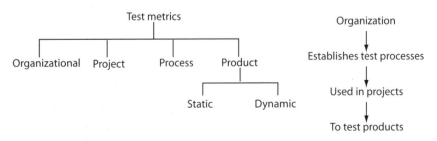

Fig. 1.9   Types of metrics used in software testing and their relationships.

be computed at the organizational, process, project, and product levels. Each set of measurements has its value in monitoring, planning, and control.

Regardless of the level at which metrics are defined and collected, there exist four general core areas that assist in the design of metrics. These are schedule, quality, resources, and size. Schedule-related metrics measure actual completion times of various activities and compare these with estimated time to completion. Quality-related metrics measure quality of a product or a process. Resource-related metrics measure items such as cost in dollars, manpower, and tests executed. Size-related metrics measure size of various objects such as the source code and number of tests in a test suite.

1.6.1 ORGANIZATIONAL METRICS

Metrics at the level of an organization are useful in overall project planning and management. Some of these metrics are obtained by aggregating compatible metrics across multiple projects. Thus, for example, the number of defects reported after product release, averaged over a set of products developed and marketed by an organization, is a useful metric of product quality at the organizational level.

Computing this metric at regular intervals and over all products released over a given duration shows the quality trend across the organization. For example, one might say "The number of defects reported in the field over all products and within 3 months of their shipping, has dropped from 0.2 defects per thousand lines of code (KLOC) to 0.04 defects per KLOC. Other organizational-level metrics include testing cost per KLOC, delivery schedule slippage, and time to complete system testing.

Organizational-level metrics allow senior management to monitor the overall strength of the organization and points to areas of weakness. Thus, these metrics help senior management in setting new goals and plan for resources needed to realize these goals.

Example 1.17: The average defect density across all software projects in a company is 1.73 defects per KLOC. Senior management has found that for the next generation of software products, which they plan to bid, they need to show that product density can be reduced to 0.1 defects per KLOC. The management thus sets a new goal.

Given the time frame from now until the time to bid, the management needs to do a feasibility analysis to determine whether this goal can be met. If a preliminary analysis shows that it can be met, then a detailed plan needs to be worked out and put into action. For example, the management might decide to train its employees in the use of new tools and techniques for defect prevention and detection using sophisticated static analysis techniques.

1.6.2 PROJECT METRICS

Project metrics relate to a specific project, for example the I/O device testing project or a compiler project. These are useful in the monitoring and control of a specific project. The ratio of actual-to-planned system test effort is one project metric. Test effort could be measured in terms of the tester-man-months. At the start of the system test phase, for example, the project manager estimates the total system test effort. The ratio of actual to estimated effort is zero prior to the system test phase. This ratio builds up over time. Tracking the ratio assists the project manager in allocating testing resources.

Another project metric is the ratio of the number of successful tests to the total number of tests in the system test phase. At any time during the project, the evolution of this ratio from the start of the project could be used to estimate the time remaining to complete the system test process.

1.6.3 PROCESS METRICS

Every project uses some test process. The *big-bang* approach is one process sometimes used in relatively small single-person projects. Several other well-organized processes exist. The goal of a process metric is to assess the goodness of the process.

When a test process consists of several phases, for example unit test, integration test, and system test, one can measure how many defects were found in each phase. It is well known that the later a defect is found, the costlier it is to fix. Hence, a metric that classifies defects according to the phase in which they are found assists in evaluating the process itself.

Example 1.18: In one software development project it was found that 15% of the total defects were reported by customers, 55% of the defects prior to shipping were found during system test, 22% during integration test, and the remaining during unit test. The large number of defects found during the system test phase indicates a possibly weak integration and unit test process. The management might also want to reduce the fraction of defects reported by customers.

1.6.4 PRODUCT METRICS: GENERIC

Product metrics relate to a specific product such as a compiler for a programming language. These are useful in making decisions related to the product, for example "Should this product be released for use by the customer?"

Product complexity-related metrics abound. We introduce two types of metrics here: the cyclomatic complexity and the Halstead metrics. The cyclomatic complexity proposed by Thomas McCabe in 1976 is based on the control flow of a program. Given the CFG G of program P containing N nodes, E edges, and p connected procedures, the cyclomatic complexity $V(G)$ is computed as follows:

$$V(G) = E - N + 2p$$

Note that P might consist of more than one procedure. The term p in $V(G)$ counts only procedures that are reachable from the main function. $V(G)$ is the complexity of a CFG G that corresponds to a procedure reachable from the main procedure. Also, $V(G)$ is not the complexity of the entire program, instead it is the complexity of a procedure in P that corresponds to G (see Exercise 1.13). Larger values of $V(G)$ tend to imply higher program complexity and hence a program more difficult to understand and test than one with a smaller values. $V(G)$ of the values 5 or less are recommended.

The now well-known Halstead complexity measures were published by late Professor Maurice Halstead in a book titled *Elements of Software Science*. Table 1.2 lists some of the software science metrics. Using program size (S) and effort (E), the following estimator has been proposed for the number of errors (B) found during a software development effort:

$$B = 7.6 \, E^{0.667} S^{0.333}$$

Table 1.2 Halstead measures of program complexity and effort

Measure	Notation	Definition
Operator count	N_1	Number of operators in a program
Operand count	N_2	Number of operands in a program
Unique operators	η_1	Number of unique operators in a program
Unique operands	η_2	Number of unique operands in a program
Program vocabulary	η	$\eta_1 + \eta_2$
Program size	N	$N_1 + N_2$
Program volume	V	$N \times \log_2 \eta$
Difficulty	D	$2/\eta_1 \times \eta_2/N_2$
Effort	E	$D \times V$

Extensive empirical studies have been reported to validate Halstead's software science metrics. An advantage of using an estimator such as **B** is that it allows the management to plan for testing resources. For example, a larger value of the number of expected errors will lead to a larger number of testers and testing resources to complete the test process over a given duration. Nevertheless, modern programming languages such as Java and C++ do not lend themselves well to the application of the software science metrics. Instead one uses specially devised metrics for object-oriented languages described next (also see Exercise 1.14).

1.6.5 Product Metrics: OO Software

A number of empirical studies have investigated the correlation between product complexity and quality. Table 1.3 lists a sample of product metrics for object-oriented (OO) and other applications. Product reliability is a quality metric and refers to the probability of product failure for a given operational profile. As explained in Section 1.4.2, product reliability of software truly measures the probability of generating a failure-causing test input. If for a given operational profile

Table 1.3 A sample of product metrics

Metric	Meaning
Reliability	Probability of failure of a software product with respect to a given operational profile in a given environment
Defect density	Number of defects per KLOC
Defect severity	Distribution of defects by their level of severity
Test coverage	Fraction of testable items, e.g. basic blocks, covered. Also a metric for test adequacy or *goodness of tests*
Cyclomatic complexity	Measures complexity of a program based on its CFG
Weighted methods per class	$\Sigma_{n=1}^{n} ci$, c_i is the complexity of method i in the class under consideration
Class coupling	Measures the number of classes to which a given class is coupled
Response set	Set of all methods that can be invoked, directly and indirectly, when a message is sent to object O
Number of children	Number of immediate descendants of a class in the class hierarchy

and in a given environment this probability is 0, then the program is perfectly reliable despite the possible presence of errors. Certainly, one could define other metrics to assess software reliability. A number of other product quality metrics, based on defects, are listed in Table 1.3.

The OO metrics in the table are due to Shyam Chidamber and Chris F. Kemerer. These metrics measure program or design complexity. These are of direct relevance to testing in that a product with a complex design is likely to require more test effort to obtain a given level of defect density than a product with less complexity.

1.6.6 PROGRESS MONITORING AND TRENDS

Metrics are often used for monitoring progress. This requires making measurements on a regular basis over time. Such measurements offer trends. For example, suppose that a browser has been coded, unit tested, and its components integrated. It is now in the system-testing phase. One could measure the cumulative number of defects found and plot these over time. Such a plot will rise over time. Eventually, it is likely to show a saturation indicating that the product is reaching stability. Figure 1.10 shows a sample plot of new defects found over time.

1.6.7 STATIC AND DYNAMIC METRICS

Static metrics are those computed without having to execute the product. Number of testable entities in an application is an example of a static product metric. Dynamic metrics require code execution. For example, the number of testable entities actually covered by a test suite is a dynamic product metric.

One could apply the notions of static and dynamic to organization and project. For example, the average number of testers working on a project is a static project metric. Number of defects remaining to be fixed could be treated as dynamic metric as it can be computed accurately only after a code change has been made and the product retested.

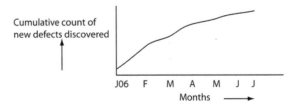

Fig. 1.10   A sample plot of cumulative count of defects found over seven consecutive months in a software project

1.6.8 Testability

According to IEEE, testability is the "degree to which a system or component facilitates the establishment of test criteria and the performance of tests to determine whether those criteria have been met." Different ways to measure testability of a product can be categorized into static and dynamic testability metrics. Software complexity is one static testability metric. The more complex an application, the lower the testability, that is, the higher the effort required to test it. Dynamic metrics for testability include various code-based coverage criteria. For example, a program for which it is difficult to generate tests that satisfy the statement-coverage criterion is considered to have low testability than one for which it is easier to construct such tests.

High testability is a desirable goal. This is best done by knowing well what needs to be tested and how, well in advance. Thus, it is recommended that features to be tested and how they are to be tested must be identified during the requirements stage. This information is then updated during the design phase and carried over to the coding phase. A testability requirement might be met through the addition of some code to a class. In more complex situations, it might require special hardware and probes in addition to special features aimed solely at meeting a testability requirement.

Example 1.19: Consider an application E required to control the operation of an elevator. E must pass a variety of tests. It must also allow a tester to perform a variety of tests. One test checks if the elevator hoist motor and the brakes are working correctly. Certainly one could do this test when the hardware is available. However, for concurrent hardware and software development, one needs a simulator for the hoist motor and brake system.

To improve the testability of E, one must include a component that allows it to communicate with a hoist motor and brake simulator and display the status of the simulated hardware devices. This component must also allow a tester to input tests such as *start the motor*.

Another test requirement for E is that it must allow a tester to experiment with various scheduling algorithms. This requirement can be met by adding a component to E that offers a tester a palette of scheduling algorithms to choose from and whether they have been implemented. The tester selects an implemented algorithm and views the elevator movement in response to different requests. Such testing also requires a random request generator and a display of such requests and the elevator response (also see Exercise 1.15).

Testability is a concern in both hardware and software designs. In hardware design, testability implies that there exist tests to detect any fault with respect to a fault model in a finished product. Thus, the aim is to verify the correctness of a finished product. Testability in software focuses on the verification of design and implementation.

1.7 SOFTWARE AND HARDWARE TESTING

There are several similarities and differences between techniques used for testing software and hardware. It is obvious that a software application does not degrade over time, any fault present in the application will remain and no new faults will creep in unless the application is changed. This is not true for hardware, such as a VLSI chip, that might fail over time due to a fault that did not exist at the time the chip was manufactured and tested.

This difference in the development of faults during manufacturing or over time leads to built-in self test (BIST) techniques applied to hardware designs and rarely, if at all, to software designs and code. BIST can be applied to software but will only detect faults that were present when the last change was made. Note that internal monitoring mechanisms often installed in software are different from BIST intended to actually test for the correct functioning of a circuit.

Fault models: Hardware testers generate tests based on fault models. For example, using a *stuck-at* fault model one can use a set of input test patterns to test whether a logic gate is functioning as expected. The fault being tested for is a manufacturing flaw or might have developed due to degradation over time. Software testers generate tests to test for correct functionality. Sometimes such tests do not correspond to any general fault model. For example, to test whether there is a memory leak in an application, one performs a combination of stress testing and code inspection. A variety of faults could lead to memory leaks.

Hardware testers use a variety of fault models at different levels of abstraction. For example, at the lower level there are transistor-level faults. At higher levels there are gate level, circuit level, and function-level fault models. Software testers might or might not use fault models during test generation even though the models exist. Mutation testing described in Chapter 7 is a technique based on software fault models. Other techniques for test generation such as condition testing, finite-state model-based testing, and combinatorial designs are also based on well-defined fault models discussed in Chapters 2, 3, and 4, respectively. Techniques for automatic generation of tests as described in several chapters in Part II of this book are based on precise fault models.

Test domain: A major difference between tests for hardware and software is in the domain of tests. Tests for a VLSI chip, for example, take the form of a bit pattern. For combinational circuits, for example a multiplexer, a

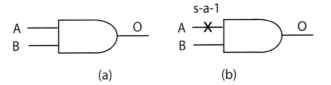

Fig. 1.11 (a) A two-input NAND gate. (b) A NAND gate with a stuck-at-1 fault in input A.

finite set of bit patterns will ensure the detection of any fault with respect to a circuit-level fault model. For sequential circuits that use flip-flops, a test may be a sequence of bit patterns that moves the circuit from one state to another and a test suite is a collection of such tests. For software, the domain of a test input is different than that for hardware. Even for the simplest of programs, the domain could be an infinite set of tuples with each tuple consisting of one or more basic data types such as integers and reals.

Example 1.20: Consider a simple two-input NAND gate in Figure 1.11(a). The stuck-at fault model defines several faults at the input and output of a logic gate. Figure 1.11(b) shows a two-input NAND gate with a stuck-at-1 fault, abbreviated as s-a-1, at input A. The truth tables for the correct and the faulty NAND gates are shown below.

Correct NAND gate			Faulty NAND gate		
A	B	O	A	B	O
0	0	1	0(1)	0	1
0	1	1	0(1)	1	0
1	0	1	1(1)	0	1
1	1	0	1(1)	1	0

A test bit vector $v: (A = 0, B = 1)$ leads to output 0, whereas the correct output should be 1. Thus v detects a single s-a-1 fault in the A input of the NAND gate. There could be multiple stuck-at faults also. Exercise 1.16 asks you to determine whether multiple stuck-at faults in a two-input NAND gate can always be detected.

Test coverage: It is practically impossible to completely test a large piece of software, for example, an OS as well as a complex integrated circuit such as a modern 32- or 64-bit microprocessor. This leads to the notion of acceptable test coverage. In VLSI testing such coverage is measured using a fraction of the faults covered to the total that might be present with respect to a given fault model.

The idea of fault coverage in hardware is also used in software testing using program mutation. A program is mutated by injecting a number of faults using a fault model that corresponds to mutation operators. The effectiveness or adequacy of a test set is assessed as a fraction of the mutants covered to the total number of mutants. Details of this technique are described in Chapter 7.

1.8 TESTING AND VERIFICATION

Program verification aims at proving the correctness of programs by showing that it contains no errors. This is very different from testing that aims at uncovering errors in a program. While verification aims at showing that a given program works for all possible inputs that satisfy a set of conditions, testing aims to show that the given program is reliable in that no errors of any significance were found.

Program verification and testing are best considered as complementary techniques. In practice, one often sheds program verification, but not testing. However, in the development of critical applications, such as smart cards or control of nuclear plants, one often makes use of verification techniques to prove the correctness of some artifact created during the development cycle, not necessarily the complete program. Regardless of such proofs, testing is used invariably to obtain confidence in the correctness of the application.

Testing is not a perfect process in that a program might contain errors despite the success of a set of tests. However, it is a process with direct impact on our confidence in the correctness of the application under test. Our confidence in the correctness of an application increases when an application passes a set of thoroughly designed and executed tests.

Verification might appear to be a perfect process as it promises to verify that a program is free from errors. However, a close look at verification reveals that it has its own weaknesses. The person who verified a program might have made mistakes in the verification process; there might be an incorrect assumption on the input conditions; incorrect assumptions might be made regarding the components that interface with the program; and so on. Thus, neither verification nor testing is a perfect technique for proving the correctness of programs.

It is often stated that programs are mathematical objects and must be verified using mathematical techniques of theorem proving. While one could treat a program as a mathematical object, one must also realize the tremendous complexity of this object that exists within the program and also in the environment in which it operates. It is this complexity that has prevented formal verification of programs such as the 5ESS switch software from the AT&T, the various versions of the Windows OS, and other monstrously complex programs. Of course, we all know that these programs are defective, but the fact remains: they are usable and provide value to users.

1.9 DEFECT MANAGEMENT

Defect management is an integral part of a development and test process in many software development organizations. It is a subprocess of the development process. It entails the following: defect prevention, discovery, recording and reporting, classification, resolution, and prediction.

Defect prevention is achieved through a variety of processes and tools. For example, good coding techniques, unit test plans, and code inspections are all important elements of any defect prevention process. Defect discovery is the identification of defects in response to failures observed during dynamic testing or found during static testing. Discovering a defect often involves debugging the code under test.

Defects found are classified and recorded in a database. Classification becomes important in dealing with the defects. For example, defects classified as *high severity* are likely to be attended to first by the developers than those classified as *low severity*. A variety of defect classification schemes exist. Orthogonal defect classification, popularly known as ODC, is one such scheme. Defect classification assists an organization in measuring statistics such as the types of defects, their frequency, and their location in the development phase and document. These statistics are then input to the organization's process improvement team that analyzes the data, identifies areas of improvement in the development process, and recommends appropriate actions to higher management.

Each defect, when recorded, is marked as *open* indicating that it needs to be resolved. One or more developers are assigned to resolve the defect. Resolution requires careful scrutiny of the defect, identifying a fix if needed, implementing the fix, testing the fix, and finally closing the defect indicating that it has been resolved. It is not necessary that every recorded defect be resolved prior to release. Only defects that are considered critical to the company's business goals, that include quality goals, are resolved; others are left unresolved until later.

Defect prediction is another important aspect of defect management. Organizations often do source code analysis to predict how many defects an application might contain before it enters the testing phase. Despite the imprecise nature of such early predictions, they are used to plan for testing resources and release dates. Advanced statistical techniques are used to predict defects during the test process. The predictions tend to be more accurate than early predictions due to the availability of defect data and the use of sophisticated models. The defect discovery data, including time of discovery and type of defect, is used to predict the count of remaining defects. Once again this information is often imprecise, though nevertheless used in planning.

Several tools exist for recording defects, and computing and reporting defect-related statistics. Bugzilla, open source, and FogBugz, commercially available, are two such tools. They provide several features for defect management, including defect recording, classification, and tracking. Several tools that compute complexity metrics also predict defects using code complexity.

1.10 EXECUTION HISTORY

Execution history of a program, also known as execution trace, is an organized collection of information about various elements of a program during a given execution. An execution slice is an executable subsequence of execution history. There are several ways to represent an execution history. For example, one possible representation is the sequence in which the functions in a program are executed against a given test input. Another representation is the sequence in which program blocks are executed. Thus, one could construct a variety of representations of the execution history of a program against a test input. For a program written in an object-oriented language such as Java, an execution history could also be represented as a sequence of objects and the corresponding methods accessed.

> Example 1.21: Consider Program P1.2 and its control-flow graph (CFG) in Figure 1.16. We are interested in finding the sequence in which the basic blocks are executed when Program P1.2 is executed with the test input $t_1 : <x=2, y=3>$. A straightforward examination of Figure 1.16 reveals the following sequence: 1, 3, 4, 5, 6, 5, 6, 5, 6, 7, 9. This sequence of blocks represents an execution history of Program P1.2 against test t_1. Another test $t_2 : <x=1, y=0>$ generates the following execution history expressed in terms of blocks: 1, 3, 4, 5, 9.

An execution history may also include values of program variables. Obviously, the more the information in the execution history, the larger the space required to save it. What gets included or excluded from an execution history depends on its desired use and the space available for saving the history. For debugging a function, one might want to know the sequence of blocks executed as well as values of one or more variables used in the function. For selecting a subset of tests to run during regression testing, one might be satisfied with only a sequence of function calls or blocks executed. For performance analysis, one might be satisfied with a trace containing the sequence in which functions are executed. The trace is then used to compute the number of times each function is executed to assess its contribution to the total execution time of the program.

A complete execution history recorded from the start of a program's execution until its termination represents a single execution path through the program. However, in some cases, such as during debugging, one might be interested only in partial execution history where program elements, such as blocks or values of variables, are recorded along a portion of the complete path. This portion might, for example, start when control enters a function of interest and end when the control exits this function.

1.11 TEST-GENERATION STRATEGIES

One of the key tasks in any software test activity is the generation of test cases. The program under test is executed against the test cases to determine whether it conforms to the requirements. The question "*How to generate test cases?*" is answered in significant detail in Part II (Test Generation) of this book. Here we provide a brief overview of the various test generation strategies.

Any form of test generation uses a source document. In the most informal of test methods, the source document resides in the mind of the tester who generates tests based on a knowledge of the requirements. In some organizations, tests are generated using a mix of formal and informal methods often directly from the requirements document serving as the source. In some test processes, requirements serve as a source for the development of formal models used for test generation.

Figure 1.12 summarizes several strategies for test generation. The top row in this figure captures techniques that are applied directly to the requirements. These may be informal techniques that assign values to input variables without the use of any rigorous or formal methods. These could also be techniques that identify input variables, capture the relationship among these variables, and use formal techniques for test generation such as random test generation and cause–effect graphing. Several such techniques are described in Chapter 2.

Another set of strategies falls under the category of *model-based test generation*. These strategies require that a subset of the requirements be modeled using a formal notation. Such a model is also known as a specification of the subset of requirements. The tests are then generated with the specification serving as the source. FSMs, statecharts, Petri nets, and timed I/O automata are some of the well-known and used formal

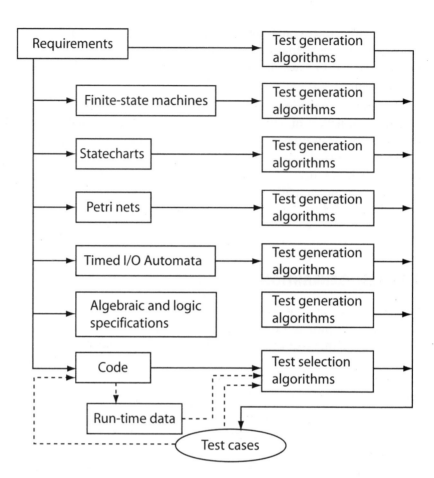

Fig. 1.12 Requirements, models, and test generation algorithms.

notations for modeling various subsets of requirements. The notations fall under the category of graphical notations, though textual equivalents also exist. Several other notations such as sequence and activity diagrams in Unified Modeling Language (UML) also exist and are used as models of subsets of requirements.

Languages based on predicate logic as well as algebraic languages are also used to express subsets of requirements in a formal manner. Each of these notational tools have their strengths and weaknesses. Usually, for any large application, one often uses more than one notation to express all requirements and generate tests. Algorithms for test generation using FSMs, statecharts and timed I/O automata are described in Chapter 3 in this volume and in two separate chapters in a subsequent volume.

There also exist techniques to generate tests directly from the code. Such techniques fall under *code-based test generation*. These techniques are useful when enhancing existing tests based on test adequacy criteria.

For example, suppose that program P has been tested against tests generated from a statechart specification. After the successful execution of all tests, one finds that some of the branches in P have not been covered, that is, there are some conditions that have never been evaluated to both true and false. One could now use code-based test generation techniques to generate tests, or modify existing ones, to generate new tests that force a condition to evaluate to true or false, assuming that the evaluations are feasible. Two such techniques, one based on program mutation and the other on control-flow coverage, are described in a chapter in a subsequent volume.

Code-based test-generation techniques are also used during regression testing when there is often a need to reduce the size of the test suite, or prioritize tests, against which a regression test is to be performed. Such techniques take four inputs—the program to be regression tested P', the program P from which P' has been derived by making changes, an existing test suite T for P, and some run-time information obtained by executing P against T. This run-time information may include items such as statement coverage and branch coverage. The test-generation algorithm then uses this information to select tests from T that must be executed to test those parts of P' that have changed or are effected by the changes made to P. The resulting test suite is usually a subset of T. Techniques for the reduction in the size of a test suite for the purpose of regression testing are described in Chapter 5.

1.12 STATIC TESTING

Static testing is carried out without executing the application under test. This is in contrast to dynamic testing that requires one or more executions of the application under test. Static testing is useful in that it may lead to the discovery of faults in the application, as well as ambiguities and errors in requirements and other application-related documents, at a relatively low cost. This is especially so when dynamic testing is expensive. Nevertheless, static testing is complementary to dynamic testing. Organizations often sacrifice static testing in favor of dynamic testing though this is not considered a good practice.

Static testing is best carried out by an individual who did not write the code, or by a team of individuals. A sample process of static testing is illustrated in Figure 1.13. The test team responsible for static testing has access to requirements document, application, and all associated documents such as design document and user manuals. The team also has access to one or more static testing tools. A static testing tool takes the application code as input and generates a variety of data useful in the test process.

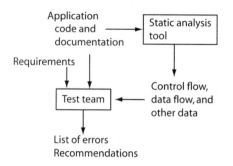

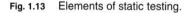

Fig. 1.13 Elements of static testing.

1.12.1 WALKTHROUGHS

Walkthroughs and inspections are an integral part of static testing. Walkthrough is an informal process to review any application-related document. For example, requirements are reviewed using a process termed requirements walkthrough. Code is reviewed using code walkthrough, also known as peer code review.

A walkthrough begins with a review plan agreed upon by all members of the team. Each item of the document, for example a source code module, is reviewed with clearly stated objectives in view. A detailed report is generated that lists items of concern regarding the document reviewed.

In requirements walkthrough, the test team must review the requirements document to ensure that the requirements match user needs, and are free from ambiguities and inconsistencies. Review of requirements also improves the understanding of the test team regarding what is desired of the application. Both functional and nonfunctional requirements are reviewed. A detailed report is generated that lists items of concern regarding the requirements.

1.12.2 INSPECTIONS

Inspection is a more formally defined process than a walkthrough. This term is usually associated with code. Several organizations consider formal code inspections as a tool to improve code quality at a lower cost than incurred when dynamic testing is used. Organizations have reported significant increases in productivity and software quality due to the use of code inspections.

Code inspection is carried out by a team. The team works according to an inspection plan that consists of the following elements: (a) statement of purpose; (b) work product to be inspected, this includes code and associated documents needed for inspection; (c) team formation, roles, and tasks to be performed; (d) rate at which the inspection task is to be completed; and (e) data collection forms where the team will record its findings such as defects discovered, coding standard violations, and time spent in each task.

Members of the inspection team are assigned roles of moderator, reader, recorder, and author. The moderator is in charge of the process and leads the review. Actual code is read by the reader, perhaps with the help of a code browser and with large monitors for all in the team to view the code. The recorder records any errors discovered or issues to be looked into. The author is the actual developer whose primary task is to help others understand code. It is important that the inspection process be friendly and nonconfrontational. Several books and articles, cited in the Bibliography section, describe various elements of the code inspection process in detail.

1.12.3 USE OF STATIC CODE ANALYSIS TOOLS IN STATIC TESTING

A variety of questions related to code behavior are likely to arise during the code-inspection process. Consider the following example: The reader asks "Variable `accel` is used at line 42 in module `updateAccel` but where is it defined?" The author might respond as "`accel` is defined in module `computeAccel`." However, a static analysis tool could give a complete list of modules and line numbers where each variable is defined and used. Such a tool with a good user interface could simply answer the question mentioned above.

Static code analysis tools can provide control-flow and data-flow information. The control-flow information, presented in terms of a CFG, is helpful to the inspection team in that it allows the determination of the flow of control under different conditions. A CFG can be annotated with data-flow information to make a data-flow graph. For example, to each node of a CFG one can append the list of variables defined and used. This information is valuable to the inspection team in understanding the code as well as pointing out possible defects. Note that a static analysis tool might itself be able to discover several data-flow-related defects.

Several such commercial as well as open source tools are available. Purify from IBM Rational and Klockwork from Klockwork, Inc. are two of the many commercially available tools for static analysis of C and Java programs. Lightweight analysis for program security in Eclipse (LAPSE) is an open source tool for the analysis of Java programs.

Example 1.22: Consider the CFGs in Figure 1.14 each of which has been annotated with data-flow information. In Figure 1.14(a), variable x is defined in block 1 and used subsequently in blocks 3 and 4.

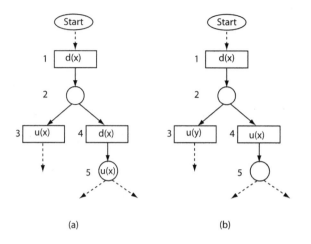

(a)   (b)

Fig. 1.14 Partial CFGs annotated with data-flow information. $d(x)$ and $u(x)$ imply the definition and use of variable x in a block, respectively. (a) CFG that indicates a possible data-flow error. (b) CFG with a data-flow error.

However, the CFG clearly shows that the definition of x at block 1 is used at bock 3 but not at block 5. In fact the definition of x at block 1 is considered killed due to its redefinition at block 4.

Is the redefinition of x at block 5 an error? This depends on what function is being computed by the code segment corresponding to the CFG. It is indeed possible that the redefinition at bock 5 is erroneous. The inspection team must be able to answer this question with the help of the requirements and the static information obtained from an analysis tool.

Figure 1.14(b) indicates the use of variable y in block 3. If y is not defined along the path from Start to block 3, then there is a data-flow error as a variable is used before it is defined. Several such errors can be detected by static analysis tools.

1.12.4 SOFTWARE COMPLEXITY AND STATIC TESTING

Often a team must decide which of the several modules should be inspected first. Several parameters enter this decision-making process. One of these being module complexity. A more complex module is likely to have more errors and must be accorded higher priority during inspection than a lower priority module.

Static analysis tools often compute complexity metrics using one or more complexity metrics discussed in Section 1.6. Such metrics could be used as a parameter in deciding which modules to inspect first. Certainly, the criticality of the function a module serves in an application could override the complexity metric while prioritizing modules.

1.13 MODEL-BASED TESTING AND MODEL CHECKING

Model-based testing refers to the acts of modeling and the generation of tests from a formal model of application behavior. Model checking refers to a class of techniques that allow the validation of one or more properties from a given model of an application.

Figure 1.15 illustrates the process of model-checking. A model, usually finite-state, is extracted from some source. The source could be the requirements, and in some cases, the application code itself. Each state of the finite-state model is prefixed with one or more properties that must hold when the application is in that state. For example, a property could be as simple as $x < 0$, indicating that variable x must hold a negative value in this state. More complex properties, such as those related to timing, may also be associated.

One or more desired properties are then coded in a formal specification language. Often, such properties are coded in temporal logic, a language for formally specifying timing properties. The model and the desired properties are then input to a model checker. The model checker attempts to verify whether the given properties are satisfied by the given model.

For each property, the checker could come up with one of the three possible answers: the property is satisfied, the property is not satisfied, or unable to determine. In the second case, the model checker provides a counterexample showing why the property is not satisfied. The third case might arise when the model checker is unable to terminate after an upper limit on the number of iterations has reached.

In almost all cases, a model is a simplified version of the actual system requirements. A positive verdict by the model checker does not

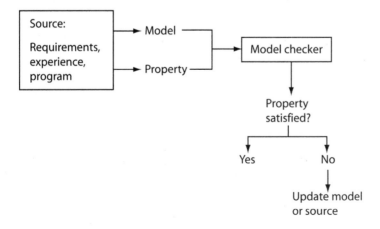

Fig. 1.15 Elements of model checking.

necessarily imply that the stated property is indeed satisfied in all cases. Hence the need for testing. Despite the positive verdict by the model checker, testing is necessary to ascertain at least for a given set of situations that the application indeed satisfies the property.

While both model-checking and model-based testing use models, model checking uses finite-state models augmented with local properties that must hold at individual states. The local properties are known as atomic propositions and the augmented models as Kripke structures.

In summary, model-checking is to be viewed as a powerful and complementary technique to model-based testing. Neither can guarantee whether an application satisfies a property under all input conditions. However, both point to useful information that helps a tester discover subtle errors.

1.14 CONTROL-FLOW GRAPH

A CFG captures the flow of control within a program. Such a graph assists testers in the analysis of a program to understand its behavior in terms of the flow of control. A CFG can be constructed manually without much difficulty for relatively small programs, say containing less than about 50 statements. However, as the size of the program grows, so does the difficulty of constructing its CFG and hence arises the need for tools.

A CFG is also known by the names *flow graph* or *program graph*. However, it is not to be confused with the program-dependence graph (PDG) introduced in Section 1.16. In the remainder of this section we explain what a CFG is and how to construct one for a given program.

1.14.1 BASIC BLOCK

Let *P* denote a program written in a procedural programming language, be it high level as C or Java or a low level such as the 80×86 assembly. A *basic block*, or simply a *block*, in *P* is a sequence of consecutive statements with a single entry and a single exit point. Thus, a block has unique entry and exit points. These points are the first and the last statements within a basic block. Control always enters a basic block at its entry point and exits from its exit point. There is no possibility of exit or a halt at any point inside the basic block except at its exit point. The entry and exit points of a basic block coincide when the block contains only one statement.

Example 1.23: The following program takes two integers x and y and outputs x^y. There are a total of 17 lines in this program including the begin and end. The execution of this program begins

at line 1 and moves through lines 2, 3, and 4 to line 5 containing an
if statement. Considering that there is a decision at line 5, control
could go to one of two possible destinations at lines 6 and 8. Thus,
the sequence of statements starting at line 1 and ending at line 5
constitutes a basic block. Its only entry point is at line 1 and the only
exit point is at line 5.

Program P1.2

```
1 begin
2    int x, y, power;
3    float z;
4    input (x, y);
5    if (y<0)
6      power=-y;
7    else
8      power=y;
9    z=1;
10   while (power!=0){
11     z=z*x;
12   power=power-1;
13   }
14   if (y<0)
15     z=1/z;
16   output(z);
17 end
```

A list of all basic blocks in Program P1.2 is given below.

Block	Lines	Entry Point	Exit Point
1	2, 3, 4, 5	1	5
2	6	6	6
3	8	8	8
4	9	9	9
5	10	10	10
6	11, 12	11	12
7	14	14	14
8	15	15	15
9	16	16	16

Program P1.2 contains a total of nine basic blocks numbered sequentially from 1 to 9. Note how the while at line 10 forms a block of its
own. Also note that we have ignored lines 7 and 13 from the listing
because these are syntactic markers, and so are begin and end that
are also ignored.

Note that some tools for program analyses place a procedure call statement in a separate basic block. If we were to do that, then we will place the input and output statements in Program P1.2 in two separate basic blocks. Consider the following sequence of statements extracted from Program P1.2.

```
1 begin
2    int x, y, power;
3    float z;
4    input (x, y);
5    if(y<0)
```

In the previous example, lines 1 through 5 constitute one basic block. The above sequence contains a call to the input function. If function calls are treated differently, then the above sequence of statements contains three basic blocks, one composed of lines 1 through 3, the second composed of line 4, and the third composed of line 5.

Function calls are often treated as blocks of their own because they cause the control to be transferred away from the currently executing function and hence raise the possibility of abnormal termination of the program. In the context of flow graphs, unless stated otherwise, we treat calls to functions like any other sequential statement that is executed without the possibility of termination.

1.14.2 FLOW GRAPH: DEFINITION AND PICTORIAL REPRESENTATION

A flow graph G is defined as a finite set N of nodes and a finite set E of directed edges. An edge (i, j) in E, with an arrow directed from i to j, connects nodes n_i and n_j in N. We often write $G = (N, E)$ to denote a flow graph G with nodes in N and edges in E. Start and End are two special nodes in N and are known as distinguished nodes. Every other node in G is reachable from Start. Also, every node in N has a path terminating at End. Node Start that has no incoming edge, and End that has no outgoing edge.

In a flow graph of program P, we often use a basic block as a node and edges indicate the flow of control across basic blocks. We label the blocks and the nodes such that block b_i corresponds to node n_i. An edge (i, j) connecting basic blocks b_i and b_j implies that control can go from block b_i to block b_j. Sometimes we will use a flow graph with one node corresponding to each statement in P.

A pictorial representation of a flow graph is often used in the analysis of the control behavior of a program. Each node is represented by a symbol, usually an oval or a rectangular box. These boxes are labeled by their corresponding block numbers. The boxes are connected by lines representing edges. Arrows are used to indicate the direction of flow. A block that ends in a decision has two edges going out of it. These edges are labeled `true` and `false` to indicate the path taken when the condition evaluates to `true` and `false`, respectively.

Example 1.24: The flow graph for Program P1.2 is defined as follows:

$N = $ {Start, 1, 2, 3, 4, 5, 6, 7, 8, 9, End}

$E = $ {(Start, 1), (1, 2), (1, 3), (2, 4), (3, 4), (4, 5), (5, 6), (6, 5), (5, 7), (7, 8), (7, 9), (9, End)}

Figure 1.16(a) depicts this flow graph. Block numbers are placed right next to or above the corresponding box. As shown in Figure 1.16(b), the contents of a block may be omitted, and nodes represented by circles, if we are interested only in the flow of control across program blocks and not their contents.

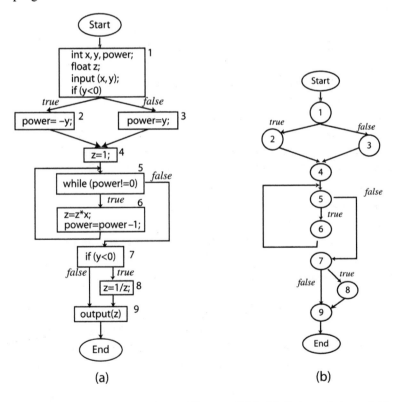

(a)   (b)

Fig. 1.16   Flow graph representations of Program P1.2. (a) Statements in each block are shown. (b) Statements within a block are omitted.

1.14.3 Path

Consider a flow graph $G = (N, E)$. A sequence of k edges, $k > 0$, $(e_1, e_2, \ldots, e_k)$, denotes a path of length k through the flow graph if the following sequence condition holds: Given that n_p, n_q, n_r, and n_s are nodes belonging to N, and $0 < i < k$, if $e_i = (n_p, n_q)$ and $e_{i+1} = (n_r, n_s)$ then $n_q = n_r$.

Thus, for example, the sequence $((1, 3), (3, 4), (4, 5))$ is a path in the flow graph shown in Figure 1.16. However, $((1, 3), (3, 5), 6, 8))$ is not a valid path through this flow graph. For brevity, we indicate a path as a sequence of blocks. For example, in Figure 1.16, the edge sequence $((1, 3), (3, 4), (4, 5))$ is the same as the block sequence $(1, 3, 4, 5)$.

For nodes $n, m \in N$, m is said to be a *descendant of n* if there is a path from n to m; in this case n is an *ancestor* of m and m its descendant. If, in addition, $n \neq m$, then n is a *proper anscestor* of m, and m a *proper descendant of n*. If there is an edge $(n, m) \in E$, then m is a *successor* of n and n the *predecessor* of m. The set of all successor and predecessor nodes of n will be denoted by *succ(n)* and *pred(n)*, respectively. Start has no ancestor and End has no descendant.

A path through a flow graph is considered *complete* if the first node along the path is Start and the terminating node is End. A path p through a flow graph for program P is considered *feasible* if there exists at least one test case which when input to P causes p to be traversed. If no such test case exists, then p is considered *infeasible*. Whether a given path p through a program P is feasible is in general an undecidable problem. This statement implies that it is not possible to write an algorithm that takes as inputs an arbitrary program and a path through that program, and correctly outputs whether this path is feasible for the given program.

Given paths $p = \{n_1, n_2, \ldots, n_t\}$ and $s = \{i_1, i_2, \ldots, i_u\}$, where s is a *subpath* of p if for some $1 \leq j \leq t$ and $j + u - 1 \leq t$, $i_1 = n_j, i_2 = n_{j+1}, \ldots, i_u = n_{j+u-1}$. In this case, we also say that s and each node i_k for $1 \leq k \leq u$ are included in p. Edge (n_m, n_{m+1}) that connects nodes n_m and n_{m+1} is considered included in p for $1 \leq m \leq (t - 1)$.

Example 1.25: In Figure 1.16, the following two are complete and feasible paths of lengths 10 and 9, respectively. The paths are listed using block numbers, the Start node, and the terminating node. Figure 1.17 shows the first of these two complete paths using edges in bold.

$p_1 = $ (Start, 1, 2, 4, 5, 6, 5, 7, 8, 9, End)
$p_2 = $ (Start, 1, 3, 4, 5, 6, 5, 7, 9, End)

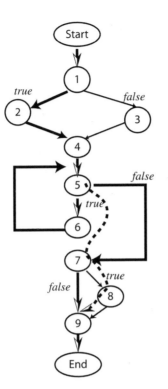

Fig. 1.17 Flow graph representation of Program P1.2. A complete path is shown using bold edges and a subpath using a dashed line.

The next two paths of lengths 4 and 5 are incomplete. The first of these two paths is shown by a dashed line in Figure 1.17.

$p_3 = (5, 7, 8, 9)$
$p_4 = (6, 5, 7, 9, \texttt{End})$

The next two paths of lengths 11 and 8 are complete but infeasible.

$p_5 = (\texttt{Start}, \; 1, \; 3, \; 4, \; 5, \; 6, \; 5, \; 7, \; 8, \; 9, \; \texttt{End})$
$p_6 = (\texttt{Start}, \; 1, \; 2, \; 4, \; 5, \; 7, \; 9, \; \texttt{End})$

Finally, the next two paths are invalid as they do not satisfy the sequence condition stated earlier.

$p_7 = (\texttt{Start}, \; 1, \; 2, \; 4, \; 8, \; 9, \; \texttt{End})$
$p_8 = (\texttt{Start}, \; 1, \; 2, \; 4, \; 7, \; 9, \; \texttt{End})$

Nodes 2 and 3 in Figure 1.17 are successors of node 1, nodes 6 and 7 are successors of node 5, and nodes 8 and 9 are successors of node 7. Nodes 6, 7, 8, 9, and End are descendants of node 5. We also have $succ(5) = \{5, 6, 7, 8, 9, End\}$ and $pred(5) = \{Start, 1, 2, 3, 4, 5, 6\}$. Note that in the presence of loops, a node can be its own ancestor or descendant.

There can be many distinct paths through a program. A program with no condition contains exactly one path that begins at node Start and terminates at node End. However, each additional condition in the program increases the number of distinct paths by at least one. Depending on their location, conditions can have an exponential effect on the number of paths.

€xample 1.26: Consider a program that contains the following statement sequence with exactly one statement containing a condition. This program has two distinct paths, one that is traversed when C_1 is true and the other when C_1 is false.

```
begin
  S₁;
  S₂;
    ⋮
  if (C₁) {...}
    ⋮
  Sₙ;
end
```

We modify the program given above by adding another if. The modified program, shown below, has exactly four paths that correspond to four distinct combinations of conditions C_1 and C_2.

```
begin
  S₁;
  S₂;
    ⋮
  if (C₁) {...}
    ⋮
  if (C₂) {...}
  Sₙ;
end
```

Note the exponential effect of adding an if on the number of paths. However, if a new condition is added within the scope of an if statement then the number of distinct paths increases only by one as is the case in the following program which has only three distinct paths.

```
begin
  S₁;
  S₂;
  ⋮
  if (C₁) {
    ⋮
    if (C₂) {...}
    ⋮
  }
  ⋮
  Sₙ;
end
```

The presence of loops can enormously increase the number of paths. Each traversal of the loop body adds a condition to the program, thereby increasing the number of paths by at least one. Sometimes, the number of times a loop is to be executed depends on the input data and cannot be determined prior to program execution. This becomes another cause of difficulty in determining the number of paths in a program. Of course, one can compute an upper limit on the number of paths based on some assumption on the input data.

Example 1.27: Program P1.3 inputs a sequence of integers and computes their product. A Boolean variable done controls the number of integers to be multiplied. A flow graph for this program appears in Figure 1.18.

Program P1.3

```
 1 begin
 2    int num, product, power;
 3    bool done;
 4    product=1;
 5    input(done);
 6    while (!done){
 7      input(num);
 8      product=product * num;
 9      input(done);
10    }
11    output(product);
12 end
```

As shown in Figure 1.18, Program P1.3 contains four basic blocks and one condition that guards the body of while. (Start, 1, 2,

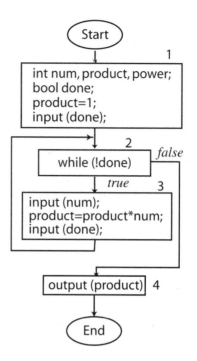

Fig. 1.18 Flow graph of Program P1.3. Numbers 1 through 4 indicate the four basic blocks in Program P1.3.

4, End) is the path traversed when `done` is `true` the first time the loop condition is checked. If there is only one value of `num` to be processed, then the path followed is (`Start`, 1, 2, 3, 2, 4, `End`). When there are two input integers to be multiplied then the path traversed is (`Start`, 1, 2, 3, 2, 3, 2, 4, `End`).

Notice that the length of the path traversed increases with the number of times the loop body is traversed. Also, the number of distinct paths in this program is the same as the number of different lengths of input sequences that are to be multiplied. Thus, when the input sequence is empty, that is of length 0, the length of the path traversed is 4. For an input sequence of length 1, it is 6, for 2 it is 8, and so on.

1.15 DOMINATORS AND POSTDOMINATORS

Let $G = (N, E)$ be a CFG for program P. Recall that G has two special nodes labeled `Start` and `End`. We define the dominator and postdominator as two relations on the set of nodes N. These relations find various applications, especially during the construction of tools for test adequacy assessment (Chapter 6) and regression testing (Chapter 5).

For nodes *n* and *m* in *N*, we say that *n* dominates *m* if *n* lies on every path from Start to *m*. We write *dom(n, m)* when *n* dominates *m*. In an analogous manner, we say that node *n* postdominates node *m* if *n* lies on every path from *m* to the End node. We write *pdom(n, m)* when *n* postdominates *m*. When $n \neq m$, we refer to these as strict dominator and strict postdominator relations. *dom(n)* and *pdom(n)* denote the sets of dominators and postdominators of node *n*, respectively.

For $n, m \in N$, n is the immediate dominator of *m* when *n* is the last dominator of *m* along a path from the Start to *m*. We write *idom(n, m)* when *n* is the immediate dominator of *m*. Each node, except for Start, has a unique immediate dominator. Immediate dominators are useful in that we can use them to build a dominator tree. A dominator tree derived from G succinctly shows the dominator relation.

For $n, m \in N$, *n* is an immediate postdominator of *m* if *n* is the first postdominator along a path from *m* to End. Each node, except for End, has a unique immediate postdominator. We write *ipdom(n, m)* when *n* is the immediate postdominator of *m*. Immediate postdominators allow us to construct a postdominator tree that exhibits the postdominator relation among the nodes in G.

Example 1.28: Consider the flow graph in Figure 1.18. This flow graph contains six nodes including Start and End. Its dominators and postdominators are shown in Figure 1.19(a) and (b), respectively. In the dominator tree, for example, a directed edge connects

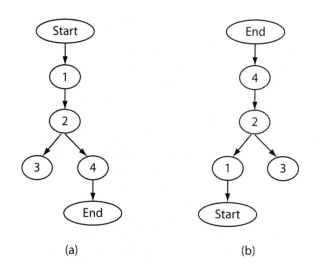

(a)   (b)

Fig. 1.19   (a) Dominator and (b) postdominator trees derived from the flow graph in Figure 1.18.

an immediate dominator to the node it dominates. Thus, among other relations, we have *idom*(1, 2) and *idom*(4, end). Similarly, from the postdominator tree, we obtain *ipdom*(4, 2) and *ipdom* (End, 4).

Given a dominator and a postdominator tree, it is easy to derive the set of dominators and postdominators for any node. For example, the set of dominators for node 4, denoted as *dom*(4), is {2, 1, Start}. *dom*(4) is derived by first obtaining the immediate dominator of 4 which is 2, followed by the immediate dominator of 2 which is 1, and finally the immediate dominator of 1 which is Start. Similarly, we can derive the set of postdominators for node 2 as {4, End}.

1.16 PROGRAM-DEPENDENCE GRAPH

A PDG for program *P* exhibits different kinds of dependencies among statements in *P*. For the purpose of testing, we consider data dependence and control dependence. These two dependencies are defined with respect to data and predicates in a program. Next, we explain data and control dependences, how they are derived from a program and their representation in the form of a PDG. We first show how to construct a PDG for programs with no procedures and then show how to handle programs with procedures.

1.16.1 DATA DEPENDENCE

Statements in a program exhibit a variety of dependencies. For example, consider Program P1.3. We say that the statement at line 8 depends on the statement at line 4 because line 8 may use the value of variable product defined at line 4. This form of dependence is known as *data dependence.*

Data dependence can be visually expressed in the form of a data-dependence graph (DDG). A DDG for program *P* contains one unique node for each statement in *P*. Declaration statements are omitted when they do not lead to the initialization of variables. Each node in a DDG is labeled by the text of the statement as in a CFG or numbered corresponding to the program statement.

Two types of nodes are used: a predicate node is labeled by a predicate such as a condition in an if or a while statement and a data node labeled by an assignment, input, or an output statement. A directed arc from node n_2 to n_1 indicates that node n_2 is data dependent on node

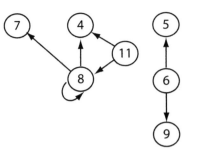

Fig. 1.20 DDG for Program P1.3. Node numbers correspond to line numbers. Declarations have been omitted.

n_1. This kind of data dependence is also known as flow dependence. A definition of data dependency follows:

> **DATA DEPENDENCE**
>
> *Let D be a DDG with nodes n_1 and n_2. Node n_2 is data dependent on n_1 if (a) variable v is defined at n_1 and used at n_2 and (b) there exists a path of nonzero length from n_1 to n_2 not containing any node that redefines v.*

Example 1.29: Consider Program P1.3 and its DDG in Figure 1.20. The graph shows seven nodes corresponding to the program statements. Data dependence is exhibited using directed edges. For example, node 8 is data dependent on nodes 4, 7, and itself because variable `product` is used at node 8 and defined at nodes 4 and 8, and variable `num` is used at node 8 and defined at node 7. Similarly, node 11, corresponding to the output statement, depends on nodes 4 and 8 because variable `product` is used at node 11 and defined at nodes 4 and 8.

Notice that the predicate node 6 is data dependent on nodes 5 and 9 because variable `done` is used at node 6 and defined through an input statement at nodes 5 and 9. We have omitted from the graph the declaration statements at lines 2 and 3 as the variables declared are defined in the input statements before use. To be complete, the data dependency graph could add nodes corresponding to these two declarations and add dependency edges to these nodes (see Exercise 1.17).

1.16.2 CONTROL DEPENDENCE

Another form of dependence is known as *control dependence.* For example, the statement at line 12 in Program P1.2 depends on the predicate at line 10. This is because control may or may not arrive at line

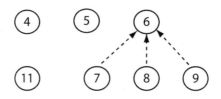

Fig. 1.21   CDG for Program P1.3.

12 depending on the outcome of the predicate at line 10. Note that the statement at line 9 does not depend on the predicate at line 5 because control will arrive at line 9 regardless of the outcome of this predicate.

As with data dependence, control dependence can be visually represented as a control-dependence graph (CDG). Each program statement corresponds to a unique node in the CDG. There is a directed edge from node n_2 to n_1 when n_2 is control dependent on n_1.

> **CONTROL DEPENDENCE**
>
> *Let C be a CDG with nodes n_1 and n_2, n_1 being a predicate node. Node n_2 is control dependent on n_1 if there is at least one path from n_1 to program exit that includes n_2 and at least one path from n_1 to program exit that excludes n_2.*

Example 1.30: Figure 1.21 shows the CDG for program P1.3. Control dependence edges are shown as dotted lines.

As shown, nodes 7, 8, and 9 are control dependent on node 6 because there exists a path from node 6 to each of the dependent nodes as well as a path that excludes these nodes. Notice that none of the remaining nodes is control dependent on node 6, the only predicate node in this example. Node 11 is not control dependent on node 6 because any path that goes from node 6 to program exit includes node 11.

Now that we know what data and control dependence is, we can show the PDG as a combination of the two dependencies. Each program statement contains one node in the PDG. Nodes are joined with directed arcs showing data and control dependence. A PDG can be considered as a combination of two subgraphs: a data dependence subgraph and a control-dependence subgraph.

Example 1.31: Figure 1.22 shows the PDG for Program P1.3. It is obtained by combining the graphs shown in Figures 1.20 and 1.21 (see Exercise 1.18).

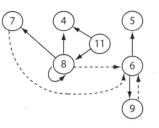

Fig. 1.22   PDG for Program P1.3.

1.17 STRINGS, LANGUAGES, AND REGULAR EXPRESSIONS

Strings play an important role in testing. As we shall see in Section 3.2, Chapter 3, strings serve as inputs to a FSM and hence to its implementation as a program. Thus a string serves as a test input. A collection of strings also forms a language. For example, a set of all strings consisting of zeros and ones is the language of binary numbers. In this section we provide a brief introduction to strings and languages.

A collection of symbols is known as an *alphabet*. We will use uppercase letters such as X and Y to denote alphabets. Though alphabets can be infinite, we are concerned only with finite alphabets. For example, $X = \{0, 1\}$ is an alphabet consisting of two symbols 0 and 1. Another alphabet is $Y = \{dog, cat, horse, lion\}$ that consists of four symbols *dog*, *cat*, *horse*, and *lion*.

A string over an alphabet X is any sequence of zero or more symbols that belong to X. For example, 0110 is a string over the alphabet $\{0, 1\}$. Also, `dog cat dog dog lion` is a string over the alphabet $\{dog, cat, horse, lion\}$. We will use lowercase letters such as p, q, r to denote strings. The length of a string is the number of symbols in that string. Given a string s, we denote its length by $|s|$. Thus, $|1011| = 4$ and $|$`dog cat dog`$| = 3$. A string of length 0, also known as an *empty string*, is denoted by ϵ.

Let s_1 and s_2 be two strings over alphabet X. We write $s_1 \cdot s_2$ to denote the *concatenation* of strings s_1 and s_2. For example, given the alphabet $X = \{0, 1\}$, and two strings 011 and 101 over X, we obtain $011 \cdot 101 = 011101$. It is easy to see that $|s_1 \cdot s_2| = |s_1| + |s_2|$. Also, for any string s, we have $s \cdot \epsilon = s$ and $\epsilon \cdot s = s$.

A set L of strings over an alphabet X is known as a *language*. A language can be finite or infinite. Given languages L_1 and L_2, we denote their catenation as $L_1 \cdot L_2$ that denotes the set L defined as:

$$L = L_1 \cdot L_2 = \{x \cdot y \mid x \in L_1, y \in L_2\}$$

The following sets are finite languages over the binary alphabet $\{0, 1\}$.

$\emptyset$ The empty set

$\{\epsilon\}$: A language consisting only of one string of length 0

$\{00, 11, 0101\}$: A language containing three strings

A regular expression is a convenient means for compact representation of sets of strings. For example, the regular expression (01)* denotes the set of strings that consists of the empty string, the string 01, and all strings obtained by concatenating the string 01 with itself one or more times. Note that (01)* denotes an infinite set. A formal definition of regular expressions follows:

Regular expression

Given a finite alphabet X, the following are regular expressions over X:

- If a belongs to X, then a is a regular expression that denotes the set $\{a\}$.
- Let r_1 and r_2 be two regular expressions over the alphabet X that denote sets L_1 and L_2, respectively. Then $r_1 \cdot r_2$ is a regular expression that denotes the set $L_1 \cdot L_2$.
- If r is a regular expression that denotes the set L, then r^+ is a regular expression that denotes the set obtained by concatenating L with itself one or more times, also written as L^+. Also, r^*, known as the *Kleene closure* of r, is a regular expression. If r denotes the set L, then r^* denotes the set $\{\epsilon\} \cup L^+$.
- If r_1 and r_2 are regular expressions that denote sets L_1 and L_2, respectively, then $r_1 \mid r_2$ is also a regular expression that denotes the set $\{\epsilon\}\ L_1 \cup L_2$.

Regular expressions are useful in expressing both finite and infinite test sequences. For example, if a program takes a sequence of zeroes and ones and flips each 0 to a 1 and a 1 to a 0, then a few possible sets of test inputs are 0*, (10)$^+$, 010 | 100. As explained in Chapter 3, regular expressions are also useful in defining the set of all possible inputs to a FSM that will move the machine from one state to another state.

1.18 TYPES OF TESTING

An answer to the question "What types of testing are performed in your organization?" often consists of a set of terms such as black-box testing, reliability testing, unit testing, and so on. There exist a number of terms that typify one or more types of testing. We abstract all these terms as *X-testing*. In this section, we present a framework for the classification of testing techniques. We then use this framework to classify a variety of testing techniques by giving meaning to the "X" in X-testing.

Our framework consists of a set of five classifiers that serve to classify testing techniques that fall under the dynamic testing category. Techniques that fall under the static testing category are discussed in Section 1.12. Dynamic testing requires the execution of the program under test. Static testing consists of techniques for the review and analysis of the program.

Each of the five classifiers is a mapping from a set of features to a set of testing techniques. Features include source of test generation, questions that define a goal, a life cycle phase, or an artifact. Here are the five classifiers labeled as C1 through C5.

1. C1: Source of test generation
2. C2: Life cycle phase in which testing takes place
3. C3: Goal of a specific testing activity
4. C4: Characteristics of the artifact under test
5. C5: Test process

Tables 1.4 through 1.8 list each classifier by specifying the mapping and provide a few examples where appropriate. While each classifier defines a mapping, there exists a hierarchy across mappings. For example, black-box testing is used in almost all goal-directed testing. As is evident from the tables, each mapping is not necessarily one-to-one. For example, pairwise testing could be used to design tests for an entire system or for a component.

Test techniques that fall under mapping C1 are more generic than others. Each technique under C1 is potentially applicable to meet the goal specified in C3 as well as to test the software objects in C4. For example, one could use pairwise testing as a means to generate tests in any goal-directed testing that falls within C3. Let us now examine each classifier in more detail.

1.18.1 CLASSIFIER C1: SOURCE OF TEST GENERATION

Black-box testing: Test generation is an essential part of testing; it is as wedded to testing as the earth is to the sun. There are a variety of ways to generate tests, some are listed in Table 1.4. Tests could be generated from informally or formally specified requirements and without the aid of the code that is under test. Such form of testing is commonly referred to as black-box testing. When the requirements are informally specified, one could use ad hoc techniques or heuristics such as equivalence partitioning and boundary-value analysis.

Table 1.4 Classification of techniques for testing computer software. Classifier C1: Source of test generation

Artifact	Technique	Example
Requirements (informal)	Black-box	Ad hoc testing
		Boundary-value analysis
		Category partition
		Classification trees
		Cause–effect graphs
		Equivalence partitioning
		Partition testing
		Predicate testing
		Random testing
		Syntax testing
Code	White-box	Adequacy assessment
		Coverage testing
		Data-flow testing
		Domain testing
		Mutation testing
		Path testing
		Structural testing
		Test minimization
Requirements and code	Black-box and White-box	
Formal model: Graphical or mathematical specification	Model-based specification	Statechart testing
		FSM testing
		Pairwise testing
		Syntax testing
Component's interface	Interface testing	Interface mutation
		Pairwise testing

Model-based or specification-based testing: Model-based or specification-based testing occurs when the requirements are formally specified, as for example, using one or more mathematical or graphical notations such as Z, statecharts, and an event sequence graph, and tests are generated using the formal specification. This is also a form of black-box testing. As listed in Table 1.4, there are a variety of techniques for generating tests for black-box and model-based testing. Part II of this book introduces several of these.

White-box testing: White-box testing refers to the test activity wherein code is used in the generation of or the assessment of test cases. It is rare, and almost impossible, to use white-box testing in isolation. As a test case consists of both inputs and expected outputs, one must use requirements to generate test cases, the code is used as an additional artifact in the generation process. However, there are techniques for generating tests exclusively from code and the corresponding expected output from requirements. For example, tools are available to generate tests to distinguish all mutants of a program under test or generate tests that force the program under test to exercise a given path. In any case, when someone claims they are using white-box testing, it is reasonable to conclude that they are using some forms of both black-box and white-box testing.

Code could be used directly or indirectly for test generation. In the direct case, a tool, or a human tester, examines the code and focuses on a given path to be covered. A test is generated to cover this path. In the indirect case, tests generated using some black-box technique are assessed against some code-based coverage criterion. Additional tests are then generated to cover the uncovered portions of the code by analyzing which parts of the code are feasible. Control flow, data flow, and mutation testing can be used for direct as well as indirect code-based test generation.

Interface testing: Tests are often generated using a component's interface.

Certainly, the interface itself forms a part of the component's requirements and hence this form of testing is black-box testing. However, the focus on interface leads us to consider interface testing in its own right. Techniques such as pairwise testing and interface mutation are used to generate tests from a component's interface specification. In pairwise testing, the set of values for each input is obtained from the component's requirement. In interface mutation, the interface itself, such as a function coded in C or a CORBA component written in an IDL, serves to extract the information needed to perform interface mutation. While pairwise testing is clearly a black-box-testing technique, interface mutation is a white-box technique though it focuses on the interface-related elements of the component under test.

Ad hoc testing is not to be confused with random testing. In ad hoc testing, a tester generates tests from requirements but without the use of any systematic method. Random testing uses a systematic method to generate tests. Generation of tests using random testing requires modeling the input space and then sampling data from the input space randomly.

In summary, black-box and white-box are the two most fundamental test techniques that form the foundation of software testing. Test-generation and assessment techniques (TGAT) are at the foundation of software testing. All the remaining test techniques classified by C2 through C4 fall into either the black-box or the white-box category.

1.18.2 Classifier C2: Life Cycle Phase

Testing activities take place throughout the software life cycle. Each artifact produced is often subject to testing at different levels of rigor and using different testing techniques. Testing is often categorized based on the phase in which it occurs. Table 1.5 lists various types of testing depending on the phase in which the activity occurs.

Programmers write code during the early coding phase. They test their code before it is integrated with other system components. This type of testing is referred to as unit testing. When units are integrated and a large component or a subsystem formed, programmers do integration testing of the subsystem. Eventually when the entire system has been built, its testing is referred to as system testing.

Test phases mentioned above differ in their timing and focus. In unit testing, a programmer focuses on the unit or a small component that has been developed. The goal is to ensure that the unit functions correctly in isolation. In integration testing, the goal is to ensure that a collection of components function as desired. Integration errors are often discovered at this stage. The goal of system testing is to ensure that all the desired functionality is in the system and works as per its requirements. Note that tests designed during unit testing are not likely to be used during integration and system testing. Similarly, tests designed for integration testing might not be useful for system testing.

Table 1.5   Classification of techniques for testing computer software. Classifier C2: Life cycle phase

Phase	Technique
Coding	Unit testing
Integration	Integration testing
System integration	System testing
Maintenance	Regression testing
Postsystem, prerelease	Beta-testing

Often a carefully selected set of customers is asked to test a system before commercialization. This form of testing is referred to as beta-testing. In the case of contract software, the customer who contracted the development performs acceptability testing prior to making the final decision as to whether to purchase the application for deployment.

Errors reported by users of an application often lead to additional testing and debugging. Often changes made to an application are much smaller in their size when compared to the entire application, thus obviating the need for a complete system test. In such situations, one performs a regression test. The goal of regression testing is to ensure that the modified system functions as per its specifications. However, regression testing may be performed using a subset of the entire set of test cases used for system testing. Test cases selected for regression testing include those designed to test the modified code and any other code that might be affected by the modifications.

It is important to note that all black-box and white-box-testing techniques mentioned in Table 1.4 are applicable during each life cycle phase when code is being tested. For example, one could use the pairwise testing technique to generate tests for integration testing. One could also use any white-box technique, such as test assessment and enhancement, during regression testing.

1.18.3 CLASSIFIER C3: GOAL-DIRECTED TESTING

Goal-directed testing leads to a large number of terms in software testing. Table 1.6 lists a sample of goals commonly used in practice and the names of the corresponding test techniques.

There exist a variety of goals. Of course, finding any hidden errors is the prime goal of testing, goal-oriented testing looks for specific types of failures. For example, the goal of vulnerability testing is to detect if there is any way by which the system under test can be penetrated by unauthorized users. Suppose that an organization has set up security policies and taken security measures. Penetration testing aims at evaluating how good these policies and measures are. Again, both black-box and white-box techniques for the generation and evaluation of tests are applicable to penetration testing. Nevertheless, in many organizations, penetration and other forms of security testing remain ad hoc.

Robustness testing: Robustness testing refers to the task of testing an application for robustness against unintended inputs. It differs from functional testing in that the tests for robustness are derived from outside of the valid (or expected) input space, whereas in the former the tests are derived from the valid input space.

Table 1.6 Classification of techniques for testing computer software. Classifier: C3: Goal directed testing

Goal	Testing technique	Example
Advertised features	Functional	
Security	Security	
Invalid inputs	Robustness	
Vulnerabilities	Vulnerability	Penetration testing
Errors in GUI	GUI	Capture/playback
		Event sequence graphs
		Complete interaction sequence
Operational correctness	Operational	Transactional flow
Reliability assessment	Reliability	
Resistance to penetration	Penetration	
System performance	Performance	Stress testing
Customer acceptability	Acceptance	
Business compatibility	Compatibility	Interface testing
		Installation testing
Peripherals compatibility	Configuration	
Foreign language compatibility	Foreign language	

Each goal is listed briefly. It is easy to examine each listing by adding an appropriate prefix such as *Check for*, *Perform*, *Evaluate*, and *Check against*. For example, the goal *Vulnerabilities* is to be read as *Check for Vulnerabilities*.

As an example of robustness testing, suppose that an application is required to perform a function for all values of $x \geq 0$. However, there is no specification of what the application must do for $x < 0$. In this case, robustness testing would require that the application be tested against tests where $x < 0$. As the requirements may not specify behavior outside the valid input space, a clear understanding of what robustness means is needed for each application. In some applications, robustness might simply mean that the application displays an error message and exits, while in others it might mean that the application brings an aircraft to a safe landing!

Stress testing: In stress testing one checks for the behavior of an application under stress. Handling of overflow of data storage, for example buffers, can be checked with the help of stress testing. Web applications can be tested by stressing them with a large number and variety of requests. The goal here is to find if the application continues to function correctly under stress.

One needs to quantify *stress* in the context of each application. For example, a Web service can be stressed by sending it an unusually large number of requests. The goal of such testing would be to check if the application continues to function correctly and performs its services at the desired rate. Thus, stress testing checks an application for conformance to its functional requirements as well as to its performance requirements when under stress.

Performance testing: The term *performance testing* refers to that phase of testing where an application is tested specifically with performance requirements in view. For example, a compiler might be tested to check if it meets the performance requirements stated in terms of number of lines of code compiled per second.

Often performance requirements are stated with respect to a hardware and software configuration. For example, an application might be required to process 1,000 billing transactions per minute on a specific Intel processor-based machine and running a specific OS.

Load testing: The term *load testing* refers to that phase of testing in which an application is *loaded* with respect to one or more operations. The goal is to determine if the application continues to perform as required under various load conditions. For example, a database server can be loaded with requests from a large number of simulated users. While the server might work correctly when one or two users use it, it might fail in various ways when the number of users exceeds a threshold.

During load testing one can determine whether the application is handling exceptions in an adequate manner. For example, an application might maintain a dynamically allocated buffer to store user IDs. The buffer size increases with an increase in the number of simultaneous users. There might be a situation when additional memory space is not available to add to the buffer. A poorly designed, or incorrectly coded, application might crash in such a situation. However, a carefully designed and correctly coded application will handle the *out of memory* exception in a graceful manner such as by announcing the high load through an apology message.

In a sense, load testing is yet another term for stress testing. However, load testing can be performed for ascertaining an application's performance as well as the correctness of its behavior. It is a form of stress testing when the objective is to check for correctness with respect to the functional requirements under load. It is a form of performance testing when the objective is to assess the time it takes to perform certain operations under a range of given conditions.

Load testing is also a form of robustness testing, that is testing for unspecified requirements. For example, there might not be any explicitly stated requirement related to the maximum number of users an application can handle and what the application must do when the number of users exceeds a threshold. In such situations, load testing allows a tester to determine the threshold beyond which the application under test fails through, for example, a crash.

Terminology overlap: Note that there is some overlap in the terminology. For example, vulnerability testing is a form of security testing. Also, testing for compatibility with business goals might also include vulnerability testing. Such overlaps abound in testing-related terminology.

Once again we note that formal techniques for test generation and test-adequacy assessment apply to all forms of goal-directed testing. A lack of examples in almost the entire Table 1.6 is because TGAT listed in Table 1.4 are applicable to goal-directed testing. It is technically correct to confess "We do ad hoc testing" when none of the formal test-generation techniques is used.

1.18.4 CLASSIFIER C4: ARTIFACT UNDER TEST

Testers often say "We do X-testing" where X corresponds to an artifact under test. Table 1.7 is a partial list of testing techniques named after the artifact that is being tested. For example, during the design phase one might generate a design using the SDL notation. This design can be tested before it is committed to code. This form of testing is known as design testing.

As another example, you might have seen articles and books on OO-testing. Again, OO-testing refers to testing of programs that are written in an OO language such as C++ or Java. Yet again, there exists a variety of test-generation and adequacy-assessment techniques that fall under black-box and white-box category and that are applicable to the testing of OO software.

It is important to note that specialized black-box and white-box test techniques are available for specialized software. For example, timed automata- and Petri net-based test-generation techniques are intended for the generation of tests for real-time software.

Table 1.7 Classification of techniques for testing computer software.
Classifier C4: Artifact under test

Characteristic	Technique
Application component	Component testing
Batch processing	Equivalence partitioning, finite-state model-based testing, and most other test-generation techniques discussed in this book
Client and server	Client–server testing
Compiler	Compiler testing
Design	Design testing
Code	Code testing
Database system	Transaction-flow testing
OO software	OO-testing
Operating system	OS testing
Real-time software	Real-time testing
Requirements	Requirement testing
Software	Software testing
Web service	Web-service testing

Batch processing applications pose a special challenge in testing. Payroll processing in organization and student record processing in academic institutions are two examples of batch processing. Often these applications perform the same set of tasks on a large number of records, for example, an employee record or a student record. Using the notions of equivalence partitioning and other requirements-based test-generation techniques discussed in Chapter 2, one must first ensure that each record is processed correctly. In addition, one must test for performance under heavy load which can be done using load testing. While testing a batch-processing application, it is also important to include an oracle that will check the result of executing each test script. This oracle might be a part of the test script itself. It could, for example, query the contents of a database after performing an operation that is intended to change the status of the database.

Sometimes an application might not be batch-processing application, but a number of tests may need to be run in a batch. An embedded application, such as a cardiac pacemaker is where there is a need to develop a set of tests that need to be run in a batch. Often organizations develop a specialized tool to run a set of tests as a batch. For example, the tests might be encoded as scripts. The tool takes each test script and applies the test to the application. In a situation like this, the tool must have facilities such as interrupt test, suspend test, resume test, check test status, and scheduling the batch test. IBM's WebSphere Studio is one of several tools available for the development and testing of batch-processing applications built using the J2EE environment.

1.18.5 Classifier C5: Test Process Models

Software testing can be integrated into the software development life cycle in a variety of ways. This leads to various models for the test process listed in Table 1.8. Some of the models are described in the following paragraphs.

Testing in the waterfall model: The waterfall model is one of the earliest, and least used, software life cycle models. Figure 1.23 shows the different phases in a development process based on the waterfall model. While verification and validation of documents produced in each phase is an essential activity, static as well as dynamic testing occurs toward the end of the process. Further, as the waterfall model requires adherence to an inherently sequential process, defects introduced in the early phases and discovered in the later phases could be costly to correct. There is very little iterative or incremental development when using the waterfall model.

Testing in the V-model: The V-model, as shown in Figure 1.24, explicitly specifies testing activities associated with each phase of the development

Table 1.8 Classification of techniques for testing computer software. Classifier C5: Test process models

Process	Attributes
Testing in waterfall model	Usually done toward the end of the development cycle
Testing in V-model	Explicitly specifies testing activities in each phase of the development cycle
Spiral testing	Applied to software increments, each increment might be a prototype that eventually leads to the application delivered to the customer. Proposed for evolutionary software development
Agile testing	Used in agile development methodologies such as eXtreme Programming (XP)
Test-driven development (TDD)	Requirements specified as tests

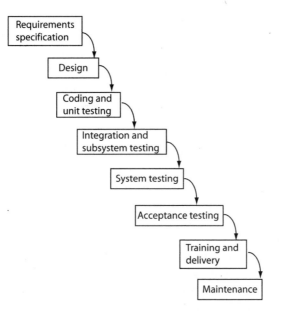

Fig. 1.23 Testing in the waterfall model. Arrows indicate the *flow* of documents from one to the next. For example, design documents are input to the coding phase. The waterfall nature of the flow led to the name of this model.

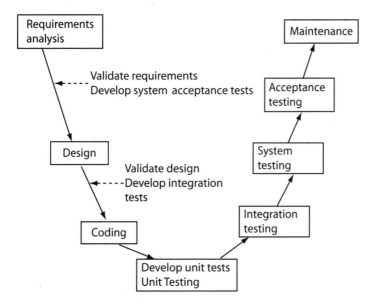

Fig. 1.24 Testing in the V-model.

cycle. These activities begin from the start and continue until the end of the life cycle. The testing activities are carried out in parallel with the development activities. Note that the V-model consists of the same development phases as in the waterfall model, the visual layout and an explicit specification of the test activities are the key differentiators. It is also important to note that test design begins soon after the requirements are available.

Spiral testing: The term *spiral testing* is not to be confused with spiral model, though they both are similar in that both can be visually represented as a spiral of activities as in Figure 1.25. The spiral model is a generic model that can be used to derive process models such as the waterfall model, the V-model, and the incremental development model. While testing is a key activity in the spiral model, spiral testing refers to a test strategy that can be applied to any incremental software development process, especially where a prototype evolves into an application. In spiral testing, the sophistication of test activities increases with the stages of an evolving prototype.

In the early stages, when a prototype is used to evaluate how an application must evolve, one focuses on test planning. The focus at this stage is on how testing will be performed in the remainder of the project. Subsequent iterations refine the prototype based on a more precise set of requirements. Further test planning takes place and unit and integration tests are performed. In the final stage, when the requirements are well defined, testers focus on system and acceptance testing. Note that all test-generation techniques described in this book are applicable in the spiral testing paradigm. Note from Figure 1.25 that

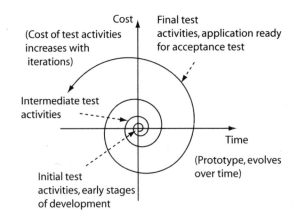

Fig. 1.25   A visual representation of spiral testing. Test activities evolve over time and with the prototype. In the final iteration, the application is available for system and acceptance testing.

the cost of the testing activities (vertical axis) increases with subsequent iterations.

Agile testing: This is a name given to a test process that is rarely well defined. One way to define it is to specify what agile testing involves in addition to the usual steps such as test planning, test design, and test execution. Agile testing promotes the following ideas: (a) include testing-related activities throughout a development project starting from the requirements phase, (b) work collaboratively with the customer who specifies requirements in terms of tests, (c) testers and developers must collaborate with each other rather than serve as adversaries, and (d) test often and in small chunks.

While there exist a variety of models for the test process, the test-generation and adequacy techniques described in this book are applicable to all. Certainly, focus on test process is an important aspect of the management of any software development process.

The next example illustrates how some of the different types of testing techniques can be applied to test the same piece of software. The techniques so used can be easily classified using one or more of the classifiers described above.

Example 1.32: Consider a Web service W to be tested. When executed, W converts a given value of temperature from one scale to another, for example from Fahrenheit scale to the Celsius scale. Regardless of the technique used for test generation, we can refer to the testing of W as Web-services testing. This reference uses the C4 classifier to describe the type of testing.

Next, let us examine various types of test-generation techniques that could be used for testing W. First, suppose that tester A tests W by supplying sample inputs and checking the outputs. No specific method is used to generate the inputs. Using classifier C1, we say that A has performed black-box testing and used an ad hoc, or exploratory method for test-data generation. Using classifier C2 we can say that A has performed unit testing on W, assuming that W is a unit of a larger application. Given that W has a GUI to interface with a user, we can use classifier C3 and say that A has performed GUI testing.

Now suppose that another tester B writes a set of formal specifications for W using the Z notation. The tester generates, and uses, tests from the specification. In this case, again using classifier C1, we say that tester B has performed black-box testing and used a set of specification-based algorithms for test-data generation.

Let us assume that we have a smarter tester C who generates tests using the formal specifications for W. C then tests W and evaluates the code coverage using one of the several code-coverage criteria. C finds that the code coverage is not 100%, that is, some parts of the code inside W have remained uncovered, that is untested, by the tests generated using the formal specification. C then generates and runs additional tests with the objective of exercising the uncovered portions of W. We say that C has performed both black-box and white-box testing. C has used specification-based test generation and enhanced the tests so generated to satisfy some control-flow-based code-coverage criteria.

Now suppose that tester D tests W as a component of a larger application. Tester D does not have access to the code for W and hence uses only its interface, and interface mutation, to generate tests. Using classifier C1 we say that tester D has performed black-box testing and used interface mutation to generate tests (also see Exercise 1.20).

It should be obvious from the above example that simply using one classifier to describe a test technique might not provide sufficient information regarding details of the testing performed. To describe the set of testing techniques used to test any software object, one must clearly describe the following.

1. Test-generation methods used; number of tests generated; number of tests run; number of tests failed, and number of tests passed.
2. Test adequacy assessment criteria used; results of test assessment stated in quantitative terms.
3. Test enhancement: number of additional tests generated based on the outcome adequacy assessment; number of additional tests run; number of additional failures discovered.

Note that test generation, adequacy assessment, and enhancement must be treated as a set of integrated activities. It is the sophistication of these activities, and their execution, that constitutes one important determinant of the quality of the delivered product.

1.19 THE SATURATION EFFECT

The saturation effect is an abstraction of a phenomenon observed during the testing of complex software systems. We refer to Figure 1.26 to understand this important effect. The horizontal axis in the figure refers to the test effort that increases over time. The test effort can be measured as, for example, the number of test cases executed or total person days

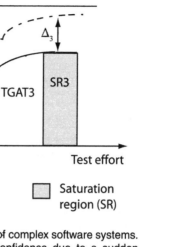

Fig. 1.26 The saturation effect observed during testing of complex software systems. Asterisk (*) indicates the point of drop in confidence due to a sudden increase in failures found; TGAT stands for test-generation and assesment techniques.

spent during the test and debug phase. The vertical axis refers to the true reliability (solid lines) and the confidence in the correct behavior (dotted lines) of the application under test. Note that the application under test evolves with an increase in test effort due to error correction.

The vertical axis can also be labeled as the *cumulative count of failures* that are observed over time, that is, as the test effort increases. The error correction process usually removes the cause of one or more failures. However, as the test effort increases, additional failures may be found that causes the cumulative failure count to increase though it saturates as shown in the figure.

1.19.1 CONFIDENCE AND TRUE RELIABILITY

Confidence in Figure 1.26 refers to the confidence of the test manager in the true reliability of the application under test. An estimate of reliability, obtained using a suitable statistical method, can be used as a measure of confidence. Reliability in the figure refers to the probability of failure-free operation of the application under test in its intended environment. The true reliability differs from the estimated reliability in that the latter is an estimate of the application reliability obtained by using one of the many statistical methods. A 0 indicates lowest possible confidence and a 1 the highest possible confidence. Similarly, a 0 indicates the lowest possible true reliability and a 1 the highest possible true reliability.

1.19.2 Saturation Region

Now suppose that application A is in the system test phase. The test team needs to generate tests, encapsulate them into appropriate scripts, set up the test environment, and run A against the tests. Let us assume that the tests are generated using a suitable test generation method (referred to as TGAT1 in Figure 1.26) and that each test either passes or fails. Each failure is analyzed and fixed, perhaps by the development team, if it is determined that A must not be shipped to the customer without fixing the cause of this failure. Whether the failure is fixed soon after it is detected or later does not concern us in this discussion.

The true reliability of A, with respect to the operational profile used in testing, increases as errors are removed. Certainly, the true reliability could decrease in cases where fixing an error introduces additional errors—a case that we ignore in this discussion. If we measure the test effort as the combined effort of testing, debugging, and fixing the errors, the true reliability increases as shown in Figure 1.26 and eventually saturates, that is stops increasing. Thus, regardless of the number of tests generated, and given the set of tests generated using TGAT1, the true reliability stops increasing after a certain amount of test effort has been spent. This saturation in the true reliability is shown in Figure 1.26 as the shaded region labeled SR1. Inside SR1, the true reliability remains constant while the test effort increases.

No new faults are found and fixed in the saturation region. Thus, the saturation region is indicative of wasted test effort under the assumption that A contains faults not detected while the test phase is in the saturation region.

1.19.3 False Sense of Confidence

The discovery and fixing of previously undiscovered faults might increase our confidence in the reliability of A. It also increases the true reliability of A. However, in the saturation region when the expenditure of test effort does not reveal new faults, the true reliability of A remains unchanged though our confidence is likely to increase due to a lack of observed failures. While in some cases this increase in confidence might be justified, in others it is a false sense of confidence.

This false sense of confidence is due to the lack of discovery of new faults, which in turn is due to the inability of the tests generated using TGAT1 to exercise the application code in ways significantly different from what has already been exercised. Thus, in the saturation region, the robust states of the application are being exercised, perhaps repeatedly, whereas the faults lie in other states.

Δ_1 in Figure 1.26 is a measure of the deviation from the true reliability of A and a test manager's confidence in the correctness of A. While one might suggest that Δ_1 can be estimated given an estimate of the confidence and the true reliability, in practice it is difficult to arrive at such an estimate due to the fuzzy nature of the confidence term. Hence, we must seek a quantitative metric that replaces human confidence.

1.19.4 REDUCING Δ

Empirical studies reveal that every single test generation method has its limitations in that the resulting test set is unlikely to detect all faults in an application. The more complex an application, the more unlikely it is that tests generated using any given method will detect all faults. This is one of the prime reasons why testers use, or must use, multiple techniques for test generation.

Suppose now that a black-box test generation method is used to generate tests. For example, one might express the expected behavior of A using a finite-state model and generate tests from the model as described in Chapter 3. Let us denote this method as TGAT1 and the test set so generated as T1.

Now suppose that after having completed the test process using T1 we check how much of the code in A has been exercised. There are several ways to perform this check, and suppose that we use a control-flow-based criterion, such as the modified condition/decision coverage (MC/DC) criterion described in Chapter 6. It is likely that T1 is inadequate with respect to the MC/DC criterion. Thus, we enhance T1 to generate T2, which is adequate with respect to the MC/DC criterion and T1 $\subset$ T2. We refer to this second method of test generation as TGAT2.

Enhancement of tests based on feedback received from adequacy assessment leads to tests that are guaranteed to move A to at least a few states that were never covered when testing using T1. This raises the possibility of detecting faults that might lie in the newly covered states. In the event a failure occurs as a consequence of executing A against one or more tests in T2, the confidence exhibits a dip while the true reliability increases, assuming that the fault that caused the failure is removed and none introduced. Nevertheless, the true reliability once again reaches the saturation region, this time SR2.

The process described above for test enhancement can be now repeated using a different and perhaps a more powerful test adequacy criterion. The new test-generation and assessment technique is referred to in Figure 1.26 as TGAT3. The test set generated due to enhancement is T3 and T2 $\subset$ T3. Once again we observe a dip in confidence, an increase in the true reliability, and eventually entry into the saturation region—SR3 in this case. Note that it is not always necessary that enhancement of a test set using an adequacy criteria will lead to a larger test set. It is certainly possible that T1 = T2 or that T2 = T3. However, this is unlikely to happen in a large application.

Theoretically, the test-generation and enhancement procedure described above can proceed almost forever, especially when the input domain is astronomical in size. In practice, however, the process must terminate so that the application can be released. Regardless of when the application is released, it is likely that $\Delta > 0$ implying that while the confidence may be close to the true reliability, it is unlikely to be equal.

1.19.5 Impact on Test Process

A knowledge and appreciation of the saturation effect are likely to be of value to any test team while designing and implementing a test process. Given that any method for the construction of functional tests is likely to lead to a test set that is inadequate with respect to code-based coverage criteria, it is important that tests be assessed for their goodness.

Various goodness measures are discussed in Chapters 6 and 7. It is some code-coverage criterion that leads to saturation shown in Figure 1.26. For example, execution of additional tests might not lead to the coverage of any uncovered conditions. Enhancing tests using one or more code-based coverage criteria is likely to help in moving out of a saturation region.

As the assessment of the goodness of tests does not scale well with the size of the application, it is important that this be done incrementally and using the application architecture. This aspect of test assessment is also covered in Chapters 6 and 7.

Summary

In this chapter, we have presented some basic concepts and terminology very likely to be encountered by any tester. The chapter begins with a brief introduction to errors and the reason for testing. A chapter in Volume II examines this topic in detail. Next we define input domain, also known as input space, as an essential source of test cases needed to test any program. The notions of correctness, reliability, and operational profiles are dealt with in subsequent section.

Testing requires the generation and specification of tests. Section 1.5 covers this topic in some detail. The interaction between testing and debugging is also explained in this section. The IEEE standard for the specification of tests is covered in Section 1.5.

CFGs represent the flow of control in a program. These graphs find use in program analysis. Many test tools transform a program into its CFG for the purpose of analysis. Section 1.14 explains what a CFG is and how to construct one.

Model-based testing is explained in Section 1.11. A growing number of organizations are resorting to model-based testing for various reasons, two of them being the desire for high quality and automation of the test-generation process. All of Part II of this book is devoted to model-based testing.

Sections 1.17 covers concepts and definitions essential to the understanding of material presented in subsequent chapters and in chapters in Volume II of the book.

Section 1.18 presents a framework for classifying a large number of testing techniques. The classification also helps to understand what lies at the foundation of software testing. Our view is that test generation, assessment, and enhancement lies at the foundation of software testing. It is this foundation that is the focus of the book you are holding. We hope that the material in this section will help you understand the complex relationship between various testing techniques and their use in different test scenarios.

Finally, Section 1.19 introduces an important observation from large-scale test processes. This observation, named as the saturation effect, might lead to a false sense of confidence in application reliability. Hence, it is important to understand the saturation effect, its impact on software reliability, and ways to overcome its shortcomings.

BIBLIOGRAPHIC NOTES

Early work: As an activity, software testing is as old as software. Programs came hand-in-hand with programmable computers and so did testing. Early work on testing of computer programs includes that of Gill [169] and Miller and Maloney [329]. Gill suggested ways to use hardware features to check computer programs on the EDSAC computer. Miller and Maloney proposed a systematic method for the analysis of programs and generation of test data.They proposed that all interactions among the branches must be tested and that each loop must be traversed at least once and entered from every possible point in the program. Thus, Miller and Maloney laid the foundation for the path-oriented test adequacy criteria discussed in Chapter 6.

Graph models: The application of graph theoretical tools to represent programs was proposed by Karp [253] and a slightly modified version used by Miller and Maloney [329]. Subsequently, several other researchers proposed testing techniques and path-oriented test completeness criteria [175, 233, 383, 405]. Concepts used in the construction of CFGs are found in most books on compilers including the classic *dragon book* by Aho *et al.* [16].

Dominators and postdominators are standard concepts covered in almost every course in compilers. A simple algorithm for computing dominators in a flow graph appears on page 671 in a book by Aho *et al.* [17]. A faster algorithm was developed by Lengauer and Tarjan [286] and is explained in detail by Appel [26]. Buchsbaum *et al.* reported an

implementation of a linear time algorithm for computing dominators in a CFG [60]. Note that the postdominators, needed for computing control dependences in a PDG, can be computed by applying the dominators algorithm to the reverse flow graph.

Software testing discipline: Software testing as a discipline is relatively new. A pioneering publication on software testing by Elmendorf appeared in 1969. Elmendorf introduced the notion of systematic testing through cause–effect graphs [140]. This technique was applied to the testing of an operating system. Three early books on software testing are by Hetzel [216], Miller and Howden [328], and Myers [340]. Software quality attributes have been defined by several researchers such as Boehm, Brown, and Lipow [53], McCall, Richards, and Walters [323], and Adrion, Barnstad, and Cherniavsky [4]. Quality attributes for software requirements have been proposed by Moreira, Araújo, and Brito [333], and others.

Another piece of early work related to the testing of operating systems appeared in a publication by Brinch Hansen describing the testing of a multiprogramming system [194]. In this paper, Hansen describes a test method and a mechanism to test the experimental OS for the RC 4000 computer. Test cases were created to test the multiplexing mechanism of RC 4000. The notions of a test case, test output, and incremental testing are all evident in Hansen's work. It is also interesting to note that the program being tested was written after the test mechanism had been selected. Hansen's work seems to indicate that Naur had made use of simple and systematic testing techniques in the testing of the Gier Algol compiler [347].

Terminology: The terms error, defect, fault, and failure are defined in the ANSI/IEEE standard on Software Engineering Terminology [243]. The ANSI/IEEE standard on Software Test Documentation [452] details formats for writing test specifications and test plans. ANSI/IEEE standards for unit testing appear in ANSI/IEEE Std 1008–1987 [242]. Prior to standardization, and even now during informal conversations, the term bug was used instead of, or in addition to, error, defect, or fault (see Figure 1 in [405]). The term bug has been in use since long, though it shot into prominence after Rear Admiral Dr. Grace Murray Hopper used it in one of the moth-related incidents at Harvard University in 1945.

A number of studies have analyzed programmer errors, both syntactic and semantic [54, 133, 206, 208, 263, 294, 418, 427, 492, 541]. Some of these studies are discussed in Volume 2. The T experiments by Hatton is specially significant in that it is a large scale study involving about 5 million lines of scientific software written in Fortran and C languages and report faults and failures [207].

Test generation: Howden proposed a methodology for the generation of test data and propounded the notion of test completeness through boundary-interior testing [233]. Goodenough and Gerhart wrote a remarkable paper paving the way for a theory of test-data selection [174–176]. They formalized the notion of test completeness through the notions of reliable and valid test-selection criteria.

They also analyzed a published, and proven-correct, text formatter program by Naur [348]. The analysis revealed seven errors and problems with Naur's program and added evidence to the belief that testing and verification are complementary activities and that proving a program correct does not necessarily mean that the program is indeed correct. The debate on testing versus proofs of correctness is highly recommended reading for all testers [120, 121, 162, 239, 257].

Oracles: Construction of program oracles is an important and difficult problem in software testing. Several techniques have been reported for the construction of oracles from specifications. Peters and Parnas have proposed an approach to generate oracles from program documentation [393]. The documentation itself is formal and created using LD-relations described by the authors. Memon and Qing have proposed a technique to construct oracles for event-driven systems, that is systems for which a test case consists of a sequence of events as inputs [326]. McDonald *et al.* [324] describe tool support to generate passive C++ oracles from formal specifications written in Object-Z [451].

A significant research effort has been devoted to model checking. While this book does not deal with model checking, several excellent books and references are available. An introductory book on model checking illustrated with examples is by Clarke *et al.* [92]. The popular SPIN model is described in a book by Holzmann [222].

We have mentioned several testing techniques in Section 1.18. Beizer's book is

BIBLIOGRAPHIC NOTES

a good compendium on various testing techniques [35]. Almost every technique mentioned in Section 1.18 is covered by Beizer though in varying detail and focus. Juristo *et al.* also present a classification of testing techniques [249]. They provide seven distinct families where each family contains one or more testing techniques. For example, *functional testing* is a family consisting of equivalence partitioning and boundary-value analysis as two techniques. In addition to providing a classification of testing techniques, Juristo *et al.* also report a critical examination of various empirical studies of the effectiveness and complexity of various testing techniques.

Metrics: A significant amount of research has gone into the definition and evaluation of metrics. The popular cyclomatic complexity is due to McCabe [322]. Baker and Zweben compared various measures of software complexity [27]. Halstead's software science metrics are described in detail, with examples, in an excellent book by Conte *et al.* [104]. The formula in Section 1.6.4 for the estimate of the number of errors found during software development is due to Schneider [436]. Halstead's software science metrics have been controversial [549]. Kavi and Jackson report a study that examined the impact of counting declarations on metrics [255].

Weyuker has proposed a set of properties against which to evaluate metrics derived from program syntax [508]. Gustafson and Prasad have also examined properties of software metrics [186]. Chidamber and Kemerer proposed a set of complexity metrics for object-oriented designs known as the CK metrics [81]. Voas proposed a dynamic testing

complexity metric, named revealing ability, based on a program's ability to hide faults related to semantic mutants [487]. A semantic mutant is created by making a state change during program execution, a technique different from that used to create syntactic mutants described in Chapter 7.

Chidamber *et al.* have also described managerial uses of OO metrics [80]. Darcy and Kemerer report the application of a subset of the CK metrics to various commercial software. They also list a set of commercially available tools to collect OO metrics for C++, Java, and Visual Basic. Metrics are now in wide use at all levels within organizations. Natwick, for example, describes the use of metrics at Harris Corporation in the context of the Capability Maturity Model® [346].

Xu *et al.* propose a process model for implementing CMMI-based process metrics in an organization [536]. Li offers a tutorial on product metrics [291]. Kan *et al.* describe in-process metrics for testing [250]. They report on the usefulness of in-process metrics in testing observed at IBM Rochester AS/400® software development laboratory. Rosenberg *et al.* investigate the relation between requirements, testing, and metrics [420].

A number of empirical studies investigated the predictive ability of metrics. Basili *et al.* studied the correlation between OO metrics and software quality [32]. Nagappan *et al.* report on early estimation of software quality using in-process testing metrics [342]. Li and Henry investigated the ability to predict maintenance effort using OO metrics [292].

Test process: Several basic terms and concepts related to the software test process are mentioned in this chapter. The concept of spiral testing was proposed by Davis [109] in the context of prototyping-based application development. Manhart and Schneider [306] describe the use of agile processes and testing in a commercial development project at Daimler-Chrysler. A number of tools and processes exist for defect management. Chillarege *et al.* report Orthogonal Defect Classification (ODC), a popular method for defect classification. Krawczyk and Wiszniewski have reported a defect classification scheme for parallel programs [273]. Li *et al.* report experience with defect prediction techniques [290] at ABB. Biffl has compared various defect estimation models [47]. Grossman *et al.* [183]. report experience with eXtreme Programming (XP) and agile development in a Web development environment. Müller and Padberg [335] report an economic evaluation of XP projects.

Testability: The definition of testability in this chapter is from an IEEE glossary of terms [244]. Several studies report ways to measure testability of a software product. Voas defined a dynamic complexity metric for testability analysis [487] and a tool to estimate it [488]. Voas and Miller provide a slightly different definition of testability than given earlier in this chapter [489]. According to Voas and Miller, "software testability is the tendency of code to reveal existing faults during random testing." Based on this definition, they suggest ways to improve the software development process. Voas and Miller have also discussed testability and verification [490].

Bieman and Yin suggest improving testability through the use of automated oracles [46]. Yin and Bieman show how to improve testability with the help of assertions [540]. A National Institute of Standards and Technology (NIST) report discusses testability of OO systems [351].

A significant amount of research has been devoted to the definition and improvement of testability of hardware designs. Keiner *et al.* have proposed testability measures for hardware designs. Trischler provides an overview of design for testability (DFT) and automatic test pattern generation [477]. Raik *et al.* describe a way to calculate testability measures and a procedure for testability-guided generation of test patterns [403]. Ockunzzi and Papachristou describe how to improve testability of circuits that exhibit control-flow behaviors such as that implied by if-then-else and looping constructs [356]. Vranken *et al.* discuss ways to arrive at techniques for DFT that apply to both hardware and software designs [136].

Hardware testing: This is a very well developed field. A number of books cover principles and techniques of VLSI testing [500, 548]. Abraham and Fuchs provide an easy-to-read tutorial on fault models for VLSI [2]. The issue of fault coverage and requirements in VLSI testing is covered, among several others, by Agrawal *et al.* [13].

Saturation effect: The saturation effect was formulated as described in the chapter by Horgan and Mathur (Chapter 13 in [227]). This description is in the context of an analysis of the shortcomings of the theory of reliability estimation based exclusively on estimated operational profiles. Ramamoorthy *et al.* have also observed a similar behavior of error detection and failure saturation during their experiments with an automated software evaluation system [405].

Schick and Wolverton have reported an error reduction similar to the one in Figure 1.26, where they show that errors found reduce to almost zero and increase when a new test phase begins [435]. Wood *et al.* compared code reading, functional testing using equivalence partitioning and boundary-value analysis, and branch coverage[526]. They observed that " . . . these techniques are consistently more effective when used in combination with each other." Several empirical studies have demonstrated the existence of the saturation effect [372, 373].

EXERCISES

1.1 The following statement is often encountered: "It is impossible to test a program completely." Discuss the context in which this statement is true. Under what definition of *completely* is the statement true? (Note: Try answering this question now and return to it after having read Chapter 6.)

1.2 Describe at least one case in which a *perceived* incorrect behavior of a product is not due to an error in the product.

1.3 How many years will it take to test max exhaustively on a computer that takes 1 ps ($=10^{-12}$s) to input a pair of integers and execute max?

1.4 It is required to develop a strategy to test whether a joke is excellent, good, or poor. What strategy would you propose? Would statistical techniques be useful in joke categorization?

1.5 Estimate the reliability of P of Example 1.9 given that (a) the input pair (0, 0) appears with probability 0.6 and the remaining two pairs appear with probability 0.2 each and (b) P fails on the input $(-1, 1)$.

1.6 According to the ANSI/IEEE Std 729-1983, is it possible for a program to have a reliability of 1.0 even when it is infected with a number of defects? Explain your answer.

1.7 Suppose that the sort program in Example 1.10 is known to fail with probability 0.9 when alphanumeric strings are input and that it functions correctly on all numeric inputs. Find the reliability of sort with respect to the two operational profiles in Example 1.10.

1.8 Suggest one possible coding of sort that will lead to the behavior given in Example 1.6.

1.9 Consider a Web site that allows its visitors to search for items in a database using arbitrary search strings. Suppose we focus our attention only on three operations allowed by this site: search, previous, and next. To invoke the search operation, a search string is typed and a Go button clicked. When the search results are displayed, the Previous and Next buttons show up and may be clicked to move to the next or the previous page of search results. Describe how an oracle will determine whether the three functions of the Web site are implemented correctly. Can this oracle be automated?

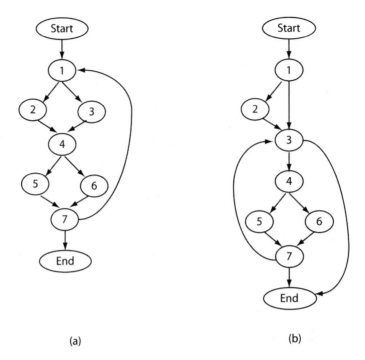

Fig. 1.27   CFGs for Exercise 1.11.

1.10 (a) Calculate the length of the path traversed when program P1.3 in Section 1.14.3 (Example 1.27) is executed on an input sequence containing N integers. (b) Suppose that the statement on line 8 of Program P1.3 is replaced by the following.

```
if(num>0)product = product*num;
```

Calculate the number of distinct paths in the modified Program P1.3 if the length of the input sequence can be 0, 1, or 2. (c) For an input sequence of length N, what is the maximum length of the path traversed by the modified Program P1.3?

1.11 Construct the dominator and postdominator trees for the CFG in Figure 1.16 and for each of the CFGs in Figure 1.27.

1.12 Let $pred(n)$ be the set of all predecessors of node n in a CFG $G = (N, E)$. The set of dominators of n can be computed using the following equations:

$$Dom(\texttt{Start}) = \{\texttt{Start}\}$$

$$Dom(n) = \{n\} \cup \{ \bigcap_{p \in pred(n)} Dom(p) \}$$

Using the above equation, develop an algorithm to compute the dominators of each node in *N*. *(Note: There exist several algorithms for computing the dominators and postdominators in a CFG. Try developing your own and then study the algorithms in relevant citations under the heading Bibliographic Notes).*

1.13 (a) Compute the cyclomatic complexity of the CFG in Figure 1.16. (b) Prove that for CFGs of structured programs, the cyclomatic complexity is the number of conditions plus one. A structured program is one that uses only single entry and single exit constructs. GOTO statements are not allowed in a structured program.

1.14 For the two Programs P1.2 and P1.3, compute Halstead's software science metrics. Discuss the relative complexity of the two programs using the metrics you have computed. Note the following while computing the software science metrics: (i) each token in a program, excluding semicolon (;) and braces, is to be considered either as an operator or an operand, and (ii) each declaration keyword is an operator and the variable declared an operand. Thus, for example, keywords such as `if` and `else`, and function calls, are operators and so are the traditional arithmetic and relational symbols such as < and +.

1.15 Consider two applications A_1 and A_2. Suppose that the testability of these applications is measured using a static complexity measure such as the cyclomatic complexity. Now suppose that the cyclomatic complexity of both applications is the same. Construct an example to show that despite the same cyclomatic complexity the testability of A_1 and A_2 might differ significantly. *(Hint: Think of embedded applications.)*

1.16 Consider a two-input NAND gate in Figure 1.11(a) with the following faults: (i) input A stuck at 0 and output O stuck at 1, (ii) input A stuck at 0 and output O stuck at 0, (iii) inputs A and B stuck at 1, (iv) inputs A and B stuck at 1, and (v) input A stuck at 1 and B stuck at 0. For each of the five cases enumerated above, does there exist a test vector that reveals that the gate is faulty?

1.17 (a) Modify the dependence graph in Figure 1.20 by adding nodes corresponding to the declarations at lines 2 and 3 in Program P1.3 and the corresponding dependence edges. (b) Can you offer a reason why for Program P1.3 the addition of nodes corresponding to the declarations is redundant? (c) Under what condition would it be useful to add nodes corresponding to declarations to the data-dependence graph?

1.18 Construct a PDG for the exponentiation Program P1.2 in Section 1.14.1 (Example 1.23).

1.19 Why would tests designed for testing a component of a system might not be usable during system test?

1.20 Company X is renowned for making state-of-the-art steam boilers. The latest model of gas- or oil-fired boiler comes with a boiler control package that is being marketed as an ultra-reliable piece of software. The package provides software for precise control of various boiler parameters such as combustion. The package has a user-friendly GUI to help with setting the appropriate control parameters. Study the following description and identify the test techniques used.

When contacted, the company revealed that the requirements for portions of the entire package were formally specified using the statechart graphical notation. The remaining portions were specified using the Z notation. Several test teams were assembled to test each component of the package.

The GUI test team's responsibility was to ensure that the GUI functions correctly and is user-friendly. The statechart and the Z specification served as a source of tests for the entire system. The tests generated from these specifications were assessed for adequacy using the MC/DC control-flow-based coverage criterion. New tests were added to ensure that all feasible conditions were covered and the MC/DC criterion was satisfied. In addition to the tests generated from formal and graphical specifications, one test team used combinatorial designs to generate tests that would exercise the software for a variety of combinations of input parameters.

Individual components of the package were tested separately prior to integration. For each component, tests were designed using the traditional techniques of equivalence partitioning and boundary-value analysis. Cause–effect graphing was used for some components. System test was performed with the help of tests generated.

1.21 List a few reasons that underlie the existence of the saturation effect.

Part II

Test
GENERATION

Generation of test inputs and the corresponding expected outputs is an essential activity in any test organization. The input data and the corresponding expected output are wedded into a test case. A collection of test data becomes a test set or a test suite.

There exist a wide range of guidelines, techniques, and supporting tools to generate test cases. On one extreme, these include guidelines such as the use of boundary-value analysis, while on the other there exist techniques for generating test data from formal specifications such as those specified in the Z notation. In addition, there are test-generation techniques that rely exclusively on the code under test and generate tests that satisfy some code-coverage criteria.

Chapters in this part of the book bring to you a varied collection of guidelines and techniques for the generation of test sets. While some techniques presented herein are widely applicable, such as equivalence partitioning, others such as test generation from finite automata find uses in specific domains.

2

Test
Generation
from
Requirements

CONTENT ▪▪

The purpose of this chapter is to introduce techniques for the generation of test data from informally and formally specified requirements. Some of these techniques can be automated while others may require significant manual effort for large applications. Most techniques presented here fall under the category "black-box" testing in that tests are generated without access to the code to be tested.

2.1 INTRODUCTION

Requirements serve as the starting point for the generation of tests. During the initial phases of development, requirements may exist only in the minds of one or more people. These requirements, more aptly ideas, are then specified rigorously using modeling elements such as use cases, sequence diagrams, and statecharts in UML. Rigorously specified requirements are often transformed into formal requirements using requirements specification languages such as Z, S, and RSML.

While a complete formal specification is a useful document, it is often the case that aspects of requirements are captured using appropriate modeling formalisms. For example, Petri nets and its variants are used for specifying timing and concurrency properties in a distributed system, timed input automata to specify timing constraints in a real-time system, and FSMs to capture state transitions in a protocol. UML is an interesting formalism in that it combines into a single framework several different notations used for rigorously and formally specifying requirements.

A requirement specification can thus be informal, rigorous, formal, or a mix of these three approaches. Usually, requirements of commercial applications are specified using a mix of the three approaches. In either case, it is the task of the tester, or a test team, to generate tests for the entire application regardless of the formalism in which the specifications are available. The more formal the specification, the higher are the chances of automating the test-generation process. For example, specifications using FSMs, timed automata, and Petri nets can be input to a programmed test generator and tests generated automatically. However, a significant manual effort is required when generating test cases from use cases.

Often, high-level designs are also considered as part of requirement specification. For example, high-level sequence and activity diagrams in UML are used for specifying interaction among high-level objects. Tests can also be generated from such high-level designs.

In this chapter we are concerned with the generation of tests from informal as well as rigorously specified requirements. These requirements serve as a source for the identification of the input domain of the application to be developed.

A variety of test-generation techniques are available to select a subset of the input domain to serve as test set against which the application will be tested.

Figure 2.1 lists the techniques described in this chapter. The figure shows requirements specification in three forms: informal, rigorous, and

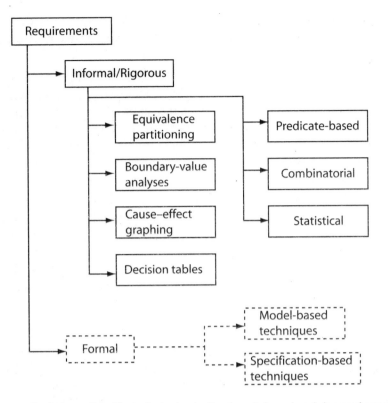

Fig. 2.1 Techniques listed here for test selection from informal and rigorously specified requirements are introduced in this chapter. Techniques from formally specified requirements using graphical models and logic-based languages are discussed in other chapters.

formal. The input domain is derived from the informal and rigorous specifications. The input domain then serves as a source for test selection. Various techniques listed in the figure are used to select a relatively small number of test cases from a usually very large input domain.

The remainder of this chapter describes each of the techniques listed in the figure. All techniques described here fall under the *black-box* testing category. However, some could be enhanced if the program code is available. Such enhancements are discussed in Part III of this book.

2.2 THE TEST-SELECTION PROBLEM

Let D denote the input domain of program p. The test-selection problem is to select a subset T of tests such that execution of p against each element of T will reveal all errors in p. In general, there does not exist any algorithm to construct such a test set. However, there are heuristics and model-based methods that can be used to generate tests that will reveal certain type of faults. The challenge is to construct a test set $T \subseteq D$ that will reveal as many errors in p as possible. As discussed below, the problem of test selection is difficult primarily because of the size and complexity of the input domain of p.

An input domain for a program is the set of all possible *legal* inputs that the program may receive during execution. The set of legal inputs is derived from the requirements. In most practical problems, the input domain is large, that is has many elements, and often complex, that is the elements are of different types such as integers, strings, reals, Boolean, and structures.

The large size of the input domain prevents a tester from exhaustively testing the program under test against all possible inputs. By exhaustive testing we mean testing the given program against every element in its input domain. The complexity makes it harder to select individual tests. The following two examples illustrate what is responsible for large and complex input domains.

Example 2.1: Consider program P that is required to sort a sequence of integers into ascending order. Assuming that P will be executed on a machine in which integers range from -32768 to 32767, the input domain of p consists of all possible sequences of integers in the range $[-32768, 32767]$.

If there is no limit on the size of the sequence that can be input, then the input domain of P is infinitely large and P can never be tested exhaustively. If the size of the input sequence is limited to, say $N > 1$, then the size of the input domain depends on the value of N. In general, denoting the size of the input domain by S, we get

$$S = \sum_{i=0}^{N} v^i$$

where v is the number of possible values each element of the input sequence may assume, which is 65536. Using the formula given above, one can easily verify that the size of the input domain for this simple sort program is enormously large even for small values of N. For small values of N, say $N = 3$, the size of the input space is large enough to prevent exhaustive testing.

Example 2.2: Consider a procedure P in a payroll-processing system that takes an employee's record as input and computes the weekly salary. For simplicity, assume that the employee's record consists of the following items with their respective types and constraints:

ID: `int`;   ID is three-digit long from 001 to 999.

name: `string`;   name is 20-character long; each character belongs to the set of 26 letters and a space character.

rate: `float`;   rate varies from $5 to $10 per hour; rates are in multiples of a quarter.

hoursWorked: `int`;   `hoursWorked` varies from 0 to 60.

Each element of the input domain of P is a record that consists of four items listed above. This domain is large as well as complex. Given that there are 999 possible values of ID, 27^{20} possible character strings representing names, 21 hourly pay rates, and 61 possible work hours, the number of possible records is

$$999 \times 27^{20} \times 21 \times 61 \approx 5.42 \times 10^{34}.$$

Once again, we have a huge input domain that prevents exhaustive testing. Note that the input domain is large primarily because of the large number of possible names that represent strings and the combinations of the values of different fields.

For most useful software, the input domains are even larger than the ones in the examples given above. Further, in several cases, it is often difficult to even characterize the complete input domain due to relationships between the inputs and timing constraints. Thus, there is a need to use methods that will allow a tester to be able to select a much smaller subset of the input domain for the purpose of testing a given program. Of course, as we will learn in this book, each test-selection method has its strengths and weaknesses.

2.3 EQUIVALENCE PARTITIONING

Test selection using equivalence partitioning allows a tester to subdivide the input domain into a relatively small number of subdomains, say $N > 1$, as shown in Figure 2.2(a). In strict mathematical terms, the subdomains by definition are disjoint. The four subsets shown in Figure 2.2(a) constitute a partition of the input domain while the subsets in Figure 2.2(b) are not. Each subset is known as an *equivalence class*.

The equivalence classes are created assuming that the program under test exhibits the same behavior on all elements, that is tests, within a

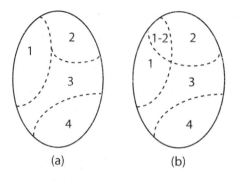

Fig. 2.2   Four equivalence classes created from an input domain. (a) Equivalence classes together constitute a partition as they are disjoint. (b) Equivalence classes are not disjoint and do not form a partition. 1–2 indicates the region where subsets 1 and 2 overlap. This region contains test inputs that belong to subsets 1 and 2.

class. This assumption allows a tester to select exactly one test from each equivalence class, resulting in a test suite of exactly *N* tests.

Of course, there are many ways to partition an input domain into equivalence classes. Hence, the set of tests generated using the equivalence partitioning technique is not unique. Even when the equivalence classes created by two testers are identical, the testers might select different tests. The fault-detection effectiveness of the tests so derived depends on the tester's experience in test generation, familiarity with the requirements, and when the code is available, familiarity with the code itself. In most situations, equivalence partitioning is used as one of the several test-generation techniques.

2.3.1 Faults Targeted

The entire set of inputs to any application can be divided into at least two subsets: one containing all expected, (*E*) or legal, inputs and the other containing all unexpected, (*U*) or illegal, inputs. Each of the two subsets, *E* and *U*, can be further subdivided into subsets on which the application is required to behave differently. Equivalence class partitioning selects tests that target any faults in the application that cause it to behave incorrectly when the input is in either of the two classes or their subsets. Figure 2.3 shows a sample subdivision of all possible inputs to an application.

For example, consider an application *A* that takes an integer denoted by *age* as input. Let us suppose that the only legal values of *age* are in the range [1 . . . 120]. The set of input values is now divided into a set *E* containing all integers in the range [1 . . . 120] and a set *U* containing the remaining integers.

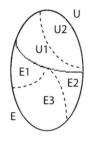

Fig. 2.3 Set of inputs partitioned into two regions one containing expected (*E*), or legal, and the other containing unexpected (*U*), or illegal, inputs. Regions *E* and *U* are further subdivided based on the expected behavior of the application under test. Representative tests, one from each region, is targeted at exposing faults that cause the application to behave incorrectly in their respective regions.

Furthermore, assume that the application is required to process all values in the range $[1 \ldots 61]$ in accordance with requirement R_1 and those in the range $[62 \ldots 120]$ according to requirement R_2. Thus, E is further subdivided into two regions depending on the expected behavior. Similarly, it is expected that all invalid inputs less than or equal to 1 are to be treated in one way while all greater than 120 are to be treated differently. This leads to a subdivision of U into two categories.

Tests selected using the equivalence partitioning technique aim at targeting faults in A with respect to inputs in any of the four regions, that is, two regions containing expected inputs and two regions containing the unexpected inputs. It is expected that any single test selected from the range $[1 \ldots 61]$ will reveal any fault with respect to R_1. Similarly, any test selected from the region $[62 \ldots 120]$ will reveal any fault with respect to R_2. A similar expectation applies to the two regions containing the unexpected inputs.

The effectiveness of tests generated using equivalence partitioning for testing application A is judged by the ratio of the number of faults these tests are able to expose to the total faults lurking in A. As is the case with any test-selection technique in software testing, the effectiveness of tests selected using equivalence partitioning is less than one for most practical applications. However, the effectiveness can be improved through an unambiguous and complete specification of the requirements and carefully selected tests using the equivalence partitioning technique described in the following sections.

2.3.2 Relations and Equivalence Partitioning

Recalling from our knowledge of sets, a relation is a set of n-ary-tuples. For example, a method `addList` that returns the sum of elements in a list of integers defines a binary relation. Each pair in this relation consists of a list and an integer that denotes the sum of all elements in the list. Sample pairs in this relation include ((1, 5), 6) and ((−3, 14, 3), 14), and (( ), 0). Formally, the relation computed by addList is defined as follows:

$$\text{addList}: \mathcal{L} \rightarrow \mathbb{Z}$$

where $\mathcal{L}$ is the set of all lists of integers and $\mathbb{Z}$ denotes the set of integers. Taking the example from the above paragraph as a clue, we can argue that every program, or method, defines a relation. Indeed, this is true provided the domain, that is the input set, and the range, that is the output set, are defined properly.

For example, suppose that the addList method has an error because of which it crashes when supplied with an empty list. In this case, even though addList is required to compute the relation defined in the above paragraph, it does not do so because of the error. However, it does compute the following relation:

$$\text{addList}: \mathcal{L} \rightarrow \mathbb{Z} \cup \{error\}$$

Relations that help a tester partition the input domain of a program are usually of the kind

$$R: \mathcal{I} \rightarrow \mathcal{I},$$

where $\mathcal{I}$ denotes the input domain. Relation R is on the input domain. It defines an *equivalence class* that is a subset of $\mathcal{I}$. The following examples illustrate several ways of defining R on the input domain.

Example 2.3: Consider a method gPrice that takes the name of a grocery item as input, consults a database of prices, and returns the unit price of this item. If the item is not found in the database, it returns with a message *Price information not available*.

The input domain of gPrice consists of names of grocery items that are of type string. Milk, Tomato, Yogurt, and Cauliflower are sample elements of the input domain. Obviously, there are many others. For this example, we assume that the price database is accessed through another method and hence is not included in the input domain of gPrice. We now define the following relation on the input domain of gPrice:

$$pFound: \mathcal{I} \rightarrow \mathcal{I}$$

The *pFound* relation associates elements t_1 and t_2 if gPrice returns a unit price for each of these two inputs. It also associates t_3 and t_4 if gPrice returns an error message on either of the two inputs. Now suppose that the price database is given as in the following table:

Item	Unit price
Milk	2.99
Tomato	0.99
Kellog Cornflakes	3.99

The inputs Milk, Tomato, and Kellog Cornflakes are related to each other through the relation *pFound*. For any of these inputs, gPrice is required to return the unit price. However, for input Cauliflower, and all other strings representing the name of a grocery item not on the list above, gPrice is required to return an error message. Arbitrarily constructed strings that do not name any grocery item belong to another equivalence class defined by *pFound*.

Any item that belongs to the database can be considered as a representative of the equivalence class. For example, Milk is a representative of one equivalence class denoted as [Milk] and Cauliflower is a representative of another equivalence class denoted as [Cauliflower].

Relation *pFound* defines equivalence classes, say *pF* and *pNF*, respectively. Each of these classes is a subset of the input domain $\mathcal{I}$ of gPrice. Together, these equivalence classes form a partition of the input domain $\mathcal{I}$ because $pF \cup pNF = \mathcal{I}$ and $pF \cap pNF = \emptyset$.

In the previous example, the input assumes discrete values such as Milk and Tomato. Further, we assumed that gPrice behaves in the same way for all valid values of the input. There may be situations where the behavior of the method under test depends on the value of the input that could fall into any of several categories, most of them being valid. The next example shows how, in such cases, multiple relations can be defined to construct equivalence classes.

Example 2.4: Consider an automatic printer testing application named pTest. The application takes the manufacturer and model of a printer as input and selects a test script from a list. The script is then executed to test the printer. Our goal is to test if the script selection part of the application is implemented correctly.

The input domain $\mathcal{I}$ of pTest consists of strings representing the printer manufacturer and model. If pTest allows textual input through a keyboard, then strings that do not represent any printer recognizable by pTest also belong to $\mathcal{I}$. However, if pTest provides a graphical user interface to select a printer, then $\mathcal{I}$ consists exactly of the strings offered in the pulldown menu.

The selected script depends on the type of the printer. For simplicity we assume that the following three types are considered: color inkjet (ci), color laserjet (cl), and color multifunction (cm). Thus, for example, if the input to pTest is *HP Deskjet 6840*, the script selected will be the one to test a color inkjet printer. The input domain of pTest consists of all possible strings, representing valid and invalid printer names. A valid printer name is one that exists in the database of printers used by pTest for the selection of scripts, while an invalid printer name is a string that does not exist in the database.

For this example, we define the following four relations on the input domain. The first three relations below correspond to the three printer categories while the fourth relation corresponds to an invalid printer name.

$$ci : \mathcal{I} \to \mathcal{I}$$
$$cl : \mathcal{I} \to \mathcal{I}$$
$$cm : \mathcal{I} \to \mathcal{I}$$
$$invP : \mathcal{I} \to \mathcal{I}$$

Each of the four relations above defines an equivalence class. For example, relation *cl* associates all color laserjet printers into one equivalence class and all other printers into another equivalence class. Thus, each of the four relations defines two equivalence classes for a total of eight equivalence classes. While each relation partitions the input domain of pTest into two equivalence classes, the eight classes overlap. Note that relation *invP* might be empty if pTest offers a list of printers to select from.

We can simplify our task of partitioning the input domain by defining a single equivalence relation *pCat* that partitions the input domain of pTest into four equivalence classes corresponding to the categories *ci*, *cl*, *cm*, and *invP*.

The example above shows that equivalence classes may not always form a partition of the input domain due to overlap. The implication of such an overlap on test generation is illustrated in the next subsection.

The two examples above show how to define equivalence classes based on the knowledge of requirements. In some cases the tester has access to both the program requirements and its code. The next example shows a few ways to define equivalence classes based on the knowledge of requirements and the program text.

Example 2.5: The wordCount method takes a word w and a filename f as input and returns the number of occurrences of w in the text contained in the file named f. An exception is raised if there is no file with name f. Using the partitioning method described in the examples above, we obtain the following equivalence classes:

E1: Consists of pairs (w, f), where w is a string and f denotes a file that exists.

E2: Consists of pairs (w, f), where w is a string and f denotes a file that does not exist.

Now suppose that the tester has access to the code for wordCount. The partial pseudo-code for wordCount is given below.

Program P2.1

```
1 begin
2   string w, f;
3   input (w, f);
4   if (¬ exists(f)) {raise exception; return(0)};
5   if (length(w)==0) return(0);
6   if (empty(f)) return(0);
7   return(getCount(w, f));
8 end
```

The code above contains eight distinct paths created by the presence of the three if statements. However, as each if statement could terminate the program, there are only six feasible paths. We can define a relation named *covers* that partitions the input domain of wordCount into six equivalence classes depending on which of the six paths is covered by a test case. These six equivalence classes are defined in the following table.

Equivalence class	w	f
E1	non-null	exists, nonempty
E2	non-null	does not exist
E3	non-null	exists, empty
E4	null	exists, nonempty
E5	null	does not exist
E6	null	exists, empty

We note that the number of equivalence classes without any knowledge of the program code is 2, whereas the number of equivalence classes derived with the knowledge of partial code is 6. Of course, an experienced tester is likely to derive the six equivalence classes given above, and perhaps more, even before the code is available (see Exercise 2.6).

In each of the examples above, we focused on the inputs to derive the equivalence relations and, hence, equivalence classes. In some cases the equivalence classes are based on the output generated by the program. For example, suppose that a program outputs an integer. It is worth asking: "Does the program ever generate a 0? What are the maximum and minimum possible values of the output?" These two questions lead to the following equivalence classes based on outputs:

E1: Output value v is 0.
E2: Output value v is the maximum possible.
E3: Output value v is the minimum possible.
E4: All other output values.

Based on the output equivalence classes, one may now derive equivalence classes for the inputs. Thus, each of the four classes given above might lead to one equivalence class consisting of inputs. Of course, one needs to carry out such output-based analysis only if there is sufficient reason to believe that it is likely to generate equivalence classes in the input domain that cannot be generated by analyzing the inputs and program requirements.

2.3.3 EQUIVALENCE CLASSES FOR VARIABLES

Tables 2.1 and 2.2 offer guidelines for partitioning variables into equivalence classes based on their type. The examples given in the table are assumed to be derived from the application requirements. As explained in the following section, these guidelines are used while deriving equivalence classes from the input domain of an entire application that uses several input variables. Below we discuss the entries listed in Tables 2.1 and 2.2.

Range: A range may be specified implicitly or explicitly. For example, the value of *speed* is in the explicitly specified range [60...90] whereas the range for the values of *area* is specified implicitly. In the former case, one can identify values outside of the range. In the case of *area*, even though it is possible to identify values outside of the range, it may be impossible to input these values to the application because of representational constraints imposed by the underlying hardware and software of the machine on which the application is being tested.

The range for the values of *age* has also been specified implicitly. However, if, for example, *age* represents the age of an employee in a payroll-processing application, then the tester must be able to identify the range of values from the knowledge of the semantics of *age*. In this case, *age* cannot be less than 0, and 120 is a reasonable upper limit. The

Table 2.1 Guidelines for generating equivalence classes for variables: range and strings

Kind	Equivalence classes	Example	
		Constraint	Class representatives[a]
Range	One class with values inside the range and two with values outside the range	$speed \in [60 \dots 90]$	$\{\{50\}\downarrow, \{75\}\uparrow,$ $\{92\}\downarrow\}$
		$area$:float; $area \geq 0$	$\{\{-1.0\}\downarrow, \{15.52\}\uparrow\}$
		age:int; $0 \leq age \leq 120$	$\{\{-1\}\downarrow, \{56\}\uparrow,$ $\{132\}\downarrow\}$
		$letter$:char;	$\{\{J\}\uparrow, \{3\}\downarrow\}$
String	At least one containing all legal strings and one containing all illegal strings. Legality is determined based on constraints on the length and other semantic features of the string	$fname$: string;	$\{\{\epsilon\}\downarrow, \{Sue\}\uparrow,$ $\{Sue2\}\downarrow, \{Too$ $Long \ a \ name\}\downarrow\}$
		$vname$: string;	$\{\{\epsilon\}\downarrow, \{shape\}\uparrow,$ $\{address1\}\uparrow\},$ $\{Long$ $variable\}\downarrow$

[a]Symbols following each equivalence class: ↓, Representative from an equivalence class containing illegal inputs; ↑, representative from an equivalence class containing legal inputs.

equivalence classes for *letter* have been determined based on the assumption that *letter* must be one of 26 letters A through Z.

In some cases an application might subdivide an input into multiple ranges. For example, in an application related to social security, *age* may be processed differently depending on which of the following four ranges

Table 2.2 Guidelines for generating equivalence classes for variables: Enumeration and arrays

		Example[a]	
Kind	**Equivalence classes**	**Constraint**	**Class representatives[b]**
Enumeration	Each value in a separate class	$auto\_color \in$ {red, blue, green}	{{red}↑, {blue}↑, {green}↑}
		up: boolean	{{true}↑, {false}↑}
Array	One class containing all legal arrays, one containing only the empty array, and one containing arrays larger than the expected size	$Java\ array$: int[] $aName = $ new int[3];	{{[]}↓, {[−10, 20]}↑, {[−9, 0, 12, 15]}↓}

[a]See text for an explanation of various entries.
[b]Symbols following each equivalence class: ↓, representative from an equivalence class containing illegal inputs, ↑, representative from an equivalence class containing legal inputs.

it falls into: [1 ... 61], [62 ... 65], [67 ... 67], and [67 ... 120]. In this case, there is one equivalence class for each range and one each for values less than the smallest value and larger than the highest value in any range. For this example, we obtain the following representatives from each of the six equivalence classes: 0 (↓), 34 (↑), 64 (↑), 67 (↑), 72 (↑), and 121 (↓). Further, if there is reason to believe that 66 is a special value and will be processed in some special way by the application, then 66 (↓) must be placed in a separate equivalence class, where, as before, ↓ and ↑ denote, respectively, values from equivalence classes containing illegal and legal inputs.

Strings: Semantic information has also been used in the table to partition values of *fname,* which denotes the first name of a person, and *vname,* which denotes the name of a program variable. We have assumed that the first name must be a non-empty string of length at most 10 and must contain only alphabetic characters; numerics and other characters are not allowed. Hence ϵ, denoting an empty string, is an invalid value in its own equivalence class, while *Sue29* and *Too Long a name* are two more invalid values in their own equivalence classes. Each of these three invalid values has been placed in its own class as these values have been derived from different semantic constraints. Similarly, valid and invalid values have been selected for *vname*. Note that while the value *address1*, which contains a digit, is a legal value for *vname*, *Sue2*, which also contains digit, is illegal for *fname*.

Enumerations: The first set of rows in Table 2.2 offer guidelines for partitioning a variable of enumerated type. If there is a reason to believe that the application is to behave differently for each value of the variable, then each value belongs to its own equivalence class. This is most likely to be true for a Boolean variable. However, in some cases, this may not be true. For example, suppose that *auto_color* may assume three different values, as shown in the table, but will be processed only for printing. In this case, it is safe to assume that the application will behave the same for all possible values of *auto_color* and only one representative needs to be selected. When there is reason to believe that the application does behave differently for different values of *auto_color* then each value must be placed in a different equivalence class as shown in the table.

In the case of enumerated types, as in the case of some range specifications, it might not be possible to specify an illegal test input. For example, if the input variable *up* is of type Boolean and can assume both `true` and `false` as legal values, then all possible equivalence classes for *up* contain legal values.

Arrays: An array specifies the size and the type of each element. Both of these parameters are used in deriving equivalence classes. In the example shown, the array may contain at least one and at most three elements. Hence, the empty array and the one containing four elements are the illegal inputs. In the absence of any additional information, we do not have any constraint on the elements of the array. In case we do have any such constraint, then additional classes could be derived. For example, if each element of the array must be in the range $[-3 \ldots 3]$ then each of the values specified in the example are illegal. A representative of the equivalence class containing legal values is [2, 0, 3].

Compound data types: Input data may also be modeled as a compound type. Any input data value that has more than one independent attribute is a compound type. For example, arrays in Java and records, or structures, in C++, are compound types. Such input types may arise while testing components of an application such as a function or an object. While generating equivalence classes for such inputs, one must consider legal and illegal values for each component of the structure.

The next example illustrates the derivation of equivalence classes for an input variable that has a compound type.

Example 2.6: A student record system, say S, maintains and processes data on students in a university. The data is kept in a database in the form of student records, one record for each student, and is read into appropriate variables prior to processing and rewriting back into the database. Data for newly enrolled students is input via a combination of mouse and keyboard.

One component of S, named *transcript*, takes a student record R and an integer N as inputs and prints N copies of the student's transcript corresponding to R. For simplicity, let us assume the following structure for R:

Program P2.2

```
1 struct R
2   {
3     string fName; // First name.
4     string lName; // Last name.
5     string cTitle [200]; // Course titles.
6     char grades [200]; // Letter grades
           corresponding to course titles.
7   }
```

Structure R contains a total of four data components. The first two of these components are of a primitive type while the last two being arrays are of compound types. A general procedure for determining the equivalence classes for *transcript* is given in the following section. For now, it should suffice to mention that one step in determining the equivalence classes for *transcript* is to derive equivalence classes for each component of R. This can be done by referring to Tables 2.1 and 2.2 and following the guidelines as explained. The classes so derived are then combined using the procedure described in the next section (see Exercise 2.7).

Most objects, and applications, require more than one input. In this case, a test input is a collection of values, one for each input. Generating such tests requires partitioning the input domain of the object, or the application, and not simply the set of possible values for one input variable. However, the guidelines in Tables 2.1 and 2.2 assist in partitioning individual variables. The equivalence classes so created are then combined to form a partition of the input domain.

2.3.4 UNIDIMENSIONAL VERSUS MULTIDIMENSIONAL PARTITIONING

The input domain of a program can be partitioned in a variety of ways. Here we examine two generic methods for partitioning the input domain and point out their advantages and disadvantages. Examples of both methods are found in the subsequent sections. We are concerned with programs that have two or more input variables.

One way to partition the input domain is to consider one input variable at a time. Thus each input variable leads to a partition of the input domain. We refer to this style of partitioning as *unidimensional* equivalence partitioning or simply *unidimensional* partitioning. In this case, there is some relation R, one for the input domain of each variable. The input domain of the program is partitioned based on R; the number of partitions being equal to the number of input variables, and each partition usually contains two or more equivalence classes.

Another way is to consider the input domain $\mathcal{I}$ as the set product of the input variables and define a relation on $\mathcal{I}$. This procedure creates one partition consisting of several equivalence classes. We refer to this method as *multidimensional* equivalence partitioning or simply *multidimensional* partitioning.

Test case selection has traditionally used unidimensional partitioning due to its simplicity and scalability. Multidimensional partitioning leads to a large, sometimes too large, number of equivalence classes that are difficult to manage manually. Many of the classes so created might be infeasible in that a test selected from such a class does not satisfy the constraints among the input variables. Nevertheless, equivalence classes created using multidimensional partitioning offer an increased variety of tests as is illustrated in the next section. The next example illustrates both unidimensional and multidimensional partitioning.

Example 2.7: Consider an application that requires two integer inputs x and y. Each of these inputs is expected to lie in the following ranges: $3 \leq x \leq 7$ and $5 \leq y \leq 9$. For unidimensional partitioning, we apply the partitioning guidelines in Tables 2.1 and 2.2 x and y individually. This leads to the following six equivalence classes:

$$\text{E1: } x < 3 \qquad \text{E2: } 3 \leq x \leq 7 \qquad \text{E3: } x > 7$$
$$\text{E4: } y < 5 \qquad \text{E5: } 5 \leq y \leq 9 \qquad \text{E6: } y > 9$$

Figures 2.4(a) and (b) show the partitions of the input domain based on, respectively, x and y. However, we obtain the following nine equivalence classes if we consider the input domain to be the product of X and Y, where X and Y denote, respectively, the set of values of variables x and y.

$$\text{E1: } x < 3, y < 5 \qquad \text{E2: } x < 3, 5 \leq y < 9 \qquad \text{E3: } x < 3, y > 9$$
$$\text{E4: } 3 \leq x \leq 7, y < 5 \quad \text{E5: } 3 \leq x \leq 7, 5 \leq y \leq 9 \quad \text{E6: } 3 \leq x \leq 7, y > 9$$
$$\text{E7: } x > 7, y < 5 \qquad \text{E8: } x > 7, 5 \leq y \leq 9 \qquad \text{E9: } x > 7, y > 9$$

From the test-selection perspective, the two unidimensional partitions generate six representative tests, one for each equivalence class.

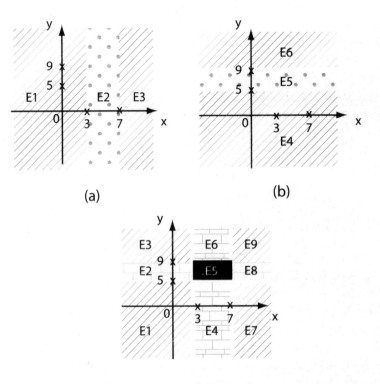

Fig. 2.4 Geometric representation of equivalence classes derived using unidimensional partitioning based on *x* and *y* in (a) and (b), respectively, and using multidimensional partitioning as in (c).

However, we obtain nine representative tests when using multidimensional partitioning. Which set of tests is better in terms of fault detection depends on the type of application.

The tests selected using multidimensional partitioning are likely to test an application more thoroughly than those selected using unidimensional partitioning. On the other hand, the number of equivalence classes created using multidimensional partitioning increases exponentially in the number of input variables (see Exercises 2.8, 2.9, 2.10, and 2.11).

2.3.5 A SYSTEMATIC PROCEDURE FOR EQUIVALENCE PARTITIONING

Test selection based on equivalence partitioning can be used for small and large applications. For applications or objects involving a few variables, say 3–5, test selection could be done manually. However, as the application or object size increases to say 25 or more input variables, manual application becomes increasingly difficult and error prone. In such situations, the use of a tool for test selection is highly recommended.

The following steps are helpful in creating the equivalence classes given program requirements. The second and third steps could be followed manually or automated. The first step below, identification of the input domain, is likely to be executed manually unless the requirements have been expressed in a formal specification language such as Z in which case this step can also be automated.

1. *Identify the input domain*: Read the requirements carefully and identify all input and output variables, their types, and any conditions associated with their use. Environment variables, such as class variables used in the method under test and environment variables in Unix, Windows, and other operating systems, also serve as input variables. Given the set of values each variable can assume, an approximation to the input domain is the product of these sets. As we will see in Step 4, constraints specified in requirements and the design of the application to be tested, is likely to eliminate several elements from the input domain derived in this step.

2. *Equivalence classing*: Partition the set of values of each variable into disjoint subsets. Each subset is an equivalence class. Together, the equivalence classes based on an input variable partition the input domain. Partitioning the input domain using values of one variable is done based on the the expected behavior of the program. Values for which the program is expected to behave in the *same way* are grouped together. Note that *same way* needs to be defined by the tester. Examples given above illustrate such grouping.

3. *Combine equivalence classes*: This step is usually omitted, and the equivalence classes defined for each variable are directly used to select test cases. However, by not combining the equivalence classes, one misses the opportunity to generate useful tests.

    The equivalence classes are combined using the multidimensional partitioning approach described earlier. For example, suppose that program P takes two integer-valued inputs denoted by X and Y. Suppose also that the values of X have been partitioned into sets X_1 and X_2 while the values of Y have been partitioned into sets Y_1, Y_2, and Y_3. Taking the set product of sets $\{X_1, X_2\}$ and $\{Y_1, Y_2, Y_3\}$, we get the following set E of six equivalence classes for P; each element of E is an equivalence class obtained by combining one equivalence class of X with another of Y.

$$E = \{X_1 \times Y_1, X_1 \times Y_2, X_1 \times Y_3, X_2 \times Y_1, X_2 \times Y_2, X_2 \times Y_3\}$$

Note that this step might lead to an unmanageably large number of equivalence classes and hence is often avoided in practice. Ways to handle such an explosion in the number of equivalence classes are discussed in Sections 2.2, 2.6, and in Chapter 4.

4. *Identify infeasible equivalence classes*: An infeasible equivalence class is one that contains a combination of input data that cannot be generated during test. Such an equivalence class might arise due to several reasons. For example, suppose that an application is tested via its GUI, that is data is input using commands available in the GUI. The GUI might disallow invalid inputs by offering a palette of valid inputs only. There might also be constraints in the requirements that render certain equivalence class infeasible.

Infeasible data is a combination of input values that cannot be input to the application under test. Again, this might happen due to the filtering of the invalid input combinations by a GUI. While it is possible that some equivalence classes are wholly infeasible, the likely case is that each equivalence class contains a mix of testable and infeasible data.

In this step we remove from E equivalence classes that contain infeasible inputs. The resulting set of equivalence classes is then used for the selection of tests. Care needs to be exercised while selecting tests as some data in the reduced E might also be infeasible.

Example 2.8: Let us now apply the equivalence partitioning procedure described earlier to generate equivalence classes for the software control portion of a boiler controller. A simplified set of requirements for the control portion are as follows:

Consider a boiler control system (BCS). The control software of BCS, abbreviated as CS, is required to offer one of several options. One of the options, C (for control), is used by a human operator to give one of the three commands (cmd): change the boiler temperature (temp), shut down the boiler (shut), and cancel the request (cancel). Command temp causes CS to ask the operator to enter the amount by which the temperature is to be changed (tempch). Values of tempch are in the range [−10...10] in increments of 5 degrees Fahrenheit. A temperature change of 0 is not an option.

Selection of option C forces the BCS to examine V. If V is set to GUI, the operator is asked to enter one of the three commands via a GUI. However, if V is set to file, BCS obtains the command from a command file.

The command file may contain any one of the three commands, together with the value of the temperature to be changed if the command is temp. The file name is obtained from variable F. Values of V and F can be altered by a different module in BCS. In response to

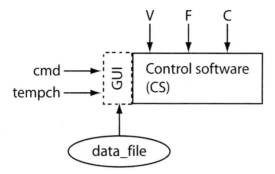

Fig. 2.5 Inputs for the boiler-control software. *V* and *F* are environment variables. Values of *cmd* (command) and *tempch* (temperature change) are input via the GUI or a data file depending on *V*. *F* specifies the data file.

> *temp and shut commands, the control software is required to generate appropriate signals to be sent to the boiler heating system.*
>
> •

We assume that the control software is to be tested in a simulated environment. The tester takes on the role of an operator and interacts with the CS via a GUI. The GUI forces the tester to select from a limited set of values as specified in the requirements. For example, the only options available for the value of *tempch* are −10, −5, 5, and 10. We refer to these four values of *tempch* as *t_valid* while all other values as *t_invalid*. Figure 2.5 is a schematic of the GUI, the control software under test, and the input variables.

Identify the input domain: The first step in generating equivalence partitions is to identify the (approximate) input domain. Recall that the domain identified in this step is likely to be a superset of the true input domain of the control software. First we examine the requirements, identify input variables, their types, and values. These are listed in the following table:

Variable	Kind	Type	Value(s)
V	Environment	Enumerated	{*GUI, file*}
F	Environment	String	A file name
cmd	Input via GUI or file	Enumerated	{*temp, cancel, shut*}
tempch	Input via GUI or file	Enumerated	{−10, −5, 5, 10 }

Considering that each variable name defines a set, we derive the following set as a product of the four variables listed above:

$$S = V \times F \times cmd \times tempch.$$

The input domain of *BCS*, denoted by $\mathcal{I}$, contains *S*. Sample values in $\mathcal{I}$, and in *S*, are given below where the lone underscore character (_) denotes a *don't care* value.

$$(GUI, \_, \ temp, -5), (GUI, \_, \ cancel, \_), (file, \ cmd\_file, \ shut, \_)$$

The following 4-tuple belongs to $\mathcal{I}$ but not to *S*:

$$(file, \ cmd\_file, \ temp, 0)$$

Equivalence classing: Equivalence classes for each variable are given in the table below. Recall that for variables that are of an enumerated type, each value belongs to a distinct class.

Variable	Partition
V	{{*GUI*}, {*file*}, {*undefined*}}
F	*f*_valid, *f_invalid*
cmd	{{*temp*}, {*cancel*}, {*shut*}, {*c_invalid*}
tempch	{*t_valid*}, {*t_invalid*}

f_valid denotes a set of names of files that exist, *f_invalid* denotes the set of names of nonexistent files, *c_invalid* denotes the set of invalid commands specified in *F*, *t_invalid* denotes the set of out-of-range values of *tempch* in the file, and *undefined* indicates that the environment variable *V* is undefined. Note that *f_valid, f_invalid, c_invalid,* and *t_invalid* denote sets of values whereas *undefined* is a singleton indicating that *V* is undefined.

Combine equivalence classes: Variables *V, F, cmd,* and *tempch* have been partitioned into 3, 2, 4, and 2 subsets, respectively. Set product of these four variables leads to a total of $3 \times 2 \times 4 \times 5 = 120$ equivalence classes. A sample follows:

{(*GUI, f_valid, temp,* −10)}, {(*GUI, f_valid, temp, t_invalid*)},
{(*file, f_invalid, c_invalid,* 5)}, {(*undefined, f_valid, temp, t_invalid*)},
{(*file, f_valid, temp,* −10)}, {(*file, f_valid, temp,* −5)}

Note that each of the classes listed above represents an infinite number of input values for the control software. For example, {(*GUI, f_valid, temp,* −10)} denotes an infinite set of values obtained by replacing *f_valid* by a string that corresponds to the name of an existing file. As we shall see later, each value in an equivalence class is a potential test input for the control software.

Discard infeasible equivalence classes: Note that the amount by which the boiler temperature is to be changed is needed only when the operator selects *temp* for *cmd*. Thus all equivalence classes that match the following template are infeasible.

$$\{(V, F, \{cancel, shut, c\_invalid\}, t\_valid \cup t\_invalid)\}$$

This parent–child relationship between *cmd* and *tempch* renders infeasible a total of $3 \times 2 \times 3 \times 5 = 90$ equivalence classes.

Next, we observe that the GUI does not allow invalid values of temperature change to be input. This leads to two more infeasible equivalence classes given below.

$\{(GUI, f\_valid, temp, t\_invalid)\}$ *The GUI does not allow invalid values of temperature change to be input.*

$\{(GUI, f\_invalid, temp, t\_invalid)\}$

Continuing with similar argument, we observe that a carefully designed application might not ask for the values of *cmd* and *tempch* when $V = file$ and F contains a file name that does not exist. In this case, five additional equivalence classes are rendered infeasible. Each of these five classes is described by the following template:

$$\{(file, f\_invalid, temp, t\_valid \cup t\_invalid)\}.$$

Along similar lines as above, we can argue that the application will not allow values of *cmd* and *tempch* to be input when V is undefined. Thus, yet another five equivalence classes that match the following template are rendered infeasible.

$$\{(undefined, \_, temp, t\_valid \cup t\_invalid)\}$$

Note that even when V is undefined, F can be set to a string that may or may not represent a valid file name.

The above discussion leads us to discard a total of $90 + 2 + 5 + 5 = 102$ equivalence classes. We are now left with only 18 testable equivalence classes. Of course, our assumption in discarding 102 classes is that the application is designed so that certain combinations of input values are impossible to achieve while testing the control software. In the absence of this assumption, all 120 equivalence classes are potentially testable.

The set of 18 testable equivalence classes match the seven templates listed below. The "_" symbol indicates, as before, that the data can be input but is not used by the control software, and the "*NA*" indicates that the data cannot be input to the control software because the GUI does not ask for it.

{(GUI, f_valid, temp, t_valid)}	four equivalence classes.
{(GUI, f_invalid, temp, t_valid)}	four equivalence classes.
{(GUI,_,cancel, NA)}	two equivalence classes.
{(file, f_valid, temp, t_valid ∪ t_invalid)}	five equivalence classes.
{(file, f_valid, shut, NA)}	one equivalence class.
{(file, f_invalid, NA, NA)}	one equivalence class.
{(undefined, NA, NA, NA)}	one equivalence classes.

There are several input data tuples that contain don't care values. For example, if $V = GUI$, then the value of F is not expected to have any impact on the behavior of the control software. However, as explained in the following section, a tester must interpret such requirements carefully.

2.3.6 Test Selection Based on Equivalence Classes

Given a set of equivalence classes that form a partition of the input domain, it is relatively straightforward to select tests. However, complications could arise in the presence of infeasible data and don't care values. In the most general case, a tester simply selects one test that serves as a representative of each equivalence class. Thus, for example, we select four tests, one from each equivalence class defined by the *pCat* relation in Example 2.4. Each test is a string that denotes the make and model of a printer belonging to one of the three classes or is an invalid string. Thus, the following is a set of four tests selected from the input domain of program *pTest*.

```
T = {HP cp1700, Canon Laser Shot LBP 3200,
     Epson Stylus Photo RX600, My Printer
     }
```

While testing pTest against tests in T we assume that if pTest correctly selects a script for each printer in T, then it will select correct scripts for all printers in its database. Similarly, from the six equivalence classes in Example 2.5, we generate the following set T consisting of six tests each of the form $(w,\ f)$, where w denotes the value of an input word and f a filename.

```
T = { (Love, my-dict), (Hello, does-not-exist),
      (Bye, empty-file), (ε, my-dict),
      (ε, does-not-exist), (ε, empty-file)
      }
```

In the test above, ϵ denotes an empty, or a null, string, implying that the input word is a null string. Following values of f *my-dict, does-not-exist,* and *empty-file* correspond to names of files that are, respectively, *exists*, *does-not-exist*, and *exists* but is empty.

Selection of tests for the boiler-control software in Example 2.8 is a bit more tricky due to the presence of infeasible data and don't care values. The next example illustrates how to proceed with test selection for the boiler-control software.

Example 2.9: Recall that we began by partitioning the input domain of the boiler-control software into 120 equivalence classes. A straightforward way to select tests would have been to pick one representative of each class. However, due to the existence of infeasible equivalence classes, this process would lead to tests that are infeasible. We, therefore, derive tests from the reduced set of equivalence classes. This set contains only feasible classes. Table 2.3 lists

Table 2.3 Test data for the control software of a boiler control system in Example 2.8.

ID	Equivalence class[a] {(V, F, cmd, tempch)}	Test data[b] (V, F, cmd, tempch)
E1	{(*GUI*, *f_valid*, *temp*, *t_valid*)}	(*GUI*, *a_file*, *temp*, −10)
E2	{(*GUI*, *f_valid*, *temp*, *t_valid*)}	(*GUI*, *a_file*, *temp*, −5)
E3	{(*GUI*, *f_valid*, *temp*, *t_valid*)}	(*GUI*, *a_file*, *temp*, 5)
E4	{(*GUI*, *f_valid*, *temp*, *t_valid*)}	(*GUI*, *a_file*, *temp*, 10)
E5	{(*GUI*, *f_invalid temp*, *t_valid*)}	(*GUI*, *no_file*, *temp*, −10)
E6	{(*GUI*, *f_invalid temp*, *t_valid*)}	(*GUI*, *no_file*, *temp*, −10)
E7	{(*GUI*, *f_invalid temp*, *t_valid*)}	(*GUI*, *no_file*, *temp*, −10)
E8	{(*GUI*, *f_invalid temp*, *t_valid*)}	(*GUI*, *no_file*, *temp*, −10)
E9	{(*GUI*,_, *cancel*, NA)}	(*GUI*, *a_file*, *cancel*, −5)
E10	{(*GUI*,_, *cancel*, NA)}	(*GUI*, *no_file*, *cancel*, −5)
E11	{(*file*, *f_valid*, *temp*, *t_valid*)}	(*file*, *a_file*, *temp*, −10)
E12	{(*file*, *f_valid*, *temp*, *t_valid*)}	(*file*, *a_file*, *temp*, −5)
E13	{(*file*, *f_valid*, *temp*, *t_valid*)}	(*file*, *a_file*, *temp*, 5)
E14	{(*file*, *f_valid*, *temp*, *t_valid*)}	(*file*, *a_file*, *temp*, 10)
E15	{(*file*, *f_valid*, *temp*, *t_invalid*)}	(*file*, *a_file*, *temp*, −25)
E16	{(*file*, *f_valid*, *temp*, NA)}	(*file*, *a_file*, *shut*, 10)
E17	{(*file*, *f_invalid*, NA, ,NA)}	(*file*, *no_file*, *shut*, 10)
E18	{(*undefined*, _, NA, NA)}	(*undefined*, *no_file*, *shut*, 10)

[a]—, don't care; NA, input not allowed.
[b]*a_file*, file exists; *no_file*, file does not exist.

18 tests derived from the 18 equivalence classes listed in Example 2.8. The equivalence classes are labeled as E1, E2, and so on for ease of reference.

While deriving the test data in Table 2.3, we have specified arbitrary values of variables that are not expected to be used by the control software. For example, in E9, the value of F is not used. However, to generate a complete test data item, we have arbitrarily assigned to F a string that represents the name of an existing file. Similarly, the value of *tempch* is arbitrarily set to 10.

The don't care values in an equivalence class must be treated carefully. It is from the requirements that we conclude that a variable is or is not don't care. However, an incorrect implementation might actually make use of the value of a don't care variable. In fact, even a correct implementation might use the value of a variable marked as don't care. This latter case could arise if the requirements are incorrect or ambiguous. In any case, it is recommended that one assign data to don't care variables, given the possibility that the program may be erroneous and hence make use of the assigned data value.

In Step 3 of the procedure to generate equivalence classes of an input domain, we suggested the product of the equivalence classes derived for each input variable. This procedure may lead to a large number of equivalence classes. One approach to test selection that avoids the explosion in the number of equivalence classes is to cover each equivalence class of each variable by a small number of tests. We say that a test input covers an equivalence class E for some variable V, if it contains a representative of E. Thus, one test input may cover multiple equivalence classes, one for each input variable. The next example illustrates this method for the boiler example.

Example 2.10: In Example 2.8 we derived 3, 2, 4, and 5 equivalence classes, respectively, for variables V, F, *cmd*, and *tempch*. The total number of equivalence classes is only 15; compare this with 120 derived using the product of individual equivalence classes. Note that we have five equivalence classes, and not just two, for variable *tempch*, because it is an enumerated type. The following set T of 5 tests cover each of the 14 equivalence classes.

```
T = {(GUI, a file, temp, −10), (GUI, no_ file, temp, −5),
     (file, a_ file, temp, 5), (file, a_ file, cancel, 10),
     (undefined, a_ file, shut, −10)
    }
```

You may verify that the tests listed above cover each equivalence classes of each variable. Though small, the above test set has several weaknesses. While the test covers all individual equivalence classes, it fails to consider the semantic relations among the different variables. For example, the last of the tests listed above will not be able to test the *shut* command assuming that the value *undefined* of the environment variable V is processed correctly.

Several other weaknesses can be identified in T of Example 2.10. The lesson to be learned from this example is that one must be careful, that is consider the relationships among variables, while deriving tests that cover equivalence classes for each variable. In fact, it is easy to show that a small subset of tests from Table 2.3 will cover all equivalence classes of each variable and satisfy the desired relationships among the variables (see Exercise 2.13).

2.3.7 GUI DESIGN AND EQUIVALENCE CLASSES

Test selection is usually affected by the overall design of the application under test. Prior to the development of GUI, data was input to most programs in textual forms through typing on a keyboard, and many years ago, via punched cards. Most applications of today, either new or refurbished, exploit the advancements in GUIs to make interaction with programs much easier and safer than before. Test design must account for the constraints imposed on data by the front-end application GUI.

While designing equivalence classes for programs that obtain input exclusively from a keyboard, one must account for the possibility of errors in data entry. For example, the requirement for an application A places a constraint on an input variable X such that it can assume integral values in the range $0 \ldots 4$. However, a user of this application may inadvertently enter a value for X that is out of range. While the application is supposed to check for incorrect inputs, it might fail to do so. Hence, in test selection using equivalence partitioning, one needs to test the application using at least three values of X, one that falls in the required range and two that fall outside the range on either side. Thus three equivalence classes for X are needed. Figure 2.6(a) illustrates this situation where the *incorrect values* portion of the input domain contains the out-of-range values for X.

However, suppose that all data entry to application A is via a GUI front-end. Suppose also that the GUI offers exactly five correct choices to the user for X. In such a situation, it is impossible to test A with a value of X that is out of range. Hence, only the correct values of X will be input to A. This situation is illustrated in Figure 2.6(b).

Of course, one could dissect the GUI from the core application and test the core separately with correct and incorrect values of X. But any error so discovered in processing incorrect values of X will be

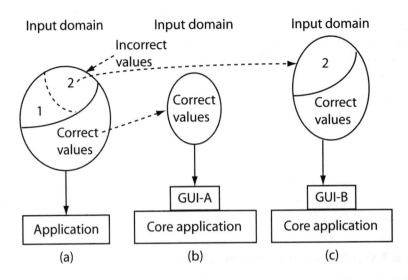

Fig. 2.6 Restriction of the input domain through careful design of the GUI. Partitioning of the input domain into equivalence classes must account for the presence of GUI as shown in (b) and (c). GUI-A protects all variables against incorrect input while GUI-B does allow the possibility of incorrect input for some variables.

meaningless because, as a developer may argue, in practice the GUI would prevent the core of A from receiving an invalid input for X. In such a situation, there is no need to define an equivalence class that contains incorrect values of an input variable.

In some cases a GUI might ask the user to type in the value of a variable in a text box. In a situation like this, one must certainly test the application with one or more incorrect values of the input variable. For example, while testing it is recommended that one use at least three values for X. In case the behavior of A is expected to be different for each integer within the range $0\ldots4$, then A should be tested separately for each value in the range as well as at least two values outside the range. However, one need not include incorrect values of variables in a test case if the variable is protected by the GUI against incorrect input. This situation is illustrated in Figure 2.6(c) where the subset labeled 1 in the set of incorrect values need not be included in the test data while values from subset labeled 2 must be included.

The discussion above leads to the conclusion that test design must take into account GUI design. In some cases, GUI design requirements could be dictated by test design. For example, the test design process might require the GUI to offer only valid values of input variables whenever possible. Certainly, GUI needs to be tested separately against such requirements. The boiler control example given earlier shows that the number of tests can be reduced significantly if the GUI prevents invalid inputs from getting into the application under test.

Note that the tests derived in the boiler example make the assumption that the GUI has been correctly implemented and does prohibit incorrect values from entering the control software.

2.4 BOUNDARY-VALUE ANALYSIS

Experience indicates that programmers make mistakes in processing values at and near the boundaries of equivalence classes. For example, suppose that method M is required to compute a function f_1 when the condition $x \leq 0$ is satisfied by input x and function f_2 otherwise. However, M has an error due to which it computes f_1 for $x < 0$ and f_2 otherwise. Obviously, this fault is revealed, though not necessarily, when M is tested against $x = 0$ but not if the input test set is, for example, $\{-4, 7\}$ derived using equivalence partitioning. In this example, the value $x = 0$, lies at the boundary of the equivalence classes $x \leq 0$ and $x > 0$.

Boundary-value analysis is a test-selection technique that targets faults in applications at the boundaries of equivalence classes. While equivalence partitioning selects tests from within equivalence classes, boundary-value analysis focuses on tests at and near the boundaries of equivalence classes. Certainly, tests derived using either of the two techniques may overlap.

Test selection using boundary-value analysis is generally done in conjunction with equivalence partitioning. However, in addition to identifying boundaries using equivalence classes, it is also possible and recommended that boundaries be identified based on the relations among the input variables. Once the input domain has been identified, test selection using boundary-value analysis proceeds as follows:

1. Partition the input domain using unidimensional partitioning. This leads to as many partitions as there are input variables. Alternately, a single partition of an input domain can be created using multidimensional partitioning.
2. Identify the boundaries for each partition. Boundaries may also be identified using special relationships among the inputs.
3. Select test data such that each boundary value occurs in at least one test input. A procedure to generate tests using boundary value-analysis and an illustrative example follows.

Example 2.11: This simple example is to illustrate the notion of boundaries and selection of tests at and near the boundaries. Consider a method *fP*, brief for *findPrice*, that takes two inputs *code* and *qty*. The item code is represented by the integer *code* and the quantity purchased by another integer variable *qty*. *fP* accesses a database to find and display the unit price, the description, and the total price of the item corresponding to *code*. *fP* is required to display an error message, and return, if either of the two inputs is incorrect. We are required to generate test data to test *fP*.

We start by creating equivalence classes for the two input variables. Assuming that an item code must be in the range 99...999 and quantity in the range 1...100, we obtain the following equivalence classes.

Equivalence classes for *code* :   E1: Values less than 99.
                                   E2: Values in the range.
                                   E3: Values greater than 999.

Equivalence classes for *qty*:   E4: Values less than 1.
                                   E5: Values in the range.
                                   E6: Values greater than 100.

Figure 2.7 shows the equivalence classes for *code* and *qty* and the respective boundaries. Notice that there are two boundaries each for *code* and *qty*. Marked in the figure are six points for each variable, two at the boundary marked "x" and four near the boundaries marked "*". Test selection based on the boundary-value analysis technique requires that tests must include, for each variable, values

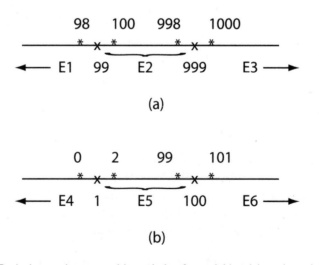

Fig. 2.7   Equivalence classes and boundaries for variables (a) *code* and (b) *qty* in Example 2.11. Values at and near the boundary are listed and marked with an "x" and "*", respectively.

at and around the boundary. Usually, several sets of tests will satisfy this requirement. Consider the following set:

$$T = \{ \; t_1 : (code = 98, \; qty = 0),$$
$$t_2 : (code = 99, \; qty = 1),$$
$$t_3 : (code = 100, \; qty = 2),$$
$$t_4 : (code = 998, \; qty = 99),$$
$$t_5 : (code = 999, \; qty = 100),$$
$$t_6 : (code = 1000, \; qty = 101)$$
$$\}$$

Each of the six values for each variable are included in the tests above. Notice that the illegal values of *code* and *qty* are included in the same test. For example, tests t_1 and t_6, contain illegal values for both *code* and *qty* and require that *fP* display an error message when executed against these tests. Tests t_2, t_3, t_4, and t_5 contain legal values.

While *T* is a minimal set of tests that include all boundary and near-boundary points for *code* and *qty*, it is not the best when evaluated against its ability to detect faults. Consider, for example, the following faulty code skeleton for method *fP*.

```
1    public void fP(int code, qty)
2    {
3      if (code<99 && code>999)
4        {display_error("Invalid code"); return;}
5      // Validity check for  qty is missing !
6      // Begin processing  code  and qty.

7        :
8    }
```

When *fP* that includes the above code segment, is executed against t_1 or t_6, it will correctly display an error message. This behavior would indicate that the value of *code* is incorrect. However, these two tests fail to check that the validity check on *qty* is missing from the program. None of the other tests will be able to reveal the missing-code error. By separating the correct and incorrect values of different input variables, we increase the possibility of detecting the missing-code error.

It is also possible that the check for the validity of *code* is missing but that for checking the validity of *qty* exists and is correct. Keeping the two possibilities in view, we generate the following four tests that can safely replace t_1 and t_6 listed above. The following four tests are also derived using boundary-value analysis:

$$t_7 = (code = 98, \quad qty = 45)$$
$$t_8 = (code = 1000, \quad qty = 45)$$
$$t_9 = (code = 250, \quad qty = 0)$$
$$t_{10} = (code = 250, \quad qty = 101)$$

A test suite for fP, derived using boundary-value analysis, now consists of t_2, t_3, t_4, t_5, t_7, t_8, t_9, and t_{10}. If there is a reason to believe that tests that include boundary values of both inputs might miss some error, then tests t_2 and t_6 must also be replaced to avoid the boundary values of *code* and *qty* from appearing in the same test (see Exercise 2.17).

Example 2.12: Consider a method named *textSearch* to search for a nonempty string s in text *txt*. Position of characters in *txt* begins with 0 representing the first character, 1 the next character, and so on. Both s and *txt* are supplied as parameters to *textSearch*. The method returns an integer x such that if $x \geq 0$ then p denotes the starting position of s in *txt*. A negative value of x implies that s is not found in *txt*.

To apply boundary-value analysis technique, we first construct the equivalence classes for each input variable. In this case, both inputs are strings and no constraints have been specified on their length or contents. Based on the guidelines in Tables 2.1 and 2.2, we arrive at the following four equivalence classes for s and *txt*.

Equivalence classes for s: E1: empty string, E2: nonempty string.
Equivalence classes for *txt*: E3: empty string, E4: nonempty string.

It is possible to define boundaries for a string variable based on its length and semantics. In this example, the lower bound on the lengths of both s and *txt* is 0 and hence this defines one boundary for each input. No upper bound is specified on lengths of either variable. Hence we obtain only one boundary case for each of the two inputs. However, as it is easy to observe, E1 and E2 contain exactly the boundary case. Thus, tests derived using equivalence partitioning on input variables are the same as those derived by applying boundary-value analysis.

Let us now partition the output space of *textSearch* into equivalence classes. We obtain the following two equivalence classes for x:

$$E5: x < 0, \quad E6: x \geq 0.$$

To obtain an output that belongs to E5, the input string s must not be in *txt*. Also, to obtain an output value that falls into E6, input s must be in *txt*. As both E5 and E6 are open ranges, we obtain only one boundary, $x = 0$ based on E5 and E6. A test input that causes a correct *textSearch* to output $x = 0$ must satisfy two conditions: (i) s must be in *txt* and (ii) s must appear at the start of *txt*. These two conditions allow us to generate the following test input based on boundary-value analysis:

$s =$ "Laughter" and

$txt =$ "Laughter is good for the heart."

Based on the six equivalence classes and two boundaries derived, we obtain the following set T of four test inputs for *textSearch*.

```
T = { t₁ : (s = ε,
        txt = "Laughter is good for the heart."),
      t₂ : (s = "Laughter", txt = ε),
      t₃ : (s = "good for",
        txt = "Laughter is good for the heart."),
      t₄ : (s = "Laughter",
        txt = "Laughter is good for the heart.")}
```

It is easy to verify that tests t_1 and t_2 cover equivalence classes E1, E2, E3, E4, and E5, and t_3 covers E6. Test t_4 is necessitated by the conditions imposed by boundary-value analysis. Note that none of the six equivalence classes requires us to generate t_3. However, boundary-value analysis, based on output equivalence classes E5 and E6, requires us to generate a test in which s occurs at the start of *txt*.

Test t_4 suggests that we add to T yet another test t_5 in which s occurs at the end of *txt*.

```
t₅ : (s = "heart.",
      txt = "Laughter is good for the heart.")
```

None of the six equivalence classes derived above, or the boundaries of those equivalence classes, directly suggest t_5. However, both t_4 and t_5 aim at ensuring that *textSearch* behaves correctly when s occurs at the boundaries of *txt*.

Having determined tests on the two boundaries using s and *txt*, we now examine test inputs that are near the boundaries. Four such cases are listed below:

- s starts at position 1 in *txt*. Expected output: $p = 1$.
- s ends at one character before the last character in *txt*. Expected output: $p = k$, where k is the position from where s starts in *txt*.
- All but the first character of s occur in *txt* starting at position 0. Expected output: $p = -1$.
- All but the last character of s occur in *txt* at the end. Expected output: $p = -1$.

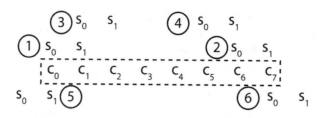

Fig. 2.8 c_0 through c_7 are the eight characters in *txt* starting at the leftmost position 0. $s_0 s_1$ is the input string *s*. Shown here is the positioning of *s* with respect to *txt* at the two boundaries, labeled 1 and 2, and at four points near the boundary, labeled 3 through 6.

The following tests, added to T, satisfy the four conditions listed above.

$t_6 : (s = \text{``Laughter''},$
$\quad txt = \text{``Laughter is good for the heart.''},)$
$t_7 : (s = \text{``heart''},$
$\quad txt = \text{``Laughter is good for the heart.''},)$
$t_8 : (s = \text{``gLaughter''},$
$\quad txt = \text{``Laughter is good for the heart.''}),$
$t_9 : (s = \text{`` heard.''},$
$\quad txt = \text{``Laughter is good for the heart.''}.)$

We now have a total of nine tests of which six are derived using boundary-value analysis. Points on and off the boundary are shown in Figure 2.8. Two boundaries are labeled 1 and 2, and four points off the boundaries are labeled 3, 4, 5, and 6.

Next, one might try to obtain additional test by combining the equivalence classes for *s* and *txt*. This operation leads to four equivalence classes for the input domain of *textSearch* as listed below.

$$E_1 \times E_3, \ E_1 \times E4, \ E_2 \times E3, \ E_2 \times E4.$$

Tests $t_1, t_2,$ and t_3 cover all four equivalence classes except for $E_1 \times E_3$. We need the following test to cover $E_1 \times E_3$.

$$t_{10} : (s = \epsilon, \ txt = \epsilon)$$

Thus, combining the equivalence classes of individual variables has led to the selection of an additional test case. Of course, one could have derived t_{10} based on E_1 and E_3. However, coverage of $E_1 \times E_3$ *requires* t_{10} whereas coverage of E_1 and E_3 separately does not. Note also that test t_4 has a special property that is not required to hold if we were to generate a test that covers the four equivalence classes obtained by combining the equivalence classes for individual variables.

The previous example leads to the following observations:

- Relationships among the input variables must be examined carefully while identifying boundaries along the input domain. This examination may lead to boundaries that are not evident from equivalence classes obtained from the input and output variables.
- Additional tests may be obtained when using a partition of the input domain obtained by taking the product of equivalence classes created using individual variables.

2.5 CATEGORY-PARTITION METHOD

The category-partition method is a systematic approach to the generation of tests from requirements. The method consists of a mix of manual and automated steps. Here we describe the various steps in using the category-partition method and illustrate with a simple running example.

2.5.1 STEPS IN THE CATEGORY-PARTITION METHOD

The category-partition method consists of eight steps as shown in Figure 2.9. In essence, a tester transforms requirements into test specifications. These test specifications consist of categories corresponding to program inputs and environment objects.

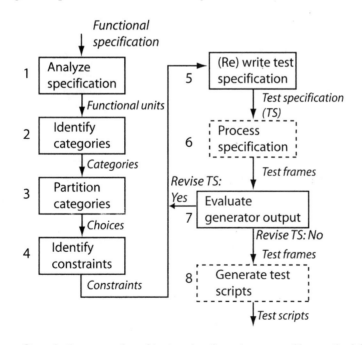

Fig. 2.9 Steps in the generation of tests using the category-partition method. Tasks in solid boxes are performed manually and generally difficult to automate. Dashed boxes indicate tasks that can be automated.

Each category is partitioned into choices that correspond to one or more values for the input or the state of an environment object. Test specifications also contain constraints on the choices so that only reasonable and valid sets of tests are generated. Test specifications are input to a test-frame generator that produces a number of test frames from which test scripts are generated. A test frame is a collection of choices, one corresponding to each category. A test frame serves as a template for one or more test cases that are combined into one or more test scripts.

A running example is used here to describe the steps shown in Figure 2.9. We use the *findPrice* function used in Example 2.11. The requirements for the *findPrice* function are expanded below for the purpose of illustrating the category-partition method.

Function: findPrice

Syntax: fP(code, quantity, weight)

Function:

findPrice takes three inputs: *code, qty,* and *weight.* Item code is represented by a string of eight digits contained in variable *code.* The quantity purchased is contained in *qty.* The weight of the item purchased is contained in *weight.*

Function *fP* accesses a database to find and display the unit price, the description, and the total price of the item corresponding to code. *fP* is required to display an error message, and return, if either of the three inputs is incorrect. As indicated below, the leftmost digit of *code* decides how the values of *qty* and *weight* are to be used. *code* is an eight digit string that denotes product type. *fP* is concerned with only the leftmost digit that is interpreted as follows:

Leftmost digit	Interpretation
0	Ordinary grocery items such as bread, magazines, and soup.
2	Variable-weight items such as meats, fruits, and vegetables.
3	Health-related items such as tylenol, bandaids, and tampons.
5	Coupon; digit 2 (dollars), 3 and 4(cents) specify the discount.
1, 6–9	Unused

The use of parameters *qty* and *weight* depends on the leftmost digit in *code*. *qty* indicates the quantity purchased, an integer, when the leftmost digit is 0 or 3; *weight* is ignored. *weight* is the weight of the item purchased when the leftmost digit is 2; *qty* is ignored. *qty* is the value of the discount when the leftmost digit is 5; again *weight* is ignored. We assume that digits 1 and 6 through 9, are ignored. When the leftmost digit is 5, the second digit from the left specifies the dollar amount and the third and fourth digits the cents.

STEP 1: ANALYZE SPECIFICATION

In this step, the tester identifies each functional unit that can be tested separately. For large systems, a functional unit may correspond to a subsystem that can be tested independently. The subsystem can be further subdivided leading eventually to independently testable subunits. The subdivision process terminates depending on what is to be tested.

> Example 2.13: In this example we assume that *fP* is an independently testable subunit of an application. Thus we will derive tests for *fP*.

STEP 2: IDENTIFY CATEGORIES

For each testable unit, the given specification is analyzed and the inputs isolated. In addition, objects in the environment, for example a file, also need to be identified.

Next, we determine characteristics of each parameter and environmental object. A characteristic is also referred to as a *category*. While some characteristics are stated explicitly, others might need to be derived by a careful examination of the specification.

> Example 2.14: We note that *fP* has three input parameters: *code*, *qty*, and *weight*. The specification mentions various characteristics of these parameters such as their type and interpretation. Notice that *qty* and *weight* are related to *code*. The specification does mention the types of different parameters but does not indicate bounds on *qty* and *weight*.
>
> The database accessed by *fP* is an environment object. No characteristics of this object are mentioned in the specification. However, for a thorough testing of *fP*, we need to make assumptions about the

existence, or nonexistence of items in the database. We identify the following categories for *fP*:

code: length, leftmost digit, remaining digits

qty: integer quantity

weight: float quantity

database: contents

Note that we have only one category each for *qty*, *weight*, and *database*. In the next step we see how to partition these categories.

STEP 3: PARTITION CATEGORIES

For each category the tester determines different cases against which the functional unit must be tested. Each case is also referred to as a *choice*. One or more cases are expected for each category. It is useful to partition each category into at least two subsets, a set containing correct values and another consisting of erroneous values.

In the case of a networked application, cases such as network failure ought to be considered. Other possible cases of failure, for example database unavailable, also need to be considered. It is for the tester to think of reasonable situations, both valid and invalid, that might arise when the unit under test is in actual use.

Example 2.15: A summary of various inputs, environment object, categories, and partitions follows:

Parameters:
code:
   Length
     Valid (eight digits)
     Invalid (less than or greater than eight digits)
   leftmost digit
     0
     2
     3
     5
     Others
   remaining digits

valid string
    invalid string (e.g., 0X5987Y)

qty:
  integer quantity
    valid quantity
    invalid quantity (e.g., 0)

weight:
  float quantity
    valid weight
    invalid weight (e.g., 0)

Environments:

database:
  Contents
    item exists
    item does not exist

Note that if *fP* were to operate in a networked environment, then several other cases are possible. We leave these to Exercise 2.18.

STEP 4: IDENTIFY CONSTRAINTS

A test for a functional unit consists of a combination of choices for each parameter and environment object. Certain combinations might not be possible while others must satisfy specific relationships. In any case, constraints among choices are specified in this step. These constraints are used by the test generator to produce only the valid test frames in Step 6.

A constraint is specified using a property list and a selector expression. A property list has the following form:

$$[\text{property} \quad P1, P2, \ldots]$$

where *property* is a key word and P1, P2, etc. are names of individual properties. Each choice can be assigned a property. A selector expression is a conjunction of pre-defined properties specified in some property list. A selector expression takes one of the following forms:

[if P]

[if P and P2 and...]

The above two forms can be suffixed to any choice. A special property written as [error] can be assigned to choices that represent error conditions. Another special property written as [single] allows the tester to specify that the associated choice is not to be combined with choices of other parameters, or environment objects, while generating test frames in Step 6.

Example 2.16: Properties and selector expressions assigned to a few choices sampled from Example 2.16 follow; comment lines start with #.

Leftmost digit of code
0	[property ordinary-grocery]
2	[property variable-weight]

Remaining digits of code
valid string	[single]

Valid value of *qty*
valid quantity	[if ordinary-grocery]

Incorrect value of *qty*
invalid quantity	[error]

STEP 5: (RE)WRITE TEST SPECIFICATION

Having assigned properties and selector expressions to various choices, the tester now writes a complete test specification. The specification is written in a test specification language (TSL) conforming to a precise syntax.

This step may need to be executed more than once in the event the tester is not satisfied with the test frames generated in Step 6. This happens when the tester evaluates the test frames in Step 7 and finds that some test frames are redundant. Such frames may have been generated by combining choices that are either impractical or unlikely to arise in practice. In such an event, the tester rewrites the specification and inputs them for processing in Step 6.

Example 2.17: A complete test specification for *fP* follows; we have ignored the processing coupon category (see Exercise 2.19). We have used a slight variation of the TSL syntax given by Ostrand and Balcer (also see Bibliographic Notes).

Parameters:
Code
  length
    valid
    invalid   [error]
  Leftmost digit
    0   [property Ordinary-grocery]
    2   [property Variable-weight]

3	[property Health-related]
5	[property Coupon]

Remaining digits
    valid string   [single]
    invalid string   [error]

qty
    valid quantity   [if Ordinary-grocery]
    invalid quantity   [error]

weight:
    valid weight   [if Variable-weight]
    invalid weight   [error]

Environments:
database:
    item exists
    item does not exist   [error]

STEP 6: PROCESS SPECIFICATION

The TSL specification written in Step 5 is processed by an automatic test-frame generator. This results in a number of test frames. The test frames are analyzed by the tester for redundancy, that is they might test the application in the same way. In such cases, one either rewrites the test specifications or simply ignores the redundant frames.

Example 2.18: A sample test frame generated from the test specification in Example 2.17 follows:

Test case 2: (Key = 1.2.1.0.1.1)
Length:	valid
Leftmost digit:	2
Remaining digits:	valid string
qty:	ignored
weight:	3.19
database:	item exists

A test number identifies the test. The key in a test frame indicates the choices used, a 0 indicating no choice. *qty* is ignored as the leftmost digit corresponds to a variable weight item that is priced by weight and not by quantity. (Note that the terminology used in this example differs from that in the original TSL.)

A test frame is not a test case. However, a test case consisting of specific input values and expected outputs can be easily derived from a test frame. It is important to note that the test frame contains information about the environment objects. Hence, it is useful in setting up the environment prior to a test.

Test frames are generated by generating all possible combinations of choices while satisfying the constraints. Choices that are marked error or single are not combined with others and produce only one test case. It is easy to observe that without any constraints (selector expressions), a total of 160 test frames will be generated from the specification in Example 2.17.

STEP 7: EVALUATE GENERATOR OUTPUT

In this step the tester examines the test frames for any redundancy or missing cases. This might lead to a modification in the test specification (Step 5) and a return to Step 6.

STEP 8: GENERATE TEST SCRIPTS

Test cases generated from test frames are combined into test scripts. A test script is a grouping of test cases. Generally, test cases that do not require any changes in settings of the environment objects are grouped together. This enables a test driver to efficiently execute the tests.

That completes our description of the category-partition method. As you may have noticed, the method is essentially a systematization of the equivalence partitioning and boundary-value techniques discussed earlier.

Writing a test specification allows a test team to take a close look at the program specifications. For large systems, this task can be divided among members of the test team. While a significant part of the method requires manual work, availability of a tool that processes TSL specifications helps in test generation and documentation. It also reduces the chances of errors in test cases.

2.6 CAUSE–EFFECT GRAPHING

We described two techniques for test selection based on equivalence partitioning and boundary-value analysis. One is based on unidimensional partitioning and the other on multidimensional partitioning of the input domain. While equivalence classes created using multidimensional partitioning allow the selection of a large number of input combinations, the number of such combinations could be astronomical. Further, many of these combinations, as in Example 2.8, are infeasible and make the test-selection process tedious.

Cause–effect graphing, also known as dependency modeling, focuses on modeling dependency relationships among program input conditions, known as *causes*, and output conditions, known as *effects*. The relationship is expressed visually in terms of a cause–effect graph. The graph is a visual representation of a logical relationship among inputs and outputs that can be expressed as a Boolean expression. The graph allows selection of various combinations of input values as tests. The combinatorial explosion in the number of tests is avoided by using certain heuristics during test generation.

A cause is any condition in the requirements that may effect the program output. An effect is the response of the program to some combination of input conditions. It may be, for example, an error message displayed on the screen, a new window displayed, or a database updated. An effect need not be an *output* visible to the user of the program. Instead, it could also be an internal *test point* in the program that can be probed during testing to check if some intermediate result is as expected. For example, the intermediate test point could be at the entrance to a method to indicate that indeed the method has been invoked.

A requirement such as "Dispense food only when the DF switch is ON" contains a cause "DF switch is ON" and an effect "Dispense food". This requirement implies a relationship between the "DF switch is ON" and the effect "Dispense food". Of course, other requirements might require additional causes for the occurrence of the "Dispense food" effect. The following generic procedure is used for the generation of tests using cause–effect graphing:

1. Identify causes and effects by reading the requirements. Each cause and effect is assigned a unique identifier. Note that an effect can also be a cause for some other effect.
2. Express the relationship between causes and effects using a cause–effect graph.
3. Transform the cause–effect graph into a limited entry decision table, hereafter referred to simply as decision table.
4. Generate tests from the decision table.

The basic notation used in cause–effect graphing and a few illustrative examples are given below.

2.6.1 NOTATION USED IN CAUSE–EFFECT GRAPHING

The basic elements of a cause–effect graph are shown in Figure 2.10. A typical cause–effect graph is formed by combining the basic elements so as to capture the relations between causes and effects derived from

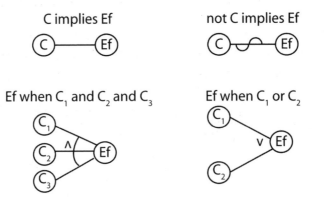

Fig. 2.10 Basic elements of a cause–effect graph: *implication, not (∼), and (∧), or (∨)*. C, C_1, C_2, C_3 denote causes and *Ef* denotes effect. An arc is used, for example in the *and* relationship, to group three or more causes.

the requirements. The semantics of the four basic elements shown in Figure 2.10 is expressed below in terms of the if-then construct; C, C_1, C_2, and C_3 denote causes, and *Ef* denotes an effect.

C implies *Ef*:	if(C) then *Ef*;
not C implies *Ef*:	if ($\neg C$) then *Ef*;
Ef when C_1 and C_2 and C_3:	if(C_1 && C_2 && C_3) then *Ef*;
Ef when C_1 or C_2:	if($C_1 \| \| C_2$) then *Ef*;

There often arise constraints among causes. For example, consider an inventory-control system that tracks the inventory of various items that are stocked. For each item, an inventory attribute is set to *Normal, Low, and Empty*. The inventory control software takes actions as the value of this attribute changes. When identifying causes, each of the three inventory levels will lead to a different cause listed below.

C_1 : "Inventory is normal"
C_2 : "Inventory is low"
C_3 :"Inventory is zero"

However, at any instant, exactly one of C_1, C_2, and C_3 can be true. This relationship among the three causes is expressed in a cause–effect graph using the *Exclusive (E)* constraint shown in Figure 2.11. In addition, shown in this figure are the *Inclusive (I)*, *Requires (R)*, and *One and only one (O)* constraints. The *I* constraint between two causes C_1 and C_2 implies that at least one of the two must be present. The *R* constraint between C_1 and C_2 implies the C_1 requires C_2. The *O*-constraint models the condition that one, and only one, of C_1 and C_2 must hold.

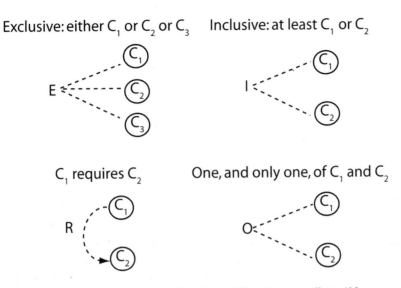

Exclusive: either C_1 or C_2 or C_3 Inclusive: at least C_1 or C_2

C_1 requires C_2 One, and only one, of C_1 and C_2

Fig. 2.11 Constraints among causes (*E*, *I*, *O*, and *R*) and among effects (*M*).

The table below lists all possible values of causes constrained by E, I, R, and O. A 0 or a 1 under a cause implies that the corresponding condition is, respectively, false and true. The arity of all constraints, except R, is greater than 1, that is all except the R constraint can be applied to two or more causes; the R constraint is applied to two causes.

		Possible values		
Constraint	**Arity**	C_1	C_2	C_3
$E(C_1,\ C_2,\ C_3)$	$n > 1$	0	0	0
		1	0	0
		0	1	0
		0	0	1
$I(C_1,\ C_2)$	$n > 1$	1	0	–
		0	1	–
		1	1	–
$R(C_1,\ C_2)$	$n > 1$	1	1	–
		1	1	–
		0	0	–
		0	1	–
$O(C_1,\ C_2,\ C_3)$	$n > 1$	1	0	0
		0	1	0
		0	0	1

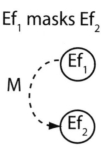

Ef_1 masks Ef_2

M

Fig. 2.12 The masking constraint among effects.

In addition to constraints on causes, there could also be constraints on effects. The cause–effect graphing technique offers one constraint, known as *Masking (M)* on effects. Figure 2.12 shows the graphical notation for the masking constraint. Consider the following two effects in the inventory example mentioned earlier.

Ef_1 : Generate "Shipping invoice".

Ef_2 : Generate an "Order not shipped" regret letter.

Effect Ef_1 occurs when an order can be met from the inventory. Effect Ef_2 occurs when the order placed cannot be met from the inventory or when the ordered item has been discontinued after the order was placed. However, Ef_2 is masked by Ef_1 for the same order, that is both effects cannot occur for the same order.

A condition that is false (true) is said to be in the "0-state" (1-state). Similarly, an effect can be *present* (1-state) or *absent* (0-state).

2.6.2 Creating Cause–Effect Graphs

The process of creating a cause–effect graph consists of two major steps. First, the causes and effects are identified by a careful examination of the requirements. This process also exposes the relationships among various causes and effects as well as constraints among the causes and effects. Each cause and effect is assigned a unique identifier for ease of reference in the cause–effect graph.

In the second step, the cause–effect graph is constructed to express the relationships extracted from the requirements. When the number of causes and effects is large, say over 100 causes and 45 effects, it is appropriate to use an incremental approach. An illustrative example follows:

$$\begin{Bmatrix} \text{CPU 1} \\ \text{CPU 2} \\ \text{CPU 3} \end{Bmatrix} \quad \begin{Bmatrix} \text{PR 1} \\ \text{PR 2} \end{Bmatrix} \quad \begin{Bmatrix} \text{M 20} \\ \text{M 23} \\ \text{M 30} \end{Bmatrix} \quad \begin{Bmatrix} \text{RAM 256} \\ \text{RAM 512} \\ \text{RAM 1G} \end{Bmatrix}$$

Fig. 2.13 Possible configurations of a computer system sold by a web-based company: CPU: CPU configuration; PR, printer; M, monitor and RAM, memory upgrade.

Example 2.19: Let us consider the task of test generation for a GUI-based computer purchase system. A Web-based company is selling computers (CPU), printers (PR), monitors (M), and additional memory (RAM). An order configuration consists of one to four items as shown in Figure 2.13. The GUI consists of four windows for displaying selections from CPU, Printer, Monitor, and RAM and one window where any free giveaway items are displayed.

For each order, the buyer may select from three CPU models, two printer models, and three monitors. There are separate windows one each for CPU, printer, and monitor that show the possible selections. For simplicity we assume that RAM is available only as an upgrade and that only one unit of each item can be purchased in one order.

Monitors M 20 and M 23 can be purchased with any CPU or as a standalone item. M 30 can only be purchased with CPU 3. PR 1 is available free with the purchase of CPU 2 or CPU 3. Monitors and printers, except for M 30, can also be purchased separately without purchasing any CPU. Purchase of CPU 1 gets RAM 256 upgrade and purchase of CPU 2 or CPU 3 gets a RAM 512 upgrade. The RAM 1G upgrade and a free PR 2 is available when CPU 3 is purchased with monitor M 30.

When a buyer selects a CPU, the contents of the printer and monitor windows are updated. Similarly, if a printer or a monitor is selected, contents of various windows are updated. Any free printer and RAM available with the CPU selection is displayed in a different window marked "Free". The total price, including taxes, for the items purchased is calculated and displayed in the "Price" window. Selection of a monitor could also change the items displayed in the "Free" window. Sample configurations and contents of the "Free" window are given below.

Items purchased	"Free" window	Price
CPU 1	RAM 256	$499
CPU 1. PR 1	RAM 256	$628
CPU 2. PR 2. M 23	PR 1, RAM 512	$2257
CPU 3. M 30	PR 2, RAM 1G	$3548

The first step in cause–effect graphing is to read the requirements carefully and make a list of causes and effects. For this example, we will consider only a subset of the effects and leave the remaining as an exercise. This strategy also illustrates how one could generate tests using an incremental strategy.

A careful reading of the requirements is used to extract the following causes. We have assigned a unique identifier, C 1 through C 8 to each cause. Each cause listed below is a condition that can be true or false. For example, C 8 is true if monitor M 30 is purchased.

C 1:   Purchase CPU 1.
C 2:   Purchase CPU 2.
C 3:   Purchase CPU 3.
C 4:   Purchase PR 1.
C 5:   Purchase PR 2.
C 6:   Purchase M 20.
C 7:   Purchase M 23.
C 8:   Purchase M 30.

Note that while it is possible to order any of the items listed above, the GUI will update the selection available depending on what CPU or any other item is selected. For example, if CPU 3 is selected for purchase, then monitors M 20 and M 23 will not be available in the monitor-selection window. Similarly, if monitor M 30 is selected for purchase, then CPU 1 and CPU 2 will not be available in the CPU window.

Next, we identify the effects. In this example, the application software calculates and displays the list of items available free with the purchase and the total price. Hence, the effect is in terms of the contents of the "Free" and "Price" windows. There are several other effects related to the GUI update actions. These effects are left for the exercise (see Exercise 2.21).

Calculation of the total purchase price depends on the items purchased and the unit price of each item. The unit price is obtained by the application from a price database. The price calculation and display is a cause that creates the effect of displaying the total price.

For simplicity, we ignore the price-related cause and effect. The set of effects in terms of the contents of the "Free" display window are listed below.

Ef₁ : RAM 256.

Ef₂ : RAM 512 and PR 1.

Ef₃ : RAM 1G and PR 2.

Ef₄ : No giveaway with this item.

Now that we have identified causes, effects, and their relationships, we begin to construct the cause–effect graph. Figure 2.14 shows the complete graph that expresses the relationships between C_1 through C_8 and effects E1 through E4.

From the cause–effect graph in Figure 2.14, we notice that C_1, C_2, and C_3 are constrained using the E (exclusive) relationship. This

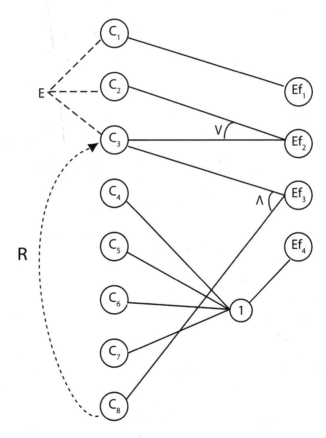

Fig. 2.14 Cause–effect graph for the web-based computer sale application. C_1, C_2, and C_3 denote the purchase of, respectively, CPU 1, CPU 2, and CPU 3. C_4 and C_5 denote the purchase of printers PR 1 and PR 2, respectively. C_6, C_7, and C_8 denote the purchase of monitors M 20, M 23, and M 30, respectively.

expresses the requirement that only one CPU can be purchased in one order. Similarly, C_3 and C_8 are related via the R (requires) constraint to express the requirement that monitor M 30 can only be purchased with CPU 3. Relationships among causes and effects are expressed using the basic elements shown earlier in Figure 2.10.

Note the use of an intermediate node labeled 1 in Figure 2.14. Though not necessary in this example, such intermediate nodes are often useful when an effect depends on conditions combined using more than one operator, for example $(C_1 \wedge C_2) \vee C_3$. Note also that purchase of printers and monitors without any CPU leads to no free item (Ef_4).

The relationships between effects and causes shown in Figure 2.14 can be expressed in terms of Boolean expressions as follows:

$$Ef_1 = C_1$$
$$Ef_2 = C_2 \vee C_3$$
$$Ef_3 = C_3 \wedge C_8$$
$$Ef_4 = C_4 \vee C_5 \vee C_6 \vee C_7$$

2.6.3 DECISION TABLE FROM CAUSE–EFFECT GRAPH

We will now see how to construct a decision table from a cause–effect graph. Each column of the decision table represents a combination of input values, and hence a test. There is one row for each condition and effect. Thus, the decision table can be viewed as an $N \times M$ matrix with N being the sum of the number of conditions and effects and M the number of tests.

Each entry in the decision table is a 0 or a 1 depending on whether or not the corresponding condition is false or true, respectively. For a row corresponding to an effect, an entry is 0 or 1 if the effect is not present or present, respectively. The following is a procedure to generate a decision table (DT) from a cause–effect graph (CEG) or CEGDT.

Procedure for generating a decision table from a cause—effect graph.

Input: (a) A cause–effect graph containing causes $C_1, C_2, \ldots, C_p$ and affects $Ef_1, Ef_2, \ldots, Ef_q$.

Output: A decision table DT containing $N = p + q$ rows and M columns, where M depends on the relationship between the causes and effects as captured in the cause–effect graph.

Procedure: CEGDT

/* `i` is the index of the next effect to be considered.

`next_dt_col` is the next empty column in the decision table.

V_k: a vector of size $p + q$ containing 1s and 0s. V_j, $1 \leq j \leq p$, indicates the state of condition C_j and $V_1, p < 1 \leq p + q$, indicates the presence or absence of effect Ef_{1-p}.

*/

Step 1 *Initialize DT to an empty decision table.*

next_ dt_col = 1.

Step 2 Execute the following steps for $i = 1$ to q.

  2.1 *Select the next effect to be processed.*

Let e = Ef_i.

  2.2 *Find combinations of conditions that cause e to be present.*

Assume that *e* is present. Starting at *e*, trace the cause–effect graph backward and determine the combinations of conditions $C_1, C_2, \ldots, C_p$ that lead to *e* being present. Avoid combinatorial explosion by using the heuristics given in the text following this procedure. Make sure that the combinations satisfy any constraints among the causes.

Let $V_1, V_2, \ldots, V_{m_i}$ be the combinations of causes that lead to *e* being present. There must be at least one combination that makes *e* to be present, that is in 1-state, and hence $m_i \geq 1$. Set $V_k(l)$, $p < l \leq p + q$ to 0 or 1 depending on whether effect Ef_{l-p} is present for the combination of all conditions in V_k.

  2.3 *Update the decision table.*

Add $V_1, V_2, \ldots, V_{m_i}$ to the decision table as successive columns starting at *next_dt_col*.

  2.4 *Update the next available column in the decision table.*

next_dt_col = *next_dt_col* + m_i. At the end of this procedure, *next_dt_col* − 1 is the number of tests generated.

End of Procedure CEGDT

Procedure CEGDT can be automated for the generation of tests. However, as indicated in Step 2.2, one needs to use some heuristics in order to avoid combinatorial explosion in the number of tests generated.

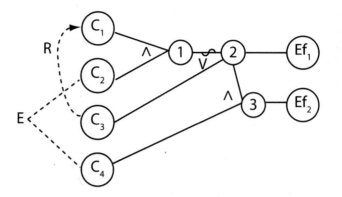

Fig. 2.15 A cause-effect graph to illustrate procedure CEGDT.

Before we introduce the heuristics, we illustrate through a simple example the application of Procedure CEGDT *without* applying the heuristics in Step 2.

Example 2.20: Consider the cause–effect graph in Figure 2.15. It shows four causes labeled C_1, C_2, C_3, and C_4 and two effects labeled Ef_1 and Ef_2. There are three intermediate nodes labeled 1, 2, and 3. Let us now follow procedure CEGDT step-by-step to generate a decision table.

In Step 1 we set *next_dt_col* = 1 to initialize the decision table to empty. Next, $i = 1$ and, in accordance with Step 2.1, $e = Ef_1$. Continuing further and in accordance with Step 2, we trace backward from e to determine combinations that will cause e to be present. e must be present when node 2 is in 1-state. Moving backward from node 2 in the cause–effect graph, we note that any of the following three combinations of states of nodes 1 and C_3 will lead to e being present: (0, 1), (1, 1), and (0, 0).

Node 1 is also an internal node and hence we move further back to obtain the values of C_1 and C_2 that effect node 1. Combination of C_1 and C_2 that brings node 1 to 1-state is (1, 1) and combinations that bring to 0-state are (1, 0), (0, 1), and (0, 0). Combining this information with that derived earlier for nodes 1 and C_3, we obtain the following seven combinations of C_1, C_2, and C_3 that cause e to be present.

1	0	1
0	1	1
0	0	1
1	1	1
1	0	0
0	1	0
0	0	0

Next, from Figure 2.15, we note that C_3 requires C_1, which implies that C_1 must be in 1-state for C_3 to be in 1-state. This constraint makes infeasible the second and third combinations above. In the end, we obtain the following five combinations of the four causes that lead to e being present.

$$
\begin{array}{ccc}
1 & 0 & 1 \\
1 & 1 & 1 \\
1 & 0 & 0 \\
0 & 1 & 0 \\
0 & 0 & 0
\end{array}
$$

Setting C_4 to 0 and appending the values of Ef_1 and Ef_2, we obtain the following five vectors. Note that $m_1 = 5$ in Step 2. This completes the application of Step 2.2, without the application of any heuristics, in the CEGDT procedure.

$$
\begin{array}{ccccccc}
V_1 & 1 & 0 & 1 & 0 & 1 & 0 \\
V_2 & 1 & 1 & 1 & 0 & 1 & 0 \\
V_3 & 1 & 0 & 0 & 0 & 1 & 0 \\
V_4 & 0 & 1 & 0 & 0 & 1 & 0 \\
V_5 & 0 & 0 & 0 & 0 & 1 & 0
\end{array}
$$

The five vectors are transposed and added to the decision table starting at column *next_dt_ col*, which is 1. The decision table at the end of Step 2.3 is as follows:

	1	2	3	4	5
C_1	1	1	1	0	0
C_2	0	1	0	1	0
C_3	1	1	0	0	0
C_4	0	0	0	0	0
Ef_1	1	1	1	1	1
Ef_2	0	0	0	0	0

We update *next_dt_col* to 6, increment i to 2, and get back to Step 2.1. We now have $e = Ef_2$. Tracing backward we find that for e to be present, node 3 must be in the 1-state. This is possible with only one combination of node 2 and C_4, which is (1, 1).

Earlier we derived the combinations of C_1, C_2, and C_3 that lead node 2 into the 1-state. Combining these with the value of C_4, we arrive at the following combination of causes that lead to the presence of Ef_2.

$$
\begin{array}{cccc}
1 & 0 & 1 & 1 \\
1 & 1 & 1 & 1 \\
1 & 0 & 0 & 1 \\
0 & 1 & 0 & 1 \\
0 & 0 & 0 & 1
\end{array}
$$

From Figure 2.15, we note that C_2 and C_4 cannot be present simultaneously. Hence, we discard the first and the fourth combinations from the list above and obtain the following three feasible combinations.

$$
\begin{array}{cccc}
1 & 0 & 1 & 1 \\
1 & 0 & 1 & 0 \\
0 & 0 & 0 & 1
\end{array}
$$

Appending the corresponding values of Ef_1 and Ef_2 to each of the above combinations, we obtain the following three vectors.

$$
\begin{array}{ccccccc}
V_1 & 1 & 0 & 1 & 1 & 1 & 1 \\
V_2 & 1 & 0 & 0 & 1 & 1 & 1 \\
V_3 & 0 & 0 & 0 & 1 & 1 & 1
\end{array}
$$

Transposing the vectors listed above and appending them as three columns to the existing decision table, we obtain the following.

	1	2	3	4	5	6	7	8
C_1	1	1	1	0	0	1	1	0
C_2	0	1	0	1	0	0	0	0
C_3	1	1	0	0	0	1	0	0
C_4	0	0	0	0	0	1	1	1
Ef_1	1	1	1	1	1	1	1	1
Ef_2	0	0	0	0	0	1	1	1

Next we update *nxt_dt_col* to 9. Of course, doing so is useless as the loop set up in Step 2 is now terminated. The decision table listed

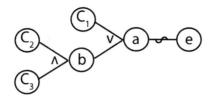

Fig. 2.16 Cause–effect graph for Example 2.21.

above is the output obtained by applying procedure CEGDT to the cause–effect graph in Figure 2.15.

2.6.4 HEURISTICS TO AVOID COMBINATORIAL EXPLOSION

While tracing back through a cause–effect graph, we generate combinations of causes that set an intermediate node, or an effect, to 0-state or a 1-state. Doing so in a brute-force manner could lead to a large number of combinations. In the worst case, if n causes are related to an effect e, then the maximum number of combinations that bring e to a 1-state is 2^n.

As tests are derived from the combinations of causes, large values of n could lead to an exorbitantly large number of tests. We avoid such a combinatorial explosion by using simple heuristics related to the "AND" ($\wedge$) and "OR" ($\vee$) nodes.

Certainly, the heuristics described below are based on the assumption that certain types of errors are less likely to occur than others. Thus, while applying the heuristics to generate test inputs is likely to lead to a significant reduction in the number of tests generated, it may also discard tests that would have revealed a program error. Hence, one must apply the heuristics with care and only when the number of tests generated without their application is too large to be useful in practice.

A set of four heuristics labeled H_1 through H_4 is given in Table 2.4. The leftmost column shows the node type in the cause–effect graph, the center column is the desired state of the dependent node, and the rightmost column is the heuristic for generating combinations of inputs to the nodes that effect the dependent node e.

For simplicity we have shown only two nodes n_1 and n_2 and the corresponding effect e; in general there could be one or more nodes related to e. Also, each of n_1 and n_2 might represent a cause or may be an internal node with inputs, shown as dashed lines, from causes or other internal nodes. The next example illustrates the application of the four heuristics shown in Table 2.4.

Table 2.4 Heuristics used during the generation of input combinations from a cause–effect graph

Node type	Desired state of e	Input combinations
	0	H_1: Enumerate all combinations of inputs to n_1 and n_2 such that $n_1 = n_2 = 0$
	1	H_2: Enumerate all combinations of inputs to n_1 and n_2 other than those for which $n_1 = n_2 = 1$
	0	H_3: Enumerate all combinations of inputs to n_1 and n_2 such that each of the possible combinations of n_1 and n_2 appears exactly once and $n_1 = n_2 = 1$ does not appear. Note that for two nodes, as in the figure on the left, there are three such combinations: $(1, 0)$, $(0, 1)$, and $(1, 0)$. In general, for k nodes anded to form e, there are $2^k - 1$ such combinations
	1	H_4: Enumerate all combinations of inputs to n_1 and n_2 such that $n_1 = n_2 = 1$

Example 2.21: Consider the cause–effect graph in Figure 2.16. We have at least two choices while tracing backward to derive the necessary combinations: derive all combinations first and then apply the heuristics and derive combinations while applying the heuristics. Let us opt for the first alternative as it is a bit simple to use in this example.

Suppose that we require node e to be 1. Tracing backward, this requirement implies that node a must be a 0. If we trace backward further, without applying any heuristic, we obtain the following seven combinations of causes that bring e to 1-state. The last column lists the inputs to node a. The combinations that correspond to the inputs to node a listed in the rightmost column are separated by horizontal lines.

	C_1	C_2	C_3	Inputs to node a
1	0	0	0	$C_1 = 0, b = 0$
2	0	0	1	
3	0	1	0	
4	0	1	1	$C_1 = 0, b = 1$
5	1	0	0	$C_1 = 1, b = 0$
6	1	0	1	
7	1	1	0	

Let us now generate tests using the heuristics applicable to this example. First we note that node a matches the OR-node shown in the top half of Table 2.4. As we want the state of node a to be 0, heuristic H_1 applies in this situation. H_1 asks us to enumerate all combinations of inputs to node a such that C_1 and node b are 0. There are two such combinations: $(0, 0)$ and $(0, 1)$. These two combinations are listed in the last column of the preceding table.

Next we consider each combination of nodes C_1 and b, one at a time. Let us begin with $(0, 0)$. No heuristic applies to C_1 as it has no preceding nodes. Node b is an AND-node as shown in the bottom half of Table 2.4. We want node b to be 0 and, therefore, heuristic H_3 applies. In accordance with H_3, we generate three combinations of inputs to node b: $(0, 0)$, $(0, 1)$, and $(1, 0)$. Note that combination $(1, 1)$ is forbidden. Joining these combinations of C_1 and C_2 with $C_1 = 0$, we obtain the first three combinations listed in the preceding table.

Next we consider $C_1 = 0$, $b = 1$. Heuristic H_4 applies in this situation. As both C_2 and C_3 are causes with no preceding nodes, the only combination we obtain now is $(1, 1)$. Combining this with $C_1 = 0$, we obtain sequence 4 listed in the preceding table.

We have completed the derivation of combinations using the heuristics listed in Table 2.4. Note that the combinations listed above for $C_1 = 1$, $b = 0$ are not required. Thus, we have obtained only four combinations instead of the seven enumerated earlier. The reduced set of combinations is listed below.

	C_1	C_2	C_3	Inputs to node a
1	0	0	0	$C_1 = 0, b = 0$
2	0	0	1	
3	0	1	0	
4	0	1	1	$C_1 = 0, b = 1$

Let us now examine the rationale underlying the various heuristics for reducing the number of combinations. Heuristic H_1 does not save us on any combinations. The only way an OR-node can cause its effect e to be 0 is for all its inputs to be 0. H_1 suggests that we enumerate all such combinations. Heuristic H_2 suggests that we use all combinations that cause e to be 1 except those that cause $n_1 = n_2 = 1$. To understand the rationale underlying H_2, consider a program required to generate an error message when condition c_1 or c_2 is true. A correct implementation of this requirement is given below.

$$\text{if } (c_1 \vee c_2) \, \text{print}(\text{``Error''});$$

Now consider the following erroneous implementation of the same requirement.

$$\text{if } (c_1 \vee \neg c_2) \, \text{print}(\text{``Error''});$$

A test that sets both c_1 and c_2 true will not be able to detect an error in the implementation above if short circuit evaluation is used for Boolean expressions. However, a test that sets $c_1 = 0$ and $c_2 = 1$ will be able to detect this error. Hence, H_2 saves us from generating all input combinations that generate the pair $(1, 1)$ entering an effect in an OR-node (see Exercise 2.23).

Heuristic H_3 saves us from repeating the combinations of n_1 and n_2. Once again, this could save us a lot of tests. The assumption here is that any error in the implementation of e will be detected by combinations that cover different combinations of n_1 and n_2. Thus, there is no need to have two or more combinations that contain the same combination of n_1 and n_2.

Finally, H_4 for the AND-node is analogous to H_1 for the OR-node. The only way an AND-node can cause its effect e to be 1 is for all its inputs to be 1. H_4 suggests that we enumerate all such combinations. We stress, once again, that while the heuristics discussed above are likely to reduce the set of tests generated using cause–effect graphing, they might also lead to useful tests being discarded. Of course, in general and prior to the start of testing, it is almost impossible to know which of the test cases discarded will be useless and which ones useful.

2.6.5 TEST GENERATION FROM A DECISION TABLE

Test generation from a decision table is relatively straightforward. Each column in the decision table generates at least one test input. Note that each combination might be able to generate more than one test when a condition in the cause–effect graph can be satisfied in more than one way. For example, consider the following cause:

$$C : x < 99.$$

The condition above can be satisfied by many values such as $x = 1$ and $x = 49$. Also, C can be made false by many values of x such as $x = 100$ and $x = 999$. Thus, while generating tests using columns from a decision table, one might have a choice of values or input variables.

While one could always select values arbitrarily as long as they satisfy the requirement in the decision table, it is recommended that the choice be made so that tests generated are different from those that may have already been generated using some other technique such as, boundary-value analysis. Exercise 2.25 asks you to develop tests for the GUI-based computer purchase system in Example 2.19.

2.7 TEST GENERATION FROM PREDICATES

In this section, we introduce techniques for generating tests that are guaranteed to detect certain faults in the coding of conditions. The conditions from which tests are generated might arise from requirements or might be embedded in the program to be tested.

A condition is represented formally as a predicate. For example, consider the requirement "if the printer is ON and has paper then send the document for printing." This statement consists of a condition part and an action part. The following predicate, denoted as p_r, represents the condition part of the statement.

```
pᵣ: (printer_status=ON) ∧ (printer_tray = ¬empty)
```

The predicate p_r consists of two relational expressions joined with the $\land$ Boolean operator. Each of the two relational expressions uses the equality (=) symbol. A programmer might code p_r correctly or might make an error, thus creating a fault in the program. We are interested in generating test cases from predicates such that any fault, that belongs to a class of faults, is guaranteed to be detected during testing. Testing to ensure that there are no errors in the implementation of predicates is also known as *predicate testing.*

We begin our move toward the test-generation algorithm by first defining some basic terms related to predicates and Boolean expressions. Then we will examine the fault model that indicates what faults are the targets of the tests generated by the algorithms we will examine. This is followed by an introduction to constraints and tests and then the algorithm for which you would have waited so long.

2.7.1 Predicates and Boolean Expressions

Let *relop* denote a relational operator in the set $\{<, >, \leq, \geq, =, \neq\}$. Let *bop* denote a Boolean operator in the set $\{\wedge, \vee, \veebar, \neg\}$, where $\wedge$, $\vee$, and $\veebar$ are binary Boolean operators and $\neg$ is a unary Boolean operator. A *Boolean variable* takes on values from the set $\{true, false\}$. Given a Boolean variable a, $\neg a$ and $\bar{a}$ denote the complement of a.

A *relational expression* is an expression of the form e_1 *relop* e_2, where e_1 and e_2 are expressions that assume values from a finite or infinite set S. It should be possible to order the elements of S so that a and b can be compared using any one of the relational operators.

A condition can be represented as a *simple predicate* or a *compound predicate*. A simple predicate is a Boolean variable or a relational expression, where any one or more variables might be negated. A compound predicate is a simple predicate or an expression formed by joining two or more simple predicates, possibly negated, with a binary Boolean operator. Parentheses in any predicate indicate groupings of variables and relational expressions. Examples of predicates and of other terms defined in this section are given in Table 2.5.

Table 2.5 Examples of terms defined in Section 2.7.1

Item	Examples	Comment
Simple predicate	p $q \wedge r$ $a + b < c$	p, q, and r are Boolean variables; a, b, and c are integer variables.
Compound predicate	$\neg(a + b < c)$ $(a + b < c) \wedge (\neg p)$	Parentheses are used to make explicit the grouping of simple predicates.
Boolean expression	$p, \neg p$ $p \wedge q \vee r$	
Singular Boolean expression	$p \wedge q \vee \bar{r} \wedge s$	p, q, r, and s are Boolean variables.
Nonsingular Boolean expression	$p \wedge q \vee \bar{r} \wedge p$	

A *Boolean expression* is composed of one or more Boolean variables joined by Boolean operators. In other words, a Boolean expression is a predicate that does not contain any relational expression. When it is clear from the context, we omit the $\wedge$ operator and use the $+$ sign instead of $\vee$. For example, Boolean expression $p \wedge q \vee \bar{r} \wedge s$ can be written as $pq + \bar{r}s$.

Note that the term pq is also known as a product of variables p and q. Similarly, the term rs is the product of Boolean variables r and s. The expression $pq + \bar{r}s$ is a sum of two product terms pq and $\bar{r}s$. We assume left-to-right associativity for operators. Also, and takes precedence over or.

Each occurrence of a Boolean variable, or its negation, inside a Boolean expression, is considered as a literal. For example, p, q, r, and p are four literals in the expression $p \wedge q \vee \bar{r} \wedge p$.

A predicate p_r can be converted to a Boolean expression by replacing each relational expression in p_r by a distinct Boolean variable. For example, the predicate $(a + b < c) \wedge (\neg d)$ is equivalent to the Boolean expression $e_1 \wedge e_2$, where $e_1 = a + b < c$ and $e_2 = \neg d$.

A Boolean expression is considered singular if each variable in the expression occurs only once. Consider the following Boolean expression E that contains k distinct Boolean expressions $e_1, e_2, \ldots, e_k$.

$$E = e_1 \; bop \; e_2 \; bop \; \ldots \; e_{k-1} \; bop \; e_k.$$

For $1 < (i, j) \leq k, i \neq j$, we say that e_i and e_j are mutually singular if they do not share any variable. e_i is considered a singular component of E if and only if e_i is singular and is mutually singular with each of the other $k - 1$ components of E. e_i is considered nonsingular if and only if it is nonsingular by itself and is mutually singular with the remaining $k - 1$ elements of E.

A Boolean expression is in *disjunctive normal form,* also referred to as DNF, if it is represented as a sum of product terms. For example, $pq + \bar{r}s$ is a DNF expression. A Boolean expression is in *conjunctive normal form,* also referred to as CNF, if it is written as a product of sums. For example, the expression $(p + \bar{r})(p + s)(q + \bar{r})(q + s)$ is a CNF equivalent of expression $pq + \bar{r}s$. Note that any Boolean expression in CNF can be converted to an equivalent DNF and vice versa.

A Boolean expression can also be represented as an abstract syntax tree as shown in Figure 2.17. We use the term $AST(p_r)$ for the abstract syntax tree of a predicate p_r. Each leaf node of $AST(p_r)$ represents a Boolean variable or a relational expression. An internal node of $AST(p_r)$ is a Boolean operator such as $\wedge, \vee, \veebar$, and, $\neg$ and

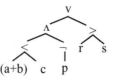

Fig. 2.17 An abstract syntax tree for compound predicate $(a + b < c) \wedge (\neg p) \vee (r > s)$.

is known as an *AND*-node, *OR*-node, *XOR*-node, and a *NOT*-node, respectively.

2.7.2 FAULT MODEL FOR PREDICATE TESTING

Predicate testing, as introduced in this chapter, targets three classes of faults: Boolean operator fault, relational operator fault, and arithmetic expression fault. A Boolean operator fault is caused when (i) an incorrect Boolean operator is used, (ii) a negation is missing or placed incorrectly, (iii) parentheses are incorrect, and (iv) an incorrect Boolean variable is used. A relational operator fault occurs when an incorrect relational operator is used. An arithmetic expression fault occurs when the value of an arithmetic expression is off by an amount equal to ϵ.

Given a predicate p_r and a test case t, we write $p(t)$ as an abbreviation for the truth value obtained by evaluating p_r on t. For example, if p_r is $a < b \wedge r > s$ and t is $< a = 1, b = 2, r = 0, s = 4 >$, then $p(t) = \texttt{false}$. Let us now examine a few examples of the faults in the fault model used in this section.

Boolean operator fault: Suppose that the specification of a software module requires that an action be performed when the condition $(a < b) \vee (c > d) \wedge e$ is true. Here $a, b, c,$ and d are integer variables and e a Boolean variable. Four incorrect codings of this condition, each containing a Boolean operator fault, are given below.

$(a < b) \wedge (c > d) \wedge e$	Incorrect Boolean operator
$(a < b) \vee \neg(c > d) \wedge e$	Incorrect negation operator
$(a < b) \wedge (c > d) \vee e$	Incorrect Boolean operators
$(a < b) \vee (c > d) \wedge f$	Incorrect Boolean variable (f instead of e).

Note that a predicate might contain a single or multiple faults. The third example above is a predicate containing two faults.

Relational operator fault: Examples of relational operator faults follow.

$(a = b) \lor (c > d) \land e$ Incorrect relational operator; $<$ replaced by $=$.

$(a = b) \lor (c \leq d) \land e$ Two relational operator faults.

$(a = b) \lor (c > d) \lor e$ Incorrect relational and Boolean operators.

Arithmetic expression fault: We consider three types of off-by-ϵ fault in an arithmetic expression. These faults are referred to as off-by-ϵ, off-by-ϵ^*, and off-by-ϵ^+. To understand the differences between these three faults, consider a correct relational expression E_c to be e_1 $relop_1$ e_2 and an incorrect relational expression E_i to be e_3 $relop_2$ e_4. We assume that the arithmetic expressions e_1, e_2, e_3, and e_4 contain the same set of variables. The three fault types are defined below.

- E_i has an off-by-ϵ fault if $| e_3 - e_4 | = \epsilon$ for any test case for which $e_1 = e_2$.

- E_i has an off-by-ϵ^* fault if $| e_3 - e_4 | \geq \epsilon$ for any test case for which $e_1 = e_2$.

- E_i has an off-by-ϵ^+ fault if $| e_3 - e_4 | > \epsilon$ for any test case for which $e_1 = e_2$.

Suppose that the correct predicate E_c is $a < b + c$, where a and b are integer variables. Assuming that $\epsilon = 1$, three incorrect versions of E_c follow.

$a < b$ Assuming that $c = 1$, there is an off-by-1 fault in E_i as $|a - b| = 1$ for any value of a and b that makes $a = b + c$.

$a < b + 1$ Assuming that $c \geq 2$, there is an off-by-1* fault in E_i as $| a - (b + 1) | \geq 1$ for any value of a and b that makes $a = b + c$.

$a < b - 1$ Assuming that $c > 0$, there is an off-by-1$^+$ fault in E_i as $| a - (b - 1) | > 1$ for any value of a and b that makes $a = b + c$

Given a correct predicate p_c, the goal of predicate testing is to generate a test set T such that there is at least one test case $t \in T$ for which p_c and its faulty version p_i evaluate to different truth values. Such a test set is said to guarantee the detection of any fault of the kind in the fault model introduced above.

As an example, suppose that $p_c : a < b + c$ and $p_i : a > b + c$. Consider a test set $T = \{t_1, t_2\}$, where $t_1 : <a = 0, b = 0, c = 0>$ and $t_2 : < a = 0, b = 1, c = 1 >$. The fault in p_i is not revealed by t_1 as both p_c and p_i evaluate to `false` when evaluated against t_1. However, the fault is revealed by the test case t_2 as p_c evaluates to `true` and p_i to `false` when evaluated against t_2.

2.7.2.1 Missing or Extra Boolean Variable Faults

Two additional types of common faults have not been considered in the fault model described above. These are the missing Boolean variable and the extra Boolean variable faults.

As an illustration, consider a process-control system in which the pressure P and temperature T of a liquid container is being measured and transmitted to a control computer. The emergency check in the control software is required to raise an alarm when any one of the following conditions is true: $T > T_{max}$ and $P > P_{max}$. The alarm specification can be translated to a predicate $p_r : T > T_{max} \lor P > P_{max}$, which when true must cause the computer to raise the alarm, and not otherwise.

Note that p_r can be written as a Boolean expression $a + b$, where $a = T > T_{max}$ and $b = P > P_{max}$. Now suppose that the implementation of the control software codes p_r as a and not as $a \lor b$. Obviously, there is a fault in coding p_r. We refer to this fault as the *missing Boolean variable* fault.

Next, assume that the predicate p_r has been incorrectly coded as $a + b + c$, where c is a Boolean variable representing some condition. Once again we have a fault in the coding of p_r. We refer to this fault as *extra Boolean variable* fault.

The missing and extra Boolean variable faults are not guaranteed to be detected by tests generated using any of the procedures introduced in this chapter. In Chapter 7, we will show under what conditions such faults are guaranteed to be detected using a test generation method based on program mutation.

2.7.3 PREDICATE CONSTRAINTS

Let BR denote the following set of symbols $\{t, f, <, =, >, +\epsilon, -\epsilon\}$. Here "BR" is an abbreviation for *Boolean and relational*. We shall refer to an element of the BR set as a BR-symbol.

A BR symbol specifies a *constraint* on a Boolean variable or a relational expression. For example, the symbol "$+\epsilon$" is a constraint on the expression $E' : e_1 < e_2$. Satisfaction of this constraint requires that a test case for E' ensure that $0 < e_1 - e_2 \leq \epsilon$. Similarly, the symbol "$-\epsilon$" is another constraint on E'. This constraint can be satisfied by a test for E' such that $-\epsilon \leq e_1 - e_2 < 0$.

A constraint C is considered *infeasible* for predicate p_r if there exist no input values for the variables in p_r that satisfy C. For example, constraint $(>, >)$ for predicate $a > b \land b > d$ requires the simple predicates $a > b$ and $b > d$ to be true. However, this constraint is infeasible if it is known that $d > a$.

> **Example 2.22:** As a simple example of a constraint, consider the relational expression $E : a < c + d$. Consider constraint "$C : (=)$" on E. While testing E for correctness, satisfying C requires at least one test case such that $a = c + d$. Thus, the test case $<a = 1, c = 0, d = 1>$ satisfies the constraint C on E.
>
> As another example, consider the constraint $C : (+\epsilon)$ on expression E given in Example 2.22. Let $\epsilon = 1$. A test to satisfy C requires that $0 < a - (c + d) \leq 1$. Thus, the test case $<a = 4, c = 2, d = 1>$ satisfies constraint $(+\epsilon)$ on expression E.
>
> Similarly, given a Boolean expression $E : b$, the constraint "**t**" is satisfied by a test case that sets variable b to `true`.

BR symbols **t** and **f** are used to specify constraints on Boolean variables and expressions. A constraint on a relational expression is specified using any of the three symbols $<$, $=$, and $>$. Symbols **t** and **f** can also be used to specify constraints on a simple relational expression when the expression is treated as a representative of a Boolean variable. For example, expression $p_r : a < b$ could serve as a representative of a Boolean variable z in which case we can specify constraints on p_r using **t** and **f**.

We will now define constraints for entire predicates that contain Boolean variables and relational expressions joined by one or more Boolean operators.

Let p_r denote a predicate with $n, n > 0$, $\land$ and $\lor$ operators. A *predicate constraint* C for predicate p_r is a sequence of $(n+1)$ BR symbols, one for each Boolean variable or relational expression in p_r. When clear from context, we refer to *predicate constraint* as simply *constraint*.

We say that a test case t satisfies C for predicate p_r, if each component of p_r satisfies the corresponding constraint in C when evaluated against t. Constraint C for predicate p_r guides the development of a test for p_r, that is it offers hints on the selection of values of the variables in p_r.

> **Example 2.23:** Consider the predicate $p : b \land r < s \lor u \geq v$. One possible BR constraint for p_r is $C : (t, =, >)$. Note that C contains three constraints one for each of the three components of p_r.

Constraint t applies to b, = to $r < s$, and > to $u \geq v$. The following test case satisfies C for p_r.

```
<b = true, r = 1, s = 1, u = 1, v = 0>
```

Several other test cases also satisfy C for p_r. However, the following test case does not satisfy C for p_r.

```
<b = true, r = 1, s = 1, u = 1, v = 2>
```

as the last of the three elements in C is not satisfied for the corresponding component of p_r, which is $u \geq v$.

Given a constraint C for predicate p_r, any test case that satisfies C makes p_r either `true` or `false`. Thus, we write $p_r(C)$ to indicate the value of p_r obtained by evaluating it against any test case that satisfies C. A constraint C for which $pr(C) = $ `true` is referred to as a *true constraint* and the one for which $p_r(C)$ evaluates to `false` is referred to as a *false constraint*. We partition a set of constraints S into two sets S^t and S^f such that $S = S^t \cup S^f$. The partition is such that for each $C \in S^t$, $p_r(C) = $ `true` and for each $C \in S^f$, $p_r(C) = $ `false`.

Example 2.24: Consider the predicate $p_r : (a < b) \wedge (c > d)$ and constraint $C_1 : (=, >)$ on p_r. Any test case that satisfies C_1 on p_r, makes p_r evaluate to `false`. Hence C_1 is a false constraint. Consider another constraint $C_2 : (<, +\epsilon)$ for $\epsilon = 1$ on predicate p_r. Any test case that satisfies C_2 on p_r, makes p_r evaluate to `true`. Hence, C_2 is a true constraint. Now, if $S = \{C_1, C_2\}$ is a set of constraints on predicate p_r, then we have $S^t = \{C_2\}$ and $S^f = \{C_1\}$.

2.7.4 PREDICATE-TESTING CRITERIA

We are interested in generating a test set T from a given predicate p_r such that (a) T is minimal and (b) T guarantees the detection of any fault in the implementation of p_r that conforms to the fault model described earlier. Toward the goal of generating such a test set, we define three criteria commonly known as the BOR-, BRO-, and BRE-testing criteria. The names BOR, BRO, and BRE correspond to, respectively, *Boolean operator*, *Boolean and relational operator*, and *Boolean and relational expression*. Formal definitions of the three criteria are as follows.

- *A test set T that satisfies the BOR-testing criterion for a compound predicate p_r, guarantees the detection of single or multiple Boolean operator faults in the implementation of p_r. T is referred to as a BOR-adequate test set and sometimes written as T_{BOR}.*

- *A test set T that satisfies the BRO-testing criterion for a compound predicate p_r, guarantees the detection of single or multiple Boolean operator and relational operator faults in the implementation of p_r. T is referred to as a BRO-adequate test set and sometimes written as T_{BRO}.*

- *A test set T that satisfies the BRE-testing criterion for a compound predicate p_r guarantees the detection of single or multiple Boolean operator, relational expression, and arithmetic expression faults in the implementation of p_r. T is referred to as a BRE-adequate test set and sometimes written as T_{BRE}.*

The term "guarantees the detection of" is to be interpreted carefully. Let T_x, $x \in \{BOR, BRO, BRE\}$ be a test set derived from predicate p_r. Let p_f be another predicate obtained from p_r by injecting single or multiple faults of one of three kinds: Boolean operator fault, relational operator fault, and arithmetic expression fault. T_x is said to guarantee the detection of faults in p_f if for some $t \in T_x$, $p(t) \neq p_f(t)$. The next example shows a sample BOR-adequate test set and its fault detection effectiveness.

Example 2.25: Consider the compound predicate $p_r : a < b \wedge c > d$. Let S denote a set of constraints on p_r; $S = \{(\mathbf{t}, \mathbf{t}), (\mathbf{t}, \mathbf{f}), (\mathbf{f}, \mathbf{t})\}$. The following test set T satisfies constraint set S and the BOR-testing criterion.

```
T = {  t₁: < a = 1, b = 2, c = 1, d = 0 >;
          Satisfies (t, t),
       t₂: < a = 1, b = 2, c = 1, d = 2 >;
          Satisfies (t, f),
       t₃: < a = 1, b = 0, c = 1, d = 0 >;
          Satisfies (f, t).
    }
```

As T satisfies the BOR-testing criterion, it guarantees that all single and multiple Boolean operator faults in p_r will be revealed. Let us check this by evaluating p_r, and all its variants created by inserting Boolean operator faults, against T.

Table 2.6 lists p_r and a total of seven faulty predicates obtained by inserting single and multiple Boolean operator faults in p_r. Each predicate is evaluated against the three test cases in T. Note that each faulty predicate evaluates to a value different from that of p_r for at least one test case.

Table 2.6 Fault detection ability of a BOR-adequate test set T of Example 2.25 for single and multiple Boolean operator faults. Results of evaluation that distinguish the faulty predicate from the correct one are italicised

	Predicate	t_1	t_2	t_3
	$a < b \wedge c > d$	true	false	false
Single Boolean operator fault				
1	$a < b \vee c > d$	true	*true*	*true*
2	$a < b \wedge \neg c > d$	*false*	*true*	false
3	$\neg a < b \wedge c > d$	*false*	false	*true*
Multiple Boolean operator faults				
4	$a < b \vee \neg c > d$	true	*true*	false
5	$\neg a < b \vee c > d$	true	false	*true*
6	$\neg a < b \wedge \neg c > d$	*false*	false	false
7	$\neg a < b \vee \neg c > d$	true	*true*	*true*

It is easily verified that if any column is removed from Table 2.6, at least one of the faulty predicates will be left indistinguishable by the tests in the remaining two columns. For example, if we remove test t_2 then the faulty predicate 4 cannot be distinguished from p_r by tests t_1 and t_3. We have thus shown that T is minimal and BOR adequate for predicate p_r.

Exercise 2.28 is similar to the one above and asks you to verify that the two given test sets are BRO and BRE adequate, respectively. In the next section we provide algorithms for generating BOR-, BRO-, and BRE-adequate tests.

2.7.5 GENERATING BOR-, BRO-, AND BRE-ADEQUATE TESTS

We are now ready to describe the algorithms that generate constraints to test a predicate. The actual tests cases are generated using the constraints. Recall that a feasible constraint can be satisfied by one or more test cases. Thus, the algorithms we describe are to generate constraints and do not focus on the generation of the specific test cases. The test cases to satisfy the constraints can be generated manually or automatically. Let us begin by describing how to generate a BOR-constraint set for a given predicate.

Let us first review the following two definitions of set products. The product of two finite sets A and B, denoted as $A \times B$, is defined as follows:

$$A \times B = \{ (a, b) \mid a \in A, b \in B \} \qquad (2.1)$$

We need another set product in order to be able to generate minimal sets of constraints. The *onto* set product operator, written as $\otimes$, is defined as follows; For finite sets A and B, $A \otimes B$ is a minimal set of pairs (u, v) such that $u \in A$, $v \in B$, and each element of A appears at least once as u and each element of B appears at least once as v. Note that there are several ways to compute $A \otimes B$ when both A and B contain two or more elements.

> **Example 2.26:** Let $A = \{t, =, >\}$ and $B = \{f, <\}$. Using the definitions of set product and the onto product, we get the following sets.

$$A \times B = \{(\mathbf{t}, \mathbf{f}), (\mathbf{t}, <), (=, \mathbf{f}), (=, <), (>, \mathbf{f}), (>, <)\}$$
$$A \otimes B = \{(\mathbf{t}, \mathbf{f}), (=, <), (>, <)\}; \text{ First possibility.}$$
$$A \otimes B = \{(\mathbf{t}, <), (=, \mathbf{f}), (>, <)\}; \text{ Second possibility.}$$
$$A \otimes B = \{(\mathbf{t}, \mathbf{f}), (=, <), (>, \mathbf{f})\}; \text{ Third possibility.}$$
$$A \otimes B = \{(\mathbf{t}, <), (=, <), (>, \mathbf{f})\}; \text{ Fourth possibility.}$$
$$A \otimes B = \{(\mathbf{t}, <), (=, \mathbf{f}), (>, \mathbf{f})\}; \text{ Fifth possibility.}$$
$$A \otimes B = \{(\mathbf{t}, \mathbf{f}), (=, \mathbf{f}), (>, <)\}; \text{ Sixth possibility.}$$

Note that there are six different ways to compute $A \otimes B$. In the algorithms described next, we select any one of the different sets that result when computing $A \otimes B$.

Given a predicate p_r, the generation of the BOR-, BRO-, and BRE-constraint sets requires the abstract syntax tree for p_r denoted as $AST(p_r)$. Recall that (a) each leaf node of $AST(p_r)$ represents a Boolean variable or a relational expression and (b) internal node of $AST(p_r)$ is a Boolean operator such as $\wedge$, $\vee$, and $\neg$ and is known as an *AND*-node, *OR*-node, and a *NOT*-node, respectively.

We now introduce four procedures for generating tests from a predicate. The first three procedures generate BOR-, BRO-, and BRE-adequate tests for predicates that involve only singular expressions. The last procedure, named BOR-MI, generates tests for predicates that contain at least one nonsingular expression. See Exercise 2.37 for an example that illustrates the problem in applying the first three procedures below to a nonsingular expression.

2.7.5 Generating the BOR-constraint set

Let p_r be a predicate and $AST(p_r)$ its abstract syntax tree. We use letters such as N, N_1, and N_2 to refer to various nodes in the $AST(p_r)$. S_N denotes the constraint set attached to node N. As explained earlier, S_N^t and S_N^f denote, respectively, the true and false constraints associated with node N; $S_N = S_N^t \cup S_N^f$. The following algorithm generates the BOR-constraint set (CSET) for p_r.

```
Procedure for generating a minimal BOR-constraint
set from an abstract syntax tree of a predicate p_r
```

Input: An abstract syntax tree for predicate p_r, denoted by $AST(p_r)$. p_r contains only singular expressions.

Output: BOR-constraint set for p_r attached to the root node of $AST(p_r)$.

Procedure: BOR-CSET

Step 1 Label each leaf node N of $AST(p_r)$ with its constraint set $S(N)$. For each leaf $S_N = \{t, f\}$

Step 2 Visit each nonleaf node in $AST(p_r)$ in a bottom up manner. Let N_1 and N_2 denote the direct descendants of node N, if N is an AND or an OR-node. If N is a NOT-node, then N_1 is its direct descendant. S_{N_1} and S_{N_2} are the BOR-constraint sets for nodes N_1 and N_2, respectively. For each nonleaf node N, compute S_N as follows:

2.1 *N is an OR-node:*

$$S_N^f = S_{N_1}^f \otimes S_{N_2}^f$$
$$S_N^t = \left(S_{N_1}^t \times \{f_2\}\right) \cup \left(\{f_1\} \times S_{N_2}^t\right)$$
$$\text{where } f_1 \in S_{N_1}^f \text{ and } f_2 \in S_{N_2}^f$$

2.2 *N is an AND-node:*

$$S_N^t = S_{N_1}^t \otimes S_{N_2}^t$$
$$S_N^f = \left(S_{N_1}^f \times \{t_2\}\right) \cup \left(\{t_1\} \times S_{N_2}^f\right)$$
$$\text{where } t_1 \in S_{N_1}^t \text{ and } t_2 \in S_{N_2}^t$$

2.3 *N is NOT-node:*

$$S_N^t = S_{N_1}^f$$
$$S_N^f = S_{N_1}^t$$

Step 3 The constraint set for the root of $AST(p_r)$ is the desired BOR-constraint set for p_r.

```
End of Procedure BOR-CSET
```

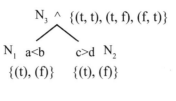

(a)

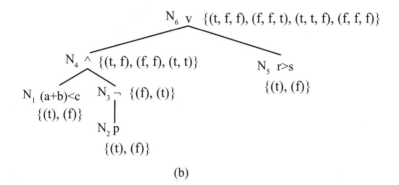

(b)

Fig. 2.18 BOR-constraint sets for predicates (a) $a < b \wedge c > d$ and (b) $(a + b) < c \wedge \neg p \vee (r > s)$. The constraint sets are listed next to each node. See the text for the separation of each constraint set into its true and false components.

Example 2.27: Let us apply the procedure described above to generate the BOR-constraint sets for the predicate $p_1 : a < b \wedge c > d$ used in Example 2.25. The abstract syntax tree for p_1 is shown in Figure 2.18(a).

N_1 and N_2 are the leaf nodes. The constraint sets for these two nodes are given below.

$$S_{N_1}^t = \{\mathbf{t}\}, \quad S_{N_1}^f = \{\mathbf{f}\}$$
$$S_{N_2}^t = \{\mathbf{t}\}, \quad S_{N_2}^f = \{\mathbf{f}\}$$

Traversing $AST(p_1)$ bottom up, we compute the constraint set for nonleaf N_3 which is an AND-node.

$$\begin{aligned}
S_{N_3}^t &= S_{N_1}^t \otimes S_{N_2}^t \\
&= \{\mathbf{t}\} \otimes \{\mathbf{t}\} \\
&= \{(\mathbf{t}, \mathbf{t})\} \\
S_{N_3}^f &= \left(S_{N_1}^f \times \{t_2\}\right) \cup \left(\{t_1\} \times S_{N_2}^f\right) \\
&= (\{\mathbf{f}\} \times \{(\mathbf{t})\}) \cup (\{\mathbf{t}\} \times \{\mathbf{f}\}) \\
&= \{(\mathbf{f}, \mathbf{t}), (\mathbf{t}, \mathbf{f})\}
\end{aligned}$$

Thus, we obtain $S_{N_3} = \{(\mathbf{t}, \mathbf{t}), (\mathbf{f}, \mathbf{t}), (\mathbf{t}, \mathbf{f})\}$, which is the BOR-constraint set for predicate p_1. We have now shown how S_{N3}, used in Example 2.25, is derived using a formal procedure.

Example 2.28: Let us compute the BOR-constraint set for predicate $p_2 : (a + b < c) \land \neg p \lor (r > s)$, which is a bit more complex than predicate p_1 from the previous example. Note that the $\land$ operator takes priority over the $\lor$ operator. Hence, p_2 is equivalent to the expression $((a + b < c) \land (\neg p)) \lor (r > s)$.

First, as shown in Figure 2.18(b), we assign the default BOR-constraint sets to the leaf nodes N_1, N_2, and N_5. Next we traverse $AST(p_2)$ bottom up and breadth first. Applying the rule for a NOT node, we obtain the BOR-constraint set for N_3 as follows:

$$S_{N_3}^t = S_{N_2}^f = \{\mathbf{f}\}$$
$$S_{N_3}^f = S_{N_2}^t = \{\mathbf{t}\}$$

We apply the rule for the AND-node and obtain the BOR-constraint set for node N_4 as follows:

$$S_{N_1}^t = S_{N_1}^t \otimes S_{N_3}^t$$
$$= \{\mathbf{t}\} \otimes \{\mathbf{f}\}$$
$$= \{(\mathbf{t}, \mathbf{f})\}$$
$$S_{N_1}^f = \left(S_{N_1}^f \times \{t_{N_3}\}\right) \cup \{t_{N_1}\} \times S_{N_3}^f\right)$$
$$= (\{\mathbf{f}\} \times \{\mathbf{f}\}) \cup (\{\mathbf{t}\} \times \{\mathbf{t}\})$$
$$= \{(\mathbf{f}, \mathbf{f}), (\mathbf{t}, \mathbf{t})\}$$
$$S_{N_1} = \{(\mathbf{t}, \mathbf{f}), (\mathbf{f}, \mathbf{f}), (\mathbf{t}, \mathbf{t})\}$$

Using the BOR-constraint sets for nodes N_4 and N_5 and applying the rule for OR-node, we obtain the BOR-constraint set for node N_6 as follows:

$$S_{N_6}^f = S_{N_4}^f \otimes S_{N_5}^f$$
$$= \{(\mathbf{f}, \mathbf{f}), (\mathbf{t}, \mathbf{t})\} \otimes \{\mathbf{f}\}$$
$$= \{(\mathbf{f}, \mathbf{f}, \mathbf{f}), (\mathbf{t}, \mathbf{t}, \mathbf{f})\}$$
$$S_{N_6}^t = \left(S_{N_4}^t \times \{f_{N_5}\}\right) \cup \{f_{N_4}\} \times S_{N_5}^t\right)$$
$$= (\{(\mathbf{t}, \mathbf{f})\} \times \{\mathbf{f}\}) \cup (\{(\mathbf{f}, \mathbf{f})\} \times \{\mathbf{t}\})$$
$$= \{(\mathbf{t}, \mathbf{f}, \mathbf{f}), (\mathbf{f}, \mathbf{f}, \mathbf{t})\}$$
$$S_{N_6} = \{(\mathbf{t}, \mathbf{f}, \mathbf{f}), (\mathbf{f}, \mathbf{f}, \mathbf{t}), (\mathbf{t}, \mathbf{t}, \mathbf{f}), (\mathbf{f}, \mathbf{f}, \mathbf{f})\}$$

Note that we could select any one of the constraints $(\mathbf{f}, \mathbf{f})$ or $(\mathbf{t}, \mathbf{t})$ for f_{N_4}. Here we have arbitrarily selected $(\mathbf{f}, \mathbf{f})$. Sample tests for p_2 that satisfy the four BOR constraints are given in Table 2.7. Exercise 2.30 asks you to confirm that indeed the test set in Table 2.7 is adequate with respect to the BOR-testing criterion.

Generating the BRO-constraint set

Recall that a test set adequate with respect to a BRO-constraint set for predicate p_r, guarantees the detection of all combinations of single or

Table 2.7 Sample test cases that satisfy the BOR constraints for predicate p_2 derived in Example 2.28

	$a + b < c$	p	$r > s$	Test case
t_1	t	f	f	$< a = 1, b = 1, c = 3,$ $p = \texttt{false}, r = 1, s = 2 >$
t_2	f	f	t	$< a = 1, b = 1, c = 1,$ $p = \texttt{false}, r = 1, s = 0 >$
t_3	t	t	f	$< a = 1, b = 1, c = 3,$ $p = \texttt{true}, r = 1, s = 1 >$
t_4	f	f	f	$< a = 1, b = 1, c = 0,$ $p = \texttt{false}, r = 0, s = 0 >$

multiple Boolean operator and relational operator faults. The BRO-constraint set S for a relational expression e_1 *relop* e_2 is $\{(>), (=), (<)\}$. As shown below, the separation of S into its true and false components depends on *relop*.

```
relop :>   S^t = {(>)}        S^f = {(=),(<)}
relop :≥   S^t = {(>),(=)}    S^f = {(<)}
relop :=   S^t = {(=)}        S^f = {(<),(>)}
relop :<   S^t = {(<)}        S^f = {(=),(>)}
relop :≤   S^t = {(<),(=)}    S^f = {(>)}
```

We now modify Procedure BRO-CSET introduced earlier for the generation of the minimal BOR-constraint set to generate a minimal BRO-constraint set. The modified procedure follows:

```
Procedure for generating a minimal BRO-constraint
set from abstract syntax tree of a predicate p_r.
```

Input : An abstract syntax tree for predicate p_r denoted by $AST(p_r)$. p_r contains only singular expressions.

Output : BRO-constraint set for p_r attached to the root node of $AST(p_r)$.

Procedure: BRO-CSET

Step 1 Label each leaf node N of $AST(p_r)$ with its constraint set $S(N)$. For each leaf node that represents a Boolean variable, $S_N = \{\texttt{t}, \texttt{f}\}$. For each leaf node that is a relational expression, $S_N = \{(>), (=), (<)\}$.

Step 2 Visit each nonleaf node in $AST(p_r)$ in a bottom up manner. Let N_1 and N_2 denote the direct descendants of node N, if N is an AND- or an OR-node. If N is a NOT-node, then N_1

is its direct descendant. S_{N_1} and S_{N_2} are the BRO-constraint sets for nodes N_1 and N_2, respectively. For each nonleaf node N, compute S_N as per Steps 2.1, 2.2, and 2.3 in Procedure BRO-CSET.

Step 3 The constraint set for the root of $AST(p_r)$ is the desired BRO-constraint set for p_r.

End of Procedure BRO-CSET

Example 2.29: Let us construct the BRO-constraint set for predicate $p_r : (a + b) < c \land \neg p \lor (r > s)$. Figure 2.19 shows the abstract syntax tree for p_r with nodes labeled by the corrresponding BRO-constraint sets. Let us derive these sets using Procedure BRO-CSET.

First, the leaf nodes are labeled with the corresponding BRO-constraint sets depending on their type. Next we traverse the tree bottom up and derive the BRO-constraints for each node from those of its immediate descendants. The BRO-constraint set for node N_3,

$$
\begin{aligned}
S_{N_4}^t &= S_{N_1}^t \land S_{N_3}^t \\
&= \{(<)\} \land \{\mathbf{f}\} \\
&= \{(<, \mathbf{f})\} \\
S_{N_4}^f &= (S_{N_1}^f \times \{t_{N_3}\}) < (\{t_{N_1}\} \times S_{N_3}^f) \\
&= (\{(>), (=)\} \times \{\mathbf{f}\}) < (\{(<)\} \times \{\mathbf{t}\}) \\
&= \{(>, \mathbf{f}), (=, \mathbf{f}), (<, \mathbf{t})\} \\
S_{N_4} &= \{(<, \mathbf{f}), (>, \mathbf{f}), (=, \mathbf{f}), (<, \mathbf{t})\}
\end{aligned}
$$

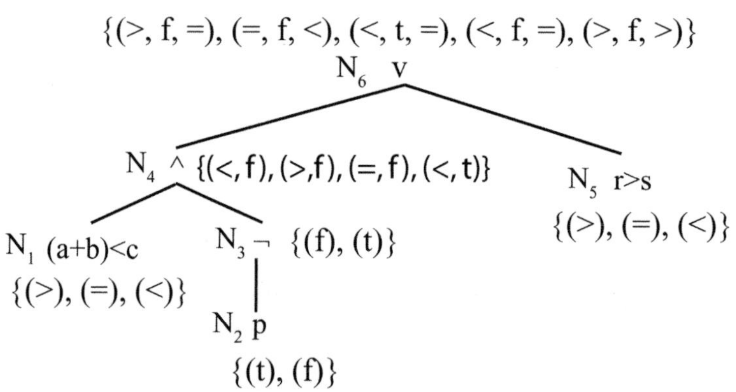

Fig. 2.19 BRO-constraint set for predicate $(a + b) < c \land \neg p \lor (r > s)$. The constraint sets are listed next to each node. See the text for the separation of each constraint set into its true and false components.

as shown in Figure 2.19, is derived using Step 2.3 of Procedure BOR-CSET.

Next we construct the BRO-constraint set for the AND-node N_4 using Step 2.2.

Finally, we construct the BRO-constraint set for the root node N_6 by applying Step 2.1 to the BRO-constraint sets of nodes N_4 and N_5.

$$S_{N_6}^f = S_{N_4}^f \otimes S_{N_5}^f$$
$$= \{(>,,\mathbf{f}),(=,\mathbf{f}),(<,\mathbf{t})\} \otimes \{(=),(<)\}$$
$$= \{(>,\mathbf{f},=),(=,\mathbf{f},<),(<,\mathbf{t},=)\}$$
$$S_{N_6}^t = \left(S_{N_4}^t \times \{f_{N_5}\}\right) \cup \left(\{f_{N_4}\} \times S_{N_5}^t\right)$$
$$= (\{(<,\mathbf{f})\} \times \{(=)\}) \cup (\{(>,\mathbf{f})\} \times \{(>)\})$$
$$= \{(<,\mathbf{f},=),(>,\mathbf{f},>)\}$$
$$S_{N_6} = \{(>,\mathbf{f},=),(=,\mathbf{f},<),(<,\mathbf{t},=),(<,\mathbf{f},=),(>,\mathbf{f},>)\}$$

Sample tests for p_r that satisfy the four BRO-constraints are given in Table 2.8. Exercise 2.31 asks you to confirm that indeed the test set in Table 2.7 is adequate with respect to the BRO-testing criterion.

2.7.5.3 Generating the BRE-constraint set

We now show how to generate BRE-constraints that lead to test cases which guarantee the detection of any Boolean operator, relation operator, arithmetic expression, or a combination thereof, faults in a predicate. The BRE-constraint set for a Boolean variable remains $\{\mathbf{t}, \mathbf{f}\}$ as

Table 2.8 Sample tests cases that satisfy the BOR-constraints for predicate p_2 derived in Example 2.28

	$a+b<c$	p	$r>s$	Test case
t_1	$>$	$\mathbf{f}$	$=$	$< a = 1, b = 1, c = 1,$ $p = \text{false}, r = 1, s = 1 >$
t_2	$=$	$\mathbf{f}$	$<$	$< a = 1, b = 0, c = 1,$ $p = \text{false}, r = 1, s = 2 >$
t_3	$<$	$\mathbf{t}$	$=$	$< a = 1, b = 1, c = 3,$ $p = \text{true}, r = 1, s = 1 >$
t_4	$<$	$\mathbf{f}$	$=$	$< a = 0, b = 2, c = 3,$ $p = \text{false}, r = 0, s = 0 >$
t_5	$>$	$\mathbf{f}$	$>$	$< a = 1, b = 1, c = 0,$ $p = \text{false}, r = 2, s = 0 >$

with the BOR- and BRO-constraint sets. The BRE-constraint set for a relational expression is $\{(+\epsilon), (=), (-\epsilon)\}, \epsilon > 0$. The BRE-constraint set S for a relational expression e_1 *relop* e_2 is separated into subsets S^t and S^f based on the following relations:

Constraint	Satisfying condition
$+\epsilon$	$0 < e_1 - e_2 \leq +\epsilon$
$-\epsilon$	$-\epsilon \leq e_1 - e_2 < 0$

Based on the conditions listed above, we can now separate the BRE-constraint S into its true and false components as follows:

```
relop :>   St = {(+ ε)}          Sf = {(=),(−ε)}
relop :≥   St = {(+ ε),(=)}      Sf = {(−ε)}
relop :=   St = {(=)}            Sf = {(+ε),(−ε)}
relop :<   St = {(−ε)}           Sf = {(=),(+ε)}
relop :≤   St = {(−ε),(=)}       Sf = {(+ε)}
```

The procedure to generate a minimal BRE-constraint set is similar to Procedure BRO-CSET. The only difference in the two procedures lies in the construction of the constraint sets for the leaves. Procedure BRE-CSET is as follows:

Procedure for generating a minimal BRE-constraint set from an abstract syntax tree of a predicate p_r.

Input: An abstract syntax tree for predicate p_r, denoted by $AST(p_r)$. p_r contains only singular expressions.

Output: BRE-constraint set for p_r attached to the root node of $AST(p_r)$.

Procedure: BRE-CSET

Step 1 Label each leaf node N of $AST(p_r)$ with its constraint set $S(N)$. For each leaf node that represents a Boolean variable, $S_N = \{\mathbf{t}, \mathbf{f}\}$. For each leaf node that is a relational expression, $S_N = \{(+\epsilon), (=), (-\epsilon)\}$.

Step 2 Visit each nonleaf node in $AST(p_r)$ in a bottom up manner. Let N_1 and N_2 denote the direct descendants of node N, if N is an AND-or an OR-node. If N is a NOT-node, then N_1 is its direct descendant. S_{N_1} and S_{N_2} are the BRE-constraint sets for nodes N_1 and N_2, respectively. For each nonleaf node N, compute S_N as in Steps 2.1, 2.2, and 2.3 in Procedure BOR-CSET.

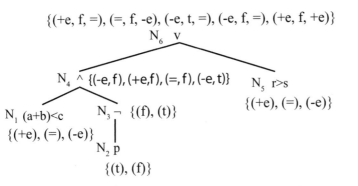

$\{(+e, f, =), (=, f, -e), (-e, t, =), (-e, f, =), (+e, f, +e)\}$
N_6 v

N_4 ∧ $\{(-e, f), (+e, f), (=, f), (-e, t)\}$ N_5 r>s
$\{(+e), (=), (-e)\}$

N_1 (a+b)<c N_3 ¬ $\{(f), (t)\}$
$\{(+e), (=), (-e)\}$ |
N_2 p
$\{(t), (f)\}$

Fig. 2.20 BRE-constraint set for the predicate $(a + b) < c \wedge \neg p \vee (r > s)$.

Step 3 The constraint set for the root of $AST(p_r)$ is the desired BRE-constraint set for p_r.

End of Procedure BRE-CSET

Example 2.30: Consider the predicate $p : (a + b) < c \wedge \neg p \vee r > s$. The BRE-constraint set for p_r is derived in Figure 2.20. Notice the similarity of BRE and BRO-constraints listed against the corresponding nodes in Figures 2.19 and 2.20.

Note that tests t_1 through t_4 in Table 2.9 are identical to the corresponding tests in Table 2.8. However, t_5 in Table 2.8 does not satisfy the $(+\epsilon)$ constraint.

Hence, we have a different t_5 in Table 2.9. Exercise 2.34 asks you to compare the test cases derived from constraints using BRO-CSET and BRE-CSET.

Table 2.9 Sample test cases that satisfy the BRE-constraints for predicate p_r derived in Example 2.30. $\epsilon = 1$

	$a+b<c$	p	$r>s$	Test case
t_1	$+\epsilon$	f	$=$	$< a = 1, b = 1, c = 1,$ $p = \texttt{false}, r = 1, s = 1 >$
t_2	$=$	f	$-\epsilon$	$< a = 1, b = 0, c = 1,$ $p = \texttt{false}, r = 1, s = 2 >$
t_3	$-\epsilon$	t	$=$	$< a = 1, b = 1, c = 3,$ $p = \texttt{true}, r = 1, s = 1 >$
t_4	$-\epsilon$	f	$=$	$< a = 0, b = 2, c = 3,$ $p = \texttt{false}, r = 0, s = 0 >$
t_5	$+\epsilon$	f	$+\epsilon$	$< a = 1, b = 1, c = 1,$ $p = \texttt{false}, r = 2, s = 0 >$

2.7.5.4 Generating BOR constraints for nonsingular expressions

As mentioned earlier, the test-generation procedures described in the previous sections generate BOR-, BRO-, and BRE-adequate tests for predicates that do not contain any nonsingular expressions. However, the presence of nonsingular expressions might create conflicts while merging constraints during the traversal of the abstract syntax tree (see Exercise 2.37). Resolution of such conflicts leads to a constraint set that is not guaranteed to detect all Boolean operator faults that might arise in the implementation of the predicate under test. In this section we generalize the BOR-CSET procedure to handle predicates that might contain nonsingular expressions.

Recall from Section 2.7.1 that a nonsingular expression is one that contains multiple occurrences of a Boolean variable. For example, we list below a few nonsingular expressions and their disjunctive normal forms; note that we have omitted the AND operator, used $+$ to indicate the OR operator, and the over bar symbol to indicate the complement of a literal.

Predicate (p_r)	DNF	Mutually singular components of p_r
$ab(b+c)$	$abb + abc$	$a; b(b+c)$
$a(bc+bd)$	$abc + abd$	$a; (bc+bd)$
$a(bc+\bar{b}+de)$	$abc + a\bar{b} + ade$	$a; bc + \bar{b}; de$

The modified BOR strategy to generate tests from predicate p_r uses the BOR-CSET procedure and another procedure that we refer to as the Meaning Impact, or simply MI, procedure. Before we illustrate the BOR-MI strategy, we introduce the MI procedure for generating tests from any Boolean expression p_r, singular or nonsingular. The predicate p_r must be in its normal DNF. If p_r is not in DNF, then it needs to be transformed into one prior to the application of the MI-CSET procedure described next; there are standard algorithms for transforming any Boolean expression into an equivalent minimal DNF.

```
Procedure for generating a minimal constraint set
from a predicate possibly containing nonsingular
expressions.
```

Input: A Boolean expression $E = e_1 + e_2 + \ldots e_n$ in minimal disjunctive normal form containing n terms. Term e_i, $1 \leq i \leq n$ contains $l_i > 0$ literals.

Output: A set of constraints S_E that guarantees the detection of missing or extra NOT operator fault in a faulty version of E.

Procedure: `MI-CSET`

Step 1 For each term e_i, $1 \leq i \leq n$, construct T_{e_i} as the set of constraints that make e_i true.

Step 2 Let $TS_{e_i} = T_{e_i} - \cup_{j=1,i\neq j}^{n} T_{e_j}$. Note that for $i \neq j$, $TS_{e_i} \cap TS_{e_j} = \emptyset$.

Step 3 Construct S_E^t by including one constraint from each TS_{e_i}, $1 \leq i \leq n$. Note that for each constraint $c \in S_E^t$, $p(c) =$ `true`.

Step 4 Let e_i^j denote the term obtained by complementing the jth literal in term e_i, for $1 \leq i \leq n$ and $1 \leq j < l_j$. We count the literals in a term from left to right, the leftmost literal being the first. Construct $F_{e_i^j}$ as the set of constraints that make e_i^j true.

Step 5 Let $FS_{e_i^j} = F_{e_i^j} - \cup_{k=1}^{n} T_{ek}$. Thus, for any constraint $c \in FS_{e_i^j}$, $p(c) =$ `false`.

Step 6 Construct S_E^f that is minimal and covers each $FS_{e_i^j}$ at least once.

Step 7 Construct the desired constraint set for E as $S_E = S_E^t \cup S_E^f$.

`End of Procedure MI-CSET`

Example 2.31: Let $E = a(bc + \bar{b}d)$, where a, b, c, and d are Boolean variables. Note that E is nonsingular as variable b occurs twice. The DNF equivalent of E is $e_1 + e_2$, where $e_1 = abc$ and $e_2 = a\bar{b}d$. We now apply Procedure MI-CSET to generate sets S_E^t and S_E^f. First, let us construct T_{e_1} and T_{e_2}.

$$T_{e_1} = \{(\mathbf{t,t,t,t}), (\mathbf{t,t,t,f})\}$$
$$T_{e_2} = \{(\mathbf{t,f,t,t}), (\mathbf{t,f,f,t})\}$$

Next we construct TS_{e_1} and TS_{e_2}.

$$TS_{e_1} = \{(\mathbf{t,t,t,t}), (\mathbf{t,t,t,f})\{$$
$$TS_{e_2} = \{(\mathbf{t,f,t,t}), (\mathbf{t,f,f,t})\}$$

Note that as T_{e_1} and T_{e_2} are disjoint, we get $TS_{e_1} = T_{e_1}$ and $TS_{e2} = T_{e2}$. Selecting one test each from TS_{e_1} and TS_{e_2}, we obtain a minimal set of tests that make E true and cover each term of E as follows:

$$S_E^t = \{\,(\mathbf{t},\mathbf{t},\mathbf{t},\mathbf{f})\,,\,(\mathbf{t},\mathbf{f},\mathbf{f},\mathbf{t})\,\}$$

Note that there exist four possible S_E^t. Next we construct tests $F_{e_i^j}, 1 \le i \le 2, 1 \le j \le 3$. We have three terms corresponding to e_1, namely $e_1^1 = \bar{a}bc$, $e_1^2 = a\bar{b}c$, and $e_1^3 = ab\bar{c}$. Similarly, we get three terms for e_2, namely, $e_2^1 = \bar{a}bd$, $e_2^2 = abd$, and $e_2^3 = ab\bar{d}$.

$$F_{e_1^1} = \{\,(\mathbf{f},\mathbf{t},\mathbf{t},\mathbf{t})\,,\,(\mathbf{f},\mathbf{t},\mathbf{t},\mathbf{f})\,\}$$

$$F_{e_1^2} = \{\,(\mathbf{t},\mathbf{f},\mathbf{t},\mathbf{t})\,,\,(\mathbf{t},\mathbf{f},\mathbf{t},\mathbf{f})\,\}$$

$$F_{e_1^3} = \{\,(\mathbf{t},\mathbf{t},\mathbf{f},\mathbf{t})\,,\,(\mathbf{t},\mathbf{t},\mathbf{f},\mathbf{f})\,\}$$

$$F_{e_2^1} = \{\,(\mathbf{f},\mathbf{f},\mathbf{t},\mathbf{t})\,,\,(\mathbf{f},\mathbf{f},\mathbf{f},\mathbf{t})\,\}$$

$$F_{e_2^2} = \{\,(\mathbf{t},\mathbf{t},\mathbf{t},\mathbf{t})\,,\,(\mathbf{t},\mathbf{t},\mathbf{f},\mathbf{t})\,\}$$

$$F_{e_2^3} = \{\,(\mathbf{t},\mathbf{f},\mathbf{t},\mathbf{f})\,,\,(\mathbf{t},\mathbf{f},\mathbf{f},\mathbf{f})\,\}$$

Next we remove from the above six sets any test cases that belong to any of the sets $T_{e_k}, 1 \le k \le n$ sets.

$$FS_{e_1^1} = F_{e_1^1}$$

$$FS_{e_1^2} = \{\,(\mathbf{t},\mathbf{f},\mathbf{t},\mathbf{f})\,\}$$

$$FS_{e_1^3} = F_{e_1^3}$$

$$FS_{e_2^1} = FS_{e_2^1}$$

$$FS_{e_2^2} = \{\,(\mathbf{t},\mathbf{t})\,\}$$

$$FS_{e_2^3} = FS_{e_2^3}$$

The test set that makes E false is now constructed by selecting tests from the six sets listed above such that S_E^f is minimal and covers each FS.

$$S_E^f = \{\,(\mathbf{f},\mathbf{t},\mathbf{t},\mathbf{f})\,,\,(\mathbf{t},\mathbf{f},\mathbf{t},\mathbf{f})\,\,(\mathbf{t},\mathbf{t},\mathbf{f},\mathbf{t})\,,\,(\mathbf{f},\mathbf{f},\mathbf{t},\mathbf{t})\,\}$$

The set of constraints S_E generated by the MI-CSET procedure for expression E contain a total of six constraints as follows:

$$S_E = \{\,(\mathbf{t},\mathbf{t},\mathbf{t},\mathbf{f})\,,\,(\mathbf{t},\mathbf{f},\mathbf{f},\mathbf{t})\,,\,(\mathbf{f},\mathbf{t},\mathbf{t},\mathbf{f})\,,\,(\mathbf{t},\mathbf{f},\mathbf{t},\mathbf{f})\,,\,(\mathbf{t},\mathbf{t},\mathbf{f},\mathbf{t})\,,$$
$$(\mathbf{f},\mathbf{f},\mathbf{t},\mathbf{t})\,\}$$

We are now ready to introduce the BOR-MI-CSET procedure for generating a minimal constraint set from a possibly nonsingular expression. The procedure described next uses the BOR-CSET and the MI-CSET procedures described earlier.

Procedure for generating a minimal constraint set for a predicate possibly containing nonsingular expressions.

Input: A Boolean expression E.

Output: A set of constraints S_E that guarantees the detection of Boolean operator faults in E.

Procedure: BOR-MI-CSET

Step 1 Partition E into a set of n mutually singular components, $E = \{E_1, E_2, \ldots E_n\}$.

Step 2 Generate the BOR-constraint set for each singular component in E using the BOR-CSET procedure.

Step 3 Generate the MI-constraint set for each singular component in E using the BOR-CSET procedure.

Step 4 Combine the constraints generated in the previous two steps using Step 2 from the BOR-CSET procedure to obtain the constraint set for E.

End of Procedure BOR-MI-CSET

The following example illustrates the BOR-MI-CSET procedure:

Example 2.32: As in Example 2.31, let $E = a(bc + \bar{b}d)$, where a, b, c, and d are Boolean variables. Note that E is nonsingular as variable b occurs twice. We follow the BOR-MI-CSET procedure to generate the constraint set S_E.

From Step 1, we partition E into components e_1 and e_2, where $e_1 = a$ is a singular expression and $e_2 = (bc + \bar{b}d)$ is a nonsingular expression. In accordance with Step 2, we use the BOR-CSET procedure to find S_{e_1} as follows:

$$S_{e_1}^t = \{(\mathbf{t})\}; \; S_{e_1}^f = \{(\mathbf{f})\}$$

Next, we apply the MI-CSET procedure to generate the MI-constraints for e_2. Note that e_2 is a DNF expression and can be written as $e_2 = u + v$, where $u = bc$ and $v = \bar{b}d$. Applying Step 1 we obtain the following.

$$T_u = \{(\mathbf{t}, \mathbf{t}, \mathbf{t}), (\mathbf{t}, \mathbf{t}, \mathbf{f})\}$$
$$T_v = \{(\mathbf{f}, \mathbf{t}, \mathbf{t}), (\mathbf{f}, \mathbf{f}, \mathbf{t})\}$$

Applying Step 2 from the MI-CSET procedure to T_u and T_v, and then Step 3, we obtain the following sets.

$$TS_u = T_u$$
$$TS_v = T_v$$
$$S_{e_2}^t = \{\,(\mathbf{t},\mathbf{t},\mathbf{f}),\,(\mathbf{f},\mathbf{t},\mathbf{t})\,\}$$

Note that we have several alternatives for $S_{e_2}^t$ from which we need to select one. Next, we derive the false constraint set S_{e_2} by applying Steps 4, 5, and 6. The complemented subexpressions needed in these steps are $u^1 = \bar{b}c$, $u^2 = b\bar{c}$, $v^1 = bd$, and $v^2 = \bar{b}\bar{d}$.

$$F_{u_1} = \{\,(\mathbf{f},\mathbf{t},\mathbf{t}),\,(\mathbf{f},\mathbf{t},\mathbf{f})\,\}$$
$$F_{u_2} = \{\,(\mathbf{t},\mathbf{f},\mathbf{t}),\,(\mathbf{t},\mathbf{f},\mathbf{f})\,\}$$
$$F_{v_1} = \{\,(\mathbf{t},\mathbf{t},\mathbf{t}),\,(\mathbf{t},\mathbf{f},\mathbf{t})\,\}$$
$$F_{v_2} = \{\,(\mathbf{f},\mathbf{t},\mathbf{f}),\,(\mathbf{f},\mathbf{f},\mathbf{f})\,\}$$
$$FS_{u_1} = \{\,(\mathbf{f},\mathbf{t},\mathbf{f})\,\}$$
$$FS_{u_2} = \{\,(\mathbf{t},\mathbf{f},\mathbf{t}),\,(\mathbf{t},\mathbf{f},\mathbf{f})\,\}$$
$$FS_{v_1} = \{\,(\mathbf{t},\mathbf{f},\mathbf{t})\,\}$$
$$FS_{v_2} = \{\,(\mathbf{f},\mathbf{f},\mathbf{f}),\,(\mathbf{f},\mathbf{f},\mathbf{f})\,\}$$
$$S_{e_2}^f = \{\,(\mathbf{f},\mathbf{t},\mathbf{f}),\,(\mathbf{t},\mathbf{f},\mathbf{t})\,\}$$

Here is a summary of what we have derived so far by applying Steps 1, 2, and 3 from procedure BOR-MI-CSET.

$$S_{e_4}^t = \{\mathbf{t}\} \qquad\qquad \text{From procedure BOR-CSET.}$$
$$S_{e_4}^f = \{\mathbf{f}\} \qquad\qquad \text{From procedure BOR-CSET.}$$
$$S_{e_2}^t = \{\,(\mathbf{t},\mathbf{t},\mathbf{f}),\,(\mathbf{f},\mathbf{t},\mathbf{t})\,\} \quad \text{From procedure MI-CSET.}$$
$$S_{e_2}^f = \{\,(\mathbf{f},\mathbf{t},\mathbf{f}),\,(\mathbf{t},\mathbf{f},\mathbf{t})\,\} \quad \text{From procedure MI-CSET.}$$

We can now apply Step 4 to the constraint sets generated for subexpressions e_1 an e_2 and obtain the BOR-constraint set for the entire expression E. This process is illustrated in Figure 2.21. The sets S_E^t, S_E^f, and S_E are listed below.

$$S_E^t = S_{e_4}^t \otimes S_{e_2}^t$$
$$= \{\,(\mathbf{t},\mathbf{t},\mathbf{t},\mathbf{f}),\,(\mathbf{t},\mathbf{f},\mathbf{t},\mathbf{t})$$
$$S_E^f = \left(S_{e_4}^f \times \{\mathbf{t}\}\right) \cup \left(\{\mathbf{t}\} \times S_{e_2}^f\right)$$
$$= \{\,(\mathbf{f},\mathbf{t},\mathbf{t},\mathbf{f}),\,(\mathbf{t},\mathbf{f},\mathbf{t},\mathbf{f}),\,(\mathbf{t},\mathbf{t},\mathbf{f},\mathbf{t})\,\}$$
$$S_E = \{\,(\mathbf{t},\mathbf{t},\mathbf{t},\mathbf{f}),\,(\mathbf{t},\mathbf{f},\mathbf{t},\mathbf{t}),\,(\mathbf{f},\mathbf{t},\mathbf{t},\mathbf{f}),\,(\mathbf{t},\mathbf{f},\mathbf{t},\mathbf{f}),$$
$$(\mathbf{t},\mathbf{t},\mathbf{f},\mathbf{t}),\,\}$$

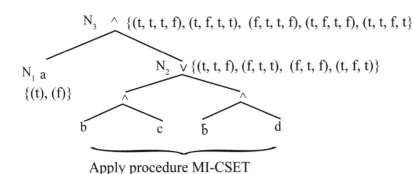

Fig. 2.21 Constraint set for predicate $a(bc + \bar{b}d)$ derived using the BOR-MI-CSET procedure.

Note that constraint set S_E derived using the BOR-MI-CSET procedure contains only five constraints as compared to the six constraints in S_E derived using the MI-CSET procedure in Example 2.31. It is generally the case that the constraint sets derived using the BOR-MI-CSET procedure are smaller, and more effective in detecting faults, than those derived using the MI-CSET procedure. Exercises 2.40 and 2.41 should help you sharpen your understanding of the BOR-MI-CSET procedure and the effectiveness of the tests generated.

2.7.6 CAUSE–EFFECT GRAPHS AND PREDICATE TESTING

Cause–effect graphing, as described in Section 2.6, is a requirement modeling and test-generation technique. Cause–effect relations are extracted from the requirements. Each *cause* portion of a cause–effect relation can be expressed as predicate. The *effect* portion is used to construct the oracle, which decides if the effect does occur when the corresponding cause exists.

To test if the condition representing the cause in a cause–effect graph has been implemented correctly, one could generate tests using either the decision table technique described in Section 2.6.3 or one of the four procedures described in this section.

Several studies have revealed that the BOR-CSET procedure generates significantly smaller tests sets than the CEGDT procedure described in Section 2.6.3. The fault detection effectiveness of the tests generated using the BOR-CSET procedure is only slightly less than that of tests generated using the CEGDT procedure.

The combination of cause–effect graphs and predicate testing procedures described in this section is considered useful for two reasons, First, the cause–effect graphs are a useful tool for modeling requirements.

Once the graphical model has been built, any one of the four predicate-based test-generation procedures introduced in this section can be applied for test generation. Exercise 2.42 is to help you understand how a combination of cause–effect graphs and predicate testing works.

2.7.7 FAULT PROPAGATION

We now explain the notion of *fault propagation* that forms the basis of the four predicate test-generation algorithms described in this section. Let p_r be a predicate, simple or compound, and p_c a component of p_r. Each node in the abstract syntax tree of a predicate is a component of that predicate. For example, as in Figure 2.17, predicate $p : (a + b) < c \land \neg p \lor r > s$ contains the following six components: $a + b < c, \land, \neg, p, \lor,$ and $r > s$.

Let p_f be a faulty version of p_r. We say that a fault in any component of p_f propagates to the root node of $AST(p_f)$, that is effects the outcome of p_f, if $p(t) \neq p_f(t)$ for some test case t. Test t is also known as an *error-revealing* or *fault-revealing* test for p_f.

In predicate testing, we are interested in generating at least one test case t that ensures the propagation of the fault in p_f. The BOR-, BRO-, and BRE-adequate test sets guarantee that certain kinds of faults, mentioned in earlier sections, propagate to the root node of the predicate under test. The next example illustrates the notion of fault propagation.

Example 2.33: Let $p : (a + b) < c \land \neg p \lor r > s$ and $p_f : (a + b) < c \lor \neg p \lor r > s$ be two predicates, where p_f is a faulty version of p_r. p_f has a Boolean operator fault created by the incorrect use of the $\lor$ operator. Table 2.7 lists four test cases that form a BOR-adequate test set.

Figure 2.22(a) and (b) show that test t_1 in Table 2.7 fails to cause the $\land$ operator fault to propagate to the root node of $AST(p_f)$ and thus we have $p(t_1) = p_f(t_1)$. However, as shown in Figure 2.22(c) and (d), test t_4 does cause the fault to propagate to the root node of $AST(p_f)$ and thus we have $p(t_4) \neq p_f(t_4)$.

Given a predicate p_r containing n AND/OR operators and Boolean variables, one can use a brute-force method to generate a test set T with 2^n tests. For example, predicate $p : (a + b) < c \land \neg p \lor r > s$ contains two Boolean AND/OR operators and one Boolean variable; thus $n = 3$. A test set T generated in a brute-force manner will contain a total of eight test cases that satisfy the following set S of eight constraints:

$$S = \{ (\mathbf{f,f,f}), (\mathbf{f,f,t}), (\mathbf{f,t,f}), \{ (\mathbf{f,t,t}), (\mathbf{t,f,f}), (\mathbf{t,f,t}),$$
$$\{ (\mathbf{t,t,f}), (\mathbf{t,t,t}) \}$$

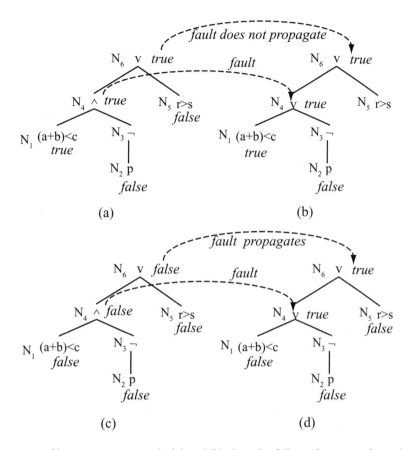

Fig. 2.22 Abstract syntax trees in (a) and (b) show the failure of test t_1 to force the propagation of the $\wedge$ operator fault. (c) and (d) show how test t_4 ensures the propagation of the $\wedge$ operator fault.

These eight constraints ensure that each relational expression and a Boolean variable in p_r will evaluate to `true` and `false` against at least one test case in T. Thus, T is obviously BOR-, BRO-, and BRE-adequate. However, T is not minimal. Note that while T contains eight test cases, a BRE-adequate test set derived in Example 2.30 contains only five test cases.

It can be shown that if a predicate p_r contains n AND/OR operators, then the maximum size of the BRO-adequate test set is $n + 2$. The maximum size of a BRO or BRE adequate test set for p_r is $2 * n + 3$ (see Exercise 2.35).

As indicated above, the size of BOR-, BRO-, and BRE-adequate tests grows linearly in the number of AND/OR and Boolean variables in a predicate. It is this nice property of the test-generation procedures introduced in this section, in addition to fault detection effectiveness, that distinguishes them from the brute-force method and the cause–effect graph-based test generation introduced earlier in Section 2.6.

The linearity property mentioned above is the result of (a) using the abstract syntax tree of a predicate to propagate the constraints from leaves to the root node and (b) using the **onto** ($\otimes$) product of two sets, instead of the set product ($\times$), while propagating the constraints up through the abstract syntax tree (see Exercise 2.36).

2.7.8 Predicate Testing in Practice

Predicate testing is used to derive test cases both from the requirements and from the application under test. Thus, it can be used for generating *specification*-based and *program*-based tests.

2.7.8.1 Specification-based predicate test generation

An analysis of application requirements reveals conditions under which the application must behave in specific ways. Thus, analysis of application requirements might yield the following list of n conditions and the associated tasks.

Condition	Task
C_1	$Task_1$
C_2	$Task_2$
$\vdots$	
C_n	$Task_n$

Such a list can be used to generate a test set T for the application under test. Note that each condition is represented by a predicate. The condition–task pairs in the list above are assumed independent in the sense that each task depends exclusively on the condition associated with it. The independence assumption does not hold when, for example, a condition, say C_2, depends on C_1 in the sense that C_2 cannot be true if C_1 is true. For example, two such dependent conditions are: $C_1 : a < b$ and $C_2 : a > b$. Obviously, if $Task_1$ and $Task_2$ are associated exclusively with conditions C_1 and C_2, respectively, then only one of them can be performed for a given input.

As conditions can be compound and tasks can be conjoined, the independence requirement does not exclude the specification of two tasks to be performed when a condition is true, or that one task requires two conditions to hold. Two tasks could be conjoined to form one task corresponding to a condition. Similarly, two conditions could be combined to form a single condition associated with a single task.

For test generation, one first selects an appropriate test-generation algorithm described in this section. Different algorithms could be used for different conditions. For example, if condition C_2 is represented by a nonsingular predicate, then the BOR-MI-CSET algorithm is likely to be preferred.

Once the test-generation procedure is selected for a predicate, one generates a distinct test set. The union of the test sets so generated is a consolidated test set T for the application. It is certainly possible that two conditions yield the same test set.

Testing the application against test cases in T guarantees the detection of certain faults, indicated in Section 2.7.2, due to the incorrect coding of conditions from which the tests are derived. However, such a guarantee is valid only under certain conditions. The next example illustrates why a test set might fail.

Example 2.34: Suppose that we are to test system X. Requirements for X indicate that task $Task_1$ is to be performed when condition $C_1 : a < b \land c > d$ is true. Tests for C_1 are derived in Example 2.27 and are guaranteed to detect any Boolean operator fault in C_1.

Now consider an implementation of X whose structure is abstracted in Figure 2.23. Statement S_1 contains a fault in the coding of C_1. The condition coded is $C_f : a < b \lor c > d$. Let us assume that S_1 is unreachable for any test input.

Suppose that statement S_2 has been added by mistake, it should not be in the program. The condition C in S_2 is $C_1 \land u$, where u is a Boolean variable input to X. Now suppose that u is set to true while testing X to check for the correct execution of $Task_1$.

The first three rows in the table below show that the observed behavior of X for each of the tests derived using the BOR-CSET procedure for condition C is identical to the expected behavior. However, when X is tested with $u = $ false and the BOR constraint $(\mathbf{t}, \mathbf{t})$, the error is revealed.

	Test		
u	$a < b \land c > d$	Observed behavior	Expected behavior
true	$(\mathbf{t}, \mathbf{t})$	Execute $Task_1$	Execute $Task_1$.
true	$(\mathbf{t}, \mathbf{f})$	$Task_1$ not executed.	Do not execute $Task_1$.
true	$(\mathbf{f}, \mathbf{t})$	$Task_1$ not executed.	Do not execute $Task_1$.
false	$(\mathbf{t}, \mathbf{t})$	$Task_1$ not executed.	Execute $Task_1$.

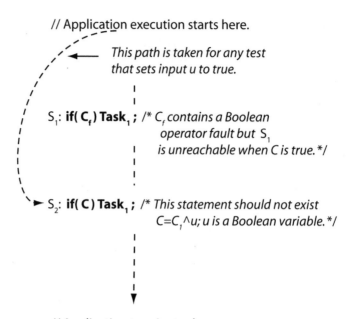

// Application execution starts here.

This path is taken for any test
that sets input u to true.

S_1: **if(C_f) Task$_1$;** /* C_f contains a Boolean
operator fault but S_1
is unreachable when C is true. */

S_2: **if(C) Task$_1$;** /* This statement should not exist
$C = C_1 \wedge u$; u is a Boolean variable. */

// Application terminates here.

Fig. 2.23 An implementation to illustrate why a predicate test that is theoretically guaranteed to detect any Boolean operator fault might fail to do so in practice.

Thus, we have shown an instance where a test generated using the BOR-CSET procedure is unable to reveal the error. Certainly, this example is not demonstrating any weakness in the error-detection effectiveness of the BOR-CSET procedure. Instead, it demonstrates that some errors in the program might mask an error in the implementation of a predicate.

2.7.8.2 Program-based predicate test generation

Test sets can also be derived from predicates in the program. Test sets so derived are often referred to as *white-box tests*. When executing such tests, one needs to ensure that the flow of control reaches the region in the program that implements the predicate being tested. As illustrated in the next example, this might cause some difficulty as several other conditions may need to be satisfied for the control to reach the desired region in the program.

Example 2.35: Consider the following program that uses two conditions to control the execution of three tasks named task1, task2, and task3. Using inputs r and e, the program determines values of parameters a, b, c, and d.

Program P2.3

```
1 begin
2    int a, b, c, d, r, e;
3    input (r, e);
4    getParam(r, e);
5    if(e < 0)
6    then
7       task1(a, b);
8    else
9       if(a < b&&c > d)
10      then
11         task2(C, D);
12      else
13         task3(c, d);
14 end
```

Suppose that the BOR-CSET procedure has been used to generate BOR constraints from the predicate $a < b\&\&c > d$. Satisfying these constraints would be relatively easier if the parameters a, b, c, and d were program inputs. However, as is the case in our example program, these four parameters depend on the values of r and e. Thus, satisfying these constraints will require a determination of the relationship between r, e, and the four parameters.

Further, one must ensure that all tests of P2.3 that correspond to the constraints force the program to reach the statement containing the predicate, that is line 9. While this seems easy for our example program, it might not be so in most real-life programs.

SUMMARY

In this chapter we have introduced two classes of test-generation techniques. The techniques using equivalence partitioning, boundary-value analysis, and cause–effect graphing fall under the category best known as partition testing.

A fault model for predicate testing is introduced. The BOR and BRO techniques fall under the general category of predicate testing. Test generation using partition testing is perhaps the most commonly used method. Predicate testing is a bit more advanced though highly effective in the detection of faults that fall under a fault model.

BIBLIOGRAPHIC NOTES

Partition testing is as ancient as software testing. Here we focus on equivalence partitioning and boundary-value analysis as the two techniques that belong to the partition testing category. Works by Myers [338–341] and Howden [236] contain early descriptions of equivalence partitioning and boundary-value analysis.

Richardson and Clarke argued in support of using program specifications and code to derive test inputs [416]. They propose and illustrate a procedure to derive tests by partitioning the domains derived from specifications and from the program code. Partition analysis is used by the authors for program verification, that is, showing the equivalence of the program and its specification, as well as for the generation of test cases. Vagoun and Hevner discuss the use of input domain partitioning arrived at using state design in the context of a revison control system (RCS) application [485].

Hamlet and Taylor wrote a rather mind boggling paper arguing that "partition testing does not inspire confidence" and that random testing appears to be better alternative [191]. Several years later, Ntafos showed that proportional partition testing can guarantee that partition testing performs better than random testing [355]. Chen and Yu have reported a careful study of the relationship between random and partition testing strategies [77, 78].

Elmendorf used cause–effect graphing in the design of tests while testing an operating system [140]. The technique is illustrated in detail by Myers [340].

Paradkar formalized the idea of specification-based test generation using cause–effect graphs [385]. Tai, Paradkar, Su, and Vouk applied formal predicate-based test-generation techniques to the generation of tests from cause–effect graphs [468]. Paradkar, Tai, and Vouk also developed the idea of specification-based test generation using cause–effect graphs [391].

The term *syntax testing* refers to testing techniques that specify the space of test inputs using a formal grammar. Such techniques have been used to specify tests for compilers as well as for other types of applications, for example sorting. Early work in this area is reported by several researchers. Sauder described a grammar-based test-data generator for COBOL programs [434]. Purdom proposed a sentence generator for testing parsers for high-level languages [402]. Celantano *et al.* describe the use of a sentence generator for testing a compiler [72]. Bazzichi and Spadafora also proposed a grammar-based test generator for the automatic testing of compilers [34]. Duncan and Hutchison proposed an attribute grammar-based method for formally describing the classes of test inputs and outputs [134]. The specification is used to generate a large class of test inputs and expected outputs. Tests so generated are then used in conjunction with a test driver, or a test harness, to drive the program under test.

Equivalence partitioning is one of the earliest techniques for test-data generation and is also known as *range-testing*. The technique has been formally described by Meyer [340]. A similar and more formal technique is known as the *category-partition method* was proposed by

Ostrand and Balcer [379]. They provide a formal notation for concisely specifying tests. They also report a detailed case study using a component of a version and configuration management system. Concise specifications, written in a Test Specification Language (TSL), are input to a tool that uses partitioning and boundary-value techniques to generate test frames and eventually test cases. Specification in TSL allows for achieving specification coverage and the generation of test scripts and test cases [28].

Grochtmann and Grimm have proposed the classification tree method for the generation of tests using domain partitioning [181, 182]. Singh, Conrad, and Sadeghipour have applied the classification tree method to the generation of tests from Z specifications [447].

Partition testing strategies have received much attention from researchers. Jeng and Weyuker present a theoretical analysis of partition testing strategies [247]. Gutjahr [187] and Reid [412] have studied the fault detection effectiveness of partition testing strategies. Amla and Amman [20], Stocks [460], and several other researchers have applied partition testing to the generation of tests from Z specifications. Offutt and Irvine propose the use of category-partition method for testing OO programs [362].

Testing strategies for Boolean and relational expressions has been proposed by several researchers. Howden proposed testing relational operators such that three tests are generated corresponding to a relational expression $E_1 < relop > E_2$, where *relop* denotes a relational operator and E_1 and E_2 are arithmetic expressions [238]. Foster [150] and

Howden [238] also proposed testing relational expressions for off-by-ϵ errors. Foster showed that a predicate with n Boolean variables can be tested with less than 2^n test cases to reveal coding faults and that exhaustive testing was not needed in all cases [151].

White and Cohen applied domain testing to the testing of relational expressions [515]. Their strategy is based on the domain boundaries determined by the relational expression $E_1 < relop > E_2$. Padmanabhan has reported a divide and conquer strategy-based on domain testing [382].

Tai [464] and Tai and Su [469] did the early work on formalizing the generation of tests from Boolean and relational expressions. The BOR and BRO techniques were proposed by Tai [466, 467]. Paradkar and Tai [389], Paradkar [384], Paradkar, Tai, and Vouk [390], and Tai, Vouk, Paradkar and Lu [470] further developed the BOR and BRO techniques and conducted empirical studies to assess their fault-detection effectiveness. The term *BRE strategy* is due to Tai [465, 467].

The Meaning Impact (MI) strategy, originally named as *Meaningful impact* strategy, is due to Weyuker, Gordia, and Singh [512]. As proposed originally, a test set generated using the MI strategy is able to detect faults due to variable negation in DNF expressions. Paradkar and Tai extended the MI strategy to MI-MIN strategy and combined it with BOR strategy [389]. Paradkar and Tai's method improves upon the MI strategy in the size of tests generated and their fault detection effectiveness. Stamelos has studied the ability of predicate testing to detect associative shift faults [459].

The work of Weyuker *et al.* on test generation from Boolean expressions [512] has been extended by Chen and Lau [75]. Chen and Lau's methods for generating tests from Boolean expressions guarantee the detection of literal insertion and reference faults in Boolean expressions. Their methods are named MUTP, MNFP, and CUTPNFP. Their methods are applied to an irredundant Boolean expression, that is one that contains no redundant literals. Chen, Lu, and Yu integrated the MUTP, MNFP, and CUTPNFP strategies into the MUMCUT strategy that guarantees the detection of seven types of faults in Boolean expressions [76]. Their fault model is more detailed than the one provided in Section 2.7.2.

BIBLIOGRAPHIC NOTES

EXERCISES

2.1 Let N be the size of a sequence s of integers. Assume that an element of s can be any one of v distinct values. Show that the number of possible sequences is $\Sigma_{i=0}^{N} v^i$.

2.2 An equivalence relation R on set S is reflexive, symmetric, and transitive. Also, R partitions S into equivalence classes. Show that each of the relations defined in Exercises 2.3 and 2.4 is an equivalence relation.

2.3 Derive equivalence classes for the input variables listed below.

    1. `int` *pen_inventory*; Current inventory level of writing pens.
    2. `string` *planet_name*; Planet name.
    3. *operating system*={"OS X", "Windows XP",
                        "Windows 2000", "Unix", "Linux",
                        "Xinu", "VxWorks"};
                        ;Name of an operating system.
    4. `printer_class=set printer_ name`; Set of printer names.
       `printer_class p`;
    5. `int` *name* [1 … 10]; An array of at most 10 integers.

2.4 In Example 2.4, suppose now that we add another category of printers, say "Home and home office (hb)". Define a suitable relation *hb* that partitions the input domain of `pTest` into two equivalence classes. Discuss the overlap of the equivalence classes induced by *hb* with the remaining eight classes defined by the four relations in Example 2.4.

2.5 Consider the following relation

$$cl : \mathcal{I} \to \{yes, no\}$$

cl maps an input domain $\mathcal{I}$ of *pTest* in Example 2.4 to the set {*yes, no*}. A printer make and model is mapped to *yes* if it is a color laserjet, else it is mapped to *no*. Is *cl* an equivalence relation?

2.6 (a) Why consider classes E2–E6 in Example 2.5 when the correctness of the program corresponding to tests in these classes can be verified by simple inspection? Offer at least two reasons.
(b) Are there any additional equivalance classes that one ought to consider while partitioning the input domain of `wordCount`?

2.7 Partition the input domain of the *transcript* component described in Example 2.6 into equivalence classes using the guidelines in Tables 2.1 and 2.2. Note that *transcript* takes two inputs, a record R and an integer N.

2.8 (a) Generate two sets of tests T_1 and T_2 from the partitions created in Example 2.7 using, respectively, unidimensional and multidimensional testing. Which of the following relations holds among T_1 and T_2 that you have created: $T_1 = T_2$, $T_1 \subset T_2$, $T_1 \subseteq T_2$, $T_1 \supset T_2$, $T_1 \supseteq T_2$, and $T_1 \neq T_2$? (b) Which of the six relations mentioned could hold between T_1 and T_2 assuming that T_1 is derived from equivalence classes constructed using unidimensional partitioning and T_2 using multidimensional partitioning?

2.9 Consider an application *App* that takes two inputs *name* and *age*, where *name* is a nonempty string containing at most 20 alphabetic characters and *age* is an integer that must satisfy the constraint $0 \leq age \leq 120$. The *App* is required to display an error message if the input value provided for *age* is out of range. The application truncates any name that is more than 20-character in length and generates an error message if an empty string is supplied for *name*.

Partition the input domain using (a) unidimensional partitioning and (b) multidimensional partitioning. Construct two sets of test-data test for *App* using the equivalence classes derived in (a) and in (b).

2.10 Suppose that an application has m input variables and that each variable partitions the input space into n equivalence classes. The multidimensional partitioning approach will divide the input domain into how many equivalence classes?

2.11 An application takes two inputs x and y where $x \leq y$ and $-5 \leq y \leq 4$. (a) Partition the input domain using unidimensional and multidimensional partitioning. (b) Derive test sets based on the partitions created in (a).

2.12 In Example 2.8, we started out by calculating the number of equivalence classes to be 120. We did so because we did not account for the parent–child relationship between *cmd* and *tempch*. Given this relationship, how many equivalence classes should we start out within the first step of the procedure for partitioning the input domain into equivalence classes?

2.13 (a) Identify weaknesses, as many as you can, of the test T derived in Example 2.10.

(b) Derive a test set that covers each individual equivalence class derived for the four variables in Example 2.8 while ensuring that the semantic relations between different variables are maintained.

(c) Compare the test set derived in (b) with that in Table 2.3 in terms of their respective sizes and error-detection effectiveness. If you believe that the error-detection effectiveness of the test set you derived is less than that of the test set in Table 2.3, then offer an example of an error in the boiler-control software that is likely not to be detected by your test set but is likely to be detected by the test set in Table 2.3.

2.14 An object named *compute* takes an integer x as input. It is required to send a message to another object O_1 if $x \leq 0$ and message to object O_2 if $x > 0$. However, due to an error in *compute*, a message is sent to O_1 when $x < 0$ and to O_2 otherwise. Under what condition(s) will the input $x = 0$ *not* reveal the error in *compute*?

2.15 For each test $t \in T$ in Example 2.12, construct one example of a fault in *textSearch* that is guaranteed to be detected only by t. Hint: Avoid trivial examples!

2.16 A method named *cC* takes three inputs: *from*, *to*, and *amount*. Both *from* and *to* are strings and denote the name of a country. Variable *amount* is of type `float`. Method *cC* converts *amount* in the currency of the country specified by *from* and returns the equivalent amount, a quantity of type `float`, in the currency of the country specified by *to*. Here is an example prepared on July 26, 2004:

Inputs: *from* = "USA", *to* = "Japan", *amount* = 100
Returned value: 11,012.0

(a) Derive a set of tests for *cC* using equivalence partitioning and boundary-value analysis. (b) Suppose that a GUI encapsulates *cC* and allows the user to select the values of *from* and *to* using a palette of country names. The user types in the amount to be converted in a text box before clicking on the button labeled `Convert`. Will the presence of the GUI change the tests you derived in (a)? If so, how? If not, why?
You may find that the requirement specification given for *cC* is incomplete in several respects. While generating tests, it is recommended that you resolve any ambiguities in the

requirements and complete the information not available by using common sense and/or discussing the problem with appropriate members of the design/development team.

2.17 Recall the boundary-value analysis in Example 2.11. (a) Construct one example of a boundary error in fP that may go undetected unless tests t_2 and t_5 are replaced so that computation at the boundaries of *code* and *qty* is checked in separate tests. (b) Replace t_2 and t_5 by an appropriate set of tests that test fP at the boundaries of *code* and *qty* in separate tests.

2.18 In Example 2.15, suppose that fP is to be used in a checkout counter. The cash register at the counter is connected to a central database from where fP obtains the various attributes of an item such as name and price. Does this use of fP in a networked environment add to the list of environment objects? Can you think of any additional categories and different partitions?

2.19 The coupon field was ignored in the test specification derived in Example 2.17. Given the specifications on page 114, modify the test specifications in Example 2.17 so that test generated test for correct processing of the coupon field.

2.20 An Internet-enabled automatic Dog Food Dispenser, referred to as iDFD, consists of two separate dispensers: a food dispenser (FD) and a water dispenser (WD). Each dispenser is controlled by a separate timer that has a default setting of 8 h and can also be set to a different period. Upon a timer interrupt, the iDFD dispenses water or food depending on whether it is a water-timer or a food-timer interrupt. A fixed amount of food or water is dispensed.

The iDFD has two sets of three identical indicators, one for the food and the other for water. The indicators are labeled *Okay*, *Low*, and *Empty*. After each dispensation, the iDFD checks the food and water levels and updates the indicators.

The iDFD can be connected to the internet via a secure connection. It allows an authorized user to set or reset the timers and also determine the water and food level in the respective containers. An email message is sent to the authorized dog sitter when food or water dispensation results in the corresponding indicators to show *Low* or *Empty*.

The iDFD is controlled by an embedded microprocessor, and the iDFD control software, that is responsible for the correct operation of all the functions mentioned above. You are required to generate test inputs to test the control software in the following

three steps:
(a) Identify all causes and effects.
(b) Relate the causes and effects through a cause–effect graph.
(c) Create a decision table from the cause–effect graph you have generated.
(d) Generate test inputs from the decision table.
While executing the steps above, you may need to resolve any ambiguities in the requirements. Also, consider separating the test inputs from water and food dispensers.

2.21 In Example 2.19, we ignored the effects of buyer selections on the GUI updates. For example, when a user selects CPU3, the monitor window contents change from displaying all three monitors to displaying only monitor M 30. (a) Identify all such GUI-related effects in the GUI-based computer purchase system in Example 2.19. (b) Draw a cause–effect graph that relates the causes given in the example to the effects you have identified. (c) Transform your cause-effect graph to a decision table. (d) Generate test data from the decision table.

2.22 Consider the four cause–effect graphs in Figure 2.24. (a) For each graph in the figure, generate combinations of input conditions (causes) that bring Ef to 1-state. Do not apply the heuristics given in Section 2.6.4. (b) Now reduce the combinations generated in (a) by applying the heuristics. How much reduction, measured in terms of the number of combinations discarded, do you achieve in

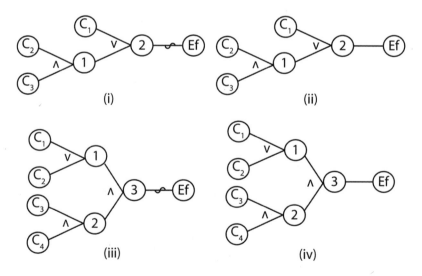

Fig. 2.24 Cause–effect graphs for Exercise 2.22.

each case? (c) Are the combinations generated in (b) unique in the sense that another set of combinations would also be satisfactory and as small in number?

2.23 Construct a sample implementation $\mathcal{I}$ to show that the application of heuristic H_2 from Table 2.4 will leave out at least one test that would have detected the error in $\mathcal{I}$.

2.24 Consider the following modified versions of heuristics H_1 and H_4 given in Table 2.4.

H_1: Enumerate any one combination of inputs to n_1 and n_2 such that $n_1 = n_2 = 0$.
H_4: Enumerate all combinations of inputs to n_1 and n_2 such that $n_1 = n_2 = 1$.

Discuss why the above modifications are undesirable (or desirable).

2.25 Complete Example 2.19 by (a) creating a decision table using procedure CEGDT in Section 2.6.3; apply heuristics from Table 2.4 while generating the decision table. (b) Generate a set of tests from the decision table.

2.26 Complete Example 2.20 by reducing the combinations in the decision table using heuristics given in Table 2.4. Generate a set of tests given the following causes:

C_1: A user selects Save As.
C_2: A user selects Open.
C_1: A user types in an integer greater than 99 in the relevant window.
C_1: A user selects any one of the following values from a list: High or Medium.

2.27 Consider the following relational expression $E_c : 2 * r < s + t$, where r, s, and t are floating point variables. Construct three faulty versions of E_c that contain, respectively, the off-by-ϵ, off-by-ϵ^*, and off-by-ϵ^+ faults. Select a suitable value for ϵ.

2.28 Consider the condition $C : (a + 1 > b) \wedge (c == d)$, where a, b, c, and d are type-compatible variables. (a) Let $S_1 = \{ (>, =) , (>, >) , (>, <) , (=, =) , (<, =) \}$ be a set of constraints on C. As in Example 2.25, construct a test set T_1 that satisfies S_1 and show that T is BRO adequate. (b) Now consider the constraint set $S_2 = \{ (+\epsilon, =), (=, -\epsilon), (-\epsilon, =), (+\epsilon, +\epsilon) \}$ on C. Construct a test set T_2 that satisfies S_2. Is T BRE adequate? Assume that $\epsilon = 1$.

2.29 Let $A = \{ (<, =), (>, <) \}$ and $B = \{ (\mathbf{t}, =), (\mathbf{t}, >), (\mathbf{f}, <) \}$ be two constraint sets. Compute $A \times B$ and $A \otimes B$.

2.30 Consider the predicate $p_2 : (a + b) < c \wedge \neg p \vee (r > s)$ in Example 2.28. Confirm that any predicate obtained by inserting a Boolean operator fault in p_2 will evaluate to a value different from that of p_2 on at least one of the four test cases derived in Example 2.28.

2.31 Consider the predicate $p : (a + b) < c \wedge \neg p \vee (r > s)$ in Example 2.29. Confirm that any predicate obtained by inserting single or multiple Boolean operator and relational operator faults in p_r will evaluate to a value different from that of p_r on at least one of the four test cases derived in Example 2.29.

2.32 For predicate p_r, the BRO-adequate test set T_{BOR} in Table 2.7 contains one more test case than the BOR-adequate test set T_{BRO} in Table 2.8. (a) Is there a faulty predicate obtained from p_r that will be distinguished from p_r by T_{BRO} and not by T_{BOR}? (b) Is there a faulty predicate obtained from p_r that will be distinguished from p_r by T_{BOR} and not by T_{BRO}? Constrain your answer to the fault model in Section 2.7.2.

2.33 Consider a predicate p_r and test sets T_{BRO} and T_{BRE} that are, respectively, BRO- and BRE-adequate for p_r. For what value of ϵ are T_{BRO} and T_{BRE} equivalent in their fault-detection abilities?

2.34 (a) Show that a BRE-constraint set can be derived from a BOR-constraint set simply by replacing constraint $(>)$ by $(+\epsilon)$ and $(<)$ by $(-\epsilon)$ and retaining $(=)$.
(b) Explain why a BRO-adequate test set might not be BRE adequate.
(c) Is a BRE-adequate test set always BRO-adequate or is it BOR adequate?
(d) Is a BRO-adequate test set always BOR adequate?

2.35 Let p_r be a predicate that contains at most n AND/OR operators. Show that $|T_{BOR}| \le n + 2$, $|T_{BRO}| \le 2 * n + 3$, and $|T_{BRE}| \le 2 * n + 3$.

2.36 Procedures BOR-CSET, BRO-CSET, and BRE-CSET use the $\otimes$ operator while propagating the constraints up through the abstract syntax tree. Show that larger test sets would be generated if instead the $\times$ operator is used.

2.37 What conflict might arise when applying any of procedures BOR-CSET, BRO-CSET, and BRE-CSET to a predicate containing one or more nonsingular expressions? Answer this question using predicate $p : (a + b)(bc)$ and applying any of the three procedures.

2.38 Use the BOR-CSET procedure to generate tests from the predicate $p : a + b$. Do the tests generated guarantee the detection of the missing Boolean variable fault that causes the implementation of p_r to be a? (b) Do the tests generated guarantee the detection of the extra Boolean variable fault in coding p_r that causes the implementation to be $a + b + c$, where c is the extra Boolean variable?

2.39 In procedure MI-CSET on page 153, show that (a) $S_E^t \neq \emptyset$ for $1 \leq i \leq n$ and (b) the $FS_{e_j^i}$ for different terms in p_r may not be disjoint and may be empty.

2.40 Use the constraint set S_E derived in Example 2.32 to show that the following faulty versions of the predicate $E = a(bc + \bar{b}d)$ evaluate differently than E on at least one test case derived from S_E.

(i)	$a(bc + bd)$	Missing NOT operator.
(ii)	$a(\bar{b}c + \bar{b}d)$	Incorrect NOT operator.
(iii)	$a + (bc + \bar{b}d)$	Incorrect OR operator.
(iv)	$a(bc\bar{b}d)$	Incorrect AND operator.
(iii)	$a + (\bar{b}c + \bar{b}d)$	Incorrect OR and NOT operators.

2.41 (a) Use the BOR-MI-CSET procedure to derive the constraint set for the following predicate p_r.

$$(a < b) \wedge (((r > s) \wedge u) \vee (a \geq b) \vee ((c < d) \vee (f = g)) \wedge (v \wedge w)),$$

where $a, b, c, d, f, g, r,$ and s are integer variables and $u, v,$ and w are Boolean variables.

(b) Using the constraint set derived in (a), construct a test set T for p_r.

(c) Verify that T is able to distinguish the following faulty versions from p_r.

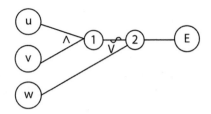

Fig. 2.25   A cause–effect effect graph for Exercise 2.42. Variables a, b, c and d are integers, $u : a < b$, $v : c > d$, and w is a Boolean variable.

   (i) $(a < b) \wedge ((\neg(r > s) \wedge u) \vee (a \geq b) \vee ((c < d) \vee (f = g)) \wedge (v \wedge w))$; Incorrect NOT operator.

  (ii) $(a < b) \wedge (((r > s) \wedge u) \vee (a \geq b) \vee ((c < d) \vee (f = g)) \wedge (v \wedge w))$; Incorrect NOT operator.

 (iii) $(a < b) \vee (((r > s) \vee u) \vee (a \geq b) \vee ((c < d) \vee (f = g)) \wedge (v \wedge w))$; Two incorrect OR operators.

 (iv) $(a < b) \vee (((r > s) \wedge \bar{u}) \vee (a \geq b) \vee ((c < d) \vee (f = g)) \wedge (v \wedge w))$; Incorrect OR and NOT operators.

2.42 Consider the cause–effect graph shown in Figure 2.25 that exhibits the relationship between several causes and effect E.
(a) Derive a test set T_{CEG} to test the implementation of E using the test-generation procedure described in Section 2.6.3.
(b) Construct a Boolean expression p_r from the Figure 2.25 that represents the condition for the effect to occur. Select one of the four procedures BOR-CSET, BRO-CSET, BRE-CSET, and BRO-MI-CSET, and apply it to construct a test set from p_r. Assume that there might be errors in the relational expressions that represent various causes effecting E. Construct a test set T_B from the constraints you derive.
(c) Suppose that u is incorrectly implemented as $a < b + 1$. Does T_{CEG} contains an error-revealing test case for this error? How about T_B?

3

Test Generation from Finite-State Models

CONTENT ■■

The purpose of this chapter is to introduce techniques for the generation of test data from finite-state models of software designs. A fault model and three test-generation techniques are presented. The test-generation techniques presented are: the W-method, the Unique Input/Output method and the Wp-method.

3.1 SOFTWARE DESIGN AND TESTING

Development of most software systems includes a design phase. In this phase the requirements serve as the basis for a design of the application to be developed. The design itself can be represented using one or more notations. FSMs, is the design notation used in this chapter.

A simplified software development process is shown in Figure 3.1. Software analysis and design is a step that ideally follows requirement gathering. The end result of the design step is the design artifact that expresses a high-level application architecture and interactions among low-level application components. The design is usually expressed using a variety of notations such as those embodied in the UML-design language. For example, UML statecharts are used to represent the design of the real-time portion of the application, and UML-sequence diagrams are used to show the interactions between various application components.

The design is often subjected to test prior to its input to the coding step. Simulation tools are used to check if the state transitions depicted

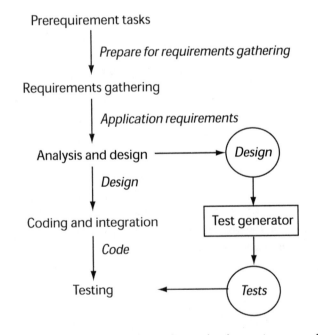

Fig. 3.1   Design and test-generation in a software development process. A *design* is an artifact generated in the analysis and design phase. This artifact becomes an input to the test generator algorithm that generates tests for input to the code during testing.

in the statecharts do conform to the application requirements. Once the design has passed the test, it serves as an input to the coding step. Once the individual modules of the application have been coded, successfully tested, and debugged, they are integrated into an application and another test step is executed. This test step is known by various names such as *system test* and *design verification test*. In any case, the test cases against which the application is run can be derived from a variety of sources, design being one of them.

In this chapter, we will show how a design can serve as source of tests that are used to test the application itself. As shown in Figure 3.1, the design generated at the end of the analysis and the design phase serve as an input to a *test-generation* procedure. This test-generation procedure generates a number of tests that serve as inputs to the code in the test phase. Note that though Figure 3.1 seems to imply that the test-generation procedure is applied to the entire design, this is not necessarily true; tests can be generated using portions of the design.

We introduce several test-generation procedures to derive tests from FSMs and statecharts. The FSM offers a simple way to model state-based behavior of applications. The statechart is a rich extension of the FSM and needs to be handled differently when used as an input to a test-generation algorithm. The Petri net is a useful formalism to express concurrency and timing and leads to yet another set of algorithms for generating tests. All test-generation methods described in this chapter can be automated though only some have been integrated into commercial test tools.

There exist several algorithms that take an FSM and some attributes of its implementation as inputs to generate tests. Note that the FSM serves as a source for test-generation and is not the item under test. It is the implementation of the FSM that is under test. Such an implementation is also known as *implementation under test* and abbreviated as IUT. For example, an FSM may represent a model of a communication protocol while an IUT is its implementation. The tests generated by the algorithms we introduce in this chapter are input to the IUT to determine if the IUT behavior conforms to the requirements.

In this chapter we introduce the following methods: the W-method, the unique input/output (UIO) method, and the partial W-method. In Section 3.9, we shall compare the various methods introduced. Before we proceed to describe the test-generation procedures, we introduce a fault model for FSMs, the characterization set of an FSM, and a procedure to generate this set. The characterization set is useful in understanding and implementing the test-generation methods introduced subsequently.

3.2 FINITE-STATE MACHINES

Many devices used in daily life contain embedded computers. For example, an automobile has several embedded computers to perform various tasks, engine control being one example. Another example is a computer inside a toy for processing inputs and generating audible and visual responses. Such devices are also known as *embedded systems*. An embedded system can be as simple as a child's musical keyboard or as complex as the flight controller in an aircraft. In any case, an embedded system contains one or more computers for processing inputs.

An embedded computer often receives inputs from its environment and responds with appropriate actions. While doing so, it moves from one state to another. The response of an embedded system to its inputs depends on its current state. It is this behavior of an embedded system in response to inputs that is often modeled by an FSM. Relatively simpler systems, such as protocols, are modeled using the FSMs. More complex systems, such as the engine controller of an aircraft, are modeled using *statecharts* that can be considered as a generalization of the FSMs. In this section we focus on the FSMs; statecharts are described in a chapter in Volume II. The next example illustrates a simple model using an FSM.

Example 3.1: Consider a traditional table lamp that has a three-way rotary switch. When the switch is turned to one of its positions, the lamp is in the OFF state. Moving the switch clockwise to the next position, one moves the lamp to an ON_DIM state. Moving the switch further clockwise one moves the lamp to the ON_BRIGHT state. Finally, moving the switch clockwise, one brings the lamp back to the OFF state. The switch serves as the input device that controls the state of the lamp. The change of lamp state in response to the switch position is often illustrated using a state diagram as in Figure 3.2(a).

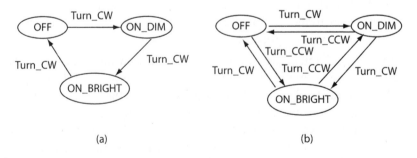

(a)   (b)

Fig. 3.2   Change of lamp state in response to the movement of a switch. (a) Switch can only move one notch clockwise (CW). (b) Switch can move one notch clockwise and counterclockwise (CCW).

Our lamp has three states, OFF, ON_DIM, and ON_BRIGHT, and one input. Note that the lamp switch has three distinct positions, though from a lamp user's perspective the switch can only be turned clockwise to its next position. Thus, "turning the switch one notch clockwise" is the only input. Suppose that the switch can also be moved counterclockwise. In this latter case, the lamp has two inputs: one corresponding to the clockwise motion and the other to the counterclockwise motion. The number of distinct states of the lamp remains three, but the state diagram is now as in Figure 3.2(b).

In the example above, we have modeled the table lamp in terms of its states, inputs and transitions. In most practical embedded systems, the application of an input might cause the system to perform an action in addition to performing a state transition. The action might be as trivial as "do nothing" and simply move to another state, or a complex function might be executed. The next example illustrates one such system.

Example 3.2: Consider a machine that takes a sequence of one or more unsigned decimal digits as input and converts the sequence to an equivalent integer. For example, if the sequence of digits input is 3, 2, and 1, then the output of the machine is 321. We assume that the end of the input-digit sequence is indicated by the asterisk (*) character. We shall refer to this machine as the DIGDEC machine. The state diagram of DIGDEC is shown in Figure 3.3.

The DIGDEC machine can be in any one of three states. It begins its operation in state q_0. Upon receiving the first digit, denoted by d in the figure, it invokes the function INIT to initialize variable num to d. In addition, the machine moves to state q_1 after performing the INIT operation. In q_1, DIGDEC can receive a digit or an end-of-input character which in our case is the asterisk. If it receives a digit, it updates num to 10 * num + d and remains in state q_1. Upon receiving an asterisk, the machine executes the OUT operation to output the current value of num and moves to state q_2. Note the double circle around state q_2, often such a double circle is used to indicate a final state of an FSM.

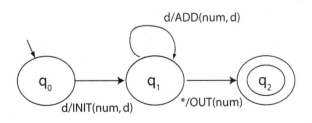

Fig. 3.3 State diagram of the DIGDEC machine that converts sequence of decimal digits to an equivalent decimal number.

Historically, FSMs that do not associate any action with a transition are known as *Moore* machines. In Moore machines, actions depend on the current state. In contrast, FSMs that do associate actions with each state transition are known as *Mealy* machines. In this book we are concerned with Mealy machines. In either case, an FSM consists of a finite set of states, a set of inputs, a start state, and a transition function that can be defined using the state diagram. In addition, a Mealy machine has a finite set of outputs. A formal definition of a Mealy machine is as follows:

Finite-state machine:

A finite-state machine is a six-tuple $(X, Y, Q, q_0, \delta, O)$, where

- X is a finite set of input symbols also known as the *input alphabet*.
- Y is a finite set of output symbols also known as the *output alphabet*.
- Q is a finite set of states.
- $q_0 \in Q$ is the initial state.
- $\delta : Q \times X \rightarrow Q$ is a next state or state transition function.
- $O : Q \times X \rightarrow Y$ is an output function.

In some variants of FSM, more than one state could be specified as an initial state. Also, sometimes it is convenient to add $F \subseteq Q$ as a set of *final* or *accepting* states while specifying an FSM. The notion of accepting states is useful when an FSM is used as an automaton to recognize a language. Also, note that the definition of the transition function δ implies that for any state q in Q, there is at most one next state. Such FSMs are also known as *deterministic* FSMs. In this book, we are concerned only with deterministic FSMs. The state transition function for nondeterministic FSMs is defined as

$$\delta : Q \times X \rightarrow 2^Q$$

which implies that such an FSM can have more than one possible transition out of a state on the same symbol. Nondeterministic FSMs are usually abbreviated as NFSM or NDFSM or simply as NFA for nondeterministic finite automata. We will use variants of NFSMs in Volume II in the context of algorithms for generating test cases to test for the timing constraints in real-time systems.

The state transition and the output functions are extended to strings as follows: Let q_i and q_j be two, possibly same, states in Q, and $s = a_1a_2 \ldots a_n$ a string over the input alphabet X of length $n \geq 0$.

Table 3.1 Formal description of three FSMs from Figures 3.2 and 3.3

	Figure 3.2 (a)	Figure 3.2 (b)	Figure 3.3
X	{Turn-CW}	{Turn-CW, Turn-CCW}	{0, 1, 2, 3, 4, 5, 6, 7, 8, 9, *}
Y	None	None	{INIT, ADD, OUT}
Q	{OFF, ON_DIM, ON_BRIGHT}	{OFF, ON_DIM, ON_BRIGHT}	{q_0, q_1, q_2}
q_0	{OFF}	{OFF}	q_0
F	None	None	q_2
δ	See Figure 3.2(a)	See Figure 3.2(b)	See Figure 3.3
O	Not applicable	Not applicable	See Figure 3.3

$\delta(q_i, s) = q_j$ if $\delta(q_i, a_1) = q_k$ and $\delta(q_k, a_2 a_3 \ldots a_n) = q_j$. The output function is extended similarly. Thus, $O(q_i, s) = O(q_i, a_1)$. $O(\delta(q_i, a_1), a_2, \ldots, a_n)$. Also, $\delta(q_i, e) = q_i$ and $O(q_i, e) = e$.

Table 3.1 contains a formal description of the state and output functions of FSMs given in Figures 3.2 and 3.3. There is no output function for the table lamp. Note that the state transition function δ and the output function O can be defined by a *state diagram* as in Figures 3.2 and 3.3. Thus, for example, from Figure 3.2(a), we can derive δ(OFF, Turn_CW) = ON_DIM. As an example of the output function, we get $O(q_0, 0)$ = INIT(num, 0) from Figure 3.3.

A state diagram is a directed graph that contains nodes, representing states, and edges, representing state transitions and output functions. Each node is labeled with the state it represents. Each directed edge in a state diagram connects two states as in Fig. 3.4.

Each edge is labeled i/o, where i denotes an input symbol that belongs to the input alphabet X and o denotes an output symbol that belongs to the output alphabet Y. i is also known as the *input portion* of the edge and o its *output portion*. Both i and o might be abbreviations. As an example, the edge connecting states q_0 and q_1 in Figure 3.3 is labeled *d/INIT(num, d)*, where d is an abbreviation for any digit from 0 to 9 and INIT(num, d) is an action.

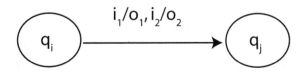

Fig. 3.4 Multiple labels for an edge connecting two states in an FSM.

Multiple labels can also be assigned to an edge. For example, the label $i_1/o_1, i_2/o_2$ associated with an edge that connects two states q_i and q_j implies that the FSM can move from q_i to q_j upon receiving either i_1 or i_2. Further, the FSM outputs o_1 if it receives input i_1, and outputs o_2 if it receives i_2. The transition and the output functions can also be defined in tabular form as explained in Section 3.2.2.

3.2.1 EXCITATION USING AN INPUT SEQUENCE

In most practical situations an implementation of an FSM is excited using a sequence of input symbols drawn from its input alphabet. For example, suppose that the table lamp whose state diagram in Figure 3.2(b) is in state ON_BRIGHT and receives the input sequence r, where

$$r = \text{Turn\_CCW Turn\_CCW Turn\_CW}.$$

Using the transition function in Figure 3.2(b), it is easy to verify that the sequence r will move the lamp from state ON_BRIGHT to state ON_DIM. This state transition can also be expressed as a sequence of transitions given below:

$$\delta(\text{ON\_BRIGHT, Turn\_CCW}) = \text{ON\_DIM}$$

$$\delta(\text{ON\_DIM, Turn\_CCW}) = \text{OFF}$$

$$\delta(\text{OFF, Turn\_CW}) = \text{ON\_DIM}$$

For brevity, we will use the notation $\delta(q_k, z) = q_j$ to indicate that an input sequence z of length 1 or more moves an FSM from state q_k to q_j. Using this notation, we can write $\delta(\text{ON\_BRIGHT}, r) = \text{ON\_DIM}$ for the state diagram in Figure 3.2(b).

We will use a similar abbreviation for the output function O. For example, when excited by the input sequence $1001*$, the DIGDEC machine ends up in state q_2 after executing the following sequence of actions and state transitions:

$$O(q_0, 1) = \text{INIT(num, 1)}, \delta(q_0, 1) = q_1$$

$$O(q_1, 0) = \text{ADD(num, 0)}, \delta(q_1, 0) = q_1$$

$$O(q_1, 0) = \text{ADD(num, 0)}, \delta(q_1, 0) = q_1$$

$$O(q_1, 1) = \text{ADD(num, 1)}, \delta(q_1, 1) = q_1$$

$$O(q_1, *) = \text{OUT(num)}, \delta(q_1, *) = q_2$$

Once again, we will use the notation $O(q, r)$ to indicate the action sequence executed by the FSM on input r when starting in state q. We also assume that a machine remains in its current state when excited with an empty sequence. Thus, $\delta(q, \epsilon) = q$. Using the abbreviation for state transitions, we can express the above action and transition sequence as follows:

$$O(q_0, 1001*) = \text{INIT(num, 1) ADD(num, 0)}$$

$$\text{ADD(num, 0) ADD(num, 1) OUT (num)}$$

$$\delta(q_0, 1001*) = q_2$$

3.2.2 TABULAR REPRESENTATION

A table is often used as an alternative to the state diagram to represent the state transition function δ and the output function O. The table consists of two subtables that consist of one or more columns each. The leftmost subtable is the *output* or the *action* subtable. The rows are labeled by the states of the FSM. The rightmost subtable is the *next state* subtable. The output subtable, which corresponds to the output function O, is labeled by the elements of the input alphabet X. The next state subtable, which corresponds to the transition function δ, is also labeled by elements of the input alphabet. The entries in the output subtable indicate the actions taken by the FSM for a single input received in a given state. The entries in the next state subtable indicate the state to which the FSM moves for a given input and in a given current state. The next example illustrates how the output and transition functions can be represented in a table.

Example 3.3: The table given below shows how to represent functions δ and O for the DIGDEC machine. In this table, the column labeled *Action* defines the output function by listing the actions taken by the DIGDEC machine for various inputs. Sometimes this column is also labeled as *Output* to indicate that the FSM generates an output symbol when it takes a transition. The column labeled *Next State* defines the transition function by listing the next state of the DIGDEC machine in response to an input. Empty entries in the table should be considered as undefined. However, in certain practical situations, the empty entries correspond to an error action. Note that in the table below, we have used the abbreviation d for the 10 digits, 0 through 9.

	Action		Next state	
Current state	d	*	d	*
q_0	INIT (num, d)		q_1	
q_1	ADD (num, d)	OUT (num)	q_1	q_2
q_2				

3.2.3 PROPERTIES OF FSM

FSMs can be characterized by one or more of several properties. Some of the properties found useful in test-generation are given below. We shall use these properties later while explaining algorithms for test-generation.

Completely specified FSM: An FSM M is said to be completely specified if from each state in M there exists a transition for each input symbol. The machine described in Example 3.1 with state diagram in Figure 3.2(a) is completely specified as there is only one input symbol and each state has a transition corresponding to this input symbol. Similarly, the machine with state diagram shown in Figure 3.2(b) is also completely specified as each state has transitions corresponding to each of the two input symbols. The DIGDEC machine in Example 3.2 is not completely specified, as state q_0 does not have any transition corresponding to an asterisk and state q_2 has no outgoing transitions.

Strongly connected: An FSM M is considered strongly connected if for each pair of states (q_i, q_j) there exists an input sequence that takes M from state q_i to q_j. It is easy to verify that the machine in Example 3.1 is strongly connected. The DIG_DEC machine in Example 3.2 is not strongly connected as it is impossible to move from state q_2 to q_0, from q_2 to q_1, and from q_1 to q_0. In a strongly connected FSM, given some state $q_i \neq q_0$, one can find an input sequence $s \in X^*$ that takes the machine from its initial state to q_i. We, therefore, say that in a strongly connected FSM, every state is reachable from the initial state.

V-equivalence: Let $M_1 = (X, Y, Q_1, m_0^1, T_1, O_1)$ and $M_2 = (X, Y, Q_2, m_0^2, T_2, O_2)$ be two FSMs. Let V denote a set of nonempty strings over the input alphabet X, that is $V \subseteq X^+$. Let q_i and q_j, $i \neq j$, be the states of machines M_1 and M_2, respectively. States q_i and q_j are considered V-equivalent if $O_1(q_i, s) = O_2(q_j, s)$ for all $s \in V$. Stated differently, states q_i and q_j are considered *V-equivalent* if M_1 and M_2 when excited in states q_i and q_j, respectively, yield identical output sequences. States q_i and q_j are said to be *equivalent* if $O_1(q_i, r) = O_2(q_j, r)$ for any set V. If q_i and q_j are not equivalent, then they are said to be *distinguishable*. This definition of equivalence also applies to states within a machine. Thus, machines M_1 and M_2 could be the same machine.

Machine equivalence: Machines M_1 and M_2 are said to be equivalent if (a) for each state σ in M_1 there exists a state σ' in M_2, such that σ and σ' are equivalent and (b) for each state σ in M_2, there exists a state σ' in M_1 such that σ and σ' are equivalent. Machines that are not equivalent are considered distinguishable. If M_1 and M_2 are strongly connected then they are equivalent if their respective initial states, m_0^1 and m_0^2, are equivalent. We write $M_1 = M_2$ if machines M_1 and M_2 are equivalent,

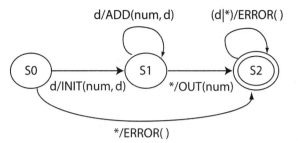

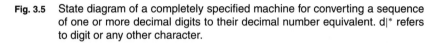

Fig. 3.5 State diagram of a completely specified machine for converting a sequence of one or more decimal digits to their decimal number equivalent. d|* refers to digit or any other character.

and $M_1 \neq M_2$ when they are distinguishable. Similarly, we write $q_i = q_j$ when states q_i and q_j are equivalent, and $q_i \neq q_j$ if they are distinguishable.

k-equivalence: Let $M_1 = (X, Y, Q_1, m_0^1, T_1, O_1)$ and $M_2 = (X, Y, Q_2, m_0^2, T_2, O_2)$ be two FSMs. States $q_t \in Q_1$ and $q_i \in Q_2$ are considered *k-equivalent* if when excited by any input of length k yield identical output sequences. States that are not *k-equivalent* are considered *k-distinguishable*. Once again M_1 and M_2 may be the same machines implying that k-distinguishability applies to any pair of states of an FSM. It is also easy to see that if two states are *k-distinguishable* for any $k > 0$, then they are also distinguishable for any $n > k$. If M_1 and M_2 are not *k-distinguishable* then they are said to be *k-equivalent*.

Minimal machine: An FSM M is considered *minimal* if the number of states in M is less than or equal to any other FSM equivalent to M.

> **Example 3.4:** Consider the DIGDEC machine in Figure 3.3. This machine is not completely specified. However, it is often the case that certain erroneous transitions are not indicated in the state diagram. A modified version of the DIGDEC machine appears in Figure 3.5. Here, we have labeled explicitly the error transitions by the output function ERROR( ).

3.3 CONFORMANCE TESTING

The term *conformance testing* is used during the testing of communication protocols. An implementation of a communication protocol is said to conform to its specification if the implementation passes a collection of tests derived from the specification. In this chapter, we introduce techniques for generating tests to test an implementation for conformance testing of a protocol modeled as an FSM. Note that the term conformance testing applies equally well to the testing of

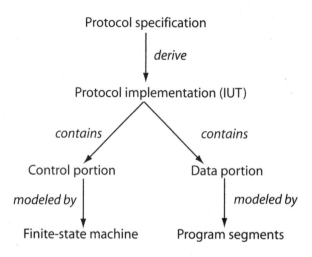

Fig. 3.6 Relationship among protocol specification, implementation, and models.

any implementation that corresponds to its specification, regardless of whether the implementation is that of a communication protocol.

Communication protocols are used in a variety of situations. For example, common use of protocols is in public data networks. These networks use access protocols such as the X.25 which is a protocol standard for wide-area network communications. The alternating bit protocol (ABP) is another example of a protocol used in the connection-less transmission of messages from a transmitter to a receiver. Musical instruments such as synthesizers and electronic pianos use the Musical Instrument Digital Interface (MIDI) protocol to communicate among themselves and a computer. These are just three examples of a large variety of communication protocols that exist and new ones are often under construction.

A protocol can be specified in a variety of ways. For example, it could be specified informally in textual form. It could also be specified more formally using an FSM, a visual notation such as a statechart, and using languages such as language of temporal ordering specification (LOTOS), Estelle, and specification and description language (SDL). In any case, the specification serves as the source for implementers and also for automatic code generators. As shown in Figure 3.6, an implementation of a protocol consists of a control portion and a data portion. The control portion captures the transitions in the protocol from one state to another. It is often modeled as an FSM. The data portion maintains information needed for the correct behavior. This includes counters and other variables that hold data. The data portion is modeled as a collection of program modules or segments.

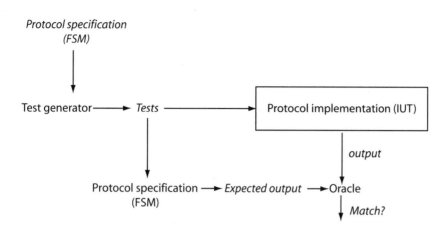

Fig. 3.7 A simplified procedure for testing a protocol implementation against an FSM model. Italicized items represent data input to some procedure. Note that the model itself serves as data input to the test generator and as a procedure for deriving the expected output.

Testing an implementation of a protocol involves testing both the control and data portions. The implementation under test is often referred to as IUT. In this chapter, we are concerned with testing the control portion of an IUT. Techniques for testing the data portion of the IUT are described in other chapters. Testing the control portion of an IUT requires the generation of test cases. As shown in Figure 3.7, the IUT is tested against the generated tests. Each test is a sequence of symbols that are input to the IUT. If the IUT behaves in accordance with the specification, as determined by an oracle, then its control portion is considered equivalent to the specification. Nonconformance usually implies that the IUT has an error that needs to be fixed. Such tests of an IUT are generally effective in revealing certain types of implementation errors discussed in Section 3.4.

A significant portion of this chapter is devoted to describing techniques for generating tests to test the control portion of an IUT corresponding to a formally specified design. The techniques described for testing IUTs modeled as FSMs are applicable to protocols and other requirements that can be modeled as FSMs. Most complex software systems are generally modeled using statecharts and not FSMs. However, some of the test-generation techniques described in this chapter are useful in generating tests from statecharts.

3.3.1 Reset Inputs

The test methods described in this chapter often rely on the ability of a tester to reset the IUT so that it returns to its start state. Thus, given a set of test cases $T = \{t_1, t_2, \ldots, t_n\}$, a test proceeds as follows:

1. Bring the IUT to its start state. Repeat the following steps for each test in T.

2. Select the next test case from T and apply it to the IUT. Observe the behavior of the IUT and compare it against the expected behavior as shown in Figure 3.7. The IUT is said to have failed if it generates an output different from the expected output.

3. Bring the IUT back to its start state by applying the reset input and repeat the above step, but with the next test input.

It is usually assumed that the application of the reset input generates a null output. Thus, for the purpose of testing an IUT against its control specification FSM $M = (X, Y, Q, q_1, \delta, O)$, the input and output alphabets are augmented as follows:

$$X = X \cup \{Re\}$$
$$Y = Y \cup \{null\}$$

where Re denotes the reset input and null the corresponding output.

While testing a software implementation against its design, a reset input might require executing the implementation from the beginning, that is restarting the implementation manually or automatically via, for example, a script. However, in situations where the implementation causes side effects, such as writing a file or sending a message over a network, bringing the implementation to its start state might be a nontrivial task if its behavior depends on the state of the environment. While testing continuously running programs, such as network servers, the application of a reset input does imply bringing the server to its initial state but not necessarily shutting it down and restarting.

The transitions corresponding to the reset input are generally not shown in the state diagram. In a sense, these are hidden transitions that are allowed during the execution of the implementation. When necessary, these transitions could be shown explicitly as in Figure 3.8.

Example 3.5: Consider the test of an application that resides inside a microwave oven. Suppose that one test, say t_1, corresponds to testing the "set clock time" function. Another test, say t_2, tests for heating ability of the oven under "low-power" setting. Finally, the third test t_3 tests the ability of the oven under "high-power" setting. In its start state, the oven has electrical power applied and is ready to receive commands from its keypad. We assume that the clock time setting is not a component of the start state. This implies that the current time

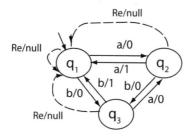

Fig. 3.8   Transitions corresponding to reset (*Re*) inputs.

on the clock, say is 1:15 p.m. or 2:09 a.m. does not have any affect on the state of the oven.

It seems obvious that the three tests mentioned above can be executed in any sequence. Further, once a test is completed and the oven application, and the oven, does not fail, the oven will be in its start state and hence no explicit reset input is required prior to executing the next test.

However, the scenario mentioned above might change after the application of, for example, t_2 if there is an error in the application under test or in the hardware that receives control commands from the application under test. For example, the application of t_2 is expected to start the oven's heating process. However, due to some hardware or software error, this might not happen and the oven application might enter a loop waiting to receive a *task completed* confirmation signal from the hardware. In this case, tests t_3 or t_1 cannot be applied unless the oven control software and hardware are reset to their start state.

It is because of situations such as the one described in the previous example that require the availability of a reset input to bring the IUT under test to its start state. Bringing the IUT to its start state gets it ready to receive the next test input.

3.3.2 The Testing Problem

There are several ways to express the design of a system or a subsystem. FSM, statecharts, and Petri nets are some of the formalisms to express various aspects of a design. Protocols, for example, are often expressed as FSMs. Software designs are expressed using statecharts. Petri nets are often used to express aspects of designs that relate to concurrency and timing. The design is used as a source for the generation of tests that are used subsequently to test the IUT for conformance to the design.

Let M be a formal representation of a design. As above, this could be an FSM, a statechart, or a Petri net. Other formalisms are possible too.

Let R denote the requirements that led to M. R may be for a communication protocol, an embedded system such as the automobile engine or a heart pacemaker. Often, both R and M are used as the basis for the generation of tests and to determine the expected output as shown in Figure 3.7. In this chapter, we are concerned with the generation of tests using M.

The testing problem is to determine if the IUT is *equivalent* to M. For the FSM representation, equivalence was defined earlier. For other representations, equivalence is defined in terms of the I/O behavior of the IUT and M. As mentioned earlier, the protocol or design of interest might be implemented in hardware, software, or a combination of the two. Testing the IUT for equivalence against M requires executing it against a sequence of test inputs derived from M and comparing the observed behavior with the expected behavior as shown in Figure 3.7. Generation of tests from a formal representation of the design and their evaluation in terms of their fault-detection ability are the key subjects of this chapter.

3.4 A FAULT MODEL

Given a set of requirements R, one often constructs a design from the requirements. An FSM is one possible representation of the design. Let M_d be a design intended to meet the requirements in R. Sometimes M_d is referred to as a *specification* that guides the implementation. M_d is implemented in hardware or software. Let M_i denote an implementation that is intended to meet the requirements in R and has been derived using M_d. Note that in practice, M_i is unlikely to be an exact analog of M_d. In embedded real-time systems and communications protocols, it is often the case that M_i is a computer program that uses variables and operations not modeled in M_d. Thus, one could consider M_d as a finite-state model of M_i.

The problem in testing is to determine whether M_i conforms to R. To do so, one tests M_i using a variety of inputs and checks for the correctness of the behavior of M_i with respect to R. The design M_d can be useful in generating a set T of tests for M_i. Tests so generated are also known as black-box tests because they have been generated with reference to M_d and not M_i. Given T, one tests M_i against each test $t \in T$ and compares the behavior of M_i with the expected behavior given by exciting M_d in the initial state with test t.

In an ideal situation, one would like to ensure that any error in M_i is revealed by testing it against some test $t \in T$ derived from M_d. One reason why this is not feasible is that the number of possible implementations of a design M_d is infinite. This gives rise to the possibility of a

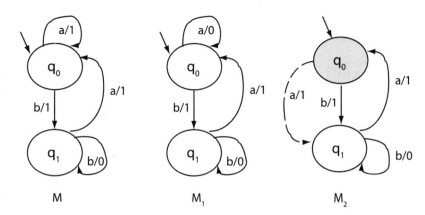

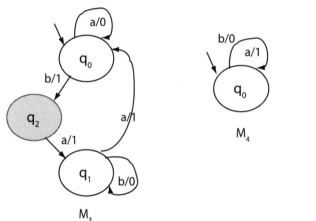

Fig. 3.9 Machine M represents the correct design. Machines M_1, M_2, M_3, and M_4 each contain an error.

large variety of errors one could be introduced in M_i. In the face of this reality, a *fault model* has been proposed. This fault model defines a small set of possible fault types that can occur in M_i. Given a fault model, the goal is to generate a test set T from a design M_d. Any fault in M_i of the type in the fault model is guaranteed to be revealed when tested against T.

A widely used fault model for FSMs is shown in Figure 3.9. This figure illustrates four fault categories.

- *Operation error*: Any error in the output generated upon a transition is an operation error. This is illustrated by machines M and M_1 in Figure 3.9, where FSM M_1 generates an output 0, instead of a 1, when symbol a is input in state q_0. More formally, an operation error implies that for some state q_i in M and some input symbol s, $O(q_i, s)$ is incorrect.

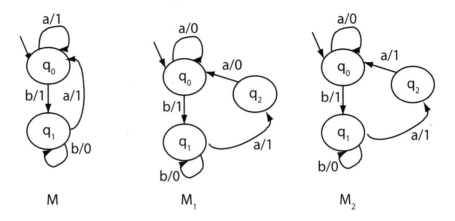

Fig. 3.10 Machine M represents the correct design. Machines M_1 and M_2 each have an extra state. However, M_1 is erroneous and M_2 is equivalent to M.

- *Transfer error*: Any error in the transition from one state to the next is a transition error. This is illustrated by machine M_2 in Figure 3.9, where FSM M_2 moves to state q_1, instead of moving to q_0 from q_0 when symbol a is input. More formally, a transfer error implies that for some state q_i in M and some input symbol s $\delta(q_i, s)$ is incorrect.

- *Extra-state error*: An extra state may be introduced in the implementation. In Figure 3.9, machine M_3 has q_2 as the extra state when compared with the state set of machine M. However, an extra state may or may not be an error. For example, in Figure 3.10, machine M represents the correct design. Machines M_1 and M_2 have one extra state each. However, M_1 is an erroneous design, but M_2 is not because M_2 is actually equivalent to M even though it has an extra state.

- *Missing-state error*: A missing state is another type of error. In Figure 3.9, machine M_4 has q_1 missing when compared with machine M_4. Given that the machine representing the design is minimal and complete a missing state implies an error in the IUT.

The above fault model is generally used to evaluate a method for generating tests from a given FSM. The faults indicated above are also known collectively as *sequencing faults* or *sequencing errors*. It may be noted that a given implementation could have more than one error of the same type. Other possibilities such as two errors one each of a different type also exist.

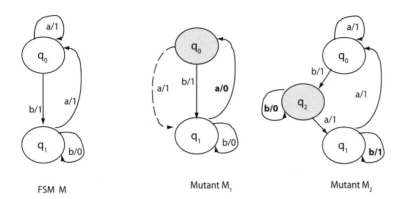

Fig. 3.11 Two mutants of machine M. Mutant M_1 is obtained by introducing into M one operation error in state q_1 and one transfer error in state q_0 for input a. Mutant M_2 has been obtained by introducing an extra state q_2 in machine M and an operation error in state q_1 on input b.

3.4.1 MUTANTS OF FSMS

As mentioned earlier, given a design M_d, one could construct many correct and incorrect implementations. Let $\mathcal{I}(M_d)$ denote the set of all possible implementations of M_d. In order to make $\mathcal{I}$ finite, we assume that any implementation in $\mathcal{I}(M_d)$ differs from M_d in known ways. One way to distinguish an implementation from its specification is through the use of *mutants*. A mutant of M_d is an FSM obtained by introducing one or more errors one or more times. We assume that the errors introduced belong to the fault model described earlier. We see in Figure 3.9 four mutants M_1, M_2, M_3, and M_4 of machine M obtained by using this method. More complex mutants can also be obtained by introducing more than one error in a machine. Figure 3.11 shows two such mutants of machine M of Figure 3.9.

Note that some mutant may be equivalent to M_d implying that the output behaviors of M_d and the mutant are identical on *all possible* inputs. Given a test set T, we say that a mutant is *distinguished* from M_d by a test $t \in T$ if the output sequence generated by the mutant is different from that generated by M_d when excited with t in their respective initial states. In this case, we also say that T distinguishes the mutant.

Using the idea of mutation, one can construct a finite set of possible implementations of a given specification M_d. Of course, this requires that some constraints be placed on the process of mutation, that is on how the errors are introduced. We caution the reader in that the technique of testing software using program mutation is a little different from the use of mutation described here. We discuss this difference in Chapter 7. The next example illustrates how to obtain one set of possible implementations.

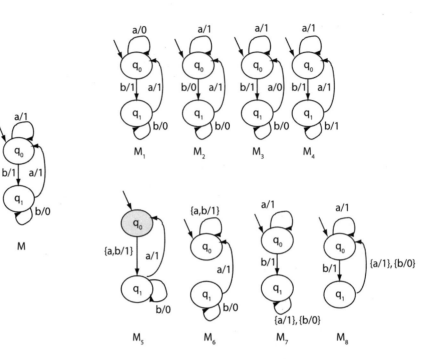

Fig. 3.12 Eight first order mutants of M generated by introducing operation and transfer errors. Mutants M_1, M_2, M_3, and M_4 are generated by introducing operation errors in M. Mutants M_5, M_6, M_7, and M_8 are generated by introducing transfer errors in M.

Example 3.6: Let M shown in Figure 3.12 denote the correct design. Suppose that we are allowed to introduce only one error at a time in M. This generates four mutants M_1, M_2, M_3, and M_4 shown in Figure 3.12 obtained by introducing an operation error. Considering that each state has two transitions, we get four additional mutants M_5, M_6, M_7, and M_8 by introducing the transfer error.

Introducing an additional state to create a mutant is more complex. First, we assume that only one extra state can be added to the FSM. However, there are several ways in which this state can interact with the existing states in the machine. This extra state can have two transitions that can be specified in 36 different ways depending on the tail state of the transition and the associated output function. We delegate to Exercise 3.10 the task of creating all the mutants of M by introducing an extra state.

Removing a state can be done in only two ways: remove q_0 or remove q_1. This generates two mutants. In general, this could be more complex when the number of states is greater than three. Removing a state will require the redirection of transitions and hence the number of mutants generated will be more than the number of states in the correct design.

Any nonempty test starting with symbol a distinguishes M from M_1. Mutant M_2 is distinguished from M by the input sequence ab. Note that when excited with ab, M outputs the string 11 whereas M_2 outputs the string 10. Input ab also distinguishes M_5 from M. The complete set of distinguishing inputs can be found using the W-method described in Section 3.6.

3.4.2 FAULT COVERAGE

One way to determine the *goodness* of a test set is to compute how many errors it reveals in a given implementation M_i. A test set that can reveal all errors in M_i is considered superior to one that fails to reveal one or more errors. Methods for the generation of test sets are often evaluated based on their fault coverage. The fault coverage of a test set is measured as a fraction between 0 and 1 and with respect to a given design specification. We give a formal definition of fault coverage in the following where the fault model presented earlier is assumed to generate the mutants.

N_t : Total number of first order mutants of the machine M used for generating tests. This is the same as $| \mathcal{I}(M) |$.

N_e: Number of mutants that are equivalent to M.

N_f: Number of mutants that are distinguished by test set T generated using some test-generation method. Recall that these are the faulty mutants.

N_l: Number of mutants that are not distinguished by T.

The fault coverage of a test suite T with respect to a design M, and an implementation set $\mathcal{I}(M)$, is denoted by $FC(T, M)$ and computed as follows:

$$FC(T, M) = \frac{\text{Number of mutants not distinguished by } T}{\text{Number of mutants that are not equivalent to } M}$$
$$= \frac{N_t - N_e - N_f}{N_t - N_e}$$

In Section 3.9, we will see how FC can be used to evaluate the goodness of various methods to generate tests from FSMs. Next, we introduce the characterization set, and its computation, useful in various methods for generating tests from FSMs.

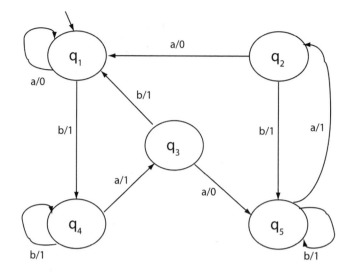

Fig. 3.13   The transition and output functions of a simple FSM.

3.5 CHARACTERIZATION SET

Most methods for generating tests from FSMs make use of an important set known as the *characterization set*. This set is usually denoted by W and is sometimes referred to as the W-set. In this section, we explain how one can derive a W-set given the description of an FSM. Let us examine the definition of the W-set.

Let $M = (X, Y, Q, q_1, \delta, O)$ be an FSM that is minimal and complete. A characterization set for M, denoted as W, is a finite set of input sequences that distinguish the behavior of any pair of states in M. Thus, if q_i and q_j are states in Q, then there exists a string s in W such that $O(q_i, s) \neq O(q_j, s)$, where s belongs to X^+.

Example 3.7: Consider an FSM $M = (X, Y, Q, q_1, \delta, O)$, where $X = \{a, b\}$, $Y = \{0, 1\}$, and $Q = \{q_1, q_2, q_3, q_4, q_5\}$, where q_1 is the initial state. The state transition function δ and the output function O are shown in Figure 3.13. The set W for this FSM is given below:

$$W = \{a, aa, aaa, baaa\}$$

Let us do a sample check to determine if indeed W is the characterization set for M. Consider the string baaa . It is easy to verify from Figure 3.13 that when M is started in state q_1 and excited with baaa, the output sequence generated is 1101. However, when M is started in state q_2 and excited with input baaa, the output sequence generated is 1100. Thus, we see that $O(q_1, baaa) \neq O(q_2, baaa)$, implying that the sequence baaa is a distinguishing sequence for states q_1 and q_2. You may now go ahead and perform similar checks for the remaining pairs of states.

The algorithm to construct a characterization set for an FSM M consists of two main steps. The first step is to construct a sequence of k-equivalence partitions $P_1, P_2, \ldots, P_m$, where $m > 0$. This iterative step converges in at most n steps, where n is the number of states in M. In the second step, these k-equivalence partitions are traversed, in reverse order, to obtain the distinguishing sequences for every pair of states. These two steps are explained in detail in the following two subsections.

3.5.1 Construction of the k-equivalence Partitions

Recall that given $M = (X, Y, Q, q_1, \delta, O)$, two states $q_i \in Q$ and $q_j \in Q$ are considered k-equivalent if there does not exist an $s \in X^k$ such that $O(q_i, s) \neq O(q_j, s)$. The notion of k-equivalence leads to the notion of k-equivalence partitions.

Given an FSM $M = (X, Y, Q, q_1, \delta, O)$, a k-equivalence partition of Q, denoted by P_k, is a collection of n finite sets of states denoted as Σ_{k_1}, $\Sigma_{k_2}, \ldots, \Sigma_{k_n}$ such that

- $\cup_{i=1}^{n} \Sigma_{ki} = Q$
- States in Σ_{kj}, for $1 \leq j \leq n$, are k-equivalent
- If $q_l \in \Sigma_{ki}$ and $q_m \in \Sigma_{kj}$, for $i \neq j$, then q_l and q_m must be k-distinguishable

We now illustrate the computation of k-equivalence partitions by computing them for the FSM of Example 3.7 using a rather long example.

Example 3.8: We begin by computing the one-equivalence partition, that is P_1, for the FSM shown in Figure 3.13. To do so, we write the transition and output functions for this FSM in a tabular form as shown below:

Current state	Output a	Output b	Next state a	Next state b
q_1	0	1	q_1	q_4
q_2	0	1	q_1	q_5
q_3	0	1	q_5	q_1
q_4	1	1	q_3	q_4
q_5	1	1	q_2	q_5

State transition and output table for M.

The next step in constructing P_1 is to regroup the states so that all states that are identical in their Output entries belong to the same group. We indicate the separation among the two groups by a horizontal line as shown in the table below. Note from this table that states q_1, q_2, and q_3 belong to one group as they share identical output entries. Similarly, states q_4 and q_5 belong to another group. Note also that we have added a Σ column to indicate group names. You may decide on any naming scheme for groups. In this example, we have labeled the groups as 1 and 2.

Σ	Current state	Output		Next state	
		a	**b**	**a**	**b**
1	q_1	0	1	q_1	q_4
	q_2	0	1	q_1	q_5
	q_3	0	1	q_5	q_1
2	q_4	1	1	q_3	q_4
	q_5	1	1	q_2	q_5

State transition and output table for M with grouping indicated.

We have now completed the construction of P_1. The groups separated by the horizontal line constitute a one-equivalence partition. We have labeled these groups as 1 and 2. Thus, we get the one-equivalence partition as follows:

$$P_1 = \{1, \ 2\}$$
$$\text{Group } 1 = \Sigma_{11} = \{q_1, q_2, q_3\}$$
$$\text{Group } 2 = \Sigma_{12} = \{q_4, q_5\}$$

In preparation to begin the construction of the two-equivalence partition, we construct the P_1 table as follows. First we copy the *Next State* subtable. Next, we rename each Next state entry by appending a second subscript that indicates the group to which that state belongs. For example, the next state entry under column "a" in the first row is q_1. As q_1 belongs to group 1, we relabel this as q_{11}. Other next state entries are relabeled in a similar way. This gives us the P_1 table as shown below:

Σ	Current state	Next state	
		a	**b**
1	q_1	q_{11}	q_{42}
	q_2	q_{11}	q_{52}
	q_3	q_{52}	q_{11}
2	q_4	q_{31}	q_{42}
	q_5	q_{21}	q_{52}

P_1 table

From the P_1 table given above, we construct the P_2 table as follows. First, regroup all rows with identical second subscripts in its row entries under the Next state column. Note that the subscript we are referring to is the group label. Thus, for example, in q_{42} the subscript we refer to is 2 and not 4 2. This is because q_4 is the name of the state in machine M and 2 is the group label under the Σ column. As an example of regrouping in the P_1 table, the rows corresponding to the current states q_1 and q_2 have next states with identical subscripts and hence we group them together. This regrouping leads to additional groups. We now relabel the groups and update the subscripts associated with the next state entries. Using this grouping scheme, we get the following P_2 table:

Σ	Current state	Next state a	b
1	q_1	q_{11}	q_{43}
	q_2	q_{11}	q_{53}
2	q_3	q_{53}	q_{11}
3	q_4	q_{32}	q_{43}
	q_5	q_{21}	q_{53}

P_2 table

Note that we have three groups in the P_2 table. We regroup the entries in the P_2 table using the scheme described earlier for generating the P_2 table. This regrouping and relabeling gives us the following P_3 table:

Σ	Current state	Next state a	b
1	q_1	q_{11}	q_{43}
	q_2	q_{11}	q_{54}
2	q_3	q_{54}	q_{11}
3	q_4	q_{32}	q_{43}
4	q_5	q_{21}	q_{54}

P_3 table

Further regrouping and relabeling of P_3 table gives us the P_4 table given below:

Σ	Current state	Next state a	b
1	q_1	q_{11}	q_{44}
2	q_2	q_{11}	q_{55}
3	q_3	q_{55}	q_{11}
4	q_4	q_{33}	q_{44}
5	q_5	q_{22}	q_{55}

P_4 table

Note that no further partitioning is possible using the scheme described earlier. We have completed the construction of k-equivalence partitions, $k = 1, 2, 3, 4$, for machine M.

Note that the process of deriving the P_k tables has converged to P_4 and no further partitions are possible. See Exercise 3.6 that asks you to show that indeed the process will always converge. It is also interesting to note that each group in the P_4 table consists of exactly one state. This implies that all states in M are distinguishable. In other words, no two states in M are equivalent.

Next, we summarize the algorithm to construct a characterization set from the k-equivalence partitions and illustrate it using an example.

3.5.2 DERIVING THE CHARACTERIZATION SET

Having constructed the k-equivalence partitions, that is the P_k tables, we are now ready to derive the W-set for machine M. Recall that for each pair of states q_i and q_j in M, there exists at least one string in W that distinguishes q_i from q_j. Thus, the method to derive W proceeds by determining a distinguishing sequence for each pair of states in M. First, we sketch the method referred to as the W-procedure, and then illustrate it by a continuation of the previous example. In the procedure given below, $G(q_i, x)$ denotes the label of the group to which the machine moves when excited using input x in state q_i. For example, in the table for P_3 in Section 3.5.1, $G(q_2, b) = 4$ and $G(q_5, a) = 1$.

The W-procedure

(A procedure to derive W from a set of partition tables.)

Begin W-procedure.

1. Let $M = (X, Y, Q, q_1, \delta, O)$ be the FSM for which $P = \{P_1, P_2, \ldots, P_n\}$ is the set of k-equivalence partition tables for $k = 1, 2, \ldots, n$. Initialize $W = \emptyset$.

2. Repeat the steps (a) through (d) given below for each pair of states (q_i, q_j), $i \neq j$, in M.

   (a) Find r, $1 \leq r < n$ such that the states in pair (q_i, q_j) belong to the same group in P_r but not in P_{r+1}. In other words, P_r is the *last* of the P tables in which (q_i, q_j) belongs to the same group. If such an r is found then move to Step (b), otherwise we find an $\eta \in X$ such that $O(q_i, \eta) \neq O(q_j, \eta)$, set $W = W \cup \{\eta\}$, and continue with the next available pair of states.

   The length of the minimal distinguishing sequence for (q_i, q_j) is $r + 1$. We denote this sequence as $z = x_0 x_1 \ldots x_r$, where $x_i \in X$ for $0 \leq i \leq r$.

   (b) Initialize $z = \epsilon$. Let $p_1 = q_i$ and $p_2 = q_j$ be the *current* pair of states. Execute steps (i) through (iii) given below for $m = r, r-1, r-2, \ldots, 1$.

   (i) Find an input symbol η in P_m such that $G(p_1, \eta) \neq G(p_2, \eta)$. In case there is more than one symbol that satisfy the condition in this step, then select one arbitrarily.

   (ii) Set $z = z\eta$

   (iii) Set $p_1 = \delta(p_1, \eta)$ and $p_2 = \delta(p_2, \eta)$.

   (c) Find an $\eta \in X$ such that $O(p_1, \eta) \neq O(p_2, \eta)$. Set $z = z\eta$.

   (d) The distinguishing sequence for the pair (q_i, q_j) is the sequence z. Set $W = W \cup \{z\}$.

End of the W-procedure

Upon termination of the W-procedure, we would have generated distinguishing sequences for all pairs of states in M. Note that the above algorithm is inefficient in that it derives a distinguishing sequence for each pair of states even though two pairs of states might share the same distinguishing sequence (see Exercise 3.7). The next example applies the W-procedure to obtain W for the FSM in Example 3.8.

Example 3.9: As there are several pairs of states in M, we illustrate how to find the distinguishing input sequences for the pairs (q_1, q_2) and (q_3, q_4). Let us begin with the pair (q_1, q_2).

According to Step 2(a) of the W-procedure we first determine r. To do so, we note from Example 3.8 that the last P-table in which q_1 and q_2 appear in the same group is P_3. Thus $r = 3$.

We now move to Step 2(b) and set $z = \epsilon$, $p_1 = q_1$, $p_2 = q_2$. Next, from P_3 we find that $G(p_1, b) \neq G(p_2, b)$ and update z to $zb = b$. Thus, b is the *first* symbol in the input string that distinguishes q_1 from q_2. In accordance with Step 2(b)(ii), we reset $p_1 = \delta(p_1, b)$ and $p_2 = \delta(p_2, b)$. This gives us $p_1 = q_4$ and $p_2 = q_5$.

Table 3.2 Distinguishing sequences for all pairs
of states in the FSM of Example 3.8

S_i	S_j	x	$o(S_i, x)$	$o(S_j, x)$
1	2	baaa	1	0
1	3	aa	0	1
1	4	a	0	1
1	5	a	0	1
2	3	aa	0	1
2	4	a	0	1
2	5	a	0	1
3	4	a	0	1
3	5	a	0	1
4	5	aaa	1	0

Going back to Step 2(b)(i), we find from the P_2 table that
$G(p_1, a) \neq G(p_2, a)$. We update z to $za = ba$ and reset p_1 and p_2 to
$p_1 = \delta(p_1, a)$ and $p_2 = \delta(p_2, a)$. We now have $p_1 = q_3$ and $p_2 = q_2$.
Hence, a is the second symbol in the string that distinguishes states
q_1 and q_2.

Once again we return to Step 2(b)(i). We now focus our attention on the P_1 table and find that states $G(p_1, a) \neq G(p_2, a)$ and also
$G(p_1, b) \neq G(p_2, b)$. We arbitrarily select a as the third symbol of
the string that will distinguish states q_1 and q_2. According to Step
2(b)(ii), we update z, p_1, and p_2 as $z = za = baa$, $p_1 = \delta(p_1, a)$, and
$p_2 = \delta(p_2, a)$. We now have $p_1 = q_1$ and $p_2 = q_5$.

Finally, we arrive at Step 2(c) and focus on the original state transition table for M. From this table, we find that states q_1 and q_5 are
distinguished by the symbol a. This is the last symbol in the string
to distinguish states q_1 and q_2. We set $z = za = baaa$. We have now
discovered baaa as the input sequence that distinguishes states q_1
and q_2. This sequence is added to W. Note that in Example 3.7, we
have already verified that indeed baaa is a distinguishing sequence
for states q_1 and q_2.

Next, we select the pair (q_3, q_4) and resume at Step 2(a). We note
that these two states are in a different group in table P_1, but in the
same group in M. Thus, we get $r = 0$. As $O(q_3, a) = O(q_4, a)$, the
distinguishing sequence for the pair (q_3, q_4) is the input sequence a.

We leave it to you to derive distinguishing sequences for the remaining pairs of states. A complete set of distinguishing sequences
for FSM M is given in Table 3.2. The leftmost two columns labeled

S_i and S_j contain pairs of states to be distinguished. The column labeled x contains the distinguishing sequence for the pairs of states to its left. The rightmost two columns in this table show the last symbol output when input x is applied to state S_i and S_j, respectively. For example, as we have seen earlier $O(q_1, \text{baaa}) = 1101$. Thus, in Table 3.2, we only show the 1 in the corresponding output column. Note that each pair in the last two columns is different, that is $o(S_i, x) \neq o(S_j, x)$ in each row. From this table, we obtain $W = \{a, aa, aaa, baaa\}$.

3.5.3 IDENTIFICATION SETS

Consider an FSM $M = (X, Y, Q, q_0, \delta, O)$ with symbols having their usual meanings and $|Q| = n$. Assume that M is completely specified and minimal. We know that a characterization set W for M is a set of strings such that for any pair of states q_i and q_j in M, there exists a string s in W such that $O(q_i, s) \neq (q_j, s)$.

Analogous to the characterization set for M, we associate an identification set with each state of M. An identification set for state $q_i \in Q$ is denoted by W_i and has the following properties: (a) $W_i \subseteq W$, $1 < i \leq n$, (b) $O(q_i, s) \neq O(q_j, s)$, for some j, $1 \leq j \leq n$, $j \neq i$, $s \in W_i$, and (c) no subset of W_i satisfies property (b). The next example illustrates the derivation of the identification sets given in W.

Example 3.10: Consider the machine given in Example 3.9 and its characterization set W shown in Table 3.2. From this table, we note, that state q_1 is distinguished from the remaining states by the strings $baaa$, aa, and a. Thus, $W_1 = \{baaa, aa, a\}$. Similarly, $W_2 = \{baaa, aa, a\}$, $W_3 = \{a, aa\}$, $W_4 = \{a, aaa\}$, and $W_5 = \{a, aaa\}$.

While the characterization sets are used in the W-method, the W_i sets are used in the Wp-method. The W- and the Wp methods are used for generating tests from an FSM. Given an FSM, we are now well-equipped to describe various methods for test-generation. We begin with a description of the W-method.

3.6 THE W-METHOD

The W-method is used for constructing a test set from a given FSM M. The test set so constructed is a finite set of sequences that can be input to a program whose control structure is modeled by M. Alternately, the tests can also be input to a design to test its correctness with respect to some specification.

The implementation modeled by M is also known as the implementation under test and abbreviated as an IUT Note that most software systems cannot be modeled accurately using an FSM. However, the global control structure of a software system can be modeled by an FSM. This also implies that the tests generated using the W-method, or any other method based exclusively on a finite-state model of an implementation, is likely to reveal only certain types of faults. Later in Section 3.9, we will discuss what kind of faults are revealed by the tests generated using the W-method.

3.6.1 ASSUMPTIONS

The W-method makes the following assumptions for it to work effectively:

1. M is completely specified, minimal, connected, and deterministic.
2. M starts in a fixed initial state.
3. M can be reset accurately to the initial state. A `null` output is generated during the reset operation.
4. M and IUT have the same input alphabet.

Later in this section, we shall examine the impact of violating the above assumptions. Given an FSM $M = (X, Y, Q, q_0, \delta, O)$, the W-method consists of the following sequence of steps:

Step 1 Estimate the maximum number of states in the correct design.

Step 2 Construct the characterization set W for the given machine M.

Step 3 Construct the testing tree for M and determine the transition cover set P.

Step 4 Construct set Z.

Step 5 $P \cdot Z$ is the desired test set.

We already know how to construct W for a given FSM. In the remainder of this section, we explain each of the remaining three steps mentioned above.

3.6.2 MAXIMUM NUMBER OF STATES

We do not have access to the correct design or the correct implementation of the given specification. Hence, there is a need to estimate the maximum number of states in the correct design. In the worst case, that is when no information about the correct design or implementation is available, one might assume that the maximum number of states is the same as the number of states in M. The impact of an incorrect estimate is discussed after we have examined the W-method.

3.6.3 COMPUTATION OF THE TRANSITION COVER SET

A transition cover set, denoted as P, is defined as follows. Let q_i and $q_j, i \neq j$, be two states in M. P consists of sequences sx such that $\delta(q_0, s) = q_i$ and $\delta(q_i, x) = q_j$. The empty sequence ϵ is also in P. We can construct P using the *testing tree* of M. A testing tree for an FSM is constructed as follows:

1. State q_0, the initial state, is the root of the testing tree.
2. Suppose that the testing tree has been constructed until level k. The $(k + 1)^{th}$ level is built as follows:
   - Select a node n at level k. If n appears at any level from 1 through $k - 1$, then n is a leaf node and is not expanded any further. If n is not a leaf node then we expand it by adding a branch from node n to a new node m if $\delta(n, x) = m$ for $x \in X$. This branch is labeled as x. This step is repeated for all nodes at level k.

The following example illustrates construction of a testing tree for the machine in Example 3.8 whose transition and output functions are shown in Figure 3.13.

Example 3.11: The testing tree is initialized with the initial state q_1 as the root node. This is level 1 of the tree. Next, we note that $\delta(q_1, a) = q_1$ and $\delta(q_1, b) = q_4$. Hence, we create two nodes at the next level and label them as q_1 and q_4. The branches from q_1 to q_1 and q_4 are labeled, respectively, a and b. As q_1 is the only node at level 1, we now proceed to expand the tree from level 2.

At level 2, we first consider the node labeled q_1. However, another node labeled q_1 already appears at level 1; hence, this node becomes a leaf node and is not expanded any further. Next, we examine the node labeled q_4. We note that $\delta(q_4, a) = q_3$ and $\delta(q_4, b) = q_4$. We, therefore, create two new nodes at level 3 and label these as q_4 and q_3 and label the corresponding branches as b and a, respectively.

We proceed in a similar manner down one level in each step. The method converges when at level 6 we have the nodes labeled q_1 and q_5, both of which appear at some level up the tree. Thus, we arrive at the testing tree for M as shown in Figure 3.14.

Once a testing tree has been constructed, we obtain the transition cover set P by concatenating labels of all partial paths along the tree. A *partial path* is a path starting from the root of the testing tree and terminating in any node of the tree. Traversing all partial paths in the

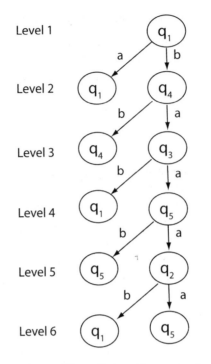

Level 1

Level 2

Level 3

Level 4

Level 5

Level 6

Fig. 3.14 Testing tree for the machine with transition and output functions shown in Figure 3.13.

tree shown in Figure 3.14, we obtain the following transition cover set:

$$P = \{\epsilon, a, b, bb, ba, bab, baa, baab, baaa, baaab, baaaa\}$$

It is important to understand the function of the elements of P. As the name *transition cover set* implies, exciting an FSM in q_0, the initial state, with an element of P, forces the FSM into some state. After the FSM has been excited with all elements of P, each time starting in the initial state, the FSM has reached every state. Thus, exciting an FSM with elements of P ensures that all states are reached, and all transitions have been traversed at least once. For example, when the FSM M of Example 3.8 is excited by the input sequence *baab* in state q_1, it traverses the branches (q_1, q_4), (q_4, q_3), (q_3, q_5), and (q_5, q_5) in that order. The empty input sequences ϵ does not traverse any branch but is useful in constructing the desired test sequence as is explained next.

3.6.4 Constructing Z

Given the input alphabet X and the characterization set W, it is straightforward to construct Z. Suppose that the number of states estimated to be in the IUT is m, and the number of states in the design specification is n, $m > n$. Given this information, we compute Z as:

$$Z = (X^0 \cdot W) \cup (X \cdot W) \cup (X^2 . W) \ldots \cup (X^{m-1-n} \cdot W) \cup (X^{m-n} \cdot W)$$

It is easy to see that $Z = W$ for $m = n$, that is when the number of states in the IUT is the same as that in the specification. For $m < n$, we use $Z = XW$. Recall that $X^0 = \{\epsilon\}$, $X^1 = X$, $X^2 = X \cdot X$, and so on, where $(\cdot)$ denotes string concatenation. For convenience, we shall use the short-hand notation $X[p]$ to denote the following set union:

$$\{\epsilon\} \cup X^1 \cup X^2 \ldots \cup X^{p-1} \cup X^p.$$

We can now rewrite Z as $Z = X[m - n]. W$ for $m > n$, where m is the number of states in the IUT and n the number of states in the design specification.

3.6.5 DERIVING A TEST SET

Having constructed P and Z, we can easily obtain a test set T as $P.Z$. The next example shows how to construct a test set from the FSM of Example 3.8.

Example 3.12: For the sake of simplicity, let us assume that the number of states in the correct design or IUT is the same as in the given design shown in Figure 3.13. Thus, we have $m = n = 5$. This leads to the following Z:

$$Z = X^0 \cdot W = \{a, aa, aaa, baaa\}$$

Catenating P with Z, we obtain the desired test set.

$T = P \cdot Z = \{e, a, b, bb, ba, bab, baa, baab, baaa, baaab, baaaa\} \cdot$

$\{a, aa, aaa, baaa\}$

$= \{a, aa, aaa, baaa,$

$aa, aaa, aaaa, abaaa,$

$ba, baa, baaa, bbaaa, bba,$

$bba, bbaa, bbaaa, bbbaaa,$

$baa, baaa, baaaa, babaaa,$

$baba, babaa, babaaa, babbaaa,$

$baaa, baaaa, baaaaa, baabaaa,$

$baaba, baabaa, baabaaa, baabbaaa,$

baaaa, baaaaa, baaaaaa, baaabaaa

baaaba, baaabaa, baaabaaa, baaabbaaa

baaaaa, baaaaaa, baaaaaaa, baaaabaaa}

If we assume that the IUT has one extra state, that is $m = 6$, then we obtain Z and the test set $P \cdot Z$ as follows:

$$Z = X^0 \cdot W \cup X^1 \cdot W = \{a, aa, aaa, baaa, aa, aaa, aaaa, abaaa,$$

$$ba, baa, baaa, bbaaa\}$$

$$T = P \cdot Z = \{\epsilon, a, b, bb, ba, bab, baa, baab, baaa, baaab, baaaa\}.$$

{a, aa, aaa, baaa, aa, aaa, aaaa, abaaa, ba, baa, baaa, bbaaa}

3.6.6 Testing Using the W-method

To test the given IUT M_i against its specification M, we do the following for each test input:

1. Find the expected response $M(t)$ to a given test input t. This is done by examining the specification. Alternately, if a tool is available, and the specification is executable, one could determine the expected response automatically.

2. Obtain the response $M_i(t)$ of the IUT when excited with t in the initial state.

3. If $M(t) = M_i(t)$, then no flaw has been detected so far in the IUT. $M(t) \neq M_i(t)$ implies the possibility of a flaw in the IUT under test, given a correct design.

Note that a mismatch between the expected and the actual response does not necessarily imply an error in the IUT. However, if we assume that (a) the specification is error free, (b) $M(t)$ and $M_i(t)$ have been determined without any error, and (c) the comparison between $M(t)$ and $M_i(t)$ is correct, then indeed $M(t) \neq M_i(t)$ implies an error in the design or the IUT under test.

> **Example 3.13:** Let us now apply the W-method to test the design shown in Figure 3.13. We assume that the specification is also given in terms of an FSM, which we refer to as the "correct design". Note that this might not happen in practice, but we make this assumption for illustration.
>
> We consider two possible implementations under test. The correct design is shown in Figure 3.15(a) and is referred to as M. We denote the two erroneous designs corresponding to two IUTs under test as M_1 and M_2, respectively, shown in Figure 3.15(b) and (c).

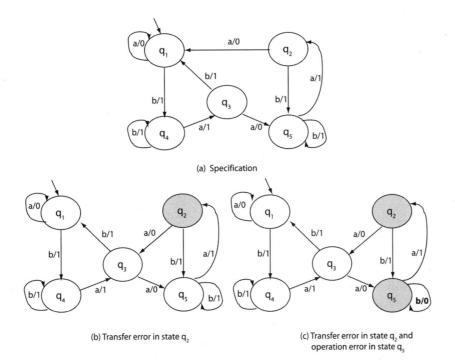

(a) Specification

(b) Transfer error in state q_2

(c) Transfer error in state q_2 and operation error in state q_5

Fig. 3.15 The transition and output functions of FSMs of the design under test denoted as M in the text and copied from Figure 3.13, and two incorrect designs in (b) and (c) denoted as M_1 and M_2 in the text.

Note that M_1 has one transfer error with respect to M. The error occurs in state q_2 where the state transition on input a should be $\delta_1(q_2, a) = q_1$ and not $\delta_1(q_2, a) = q_3$. M_2 has two errors with respect to M. There is a transfer error in state q_2 as mentioned earlier. In addition, there is an operation error in state q_5 where the output function on input b should be $O_2(q_5, b) = 1$ and not $O_2(q_5, b) = 0$.

To test M_1 against M, we apply each input t from the set $P \cdot Z$ derived in Example 3.12 and compare $M(t)$ with $M_1(t)$. However, for the purpose of this example, let us first select $t = ba$. Tracing gives us $M(t) = 11$ and $M_1(t) = 11$.

Thus, IUT M_1 behaves correctly when excited by the input sequence ba. Next, we select $t = baaaaaa$ as a test input. Tracing the response of $M(t)$ and $M_1(t)$ when excited by t, we obtain $M(t) = 1101000$ and $M_1(t) = 1101001$. Thus, the input sequence $baaaaaa$ has revealed the transfer error in M_1.

Next, let us test M_2 with respect to specification M. We select the input sequence $t = baaba$ for this test. Tracing the two designs, we obtain $M(t) = 11011$ whereas $M_2(t) = 11001$. As the two traces are different, input sequence $baaba$ reveals the operation error. We have already shown that $x = baaaaaa$ reveals the transfer error.

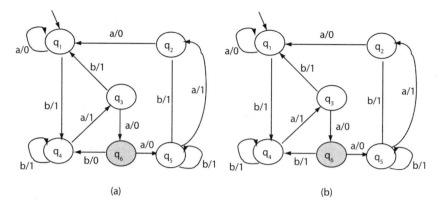

(a)   (b)

Fig. 3.16   Two implementations of the design in Figure 3.13 each having an extra state. Note that the output functions of the extra-state q_6 are different in (a) and (b).

Thus, the two input sequences *baaba* and *baaaaaa* in $P \cdot Z$ reveal the errors in the two IUTs under test.

Note that for the sake of brevity we have used only two test inputs. However, in practice, one needs to apply test inputs to the IUT in some sequence until the IUT fails or the IUT has performed successfully on all tests.

Example 3.14: Suppose we estimate that the IUT corresponding to the machine in Figure 3.13 has one extra state, that is $m = 6$. Let us also assume that the IUT, denoted as M_1, is as shown in Figure 3.16(a) and indeed has six states. We test M_1 against $t = baaba$ and obtain $M_1(t) = 11001$. The correct output obtained by tracing M against t is 11011. As $M(t) = M_1(t)$, test input t has revealed the *extra state* error in S_1.

However, test $t = baaba$ does not reveal the extra-state error in machine M_2 as $M_2(t) = 11011 = M(t)$. Consider now test $t = baaa$. We get $M(t) = 1101$ and $M_2(t) = 1100$. Thus the input *baaa* reveals the extra state error in machine M_2.

3.6.7 The Error-detection Process

Let us now carefully examine how the test sequences generated by the W-method detect operation and transfer errors. Recall that the test set generated in the W-method is the set $P \cdot W$, given that the number of states in the IUT is the same as that in the specification. Thus, each test case t is of the form $r \cdot s$, where r belongs to the transition cover set P and s to the characterization set W. We consider the application of t to the IUT as a two-phase process. In the first phase, input r moves the IUT from its initial state q_0 to state q_i. In the second phase,

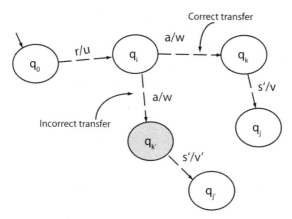

Fig. 3.17 Detecting errors using tests generated by the W-method.

the remaining input s moves the IUT to its final state q_j or $q_{j'}$. These two phases are shown in Figure 3.17.

When the IUT is started in its initial state, say q_0, and excited with test t, it consumes the string r and arrives at some state q_i as shown in Figure 3.17. The output generated so far by the IUT is u, where $u = O(q_0, r)$. Continuing further in state q_i, the IUT consumes symbols in string s and arrives at state q_j. The output generated by the IUT while moving from state q_i to q_j is v, where $v = O(q_i, s)$. If there is any operation error along the transitions traversed between states q_0 and q_i, then the output string u would be different from the output generated by the specification machine M when excited with r in its initial state. If there is any operation error along the transitions while moving from q_i to q_j, then the output wv would be different from that generated by M.

The detection of a transfer error is more involved. Suppose that there is a transfer error in state q_i and $s = as'$. Thus, instead of moving to state $q_{k'}$, where $q_{k'} = \delta(q_i, a)$, the IUT moves to state q_k, where $q_k = \delta(q_i, a)$. Eventually, the IUT ends up in state $q_{j'}$, where $q_{j'} = \delta(q_{k'}, s')$. Our assumption is that s is a distinguishing sequence in W. If s is the distinguishing sequence for states q_i and $q_{j'}$, then $wv' \neq wv$. If s is not a distinguishing sequence for q_i and $q_{j'}$, then there must exist some other input as'' in W such that $wv'' \neq wv$, where $v'' = O(q_{k'}, s'')$.

3.7 THE PARTIAL W-METHOD

The partial W-method, also known as the *Wp-method,* is similar to the W-method in that tests are generated from a minimal, complete, and connected FSM. However, the size of the test set generated using the Wp-method is often smaller than that generated using the W-method.

This reduction is achieved by dividing the test-generation process into two phases and making use of the state identification sets W_i, instead of the characterization set W, in the second phase. Furthermore, the fault-detection effectiveness of the Wp-method remains the same as that of the W-method. The two-phases used in the Wp-method are described later in Section 3.7.1.

First, we define a *state cover set* S of an FSM $M = (X, Y, Q, q_0, \delta, O)$. S is a finite nonempty set of sequences where each sequence belongs to X^* and for each state $q_i \in Q$, there exists an $r \in S$ such that $\delta(q_0, r) = q_i$. It is easy to see that the state cover set is a subset of the transition cover set and is not unique. Note that the empty string ϵ belongs to S which covers the initial state because, as per the definition of state transitions, $\delta(q_0, \epsilon) = q_0$.

Example 3.15: In Example 3.11, we constructed the following transition cover set for machine M shown in Figure 3.13:

$$P = \{\epsilon, a, b, bb, ba, bab, baa, baab, baaa, baaab, baaaa\}$$

The following subset of P forms a state cover set for M:

$$S = \{\epsilon, b, ba, baa, baaa\}$$

We are now ready to show how tests are generated using the Wp-method. As before, let M denote the FSM representation of the specification against which we are to test an IUT. We assume that M contains $n > 0$ states and the IUT contains M states. The test set T derived using the Wp-method is composed of subsets T_1 and T_2, that is $T = T_1 \cup T_2$. Below we show how to compute subsets T_1 and T_2 assuming that M and the IUT have an equal number of states, that is $m = n$.

```
Procedure for test generation using the Wp-method
```

Step 1 Compute the transition cover set P, the state cover set S, the characterization set W, and the state identification sets W_i for M. Recall that S can be derived from P and the state identification sets can be computed as explained in Example 3.10.

Step 2 $T_1 = S \cdot W$.

Step 3 Let $\mathcal{W}$ be the set of all state identification sets of M, that is $\mathcal{W} = \{W_1, W_2, \ldots, W_n\}$.

Step 4 Let $R = \{r_{i1}, r_{i2}, \ldots r_{ik}\}$ denote the set of all sequences that are in the transition cover set P but not in the state cover set S, that is $R = P - S$. Furthermore, let $r_{ij} \in R$ be such that $\delta(q_0, r_{ij}) = q_{ij}$.

Step 5 $T_2 = R \otimes \mathcal{W} = \cup_{j=1}^{k}(\{r_{ij}\}.\mathcal{W}_{ij})$, where $\mathcal{W}_{ij} \in \mathcal{W}$ is the state identification set for state q_{ij}.

End of procedure for test generation using the Wp-method

The $\otimes$ operator used in the derivation of T_2 is known as the *partial string concatenation operator.* Having constructed the test set T, which consists of subsets T_1 and T_2, one proceeds to test the IUT as described in the next section.

3.7.1 Testing Using the Wp-method for m=n

Given a specification machine M and its implementation under test, the Wp-method consists of a two-phase test procedure. In the first phase, the IUT is tested using the elements of T_1. In the second phase, the IUT is tested against the elements of T_2. Details of the two phases follow:

Phase 1: Testing the IUT against each element of T_1 tests each state for equivalence with the corresponding state in M. Note that a test sequence t in T_1 is of the kind uv, where $u \in S$ and $v \in W$. Suppose that $\delta(q_0, u) = q_i$ for some state q_i in M. Thus, the application of t first moves M to some state q_i. Continuing with the application of t to M, now in state q_i, one can generate an output different from that generated if v were applied to M in some other state q_j, that is $O(q_i, v) \neq O(q_j, v)$ for $i \neq j$. If the IUT behaves as M against each element of T_1, then the two are equivalent with respect to S and W. If not then there is an error in the IUT.

Phase 2: While testing the IUT using elements of T_1, one can check all states in the implementation against those in M, it may miss checking all transitions in the IUT. This is because T_1 is derived using the state cover set S and not the transition cover set P. Elements of T_2 complete the checking of the remaining transitions in the IUT against M.

To understand how, we note that each element t of T_2 is of the kind uv, where u is in P but not in S. Thus, the application of t to the M moves it to some state q_i, where $\delta(q_0, u) = q_i$. However, the sequence of transitions that M goes through is different from the sequence it goes through while being tested against elements of T_1 because $u \notin S$. Next, M that is now in state q_i is excited with v. Now, v belongs to W_i which is the state identification set of q_i and hence this portion of the test will distinguish q_i from all other states with respect to transitions not traversed while testing against T_1. Thus, any transfer or operation errors in the transitions not tested using T_1 will be discovered using T_2.

Example 3.16: We will now show how to generate tests using the Wp-method. For this example, let us reconsider the machine in Figure 3.13 to be the specification machine M. First, various sets needed to generate the test set T are reproduced below for convenience:

$$W = \{a, aa, aaa, baaa\}$$

$$P = \{e, a, b, bb, ba, bab, baa, baab, baaa, baaab, baaaa\}$$

$$S = \{e, b, ba, baa, baaa\}$$

$$W_1 = \{baaa, aa, a\}$$

$$W_2 = \{baaa, aa, a\}$$

$$W_3 = \{a, aa\}$$

$$W_4 = \{a, aaa\}$$

$$W_5 = \{a, aaa\}$$

Next, we compute set T_1 using Step 2.

$$
\begin{aligned}
T_1 = S \cdot W = \{ & a, aa, aaa, baaa, \\
& ba, baa, baaa, bbaaa, \\
& baa, baaa, baaa, babaaa \\
& baaa, baaaa, baaaaa, baabaaa, \\
& baaaa, baaaaa, baaaaaa, baaabaaa\}
\end{aligned}
$$

Next, in accordance with Step 4, we obtain R as

$$R = P - S = \{a, bb, bab, baab, baaab, baaaa\}.$$

With reference to Step 4 and Figure 3.13, we obtain the following state transitions for the elements in R:

$$\delta(q_1, a) = q_1$$

$$\delta(q_1, bb) = q_4$$

$$\delta(q_1, bab) = q_5$$

$$\delta(q_1, baab) = q_5$$

$$\delta(q_1, baaab) = q_5$$

$$\delta(q_1, baaaa) = q_1$$

From the transitions given above we note that when M is excited by elements *a, bb, bab, baab, baaab, baaaa,* starting on each occasion in state q_1, it moves to states, $q_1, q_4, q_5, q_5, q_5,$ and q_1, respectively. Thus, while computing T_2 we need to consider the state identification sets $W_1, W_4,$ and W_5. Using the formula in Step 5, we obtain T_2 as follows:

$$T_2 = R \otimes W = (\{a\} \cdot W_1) \cup (\{bb\} \cdot W_4) \cup (\{bab\} \cdot W_5) \cup (\{baab\} \cdot W_5) \cup$$

$$(\{baaab\} \cdot W_5) \cup (\{baaaa\} \cdot W_1)$$

$$= \{abaaa, aaa, aa\} \cup \{bba, bbaaa\} \cup \{baba, babaaa\} \cup$$

$$= \{baaba, baabaaa\} \cup \{baaaba, baaabaaa\} \cup$$

$$\{baaaabaaaa, baaaaaaa, baaaaa\}$$

$$= \{abaaa, aaa, aa, bba, bbaaa, baba, babaaa, baaba, baabaaa,$$

$$baaaba, baaabaaa, baaaabaaaa, baaaaaaa, baaaaa\}.$$

The desired test set is $T = T_1 \cup T_2$. Note that T contains a total of 34 tests, 20 from T_1 and 14 from T_2. This is in contrast to the 44 tests generated using the W-method in Example 3.12 when $m = n$.

The next example illustrates how to use the Wp-method to test an IUT.

Example 3.17: Let us assume we are given the specification M as shown in Figure 3.15(a) and are required to test IUTs that correspond to designs M_1 and M_2 in Figure 3.15(b) and (c), respectively. For each test, we proceed in two phases as required by the Wp-method.

Test M_1, phase 1: We apply each element t of T_1 to the IUT corresponding to M_1 and compare $M_1(t)$ with the expected response $M(t)$. To keep this example short, let us consider test $t = baaaaaa$. We obtain $M_1(t) = 1101001$. On the contrary, the expected response is $M(t) = 1101000$. Thus, test input t has revealed the transfer error in state q_2.

Test M_1, phase 2: This phase is not needed to test M_1. In practice, however, one would test M_1 against all elements of T_2. You may verify that none of the elements of T_2 reveals the transfer error in M_1.

Test M_2, phase 1: Test $t = baabaaa$ that belongs to T_1 reveals the error as $M_2(t) = 1100100$ and $M(t) = 110100$.

Test M_2, phase 2: Once again this phase is not needed to reveal the error in M_2.

Note that in both the cases in the example above, we do not need to apply phase 2 of the Wp-method to reveal the error. For an example that does require phase 2 to reveal an implementation error refer to

Exercise 3.15 that shows an FSM and its erroneous implementation and requires the application of phase 2 for the error to be revealed. However, in practice one would not know whether phase 1 is sufficient. This would lead to the application of both phases and hence all tests. Note that tests in phase 2 ensure the coverage of all transitions. While tests in phase 1 might cover all transitions, they might not apply the state identification inputs. Hence, all errors corresponding to the fault model in Section 3.4 are not guaranteed to be revealed by tests in phase 1.

3.7.2 TESTING USING THE WP-METHOD FOR $m > n$

The procedure for constructing tests using the Wp-method can be modified easily when the number of states in the IUT is estimated to be larger than that in the specification, that is when $m > n$. The modifications required to the procedure described in Section 3.7 are in Step 2 and Step 5.

For $m = n$ we compute $T_1 = S \cdot W$. For $m > n$ we modify this formula so that $T_1 = S \cdot Z$ where $Z = X[m - n] \cdot W$ as explained in Section 3.6.4. Recall that T_1 is used in phase 1 of the test procedure. T_1 is different from T derived from the W-method in that it uses the state cover set S and not the transition cover set P. Hence, T_1 contains fewer tests than T except when $P = S$.

To compute T_2, we first compute R as in Step 4 in Section 3.7. Recall that R contains only those elements of the transition cover set P that are not in the state cover set S. Let $R = P - S = \{r_{i_1}, r_{i_2}, \ldots r_{i_k}\}$. As before, $r_{i_j} \in R$ moves M from its initial state to state q_{i_j}, that is $\delta(q_0, r_{i_j}) = q_{i_j}$. Given R, we derive T_2 as follows:

$$T_2 = R \cdot X[m - n] \otimes W = \cup_{j=1}^{k} \{r_{i_j}\} \cdot (\cup_{u \in X[m-n]} u \cdot W_l),$$

where $\delta(q_0, r_{ij}) = q_{ij}$, $\delta(q_{ij}, u) = q_l$, and $W_l \in W$ is the identification set for state q_l.

The basic idea underlying phase 2 is explained below. The IUT under test is exercised so that it reaches some state q_i from the initial state q_0. Let u denote the sequence of input symbols that move the IUT from state q_0 to state q_i. As the IUT contains $m > n$ states, it is now forced to take an additional $(m - n)$ transitions. Of course, it requires $(m - n)$ input symbols to force the IUT for that many transitions. Let v denote the sequence of symbols that move the IUT from state q_i to state q_j in $(m - n)$ steps. Finally, the IUT inputs a sequence of symbols, say w, that belong to the state identification set W_j. Thus, one test for the IUT in phase 2 is composed of the input sequence uvw.

Note that the expression to compute T_2 consists of two parts. The first part is R and the second part is the partial string concatenation of

$X[m - n]$ and $\mathcal{W}$. Thus, a test in T_2 can be written as uvw where $u \in R$ is the string that takes the IUT from its initial state to some state q_i, string $v \in X|m - n]$ takes the IUT further to state q_j, and string $w \in W_j$ takes it to some state q_l. If there is no error in the IUT, then the output string generated by the IUT upon receiving the input uvw must be the same as the one generated when the design specification M is exercised by the same string.

Example 3.18: We will now show how to construct a test set using the Wp-method for machine M in Figure 3.13, given that the corresponding IUT contains an extra state. For this scenario, we have $n = 5$ and $m = 6$. Various sets needed to derive T are reproduced here for convenience.

$$X = \{a, b\}$$

$$W = \{a, aa, aaa, baaa\}$$

$$P = \{\epsilon, a, b, bb, ba, baa, bab, baab, baaa, baaab, baaaa\}$$

$$S = \{\epsilon, b, ba, baa, baaa\}$$

$$W_1 = \{baaa, aa, a\}$$

$$W_2 = \{baaa, aa, a\}$$

$$W_3 = \{a, aa\}$$

$$W_4 = \{a, aaa\}$$

$$W_5 = \{a, aaa\}$$

First, we derive T_1 as $S \cdot X[1] \cdot W$. Recall that $X[1]$ denotes the set $\{\epsilon\} \cup X^1$.

$$T_1 = S \cdot (\{\epsilon\} \cup X^1).W$$
$$= (S \cdot W) \cup (S \cdot X \cdot W)$$

$S \cdot W = \{a, \quad aa, \quad aaa, \quad baaa,$

$\qquad ba, \quad baa, \quad baaa, \quad bbaaa,$

$\qquad baa, \quad baaa, \quad baaaa, \quad babaaa,$

$\qquad baaa, \quad baaaa, \quad baaaaa, \quad baabaaa,$

$\qquad baaaa, \quad baaaaa, \quad baaaaaa, \quad baaabaaa\}$

$S \cdot X = \{a, \quad b, \quad ba, \quad bb, \quad baa, \quad bab, \quad baaa, \quad baab, \quad baaaa, \quad baaab\}$

$S \cdot X \cdot W = \{aa, \quad aaa, \quad aaaa, \quad abaaa,$

$\qquad ba, \quad baa, \quad baaa, \quad bbaaa,$

$$baa, \; baaa, \; baaaaa, \; babaaa,$$

$$bba, \; bbaa, \; bbaaa, \; bbbaaa,$$

$$baaa, \; baaaa, \; baaaaaa, \; baabaaa,$$

$$baba, \; babaa, \; babaaa, \; babbaaa,$$

$$baaaa, \; baaaaa, \; baaaaaa, \; baaabaaa,$$

$$baaba, \; baabaa, \; baabaaa, \; baabbaaa,$$

$$baaaaa, \; baaaaaa, \; baaaaaaa, \; baaaabaaa,$$

$$baaaba, \; baaabaa, \; baaabaaa, \; baaabaaa\}$$

T_1 contains a total of 60 tests of which 20 are in $S \cdot W$ and 40 in $S \cdot X \cdot W$. To obtain T_2, we note that $R = P - S = \{a, \; bb, \; bab, \; baab, \; baaab, \; baaaa\}$. T_2 can now be computed as follows:

$$T_2 = R \cdot X[m-n] \otimes W$$

$$= (R \otimes W) \cup R \cdot X \otimes W)$$

$$R \otimes W = (\{a\} \cdot W_1) \cup (\{bb\} \cdot W_4) \cup (\{baab\} \cdot W_5) \cup \{bab\} \cdot W_1 \cup$$

$$\{baaab\} \cdot W_1 \cup \{baaaa\} \cdot W_5$$

$$= \{abaaa, \; aaa, \; aa, \; bba, \; bbaaa, \; baaba, \; baabaaa\}$$

$$R \cdot X W = (aa \cdot W_1) \cup (ab \cdot W_4) \cup$$

$$(bba \cdot W_3(\cup(bbb \cdot W_4) \cup$$

$$(baaba \cdot W_2) \cup (baabb \cdot W_5)$$

$$(baba \cdot W_1) \cup (babb \cdot W_4)$$

$$(baaaba \cdot W_2) \cup (baaabb \cdot W_5)$$

$$(baaaaa \cdot W_1) \cup (baaaab \cdot W_5)$$

$$= \{aabaaa, \; aaaa, aaa, \; aba, \; abaaa, \; bbaa, \; bbaaa, \; bbba,$$

$$bbbaaa, \; baababaaa, \; baabaaa, \; baabaa, \; baabba,$$

$$baabbaaa\}$$

T_2 contains a total of 21 tests. In all, the entire test set $T = T_1 \cup T_2$ contains 81 tests. This is in contrast to a total of 81 tests that would be generated by the W-method (see Exercises 3.16 and 3.17):

3.8 THE UIO-SEQUENCE METHOD

The W-method uses the characterization set W of distinguishing sequences as the basis to generate a test set for an IUT. The tests so

Test Generation

generated are effective in revealing operation and transfer faults. However, the number of tests generated using the W-method is usually large. Several alternative methods have been proposed that generate fewer test cases. In addition, these methods are either as effective or nearly as effective as the W-method in their fault-detection capability. A method for test-generation based on *unique input/output sequences* is presented in this section.

3.8.1 Assumptions

The UIO-method generates tests from an FSM representation of the design. All the assumptions stated in Section 3.6.1 apply to the FSM that is input to the UIO test-generation procedure. In addition, it is assumed that the IUT has the same number of states as the FSM that specifies the corresponding design. Thus, any errors in the IUT are transfer and operation errors only as shown in Figure 3.12.

3.8.2 UIO sequences

A UIO sequence is a sequence of input and output pairs that distinguishes a state of an FSM from the remaining states. Consider FSM $M = (X, Y, Q, q_0, \delta, O)$. A UIO sequence of length k for some state $s \in Q$, is denoted as $UIO(s)$ and looks like the following sequence:

$$UIO(s) = i_1/o_1 \cdot i_2/o_2 \ldots i_{(k-1)}/o_{(k-1)} \cdot i_k/o_k.$$

In the sequence given above, each pair a/b consists of an input symbol a that belongs to the input alphabet X and an output symbol b that belongs to the output alphabet Y. The dot symbol (.) denotes string concatenation. We refer to the input portion of a $UIO(s)$ as $in(UIO(s))$ and to its output portion as $out(UIO(s))$. Using this notation for the input and output portions of $UIO(s)$, we can rewrite $UIO(s)$ as

$$in(UIO(s)) = i_1 \cdot i_2 \ldots .i_{(k-1)} \cdot i_k \text{ and}$$

$$out(UIO(s)) = o_1 \cdot o_2 \ldots .o_{(k-1)} . o_k.$$

When the sequence of input symbols that belong to $in(UIO(s))$ is applied to M in state s, the machine moves to some state t and generates the output sequence $out(UIO(s))$. This can be stated more precisely as follows:

$$\delta(s, in(UIO(s))) = out(UIO(s)).$$

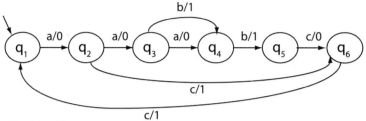

Machine M_1

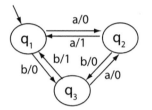

Machine M_2

Fig. 3.18 Two FSMs used in Example 3.19. There is a UIO sequence for each state in machine M_1. There is no UIO sequence for state q_1 in machine M_2.

A formal definition of UIO sequences is as follows:

Given an FSM $M = (X, Y, Q, q_0, \delta, O)$, the UIO sequence for state $s \in Q$, denoted as UIO (s), is a sequence of one or more edge labels such that the following condition holds:

$$\delta(s, in(UIO(s))) \neq \delta(t, in(UIO(s))), \text{ for all } t \in Q, t \neq s.$$

The next example offers UIO sequences for a few FSMs. The example also shows that there may not exist any UIO sequence for one or more states in an FSM.

Example 3.19: Consider machine M_1 shown in Figure 3.18. The UIO sequence for each of the six states in M_1 is given below:

State (s)	UIO (s)
q_1	a/0.c/1
q_2	c/1.c/1
q_3	b/1.b/1
q_4	b/1.c/0
q_5	c/0
q_6	c/1.a/0

Using the definition of UIO sequences, it is easy to check whether a $UIO(s)$ for some state s is indeed a UIO sequence. However, before we perform such a check, we assume that the machine generates an empty string as the output if there does not exist an outgoing edge from a state on some input. For example, in machine M_1, there is no outgoing edge from state q_2 for input c. Thus, M_1 generates an empty string when it encounters a c in state q_2. This behavior is explained in Section 3.8.3.

Let us now perform two sample checks. From the table above, we have $UIO(q_1) = a/0.c/1$. Thus, $in(UIO(q_1)) = a.c$. Applying the sequence $a.c$ to state q_2 produces the output sequence 0 which is different from 01 generated when $a.c$ is applied to M_1 in state q_1. Similarly, applying $a.c$ to machine M_1 in state q_5 generates the output pattern 0 which is, as before, different from that generated by q_1. You may now perform all other checks to ensure that indeed the UIOs given above are correct.

Example 3.20: Now consider machine M_2 in Figure 3.18. The UIO sequences for all states, except state q_1, are listed below. Note that there does not exist any UIO sequence for state q_1.

State (s)	UIO (s)
q_1	None
q_2	a/1
q_3	b/1

3.8.3 CORE AND NON-CORE BEHAVIOR

An FSM must satisfy certain constraints before it is used for constructing UIO sequences. First, there is the *connected assumption* that implies that every state in the FSM is reachable from its initial state. The second assumption is that the machine can be applied a *reset* input in any state that brings it to its start state. As has been explained earlier, a `null` output is generated upon the application of a reset input.

The third assumption is known as the completeness assumption. According to this assumption, an FSM remains in its current state upon the receipt of any input for which the state transition function δ is not specified. Such an input is known as a *noncore* input. In this situation, the machine generates a `null` output. The completeness assumption implies that each state contains a self-loop that generates a `null` output upon the receipt of an unspecified input. The fourth assumption is that the FSM must be minimal. A machine that depicts only the core behavior of

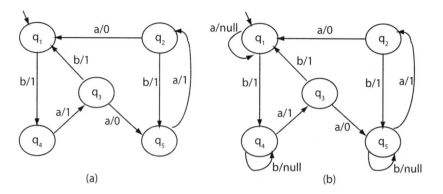

Fig. 3.19 (a) An incomplete FSM. (b) Addition of `null` transitions to satisfy the completeness assumption.

an FSM is referred to as its core-FSM. The following example illustrates the core behavior.

Example 3.21: Consider the FSM shown in Figure 3.19(a) similar to the FSM shown earlier in Figure 3.13 and contains self-loops in states q_1, q_4, and q_5. Note that states q_1, q_4, and q_5 have no transitions corresponding to inputs a, b, and b, respectively. Thus, this machine does not satisfy the completeness assumption.

As shown in Figure 3.19(b), additional edges are added to this machine in states q_1, q_4, and q_5. These edges represent transitions that generate `null` output. Such transitions are also known as erroneous transitions. Figure 3.19(a) shows the core behavior corresponding to the machine in Figure 3.19(b).

While determining the UIO sequences for a machine, only the core behavior is considered. The UIO sequences for all states of the machine shown in Figure 3.19(a) are given below:

State(s)	UIO(s)
q_1	b/1.a/1/.b/1.b/1
q_2	a/0.b/1
q_3	b/1.b/1
q_4	a/1.b/1.b/1
q_5	a/1.a/0.b/1

Note that the core behavior exhibited in Figure 3.19 is different from that in the original design in Figure 3.13. Self-loops that generate a `null` output are generally not shown in a state diagram that depicts the core behavior. The impact of removing self-loops that generate a nonnull output on the fault-detection capability of the UIO method will be discussed in Section 3.8.8. In Figure 3.19, the set of core edges is $\{(q_1, q_4), (q_2, q_1), (q_2, q_5), (q_3, q_1), (q_3, q_5), (q_4, q_3), (q_5, q_2), (q_1, q_1), (q_2, q_2), (q_3, q_3), (q_4, q_4), (q_5, q_5)\}$.

During a test, one wishes to determine if the IUT behaves in accordance with its specification. An IUT is said to conform *strongly* to its specification if it generates the same output as its specification for all inputs. An IUT is said to conform *weakly* to its specification if it generates the same output as that generated by the corresponding core-FSM.

Example 3.22: Consider an IUT that is to be tested against its specification M as in Figure 3.13. Suppose that the IUT is started in state q_1 and the one symbol sequence a is input to it and the IUT outputs a null sequence, that is the IUT does not generate any output. In this case, the IUT does not conform strongly to M. However, on input a, this is exactly the behavior of the core-FSM. Thus, if the IUT behaves exactly as the core-FSM shown in Figure 3.19, then it conforms weakly to M.

3.8.4 GENERATION OF UIO SEQUENCES

The UIO sequences are essential to the UIO-sequence method for generating tests from a given FSM. In this section, we present an algorithm for generating the UIO sequences. As mentioned earlier, a UIO sequence might not exist for one or more states in an FSM. In such a situation, a signature is used instead. An algorithm for generating UIO sequences for all states of a given FSM is as follows.

```
Procedure for generating UIO sequences
```

Input: (a) An FSM $M = (X, Y, Q, q_0, \delta, O)$, where $|Q| = n$.
 (b) State $s \in Q$.

Output: UIO[s] contains a UIO sequence for state s; $UIO(s)$ is empty if no such sequence exists.

Procedure: `gen-uio(s)`

/* *Set(l)* denotes the set of all edges with label *l*.
 label(e) denotes the label of edge *e*.
 A label is of the kind a/b, where $a \in X$ and $b \in Y$.
 head(e) and *tail(e)* denote, respectively, the head and tail states of edge *e*. */

Step 1 For each distinct edge label *el* in the FSM, compute *Set (el)*.

Step 2 Compute the set *Oedges(s)* of all outgoing edges for state *s*. Let
$NE = | Oedges |$.

Step 3 For $1 \leq i \leq NE$ and each edge $e_i \in OutEdges$, compute
Oled [i], *Opattern[i]*, and *Oend [i]* as follows:
3.1 $Oled[i] = Set\ (label\ (ei)) - \{ei\}$
3.2 $Opattern[i] = label(i)$
3.3 $Oend[i] = tail(i)$

Step 4 Apply algorithm *gen-1-uio(s)* to determine if *UIO[s]* consists
of only one label.

Step 5 If simple UIO sequence found then return *UIO[s]* and terminate this algorithm, otherwise proceed to the next step.

Step 6 Apply the *gen-long-uio(s)* procedure to generate longer *UIO[s]*.

Step 7 If longer UIO sequence found then return *UIO[s]* and terminate
this algorithm, else return with an empty *UIO[s]*

```
End of Procedure gen-uio
Procedure gen-1-uio
```

Input: State $s \in Q$.

Output: *UIO[s]* of length 1 if it exists, an empty string otherwise.

Procedure: gen-1-uio(state s):

Step 1 If $Oled[i] = \emptyset$ for $1 \leq i \leq NE$, then return $UIO[s] = label(e)$,
otherwise return $UIO[s] = $ "".

```
End of Procedure gen-1-uio

Procedure for generating longer UIO sequences
```

Input: (a) *OutEdges, Opattern, Oend*, and *Oled* as computed in *gen-1-
uio*.
(b) State $s \in Q$.

Output: *UIO[s]* contains a UIO sequence for state *s*. *UIO(s)* is empty if
no such sequence exists.

Procedure: gen-long-uio (state s)

Step 1 Let *L* denote the length of the *UIO* sequence being examined.
Set $L = 1$. Let *Oend* denote the number of outgoing edges from
some state under consideration.

Step 2 Repeat steps below while $L < 2n^2$ or the procedure is terminated prematurely.

    2.1 Set $L = L + 1$ and $k = 0$. Counter k denotes the number of distinct patterns examined as candidates for $UIO(s)$. The following steps attempt to find a $UIO[s]$ of size L.

    2.2 Repeat steps below for $i = 1$ to NE. Index i is used to select an element of $Oend$ to be examined next. Note that $Oend[i]$ is the tail state of the pattern in $Opattern[i]$.

        2.2.1 Let $Tedges(t)$ denote the set of outgoing edges from state t. We compute $Tedges(Oend[i])$.

        2.2.2 For each edge $te \in Tedges$ execute *gen-L-uio(te)* until either all edges in *Tedges* have been considered or a $UIO[s]$ is found.

    2.3 Prepare for the next iteration. Set $NE = k$ which will serve as the new maximum value of the next iteration over index i. For $1 \leq j \leq k$ set $Opattern[j] = Pattern[j]$, $Oend[j] = End[j]$, and $Oled[j] = Led[j]$. If the loop termination condition is not satisfied then go back to Step 2.1 and search for UIO of the next higher length, else return to *gen-uio* indicating a failure to find any UIO for state s.

```
End of Procedure gen-long-uio
Procedure for generating UIO sequences of Length
```
$L > 1$

    Input: Edge *te* from procedure *gen-long-uio*.

Output: $UIO[s]$ contains a UIO sequence of length L for state s of length L, $UIO(s)$ is empty if no such sequence exists.

Procedure: `gen-L-uio (edge te)`

Step 1 $k = k + 1$, $Pattern[k] = Opattarn[i]$. *label* (te). This could be a possible UIO.

Step 2 $End[k] = tail(te)$ and $Led[k] = \emptyset$.

Step 3 For each pair $oe \in Oled[i]$, where $h = head(oe)$ and $t = tail(oe)$, repeat the next step.

    3.1 Execute the next step for each edge $o \in OutEdges(t)$.

        3.1.1 If $label(o) = label(te)$ then
                $Led[k] = Led[k] \cup \{(head(oe), tail(o))\}$.

Step 4 If $Led[k] = \emptyset$ then UIO of length L has been found. Set $UIO[s] = Pattern[k]$ and terminate this and all procedures up until the main procedure for finding UIO for a state. If $Led[k] \neq 0$ then

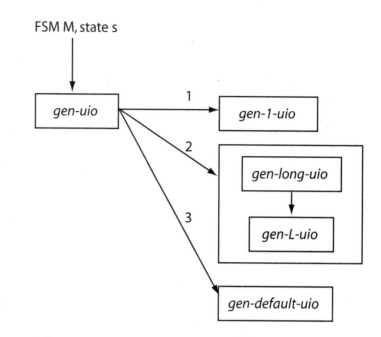

FSM M, state s

Fig. 3.20 Flow of control across various procedures in *gen-uio*.

no UIO of length L has been found corresponding to edge *te*. Return to the caller to make further attempts.

End of Procedure gen-L-uio

3.8.4.1 Explanation of gen-uio

The idea underlying the generation of a UIO sequence for state s can be explained as follows. Let M be the FSM under consideration and s a state in M for which a UIO is to be found. Let $E(s) = e_1 e_2 \ldots e_k$ be a sequence of edges in M such that $s = head(e_1)$, $tail(e_i) = head(e_{i+1})$, $1 \leq i < k$.

For $E(s)$, we define a string of edge labels as *label* $(E(s)) = l_1.l_2.\ldots.l_{k-1}.l_k$, where $l_i = label(e_i)$, $1 \leq i \leq k$, is the label of edge e_i. For a given integer $l > 0$, we find if there is a sequence $E(s)$ of edges starting from s such that $label(E(s)) \neq label(E(t))$, $s \neq t$, for all states t in M. If there is such an $E(s)$, then $label(E(s))$ is a UIO for state s. The uniqueness check is performed on $E(s)$ starting with $l = 1$ and continuing for $l = 2, 3, \ldots$ until a UIO is found or $l = 2n^2$, where n is the number of states in M. Note that there can be multiple UIOs for a given state though the algorithm generates only one UIO, if it exists.

We explain the *gen-uio* algorithm with reference to Figure 3.20. *gen-uio* for state s begins with the computation of some sets used in the subsequent steps. First, the algorithm computes *Set(el)* for all distinct labels *el* in the FSM. *Set(el)* is the set of all edges that have *el* as their label.

Next, the algorithm computes the set *Oedges(s)* that is the set of outgoing edges from state q_s. For each edge *e* in *Oedges(s)*, the set *Oled*[e] is computed. *Oled*[e] contains all edges in *Set(label(e))* except for the edge *e*. The tail state of reach edge in *Oedges* is saved in *Oend*[e]. The use of *Oled* will become clear later in Example 3.27.

Example 3.23: To find $UIO(q_1)$ for machine M_1 in Figure 3.18, *Set*, *Outedges*, and *Oled* are computed as follows:

Distinct labels in $M_1 = \{a/0, b/1, c/0, c/1\}$

$$Set(a/0) = \{(1,2), (2,3), (3,4)_{a/0}\}$$

$$Set(b/1) = \{(3,4), (4,5)\}$$

$$Set(c/0) = \{(5,6)\}$$

$$Set(c/1) = \{(2,6), (6,1)\}$$

$$Oedges(q) = \{(1,2)\}, NE = 1$$

$$Oled[1] = \{(2,3), (3,4)\}$$

$$Oend[1] = q_2$$

Next *gen-1-uio* is called in an attempt to generate a UIO of length 1. For each edge $e_i \in Oedges$, *gen-1-uio* initializes *Opattern*[i] to *label(e_i)*, and *Oend*[i] to *tail(e_i)*. *Opattern* and *Oend* are used subsequently by *gen-uio* in case a UIO of length 1 is not found. *gen-1-uio* now checks if the label of any of the outgoing edges from *s* is unique. This is done by checking if *Oled*[i] is empty for any $e_i \in Oedges(s)$. Upon return from *gen-1-uio*, *gen-uio* terminates if a UIO of length 1 was found, otherwise it invokes *gen-long-uio* in an attempt to find a UIO of length greater than 1. *gen-longer-uio* attempts to find UIO of length $L > 1$ until it finds one, or $L = 2n^2$.

Example 3.24: As an example of a UIO of length 1, consider state q_5 in machine M_1 in Figure 3.18. The set of outgoing edges for state q_5 is $\{(5, 6)\}$. The label of $\{(5, 6)\}$ is $c/0$. Thus, from *gen-uio* and *gen-1-uio*, we get *Oedges(q_5)* = $\{(5, 6)\}$, *Oled*[1] = $\emptyset$, *Oen*[1] = 6, and *Opattern*[1] = $c/0$. As *Oled*[1] = $\emptyset$, state q_5 has a UIO of length 1 which is *Opattern*[1], that is $c/0$.

Example 3.25: As an example of a state for which a UIO of length 1 does not exist, consider state q_3 in machine M_2 shown in Figure 3.18.

For this state, we get the following sets:

$$Oedges[q_3] = \{(3, 4)_{a/0}, (3, 4)_{b/1}\}, NE = 2$$

$$Oled[1] = \{(1, 2), (2, 3)\}, Oled[2] = \{(4, 5)\}$$

$$Opattern[1] = a/0, Opattern[2] = b/1$$

$$Oend[1] = q_4, Oend[2] = q_4.$$

As no element of *Oled* is empty, *gen-1-uio* concludes that state q_3 has no UIO of length 1 and returns to *gen-uio*.

In the event *gen-1-uio* fails, procedure *gen-long-uio* is invoked. The task of *gen-long-uio* is to check if a *UIO(s)* of length 2 or more exists. To do so, it collaborates with its descendant *gen-L-uio*. An incremental approach is used where UIOs of increasing length, starting at 2, are examined until either a UIO is found or one is unlikely to be found, that is a maximum length pattern has been examined.

To check if there is UIO of length L, *gen-long-uio* computes the set *Tedges(t)* for each edge $e \in Oedges(s)$, where $t = tail(e)$. For $L = 2$, *Tedges(t)* will be a set of edges outgoing from the tail state t of one of the edges of state s. However, in general, *Tedges(t)* will be the set of edges going out of a tail state of some edge outgoing from state s', where s' is a successor of s. After initializing *Tedges, gen-L-uio* is invoked iteratively for each element of *Tedges(t)*. The task of *gen-L-uio* is to find whether there exists a UIO of length L.

Example 3.26: There is no $UIO(q_1)$ of length 1. Hence *gen-long-uio* is invoked. It begins by attempting to find a UIO of length 2, that is $L = 2$. From *gen-uio*, we have $OutEdges(q_1) = \{(1, 2)\}$. For the lone edge in *Oedges*, we get $t = tail((1, 2) = q_2$. Hence *Tedges(q_2)*, which is the set of edges out of state q_2, is computed as follows:

$$Tedges(q_2) = \{(2, 3), (2, 6)\}$$

gen-L-uio is now invoked first with edge $(2, 3)$ as input to determine if there is a UIO of length 2. If this attempt fails, then *gen-L-uio* is invoked with edge $(2, 6)$ as input.

To determine if there exists a UIO of length L corresponding to an edge in *Tedges, gen-L-uio* initializes *Pattern[k]* by catenating the label of edge *te* to *Opattern[k]*. Recall that *Opattern[k]* is of length $(L-1)$ and has been rejected as a possible *UIO(s)*. *Pattern[k]* is of length L and is a candidate for *UIO(s)*. Next, the tail of *te* is saved in *End[k]*. Here, k serves as a running counter of the number of patterns of length L examined.

Next, for each element of *Oled [i]*, *gen-L-uio* attempts to determine if indeed *Pattern[k]* is a *UIO(s)*. To understand this procedure, suppose that *oe* is an edge in *Oled [i]*. Recall that edge *oe* has the same label as the edge e_t and that e_t is not in *Oled [i]*. Let *t* be the tail of state of *oe* and *OutEdges(t)* the set of all outgoing edges from state *t*. Then *Led [k]* is the set of all pairs *(head(oe), tail(o))* such that *label(te) = label(o)* for all $o \in OutEdges(t)$.

Note that an element of *Led [k]* is not an edge in the FSM. If *Led [k]* is empty after having completed the nested loops in Step 3, then *Pattern[k]* is indeed a *UIO(s)*. In this case, the *gen-uio* procedure is terminated and *Pattern[te]* is the desired UIO. If *Led [k]* is not empty then *gen-L-uio* returns to the caller for further attempts at finding *UIO(s)*.

Example 3.27: Continuing Example 3.26, suppose that *gen-L-uio* is invoked with $i = 1$ and $te = (2, 3)$. The goal of *gen-L-uio* is to determine if there is a path of length *L* starting from state *head(te)* that has its label same as *Opattern[i].label(te)*.

Pattern[i] is set to *a/0.a/0* because *Opattern[i] = a/0* and $label((2, 3)) = a/0$. *End [i]* is set to *tail(2, 3)*, which is q_3. The outer loop in Step 3 examines each element *oe* of *Oled*[1]. Let *oe* = (2, 3) for which we get $h = q_2$ and $t = q_3$. The set $OutEdges(q_3) = \{(3, 4)_{a/0}, (3, 4)_{b/1})\}$. Step 3.1 now iterates over the two elements of *OutEedges*(q_3) and updates *Led*[i]. At the end of this loop, we have *Led*[i] = {(2, 4)} because $label((3, 4)_{a/0}) = label((2, 3))$.

Continuing with the iteration over *Oled* [1] *oe* is set to $(3, 4)_{a/0}$ for which $h = q_2$ and $t = q_4$. The set $OutEdges(q_4) = \{(4, 5)\}$. Iterating over $OutEdges(q_4)$ does not alter *Led*[i] because $label ((4, 5)) \neq label((3, 4)_{a/0})$.

The outer loop in Step 3 is now terminated. In the next step, that is Step 4, *Pattern[i]* is rejected and *gen-L-uio* returns to *gen-long-uio*.

Upon return from *gen-L-uio*, *gen-long-uio* once again invokes it with $i = 1$ and $te = (2, 6)$. *Led*[2] is determined during this call. To do so, *Pattern*[2] is initialized to *a/0.c/1*, because *Opattern[i] = a/0* and $label(2, 6) = c/1$, and *End* [2] to q_6.

Once again the procedure iterates over elements *oe* of *Oled*. For $oe = (2, 3)$, we have $OutEdges(q_3) = \{(3, 4)_{a/0}, (3, 4)_{b/1})\}$ as before. Step 3.1 now iterates over the two elements of $OutEdges(q_3)$. In Step 1, none of the checks is successful as $label((2, 6))$ is not equal to $label((3, 4)_{a/0})$ or to $label((4,5))$. The outer loop in Step 3 is now terminated. In the next step, that is Step 4, *Pattern*[2] is accepted as $UIO(q_1)$.

It is important to note that *Led*[i] does not contain edges. Instead, it contains one or more pairs of states (s_1, s_2) such that a path in the

FSM from state s_1 to s_2 has the same label as *Pattern*[*i*]. Thus, at the end of the loop in Step 3 of *gen-L-uio*, an empty *Led*[*i*] implies that there is no path of length *L* from *head*(*te*) to *tail*(*tail*(*te*)) with a label same as *Pattern*[*i*].

A call to *gen-L-uio* either terminates the *gen-uio* algorithm abruptly indicating that *UIO*(*s*) has been found or returns normally indicating that *UIO*(*s*) is not found, and any remaining iterations should now be carried out. Upon a normal return from *gen-L-uio*, the execution of *gen-long-uio* resumes at Step 2.3. In this step, the existing *Pattern*, *Led*, and *End* data is transferred to *Opattern*, *Oend*, and *Oled*, respectively. This is done in preparation for the next iteration to determine if there exists a UIO of length $(L + 1)$. In case a higher-length sequence remains to be examined, the execution resumes from Step 2.2, else the *gen-long-uio* terminates without having determined a *UIO*(*s*).

Example 3.28: Consider machine M_2 in Figure 3.18. We invoke *gen-uio*(q_1) to find a UIO for state q_1. As required in Steps 1 and 2, we compute *Set* for each distinct label and the set of outgoing edges *Oedges*(q_1).

Distinct labels in $M_2 = \{a/0,\ a/1,\ b/0,\ b/1\}$

$$Set(a/0) = \{(1,2),(3,2)\}$$

$$Set(a/1) = \{(2,1)\}$$

$$Set(b/0) = \{(1,3),(2,3)\}$$

$$Set(b/1) = \{(3,1)\}$$

$$Oedges(q_1) = \{(1,2),(1,3)\}$$

$$NE = 2$$

Next, as directed in Step 3, we compute *Oled* and *Oend* for each edge in *Oedges*(q_1). The edges in *Oedges* are numbered sequentially so that edge (1, 2) is numbered 1 and edge (1, 3) is numbered 2.

$$Oled[1] = \{(3,2)\}$$

$$Oled[2] = \{(2,3)\}$$

$$Oend[1] = q_2$$

$$Oend[2] = q_3$$

$$Opattern[1] = a/0$$

$$Opattern[2] = b/0$$

gen-1-uio(q_1) is now invoked. As *Oled*[1] and *Oled*[2] are non-empty, *gen-1-uio* fails to find a UIO of length 1 and returns. We now move to Step 6 where procedure *gen-long-uio* is invoked. It begins by attempting to check if a UIO of length 2 exists. Toward this goal, the set *Tedges* is computed for each edge in *OutEdges* at Step 2.1. First, for $i = 1$, we have *Oend* [1] $= (3, 2)$ whose tail is state q_2. Thus, we obtain *Tedges*(q_2) $= \{(2, 3), (2, 1)\}$.

The loop for iterating over the elements of *Tedges* begins at Step 2.2.2. Let *te* $= (2, 3)$. *gen-L-uio* is invoked with *te* as input and the value of index *i* as 1. Inside *gen-L-uio*, *k* is incremented to 1 indicating that the first pattern of length 2 is to be examined. *Pattern* [1] is set to *a*/0.*b*/0, and *End* [1] is set to 3, and *Led* [1] initialized to the empty set.

The loop for iterating over the two elements of *Oled* begins at Step 3. Let *oe* $= (3, 2)$ for which $h = 3$, $t = 2$, and *OutEdges*(2) $= \{(2, 1), (2, 3)\}$. We now iterate over the elements of *Oedges* as indicated in Step 3.1. Let *o* $= (2, 1)$. As labels of $(2, 1)$ and $(2, 3)$ do not match, *Led* [1] remains unchanged. Next, *o* $= (2, 3)$. This time we compare labels of *o* and *te*, which are the same edges. Hence, the two labels are the same. As directed in Step 3.1.1, we set *Led*[1] $= (head(oe), tail(o)) = (3, 3)$. This terminates the iteration over *Outedges*. This also terminates the iteration over *Oled* as it contains only one element.

In Step 4, we find that *Led*[1] is not empty and therefore reject *Pattern*[1] as a UIO for state q_1. Note that *Led*[1] contains a pair (3, 3), which implies that there is a path from state q_3 to q_3 with the label identical to that in *Pattern*[1].

A quick look at the state diagram of M_2 in Figure 3.18 reveals that indeed the path $q_3 \rightarrow q_2 \rightarrow q_3$ has the label *a*/0.*b*/0 that is the same as in *Pattern*[1].

Contol now returns to Step 2.2.2 in *gen-long-uio*. The next iteration over *Tedges*(q_2) is initiated with *te* $= (2, 1)$. *gen-L-uio* is invoked once again, but this time with index $i = 1$ and *te* $= (2, 1)$. The next pattern of length 2 to be examined is *Pattern*[2] $= a/0.a/1$. We now have *End*[2] $= 1$ and *Led*[2] $= \emptyset$. Iteration over elements of *Oled*[1] begins. Once again, let *oe* $= (3, 2)$ for which $h = 3, t = 2$, and *OutEdges*(2) $= \{(2, 1), (2, 3)\}$. Iterating over the two elements of *OutEdges*, we find the label of *te* matches that of edge $(2, 1)$ and not of edge $(2, 3)$. Hence, we get *Led*[2] $= (head(oe), tail(2, 1)) = (3, 1)$, implying that *Pattern*[2] is the same as the label of the path from state q_3 to q_1. The loop over *Oled* also terminates and control returns to *gen-long-uio*.

In *gen-long-uio* the iteration over *Tedges* now terminates as we have examined both edges in *Tedges*. This also completes the iteration for $i = 1$ that corresponds to the first outgoing edge of state q_1. We now repeat Step 2.2.2 for $i = 2$. In this iteration, the second outgoing edge of state q_1, that is edge $(1, 3)$, is considered. Without going into the fine details of each step, we leave it to you to verify that at the end of the iteration for $i = 2$, we get the following:

$$Pattern\,[3] = b/0.a/0$$

$$Pattern\,[4] = b/0.b/1$$

$$End\,[3] = 2$$

$$End\,[4] = 1$$

$$Led\,[3] = (2,2)$$

$$Led\,[4] = (2,1)$$

This completes the iteration set up in Step 2.2. We now move to Step 3. This step leads to the following values of *Opattern*, *Oled*, and *Oend*:

$$Opattern[1] = Pattern[1] = a/0.b/0$$

$$Opattern[2] = Pattern[2] = a/0.a/1$$

$$Opattern[3] = Pattern[3] = b/0.a/0$$

$$Oend[1] = End[1] = 3$$

$$Oend[2] = End[2] = 1$$

$$Oend[3] = End[3] = 2$$

$$Oend[4] = End[4] = 1$$

$$Oled[1] = Led[1] = (3,3)$$

$$Oled[2] = Led[2] = (3,1)\,Oled[3] = Led[3] = (2,2)$$

$$Oled[4] = Led[4] = (2,1)$$

The while-loop is now continued with the new values of *Opattern*, *Oend*, and *Oled*. During this iteration, $L = 3$ and hence patterns of length 3 will be examined as candidates for $UIO(q_1)$. The patterns to be examined next will have at least one of the patterns in *Opattern* as their prefix. For example, one of the patterns examined for $i = 1$ is $a/0/.b/0.a/0$.

The *gen-L-uio* procedure is invoked first with $e = (1, 2)$ and $te = (2, 3)$ in Step 2.1.2. It begins with $Pattern[(2, 3)] = a/0.b/0$ and $End[(2, 3)] = 3$.

Example 3.29: This example illustrates the workings of procedure *gen-uio(s)* by tracing through the algorithm for machine M_1 in Figure 3.18. The complete set of UIO sequences for this machine is given in Example 3.19. In this example, we sequence through *gen-uio(s)* for $s = q_1$. The trace is as follows:

gen-uio Input: State q_1

Step 1 Find the set of edges for each distinct label in M_1. There are four distinct labels in M_1, namely $a/0, b/1, c/0,$ and $c/1$. The set of edges for each of these four labels is given below:

$$Set(a/0) = \{(1,2),(2,3),(3,4)\}$$

$$Set(b/1) = \{(3,4),(4,5)\}$$

$$Set(c/0) = \{(5,6)\}$$

$$Set(c/1) = \{(2,6),(6,1)\}$$

Step 2 It is easily seen from the state transition function of M_1 that the set of outgoing edges from state q_1 is $\{(1, 2)\}$. Thus, we obtain $Oedges(q_1) = \{(1, 2)\}$ and $NE = 1$.

Step 3 For each edge in *Oedges*, we compute *Oled*, *Opattern*, and *Oend*.

$$Oled[1] = \{(1,2),(2,3),(3,4)_{a/0}\} - \{(1,2)\}$$

$$= \{(2,3),(3,4)_{a/0}\}.$$

$$Opattern[1] = label((1,2)) = a/0, \text{and}$$

$$Oend[1] = tail((1,2)) = 2.$$

Step 4 Procedure *gen-1-uio* is invoked with state q_1 as input. In this step, an attempt is made to determine if there exists a UIO sequence of length 1 for state q_1.

gen-1-uio Input: State q_1

Step 1 Now check if any element of *Oled* contains only one edge. From the computation done earlier, note that there is only one element in *Oled*, and that this element, *Oled*[1], contains two edges. Hence, there is no $UIO[q_1]$ with only a single label. The *gen-1-uio* procedure is now terminated and the control returns to *gen-uio*.

gen-uio Input: State q_1

Step 5 Determine if a simple UIO sequence was found. As it has not been found move to the next step.

Step 6 Procedure *gen-long-uio* is invoked in an attempt to generate a longer $uio[q_1]$.

gen-long-uio

Input: State q_1

Step 1 $L = 1$.

Step 2 Start a loop to determine if a $UIO[q_1]$ of length greater than 1 exists. This loop terminates when a UIO is found or when $L = 2n^2$ that for a machine with $n = 6$ states translates to $L = 72$. Currently, L is less than 72 and hence continue with the next step in this procedure.

Step 2.1 $L = 2$ and $k = 0$.

Step 2.2 Start another loop to iterate over the edges in *Oedges*. Set $i = 1$ and $e_i = (1, 2)$.

Step 2.2.1 $t = tail((1, 2)) = 2$. *Tedges*(2) = {(2, 3), (2, 6)}.

Step 2.2.2 Yet another loop begins at this point. Loop over the elements of *Tedges*. First set $te = (2, 3)$ and invoke *gen-L-uio*.

gen-L-uio Input: $te = (2, 3)$

Step 1 $k = 1$, *Pattern*[1] = *Opattern*[1].*label*((2, 3)) = a/0.a/0.

Step 2 *End*[1] = 3, *Led*[1] = ∅.

Step 3 Now iterate over elements of *Oled*[1] = {(2, 3), (3, 4)$_{a/0}$}. First select $oe = (2, 3)$ for which $h = 2$ and $t = 3$.

Step 3.1 Another loop is set up to iterate over elements of *OutEdges*(q_3) = {(3, 4)$_{a/0}$, (3, 4)$_{b/1}$}. Select $o = (3, 4)_{a/0}$.

Step 3.1.1 As *label*((3, 4)$_{a/0}$) = *label*((2, 3)), set *Led*[1] = {(2, 4)}. Next select $o = (3, 4)_{b/1}$ and execute Step 3.1.1.

Step 3.1.1 As *label*((2, 3)) = *label*((3, 4)$_{b/1}$), no change is made to *Led*[1]. The iteration over *Oedges* terminates.

Next, continue from Step 3.1 with $oe = (3, 4)_{a/0}$ for which $h = 3$ and $t = 4$.

Step 3.1 Another loop is set up to iterate over elements of *OutEdges*(4) = {(4, 5)}, select $o = (4, 5)$.

Step 3.1.1 As *label*((4, 5)) = *label*((3, 4)$_{a/0}$) no change is made to *Led*[1].

The iteration over *Oedges* terminates. Also, the iteration over *Oled*[1] terminates.

Step 3.4 *Led*[1] is not empty, which implies that this attempt to find a $UIO[q_1]$ has failed. Note that in this attempt, the algorithm checked if a/0.a/0 is a valid $UIO[q_1]$. Now return to the caller.

gen-long-uio Input: State q_1

Step 2.2.2 Select another element of *Tedges* and invoke *gen-L-uio(e, te)*. For this iteration $te = (2, 6)$.

gen-L-uio Input: $te = (2, 6)$

Step 1 $k = 2$, $Pattern[2] = Opattern[1].label((2, 6)) = a/0.c/1$.

Step 2 $End[2] = 6$, $Led[2] = \emptyset$.

Step 3 Iterate over elements of $Oled[1] = \{(2, 3), (3, 4)_{a/0}\}$. First select $oe = (2, 3)$ for which $h = 2$ and $t = 3$.

Step 3.1 Another loop is set up to iterate over elements of $OutEdges(3) = \{(3, 4)_{a/0}, (3, 4)_{b/1}\}$, select $o = (3, 4)_{a/0}$.

Step 3.1.1 As $label((3, 4)_{a/0}) \neq label((2, 6))$, do not change $Led[2]$.

Next select $o = (3, 4)_{b/1}$ and once again execute Step 3.1.1.

Step 3.1.1 As $label((2, 6)) \neq label((3, 4)_{b/1})$, do not change $Led[2]$. The iteration over *Oedges* terminates.

Next, continue from Step 3.1 with $oe = (3, 4)_{a/0}$ for which $h = 3$ and $t = 4$.

Step 3.1 Another loop is set up to iterate over elements of $OutEdges(4) = 4\ \{(4, 5)\}$, select $o = (4, 5)$.

Step 3.1.1 As $label((4, 5) \neq label((3, 4)_{a/0})$, no change is made to $Led[2]$.

The iteration over *Oedges* terminates. Also, the iteration over $Oled[(1, 2)]$ terminates.

Step 3.4 $Led[2]$ is empty. Hence, $UIO[q_1] = Pattern[2] = a/0.c/1$. A UIO of length 2 for state q_1 is found and hence the algorithm terminates.

3.8.5 DISTINGUISHING SIGNATURES

As mentioned earlier, the *gen-uio* procedure might return an empty $UIO(s)$, indicating that it failed to find a UIO for state s. In this case, we compute a signature that distinguishes s from other states one by one. We use $Sig(s)$ to denote a signature of state s. Before we show the computation of such a signature, we need some definitions. Let $W(q_i, q_j)$, $i \neq j$ be a sequence of edge labels that distinguishes states q_i and q_j. Note that $W(q_i, q_j)$ is similar to the distinguishing sequence W for q_i and q_j except that we are now using edge labels of the kind a/b, where a is an input symbol and b an output symbol, instead of using only the input symbols.

Example 3.30: A quick inspection of M_2 in Figure 3.18 reveals the following distinguishing sequences:

$$W(q_1, q_2) = a/0$$
$$W(q_1, q_3) = b/0$$
$$W(q_2, q_3) = b/0$$

To check if indeed the above are correct distinguishing sequences, consider states q_1 and q_2. From the state transition function of M_2, we get $O(q_1, a) = 0 \neq O(q_2, a)$. Similarly, $O(q_1, b) = 0 \neq O(q_3, b)$ and $O(q_2, a) = 0 = O \neq (q_2, a)$. For a machine more complex than M_2, one can find $W(q_i, q_j)$ for all pairs of states q_i and q_j using the algorithm in Section 3.5 and using edge labels in the sequence instead of the input symbols.

We use $P_i(j)$ to denote a sequence of edge labels along the shortest path from state q_j to q_i. $P_i(j)$ is known as a *transfer sequence* for state q_j to move the machine to state q_i. When the inputs along the edge labels of $P_i(j)$ are applied to a machine in state q_j, the machine moves to state q_i. For $i = j$, the null sequence is the transfer sequence. As we see later, $P_i(j)$ is used to derive a signature when the *gen-uio* algorithm fails.

Example 3.31: For M_2, we have the following transfer sequences:

$$P_1(q_2) = a/1$$
$$P_1(q_3) = b/1$$
$$P_2(q_1) = a/0$$
$$P_2(q_3) = a/0$$
$$P_3(q_1) = b/0$$
$$P_3(q_2) = b/0$$

For M_1 in Figure 3.18, we get the following subset of transfer sequences (you may derive the others by inspecting the transition function of M_1).

$$P_1(q_5) = c/0.c/1$$
$$P_5(q_2) = a/0.a/0.b/1 \text{ or } P_5(2) = a/0.b/1.b/1$$
$$P_6(q_1) = a/0.c/1$$

A transfer sequence $P_i(j)$ can be found by finding the shortest path from state q_j to q_i and catenating in order the labels of the edges along this path.

To understand how the signature is computed, suppose that *gen-uio* fails to find a UIO for some state $q_i \in Q$, where Q is the set of n states in machine M under consideration. The signature for s consists of two parts. The first part of the sequence is $W(q_i, q_1)$ that distinguishes q_i from q_1.

Now suppose that the application of sequence $W(q_i, q_1)$ to state q_i takes the machine to some state t_k. The second part of the signature for q_i consists of pairs $P_i(t_k).W(q_i, q_{k+1})$ for $1 \leq k < n$. Note that the second part can be further split into two sequences.

The first sequence $P_i(t_k)$ transfers the machine from t_k back to q_i. The second sequence $W(q_i, q_{k+1})$ applies a sequence that distinguishes q_i from state q_{k+1}. Thus, in essence, the signature makes use of the sequences that distinguish q_i from all other states in the machine and the transfer sequences that move the machine back to state q_i prior to applying another distinguishing sequence. Given that $q_1 \in Q$ is the starting state of M, a compact definition of the signature for state $q_i \in Q$ follows:

$$Sig(q_i) = W(q_1, q_2).(P_1(t_1).W(q_1, q_3)).(P_1(t_2).W(q_1, q_4)).\ \ldots$$
$$(P_1(t_n).W(q_1, q_n)),\ \text{for } i = 1.$$
$$= W(q_i, q_1).(P_i(t_1).W(q_i, q_2)).(P_i(t_2).W(q_i, q_3)).\ \ldots$$
$$(P_i(t_{i-2}).W(q_i, q_{i-1})).(P_i(t_i).W(q_i, q_{i+1})).\ \ldots$$
$$(P_i(t_{n-1}).W(q_i, q_n)),\ \text{for } i \neq 1.$$

Example 3.32: We have seen earlier that *gen-long-uio* fails to generate a UIO sequence for state q_1 in M_2 shown in Figure 3.18. Let us, therefore, apply the method described above for the construction of a signature for state q_1. The desired signature can be found by substituting the appropriate values in the following formula:

$$Sig(q_1) = W(q_1, q_2).((P_1(t_1).W(q_1, q_2))$$

From Example 3.30, we have the following distinguishing sequences for state q_1.

$$W(q_1, q_2) = a/0$$
$$W(q_1, q_3) = b/0$$

The application of $W(q_1, q_2)$ to state q_1 takes M_2 to state q_2. Hence, we need the transfer sequence $P_1(q_2)$ to bring M_2 back to state q_1. From Example 3.31, we get $P_1(q_2) = a/1$. Substituting these values in the formula for $UIO(q_1)$, we obtain the desired signature.

$$Sig(q_1) = a/0.a/1.b/0$$

Later, while deriving test cases from UIO of different states, we will use signatures for states that do not possess a UIO.

3.8.6 TEST GENERATION

Let $M = (X, Y, Q, q_1, \delta, O)$ be an FSM from which we need to generate tests to test an implementation for conformance. Let E denote the set of core edges in M. m is the total number of core edges in M. Recall that edges corresponding to a reset input in each state are included in E. The following procedure is used to construct a total of m tests, each corresponding to the *tour* of an edge:

1. Find the UIO for each state in M.
2. Find the shortest path from the initial state to each of the remaining states. As mentioned earlier, the shortest path from the initial state q_1 to any other state $q_i \in Q$ is denoted by $P_i(q_1)$.
3. Construct an *edge tour* for each edge in M. Let $TE(e)$ denote a subsequence that generates a tour for edge e. $TE(e)$ is constructed as follows:

$$TE(e) = P_{head(e)}(1).label(e).UIO(tail(e)).$$

4. This step is optional. It is used to combine the m-test subsequences generated in the previous step into one test sequence that generates the tour of all edges. This sequence is denoted by TA. It is sometimes referred to as β-sequence. TA is obtained by catenating pairs of reset input and edge-tour subsequences as follows:

$$TA = \times_{e \in E}((Re/null).TE(e)).$$

TA is useful when the IUT under test can be brought automatically to its start state by applying a Re. In this case, the application of TA is likely to shorten the time to test the IUT. While testing an IUT, the application of Re might be possible automatically through a script that sends a *kill process* signal to terminate the IUT and, upon the receipt of an acknowledgment that the process has terminated, may restart the IUT for the next test.

The next example illustrates the test-generation procedure using the UIO sequences generated from M_1 shown in Figure 3.18.

> **Example 3.33:** The UIO sequences for each of the six states in M_1 are reproduced below for convenience. Also included in the rightmost column are the shortest paths from state q_1 to the state corresponding to state in the leftmost column.

State(s)	UIO(s)	$P_i(q_1)$
q_1	a/0.c/1	null
q_2	c/1.c/1	a/0
q_3	b/1.b/1	a/0.a/0
q_4	b/1.c/0	a/0.a/0.a/0
q_5	c/0	a/0.a/0.a/0.b/1
q_6	c/1.a/0	a/0.c/1

We consider only the core edges while developing tests for each edge. For example, the self-loop in state q_5 corresponding to inputs *a* and *b*, not shown in Figure 3.18, is ignored as it is not part of the core behavior of M_1. Also note that edge (q_6, q_1) will be considered twice, one corresponding to the label $c/0$ and the other corresponding to the label *Re*/null. Using the formula given above, we obtain the following tests for each of the 14 core edges.

Test count	Edge (e)	TE(e)
1	q_1, q_2	a/0.c/1.c/1
2	q_1, q_1	*Re*/null.*Re*/null.a/0.c/1
3	q_2, q_3	a/0.a/0.b/1.b/1
4	q_2, q_6	a/0.c/1.c/1.a/0
5	q_2, q_1	a/0.*Re*/null.a/0.c/1
6	q_3, q_4	a/0.a/0.a/0.b/1.c/0
7	q_3, q_4	a/0.a/0.b/1.b/1.c/0
8	q_3, q_1	a/0.a/0.*Re*/null.a/0.c/1
9	q_4, q_5	a/0.a/0.a/0.c/0
10	q_4, q_1	a/0.a/0.a/0.*Re*/null.a/0.c/1
11	q_5, q_6	a/0.a/0.b/1.c/0.c/1
12	q_5, q_1	a/0.a/0.a/0.b/1.*Re*/null.a/0.c/1
13	q_6, q_1	a/0.c/1.c/1.a/0.c/1
14	q_6, q_1	a/0.c/1.*Re*/null.a/0.c/1

The 14 tests derived above can be combined into a β-sequence and applied to the IUT. This sequence will exercise only the core edges. Thus, for example, the self-loops in state q_5 corresponding to inputs *a* and *b* will not be exercised by the tests given above. It is also important to note that each *TE(e)* subsequence is applied with the IUT in its start state, implying that a *Re* input is applied to the IUT prior to exercising it with the input portion of *TE(e)*.

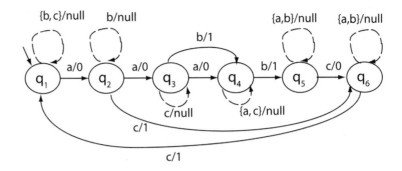

Fig. 3.21 Machine M_1 from Figure 3.18 with all noncore edges shown as dashed lines.

3.8.7 TEST OPTIMIZATION

The set of test subsequences $TE(e)$ can often be reduced by doing a simple optimization. For example, if $TE(e_1)$ is a subsequence of test $TE(e_2)$, then $TE(e_1)$ is redundant. This is because the edges toured by $TE(e_1)$ are also toured by $TE(e_2)$, and in the same order. Identification and elimination of subsequences that are fully contained in another subsequence generally leads to a reduction in the size of the test suite. In addition, if two tests are identical then one of them can be removed from further consideration (see Exercise 3.21).

Example 3.34: In an attempt to reduce the size of the test set derived in Example 3.33, we examine each test and check if it is contained in any of the remaining tests. We find that test 3 is fully contained in test 7, test 1 is contained in test 4, and test 4 is contained in test 13. Thus, the reduced set of tests consists of 11 tests: 2, 5, 6, 7, 8, 9, 10, 11, 12, 13, and 14 given in Example 3.33.

The tests derived in Example 3.33 are useful for a weak conformance test. To perform a strong conformance test of the IUT against the specification, we need to derive tests for noncore edges as well. The method for deriving such tests is the same as that given earlier for deriving $TE(e)$ for the tour of edge e except that e now includes noncore edges.

Example 3.35: We continue Example 3.33 for M_1 and derive additional tests needed for strong conformance. To do so, we need to identify the non-core edges. There are 10 noncore edges corresponding to the 6 states. Figure 3.21 shows the state diagram of M with both core and non-core edges shown. Tests that tour the noncore edges can be generated easily using the formula for TE given earlier. The 10 tests follow:

Test count	Edge (e)	*TE(e)*
1	$(q_1, q_1)_b$/null	b/null.a/0.c/1
2	$(q_1, q_1)_c$/null	c/null.a/0.c/1
3	$(q_2, q_2)_b$/null	a/0.b/null.c/1.c/1
4	$(q_3, q_3)_c$/null	a/0.a/0.c/null.b/1.b/1
5	$(q_4, q_4)_a$/null	a/0.a/0.a/0.a/null.b/1.c/0
6	$(q_4, q_4)_c$/null	a/0.a/0.a/0.c/null.b/1.c/0
7	$(q_5, q_5)_a$/null	a/0.a/0.a/0.b/1.a/null.c/0
8	$(q_5, q_5)_b$/null	a/0.a/0.a/0.b/1.b/null.c/0
9	$(q_6, q_6)_a$/null	a/0.c/1.a/null.c/1.a/0
10	$(q_6, q_6)_b$/null	a/0.c/1.b/null.c/1.a/0

Note that a test for noncore edge *e* is similar to the tests for core edges in that the test first moves the machine to *head(e)*. It then traverses the edge itself. Finally, it applies *UIO(tail(e))* starting at state *tail(e)*. Thus, in all we have 21 tests to check for strong conformance of an IUT against M.

3.8.8 FAULT DETECTION

Tests generated using the UIO sequences are able to detect all operation and transfer errors. However, combination faults such as an operation error and a transfer error might not be detectable. The next two examples illustrate the fault-detection ability of the UIO-method.

Example 3.36: Consider the transition diagram in Figure 3.22. Suppose that this diagram represents the state transitions in an IUT to be tested for strong conformance against machine M_1 in Figure 3.21. The IUT has two errors. State q_2 has a transfer error due to which

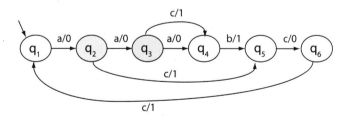

Fig. 3.22 State diagram of an IUT containing two faults. State q_2 has a transfer error and q_3 has an operation error. The behavior of this IUT is to tested against that of the machine in Figure 3.21. Noncore edges are not shown.

$\delta(q_2, c) = q_5$ instead of $\delta(q_2, c) = q_6$. State q_3 has an operation error due to which $O(q_3, b)$ is undefined.

To test the IUT against its specification as in Figure 3.21, one needs to apply the β sequence to the IUT and observe its behavior. The β sequence is obtained by combining all subsequences derived for weak and strong conformance in the earlier examples. However, as such a β sequence is too long to be presented here, we use an alternate method to show how the faults will be detected.

First, consider the transfer error in state q_2. Let us apply the input portion of test 4, which is TE (q_2, q_6), to the IUT. We assume that the IUT is in its start state, that is q_1, prior to the application of the test. From Example 3.33, we obtain the input portion as $acca$. The expected behavior of the IUT for this input is determined by tracing the behavior of the machine in Figure 3.21. Such a trace gives us $O(q_1, acca) = 0110$. However, when the same input is applied to the IUT, we obtain $O(q_1, acca) = 010\,\texttt{null}$.

As the IUT behaves differently than its specification, TE (q_2, q_6) has been able to discover the fault. Note that if test 4 has been excluded due to optimization, then test 13 can be used instead. In this case, the expected behavior is $O(q_1, accac) = 01101$, whereas the IUT generates $O(q_1, accac) = 010\,\texttt{null}1$ that also reveals a fault in the IUT.

Next, let us consider the operation error in state q_3 along the edge $(q_3, q_4)_{c/1}$. We use test 7. The input portion of this test is $aabbc$. For the specification, we have $O(q_1, aabbc) = 00110$. Assuming that this test is applied to the IUT in its start state, we get $O(q_1, aabbc) = 00\texttt{nullnull}1$, which is different from the expected output and thus test 7 has revealed the operation fault (also see Exercise 3.24).

Example 3.37: Consider the specification shown in Figure 3.23(a). We want to check if tests generated using the UIO-method will be able to reveal the transfer error in the IUT shown in Figure 3.23(b). UIO sequences and shortest paths from the start state to the remaining two states are given below:

State(s)	UIO (s)	$P_i(q_1)$
q_1	a/1	null
q_2	a/0.a/1	a/0
q_3	b/1.a/1	b/1
	(also a/0.a/0)	

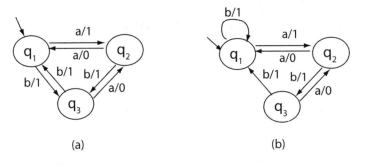

Fig. 3.23 State diagram of an FSM for which a test sequence derived using the UIO approach does not reveal the error. (a) Specification FSM. (b) State diagram of a faulty IUT.

Given below are tests for touring each of the nine core edges, including three edges that bring each state to state q_1 upon reset. Note that we have added the *Re*/null transition at the start of each test sequence to indicate explicitly that the machine starts in state q_1 prior to the test being applied.

Test count	Edge (e)	*TE(e)*
Edges (e) from each state to state q_1, label(e) = Re/null		
1	q_1, q_1	*Re*/null.*Re*/null.a/1
2	q_2, q_1	*Re*/null.a/1*Re*/null.a/1
3	q_3, q_1	*Re*/null.b/1.*Re*/null.a/1
Edges shown in Figure 3.23(a)		
4	q_1, q_2	*Re*/null.a/1.a/0.a/1
5	q_1, q_3	*Re*/null.b/1.b/1.a/1
6	q_2, q_1	*Re*/null.a/1.a/0.a/1
7	q_2, q_3	*Re*/null.a/1.b/1.b/1.a/1
8	q_3, q_1	*Re*/null.b/1.b/1.a/1
9	q_3, q_2	*Re*/null.b/1.a/0.a/0.a/1

To test the IUT, let us apply the input portion *bba* of test 5 that tours the edge (q_1, q_3). The expected output is 111. The output generated by the IUT is also 111. Hence, the tour of edge (q_1, q_3) fails to reveal the transfer error in state q_1. However, test 9 that tours edge (q_3, q_2) does reveal the error because the IUT generates the output 1101 whereas the expected output is 1001, ignoring the null output. Note that tests 4 and 6 are identical and so are tests 5 and 8. Thus, an optimal test sequence for this example is the set containing tests 1, 2, 3, 4, 5, 7, and 9.

3.9 AUTOMATA THEORETIC VERSUS CONTROL-FLOW-BASED TECHNIQUES

The test-generation techniques described in this chapter fall under the *automata-theoretic* category. There exist other techniques that fall under the control-flow-based category. Here we compare the fault-detection effectiveness of some techniques in the two categories.

Several empirical studies have aimed at assessing the fault-detection effectiveness of test sequences generated from FSMs by various test-generation methods. These studies are described in some detail in Volume II. Here, we compare the fault-detection effectiveness of the W- and Wp-methods with four control-flow-based criteria to assess the adequacy of tests. Some of the control-theoretic techniques can be applied to assess the adequacy of tests derived from FSMs against the FSM itself. In this section, we define four such criteria and show that test derived from the W- and Wp-methods are superior in terms of their fault-detection effectiveness than the four control-flow-based methods considered.

Tests generated using the W- and the Wp-methods guarantee the detection of all missing transitions, incorrect transitions, extra or missing states, and errors in the output associated with a transition given that the underlying assumptions listed in Section 3.6.1 hold. We show through an example that tests generated using these methods are more effective in detecting faults than the tests that are found adequate with respect to *state cover, branch cover, switch cover,* and the *boundary-interior* cover test-adequacy criteria. First, a few definitions are presented below before we illustrate this fact.

State cover:
> *A test set T is considered adequate with respect to the* state cover *criterion for an FSM M if the execution of M against each element of T causes each state in M to be visited at least once.*

Transition cover:
> *A test set T is considered adequate with respect to the* branch, *or* transition, *cover criterion for an FSM M if the execution of M against each element of T causes each transition in M to be taken at least once.*

Switch cover:
> *A test set T is considered adequate with respect to the* one-switch cover *criterion for an FSM M if the execution of M against each element of T causes each pair of transitions (tr_1, tr_2) in M to be taken at least once, where for some input substring $ab \in X^*$,*

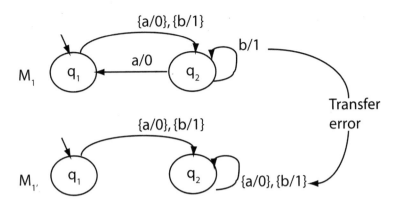

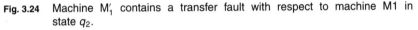

Fig. 3.24 Machine M'_1 contains a transfer fault with respect to machine M1 in state q_2.

$tr_1 : q_i = c(q_j, a)$ and $tr_2 : q_k = \delta(q_i, b,$ *and* q_i, q_j, q_k *are states in M.*

Boundary-interior cover:

A test set T is considered adequate with respect to the boundary-interior cover criterion for an FSM M if the execution of M against each element of T causes each loop body to be traversed zero times and at least once. Exiting the loop upon arrival covers the "boundary" condition and entering it and traversing the body at least once covers the "interior" condition.

The next example illustrates weaknesses of the state cover, branch cover, switch cover, and the boundary-interior cover test-adequacy criteria.

Example 3.38: Machine M_1 in Figure 3.24 represents correct design, while $M_{1'}$ has an output error in state q_2. Consider the input sequence $t = abba$. t covers all states and all transitions in M_1 and hence is adequate with respect to the state-coverage and transition-coverage criteria. However, we obtain $O_{M1}(q_1, t) = 0111 = O_{M1}(q_1, t)$. While t covers all states and all transitions (branches) in M_1 and $M_{1'}$, it does not reveal the transfer error in $M_{1'}$.

Machine M_2 in Figure 3.25 represents correct design while $M_{2'}$ has an output error in state q_3. In order for a test set to be adequate with respect to the switch cover criterion, it must cause the following set of branch pairs to be exercised:

$$S = \{(tr_1, tr_2), (tr_1, tr_3), (tr_2, tr_2), (tr_2, tr_3, (tr_3, tr_4), (tr_3, tr_5),$$

$$(tr_4, tr_4), (tr_4, tr_5, (tr_5), tr_6), (tr_5, tr_1), (tr_6, tr_4), (tr_6, tr_5)\}$$

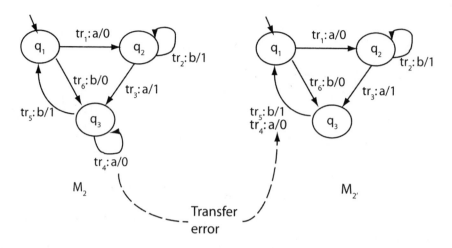

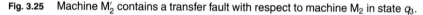

Fig. 3.25 Machine M$'_2$ contains a transfer fault with respect to machine M$_2$ in state q_3.

The following table lists a set of test sequences adequate with respect to the switch cover criterion, but do not reveal the transfer error in state q_3. The second column in the table shows the output generated and the rightmost column lists the switches covered.

Test sequence (t)	$O_{M2}(q_1, t)$ $(= O_{M2'}(q_1, t))$	Switches covered
abbaaab	0111001	$(tr_1, tr_2), (tr_2, tr_2), (tr_2, tr_3),$ $(tr_3, tr_4), (tr_4, tr_4), (tr_4, tr_5)$
aaba	0110	$(tr_1, tr_3), (tr_3, tr_5), (tr_5, tr_1)$
aabb	0110	$(tr_1, tr_3), (tr_3, tr_5), (tr_5, tr_6)$
baab	0001	$tr_6, tr_4), (tr_4, tr_4), (tr_4, tr_5)$
bb	01	(tr_6, tr_5)

A simple inspection of machine M$_2$ in Figure 3.25 reveals that all states are one-distinguishable, that is for each pair of states (q_i, q_j), there exists a string of length 1 that distinguishes q_i from q_j, $1 \leq (i, j) \leq 3, i \neq j$. Later, we define an n-switch cover and show how to construct an n-switch cover that will reveal all transfer and operation errors for an FSM that is n-distinguishable.

In Figure 3.26, we have machine M$_{3'}$ that has a transfer error in state q_2 with respect to machine M$_{3'}$. There are two loops in M$_3$, one in state q_2 and the other in q_3. Test sequence $t_1 = aab$ causes both loops to exit without ever looping in either state q_2 or q_3. Also, test sequence $t_2 = abaab$ causes each state to be entered once and exited.

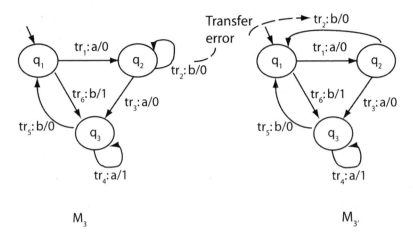

Fig. 3.26 Machine M_3' contains a transfer fault with respect to machine M_3 in state q_2.

Thus, the set $T = \{t_1, t_2\}$ is adequate with respect to the boundary-interior cover criterion. We note that $O_{M_3}(q_1, t_1) = O_{M_3'}(q_1, t_1) = 000$ and $O_{M_3}(q_1, t_2) = O_{M_3'}, (q_1, t_2) = 00010$. We conclude that T is unable to distinguish M_3 from $M_{3'}$ and hence does not reveal the error. Note that machine M_3 is one-distinguishable.

3.9.1 n-SWITCH COVER

The switch cover criterion can be generalized to an *n*-switch cover criterion as follows. An *n-switch* is a sequence of $(n + 1)$ transitions. For example, for machine M_3 in Figure 3.26, transition sequence tr_1 is a 0-switch, tr_1, tr_2 is a 1-switch, tr_1, tr_2, tr_3 is a 2-switch, and transition sequence tr_6, tr_5, tr_1, tr_3 is a 3-switch. For a given integer $n > 0$, we can define an *n*-switch set for a transition *tr* as the set of all *n*-switches with *tr* as the prefix. For example, for each of the six transitions in Figure 3.26, we have the following 1-switch sets:

$$tr_1 : \{(tr_1, tr_2), (tr_1, tr_3)\}$$

$$tr_2 : \{(tr_2, tr_2), (tr_2, tr_3)\}$$

$$tr_3 : \{(tr_3, tr_4), (tr_3, tr_5)\}$$

$$tr_4 : \{(tr_4, tr_4), (tr_4, tr_5)\}$$

$$tr_5 : \{(tr_5, tr_6), (tr_5, tr_1)\}$$

$$tr_6 : \{(tr_6, tr_4), (tr_6, tr_5)\}$$

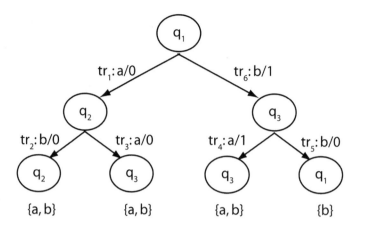

Fig. 3.27 Testing tree of machine M_3 in Figure 3.26.

An n-switch set S for a transition tr in FSM M is considered covered by a set T of test sequences if exercising M against elements of T causes each transition sequence in S to be traversed. T is considered an *n-switch set cover* if it covers all n-switch sets for FSM M. It can be shown that an n-switch set cover can detect all transfer, operation, extra, and missing-state errors in a minimal FSM that is n-distinguishable (see Exercise 3.28). Given a minimal, 1-distinguishable FSM M, the next example demonstrates a procedure to obtain a 1-switch cover using the testing tree of M.

Example 3.39: Figure 3.27 shows a testing tree for machine M_3 in Figure 3.26. To obtain the one-switch cover, we traverse the testing tree from the root and enumerate all complete paths. Each path is represented by the sequence s of input symbols that label the corresponding links in the tree. The sequence s corresponding to each path is concatenated with the input alphabet of M as $s.x$, where $x \in X$, X being the input alphabet. Traversing the testing tree in Figure 3.27 and concatenating as described give us the following one-switch cover:

$$T = \{aba, abb, aaa, aab, baa, bab, bba, bbb\}$$

We leave it for the reader to verify that T is a one-switch cover for M_3. Recall from Example 3.38 that the error in $M_{3'}$ is not revealed by a test set adequate with respect to the boundary-interior cover criterion. However, if a test set is derived using the method explained here, it will be adequate with respect to the one-switch cover criterion and will always reveal the transfer, operation, missing, and

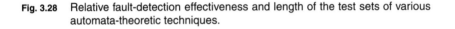

Fault-detection ability

TT   UIO   W
                    UIOv
                    DS
                    Wp

Length of test sets

TT   UIO   UIOv   W
                    DS
                    Wp

Fig. 3.28 Relative fault-detection effectiveness and length of the test sets of various automata-theoretic techniques.

extra-state errors if each state is one-distinguishable and the usual assumptions hold.

For machine $M_{2'}$, we note that test $aba \in T$ distinguishes M_3 from M'_3 as $O_{M_3}(q_1, abb) = 000 \neq O_{M3'}(q_1, abb)$. Exercise 3.30 asks for the derivation of a test set from M_2 in Figure 3.25 that is adequate with respect to one-switch cover criterion.

3.9.2 Comparing Automata-theoretic Methods

Figure 3.28 shows the relative fault-detection effectiveness of the TT-, UIO, UIOv-, distinguishing sequence (DS)-, Wp-, and W-methods. As is shown in the figure, the W-, UIOv-, Wp-, and DS-methods can detect all faults using the fault model described in Section 3.4.

The distinguishing-sequence method constructs an input sequence x from an FSM M such that $O(q_i, x)$ is different for each q_i in M. Sequences so constructed are able to detect all faults in our fault model. The UIO method is able to detect all output faults along transitions, but not necessarily all transfer faults.

Note that the TT-method has the lowest fault-detection capability. In this method, test sequences are generated randomly until all transitions in the underlying FSM are covered. Redundant sequences are removed using a minimization procedure. One reason for the low fault-detection ability of the TT-method is that it checks only whether a transition has been covered and does not check the correctness of the start and tail states of the transition (see Exercise 3.25).

The relative lengths of test seqences is shown in Figure 3.28. Once again the W-method generates the longest, and the largest, set of test sequences while the TT-method the shortest. From the relative lengths and fault-detection relationships, we observe that larger tests tend to be more powerful than shorter tests. However, we also observe that smaller tests can be more powerful in their fault-detection ability than larger tests as indicated by comparing the fault-detection effectiveness of the Wp-method with that of the W-method.

SUMMARY

The area of test-generation from finite-state models is wide. Research in this area can be categorized as follows:

- Test-generation techniques
- Empirical studies
- Test methodology and architectures

In this chapter, we have focused primarily on test-generation techniques. Of the many available techniques, we have described three techniques—the W-method, UIO-method, and the Wp-method. We selected these for inclusion due to their intrinsic importance in the field of FSM-based test-generation and their high fault-detection effectiveness. Each of these methods has also found its way into test-generation from more complex models such as statecharts and timed automata as described in Volume II. Thus, it is important for the reader to be familiar with these foundational test-generation methods and prepare for more advanced and complex test-generation methods.

Test-generation from each of the techniques introduced in this chapter has been automated by several researchers. Nevertheless, students may find it challenging to write their own test generators and conduct empirical studies on practical FSM models. Empirical studies aimed at assessing the fault-detection effectiveness of various test-generation methods and the lengths of the generated test sequences are discussed in Volume II. Test architectures and methodologies for testing based on finite-state and other models are introduced in Volume II.

BIBLIOGRAPHIC NOTES

FSMs have long been in use as models of physical systems, software systems, and hybrid systems. Almost any book on the theory of finite automata can be used to learn more about FSMs, regular expressions, and regular languages. A classic book in this area is by Hopcroft and Ullman [223]. Gill offers an excellent introduction to the theory of FSMs [168]. The algorithm for the construction of the characterization set W is found in Chapter 4, Section 4.4 of Gill's book. Several other algorithms related to the processing and testing of FSMs are also found in this book. Another useful text on the theory of FSMs is due to Hennie [215].

Testing an IUT against an FSM is known as conformance testing. A significant research effort has been directed at the generation of test sequences from FSM models. Gonenc [173] describes early work in the design of experiments to test FSMs using a set of distinguishing sequences. These sequences were constructed using the testing tree, also known as the distinguishing tree [265]. The W-method for the construction of test cases from FSMs was first proposed by Chow [88]; examples in Section 3.9 are minor modifications of those by Chow [88]. A solution to Exercise 3.28 is also found in [88].

The W-method of Chow led to a flurry of algorithms for test-generation from FSMs, mostly improvements over the W-method in the size of the generated test set and in the efficiency of the test-generation algorithm. Bernhard has proposed three variations of the W-method

that in most cases generate smaller test suits with no reduction in the fault-detection capability [43]. The partial W-method, also known as the Wp-method, was proposed by Fujiwara et al. [157] as an improvement over the W-method in terms of the size of the test set generated while retaining the fault-detection ability.

Naito and Tsunoyama [345] proposed a TT algorithm. Generation of optimal TT using the Chinese postman tour algorithm has been proposed by Uyar and Dahbura [483]. Sabnani and Dahbura [429] proposed the UIO sequence approach that generated significant research interest. Aho et al. [15] exploited the rural Chinese postman-tours to reduce the size of tests generated using the UIO-method. Chan et al. [74] suggested the UIOv-method as an improvement over the original UIO-method in terms of its fault-detection ability. Vuong and Ko [496] formulated test generation as a constraint-satisfaction problem in artificial intelligence. Their method is as good as the UIO- and W-methods in terms of its fault-detection ability and generates short test sequences.

Shen et al. proposed an optimization of the UIO-method by proposing multiple UIO (MUIO) sequences for each state in the FSM [439]. Yang and Ural [537], Ural et al. [482], and Hierons and Ural [219] describe methods for further reducing the length of test sequences generated from an FSM [537]. Miller and Paul developed an algorithm for the generation of optimal length UIO sequences under certain conditions [330]. Naik [343] proposed an efficient algorithm for the computation of minimal length UIO sequences when they exist. Pomeranz and Reddy describe an approach to test generation from FSMs for the detection of multiple state-table faults [400]. Survey articles on conformance testing include those by Wang and Hutchison [498], Lee and Yan-nakakis [283], and Sarikaya [431].

A methodology and architectures for testing protocols are described by Sarikaya *et al.* [433] and Bochmann *et al.* [52]. Bochmann *et al.* study the problem of constructing oracles that would assess the validity of a trace of an IUT derived by executing the IUT against a test sequence; the IUT in this case being an implementation of a protocol specification. Sarikaya and Bochmann [432] provide upper bounds on the length of the test sequences of Naito and Tsunoyama TT method and Chow's W-method.

Fault models for FSMs have been proposed by several researchers including Koufareva *et al.* [269] and Godskesen [172]. Several studies have been reported that assess the fault-detection ability of various test-generation methods. These include studies by Sidhu and Leung [443, 444] and Petrenko *et al.* [394]. Sidhu and Chang have proposed probabilistic testing of protocols [442]. The study reported by Sidhu and Leung [444] used the National Bureau of Standards Class 4 transport protocol [453] as the subject for the comparison of T-[345], UIO- [429], D- [173], and W-method [88]. Their results are summarized for the UIO- and the W-methods in Section 3.9. Karoui *et al.* [252] discuss factors that influence the testability and diagnostics of IUTs against FSM designs.

Several variations of FSM models and methods for testing them have been proposed. Extended finite state machines (EFSMs) are FSMs with memory. Wang and Liu [499], Kim *et al.* [261], and Uyar and Duale [484] describe algorithms for generating tests from EFSMs. The problem of generating tests from a set of communicating FSMs has been addressed by Hierons [217], Lee *et al.* [282], and Gang *et al.* [159]. Gang *et al.* [159] have also proposed an extension of the Wp-method to generate tests from a single nondeterministic FSM.

Event sequence Graphs, also known as ESGs, have been proposed by Belli and others [38, 39]. ESGs capture the behavior of a GUI in terms of a sequence of I/O event pairs.

Test-suite minimization for nondeterministic FSMs is discussed by Yevtushenko *et al.* [539]. Petrenko and Yevtushenko describe an algorithm for generating tests from partial FSMs [395]. They define a weak conformance relation between the specification FSM and the FSM corresponding to the object under test. El-Fakih *et al.* propose a method for generating tests from FSMs when the system specification and development happen incrementally [137]. They show that significant gains are obtained in the length of test suits when these are derived incrementally in contrast to directly from complete specifications. Shehady and Siewiorek [438] point to the weakness of an FSM in modeling GUIs with variables as part of their internal state and introduce variable finite state machine (VFSM) as an alternative. VFSMs are obtained from FSMs by adding variables, and simple functions on variables, to transitions. The authors provide an automata-theoretic method for test-generation from a VFSM.

BIBLIOGRAPHIC NOTES

Test-adequacy assessment and test enhancement for FSMs based on mutation coverage have been proposed by Fabbri *et al.* [142]. Fabbri *et al.* [143] also report a tool, named Proteum/FSM, for testing FSMs. Gören and Ferguson [178] propose fault coverage of a test suite as an adequacy criterion and provide an algorithm for the incremental generation of tests. This method is an extension of the method proposed by the same authors for asynchronous sequential machines [177].

The test-adequacy criteria defined in Section 3.9, and used for comparison with the W- and Wp-methods, have been considered by Howden [233], Huang [240], and Pimont and Rault [398].

The FSM-based test-generation techniques described in this chapter have also been applied to the automatic generation of tests from SDL specifications [297]. Belina and Hogrefe [36, 37] provide an introduction to the SDL specification language.

EXERCISES

3.1 Modify the DIGDEC machine shown in Figure 3.3 so that it accepts a string over the alphabet $X = \{d, *\}$. For example, strings such as $s = 324 * 41 * 9 * 199 * *230*$ are valid inputs. An asterisk causes the machine to execute the OUT(num) function where num denotes the decimal number corresponding to the digits received prior to the current asterisk but after any previous asterisk. Thus, the output of the machine for input string s will be:

OUT(324) OUT(41) OUT(9) OUT(199) OUT(230)

Note that the machine does not perform any action if it receives an asterisk following another asterisk.

3.2 Show that (a) *V-equivalence* and *equivalence* of states and machines as defined in Section 3.2.3 are equivalence relations, that is they obey the reflexive, symmetric, and transitive laws; (b) if two states are k-distinguishable for any $k > 0$, then they are also distinguishable for any $n > k$.

3.3 Show that it is not necessary for equivalent machines to have an equal number of states.

3.4 Show that the set W of Example 3.7 is a characterization set for the machine in Figure 3.13.

3.5 Prove that the FSM M must be a *minimal* machine for the existence of a characterization set.

3.6 Prove that the method for the construction of k-equivalence partitions described in Example 3.8 will always converge, that is there will be a table $P_n, n > 0$, such that $P_n = P_{n+1}$.

3.7 The W-procedure for the construction of the W-set from a set of k–equivalence partitions is given in Section 3.5.2. This is a brute-force procedure that determines a distinguishing sequence for every pair of states. From Example 3.9, we know that two or more pairs of states might be distinguishable by the same input sequence. Rewrite the W-procedure by making use of this fact.

3.8 Prove that the k-equivalence partition of a machine is unique.

3.9 Prove that in an FSM with n states, at most $n-1$ constructions of the equivalence classes are needed, that is, one needs to construct only $P_1, P_2, \ldots, P_{n-1}$.

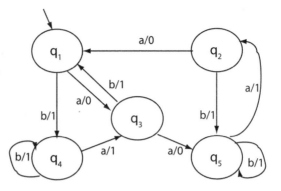

Fig. 3.29   An implementation of M shown Figure 3.15(a) with a transfer error in state q_1 on input a.

3.10 Given the FSM of Example 3.6, construct all mutants that can be obtained by adding a state to M.

3.11 Generate a set T of input sequences that distinguish all mutants in Figure 3.12 from machine M.

3.12 Show that any *extra* or *missing*-state error in the implementation of design M will be detected by at least one test generated using the W-method.

3.13 Construct the characterization set W and the transition cover for the machine in Figure 3.23(a). Using the W-method, construct set Z assuming that $m = 3$ and derive a test set T. Does any element of T reveal the transfer error in the IUT of Figure 3.23(b)? Compare T with the test set in Example 3.37 with respect to the number of tests and the average size of test sequences.

3.14 Consider the design specification M as shown in Figure 3.15(a). Further, consider an implementation M_3 of M as shown in Figure 3.29. Find all tests in T_1 and T_2 from Example 3.17 that reveal the error in M_3.

3.15 Consider the design specification in Figure 3.30(a). It contains three states q_0, q_1, and q_2. The input alphabet is $X = \{a, b, c\}$, and the output alphabet is $Y = \{0, 1\}$. (a) Derive a transition cover set P, the state cover set S, the characterization set W, and state identification sets for each of the three states. (b) From M, derive a test set T_w using the W-method and test set T_{wp} using the Wp-method. Compare the sizes of the two sets. (c) Figure 3.30(b) shows the transition diagram of an implementation of M that contains a transfer error in state q_2. Which tests in T_w and T_{wp}

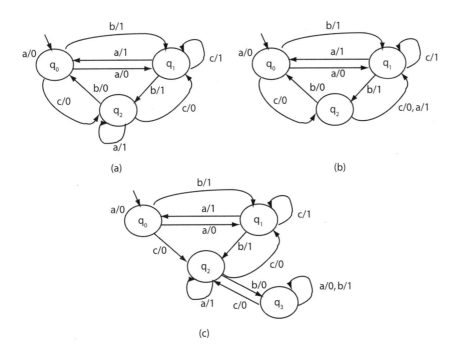

Fig. 3.30 Three FSMs. (a) Design specification machine, (b) and (c) are machine indicating an erroneous implementation of the FSM in (a).

reveal this error? (d) Figure 3.30(c) shows the transition diagram of an implementation of M that contains an extra state q_3 and a transfer error in state q_2. Which tests in T_w and T_{wp} reveal this error?

3.16 (a) Given an FSM $M = (X, Y, Q, q_0, \delta, O)$, where $|X| = n_x, |Y| = n_y, |Q| = n_z$, calculate the upper bound on the number of tests that will be generated using the W-method. (b) Under what condition(s) will the number of tests generated by the Wp-method be the same as those generated by the W-method?

3.17 Using the tests generated in Example 3.18, determine at least one test for each of the two machines in Figure 3.16 that will reveal the error. Is it necessary to apply phase 2 testing to reveal the error in each of the two machines?

3.18 What is the difference between sequences in the W set and the UIO sequences? Find UIO sequences for each state in the machine with transition diagram shown in Figure 3.13. Find the distinguishing signature for states for which a UIO sequence does not exist.

3.19 What will be the value of counter k when control arrives at Step 2.3 in procedure *gen-long-uio* given in Section 3.8.4?

3.20 For machine M_2 used in Example 3.32, what output sequences are generated when the input portion of $Sig(q_1)$ is applied to states q_2 and q_3?

3.21 Suppose that tests $TE(e_1)$ and $TE(e_2)$ are derived using the method in Section 3.8.6 for a given FSM M. Is it possible that $TE(e_1) = TE(e_2)$?

3.22 Generate UIO sequences for all states in the specification shown in Figure 3.13. Using the sequences so generated, develop tests for weak conformance testing of an IUT built that must behave as per the specification given.

3.23 Generate tests for weak conformance testing of machine M_1 in Figure 3.18. Use the UIO sequences for M_2 given in Section 3.8.2.

3.24 Consider an implementation of the machine shown in Figure 3.21. The state diagram of the implementation is shown in Figure 3.31. Note that the IUT has two errors, a transfer error in state q_2 and an operation error in state q_6. In Example 3.36, the transfer error in q_2 is revealed by test 4 (and 13). Are any of these tests successful in revealing the error in q_2? Is there any test derived earlier that will reveal the error in q_2? Which one of the tests derived in Examples 3.33 and 3.35 will reveal the error in q_b?

3.25 TT is a technique to generate tests from FSM specifications. A TT is an input sequence that when applied to an FSM in its start state traverses each edge at least once. (a) Find a TT for each of the two FSMs shown in Figure 3.18. (b) Show that a TT is able to detect all operation errors but may not be able to detect all transfer errors. Assume that the FSM specification satisfies the

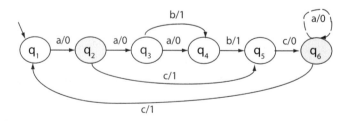

Fig. 3.31   State diagram of an erroneous implementation of the machine in Figure 3.21.

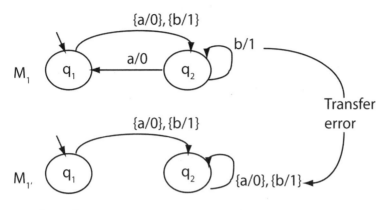

Fig. 3.32 A transfer error.

assumptions in Section 3.6.1. (c) Compare the size of tests generated using TT and the W-method.

3.26 In Example 3.38, we developed adequate tests to show that certain errors in the IUT corresponding to an FSM are not detected. Derive tests using the W-method, and then using the Wp-method, and show that each test set derived detects all errors shown in Figure 3.32.

3.27 FSM models considered in this chapter are pure in the sense that they capture only the control flow and ignore data definitions and uses. In this exercise, you will learn how to enhance a test set derived using any of the methods described in this chapter by accounting for data flows.
Figure 3.33 shows machine M, an augmented version of the FSM in Figure 3.13. We assume that the IUT corresponding to the FSM in Figure 3.33 uses a local variable Z. This variable is *defined* along transitions $tr_1 = (q_1, q_4)$ and $tr_3 = (q_3, q_5)$. Variable Z is *used* along transitions $tr_2 = (q_2, q_1)$ and $tr_4 = (q_3, q_1)$. Also, x and y are parameters of, respectively, inputs b and a. A data-flow path for variable Z is a sequence Tr of transitions such that Z is defined on one transition along Tr and, subsequently, used along another transition also in Tr. For example, tr_1, tr_4, tr_5 is a data-flow path for Z in M where Z is defined along tr_1 and used along tr_5. We consider only finite-length paths and those with only one definition and one corresponding use along a path. While testing the IUT against M, we must ensure that all data-flow paths are tested. This is to detect faults in the defining or usage transitions. (a) Enumerate all data flow paths for variable

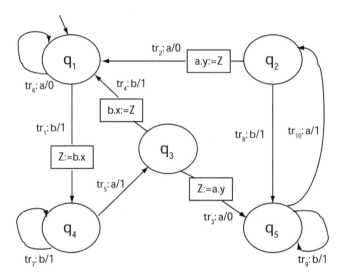

Fig. 3.33 FSM of Figure 3.13 augmented with definition and use of local variable Z.

Z in M. (b) Derive tests, that is input sequences, which will traverse all data-flow paths derived in (a). (c) Consider a test set T derived for M using the W-method. Does exercising M against all elements of T exercise all data-flow paths derived in (a)? (Note: Chapter 6 provides details of data-flow-based assessment of test adequacy and enhancement of tests.)

3.28 Let T be a set of test inputs that forms an n-switch set cover for a minimal n-distinguishable FSM M. Prove that T can detect all transfer, and operation errors, and extra and missing-state errors in M.

3.29 Show that a test set T that is adequate with respect to the boundary-interior coverage criterion may not be adequate with respect to the one-switch cover criterion.

3.30 Derive a test set T from M2 shown in Figure 3.25 that is adequate with respect to the one-switch cover criterion. Which test in T distinguishes M_2 from $M_{2'}$ and thereby reveal the error? Compare T derived in this exercise with the test given in Example 3.38 and identify a property of the method used to construct T that allows T to distinguish M_2 from $M_{2'}$.

4

Test Generation from Combinatorial Designs

CONTENT ■■

The purpose of this chapter is to introduce techniques for the generation of test configurations and test data using the combinatorial design techniques with program inputs and their values as, respectively, factors and levels. These techniques are useful when testing a variety of applications. They allow selection of a small set of test configurations from an often impractically large set, and are effective in detecting faults arising out of factor interactions.

4.1 COMBINATORIAL DESIGNS

Software applications are often designed to work in a variety of environments. Combinations of factors such as the OS, network connection, and hardware platform lead to a variety of environments. Each environment corresponds to a given set of values for each factor, known as a *test configuration*. For example, Windows XP, dial-up connection, and a PC with 512 MB of main memory is one possible configuration. To ensure high reliability across the intended environments, the application must be tested under as many test configurations, or environments, as possible. However, as illustrated in examples later in this chapter, the number of such test configurations could be exorbitantly large, making it impossible to test the application exhaustively.

An analogous situation arises in the testing of programs that have one or more input variables. Each test run of a program often requires at least one value for each variable. For example, a program to find the greatest common divisor of two integers x and y requires two values, one corresponding to x and the other to y. In earlier chapters, we have seen how program inputs can be selected using techniques such as equivalence partitioning and boundary-value analysis. While these techniques offer a set of guidelines to design test cases, they suffer from two shortcomings: (a) they raise the possibility of a large number of subdomains in the partition of the input space and (b) they lack guidelines on how to select inputs from various subdomains in the partition.

The number of subdomains in a partition of the input domain increases in direct proportion to the number and type of input variables, and especially so when multidimensional partitioning is used. Also, once a partition is determined, one selects at random a value from each of the subdomains. Such a selection procedure, especially when using unidimensional equivalence partitioning, does not account for the possibility of faults in the program under test that arise due to specific interactions among values of different input variables. While boundary-value analysis leads to the selection of test cases that test a program at the boundaries of the input domain, other interactions in the input domain might remain untested.

This chapter describes several techniques for generating test configurations or test sets that are small even when the set of possible configurations, or the input domain, and the number of subdomains in its partition, is large and complex. The number of test configurations, or the test set so generated, has been found to be effective in the discovery of faults due to the interaction of various input variables. The techniques we describe here are known by several names such as design of experiments, combinatorial designs, orthogonal designs, interaction testing, and pairwise testing.

4.1.1 Test Configuration and Test Set

In this chapter, we use the terms *test configuration* and *test set* interchangeably. Even though we use the terms interchangeably, they do have different meanings in the context of software testing. However, the techniques described in this chapter apply to the generation of both test configurations as well as test sets, we have taken the liberty of using them interchangeably. One must be aware that a test configuration is usually a static selection of factors such as the hardware platform or an OS. Such selection is completed prior to the start of the test. In contrast, a test set is a collection of test cases used as input during the test process.

4.1.2 Modeling the Input and Configuration Spaces

The input space of a program P consists of k-tuples of values that could be input to P during execution. The configuration space of P consists of all possible settings of the environment variables under which P could be used.

> **Example 4.1:** Consider program P that takes two integers $x > 0$ and $y > 0$ as inputs. The input space of P is the set of all pairs of positive nonzero integers. Now suppose that this program is intended to be executed under the Windows and the Mac OS, through the Netscape or Safari browsers, and must be able to print to a local or a networked printer. The configuration space of P consists of triples (X, Y, Z) where X represents an OS, Y a browser, and Z a local or a networked printer.

Next, consider a program P that takes n inputs corresponding to variables $X_1, X_2, \ldots, X_n$. We refer to the inputs as *factors*. The inputs are also referred to as *test parameters* or as *values*. Let us assume that each factor may be set at any one from a total of $c_i, 1 \leq i \leq n$ values. Each value assignable to a factor is known as a *level*. The notation $|F|$ refers to the number of levels for factor F.

The environment under which an application is intended to be used generally contributes one or more factors. In Example 4.1, the OS, browser, and printer connection are three factors that are likely to affect the operation and performance of P.

A set of values, one for each factor, is known as a *factor combination*. For example, suppose that program P has two input variables X and Y. Let us say that during an execution of P, X and Y may each assume a value from the set $\{a, b, c\}$ and $\{d, e, f\}$, respectively. Thus, we have two factors and three levels for each factor. This leads to a total of $3^2 = 9$ factor combinations, namely $(a, d), (a, e), (a, f), (b, d), (b, e), (b, f), (c, d), (c, e)$, and (c, f). In general, for k factors with each factor assuming a value from a set of n values, the total number of factor combinations is n^k.

Suppose now that each factor combination yields one test case. For many programs, the number of tests generated for exhaustive testing could be exorbitantly large. For example, if a program has 15 factors with 4 levels each, the total number of tests is $4^{15} \approx 10^9$. Executing a billion tests might be impractical for many software applications.

There are special combinatorial design techniques that enable the selection of a small subset of factor combinations from the complete set. This sample is targeted at specific types of faults known as *interaction* faults. Before we describe how the combinatorial designs are generated, let us look at a few examples that illustrate where they are useful.

Example 4.2: Let us model the input space of an online pizza delivery service (PDS) for the purpose of testing. The service takes orders online, checks for their validity, and schedules pizza for delivery. A customer is required to specify the following four items as part of the online order: pizza size, toppings list, delivery address, and a home phone number. Let us denote these four factors by S, T, A, and P, respectively.

Suppose now that there are three varieties for size: Large, Medium, and Small. There is a list of six toppings from which one has to select. In addition, the customer can customize the toppings. The delivery address consists of the customer name, address, city, and zip code. The phone number is a numeric string possibly containing the dash ("–") separator.

The table below lists one model of the input space for the PDS. Note that while for Size we have selected all three possible levels, we have constrained the other factors to a smaller set of levels. Thus, we are concerned with only one of the two types of values for Toppings, namely Custom or Preset, and one of the two types of values for factors Address and Phone, namely Valid and Invalid.

Factor	Levels		
Size	Large	Medium	Small
Toppings	Custom	Preset	
Address	Valid	Invalid	
Phone	Valid	Invalid	

The total number of factor combinations is $2^4 + 2^3 = 24$. However, as an alternate to the table above, we could consider $6 + 1 = 7$ levels for `Toppings`. This would increase the number of combinations to $2^4 + 5 \times 2^3 + 2^3 + 5 \times 2^2 = 84$. We could also consider additional types of values for `Address` and `Phone` that would further increase the number of distinct combinations. Note that if we were to consider each possible valid and invalid string of characters, limited only by length, as a level for `Address`, we will arrive at a huge number of factor combinations.

Later in this section, we explain the advantages and disadvantages of limiting the number of factor combinations by partitioning the set of values for each factor into a few subsets. Note also the similarity of this approach with equivalence partitioning. The next example illustrates factors in a GUI.

Example 4.3: The GUI of application T consists of three menus labeled `File`, `Edit`, and `Typeset`. Each menu contains several items listed below.

Factor	Levels			
File	New	Open	Save	Close
Edit	Cut	Copy	Paste	Select
Typeset	LaTex	BibTex	PlainTeX	MakeIndex

We have three factors in T. Each of these three factors can be set to any of four levels. Thus, we have a total of $4^3 = 64$ factor combinations.

Note that each factor in this example corresponds to a relatively smaller set of levels when compared to factors `Address` and `Phone` in the previous example. Hence, the number of levels for each factor is set equal to the cardinality of the set of the corresponding values.

Example 4.4: Let us now consider the Unix `sort` utility for sorting ASCII data in files or obtained from the standard input. The utility has several options and makes an interesting example for the identification of factors and levels. The command line for `sort` is as given below.

Tables 4.1 and 4.2 list all the factors of `sort` and their corresponding levels. Note that the levels have been derived using equivalence partitioning for each option and are not unique. We have decided to limit the number of levels for each factor to four. You

Table 4.1 Factors and levels for the Unix `sort` utility

Factor	Meaning	Levels		
-	Forces the source to be the standard input	Unused	Used	
-c	Verify that the input is sorted according to the options specified on the command line	Unused	Used	
-m	Merge sorted input	Unused	Used	
-u	Suppress all but one of the matching keys	Unused	Used	
-o *output*	Output sent to a file	Unused	Valid file	Invalid file
-T *directory*	Temporary directory for sorting	Unused	Exists	Does not exist
-y *kmem*	Use *kmem* kilobytes of memory for sorting	Unused	Valid *kmem*	Invalid *kmem*
-z recsize	Specifies record size to hold each line from the input file	Unused	Zero size	Large size
-d *fiMnr*	Perform dictionary sort	Unused	fi	Mnr	fiMnr

```
sort [ -cmu ] [ -o output ] [ -T directory ] [ -y [ kmem ]] [ -z recsz ] [ -d fiMnr ] [ - b ] [ t char ]
[ -k keydef ] [ +pos1 [ -pos2 ]] [ file . . . ]
```

could come up with a different, and possibly a larger or a smaller, set of levels for each factor.

In Tables 4.1 and 4.2, level *Unused* indicates that the corresponding option is not used while testing the `sort` command. *Used* means that the option is used. Level *Valid File* indicates that the file specified using the -o option exists, whereas *Invalid File* indicates that the specified file does not exist. Other options can be interpreted similarly.

Table 4.2 Factors and levels for the Unix `sort` utility (continued)

Factor	Meaning	Levels			
-f	Ignore case	Unused	Used		
-i	Ignore non-ASCII characters	Unused	Used		
-M	Fields are compared as months	Unused	Used		
-n	Sort input numerically	Unused	Used		
-r	Reverse the output order	Unused	Used		
-b	Ignore leading blanks when using +pos1 and −pos2	Unused	Used		
-t char	Use character c as field separator	Unused	c_1	$c_1 c_2$	
-k *keydef*	Restricted sort key definition	Unused	start	end	start*type*
+*pos1*	Start position in the input line for comparing fields	Unused	f.c	f	0.c
−*pos2*	End position for comparing fields	Unused	f.c	f	0.c
file	File to be sorted	Not specified	Exists	Does not exist	

We have identified a total of 20 factors for the `sort` command. The levels listed in Table 4.1 lead to a total of approximately 1.9×10^9 combinations.

Example 4.5: There is often a need to test a Web application on different platforms to ensure that any claim such as "Application X can be used under Windows and Mac OS X" are valid. Here we consider a combination of hardware, operating system, and a browser as a platform. Such testing is commonly referred to as *compatibility* testing.

Let us identify factors and levels needed in the compatibility testing of application X. Given that we would like X to work on a variety of hardware, OS, and browser combinations, it is easy to obtain three factors, that is hardware, OS, and browser. These are listed in the top row of Table 4.3. Notice that instead of listing factors in different rows, we now list them in different columns. The levels for each factor are listed in rows under the corresponding columns. This has been done to simplify the formatting of the table.

A quick examination of the factors and levels in Table 4.3 reveals that there are 75 factor combinations. However, some of these combinations are infeasible. For example, OS 10.2 is an OS for the Apple computers and not for the Dell Dimension Series PCs. Similarly, the Safari browser is used on Apple computers and not on the PC in the Dell Series. While various editions of the Windows OS can be used on an Apple computer using an OS bridge such as the Virtual PC or Boot Camp, we assume that this is not the case for testing application X.

The discussion above leads to a total of 40 infeasible factor combinations corresponding to the hardware–OS combination and the hardware–browser combination. Thus, in all we are left with 35 platforms on which to test X.

Note that there is a large number of hardware configurations under the Dell Dimension Series. These configurations are obtained by selecting from a variety of processor types, for example, Pentium versus Athelon, processor speeds, memory sizes, and several others. One could replace the Dell Dimension Series in Table 4.3 by a few

Table 4.3 Factors and levels for testing Web application X

Hardware	Operating system	Browser
Dell Dimension Series	Windows Server 2003- Web Edition	Internet Explorer 6.0
Apple G4	Windows Server 2003- 64-bit Enterprise Edition	Internet Explorer 5.5
Apple G5	Windows XP Home Edition	Netscape 7.3
	OS 10.2	Safari 1.2.4
	OS 10.3	Enhanced Mosaic

selected configurations. While doing so will lead to more thorough testing of application X, it will also increase the number of factor combinations, and hence the time to test.

Identifying factors and levels allows us to divide the input domain into subdomains, one for each factor combination. The design of test-cases can now proceed by selecting at least one test from each subdomain. However, as shown in examples above, the number of subdomains could be too large and hence the need for further reduction. The problem of test-case construction and reduction in the number of test cases are considered in the following sections.

4.2 A COMBINATORIAL TEST-DESIGN PROCESS

Figure 4.1 shows a three-step process for the generation of test cases and test configurations for an application under test. The process begins with a model of the input space if test cases are to be generated. The application environment is modeled when test configurations are to be generated. In either case, the model consists of a set of factors and the corresponding levels. The modeling of input space or the environment is not exclusive, and one might apply either one or both depending on the application under test. Examples in the previous section illustrate the modeling process.

In the second step, the model is input to a combinatorial design procedure to generate a combinatorial object that is simply an array of factors and levels. Such an object is also known as a *factor-covering design*. Each row in this array generates at least one test configuration or one test input. In this chapter, we have described several procedures for generating a combinatorial object. The procedures described make use of Latin squares, orthogonal arrays, mixed orthogonal arrays, covering

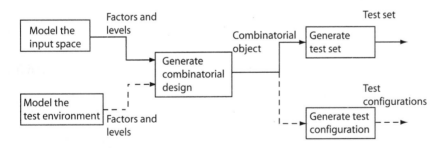

Fig. 4.1 A process for generating tests and test configurations using combinatorial designs. A combinatorial design is represented as a combinatorial object that is an array of size $N \times k$ with N rows, one corresponding to at least one test run, and k columns, one corresponding to each factor.

arrays, and mixed-level covering arrays. While all procedures, and their variants, introduced in this chapter are used in software testing, covering arrays and mixed-level covering arrays seem to be the most useful in this context.

In the final step, the combinatorial object generated is used to design a test set or a test configuration as per the requirement might be. The combinatorial object is an array of factor combinations. Each factor combination may lead to one or more test cases where each test case consists of values of input variables and the expected output. However, all combinations generated might not be feasible. Further, the sequence in which test inputs are entered is also not specified in the combinations. The next few examples illustrate how a factor combination may lead to one or more test cases, both feasible and infeasible, and assist in detecting errors.

Of the three steps shown in Figure 4.1, the second and third steps can be automated. There are commercial tools available that automate the second step, that is the generation of a combinatorial object. Generation of test configurations and test cases requires a simple mapping from integers to levels or values of factors and input variables, a relatively straightforward task.

Example 4.6: From the factor levels listed in Example 4.3, we can generate 64 test cases, one corresponding to each combination. Thus, for example, the next two test inputs are generated from the table in Example 4.3.

$$< t_1 : \texttt{File} = \texttt{Open}, \texttt{Edit} = \texttt{Paste}, \texttt{Typeset} = \texttt{MakeIndex} >$$
$$< t_2 : \texttt{File} = \texttt{New}, \texttt{Edit} = \texttt{Cut}, \texttt{Typeset} = \texttt{LaTeX} >$$

Let us assume that the values of `File`, `Edit`, and `Typeset` are set in the sequence listed. Test t_1 requires that the tester select "Open" from the `File` menu, followed by "Paste" from the `Edit` menu, and finally "MakeIndex" from the `Typeset` menu. While this sequence of test inputs is feasible, that is this can be applied as desired, the sequence given in t_2 cannot be applied.

To test the GUI using t_2, one needs to open a "New" file and then use the "Cut" operation from the `Edit` menu. However, the "Cut" operation is usually not available when a new file is opened, unless there is an error in the implementation. Thus, while t_2 is infeasible if the GUI is implemented correctly, it becomes feasible when there is an error in the implementation. While one might consider t_2 to be a useless test case, it does provide a useful sequence of input selections from the GUI menus in that it enforces a check for the correctness of certain features.

Example 4.7: Each combination obtained from the levels listed in Table 4.1 can be used to generate many test inputs. For example, consider the combination in which all factors are set to *Unused* except the $-o$ option, which is set to *Valid File* and the *file* option that is set to *Exists*. Assuming that files *afile*, *bfile*, *cfile*, and *dfile* exist, this factor setting can lead to many test cases, two of which are listed below:

$$< t_1 : \text{sort} - \text{oafile bfile} >$$
$$< t_2 : \text{sort} - \text{ocfile dfile} >$$

One might ask as to why only one of t_1 and t_2 is not sufficient. Indeed, t_2 might differ significantly from t_1 in that dfile is a very large-sized file relative to bfile. Recall that both bfile and dfile contain data to be sorted. One might want to test `sort` on a very large file to ensure its correctness and also to measure its performance relative to a smaller data file. Thus, in this example, two tests generated from the same combination are designed to check for correctness and performance.

To summarize, a combination of factor levels is used to generate one or more test cases. For each test case, the sequence in which inputs are to be applied to the program under test must be determined by the tester. Further, the factor combinations do not indicate in any way the sequence in which the generated tests are to be applied to the program under test. This sequence too must be determined by the tester. The sequencing of tests generated by most test-generation techniques must be determined by the tester and is not a unique characteristic of tests generated in combinatorial testing.

4.3 FAULT MODEL

The combinatorial design procedures described in this chapter are aimed at generating test inputs and test configurations that might reveal certain types of faults in the application under test. We refer to such faults as *interaction* faults. We say that an interaction fault is triggered when a certain combination of $t \geq 1$ input values causes the program containing the fault to enter an invalid state. Of course, this invalid state must propagate to a point in the program execution where it is observable and hence is said to reveal the fault.

Faults triggered by some value of an input variable, that is $t = 1$, regardless of the values of other input variables, are known as *simple* faults. For $t = 2$, they are known as pairwise interaction faults, and in general, for any arbitrary value of t, as t-way interaction faults. An t-way interaction fault is also known as a *t*-factor fault. For example, a pairwise interaction fault will be triggered only when two input variables are set to specific values. A three-way interaction fault will be triggered only when three input variables assume specific values. The next two examples illustrate interaction faults.

Example 4.8: Consider the following program that requires three inputs x, y, and z. Prior to program execution, variable x is assigned a value from the set $\{x_1, x_2, x_3\}$, variable y a value from the set $\{y_1, y_2, y_3\}$, and variable z a value from the set $\{z_1, z_2\}$. The program outputs the function $f(x, y, z)$ when $x = x_1$ and $y = y_2$, function $g(x, y)$ when $x = x_2$ and $y = y_1$, and function $f(x, y, z) + g(x, y)$ when $x = x_2$, and $y = y_2$ otherwise.

Program P4.1

```
1    begin
2       int x,y,z;
3       input (x,y,z);
4       if(x==x₁ and y==y₂)
5          output (f(x,y,z));
6       else if(x==x₂ and y==y₁)
7          output (g(x,y));
8       else
9          output (f(x,y,z)+g(x,y))  ← This
                statement is not protected correctly.
10   end
```

As marked, Program P4.1 contains one error. The program must output $f(x, y, z) - g(x, y)$ when $x = x_1$ and $y = y_1$ and $f(x, y, z) + g(x, y)$ when $x = x_2$ and $y = y_2$. This error will be revealed by executing the program with $x = x_1$, $y = y_1$, and any value of z, if $f(x_1, y_1, *) - g(x_1, y_1) \neq f(x_1, y_1, *) + g(x_1, y_1)$. This error is an example of a pairwise interaction fault revealed only when inputs x and y interact in a certain way. Note that variable z does not play any role in triggering the fault but it might need to take a specific value for the fault to be revealed (also see Exercises 4.2 and 4.3).

Example 4.9: A missing condition is the cause of a pairwise interaction fault in Example 4.1. Also, the input variables are compared against their respective values in the conditions governing the flow of control. Program P4.2 contains a three-way interaction fault in which an incorrect arithmetic function of three input variables is responsible for the fault.

Let the three variables assume input values from their respective domains as follows: $x, y \in \{-1, 1\}$, and $z \in \{0, 1\}$. Note that there is a total of eight combinations of the three input variables.

Program P4.2

```
1   begin
2      int x,y,z,p;
3      input (x,y,z);
4      p = (x + y)*z;   ← This statement must be
          p = (x − y)*z
5      if (p ≥ 0)
6         output (f(x,y,z));
7      else
8         output (g(x,y));
9   end
```

The program above contains a three-way interaction fault. This fault is triggered by all inputs such that $x + y \neq x - y$ and $z \neq 0$ because for such inputs the program computes an incorrect value of p, thereby entering an incorrect state. However, the fault is revealed only by the following two of the eight possible input combinations: $x = -1, y = 1, z = 1$ and $x = -1, y = -1, z = 1$.

4.3.1 FAULT VECTORS

As mentioned earlier, a t-way fault is triggered whenever a subset of $t \leq k$ factors, out of a complete set of k factors, is set to some set of levels. Given a set of k factors $f_1, f_2, \ldots, f_k$, each at $q_i, 1 \leq i \leq k$ levels, a vector V of factor levels is $l_1, l_2, \ldots, l_k$, where $l_i, 1 \leq i \leq k$ is a specific level for the corresponding factor. V is also known as a *run*.

We say that a run V is a *fault vector* for program P if the execution of P against a test case derived from V triggers a fault in P. V is considered as a t-fault vector if any $t \leq k$ elements in V are needed to trigger a fault in P. Note that a t-way fault vector for P triggers a t-way fault in P. Given k factors, there are $k - t$ don't care entries in a t-way fault vector. We indicate don't care entries with an asterisk. For example, the two-way fault vector $(2, 3, *)$ indicates that the two-way interaction fault is triggered when factor 1 is set to level 2, factor 2 to level 3, and factor 3 is the don't care factor.

Example 4.10: The input domain of Program P4.2 consists of three factors x, y, and z each having two levels. There is a total of eight runs. For example, $(1, 1, 1)$ and $(-1, -1, 0)$ are two runs. Of these eight runs, $(-1, 1, 1)$ and $(-1, -1, 1)$ are three fault vectors that trigger the three-way fault in Program P4.2. $(x_1, y_1, *)$ is a two-way fault vector given that the values x_1 and y_1 trigger the two-way fault in Program P4.2.

The goal of the test-generation techniques described in this chapter is to generate a sufficient number of runs such that tests generated from these runs reveal all t-way faults in the program under test. As we see later in this chapter, the number of such runs increases with the value of t. In many practical situations, t is set to 2 and hence the tests generated are expected to reveal pairwise interaction faults. Of course, while generating t-way runs, one also generates some $t+1, t+2, \ldots, t+k-1$ and k-way runs. Hence, there is always a chance that runs generated with $t = 2$ reveal some higher-level interaction faults.

4.4 LATIN SQUARES

In the previous sections, we have shown how to identify factors and levels in a software application and how to generate test cases from factor combinations. Considering that the number of factor combinations could be exorbitantly large, we want to examine techniques for test generation that focus on only a certain subset of factor combinations.

Latin squares and mutually orthogonal Latin squares (MOLS) are rather ancient devices found useful in selecting a subset of factor combinations from the complete set. In this section, we introduce Latin squares that are used to generate fewer factor combinations than what would be generated by the brute-force technique mentioned earlier. MOLS and the generation of a small set of factor combinations are explained in the subsequent sections.

Let S be a finite set of n symbols. A Latin square of order n is an $n \times n$ matrix such that no symbol appears more than once in a row and column. The term *Latin square* arises from the fact that the early versions used letters from the Latin alphabet A, B, C, and so on, in a square arrangement.

Example 4.11: Given $S = \{A, B\}$, we have the following two Latin squares of order 2:

$$
\begin{array}{cc} A & B \\ B & A \end{array} \qquad \begin{array}{cc} B & A \\ A & B \end{array}
$$

Given $S = \{1, 2, 3\}$, we have the following three Latin squares of order 3:

$$
\begin{array}{ccc} 1 & 2 & 3 \\ 2 & 3 & 1 \\ 3 & 1 & 2 \end{array} \qquad \begin{array}{ccc} 2 & 3 & 1 \\ 1 & 2 & 3 \\ 3 & 1 & 2 \end{array} \qquad \begin{array}{ccc} 2 & 1 & 3 \\ 3 & 2 & 1 \\ 1 & 3 & 2 \end{array}
$$

Additional Latin squares of order 3 can be constructed by permuting rows and columns and by exchanging symbols, for example by replacing all occurrences of symbol 2 by 3 and 3 by 2, of an existing Latin square.

Larger Latin squares of order n can be constructed by creating a row of n distinct symbols. Additional rows can be created by permuting the first row. For example, the following is a Latin square M of order 4 constructed by cyclically rotating the first row and placing successive rotations in subsequent rows.

$$
\begin{array}{cccc}
1 & 2 & 3 & 4 \\
2 & 3 & 4 & 1 \\
3 & 4 & 1 & 2 \\
4 & 1 & 2 & 3
\end{array}
$$

Given a Latin square M, a large number of Latin squares of order 4 can be obtained from M through row and column interchange and symbol-renaming operations. Two Latin squares M_1 and M_2 are considered *isomorphic* if one can be obtained from the other by permutation of rows, columns, and symbol exchange. However, given a Latin square of order n, not all Latin squares of order n can be constructed using the interchange and symbol renaming.

Example 4.12: Consider the following Latin square M_1 of order 4:

$$
\begin{array}{cccc}
1 & 2 & 3 & 4 \\
2 & 1 & 4 & 3 \\
3 & 4 & 1 & 2 \\
4 & 3 & 2 & 1
\end{array}
$$

M_1 cannot be obtained from M listed earlier by permutation of rows and columns or symbol exchange. Exercise 4.6 suggests how M_1 can be constructed. Note that M_1 has six 2×2 subtables that are Latin squares containing the symbol 1. However, there are no such 2×2 Latin squares in M.

A Latin square of order $n > 2$ can also be constructed easily by doing module arithmetic. For example, the Latin square M of order 4 given below is constructed such that $M(i, j) = i + j \pmod 4$, $1 \leq (i, j) \leq 4$.

	1	2	3	4
1	2	3	0	1
2	3	0	1	2
3	0	1	2	3
4	1	2	3	0

A Latin square based on integers $0, 1, \ldots, n$ is said to be in standard form if the elements in the top row and the leftmost column are arranged in order. In a Latin square based on letters A, B, ..., the elements in the top row and the leftmost column are arranged in alphabetical order.

4.5 MUTUALLY ORTHOGONAL LATIN SQUARES

Let M_1 and M_2 be two Latin squares, each of order n. Let $M_1(i, j)$ and $M_2(i, j)$ denote, respectively, the elements in the ith row and j^{th} column of M_1 and M_2. We now create an $n \times n$ matrix M from M_1 and M_2 such that the $L(i, j)$ is $M_1(i, j)M_2(i, j)$, that is we simply juxtapose the corresponding elements of M_1 and M_2. If each element of M is unique, that is it appears exactly once in M, then M_1 and M_2 are said to be MOLS of order n.

Example 4.13: There are no MOLS of order 2. Listed below are two MOLS of order 3:

$$M_1 = \begin{matrix} 1 & 2 & 3 \\ 2 & 3 & 1 \\ 3 & 1 & 2 \end{matrix} \qquad M_2 = \begin{matrix} 2 & 3 & 1 \\ 1 & 2 & 3 \\ 3 & 1 & 2 \end{matrix}$$

To check if indeed M_1 and M_2 are mutually orthogonal, we juxtapose the corresponding elements to obtain the following matrix:

$$L = \begin{matrix} 12 & 23 & 31 \\ 21 & 32 & 13 \\ 33 & 11 & 22 \end{matrix}$$

As each element of M appears exactly once, M_1 and M_2 are indeed mutually orthogonal.

Mutually orthogonal Latin squares are commonly referred to as MOLS. The term MOLS(n) refers to the set of MOLS of order n. It is known that when n is prime, or a power of prime, MOLS(n) contains $n - 1$ MOLS. Such a set of MOLS is known as a *complete* set.

MOLS do not exist for $n = 2$ and $n = 6$, but they do exist for all other values of $n > 2$. Numbers 2 and 6 are known as *Eulerian numbers* after the famous mathematician Leonhard Euler (1707–1783). The number of MOLS of order n is denoted by $N(n)$. Thus, when n is prime or a power of prime, $N(n) = n - 1$ (also see Exercise 4.9). The next example illustrates a simple procedure to construct MOLS(n) when n is prime.

Example 4.14: We follow a simple procedure to construct MOLS(5). We begin by constructing a Latin square of order 5, given the symbol set $S = \{1, 2, 3, 4, 5\}$. This can be done by the method described in the previous section, which is to generate subsequent rows of the matrix by rotating the previous row to the left by one position. The first row is a simple enumeration of all symbols in S; the order of enumeration does not matter. The following is one element of MOLS(5):

$$M_1 = \begin{matrix} 1 & 2 & 3 & 4 & 5 \\ 2 & 3 & 4 & 5 & 1 \\ 3 & 4 & 5 & 1 & 2 \\ 4 & 5 & 1 & 2 & 3 \\ 5 & 1 & 2 & 3 & 4 \end{matrix}$$

Next, we obtain M_2 by rotating rows 2 through 5 of M_1 by two positions to the left.

$$M_2 = \begin{matrix} 1 & 2 & 3 & 4 & 5 \\ 3 & 4 & 5 & 1 & 2 \\ 5 & 1 & 2 & 3 & 4 \\ 2 & 3 & 4 & 5 & 1 \\ 4 & 5 & 1 & 2 & 3 \end{matrix}$$

M_3 and M_4 are obtained similarly, but by rotating the first row of M_1 by three and four positions, respectively.

$$M_3 = \begin{matrix} 1 & 2 & 3 & 4 & 5 \\ 4 & 5 & 1 & 2 & 3 \\ 2 & 3 & 4 & 5 & 1 \\ 5 & 1 & 2 & 3 & 4 \\ 3 & 4 & 5 & 1 & 2 \end{matrix}$$

$$M_4 = \begin{matrix} 1 & 2 & 3 & 4 & 5 \\ 5 & 1 & 2 & 3 & 4 \\ 4 & 5 & 1 & 2 & 3 \\ 3 & 4 & 5 & 1 & 2 \\ 2 & 3 & 4 & 5 & 1 \end{matrix}$$

Thus, we get MOLS(5) = $\{M_1, M_2, M_3, M_4\}$. It is easy to check that indeed the elements of MOLS(5) are mutually orthogonal by superimposing them pairwise. For example, superimposing M_2 and M_4 leads to the following matrix where each element occurs exactly once.

$$\begin{matrix} 11 & 22 & 33 & 44 & 55 \\ 35 & 41 & 52 & 13 & 24 \\ 54 & 15 & 21 & 32 & 43 \\ 23 & 34 & 45 & 51 & 12 \\ 42 & 53 & 14 & 25 & 31 \end{matrix}$$

The method illustrated in the previous example is guaranteed to work only when constructing MOLS(n) for n that is prime or a power of prime. For other values of n, the maximum size of MOLS(n) is $n - 1$. However, different methods are used to construct MOLS(n) when n is not a prime or a power of prime. Such methods are beyond the scope of this book. There is no general method available to construct the largest possible MOLS(n) for n that is not a prime or a power of prime. The *CRC Handbook of Combinatorial Designs* (see the Bibliographic Notes section of this chapter) lists a large set of MOLS for various values of n.

4.6 PAIRWISE DESIGN: BINARY FACTORS

We now introduce techniques for selecting a subset of factor combinations from the complete set. First, we focus on programs whose configuration or input space can be modeled as a collection of factors where each factor assumes one or two values. We are interested in selecting a subset from the complete set of factor combinations such that all pairs of factor levels are covered in the selected subset.

Each factor combination selected will generate at least one test input or test configuration for the program under test. As discussed earlier, the complete set of factor combinations might be too large and impractical to drive a test process, and hence the need for selecting a subset.

To illustrate the process of selecting a subset of combinations from the complete set, suppose that a program to be tested requires three inputs, one corresponding to each input variable. Each variable can take only one of two distinct values. Considering each input variable as a factor, the total number of factor combinations is 2^3. Let X, Y, and Z denote the three input variables and $\{X_1, X_2\}, \{Y_1, Y_2\}$, and $\{Z_1, Z_2\}$ their respective sets of values. All possible combinations of these three factors are given below:

$$(X_1, Y_1, Z_1) \quad (X_1, Y_1, Z_2)$$
$$(X_1, Y_2, Z_1) \quad (X_1, Y_2, Z_2)$$
$$(X_2, Y_1, Z_1) \quad (X_2, Y_1, Z_2)$$
$$(X_2, Y_2, Z_1) \quad (X_2, Y_2, Z_2$$

However, we are interested in generating tests such that each pair of input values is covered, that is each pair of input values appears in at least one test. There are 12 such pairs, namely $(X_1, Y_1), (X_1, Y_2), (X_1, Z_1)$, $(X_1, Z_2), (X_2, Y_1), (X_2, Y_2), (X_2, Z_1), (X_2, Z_2), (Y_1, Z_1), (Y_1, Z_2), (Y_2, Z_1)$, and (Y_2, Z_2). In this case, the following set of four combinations suffices:

$$(X_1, Y_1, Z_2) \quad (X_1, Y_2, Z_1)$$
$$(X_2, Y_1, Z_1) \quad (X_2, Y_2, Z_2)$$

The above set of four combinations is also known as a *pairwise design*. Further, it is a balanced design because each value occurs exactly the same number of times. There are several sets of four combinations that cover all 12 pairs (see Exercise 4.8).

Note that being content with pairwise coverage of the input values reduces the required number of tests from eight to four, a 50% reduction. The large number of combinations resulting from three-way, four-way, and higher-order designs often force us to be content with pairwise coverage.

Let us now generalize the problem of pairwise design to $n \geq 2$ factors where each factor takes on one of two values. To do so, we define S_{2k-1} to be the set of all binary strings of length $2k - 1$ such that each string has exactly k 1s. There are exactly $\binom{2k-1}{k}$ strings in S_{2k-1}. Recall that $\binom{n}{k} = \frac{!n}{!(n-k)!k}$.

Example 4.15: For $k = 2$, S_3 contains $\binom{3}{2} = 3$ binary strings of length 3, each containing exactly two 1s. All strings are laid out in the following with column number indicating the position within a string and row number indicating the string count.

	1	2	3
1	0	1	1
2	1	0	1
3	1	1	0

For $k = 3$, S_5 contains $\binom{5}{3} = 10$ binary strings of length 5, each containing three 1s.

	1	2	3	4	5
1	0	0	1	1	1
2	0	1	1	1	0
3	1	1	1	0	0
4	1	0	1	1	0
5	0	1	1	0	1
6	1	1	0	1	0
7	1	0	1	0	1
8	0	1	0	1	1
9	1	1	0	0	1
10	1	0	0	1	1

Given the number of two-valued parameters, the following procedure can be used to generate a pairwise design. We have named the procedure as the *SAMNA procedure* after its authors (see Bibliographic Notes section for details).

Input: n: Number of two-valued input variables (or factors).

Output: A set of factor combinations such that all pairs of input values are covered.

Procedure: SAMNA

```
/* X₁, X₂, ..., Xₙ denote the n input variables.
```
$X_1, X_2, \ldots, X_n$ denote the n input variables.

X_i^* denotes one of the two possible values of variable X_i, for $1 \le i \le n$. One of the two values of each variable corresponds to a 0 and the other to a 1.

```
*/
```

Step 1 Compute the smallest integer k such that $n \le |S_{2k-1}|$.

Step 2 Select any subset of n strings from S_{2k-1}. Arrange these to form an $n \times (2k-1)$ matrix with one string in each row, while the columns contain different bits in each string.

Step 3 Append a column of 0s to the end of each string selected. This will increase the size of each string from $2k - 1$ to $2k$.

Step 4 Each one of the $2k$ columns contains a bit pattern from which we generate a combination of factor levels as follows. Each combination is of the kind $(X_1^*, X_2^*, \ldots, X_n^*)$, where the value of each variable is selected depending on whether the bit in column i, $1 \le i \le n$ is a 0 or a 1.

End of Procedure SAMNA

Example 4.16: Consider a simple Java applet named ChemFun that allows a user to create an in-memory database of chemical elements and search for an element. The applet has five inputs listed below with their possible values. We refer to the inputs as factors. For simplicity, we have assumed that each input has exactly two possible values.

Factor	Name	Levels	Comments
1	Operation	{Create, Show}	Two buttons
2	Name	{Empty, Nonempty}	Data field, string
3	Symbol	{Empty, Nonempty}	Data field, string
4	Atomic number	{Invalid, Valid}	Data field, data > 0
5	Properties	{Empty, Nonempty}	Data field, string

The applet offers two operations via buttons labeled `Create` and `Show`. Pressing the `Create` button causes the element-related data, for example its name and atomic number, to be recorded in the database. However, the applet is required to perform simple checks prior to saving the data. The user is notified if the checks fail and data entered is not saved. The `Show` operation searches for data that matches information typed in any of the four data fields.

Note that each of the data fields could take on an impractically large number of values. For example, a user could type almost any string using characters on the keyboard in the `Atomic number` field. However, using equivalence class partitioning, we have reduced the number of data values for which we wanted to test `ChemFun`.

Testing `ChemFun` on all possible parameter combinations would require a total of $2^5 = 32$ tests. However, if we are interested in testing against all pairwise combinations of the five parameters, then only six tests are required. We now show how these six tests are derived using procedure SAMNA.

Input: $n = 5$ factors.

Output: A set of factor combinations such that all pairs of input values are covered.

Step 1 *Compute the smallest integer k such that $n \leq \mid S_{2k-i} \mid$.*
       In this case, we obtain $k = 3$.

Step 2 *Select any subset of n strings from S_{2k-1}. Arrange these to form an $n \times (2k - 1)$ matrix with one string in each row while the columns contain bits from each string.*

       We select first 5 of the 10 strings in S_5 listed in Example 4.15. Arranging them as desired gives us the following matrix:

	1	2	3	4	5
1	0	0	1	1	1
2	0	1	1	1	0
3	1	1	1	0	0
4	1	0	1	1	0
5	0	1	1	0	1

Step 3 *Append 0s to the end of each selected string. This will increase the size of each string from $2k - 1$ to $2k$.*

Appending a column of zeroes to the matrix above leads to the following 5×6 matrix:

	1	2	3	4	5	6
1	0	0	1	1	1	0
2	0	1	1	1	0	0
3	1	1	1	0	0	0
4	1	0	1	1	0	0
5	0	1	1	0	1	0

Step 4 *Each of the 2k columns contains a bit pattern from which we generate a combination of factor values as follows. Each combination is of the kind $(X_1^*, X_2^*, \ldots, X_n^*)$, where the value of each variable is selected depending on whether the bit in column i, $1 \le i \le n$, is a 0 or a 1.*

The following factor combinations are obtained by replacing the 0s and 1s in each column of the matrix listed above by the corresponding values of each factor. Here, we have assumed that the first of two factors levels listed earlier corresponds to a 0 and the second level corresponds to a 1.

	1	2	3	4	5	6
1	Create	Create	Show	Show	Show	Create
2	Empty	NE	NE	NE	Empty	Empty
3	Nonempty	NE	NE	Empty	Empty	Empty
4	Valid	Invalid	Valid	Valid	Invalid	Invalid
5	Empty	NE	NE	Empty	NE	Empty

NE, Nonempty.

The matrix above lists six factor combinations, one corresponding to each column. Each combination can now be used to generate one or more tests as explained in Section 4.2. The following is a set of six tests for the ChemFun applet.

$T = \{\ t_1: < \text{Button} = \text{Create, Name} = \text{``''}, \text{Symbol} = \text{`C''}, \\ \text{Atomic number} = 6, \text{Properties} = \text{``''} >$

$t_2: < \text{Button} = \text{Create, Name} = \text{``Carbon''}, \text{Symbol} = \text{`C''}, \\ \text{Atomic number} = -6, \text{Properties} = \text{``Non-metal''} >$

$t_3: < \text{Button} = \text{Show, Name} = \text{``Hydrogen''}, \text{Symbol} = \text{`C''}, \\ \text{Atomic number} = 1, \text{Properties} = \text{``Non-metal''}>$

$t_4: < \text{Button} = \text{Show, Name} = \text{``Carbon''}, \text{Symbol} = \text{`C''}, \\ \text{Atomic number} = 6, \text{Properties} = \text{``''}>$

```
₅: < Button = Show, Name = "", Symbol = "",
     Atomic number = −6, Properties = "Non-metal">
₅: < Button = Create, Name = "", Symbol = "",
     Atomic number = −6 , Properties = "" >
}
```

The 5×6 array of 0s and 1s in Step 2 of procedure SAMNA is sometimes referred to as a *combinatorial object*. While procedure SAMNA is one method for generating combinatorial objects, several other methods appear in the following sections.

Each method for generating combinatorial objects has its advantages and disadvantages that are often measured in terms of the total number of test cases or test configurations generated. In the context of software testing, we are interested in procedures that allow the generation of a small set of test cases, or test configurations, while covering all interaction tuples. Usually, we are interested in covering interaction pairs, though in some cases interaction triples or even quadruples might be of interest.

4.7 PAIRWISE DESIGN: MULTIVALUED FACTORS

Many practical test configurations are constructed from one or more factors where each factor assumes a value from a set containing more than two values. In this section, we will show how to use MOLS to construct test configurations when (a) the number of factors is two or more, (b) the number of levels for each factor is more than two, and (c) all factors have the same number of levels.

Next, we list a procedure for generating test configurations in situations where each factor can be at more than two levels. The procedure uses MOLS(n) when the test configuration requires n factors.

```
Procedure for generating pairwise designs using
mutually orthogonal Latin squares
```

Input: n: Number of factors.

Output: A set of factor combinations such that all level pairs are covered.

Procedure: PDMOLS

/* F_1', F_2', ..., F_n' denote the n factors.

$X_{i,j}^*$ denotes the $j th$ level of the $i th$ factor.

*/

Step 1 Relabel the factors as $F_1, F_2, \ldots, F_n$ such that the following ordering constraint is satisfied: $| F_1 | \geq | F_2 | \geq \ldots \geq | F_{n-1} | \geq | F_n |$. Let $b = |F_1|$ and $k = |F_2|$. Note that two or more labeling are possible when two or more pairs of factors have the same number of levels.

Step 2 Prepare a table containing n columns and $b \times k$ rows divided into b blocks. Label the columns as $F_1, F_2, \ldots, F_n$. Each block contains k rows. A sample table for $n = b = k = 3$, when all factors have an equal number of labels, is shown below.

Block	Row	F_1	F_2	F_3
1	1			
	2			
	3			
2	1			
	2			
	3			
3	1			
	2			
	3			

Step 3 Fill column F_1 with 1s in Block 1, 2s in Block 2, and so on. Fill Block 1 of column F_2 with the sequence $1, 2, \ldots, k$ in rows 1 through k. Repeat this for the remaining blocks. A sample table with columns 1 and 2 filled is shown below.

Block	Row	F_1	F_2	F_3
1	1	1	1	
	2	1	2	
	3	1	3	
2	1	2	1	
	2	2	2	
	3	2	3	
3	1	3	1	
	2	3	2	
	3	3	3	

Step 4 Find $s = n(k)$ MOLS of order k. Denote these MOLS as $M_1, M_2, \ldots, M_s$. Note that $s < k$ for $k > 1$. Recall from Section 4.5 that there are at most $k - 1$ MOLS of order k, and the maximum is achieved when k is prime.

Step 5 Fill Block 1 of Column F_3 with entries from column 1 of M_1, Block 2 with entries from column 2 of M_1, and so on. If the number of blocks $b = b_1 > k$, then reuse the columns of M_1 to fill rows in the remaining $(b_1 - k)$ blocks. Repeat this procedure and fill columns F_4 through F_n using MOLS M_2 through M_s. If $s < (n-2)$, then fill the remaining columns by randomly selecting the values of the corresponding factor. The following sample table for $n = k = 3$ is created using M_1 from Example 4.13.

Block	Row	F_1	F_2	F_3
1	1	1	1	1
	2	1	2	2
	3	1	3	3
2	1	2	1	2
	2	2	2	3
	3	2	3	1
3	1	3	1	3
	2	3	2	1
	3	3	3	2

Step 6 The above table lists nine factor combinations, one corresponding to each row. Each combination can now be used to generate one or more tests as explained in Section 4.2.

In many practical situations, the table of configurations generated using the steps above will need to be modified to handle constraints on factors and to account for factors that have fewer levels than k. There is no general algorithm for handling such special cases. Examples and exercises in the remainder of this chapter illustrate ways to handle a few situations.

End of Procedure PDMOLS

The PDMOLS procedure can be used to generate test configurations that ensure the coverage of all pairwise combinations of factor levels. It is easy to check that the number of test configurations so generated is usually much less than all possible combinations. For example, the total number of combinations is 27 for 3 factors each having 3 levels. However, as illustrated above, the number of test configurations derived using MOLS is only nine.

Applications often impose constraints on factors such that certain level combinations are either not possible or desirable to achieve in practice. The next, rather long, example illustrates the use of PDMOLS in a more complex situation.

Example 4.17: DNA sequencing is a common activity among biologists and other researchers. Several genomics facilities are available that allow a DNA sample to be submitted for sequencing. One such facility is offered by the Applied Genomics Technology Center (AGTC) at the School of Medicine in Wayne State University Detroit, MI, USA. The submission of the sample itself is done using a software application available from the AGTC. We refer to this software as AGTCS.

The AGTCS is supposed to work on a variety of platforms that differ in their hardware and software configurations. Thus, the hardware platform and the operating system are two factors to be considered while developing a test plan for the AGTCS. In addition, the user of the AGTCS, referred to as PI, must either have a profile already created with the AGTCS or create a new one prior to submitting a sample. The AGTCS supports only a limited set of browsers. In all we have a total of four factors with their respective levels listed below.

304

Factor	Levels			
F_1': Hardware (H)	PC	Mac		
F_2': OS (O)	Windows 2000	Windows XP	OS 9	OS 10
F_3': Browser (B)	Explorer	Netscape 4.x	Firefox	Mozilla
F_4': PI (P)	New	Existing		

It is obvious that many more levels can be considered for each factor above. However, for the sake of simplicity, we constrain ourselves to the given list.

There are 64 combinations of the factors listed above. However, given the constraint that PCs and Macs will run their dedicated OSs, the number of combinations reduces to 32, with 16 combinations each corresponding to the PC and the Mac. Note that each combination leads to a test configuration. However, instead of testing the AGTCS for all 32 configurations, we are interested in testing under enough configurations so that all possible pairs of factor levels are covered.

We can now proceed to design test configurations in at least two ways. One way is to treat the testing on the PC and the Mac as two distinct problems and design the test configurations independently.

Exercise 4.12 asks you to take this approach and explore its advantages over the second approach used in this example.

The approach used in this example is to arrive at a common set of test configurations that obey the constraint related to the OSs. Let us now follow a modified version of procedure PDMOLS to generate the test configurations. We use $|F|$ to indicate the number of levels for factor F.

Input: $n = 4$ factors. $|F_1'| = 2$, $|F_2'| = 4$, $|F_3'| = 4$, and $|F_4'| = 2$.

Output: A set of factor combinations such that all pairwise interactions are covered.

Step 1 Relabel the factors as F_1, F_2, F_3, F_4 such that $|F_1| \geq |F_2| \geq |F_3| \geq |F_4|$. Doing so gives us $F_1 = F_2'$, $F_2 = F_3'$, $F_3 = F_1'$, $F_4 = F_4'$, $b = k = 4$. Note that a different assignment is also possible because $|F_1| = |F_4|$ and $|F_2| = |F_3|$. However, any assignment that satisfies the ordering constraint will retain the values of b and k as 4.

Step 2 Prepare a table containing 4 columns and $b \times k = 16$ rows divided into 4 blocks. Label the columns as $F_1, F_2, \ldots, F_n$. Each block contains k rows. The required table is shown below.

Block	Row	F_1(O)	F_2(B)	F_3 (H)	F_4 (P)
1	1				
	2				
	3				
	4				
2	1				
	2				
	3				
	4				
3	1				
	2				
	3				
	4				
4	1				
	2				
	3				
	4				

Step 3 Fill column F_1 with 1s in Block 1, 2s in Block 2, and so on. Fill Block 1 of column F_2 with the sequence $1, 2, \ldots, k$ in rows 1 through k. Repeat this for the remaining blocks. A sample table with columns F_1 and F_2 filled is shown below:

Block	Row	F_1(O)	F_2(B)	F_3 (H)	F_4 (P)
1	1	1	1		
	2	1	2		
	3	1	3		
	4	1	4		
2	1	2	1		
	2	2	2		
	3	2	3		
	4	2	4		
3	1	3	1		
	2	3	2		
	3	3	3		
	4	3	4		
4	1	4	1		
	2	4	2		
	3	4	3		
	4	4	4		

Step 4 Find MOLS of order 4. As 4 is not prime, we cannot use the procedure described in Example 4.13. In such a situation, one may either resort to a predefined set of MOLS of the desired order or construct ones own using a procedure not described in this book but referred to in the Bibliographic Notes section. We follow the former approach and obtain the following set of three MOLS of order 4.

$$M_1 = \begin{matrix} 1 & 2 & 3 & 4 \\ 2 & 1 & 4 & 3 \\ 3 & 4 & 1 & 2 \\ 4 & 3 & 2 & 1 \end{matrix} \qquad M_2 = \begin{matrix} 1 & 2 & 3 & 4 \\ 3 & 4 & 1 & 2 \\ 4 & 3 & 2 & 1 \\ 2 & 1 & 4 & 3 \end{matrix} \qquad M_3 = \begin{matrix} 1 & 2 & 3 & 4 \\ 4 & 3 & 2 & 1 \\ 2 & 1 & 4 & 3 \\ 3 & 4 & 1 & 2 \end{matrix}$$

Step 5 We now fill the remaining two columns of the table constructed in Step 3. As we have only two more columns to be filled, we use entries from M_1 and M_2. The final statistical design is as follows:

Block	Row	F_1(O)	F_2(B)	F_3(H)	F_4(P)
1	1	1	1	1	1
	2	[1]	2	[2]	3*
	3	1	3	3*	4*
	4	1	4	4*	2
2	1	[2]	1	[2]	2
	2	2	2	1	4*
	3	2	3	4*	3*
	4	2	4	3*	1
3	1	3	1	3*	3*
	2	3	2	4*	1
	3	[3]	3	[1]	2
	4	3	4	2	4*
4	1	4	1	4*	4*
	2	4	2	3*	2
	3	4	3	2	1
	4	[4]	4	[1]	3*

A boxed entry indicates a pair that does not satisfy the OS constraint. An entry marked with an asterisk (*) indicates an invalid level.

Step 6 Using the 16 entries in the table above, we can obtain 16 distinct test configurations for the AGTCS. However, we need to resolve two problems before we get to the design of test configurations. One problem is that factors F_3 and F_4 can only assume values 1 and 2, whereas the table above contains other infeasible values for these two factors. These infeasible values are marked with an asterisk (*). One simple way to get rid of the infeasible values is to replace them by an arbitrarily selected feasible value for the corresponding factor.

The other problem is that some configurations do not satisfy the OS constraint. Four such configurations are highlighted in the design above by enclosing the corresponding numbers in rectangles. For example, note the entry in Block 3—Row 3 indicates that factor F_3, that corresponds to Hardware is set at level PC, while factor F_1 that corresponds to Operating System is set to Mac OS 9.

Obviously we cannot delete these rows as this would leave some pairs uncovered. For example, on removing Block 3, Row 3 will leave the following five pairs uncovered: $(F_1 = 3, F_2 = 3)$, $(F_1 = 3, F_4 = 2)$, $(F_2 = 3, F_3 = 1)$, $(F_2 = 3, F_4 = 2)$, and $(F_3 = 1, F_4 = 2)$.

We follow a two-step procedure to remove the highlighted configurations and retain complete pairwise coverage. In the first step, we modify the four highlighted rows so they do not violate the constraint. However, by doing so we leave some pairs uncovered. In the second step, we add new configurations that cover the pairs that are left uncovered when we replace the highlighted rows.

In the modified design, we have replaced the infeasible entries for factors F_3 and F_4 by feasible ones (also see Exercise 4.10). Entries changed to resolve conflicts are highlighted. Also, "don't care" entries are marked with a dash (–). While designing a configuration, a don't care entry can be selected to create any valid configuration.

Block	Row	F_1(O)	F_2(B)	F_3 (H)	F_4 (P)
1	1	1	1	1	1
	2	1	2	[1]	1
	3	1	3	1	2
	4	1	4	2	2
2	1	2	1	[1]	2
	2	2	2	1	1
	3	2	3	1	2
	4	2	4	2	1
3	1	3	1	1	1
	2	3	2	4	1
	3	[1]	3	1	2
	4	3	4	2	2
4	1	4	1	2	2
	2	4	2	1	2
	3	4	3	2	1
	4	[2]	4	1	1
5	1	–	2	2	1
	2	–	1	2	2
	3	3	3	–	2
	4	4	4	–	1

Entries changed to satisfy the OS constraint are boxed. Don't care entries are marked as "–" and can be set to an appropriate level for the corresponding factor. Care must be taken not to violate the OS constraint while selecting a value for a don't care entry.

It is easy to obtain 20 test configurations from the design given above. Recall that we would get a total of 32 configurations if a brute-force method is used. However, by using the PDMOLS procedure, we have been able to achieve a reduction of 12 test configurations. A further reduction can be obtained in the number of test configurations by removing Row 2 in Block 5 as it is redundant in the presence of Row 1 in Block 4 (also see Exercise 4.11).

4.7.1 Shortcomings of Using MOLS for Test Design

While the approach of using MOLS to develop test configurations has been used in practice, it has its shortcomings as enumerated below:

1. *A sufficient number of MOLS might not exist for the problem at hand.*

   As an illustration, in Example 4.17, we needed only two MOLS of order 4 that do exist. However, if the number of factors increases, to say 6, without any change in the value of $k = 4$, then we would be short by one MOLS as there exist only three MOLS of order 4. As mentioned earlier in Step 5 in Procedure PDMOLS, the lack of sufficient MOLS is compensated by randomizing the generation of columns for the remaining factors.

2. *While the MOLS approach assists with the generation of a balanced design in which all interaction pairs are covered an equal number of times, the number of test configurations is often larger than what can be achieved using other methods.*

   For example, the application of procedure PDMOLS to the problem in Example 4.16 leads to a total of nine test cases for testing the GUI. This is in contrast to the six test cases generated by the application of procedure SAMNA.

Several other methods for generating combinatorial designs have been proposed for use in software testing. The most commonly used methods are based on the notions of orthogonal arrays, covering arrays, mixed-level covering arrays, and in-parameter order. These methods are described in the following sections.

4.8 ORTHOGONAL ARRAYS

An orthogonal array is an $N \times k$ matrix in which the entries are from a finite set S of s symbols such that any $N \times t$ subarray contains each t-tuple exactly the same number of times. Such an orthogonal array is denoted by $OA(N, k, s, t)$. The index of an orthogonal array, denoted by λ, is equal to N/s^t. N is referred to as the number of *runs* and t as the *strength* of the orthogonal array.

When using orthogonal arrays in software testing, each column corresponds to a factor and the elements of a column to the levels for the corresponding factor. Each run, or row of the orthogonal array, leads to a test case or a test configuration. The following example illustrates some properties of simple orthogonal arrays.

Example 4.18: The following is an orthogonal array having four runs and a strength of 2. It uses symbols from the set {1, 2}. Notationally, this array is denoted as $OA(4, 3, 2, 2)$. Note that the value of parameter k is 3 and hence we have labeled the columns as F_1, F_2, and F_3 to indicate the three factors.

Run	F_1	F_2	F_3
1	1	1	1
2	1	2	2
3	2	1	2
4	2	2	1

The index λ of the array shown above is $4/2^2 = 1$, implying that each pair ($t = 2$) appears exactly once ($\lambda = 1$) in any 4×2 subarray. There is a total of $s^t = 2^2 = 4$ pairs given as $(1, 1)$, $(1, 2)$, $(2, 1)$, and $(2, 2)$. It is easy to verify, by a mere scanning of the array, that each of the four pairs appears exactly once in each 4×2 subarray.

The orthogonal array shown below has nine runs and a strength of 2. Each of the four factors can be at any one of the three levels. This array is denoted as $OA(9, 4, 3, 2)$ and has an index of 1.

Run	F_1	F_2	F_3	F_4
1	1	1	1	1
2	1	2	2	3
3	1	3	3	2
4	2	1	2	2
5	2	2	3	1
6	2	3	1	3
7	3	1	3	3
8	3	2	1	2
9	3	3	2	1

There are nine possible pairs of symbols formed from the set $\{1, 2, 3\}$. Again, it is easy to verify that each of these pairs occurs exactly once in any 9×2 subarray taken out of the matrix given above.

An alternate notation for orthogonal arrays is also used. For example, L_N (s^k) denotes an orthogonal array of N runs where k factors take on any value from a set of s symbols. Here, the strength t is assumed to be 2. Using this notation, the two arrays in Example 4.18 are denoted by L_4 (2^3) and L_9 (3^3), respectively.

Sometimes a simpler notation L_N is used that ignores the remaining three parameters k, s, and t assuming that they can be determined from the context. Using this notation, the two arrays in Example 4.18 are denoted by L_4 and L_9, respectively. We prefer the notation OA (N, k, s, t).

4.8.1 Mixed-Level Orthogonal Arrays

The orthogonal arrays shown in Example 4.18 are also known as *fixed-level orthogonal arrays*. This is because the design of such arrays assumes that all factors assume values from the same set of s values. As illustrated in Section 4.1.2, this is not true in many practical situations. In many practical applications, one encounters more than one factor, each taking on a different set of values. Mixed-level orthogonal arrays are useful in designing test configurations for such applications.

A mixed, level orthogonal array of strength t is denoted by $MA(N, s_1^{k_1} s_2^{k_2} \ldots s_p^{k_p}, t)$, indicating N runs where k_1 factors are at s_1 levels, k_2 factors at s_2 levels, and so on. The total number of factors is $\Sigma_{i=1}^{p} k_i$.

The formula used for computing the index λ of an orthogonal array does not apply to the mixed-level orthogonal array as the count of values for each factor is a variable. However, the balance property of orthogonal arrays remains intact for mixed-level orthogonal arrays in that any $N \times t$ subarray contains each t-tuple corresponding to the t columns, exactly the same number of times, which is λ. The next example shows two mixed-level orthogonal arrays.

Example 4.19: A mixed-level orthogonal array $MA(8, 2^4 4^1, 2)$ is shown below. It can be used to design test configurations for an application that contains four factors each at two levels and one factor at four levels.

Run	F_1	F_2	F_3	F_4	F_5
1	1	1	1	1	1
2	2	2	2	2	1
3	1	1	2	2	2
4	2	2	1	1	2
5	1	2	1	2	3
6	2	1	2	1	3
7	1	2	2	1	4
8	2	1	1	2	4

Note that the above array is balanced in the sense that in any subarray of size 8×2, each possible pair occurs exactly the same number of times. For example, in the two leftmost columns, each pair occurs exactly twice. In columns 1 and 3, each pair also occurs exactly twice. In columns 1 and 5, each pair occurs exactly once.

The next example shows $MA(16, 2^6 4^3, 2)$. This array can be used to generate test configurations when there are six binary factors, labeled F_1 through F_6, and three factors each with four possible levels, labeled F_7 through F_9.

Run	F_1	F_2	F_3	F_4	F_5	F_6	F_7	F_8	F_9
1	1	1	1	1	1	1	1	1	1
2	2	2	1	2	1	2	1	3	3
3	1	2	2	2	2	1	3	1	3
4	2	1	2	1	2	2	3	3	1
5	1	1	2	2	2	2	1	4	4
6	2	2	2	1	2	1	1	2	2
7	1	2	1	1	1	2	3	4	2
8	2	1	1	2	1	1	3	2	4
9	2	2	1	1	2	2	4	1	4
10	1	1	1	2	2	1	4	3	2
11	2	1	2	2	1	2	2	1	2
12	1	2	2	1	1	1	2	3	4
13	2	2	2	2	1	1	4	4	1
14	1	1	2	1	1	2	4	2	3
15	2	1	1	1	2	1	2	4	3
16	1	2	1	2	2	2	2	2	1

Example 4.20: In Example 4.2, we have three factors at two levels and one factor at three levels. The following mixed array $MA(12, 2^3 3^1, 2)$ can be used to generate 12 test configurations. This implies that a total of 12 configurations are required for exhaustive testing of the pizza service.

Run	Size	Toppings	Address	Phone
1	1	1	1	1
2	1	1	2	1
3	1	2	1	2
4	1	2	2	2
5	2	1	1	2
6	2	1	2	2
7	2	2	1	1
8	2	2	2	1
9	3	1	1	2
10	3	1	2	1
11	3	2	1	1
12	3	2	2	2

Following is the set of test inputs for the pizza service derived using $MA(12, 2^3 3^1, 2)$ shown above. To arrive at the design below, we assumed that levels 1, 2, and 3 for *Size* correspond to `large`, `medium`, and `small`, respectively. Similarly, the levels 1 and 2, corresponding to the remaining three levels, are mapped to their respective values in Example 4.2 with 1 corresponding to the leftmost value and 2 to the rightmost value. Note that this assignment of integers to actual values is arbitrary and does not affect the set of test configurations generated in any way.

Run	Size	Toppings	Address	Phone
1	Large	Custom	Valid	Valid
2	Large	Custom	Invalid	Valid
3	Large	Preset	Valid	Invalid
4	Large	Preset	Invalid	Invalid
5	Medium	Custom	Valid	Invalid
6	Medium	Custom	Invalid	Invalid
7	Medium	Preset	Valid	Valid
8	Medium	Preset	Invalid	Valid
9	Small	Custom	Valid	Invalid
10	Small	Custom	Invalid	Valid
11	Small	Preset	Valid	Valid
12	Small	Preset	Invalid	Invalid

It is easy to check that all possible pairs of factor combinations are covered in the design above. Testing the pizza service under the 12 configurations mentioned above is likely to reveal any pairwise interaction errors.

So far, we have examined techniques for generating balanced combinatorial designs and explained how to use these to generate test configurations and test sets. However, while the balance requirement is often essential in statistical experiments, it is not always so in software testing. For example, if a software application has been tested once for a given pair of factor levels, there is generally no need for testing it again for the same pair unless the application is known to behave nondeterministically. One might also test the application against the same pair of values to ensure repeatability of results. Thus, for deterministic applications, and when repeatability is not the focus of the test, we can relax the balance requirement and instead use *covering arrays*, or *mixed-level covering arrays*, for obtaining combinatorial designs. This is the topic of the next section.

4.9 COVERING AND MIXED-LEVEL COVERING ARRAYS

4.9.1 COVERING ARRAYS

A covering array $CA(N, k, s, t)$ is an $N \times k$ matrix in which entries are from a finite set S of s symbols such that each $N \times t$ subarray contains each possible t-tuple at least λ times. As in the case of orthogonal arrays, N denotes the number of runs, k the number of factors, s the number of levels for each factor, t the strength, and λ the index. While generating test cases or test configurations for a software application, we use $\lambda = 1$.

Let us point to a key difference between a covering array and an orthogonal array. While an orthogonal array $OA(N, k, s, t)$ covers each possible t-tuple λ times in any $N \times t$ subarray, a covering array $CA(N, k, s, t)$ covers each possible t-tuple at least λ times in any $N \times t$ subarray. Thus, covering arrays do not meet the balance requirement that is met by orthogonal arrays. This difference leads to combinatorial designs that are often smaller in size than orthogonal arrays. Covering arrays are also referred to as *unbalanced* designs.

Of course, we are interested in *minimal* covering arrays. These covering arrays satisfy the requirement of a covering array in the least number of runs.

Example 4.21: A balanced design of strength 2 for five binary factors requires eight runs and is denoted by $OA(8, 5, 2, 2)$. However, a covering design with the same parameters requires only six runs. Thus, in this case, we will save two test configurations if we use a covering design instead of the orthogonal array. The two designs follow:

$OA(8, 5, 2, 2) =$

Run	F_1	F_2	F_3	F_4	F_5
1	1	1	1	1	1
2	2	1	1	2	2
3	1	2	1	2	1
4	1	1	2	1	2
5	2	2	1	1	2
6	2	1	2	2	1
7	1	2	2	2	2
8	2	2	2	1	1

$CA(6, 5, 2, 2) =$

Run	F_1	F_2	F_3	F_4	F_5
1	1	1	1	1	1
2	2	2	1	2	1
3	1	2	2	1	2
4	2	1	2	2	2
5	2	2	1	1	2
6	1	1	1	2	2

4.9.2 MIXED-LEVEL COVERING ARRAYS

Mixed-level covering arrays are analogous to mixed-level orthogonal arrays in that both are practical designs that allow the use of factors to assume levels from different sets. A mixed-level covering array is denoted as $MCA(N, s_1^{k_1} s_2^{k_2} \ldots s_p^{k_p}, t)$ and refers to an $N \times Q$ matrix of entries such that $Q = \Sigma_{i=1}^{p} k_i$, and each $N \times t$ subarray contains at least one occurrence of each t-tuple corresponding to the t columns.

Mixed-level covering arrays are generally smaller than mixed-level orthogonal arrays and more appropriate for use in software testing. The next example shows $MCA(6, 2^3 3^1, 2)$. Comparing this with $MA(12, 2^3 3^1, 2)$ from Example 4.20, we notice a reduction of six test inputs.

Run	Size	Toppings	Address	Phone
1	1	1	1	1
2	2	2	1	2
3	3	1	2	2
4	1	2	2	2
5	2	1	2	1
6	3	2	1	1

Note that the array above is not balanced and hence is not a mixed-level orthogonal array. For example, the pair (1, 1) occurs twice in columns *Address* and *Phone*, but the pair (1, 2) occurs only once in the same two columns. However, this imbalance is unlikely to affect the reliability of the software test process as each of the six possible pairs between *Address* and *Phone* are covered and hence will occur in a test input. For the sake of completeness, we list below the set of six tests for the pizza service:

Run	Size	Toppings	Address	Phone
1	Large	Custom	Valid	Valid
2	Medium	Preset	Valid	Invalid
3	Large	Custom	Invalid	Invalid
4	Small	Preset	Invalid	Invalid
5	Large	Custom	Invalid	Valid
6	Small	Preset	Valid	Valid

4.10 ARRAYS OF STRENGTH >2

In the previous sections, we have examined various combinatorial designs all of which have a strength $t = 2$. While tests generated from such designs are targeted at discovering errors due to pairwise interactions, designs with higher strengths are sometimes needed to achieve higher confidence in the correctness of software. Thus, for example, a design with $t = 3$ will lead to tests that target errors due to three-way interactions. Such designs are usually more expensive than designs with $t = 2$ in terms of the number of tests they generate. The next example illustrates a design with $t = 3$.

Example 4.22: Pacemakers are medical devices used for automatically correcting abnormal heart conditions. These devices are controlled by software that encodes several complicated algorithms for sensing, computing, and controlling the heart rate. Testing of a typical modern pacemaker is an intense and complex activity. Testing it against a combination of input parameters is one aspect of this activity. The table below lists only five of the several parameters, and their values, that control the operation of a pacemaker.

Parameter	Levels		
Pacing mode	AAI	VVI	DDD-R
QT interval	Normal	Prolonged	Shortened
Respiratory rate	Normal	Low	High
Blood temperature	Normal	Low	High
Body activity	Normal	Low	High

Due to the high-reliability requirement of the pacemaker, we would like to test it to ensure that there are no pairwise or three-way interaction errors. Thus, we need a suitable combinatorial object with strength 3. We could use an orthogonal array $OA(54, 5, 3, 3)$ that has 54 runs for 5 factors each at 3 levels and is of strength 3. Thus, a total of 54 tests will be required to test for all three-way interactions of the 5 pacemaker parameters (see also Exercises 4.16 and 4.17).

It is noteworthy that a combinatorial array for three or more factors that provides two-way coverage, balanced or unbalanced, also provides some n-way coverage for each $n > 2$. For example, $MA(12, 2^3 3^1, 2)$ in Example 4.20 covers all 20 of the 32 three-way interactions of the three binary and one ternary parameters. However, the mixed-level covering array $MCA(6, 2^3 3^1, 2)$ in Section 4.9.2 covers only 12 of the 20 three-way interactions. While (*Size* = Large, *Toppings* = Custom, *Address* = Invalid) is a three-way interaction covered by $MCA(12, 2^3 3^1, 2)$, the triple (*Size* = Medium, *Toppings* = Custom, *Address* = Invalid) is not covered.

4.11 GENERATING COVERING ARRAYS

Several practical procedures have been developed and implemented for the generation of various types of designs considered in this chapter.

Here, we focus on a procedure for generating mixed-level covering arrays for pairwise designs.

The procedure described below is known as *in-parameter-order*, or simply *IPO*, procedure. It takes the number of factors and the corresponding levels as inputs and generates a covering array that is, at best, near optimal. The covering array generated covers all pairs of input parameters at least once and is used for generating tests for pairwise testing. The term *parameter* in IPO is a synonym for *factor*.

The IPO procedure has several variants, of which only one is presented here. The entire procedure is divided into three parts: the main procedure, named IPO, procedure HG for horizontal growth, and procedure VG for vertical growth. While describing IPO and its subprocedures, we use parameter for factor and value for level.

Procedure for generating pairwise mixed-level
    covering designs

> *Input:* (a) $n \geq 2$: Number of input parameters and (b) number of values for each parameter
>
> *Output:* *CA:* A set of parameter combinations such that all pairs of values are covered at least once.

Procedure: IPO

/*

- $F_1, F_2, \ldots, F_n$ denote n parameters. $q_1, q_2, \ldots, q_n$ denote the number of values for the corresponding parameter.
- T holds partial or complete runs of the form $(v_1, v_2, \ldots, v_k)$, $1 \leq k \leq n$, where v_i denotes a value for parameter F_i, $1 \leq i \leq k$.
- $\mathcal{D}(F)$ denotes the domain of parameter F, that is the set of all values for parameter F.

*/

> Step 1 [*Initialize*] Generate all pairs for parameters F_1 and F_2. Set $T = \{(r, s) \mid \text{for all } r \in \mathcal{D}(F_1) \text{ and } s \in \mathcal{D}(F_2)\}$.
>
> Step 2 [*Possible termination*] if $n = 2$, then set $CA = T$ and terminate the algorithm, else continue.
>
> Step 3 [*Add remaining parameters*] Repeat the following steps for parameters F_k, $k = 3, 4, \ldots, n$.
>
>> 3.1 [*Horizontal growth*] Replace each partial run (v_1, v_2, v_{k-1}) $\in T$ with (v_1, v_2, v_{k-1}, v_k), where v_k is a suitably selected value

of parameter F_k. More details of this step are found in procedure HG described later in this section.

3.2 [*Uncovered pairs*] Compute the set U of all uncovered pairs formed by pairing parameters $F_i, 1 \leq i \leq k - 1$ and parameter F_k.

3.3 [*Vertical growth*] If U is empty, then terminate this step, else continue. For each uncovered pair $u = (v_j, v_k) \in U$, add a run $(v_1, v_2, \ldots, v_j, \ldots, v_{k-1}, v_k)$ to T. Here, v_j and v_k denote values of parameters F_j and F_k, respectively. More details of this step are found in procedure VG described later in this section.

End of Procedure IPO

Procedure for horizontal growth

Input: (a) T: A set of $m \geq 1$ runs of the kind $R = (v_1, v_2, \ldots, v_{k-1}), k > 2$, where $v_i, 1 \leq i \leq (k-1)$ is a value of parameter F_i. (b) Parameter $F \neq F_i, 1 \leq i \leq (k-1)$.

Output: T': A set of runs $(v_1, v_2, \ldots, v_{k-1}, v_k), k > 2$ obtained by extending the runs in T that cover the maximum number of pairs between parameter $F_i, 1 \leq i \leq (k-1)$ and parameter F.

318

Procedure: HG

/*

- $\mathcal{D}(F) = \{l_1, l_2, \ldots, l_q\}, q \geq 1$.
- $t_1, t_2, \ldots, t_m$ denote the $m \geq 1$ runs in T.
- For a run $t \in T$, where $t = (v_1, v_2, \ldots, v_{k-1})$, $extend(t, v) = (v_1, v_2, \ldots, v_{k-1}, v)$, where v is a value of parameter F.
- Given $t = (v_1, v_2, \ldots, v_k - 1)$ and v is a parameter value, $pairs \ (extend \ (t, v)) = \{(v_i, v_2), 1 \leq i \leq (k-1)\}$.

*/

Step 1 Let $AP = \{(r, s)|$, where r is a value of parameter $F_i, 1 \leq i \leq (k-1)$ and $s \in \mathcal{D}(F)\}$. Thus, AP is the set of all pairs formed by combining parameters $F_i, 1 \leq i \leq (k-1)$, taken one at a time, with parameter F.

Step 2 Let $T' = \emptyset$. T' denotes the set of runs obtained by extending the runs in T in the following steps:

Step 3 Let $C = min(q, m)$. Here, C is the number of elements in the set T or the set $\mathcal{D}(F)$, whichever is less.

Step 4 Repeat the next two substeps for $j = 1$ to C.

    4.1 Let $t'_j = extend(t_j, l_j)$. $T' = T' \cup t'_j$.

    4.2 $AP = AP - pairs(t'_j)$.

Step 5 If $C = m$ then return T'.

Step 6 We will now extend the remaining runs in T by values of parameter F that cover the maximum pairs in AP.

    Repeat the next four substeps for $j = C + 1$ to m.

    6.1 Let $AP' = \emptyset$ and $v' = l_1$.

    6.2 In this step, we find a value of F by which to extend run t_j. The value that adds the maximum pairwise coverage is selected.

    Repeat the next two substeps for each $v \in \mathcal{D}(F)$.

    6.2.1 $AP'' = \{(r, v)|$, where r is a value in run $t_j\}$. Here AP'' is the set of all new pairs formed when run t_j is extended by v.

    6.2.2 If $|AP''| > |AP'|$ then $AP' = AP''$ and $v' = v$.

    6.3 Let $t'_j = extend(t_j, v')$. $T' = T' \cup t'_j$.

    6.4 $AP = AP - AP'$.

Step 7 Return T'.

```
End of Procedure HG

Procedure for vertical growth
```

Input: (a) T: A set of $m \geq 1$ runs each of the kind $(v_1, v_2, \ldots, v_{k-1}, v_k)$, $k > 2$, where v_i, $1 \leq i \leq k$ is a value of parameter F_i. (b) The set MP of all pairs (r, s), where r is a value of parameter F_i, $1 \leq i \leq (k-1)$, $s \in \mathcal{D}(F_k)$, and the pair (r, s) is not contained in any run in T.

Output: A set of runs $(v_1, v_2, \ldots, v_{k-1}, v_k)$, $k > 2$ such that all pairs obtained by combining values of parameter F_i, $1 \leq i \leq (k-1)$ with parameter F_k are covered.

Procedure: VG

```
/*
```

- $\mathcal{D}(F) = \{l_1, l_2, \ldots, l_q\}$, $q \geq 1$.
- $t_1, t_2, \ldots, t_m$ denote the $m \geq 1$ runs in T.
- $(A_i.r, B_j.s)$ denotes a pair of values r and s that correspond to parameters A and B, respectively.
- In run $(v_1, v_2 \ldots, v_{i-1}, *, v_{i+1}, \ldots, v_k)$, $i < k$, an "$*$" denotes a don't care value for parameter F_i. When needed, we use dc instead of "$*$".

```
*/
```

Step 1 Let $T' = \emptyset$.

Step 2 Add new tests to cover the uncovered pairs.

For each missing pair $(F_i.r, F_k.s) \in MP$, $1 \le i < k$, repeat the next two substeps.

2.1 If there exists a run $(v_1, v_2 \ldots, v_{i-1}, *, v_{i+1}, \ldots, v_{k-1}, s) \in T'$, then replace it by the run $(v_1, v_2 \ldots, v_{i-1}, r, v_{i+1}, \ldots, s)$ and examine the next missing pair, else go to the next substep.

2.2 Let $t = (dc_1, dc_2 \ldots, dc_{i-1}, r, dc_{i+1}, \ldots, dc_{k-1}, s)$, $1 \le i < k$. Add t to T'.

Step 3 For each run $t \in T'$, replace any don't care entry by an arbitrarily selected value of the corresponding parameter. Instead, one could also select a value that maximizes the number of higher-order tuples such as triples.

Step 4 Return $T \cup T'$.

End of Procedure VG

Example 4.23: Suppose that we want to find a mixed covering design $MCA(N, 2^1 3^2, 2)$. Let us name the three parameters as A, B, and C where parameters A and C each have three values and parameter B has two values. The domains of A, B, and C are, respectively, $\{a_1, a_2, a_3\}$, $\{b_1, b_2\}$, and $\{c_1, c_2, c_3\}$.

IPO. Step 1: Note that we have $n = 3$. In this step, we construct all runs that consist of pairs of values of the first two parameters, A and B. This leads to the following set:

$T = \{(a_1, b_1), (a_1, b_2), (a_2, b_1), (a_2, b_2), (a_3, b_1), (a_3, b_2)\}$. We denote the elements of this set, starting from the first element, as $t_1, t_2, \ldots, t_6$.

As $n \ne 2$, we continue to Step 3. We will execute the loop for $k = 3$. In the first substep inside the loop, we perform HG (Step 3.1) using procedure HG. In HG. Step 1, we compute the set of all pairs between parameters A and C and parameters B and C. This leads us to the following set of 15 pairs:

$AP = \{(a_1, c_1), (a_1, c_2), (a_2, c_3), (a_2, c_1), (a_2, c_2), (a_2, c_3), (a_3, c_1),$
$(a_3, c_2), (a_3, c_3), (b_1, c_1), (b_1, c_2), (b_1, c_3), (b_2, c_1), (b_2, c_2),$
$(b_2, c_3)\}$

Next, in HG. Step 2 we initialize T' to $\emptyset$. In HG. Step 3 we compute $C = min(q, m) = min(3, 6) = 3$. (Do not confuse this C with the parameter C.) We now move to HG. Step 4 where we begin the extension of the runs in T with $j = 1$.

HG. Step 4.1: $t_1' = extend(t_1, l_1) = (a_1, b_1, c_1)$. $T' = \{(a_1, b_1, c_1)\}$.

HG. Step 4.2: The run we just created by extending t_1 has covered the pairs (a_1, c_1) and (b_1, c_1). We now update AP as follows.

$$AP = AP - \{(a_1, c_1), (b_1, c_1)\}$$
$$= \{(a_1, c_2), (a_1, c_3), (a_2, c_1), (a_2, c_2), (a_2, c_3), (a_3, c_1), (a_3, c_2), (a_3, c_3)$$
$$(b_1, c_2), (b_1, c_3), (b_2, c_1), (b_2, c_2), (b_2, c_3)\}$$

Repeating the above substeps for $j = 2$ and $j = 3$, we obtain the following.

HG. Step 4.1: $t_2' = extend(t_2, l_2) = (a_1, b_2, c_2)$. $T' = \{(a_1, b_1, c_1), (a_1, b_2, c_2)\}$.

HG. Step 4.2:

$$AP = AP - \{(a_1, c_2), (b_2, c_2)\}$$
$$= \{(a_1, c_3), (a_2, c_1), (a_2, c_2), (a_2, c_3), (a_3, c_1), (a_3, c_2), (a_3, c_3)$$
$$(b_1, c_2), (b_1, c_3), (b_2, c_1), (b_2, c_3)\}$$

HG. Step 4.1: $t_3' = extend(t_3, l_3) = (a_2, b_1, c_3)$. $T' = \{(a_1, b_1, c_1), (a_1, b_2, c_2), (a_2, b_1, c_3)\}$.

HG. Step 4.2:

$$AP = AP - \{(a_2, c_3), (b_1, c_3)\}$$
$$= \{(a_1, c_3), (a_2, c_1), (a_2, c_2), (a_3, c_1), (a_3, c_2), (a_3, c_3).$$
$$(b_1, c_2), (b_2, c_1), (b_2, c_3)\}$$

Moving to HG. Step 5, we find that $C \neq 6$ and hence we continue at HG. Step 6. We repeat the substeps for $j = 4, 5,$ and 6. Let us first do it for $j = 4$.

HG. Step 6.1: $AP' = \emptyset$ and $v' = c_1$. Next, we move to HG. Step 6.2. In this step, we find the best value of parameter C for extending run t_j. This step is to be repeated for each value of parameter C. Let us begin with $v = c_1$.

HG. Step 6.2.1: If we were to extend run t_4 by v, we get the run (a_2, b_2, c_1). This run covers two pairs in AP, namely (a_2, c_1) and (b_2, c_1). Hence, we get $AP'' = \{(a_2, c_1), (b_2, c_1)\}$.

HG. Step. 6.2.2: As $|AP''| > |AP'|$, we set $AP' = \{(a_2, c_1), (b_2, c_1)\}$ and $v' = c_1$. Next, we repeat the two substeps 6.2.1 and 6.2.2 for $v = c_2$ and then $v = c_3$.

HG. Step 6.2.1: Extending t_4 by $v = c_2$, we get the run (a_2, b_2, c_2). This extended run leads to one pair in AP. Hence, $AP'' = \{(a_2, c_2)\}$.

HG. Step 6.2.2: As $|AP''| < |AP'|$, we do not change AP'.

HG. Step 6.2.1: Now extending t_4 by $v = c_3$, we get the run (a_2, b_2, c_3). This extended run gives us (b_2, c_3) in AP. Hence, we get $AP'' = \{(b_2, c_3)\}$.

HG. Step 6.2.2: As $|AP''| < |AP'|$, we do not change AP'. This completes the execution of the inner loop. We have found that the best way to extend t_4 is to do so by c_1.

HG. Step 6.3: $t_4' = extend(t_4, c_1) = (a_2, b_2, c_1)$.

$$T' = \{(a_1, b_1, c_1), (a_1, b_2, c_2), (a_2, b_1, c_3), (a_2, b_2, c_1)\}.$$

HG. Step 6.4: Update AP by removing the pairs covered by t_4'.

$$\begin{aligned}
AP = AP &- \{(a_2, c_1), (b_2, c_1)\} \\
&= \{(a_1, c_3), (a_2, c_2), (a_3, c_1), (a_3, c_2), (a_3, c_3) \\
&\quad (b_1, c_2), (b_2, c_3)\}
\end{aligned}$$

We now move to the case $j = 5$ and find the best value of parameter C to extend t_5.

HG. Step 6.1: $AP' = \varnothing$, $v' = c_1$, and $v = c_1$.

HG. Step 6.2.1: If we were to extend run t_5 by v, we get the run (a_3, b_1, c_1). This run covers one pair in the updated AP, namely (a_3, c_1). Hence, we get $AP'' = \{(a_3, c_1)\}$.

HG. Step 6.2.2: As $|AP''| > |AP'|$, we set $AP' = \{(a_3, c_1)\}$ and $v' = c_1$.

HG. Step 6.2.1: Extending t_5 by $v = c_2$, we get the run (a_3, b_1, c_2). This extended run gives us two pairs (a_3, c_2) and (b_1, c_2) in the updated AP. Hence, $AP'' = \{(a_3, c_2), (b_1, c_2)\}$.

HG. Step 6.2.2: As $|AP''| > |AP'|$, $AP' = \{(a_3, c_2), (b_1, c_2)\}$ and $v' = c_2$.

HG. Step 6.2.1: Next, we extend t_5 by $v = c_3$ and get (a_3, b_1, c_3). This extended run gives the pair (a_3, c_3) in AP. Hence, we get $AP'' = \{(a_3, c_3)\}$.

HG. Step 6.2.2: As $|AP''| < |AP'|$, we do not change $AP' = \{(a_3, c_2), (b_1, c_2)\}$. This completes the execution of the inner loop. We have found that the best way to extend t_5 is to do so by c_2. Note that this is not the only best way to extend t_5.

HG. Step 6.3: $t_5' = extend(t_5, c_2) = (a_3, b_1, c_2)$.

$$\mathcal{T}' = \{(a_1, b_1, c_1), (a_1, b_2, c_2), (a_2, b_1, c_3), (a_2, b_2, c_1), (a_3, b_1, c_2)\}.$$

HG. Step 6.4: Update AP by removing the pairs covered by t_5'.

$$AP = AP - \{(a_3, c_2), (b_1, c_2)\}$$
$$= \{(a_1, c_3), (a_2, c_2), (a_3, c_1), (a_3, c_3), (b_2, c_3)\}$$

Finally, we move to the last iteration of the outer loop in HG, execute it for $j = 6$, and find the best value of parameter C to extend t_6.

HG. Step 6.1: $AP' = \varnothing$, $v' = c_1$, and $v = c_1$.

HG. Step 6.2.1: If we were to extend run t_6 by v, we get the run (a_3, b_2, c_1). This run covers one pair in the updated AP, namely (a_3, c_1). Hence, we get $AP'' = \{(a_3, c_1)\}$.

HG. Step 6.2.2: As $|AP''| > |AP'|$, we set $AP' = \{(a_3, c_1)\}$ and $v' = c_1$.

HG. Step 6.2.1: Extending t_6 by $v = c_2$, we get the run (a_3, b_2, c_2). This extended run gives us no pair in the updated AP. Hence $AP'' = \varnothing$.

HG. Step 6.2.2: As $|AP''| < |AP'|$, AP' and v' remain unchanged.

HG. Step 6.2.1: Next, we extend t_6 by $v = c_3$ and get (a_3, b_2, c_3). This extended run gives two pairs (a_3, c_3) and (b_2, c_3) in AP. Hence, we get $AP'' = \{(a_3, c_3), (b_2, c_3)\}$.

HG. Step 6.2.2: As $|AP''| > |AP'|$, we set $AP' = \{(a_3, c_3), (b_2, c_3)\}$ and $v' = c_3$. This completes the execution of the inner loop. We have found that c_3 is the best value of C to extend t_6.

HG. Step 6.3: $t'_6 = extend(t_6, c_3) = (a_3, b_2, c_3)$.

$$T' = \{(a_1, b_1, c_1), (a_1, b_2, c_2), (a_2, b_1, c_3), (a_2, b_2, c_1), (a_3, b_1, c_2),$$
$$(a_3, b_2, c_3)\}.$$

HG. Step 6.4: Update AP by removing the pairs covered by t'_6.

$$AP = AP - \{(a_3, c_3), (b_2, c_3)\}$$
$$= \{(a_1, c_3), (a_2, c_2), (a_3, c_1)\}$$

HG. Step 7: We return to the main IPO procedure with T' containing six runs.

IPO. Step 3.2: The set of runs T is now the same as the set T' computed in procedure HG. The set of uncovered pairs U is $\{(a_1, c_3), (a_2, c_2), (a_3, c_1)\}$. We now move to procedure VG for vertical growth.

IPO. Step 3.3: For each uncovered pair in U, we need to add runs to T.

VG. Step 1: We have $m = 6$, $F = C$, $\mathcal{D}(F) = \{c_1, c_2, c_3\}$, $MP = U$, and $T' = \emptyset$. Recall that m is the number of runs in T', F denotes the parameter to be used for vertical growth, and MP the set of missing pairs.

V.G. Step 2: We will consider each missing pair in MP and repeat the substeps. We begin with the pair $(A.a_1, C.c_3)$.

V.G. Step 2.1: As T' is empty, we move to the next step.

V.G. Step 2.2: $t = (a_1, *, c_3)$. $T' = \{(a_1, *, c_3)\}$.

V.G. Step 2: Next missing pair: $\{(A.a_2, C.c_2)\}$.

V.G. Step 2.1: No run in T' is of the kind $(*, dc, c_2)$.

V.G. Step 2.2: $t = (a_2, *, c_2)$. $T' = \{(a_1, *, c_3), (a_2, *, c_2)\}$.

V.G. Step 2: Next missing pair: $\{(A.a_3, C.c_1)\}$.

V.G. Step 2.1: No run in T' is of the kind $(*, dc, c_1)$.

V.G. Step 2.2: $t = (a_3, *, c_1)$. $T' = \{(a_1, *, c_3), (a_2, *, c_2), (a_3, *, c_1)\}$. We are done with Step 2.

V.G. Step 3: We now replace the don't cares in T' and obtain the following:

$$T' = \{(a_1, b_2, c_3), (a_2, b_1, c_2), (a_3, b_1, c_1)\}$$

V.G. Step 4: We return to procedure IPO with the following set of runs:

$$\{(a_1, b_1, c_1), (a_1, b_2, c_2), (a_2, b_1, c_3), (a_2, b_2, c_1), (a_3, b_1, c_2),$$

$$(a_3, b_2, c_3), (a_1, b_2, c_3), (a_2, b_1, c_2), (a_3, b_1, c_1)\}$$

Step 3: This loop is now terminated as there are no more parameters to be processed. The covering array we wanted to find, namely $MCA(9, 2^1 3^2, 2)$, is listed below in row–column format. We have replaced a_i and c_i by $i, 1 \leq i \leq 3$ and b_i by $i, 1 \leq i \leq 2$. Parameters A, B, and C are labeled as F_1, F_2, and F_3, respectively.

Run	$F_1(A)$	$F_2(B)$	$F_3(C)$
1	1	1	1
2	1	2	2
3	2	1	3
4	2	2	1
5	3	1	2
6	3	2	3
7	1	2	3
8	2	1	2
9	3	1	1

This completes our presentation of an algorithm to generate covering arrays. A detailed analysis of the algorithm has been given by its authors (see the Bibliographic Notes section). To be of any practical use, procedure IPO needs several modifications. Exercise 4.23 lists various types of constraints that are often found in practice and asks you to implement a revised version of procedure IPO.

SUMMARY

This chapter has covered a well-known set of techniques for the generation of tests for software applications. These techniques fall under the general umbrella of *model-based testing* and assist with the generation of tests using combinatorial designs. The primary goal of these techniques is to allow the selection of a small number of tests, or test configurations, from a potentially huge test input, or test configuration, domain. While this is also the goal of techniques such as equivalence partitioning and boundary-value analysis, test generation based on combinatorial designs is a more formal, and often complementary, discipline.

The combinatorial designs covered in this chapter include orthogonal arrays, mixed orthogonal arrays, covering arrays, and mixed-level covering arrays. In addition, we have explained how to generate tests using MOLS. Mixed-level covering arrays seem to be the most popular choice of combinatorial designs among software testers. While there exist several tools and methods for the generation of such designs, we have chosen to describe the IPO procedure due to its effectiveness in generating near-minimal mixed-level covering designs and simplicity. Several exercises, and a term project, at the end of this chapter are designed to help you to test and further sharpen your understanding of combinatorial design-based software testing.

Combinatorial designs are used in a variety of fields, such as behavioral science, biology, and agriculture, for the design of experiments. Their use in software testing was first proposed in 1985 by Mandl [305] who showed how Latin squares can be used in the design of tests for a compiler. A few years later, Brownlie *et al.* [58] used combinatorial designs in the testing of the AT&T PMX/StarMAIL application. Design of tests using orthogonal arrays has also been proposed by Phadke [396, 397] and Sherwood [440].

A concise publication by Dalal and Mallows [107] and the development of a commercial tool named Automatic Efficient Testcase Generator (AETG) [474] reported by Cohen *et al.* [96] brought the combinatorial designs into more widespread use in the software testing arena. Prior to the development of AETG, Sherwood had developed a tool named constrained Array Test System (CATS) [440] for the generation of covering designs. The primary difference between CATS and AETG, as reported by Cohen *et al.* [96], is in the way the two tools handle constraints on the factors. AETG offers the AETGSpec [105] notation in which to specify constraints on input parameters. Cohen *et al.* have reported that AETG generates smaller designs than CATS [99].

AETG and its applications are described by several authors [95, 98, 105]. Burr and Young [68] measured code coverage obtained while testing Nortel's e-mail system against tests generated using AETG and found that 97% of the branches were covered. They were able to reduce the test space from about 27 trillion test inputs needed for exhaustive testing to about 100 test inputs generated using AETG. Cohen *et al.* [95] reported structural and data-flow coverage of applications tested against tests generated by AETG.

Paradkar [388] proposed an alternate to covering arrays for generating combinatorial designs. Paradkar's algorithm generates tests from behavioral specifications written in a Specification and Abstraction Language for Testing (SALT) [386, 387]. Paradkar also gives examples of situations where combinatorial designs of strength 2 are inadequate for detecting certain types of errors.

Grindal et al. [180] compared several combinatorial test-generation strategies using the size of the generated tests and their fault detection ability. They experimented with five programs with a total of 33 known faults. Another 118 faults were injected in order to obtain meaningful differences in the fault detection capabilities of the test-generation strategies. They found that the combinatorial design strategy for $n = 1$, which they refer to as the base choice combination strategy, generated the least number of test cases (30) and revealed 90% of the faults injected as compared to the strategy using orthogonal arrays that generated 191 test cases and revealed 98% of the faults. The corresponding numbers using AETG are 181 test cases and 98% faults detected. The strategy using $n = 1$ requires that each *interesting* value of each factor is used at least once and, in addition, uses semantic information regarding the program to generate additional test cases. The additional test cases are derived using inputs that belong to the invalid input subset of the input domain of the program under test.

Other applications of the use of combinatorial designs in software testing are reported by Kuhn and Reilly [275], Kuhn et al. [276], Nair et al. [344], Heller [213], Huller [241], and Smith et al. [450]. West [507] and Cohen et al. [97] discuss interaction faults in realistic situations. As discussed in this chapter, interaction faults are the target of tests generated using combinatorial designs.

While AETG continues to be one of the popular commercial tools for the generation of combinatorial designs and test cases, other tools have also been developed. Tung and Aldiwan developed a tool named test case generator (TCG) [479] for the generation of tests using covering arrays. They conducted experiments using TCG and concluded that the number of tests generated by TCG compared favorably to those generated by AETG and were about 25% less than those generated by another tool named Remote Agent Experiment (RAX) [450]. CATS developed by Sherwood [440] has been mentioned above.

An interesting incident in the history of Latin squares dates back to 1782 when the famous mathematician Leonhard Euler [141] conjectured that MOLS of order $4n + 2$ do not exist. However, this conjecture was proven incorrect by Bose et al. [57]. An early effort in using a computer to search for MOLS is reported by Bose et al. [55, 56]. Colbourn and Dinitz [102] provide a survey of various constructions of MOLS. Another useful reference for Latin squares and various combinatorial designs is the handbook by Colbourn and Dinitz [103].

Certain combinatorial arrangements were first proposed by Rao [406] in 1946. These arrangements later became known as orthogonal arrays [70]. Hedayat et al. [211] is an excellent reference on orthogonal arrays and their relationships to MOLS and other combinatorial arrangements.

Dalal and Mallows [96, 107] argued against the balance requirement in orthogonal arrays when used in software testing. Instead, they proposed the use of covering designs and mixed-level covering designs used in the AETG system. Covering designs had been proposed earlier by Sloane [449] in the context of coding theory. While the AETG system is covered by US Patent 5, 542, 043, several nonpatented algorithms exist for the generation of covering and mixed-level covering arrays in the open literature.

Lei and Tai [285] proposed the IPO algorithm for the generation of covering designs. While only one version of this algorithm is described in this chapter, others appear in the cited publication. Lei and Tai found that the IPO algorithm performs almost as well, as the AETG in the size of the generated arrays. Procedure SAMNA described in this chapter is due to Maity et al. [302].

Cohen et al. [101] presented variable-strength covering arrays. Such arrays allow for different strengths of coverage for subsets of parameters. For example, if an application has four parameters, A, B, C, and D, one might require that all interaction pairs be covered while all triples formed by A, B, and C be covered. They offer several techniques for the construction of covering and variable-strength covering arrays, and provide an empirical comparison of arrays generated using several algorithms, including the one used in AETG. Cohen *et al.* [100] and Renè *et al.* [414] describe greedy algorithms for the generation of multilevel covering arrays. The problem of generating minimal multilevel covering arrays continues to be a topic of considerable interest among researchers.

Test generation using combinatorial designs falls under model-based testing [105, 106], a topic that has received considerable attention among researchers and practitioners alike. However, there is a large variety of test generation techniques that belong to model-based testing. Several such techniques such as test generation using FSMs and statecharts are covered in this book. Hartman offers a detailed survey of combinatorial design techniques in testing software and hardware [203].

BIBLIOGRAPHIC NOTES

EXERCISES

4.1 When and why would an infeasible test case be useful?

4.2 Program P4.1 contains two `if` statements. As explained in Example 4.8, this program contains an interaction fault. Consider a test set T that ensures that each of the two `if` statements is executed at least once and that each of the two conditions $(x == x_1$ and $y == y_2)$ and $(x == x_2$ and $y == y_1)$ evaluates to `true` and `false` in some execution on an input from T. (a) Does there exist a T that will not reveal the interaction fault? (b) Why might the value of z cause the fault to be not revealed even when the fault is triggered?

4.3 Construct an example program that contains one two-way and one three-way interaction fault. Generate a test set T that reveals the two interaction faults. Specify any conditions that must be satisfied for T to be able to reveal the faults.

4.4 A set X is known as a *quasigroup* under a binary operation *op* if (a) *op* is defined on the elements of X and (b) there exist unique elements $x, y \in X$ such that for all $a, b \in X$, a *op* $x = b$ and y *op* $a = b$. Prove that the multiplication table for the quasigroup is a Latin square. (For answer see pages 16–17 in [129].)

4.5 Construct a multiplication table of nonzero integers modulo 5. For example, in your table, $2 \times 4 = 3$. (a) Is the table you constructed a Latin square, and if so, of what order? (b) Can you generalize this method to construct a Latin square of any order $n > 2$?

4.6 Construct a 4×4 addition table of binary 2-bit strings modulo 2. For example, $01 + 11 = 10$ and $11 + 11 = 00$. Replace each element in the table by its decimal equivalent plus 1. For example, 11 is replaced by 4. Is the resulting table a Latin square? Generalize this method for constructing Latin squares of order n.

4.7 Construct MOLS(7) given $S = \{*, \circ, \bullet, \times, \Delta, \nabla\}$. (Note: You may have guessed that it is easier to write a computer program to construct MOLS(n) when n is a prime or a power of prime than to do so by hand, especially for larger values of n.)

4.8 Given three two-valued factors X and Z, list all minimal sets of factor combinations that cover all pairs of values.

4.9 *Let N(n)* denote the maximum number of MOLS. What is $N(k)$ for $k = 1, 2, 3$?

4.10 In Example 4.17, we modified the design generated using MOLS so as to satisfy the OS constraint. However, we did so by altering the values in specific entries so that all pairs are covered. Suggest other ways to resolving the infeasible values when using MOLS to generate test configurations. Discuss advantages and disadvantages of the ways you suggest.

4.11 Example 4.17 illustrates how to obtain a statistical design that covers all interaction pairs in 20 configurations instead of 32.

   (a) Enumerate all test configurations by listing the levels for each factor.
   (b) How many interaction pairs are covered more than once?
   (c) Derive an alternate design that covers all interaction pairs and satisfies the OS and hardware related constraint.
   (d) Is your design better than the design in Example 4.17 in any way?
   (e) Can you think of any error in the AGTCS software that might not be discovered by testing against the 20 configurations derived in Example 4.17?

4.12 This exercise is intended to show how constraints on factors could lead to the partitioning of the test configuration problem into two or more simpler problems that are solved independently using the same algorithm.

   (a) Design test configurations for testing the AGTCS application described in Example 4.17. Use the PDMOLS procedure to arrive at two sets of test configurations, one for the PC and the other for the Mac. Note that the PDMOLS procedure is to be applied on two sets of factors, one related to the PC and the other to the Mac.
   (b) Compare the test configurations derived in (a) with those derived in Example 4.17 in terms of their impact on the test process for AGTCS.

4.13 How many test cases will be generated if the PDMOLS procedure is applied to the GUI problem in Example 4.16?

4.14 Given three factors $x \in \{-1, 1\}$, $y \in \{-1, 1\}$, and $z \in \{0, 1\}$, construct an orthogonal array $OA(N, 3, 2, 2)$. (a) Using the array you have constructed, derive a set of N tests for the program in Example 4.9. (b) Which of the N tests triggers the fault in

EXERCISES

Program P4.2? (c) What conditions must be satisfied for the fault to be revealed, that is propagate to the output of the program? (d) Construct, if possible, nontrivial functions f and g that will prevent the triggered fault to propagate to the output.

4.15 Consider an application iAPP intended to be used from any of the three different browsers (Netscape, Internet Explorer, and Firefox) running on the three OSs (Windows, Mac, and Linux). The application must be able to connect to other devices using any of the three connection protocols (LAN, PPP, and ISDN). The application must also be able to send output to a printer that is networked or local, or to the screen.

(a) Identify the factors and levels in the problem mentioned above.

(b) Use procedure PDMOLS to generate test configurations for iAPP.

4.16 Example 4.22 suggests the use of $OA(54, 5, 3, 3)$ to cover all three-way inter actions. Look up for this array on the Internet and design all 54 tests for the pacemaker. The following URL should take you to the site containing a large number of orthogonal and mixed orthogonal arrays:

`http://www.research.att.com/~njas/oadir/`

(Should this site become unavailable, refer to the *CRC Handbook of Combinatorial Design* cited in the Bibliographic Notes section.) How many tests are required if the coverage requirement is relaxed to pairwise coverage?

4.17 As indicated in Example 4.22, a total of 54 tests are required to cover all three-way interactions. (a) What is the minimum number of tests required to test for all three-way interactions, given five parameters each assuming one of three values? (b) Design a minimal covering array $CA(N, 5, 3, 3)$, where N is the number of runs needed.

4.18 A *complete factorial* array of Q factors is a combinatorial object that contains all possible combinations of Q factors. In some cases, a combinatorial array is a minimal size array of a given strength and index. Which of the following arrays is complete factorial? (We have not specified the number of runs. For answers, visit the site mentioned in Exercise 4.16.)

(a) $MA(N, 3^1 5^1, 2)$

(b) $OA(N, 4, 3, 2)$

(c) $MA(N, 2^1 3^1, 2)$

(d) $OA(N, 5, 2, 4)$

4.19 Justify the name *in-parameter-order* for procedure IPO.

4.20 Is $MCA(10, 2^1 3^2, 2)$, generated in Example 4.23 using procedure IPO, a minimal array? Is this a mixed orthogonal array?

4.21 In Example 4.23, we assumed $F_1 = A$, $F_2 = B$, and $F_3 = C$. Would the size of the resulting array be different if we were to use the assignment $F_1 = A$, $F_2 = C$, and $F_3 = B$?

4.22 (a) At Step 3 of procedure VG, We can replace the don't care values to maximize the number of higher-order tuples. Can you replace the don't care values in Example 4.23, VG. Step 3, so that the number of triples covered is more than the number covered in the array given at the end of the Section 4 (Example 4.23)?
(b) What is the minimum array size needed to cover all possible triples of factors A, B, and C?

4.23 *This is a term project.*

(a) Consider the following types of constraints that might exist in a software test environment.

Prohibited pairs

A set of pairs that must not appear in the covering array.

Prohibited higher-order tuples

A set of n-order tuples, $n > 2$, must not appear in a covering array of strength 2.

Factor coupling

If factor A is set to r then factor B must be set to s, where s and s belong to, respectively, $\mathcal{D}(A)$ and $\mathcal{D}(B)$. This relationship can be generalized to the following.
If $X(F_1, F_2, \ldots, F_n)$, then $Y_1, Y_2, \ldots, Y_m$; $n, m \geq 1$.
Where X is a relation among one of more factors and Y s are constraints on factors. For example, a simple relation exists when $X \in \{ <, \leq, =, >, \geq, \neq \}$. Such relations might also exist among more than two factors.

Procedure IPO does not consider any factor-related constraints while generating a covering design. Rewrite IPO by including the ability to input and satisfy the constraints listed above. You might solve this problem in an incremental fashion. For example, you might start with modifying IPO so that only the *prohibited pairs* constraint is included. Then proceed to include the other constraints incrementally.

(b) Think of some practical relations that correspond to X above. Include these in the revised IPO.

(c) Write a Java applet that implements the revised IPO procedure.

(d) If you want to commercialize your applet and make some money by selling it, watch out for companies that have patented algorithms for the generation of combinatorial designs.

5

Test Selection, Minimization, and Prioritization for Regression Testing

CONTENT

The purpose of this chapter is to introduce techniques for the selection, minimization, and prioritization of tests for regression testing. The source T from which tests are selected is likely derived using a combination of black-box and white-box techniques and used for system or component testing. However, when this system or component is modified, for whatever reason, one might be able to retest it using only a subset of T and ensure that despite the changes the existing unchanged code continues to function as desired. A sample of techniques for the selection, minimization, and prioritization of this subset is presented in this chapter.

5.1 WHAT IS REGRESSION TESTING?

The word *regress* means to return to a previous, usually worse, state. Regression testing refers to that portion of the test cycle in which a program P' is tested to ensure that not only does the newly added or modified code behaves correctly, but also that code carried over unchanged from the previous version P continues to behave correctly. Thus regression testing is useful, and needed, whenever a new version of a program is obtained by modifying an existing version.

Regression testing is sometimes referred to as "program revalidation". The term "corrective regression testing" refers to regression testing of a program obtained by making corrections to the previous versions. Another term "progressive regression testing" refers to regression testing of a program obtained by adding new features. A typical regression-testing scenario often includes both corrective and progressive regression testing. In any case, techniques described in this chapter are applicable to both types of regression testing.

To understand the process of regression testing, let us examine a development cycle exhibited in Figure 5.1. The figure shows a highly simplified develop–test–release process for program P, which is referred to as Version 1. While P is in use, there might be a need to add new features, remove any reported errors, and rewrite some code to improve performance. Such modifications lead to P' referred to as Version 2. This modified version must be tested for any new functionality (Step 5 in the figure). However, when making modifications to P, developers might mistakenly add or remove code that causes the existing and unchanged

Version 1	Version 2
1. Develop P	4. Modify P to P'
2. Test P	5. Test P' for new functionality
3. Release P	6. Perform regression testing on P' to ensure that the code carried over from P behaves correctly
	7. Release P'

Fig. 5.1 Two phases of product development and maintenance. Version 1 (P) is developed, tested, and released in the first phase. In the next phase, Version 2 (P') is obtained by modifying Version 1.

functionality from P to stop behaving as desired. One performs regression testing (Step 6) to ensure that any malfunction of the existing code is detected and repaired prior to the release of P'.

It should be obvious from the above description that regression testing can be applied in each phase of software development. For example, during unit testing, when a given unit such as a class is modified by adding new methods, one needs to perform regression testing to ensure that methods not modified continue to work as required. Certainly, regression testing is redundant in cases where the developer can demonstrate through suitable arguments that the methods added can have no effect on the existing methods.

Regression testing is also needed when a subsystem is modified to generate a new version of an application. When one or more components of an application are modified, the entire application must also be subject to regression testing. In some cases, regression testing might be needed when the underlying hardware changes. In this case, regression testing is performed despite any change in the software.

In the remainder of this chapter, you will find various techniques for regression testing. It is important to note that some techniques introduced in this chapter, while sophisticated, might not be applicable in certain environments while absolutely necessary in others. Hence, it is not only important to understand the technique for regression testing but also its strengths and limitations.

5.2 REGRESSION-TEST PROCESS

A regression test process is exhibited in Figure 5.2. The process assumes that P' is available for regression testing. There is usually a long series of tasks that lead to P' from P. These tasks, not shown in Figure 5.2, include creation of one or more modification requests and the actual modification of the design and the code. A modification request might lead to a simple error fix or to a complex redesign and coding of a

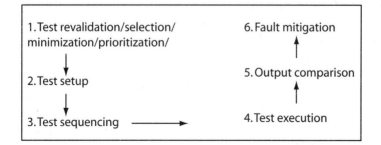

Fig. 5.2   A subset of tasks in regression testing.

component of P. In any case, regression testing is recommended after P has been modified and any newly added functionality tested and found correct.

The tasks in Figure 5.2 are shown as if they occur in the given sequence. This is not necessarily true and other sequencings are also possible. Several of the tasks shown can be completed while P is being modified to P'. It is important to note that except in some cases, for test selection, all tasks shown in the figure are performed in almost all phases of testing and are not specific to regression testing.

5.2.1 TEST REVALIDATION, SELECTION, MINIMIZATION, AND PRIORITIZATION

While it would be ideal to test P' against all tests developed for P, this might not be possible for several reasons. For example, there might not be sufficient time available to run all tests. Also, some tests for P might become invalid for P' due to reasons such as a change in the input data and its format for one or more features. In yet another scenario, the inputs specified in some tests might remain valid for P' but the expected output might not. These are some reasons that necessitate Step 1 in Figure 5.2.

Test revalidation refers to the task of checking which tests for P remain valid for P'. Revalidation is necessary to ensure that only tests that are applicable to P' are used during regression testing.

Test selection can be interpreted in several ways. Validated tests might be redundant in that they do not traverse any of the modified portions in P'. The identification of tests that traverse modified portions of P' is often referred to as the test selection and sometimes as the *regression-test selection* (RTS) problem. However, note that both test minimization and prioritization described in the following paragraphs are also techniques for test selection.

Test minimization discards tests seemingly redundant with respect to some criteria. For example, if both t_1 and t_2 test function f in P, then one might decide to discard t_2 in favor of t_1. The purpose of minimization is to reduce the number of tests to execute for regression testing.

Test prioritization refers to the task of prioritizing tests based on some criteria. A set of prioritized tests becomes useful when only a subset of tests can be executed due to resource constraints. Test selection can be achieved by selecting a few tests from a prioritized list. However, several other methods for test selection are available as discussed later in this chapter. Revalidation, followed by selection, minimization, and prioritization is one possible sequence to execute these tasks.

Example 5.1: A Web service is a program that can be used by another program over the Web. Consider a Web service named ZC, short for ZipCode. The initial version of ZC provides two services: ZtoC and ZtoA. Service ZtoC inputs a zip code and returns a list of cities and the corresponding state, while ZtoA inputs a zip code and returns the corresponding area code. We assume that while the ZC service can be used over the Web from wherever an Internet connection is available, it serves only the United States.

Let us suppose that ZC has been modified to ZC′ as follows. First, a user can select the zip code from a list of countries and supply it to obtain the corresponding city in that country. This modification is made only to the ZtoC function while ZtoA remains unchanged. Note that the term *zip code* is not universal. For example, in India, the equivalent term is *pin code* which is six-digit long as compared to the five-digit zip code used in the United States.

Second, a new service named ZtoT has been added that inputs a country and a zip code and returns the corresponding time zone.

Consider the following two tests (only inputs specified) used for testing ZC:

$$t_1 : < service = ZtoC, zip = 47906 >$$
$$t_2 : < service = ZtoA, zip = 47906 >$$

A simple examination of the two tests reveals that test t_1 is not valid for ZC′ as it does not list the required country field. Test t_2 is valid as we have made no change to ZtoA. Thus, we need to either discard t_1 and replace it by a new test for the modified ZtoC or simply modify t_1 appropriately. We prefer to modify and hence our validated regression-test suite for ZC′ is as follows:

$$t_1 : < country = USA, service = ZtoC, zip = 47906 >$$
$$t_2 : < service = ZtoA, zip = 47906 > .$$

Note that testing ZC′ requires additional tests to test the ZtoT service. However, we need only the two tests listed above for regression testing. To keep this example short, we have listed only a few tests for ZC. In practice, one would develop a much larger suite of tests for ZC that will then be the source of regression tests for ZC′.

5.2.2 TEST SETUP

Test setup refers to the process by which the application under test is placed in its intended, or simulated, environment ready to receive data and able to transfer any desired output information. This process could be as simple as double clicking on the application icon to launch it for testing and as complex as setting up the entire special-purpose hardware and monitoring equipment, and initializing the environment before the test could begin. Test setup becomes even more challenging when testing embedded software such as that found in printers, cell phones, automated teller machines, medical devices, and automobile engine controllers.

Note that test setup is not special to regression testing, it is also necessary during other stages of testing such as during integration or system testing. Often test setup requires the use of simulators that allow the replacement of a "real device" to be controlled by the software with its simulated version. For example, a heart simulator is used while testing a commonly used heart control device known as the pacemaker. The simulator allows the pacemaker software to be tested without having to install it inside a human body.

The test setup process and the setup itself are highly dependent on the application under test and its hardware and software environment. For example, the test setup process and the setup for an automobile engine control software is quite different from that of a cell phone. In the former, one needs an engine simulator or the actual automobile engine to be controlled, while in the latter, one needs a test driver that can simulate the constantly changing environment.

5.2.3 TEST SEQUENCING

The sequence in which tests are input to an application may be of concern. Test sequencing often becomes important for an application that has an internal state and is continuously running. Banking software, Web service, and engine controller are examples of such applications. Sequencing requires grouping and sequencing tests to be run together. The following example illustrates the importance of test sequencing.

> Example 5.2: Consider a simplified banking application referred to as SATM. Application SATM maintains account balances and offers users the following functionality: login, deposit, withdraw, and exit. Data for each account is maintained in a secure database.
>
> Figure 5.3 exhibits the behavior of SATM as an FSM. Note that the machine has six distinct states, some referred to as modes in the figure. These are labeled as Initialize, LM, RM, DM, UM, and WM. When launched, SATM performs initialization operations, generates an "ID?" message, and moves to the LM state. If a user enters a valid ID, SATM moves to the RM state, else it remains in the LM state and again requests for an ID.
>
> While in the RM state, the application expects a service request. Upon receiving a Deposit request, it enters the DM state and asks

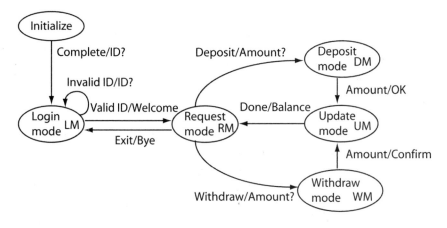

Fig. 5.3 State transition in a simplified banking application. Transitions are labeled as
X/Y, where X indicates an input and Y the expected output. "Complete" is
an internal input indicating that the application moves to the next state upon
completion of operations in its current state.

for an amount to be deposited. Upon receiving an amount, it generates a confirmatory message and moves to the UM state where it
updates the account balance and gets back to the RM state. A similar behavior is shown for the Withdraw request. SATM exits the RM
state upon receiving an Exit request.

Let us now consider a set of three tests designed to test the
Login, Deposit, Withdraw, and Exit features of SATM. The tests are
given in the following table in the form of a test matrix. Each test
requires that the application be launched fresh and the user (tester in
this case) log in. We assume that the user with ID = 1 begins with an
account balance of 0. Test t_1 checks the login module and the Exit
feature, t_2 the Deposit module, and t_3 the Withdraw module. As you
might have guessed, these tests are not sufficient for a thorough test
of SATM, but they suffice to illustrate the need for test sequencing
as explained later.

Test	Input Sequence	Expected Output Sequence	Module Tested
t_1	ID = 1, Request = Exit	Welcome, Bye	Login
t_2	ID = 1, Request = Deposit, Amount = 50	ID?, Welcome, Amount?, OK, Done, 50	Deposit
t_3	ID = 1, Request = Withdraw, Amount = 30	ID?, Welcome, Amount?, 30, Done, 20	Withdraw

Now suppose that the Withdraw module has been modified to implement a change in withdrawal policy, for example "No more than $300 can be withdrawn on any single day." We now have the modified SATM' to be tested for the new functionality as well as to check if none of the existing functionality has broken. What tests should be rerun ?

Assuming that no other module of SATM has been modified, one might propose that tests t_1 and t_2 need not be rerun. This is a risky proposition unless some formal technique is used to prove that indeed the changes made to the Withdraw module cannot affect the behavior of the remaining modules.

Let us assume that the testers are convinced that the changes in SATM will not affect any module other than Withdraw. Does this mean that we can run only t_3 as a regression test? The answer is in the negative. Recall our assumption that testing of SATM begins with an account balance of 0 for the user with $ID = 1$. Under this assumption, when run as the first test, t_3 is likely to fail because the expected output will not match the output generated by SATM' (see Exercise 5.1).

The argument above leads us to conclude that we need to run test t_3 after having run t_2. Running t_2 ensures that SATM' is brought to the state in which we expect test t_3 to be successful.

Note that the FSM shown in Figure 5.3 ignores the values of internal variables and databases used by SATM and SATM'. During regression as well as many other types of testing, test sequencing is often necessary to bring the application to a state where the values of internal variables, and contents of the databases used, correspond to the intention at the time of designing the tests. It is advisable that such intentions (or assumptions) be documented along with each test.

5.2.4 TEST EXECUTION

Once the testing infrastructure has been setup, tests selected, revalidated, and sequenced, it is time to execute them. This task is often automated using a generic or a special-purpose tool. General-purpose tools are available to run regression tests for applications such as Web service (see Section 5.10). However, most embedded systems, due to their unique hardware requirements, often require special-purpose tools that input a test suite and automatically run the application against it in a batch mode.

The importance of a tool for test execution cannot be overemphasized. Commercial applications tend to be large and the size of the regression test suite usually increases as new versions arrive. Manual execution of regression tests might become impractical and error prone.

5.2.5 OUTPUT COMPARISON

Each test needs verification. This is also done automatically with the help of the test execution tool that compares the generated output with the expected output. However, this might not be a simple process, especially in embedded systems. In such systems, often it is the internal state of the application, or the state of the hardware controlled by the software application, that must be checked. This is one reason why generic tools that offer an oracle might not be appropriate for test verification.

One of the goals for test execution is to measure an application's performance. For example, one might want to know how many requests per second can be processed by a Web service. In this case performance, and not functional correctness, is of interest. The test execution tool must have special features to allow such measurements.

5.3 RTS: THE PROBLEM

Let us examine the regression test selection problem with respect to Figure 5.4. Let P denote Version X that has been tested using test set T against specification S. Let P' be generated by modifying P. The behavior of P' must conform to specification S'. Specifications S and S' could be the same and P' is the result of modifying P to remove faults.

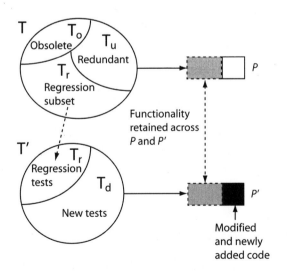

Fig. 5.4 Regression testing as a test selection problem. A subset T_r of set T is selected for retesting the functionality of P that remains unchanged in P'.

S' could also be different from S in that S' contains all features in S and a few more, or that one of the features in S has been redefined in S'.

The regression-testing problem is to find a test set T_r on which P' is to be tested to ensure that code that implements functionality carried over from P works correctly. As shown in Figure 5.4, often T_r is a subset of T used for testing P.

In addition to regression testing, P' must also be tested to ensure that the newly added code behaves correctly. This is done using a newly developed test set T_d. Thus, P' is tested against $T' = T_r \cup T_d$, where T_r is the regression-test suite and T_d the development test suite intended to test any new functionality in P'. Note that we have subdivided T into three categories: redundant tests (T_u), obsolete tests (T_o), and regression tests (T_r). While P is executed against the entire T, P' is executed only against the regression set T_r and the development set T_d. Tests in T that cause P to terminate prematurely or enter into an infinite loop might be included in T_o or in T_r depending on their purpose.

In summary, the RTS problem is stated as follows: Find a minimal T_r such that $\forall t \in T_r$ and $t' \in T_u \cup T_r$, $P(t) = P'(t) \Rightarrow P(t') = P'(t')$. In other words, the RTS problem is to find a minimal subset T_r of non-obsolete tests from T such that if P' passes tests in T_r then it will also pass tests in T_u. Note that determination of T_r requires that we know the set of obsolete tests T_o. Obsolete tests are those no longer valid for P' for some reason.

Identification of obsolete tests is a largely manual activity. As mentioned earlier, this activity is often referred to as *test-case revalidation*. A test case valid for P might be invalid for P' because the input, output, or both input and output components of the test are rendered invalid by the modification to P. Such a test case either becomes obsolete and is discarded while testing P' or is corrected and becomes a part of T_r or T_u.

Note that the notion of *correctness* in the above discussion is with respect to the correct functional behavior. It is possible that a solution to the RTS problem ignores a test case t on which P' fails to meet its performance requirement whereas P does. Algorithms for test selection in the remainder of this chapter ignore the performance requirement.

5.4 SELECTING REGRESSION TESTS

In this section, we summarize several techniques for selecting tests for regression testing. Details of some of these techniques follow in the subsequent sections.

5.4.1 Test All

This is perhaps the simplest of all regression-testing techniques. The tester is unwilling to take any risks and tests the modified program P' against all non-obsolete tests from P. Thus, with reference to Figure 5.4, we use $T' = T - T_o$ in the test-all strategy.

While the test-all strategy might be the least risky among the ones described here, it does suffer from a significant disadvantage. Suppose that P' has been developed and the added functionality verified. Assume that 1 week remains to release P'. However, the test-all strategy will require at least 3 weeks for completion. In this situation, one might want to use a smaller regression-test suite than $T - T_o$. Various techniques for obtaining smaller regression-test sets are discussed later in this chapter. Nevertheless, the test-all strategy combined with tools for automated regression-test tools is perhaps the most widely used technique in the commercial world.

5.4.2 Random Selection

Random selection of tests for regression testing is one possible method to reduce the number of tests. In this approach, tests are selected randomly from the set $T - T_o$. The tester can decide how many tests to select depending on the level of confidence required and the available time for regression testing.

Under the assumption that all tests are equally good in their fault detection ability, the confidence in the correctness of the unchanged code increases with an increase in the number of tests sampled and executed successfully. However, in most practical applications such an assumption is unlikely to hold. This is because some of the sampled tests might bear no relationship to the modified code while others might. This is the prime weakness of the random selection approach to regression testing. Nevertheless, random selection might turn out to be better than no regression testing at all.

5.4.3 Selecting Modification-traversing Tests

Several RTS techniques aim to select a subset of T such that only tests that guarantee the execution of modified code and code that might be impacted by the modified code in P' are selected, while those that do not are discarded. These techniques use methods to determine the desired subset and aim at obtaining a minimal regression-test suite. Techniques that obtain a minimal regression-test suite without discarding any test that will traverse a modified statement are known as *safe* RTS techniques.

A key advantage of modification-traversing tests is that when under time crunch, testers need to execute only a relatively smaller number of regression tests. Given that a safe technique is used, execution of such tests is likely a superior alternative to the test-all and random-selection strategies.

The sophistication of techniques to select modification-traversing tests requires automation. It is impractical to apply these techniques to large commercial systems unless a tool is available that incorporates at least one safe test minimization technique. Further, while test selection appears attractive from the test effort point of view, it might not be a practical technique when tests are dependent on each other in complex ways and that this dependency cannot be incorporated in the test selection tool.

5.4.4 TEST MINIMIZATION

Suppose that T_r is a modification-traversing subset of T. There are techniques that could further reduce the size of T_r . Such test minimization techniques aim at discarding redundant tests from T_r. A test t in T_r is considered redundant if another test u in T_r achieves the same objective as t. The objective in this context is often specified in terms of code coverage such as basic block coverage or any other form of control-flow or data-flow coverage. Requirements coverage is another possible objective used for test minimization.

While test minimization might lead to a significant reduction in the size of the regression-test suite, it is not necessarily safe. When tests are designed carefully, minimization might discard a test case whose objective does match that used for minimization. The next example illustrates this point.

Example 5.3: Consider the following trivial program P' required to output the sum of two input integers. However, due to an error, the program outputs the difference of the two integers.

```
1 int x, y;
2 input (x, y);
3 output(x-y)
```

Now suppose that T_r contains 10 tests, 9 with $y = 0$ and 1, say t_{nz}, with nonzero values of both x and y. t_{nz} is the only test that causes P' to fail.

Suppose that T_r is minimized so that the basic block coverage obtained by executing P' remains unchanged. Obviously, each of the 10 tests in T_r covers the lone basic block in P' and therefore all but 1 test will be discarded by a minimization algorithm. If t_{nz} is the one discarded then the error in P' will not be revealed by the minimized test suite.

While the above example might seem trivial, it does point to the weakness of test minimization. Situations depicted in this example could arise in different forms in realistic applications. Hence, it is recommended that minimization be carried out with caution. Tests discarded by a minimization algorithm must be reviewed carefully before being truely discarded.

5.4.5 Test Prioritization

One approach to RTS is through test prioritization. In this approach, a suitable metric is used to rank all tests in T_r (see Figure 5.4). A test with the highest rank has the highest priority, the one with the next highest rank has the second highest priority, and so on. Prioritization does not eliminate any test from T_r. Instead, it allows the tester to decide which tests to select based on their relative priority and individual relationships based on sequencing and other requirements.

> **Example 5.4:** Let R_1, R_2, and R_3 be three requirements carried over unchanged from P to P'. One approach first ranks the requirements for P' according to their criticality. For example, a ranking might be: R_2 most critical, followed by R_3, and finally R_1. Any new requirements implemented in P' but not in P are not used in this ranking as they correspond to new tests in set T_d as shown in Figure 5.4.
>
> Now suppose that the regression subset T_r from P is $\{t_1, t_2, t_3, t_4, t_5\}$ and that t_1 tests R_1, t_2 and t_3 test R_2, and t_4 and t_5 test R_3. We can now prioritize the tests in this order: t_2, t_3, t_4, t_5, t_1, where t_2 has the highest priority for execution and t_1 the lowest. It is up to the tester to decide which tests to select for regression testing. If the tester believes that changes made to P to arrive at P' are unlikely to have any effect on code that implements R_3, then tests t_4 and t_5 need not be executed. In case the tester has resources to run only three tests before P' is to be released, then t_2, t_3, and t_4 can be selected.

Several other more sophisticated techniques are available for test prioritization. Some of these use the amount of code covered as a metric to prioritize tests. These techniques, and others for test selection, are discussed in the following sections.

5.5 Test Selection Using Execution Trace

Let P be a program containing one or more functions. P has been tested against tests in T as shown in Figure 5.4. P is modified to P' by adding new functionality and fixing some known errors. The newly added functionality has been tested and found correct. Also, the corrections made have been tested and found adequate. Our goal now is to test P' to ensure that the changes made do not affect the functionality carried over from P. While this could be achieved by executing P' against all the non-obsolete tests in T, we want to select only those that are necessary to check if the modifications made do not affect functionality common to P and P'.

Our first technique for selecting a subset of T is based on the use of execution slice obtained from the execution trace of P. The technique can be split into two phases. In the first phase, P is executed and the execution slice recorded for each test case in $T_{no} = T_u \cup T_r$ (see Figure 5.4). T_{no} contains no obsolete test cases and hence is a candidate for full regression test. In the second phase, the modified program P' is compared with P, and T_r is isolated from T_{no} by an analysis of the execution slice obtained in the first phase.

5.5.1 Obtaining the Execution Trace

Let $G = (N, E)$ denote the CFG of P, N being a set of nodes and E a set of directed edges joining the nodes. Each node in N corresponds to a basic block in P. *Start* and *End* are two special elements of N such that *Start* has no ancestor and *End* has no descendant. For each function f in P, we generate a separate CFG denoted by G_f. The CFG for P is also known as the main CFG and corresponds to the main function in P. All other CFGs are known as child CFGs. When necessary, we will use the notation CFG (f) to refer to the CFG of function f.

Nodes in each CFG are numbered as 1, 2, and so on, with 1 being the number of the *Start* node. A node in a CFG is referred to by prefixing the function name to its number. For example, P.3 is node 3 in G_P and f.2 node 2 in G_f.

We execute P against each test in T_{no}. During execution against $t \in T_{no}$, the execution trace is recorded as *trace* (t). The execution trace is a sequence of nodes. We save an execution trace as a set of nodes touched during the execution of P. Such a set is also known as an execution slice of P. *Start* is the first node in an execution trace and *End* the last node. Notice that an execution trace contains nodes from functions of P invoked during its execution.

Example 5.5: Consider Program P5.1. It contains three functions: main, g1, and g2. The CFGs and child CFGs appear in Figure 5.5.

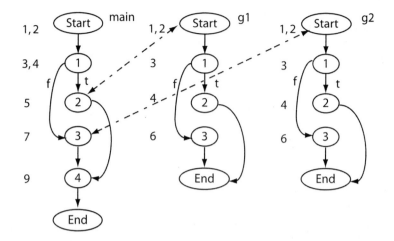

Fig. 5.5 CFG for function `main`, and its child functions `g1` and `g2` in Program P5.1. Line numbers corresponding to each basic block, represented as a node, are placed to the left of the corresponding node. Labels t and f indicate, respectively, true and false values of the condition in the corresponding node. Dotted lines indicate points of function calls.

Program P5.1

```
 1  main(){            1  int g1(int a, b){  1  int g2 (int a, b){
 2  int x,y,p;         2  int a,b;           2  int a,b;
 3  input (x,y);       3  if(a+ 1==b)        3  if(a==(b+1))
 4  if (x<y)           4      return(a*a);   4      return(b*b);
 5    p=g1(x,y);       5  else               5  else
 6  else               6      return(b*b);   6      return(a*a);
 7    p=g2(x,y);       7  }                  7  }
 8  endif
 9  output (p);
10  end
11  }
```

Now consider the following test set:

$$T = \begin{Bmatrix} t_1 :< x = 1, y = 3 > \\ t_2 :< x = 2, y = 1 > \\ t_3 :< x = 3, y = 1 > \end{Bmatrix}$$

Executing Program P5.1 against the three test cases in T results in the following execution traces corresponding to each test and the CFGs in Figure 5.5. We have shown the execution trace as a sequence of nodes traversed. However, a tool that generates the trace can, for the purpose of test selection, save it as a set of nodes, thereby conserving memory space.

Test (t)	Execution trace ($trace(t)$)
t_1	main.Start, main.1, main.2, g1.Start, g1.1, g1.3, g1.End, main.2, main.4, main.End.
t_2	main.Start, main.1, main.3, g2.Start, g2.1, g2.2, g2.End, main.3, main.4, main.End.
t_3	main.Start, main.1, main.2, g1.Start, g1.1, g1.2, g1.End, main.2, main.4, main.End.

While collecting the execution trace, we assume that P is started in its initial state for each test input. This might create a problem for continuously running programs, for example an embedded system that requires initial setup and then responds to external events that serve as test inputs. In such cases, a sequence of external events serves as test case. Nevertheless, we assume that P is brought into an initial state prior to the application of any external sequence of inputs that is considered a test case in T_{no}.

Let $test(n)$ denote the set of tests such that each test in $test(n)$ traversed node n at least once. Given the execution trace for each test in T_{no}, it is easy to find $test(n)$ for each $n \in N$. $test(n)$ is also known as test vector corresponding to node n.

Example 5.6: Test vectors for each node in the CFGs shown in Figure 5.5 can be found from the execution traces given in Example 5.5. These are listed in the following table. All tests traverse the *Start* and *End* nodes and hence the corresponding test vectors are not listed.

Function	Test vector ($test(n)$) for node n			
	1	2	3	4
main	t_1, t_2, t_3	t_1, t_3	t_2	$t_1, t_2\ t_3$
g1	t_1, t_3	t_3	t_1	–
g2	t_2	t_2	None	–

5.5.2 SELECTING REGRESSION TESTS

This is the second phase in the selection of modification-traversing regression tests. It begins when P' is ready, and has been tested and found correct in any added functionality and error fixes. The two key steps in this phase are: construct CFG and syntax trees for P' and select tests. These two steps are described in the following paragraph.

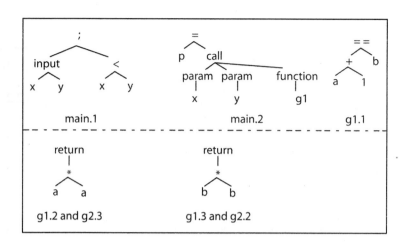

Fig. 5.6 Syntax trees for some nodes in the CFGs of functions `main`, `g1`, and `g2` of P shown in Figure 5.5. A semicolon (;) indicates left to right sequencing of two or more statements within a node.

Construct CFG and syntax trees: The first step in this phase is to get the CFG of P' denoted as $G' = (N', E'')$. We now have G and G' as the CFGs of P and P'. Recall that other than the special nodes, each node in a CFG corresponds to a basic block.

During the construction of G and G', a syntax tree is also constructed for each node. Although not mentioned earlier, syntax trees for G can be constructed during the first phase. Each syntax tree represents the structure of the corresponding basic block denoted by a node in the CFG. This construction is carried out for the CFGs of each function in P and P'.

The syntax trees for the *Start* and *End* nodes consist of exactly one node each labeled, respectively, *Start* and *End*. The syntax trees for other nodes are constructed using traditional techniques often used by compiler writers. In a syntax tree, a function call is represented by parameter nodes, one for each parameter, and a call node. The call node points to a leaf labeled with the name of the function to be called.

Example 5.7: Syntax trees for some nodes in Figure 5.5 are shown in Figure 5.6. Note the semicolon that labels the tree for node 1 in function `main`. It indicates left to right sequencing of statements or expressions.

Compare CFGs and select tests: In this step the CFGs for P and P' are compared and a subset of T selected. The comparison starts from the *Start* nodes of the `main` functions of P and P' and proceeds further

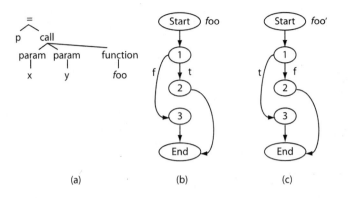

(a)   (b)   (c)

Fig. 5.7 Syntax trees with identical function call nodes but different function CFGs. (a) Syntax tree for nodes *n* and n^1, respectively in *G* and *G'*.(b) CFG for *foo* in P. (c) CFG for *foo'* in *P'*.

down recursively identifying corresponding nodes that differ in *P* and *P'*. Only tests that traverse such nodes are selected.

While traversing the CFGs, two nodes $n \in N$ and $n' \in N'$ are considered equivalent if the corresponding syntax trees are identical. Two syntax trees are considered identical when their roots have the same labels and the same corresponding descendants (see Exercise 5.4). Function calls can be tricky. For example, if a leaf node is labeled as a function name *foo*, then the CFGs of the corresponding functions in *P* and *P'* must be compared to check for the equivalence of the syntax trees.

Example 5.8: Suppose that the basic blocks in nodes *n* and *n'* in *G* and *G'* have identical syntax trees shown in Figure 5.7(a). However, these two nodes are not considered equivalent because the CFGs of function *foo* in *P*, and *foo* in *P'*, are not identical. The difference in the two CFGs is due to different labels of edges going out of node 1 in the CFGs. In Figure 5.7(b), the edge labeled *f* goes to node 3, while the edge with the same label goes to node 2 in Figure 5.7(c).

```
Procedure for selecting modification-traversing
tests
```

    Input • G, G': CFGs of programs *P* and *P'* and syntax trees corresponding to each node in a CFG.
        • Test vector *test(n)* for each node *n* in each CFG.
        • *T* : Set of non-obsolete tests for *P*.
    Output: T': A subset of *T*.
    Procedure: `SelectTestsMain`

```
/*
```

After initialization, procedure `SelectTests` is invoked. In turn `SelectTests` recursively traverses G and G' starting from their corresponding start nodes. A node n in G found to differ from its corresponding node in G' leads to the selection of all tests in T that traverse n.

```
*/
```

Step 1 Set $T' = \emptyset$. Unmark all nodes in G and in its child CFGs.

Step 2 Call procedure `SelectTests` (G. Start, G'.Start'), where G.Start and G'.Start' are, respectively, the start nodes in G and G'.

Step 3 T' is the desired test set for regression testing P'.

```
End of Procedure SelectTestsMain
```

Procedure: `SelectTests` (N, N')

Input: N, N', where N is a node in G and N' its corresponding node in G'.

Output: T'.

Step 1 Mark node N to ensure that it is ignored in the next encounter.

Step 2 If N and N' are not equivalent, then $T' = T' \cup test(N)$ and return, otherwise go to the next step.

Step 3 Let S be the set of successor nodes of N. Note that S is empty if N is the *End* node.

Step 4 Repeat the next step for each $n \in S$.
  4.1 If n is marked then return else repeat the following steps.
    4.1.1 Let $l = label(N, n)$. The value of l could be t, f, or $\in$ (for empty).
    4.1.2 $n' = getNode(l, N')$. n' is the node in G' that corresponds to n in G. Also, the label on edge (N', n') is l.
    4.1.3 `SelectTests` (n, n').

Step 5 Return from `SelectTests`.

```
End of Procedure SelectTests
```

Example 5.9: Next, we illustrate the RTS procedure using Program P5.1. The CFGs of functions `main`, `g1`, and `g2` are shown in Figure 5.5. *test(n)* for each node in the three functions is given in Example 5.6.

Now suppose that function g1 is modified by changing the condition at line 3 as shown in Program P5.2. The CFG of g1 changes only in that the syntax tree of the contents of node 1 is now different from that shown in Figure 5.5. We will use the SelectTests procedure to select regression tests for the modified program. Note that all tests in T in Example 5.5 are valid for the modified program and hence are candidates for selection.

Program P5.2

```
1  int g1(int a, b){  ← Modified g1.
2  int a, b;
3  if(a-1==b)  ← Predicate modified.
4    return(a*a),
5  else
6    return(b*b),
7  }
```

Let us follow the steps as described in SelectTestsMain. G and G' refer to, respectively, the CFGs of Program P5.1 and its modified version—the only change being in g1.

SelectTestsMain.Step 1: $T' = \emptyset$.

SelectTestsMain.Step 2: SelectTests(G.main.Start, G'.main.Start).

SelectTests.Step 1: $N =$ G.main.Start and $N' = G'$.main.Start. MarkG.main.Start.

SelectTests.Step 2 G.main.Start and G'.main.Start are equivalent hence proceed to the next step.

SelectTests.Step 3 $S = succ(G.$Start$) = \{$G.main.1$\}$.

SelectTests.Step 4: Let $n =$ G.main.1.

SelectTests.Step 4.1: n is unmarked hence proceed further.

SelectTests.Step 4.1.1: $l = label($G.main.Start, $n) = \epsilon$.

SelectTests.Step 4.1.2: $n' = getNode(\epsilon,$ G'.Start$) =$ G'.main.1.

SelectTests.Step 4.1.3: SelectTests(n, n').

SelectTests.Step 1: $N =$ G.main.1 and $N' =$ G'.main.1. Mark G.main.1.

SelectTests.Step 2 G.main.1 and G'.main.1 are equivalent hence proceed to the next step.

SelectTests.Step 3 $S = succ($G.main.1$) = \{$G.main.2, G.main.3$\}$.

SelectTests.Step 4: Let $n =$ G.main.2.

`SelectTests.`Step 4.1: n is unmarked hence proceed further.

`SelectTests.`Step 4.1.1: $l = label(G.\text{main}.1, n) = t$.

`SelectTests.`Step 4.1.2: $n' = getNode(l, G'.\text{main}.1) = G'.\text{main}.2$.

`SelectTests.`Step 4.1.3: `SelectTests` (n, n').

`SelectTests.`Step 1: $N = G.\text{main}.2$ and $N' = G'.\text{main}.2$. Mark G.main.1.

As G.main.2 contains a call to `g1`, the equivalence needs to be checked with respect to the CFGs of `g1` and `g2`. N and N' are not equivalent due to the modification in `g1`. Hence, $T' = tests(N) = tests(G.\text{main}.2) = \{t_1, t_3\}$. This call to `SelectTests` terminates. We continue with the next element of S. Exercise 5.6 asks you to complete the steps in this example.

5.5.3 HANDLING FUNCTION CALLS

The `SelectTests` algorithm compares respective syntax trees while checking for the equivalence of two nodes. In the event the nodes being checked contain a call to function f that has been modified to f', a simple check as in Example 5.9 indicates nonequivalence if f and f' differ along any one of the corresponding nodes in their respective CFGs. This might lead to selection of test cases that do not execute the code corresponding to a change in f.

355

> Example 5.10: Suppose that `g1` in Program P5.1 is changed by replacing line 4 by `return (a*a*a)`. This corresponds to a change in node 2 in the CFG for `g1` in Figure 5.5. It is easy to conclude that despite t_1 not traversing node 2, `SelectTests` will include t_1 in T'. Exercise 5.7 asks you to modify `SelectTests`, and the algorithm to check for node equivalence, to ensure that only tests that touch the modified nodes inside a function are included in T'.

5.5.4 HANDLING CHANGES IN DECLARATIONS

The `SelectTests` algorithm selects modification-traversing tests for regression testing. Suppose that a simple change is made to variable declaration and that this declaration occurs in the main function. `SelectTests` will be unable to account for the change made simply because we have not included declarations in the CFG.

One method to account for changes in declarations is to add a node corresponding to the declarations in the CFG of a function. This is done for the CFG of each function in P. Declarations for global variables belong to a node placed immediately following the `Start` node in the CFG for `main`.

The addition of a node representing declarations will force `SelectTests` to compare the corresponding declaration nodes in the CFGs for P and P'. Tests that traverse the declaration node will be included in T' if the nodes are found not equivalent. The problem now is that any change in the declaration will force the inclusion of all tests from T in T'. This is obviously due to the fact that all tests traverse the node following the `Start` node in the CFG for `main`. In the following paragraph, we present another approach to test selection in the presence of changes in declarations.

Let $declChange_f$ be the set of all variables in function f whose declarations have changed in f'. Variables removed or added are not included in $declChange_f$ (see Exercise 5.9). Similarly, we denote by $gdeclChange$ the set of all global variables in P whose declarations have changed.

Let $use_f(n)$ be the set of variable names used at node n in the CFG of function f. This set can be computed by traversing the CFG of each function and analyzing the syntax tree associated with each node. Any variable used—not assigned to—in an expression at node n in the CFG of function f is added to $use_f(n)$. Note that $declChange_f$ is empty when there has been no change in declarations of variables in f. Similarly, $use_f(n)$ is empty when node n in CFG(f) does not use any variable, for example in statement $x = 0$.

Procedure `SelectTestsMainDecl` is a modified version of procedure `SelectTestsMain`. It accounts for the possibility of changes in declarations and carefully selects only those tests that need to be run again for regression testing.

```
Procedure for selecting modification-traversing
tests while accounting for changes in variable
declarations
```

Input:
- G, G': CFGs of programs P and P' and syntax trees corresponding to each node in a CFG.
- Test vector *test(n)* for each node n in each CFG.
- For each function f, $use_f(n)$ for each node n in CFG (f).
- For each function f, $declChange_f$.
- The set of global variables whose declarations have changed: *gdeclChange*.
- T: Set of nonobsolete tests for P.

Output: T': A subset of T.

Procedure: `SelectTestsMainDecl`

/*

Procedure `SelectTestsDecl` is invoked repeatedly after the initialization step. In turn, `SelectTestsDecl` looks for any changes in declarations and selects those tests from T that traverse nodes affected by the changes. Procedure `SelectTests`, decribed earlier, is called upon the termination of the previous step.

*/

Step 1 Set $T' = \emptyset$. Unmark all nodes in G and in its child CFGs.

Step 2 For each function f in G, call procedure `SelectTestsDecl` $(f,\ declChange_f,\ gdeclChange)$. Each call updates T'.

Step 3 Call procedure `SelectTests` (G.Start, G'.Start'), where G.Start and G'.Start are, respectively, the start nodes in G and $G\prime$. This procedure may add new tests to T'.

Step 4 T' is the desired test set for regression testing P'.

End of Procedure `SelectTestsMainDecl`

Procedure: `SelectTestsDecl` *(f, declChange, gdeclChange)*

Input: f is function name and *declChange* is a set of variable names in f whose declarations have changed.

Output: T'.

Step 1 Repeat the following step for each node $n \in \text{CFG}(f)$.

1.1 `if` *use(n)* $\cap$ *declChange* $\neq \emptyset$ or *use(n)* $\cap$ *gdeclChange* $\neq \emptyset$, then $T' = T' \cup test(n)$.

End of Procedure `SelectTestsDecl`

The `SelectTests` procedure remains unchanged. Note that in the approach described above, the CFG of each function does not contain any nodes corresponding to declarations in the function. Declarations involving explicit variable initializations are treated in two parts: a pure declaration part followed by an initialization part. Initializations are included in a separate node placed immediately following the `Start` node. Thus, any change in the initialization part of a variable declaration, such as "int x=0;" changed to "int x=1;" is processed by `SelectTests`.

Example 5.11: Consider Program P5.3 and its CFG shown next to the code in Figure 5.8. As indicated, suppose that the type of variable

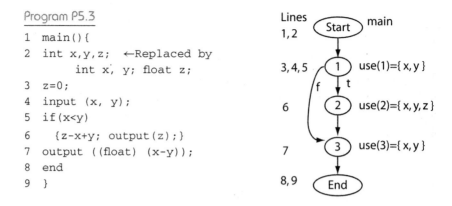

Program P5.3

```
1  main(){
2  int x,y,z;    ←Replaced by
        int x, y; float z;
3  z=0;
4  input (x, y);
5  if(x<y)
6    {z-x+y; output(z);}
7  output ((float) (x-y));
8  end
9  }
```

Fig. 5.8 Program and its CFG for Example 5.11.

z is changed from int to float. We refer to the original and the modified programs as P and P', respectively. It is easy to see that $gdeclChange = \emptyset$ and $declChange_{main} = \{z\}$. Suppose the following test set is used for testing P:

$$T = \begin{cases} t_1 :< x = 1, y = 3 > \\ t_2 :< x = 2, y = 1 > \\ t_3 :< x = 3, y = 4 > \end{cases}$$

We can easily trace $\text{CFG}(P)$ for each test case to find the test vectors. These are listed below.

$$\begin{aligned} test(1): &\quad \{t_1, t_2, t_3\} \\ test(2): &\quad \{t_1, t_3\} \\ test(3): &\quad \{t_1, t_2, t_3\} \end{aligned}$$

Step 1 in procedure SelectTestsDecl proceeds as follows:
node 1: $use(1) \cap declChange_{main} = \emptyset$. Hence, T' does not change.
node 2: $use(2) \cap declChange_{main} = \{z\}$. Hence, $T' = T' \cup tests(2) = \{t_1, t_3\}$.
node 3: $use(3) \cap declChange_{main} = \emptyset$. Hence, T' does not change.

Procedure SelectTestsDecl terminates at this point. Procedure SelectTests does not change T', as all the corresponding nodes in $\text{CFG}(P)$ and $\text{CFG}(P')$ are equivalent. Hence, we obtain the regression test $T' = \{t_1, t_3\}$.

5.6 TEST SELECTION USING DYNAMIC SLICING

Selection of modification-traversing tests using execution trace may lead to regression tests that are really not needed. Consider the following

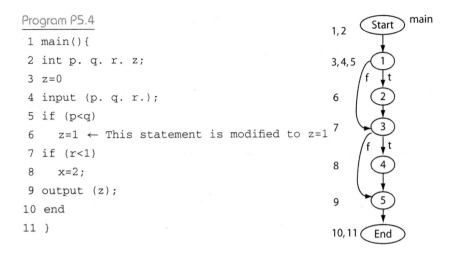

Program P5.4

```
1  main(){
2  int p. q. r. z;
3  z=0
4  input (p. q. r.);
5  if (p<q)
6     z=1  ← This statement is modified to z=1
7  if (r<1)
8     x=2;
9  output (z);
10 end
11 }
```

Fig. 5.9 A program and its CFG for Example 5.12.

scenario. Program P has been modified by changing the statement at line l. There are two tests t_1 and t_2 used for testing P. Suppose that both traverse l. The execution slice technique described earlier will select both t_1 and t_2.

Now suppose that whereas t_1 traverses l, the statement at l does not affect the output of P along the path traversed from the Start to the End node in CFG(P). On the contrary, traversal of l by t_2 does affect the output of P. In this case, there is no need to test P' on t_1.

Example 5.12: Consider Program P5.4 that takes three inputs, computes, and outputs z. Suppose that P is modified by changing the statement at line 6 as shown.

Consider the following test set used for testing P.

$$T = \begin{cases} t_1 : < p = 1, q = 3, r = r > \\ t_2 : < p = 3, q = 1, r = 0 > \\ t_3 : < p = 1, q = 3, r = 0 > \end{cases}$$

Tests t_1 and t_3 traverse node 2 in CFG(P) shown in Figure 5.9, t_2 does not. Hence, if we were to use SelectTests described earlier, then $T' = \{t_1, t_3\}$. This T' is a set of modification-traversing tests. However, it is easy to check that even though t_1 traverses node 2, output z does not depend on the value of z computed at this node. Hence, there is no need to test P' against t_1; it needs to be tested only against t_3.

We will now present a technique for test selection that makes use of PDG and dynamic slicing to select regression tests. The main advantage of this technique over the technique based exclusively on the execution slice is that it selects only those tests that are modification traversing and might affect the program output.

5.6.1 Dynamic Slicing

Let P be the program under test and t a test case against which P has been executed. Let l be a location in P where variable v is used. The dynamic slice of P with respect to t and v is the set of statements in P that lie in *trace(t)* and did effect the value of v at l. Obviously, the dynamic slice is empty if location l was not traversed during this execution. The notion of a dynamic slice grew out of that of a static slice based on program P and not on its execution.

> **Example 5.13:** Consider P to be Program P5.4 in Figure 5.9 and test $t_1 :< p = 1,\ q = 3,\ r = 2 >$. The dynamic slice of P with respect to variable z at line 9 and test t consists of statements at lines 4, 5, 7, and 8. The static slice of z at line 9 consists of statements at lines 3, 4, 5, 6, 7, and 8. It is generally the case that a dynamic slice for a variable is smaller than the corresponding static slice. For $t_2 :< p = 1,\ q = 0,\ r = 0 >$, the dynamic slice contains statements 3, 4, and 5. The static slice does not change.

5.6.2 Computation of Dynamic Slices

There are several algorithms for computing a dynamic slice. These vary across attributes such as the precision of the computed slice and the amount of computation and memory needed. A precise dynamic slice is one that contains exactly those statements that might affect the value of variable v at the given location and for a given test input. We use $DS(t, v, l)$ to denote the dynamic slice of variable v at location l with respect to test t. When the variable and its location are easily identified from the context, we simply write DS to refer to the dynamic slice.

Next we present an algorithm for computing dynamic slices based on the dynamic program dependence graph. Several other algorithms are cited in the Bibliographic Notes section. Given program P, test t, variable v, and location l, computation of a dynamic slice proceeds in the following steps:

Procedure: DSLICE

Step 1 Execute P against test case t and obtain *trace(t)*.

Step 2 Construct the dynamic dependence graph G from P and *trace(t)*.

Step 3 Identify in G the node n labeled l and containing the last assignment to v. If no such node exists then the dynamic slice is empty, otherwise proceed to the next step.

Step 4 Find in G the set $DS(t, v, n)$ of all nodes reachable from n, including n. $DS(v, n)$ is the dynamic slice of P with respect to variable v at location l for test t.

End of Procedure DSLICE

In Step 2 of DSLICE, we construct the dynamic-dependence graph (DDG). This graph is similar to the PDG introduced in Chapter 1. Given program P, a PDG is constructed from P, whereas a DDG is constructed from the execution trace *trace*(*t*) of P. Thus, statements in P that are not in *trace*(*t*) do not appear in the DDG.

Construction of G begins by initializing it with one node for each declaration. These nodes are independent of each other and no edge exists between them. Then a node corresponding to the first statement in *trace*(*t*) is added. This node is labeled with the line number of the executed statement. Subsequent statements in *trace*(*t*) are processed one by one. For each statement, a new node n is added to G. Control and data-dependence edges from n are then added to the existing nodes in G. The next example illustrates the process.

Example 5.14: Consider the program in Figure 5.10. We have ignored the function header and declarations as these do not affect the computation of the dynamic slice in this example (see Exercise 5.13). Suppose now that P5.5 is executed against test case $t : < x = 2, \ y = 4 >$. Also, we assume that successive values of x are 0 and 5. Function $f1(x)$ evaluates to 0, 2, and 3, respectively,

361

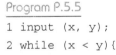

```
1 input (x, y);
2 while (x < y){
3   if (f1(x)==)0
4     z=f2(x);
    else
5     z=f3(x);
6   x=f4(x);
7   w=f5(z);
}
8 output (w)
  end
```

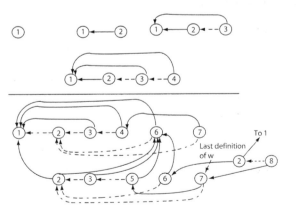

Fig. 5.10 A program and its DDG for Example 5.14 and test $< x = 2, \ y = 4 >$. Function header and declarations omitted for simplicity. Construction process for the first four nodes is shown above the solid line.

for $x = 2$, 0, and 5. Under these assumptions we get *trace(t)* = $(1, 2^1, 3^1, 4, 6^1, 7^1, 2^2, 3^2, 5, 6^2, 7^2, 2^3, 8)$; superscripts differentiate multiple occurrences of a node.

The construction of the DDG is exhibited in Figure 5.10 above the solid line. To begin with, node labeled 1 is added to G. Node 2 is added next. This node is data independent on node 1 and hence an edge, indicated as a solid line, is added from node 2 to node 1.

Next, node 3 is added. This node is data dependent on node 1 as it uses variable x defined at node 1. Hence, an edge is added from node 3 to node 1. Node 3 is also control dependent on node 2 and hence an edge, indicated as a dotted line, is added from node 3 to node 2. Node 4 is added next and data and control-dependence edges are added, respectively, from node 4 to node 1 and to node 3. The process continues as described until the node corresponding to the last statement in the trace, that is at line 8, is added. The final DDG is shown in Figure 5.10 below the solid line.

The DDG is used for the construction of a dynamic slice as mentioned in Steps 3 and 4 of procedure DSLICE. When computing the dynamic slice for the purpose of RTS, this slice is often based on one or more output variables which is w in program P5.5.

Example 5.15: To compute the dynamic slice for variable w at line 8, we identify the last definition of w in the DDG. This occurs at line 7 and, as marked in the figure, corresponds to the second occurrence of node 7 in Figure 5.10. We now trace backward starting at node 7 and collect all reachable nodes to obtain the desired dynamic slice as $\{1, 2, 3, 5, 6, 7, 8\}$ (also see Exercise 5.12).

5.6.3 SELECTING TESTS

Given a test set T for P, we compute the dynamic slice of all, or a selected set of, output variables for each test case in T. Let $DS(t)$ denote such a dynamic slice for $t \in T$. $DS(t)$ is computed using the procedure described in the previous section. Let n be a node in P modified to generate P'. Test $t \in T$ is added to T' if n belongs to $DS(t)$.

We can use SelectTests to select regression tests but with a slightly modified interpretation of *test(n)*. We now assume that *test(n)* is the set of tests $t \in T$ such that $n \in DS(t)$. Thus, for each node n in CFG(P), only those tests that traverse n and might have effected the value of at least one of the selected output variables are selected and added to T'.

Example 5.16: Suppose that line 4 in Program P5.5 is changed to obtain P'. Should t from Example 5.14 be included in T'? If we were to use only the execution slice, then t will be included in T' because it causes the traversal of node 4 in Figure 5.10. However, the traversal of node 4 does not affect the computation of w at node 8 and hence, when using the dynamic slice approach, t is not included in T'. Note that node 4 is not in $DS(t)$ with respect to variable w at line 8 and hence t should not be included in T'.

5.6.4 POTENTIAL DEPENDENCE

The dynamic slice contains all statements in $trace(t)$ that had an affect on program output. However, there might be a statement s in the trace that did not affect program output but may affect if changed. By not including s in the dynamic slice we exclude t from the regression tests. This implies that an error in the modified program due to a change in s might go undetected.

> **Example 5.17:** Let P denote Program P5.6. Suppose P is executed against test case $t :< N = 1, \ x = 1 >$ and that $f(x) \quad < 0$ during the first and only iteration of the loop in P. We obtain $trace(t) = (1, 2, 3, 4, 5, 6, 8, 10, 4, 11)$. The DDG for this trace is shown in Figure 5.11; for this example ignore the edges marked as "p" . The dynamic slice $DS(t, z, 11) = \{3, 11\}$ for output z at location 11.

Program P5.6

```
    int x, z, i, N;
1   input (N);
2   i=1;
3   z=0;
4   while (i ≤ N){
5     input (x);
6     if (f(x)==0)← Erroneous condition.
7       z=1;
8     if (f(x)>0)
9       z=2;
10    i++;
    }
11  output (z);
    end
```

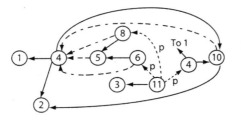

Fig. 5.11 DDG for Program P5.6 obtained from $trace(t)$, $t :< N = 1, \ x = 1 >$. Unmarked dotted edges indicate control dependence. Edges marked "p" indicate potential dependence.

Note that $DS(t, z, 11)$ does not include the node corresponding to line 6. Hence, t will not be selected for regression testing of P' obtained by modifying the if statement at line 6. But, of course, t must be included in the regression test.

We define the concept of *potential dependence* to overcome the problem illustrated in the previous example. Let *trace(t)* be a trace of P on test t. Let v be a variable used at location L_v and p a predicate that appears at location L_p prior to the traversal of location L_v. A potential dependency is said to exist between v and p when the following two conditions hold:

1. v is never defined on the subpath traversed from L_p to L_v but there exists another path, say r, from L_p to L_v where v is defined.
2. Changing the evaluation of p may cause path r to be executed.

The following example illustrates how to use the above definition to identify potential dependencies.

Example 5.18: Let us apply the above definition of potential dependence to Program P5.6 when executed against t as in Example 5.17. The subpath traversed from node 6 to node 11 contains nodes in the following sequence: 6, 8, 10, 4, 11. Node 11 has a potential dependency on node 6 because (i) z is never defined on this subpath but there exists a path r from node 6 to node 11 along which z is defined and (ii) changing the evaluation of the predicate at node 6 causes r to be executed. This potential dependency is shown in Figure 5.11. Note that one possible subpath r contains nodes in the following sequence: 6, 7, 8, 10, 4, 11.

Using a similar argument, it is easy to show the existence of potential dependency between nodes 8 and 11. The two potential dependencies are shown by dotted edges labeled "p" in Figure 5.11.

Procedure to compute potential dependencies

    Input: • Program P and its CFG G. There is exactly one node in G for each statement in P.
           • *trace(t)* for test t obtained by executing P against t.
           • DDG(t).
           • Location L and variable v in P for which the potential dependencies are to be computed.
    Output: PD: Set of edges indicating potential dependencies between L and other nodes in DDG(t).
    Procedure: ComputePotentialDep

/*

Procedure `ComputePotentialDep` is invoked after the construction of the DDG corresponding to a given trace. It uses G to determine reaching definitions of v at location L. These definitions are then used to iteratively compute PD.

*/

Step 1 Using P and G, compute the set S of all nodes in G that contain (static) reaching definitions of v at location L. A *reaching definition* of v at node L is a node L_v in G that assigns a value to v, and there is a path from the start node in G to the end node that reaches L_v and then L without redefining v. We refer to these as *static* reaching definitions because they are computed from P and not from the execution trace of P.

Step 2 Compute the set C of direct and indirect control nodes. A direct control node n is a predicate node in G such that some node $m \in S$ has control dependency on n. All nodes that are control dependent on nodes in C are indirect control nodes and also added to C.

Step 3 Find node D in G that contains the last definition of v before control arrives at L in *trace(t)*. In the absence of such a node, D is the declaration node corresponding to v.

Step 4 Let PD $= \emptyset$.

Step 5 Let *nodeSeq* be the sequence of nodes in *trace(t)* contained between the occurrences of L_v and L, and including L_v and L. Mark each node in *nodeSeq* as "NV".

Step 6 Repeat the following steps for each n in *nodeSeq* starting with $n = L$ and moving backward.
   6.1 Execute the following steps if n is marked "NV".
      6.1.1 Mark n as "V".
      6.1.2 If $n \in C$, then do the following:
         (a) PD $=$ PD $\cup \{n\}$.
         (b) Let M be the set of nodes in *nodeSeq* between n and D. For each node $n' \in M$, mark as "V" all nodes $m \in G$ such that n' is control dependent on m.

End of Procedure ComputePotentialDep

Example 5.19: Let us apply procedure `ComputePotentialDep` to compute potential dependencies for variable z at location 11 for $trace(t) = (1, 2, 3, 4^1, 5, 6, 8, 10, 4^2, 11)$ as in Example 5.17. The inputs to `ComputePotentialDep` include program P5.6, DDG shown in Figure 5.11, *trace (t)*, location L = 11, and variable $v = z$.

Step 1: From P, we get the static reaching definitions of v at L as $S = \{3, 7, 9\}$. Note that in general this is a difficult task for large programs and especially those that contain pointer references (see Bibliographic Notes for general algorithms for computing static reaching definitions).

Step 2: Node 3 has no control dependency. Noting from P, nodes 7 and 9 are control dependent on, respectively, nodes 6 and 8. Each of these nodes is in turn control dependent on node 4. Thus, we get $C = \{4, 6, 8\}$.

Step 3: Node 3 contains the last definition of z in *trace(t)*. Hence, $D = s$.

Step 4: PD $= \emptyset$.

Step 5: $L_v = 3$. *nodeSeq* $= (3, 4, 5, 6, 8, 10, 4^2, 11)$. Each node in *nodeSeq* is marked NV. We show this as *nodeSeq* $= (3^{NV}, 4^{NV}, 5^{NV}, 6^{NV}, 8^{NV}, 10^{NV}, 4^{NV}, 11^{NV})$.

Step 6: Select $n = L = 11$.

Step 6.1: n is marked NV; hence, we consider it.

Step 6.1.1: *nodeSeq* $= (3^{NV}, 4^{NV}, 5^{NV}, 6^{NV}, 8^{NV}, 10^{NV}, 4^{NV}, 11^{V})$. We have omitted the superscript 2 on the second occurrence of 4.

Step 6.1.2: As n is not in C, we ignore it and continue with the loop.

Step 6: Select $n = L = 4$.

Step 6.1: n is marked NV hence we consider it.

Step 6.1.1: *nodeSeq* $= (3^{NV}, 4^{NV}, 5^{NV}, 6^{NV}, 8^{NV}, 10^{NV}, 4^{V}, 11^{V})$.

Step 6.1.2: As n is in C, we process it. (a) PD $= \{4\}$. (b) Nodes 4 and 11 are not control dependent on any node and hence no other node needs to be marked.

Steps 6, 6.1, 6.1.1: Select $n = 10$. As n is marked NV, we consider it and mark it V. *nodeSeq* $= (3^{NV}, 4^{NV}, 5^{NV}, 6^{NV}, 8^{NV}, 10^{V}, 4^{V}, 11^{V})$.

Step 6.1.2: Node 10 is not a control node; hence, we ignore it and move to the next iteration.

Steps 6, 6.1, 6.1.1: Select $n = 8$. This node is marked NV; hence, we mark it V and process it. *nodeSeq* $= (3^{NV}, 4^{NV}, 5^{NV}, 6^{NV}, 8^{V}, 10^{V}, 4^{V}, 11^{V})$.

Step 6.1.2: Node 8 is in C; hence, (a) we add it to PD to get PD $= \{4, 8\}$ and (b) mark node 4 as V because 8 is control dependent on these nodes. *nodeSeq* $= (3^{NV}, 4^{V}, 5^{NV}, 6^{NV}, 8^{V}, 10^{V}, 4^{V}, 11^{V})$.

Steps 6, 6.1, 6.1.1: Select $n = 6$. This node is marked NV; hence, we mark it V and process it. $nodeSeq = (3^{NV}, 4^{NV}, 5^{NV}, 6^V, 8^V, 10^V, 4^V, 11^V)$.

Step 6.1.2: Node 6 is in C; hence, (a) we add it to PD to get PD = {4, 6, 8} and (b) there are no new nodes to be marked.

Steps 6, 6.1, 6.1.1, 6.1.2: Select $n = 5$. This node is marked NV, hence we mark it V and process it. $nodeSeq = (3^{NV}, 4^{NV}, 5^V, 6^V, 8^V, 10^V, 4^V, 11^V)$. We ignore 5 as it is not in C.

The remaining nodes in *nodeSeq* are either marked V or are not in C and hence will be ignored. The output of procedure `ComputePotentialDep` is PD = {4, 6, 8}.

Computing potential dependences in the presence of pointers requires a complicated algorithm. See the Bibliographic Notes section for references to algorithms for computing dependence relationships in C programs.

5.6.5 COMPUTING THE RELEVANT SLICE

The *relevant slice RS(t, v, n)* with respect to variable v at location n for a given test case t is the set of all nodes in the *trace(t)*, which if modified may alter the program output. Given *trace(t)*, the following steps are used to compute the relevant slice with respect to variable v at location n.

Step 1 Using the DDG, compute the dynamic slice *DS(t, v, n)* corresponding to node n that contains the output variable v.

Step 2 Modify the DDG by adding edges corresponding to all potential dependencies from node n to a predicate node.

Step 3 Find the set S of all nodes reachable from any node in *DS(t, v, n)* by following the data and potential-dependence (not control-dependence) edges.

Step 4 The relevant slice *RS(t, v, n)* = $S \cup DS(t, v, n)$.

Example 5.20: Continuing with Example 5.19 and referring to Figure 5.11 that indicates the potential dependence, we obtain $S = \{1, 2, 4, 5, 6, 8, 10\}$, and hence $RS(t, z, 11) = S \cup DS(t, z, 11) = \{1, 2, 3, 4, 5, 6, 8, 10, 11\}$. If the relevant slice is used for test selection, test t in Example 5.17 will be selected if any statement on lines 1, 3, 4, 5, 6, 8, 10, and 11 is modified.

5.6.6 ADDITION AND DELETION OF STATEMENTS

Statement addition: Suppose that program P is modified to P' by adding statement s. Obviously, no relevant slice for P would include the node corresponding to s. However, we do need to find tests in T, used for testing P, that must be included in the regression test set T' for P'. To do so, suppose that (a) s defines variable x, as for example through an assignment statement, and (b) $RS(t, x, l)$ is the relevant slice for variable x at location l corresponding to test case $t \in T$. We use the following steps to determine whether t needs to be included in T'.

Step 1 Find the set S of statements $s_1, s_2, \ldots, s_k$, $k \geq 0$ that use x. Let n_i, $1 \leq i \leq k$ denote the node corresponding to statement s_i in the DDG of P. A statement in S could be an assignment that uses x in an expression, an output statement, or a function or method call. Note that x could also be a global variable in which case all statements in P that refer to x must be included in S. It is obvious that if $k = 0$ then the newly added statement s is useless and need not be tested.

Step 2 For each test $t \in T$, add t to T' if for any $j, 1 \leq j \leq k, n_j \in RS(t, x, l)$.

Example 5.21: Suppose that Program P5.5 is modified by adding the statement $x = g(w)$ immediately following line 4 as part of the then clause. The newly added statement will be executed when control arrives at line 3 and $f1(x) = 0$.

Set S of statements that use x is {2, 3, 4, 5, 6}. Now consider test t from Example 5.14. You may verify that the dynamic slice of t with respect to variable w at line 8 is the same as its relevant slice $RS(8)$, which is {1, 2, 3, 5, 6, 7, 8} as computed in Example 5.15. Several statements in S belong to $RS(t, w, 8)$ and hence t must be included in T' (also see Exercise 5.19).

Statement deletion: Now suppose that P' is obtained by deleting statement s from P. Let n be the node corresponding to s in the DDG of P. It is easy to see that all tests from T whose relevant slice includes n must be included in T'.

Statement deletion and addition: An interesting case arises when P' is obtained by replacing some statement s in P by S' such that the left side of S' is different from that of s. Suppose that node n in the DDG of P corresponds to s and that S' modifies variable x. This case can be handled by assuming that s has been deleted and S' added. Hence, all tests $t \in T$ satisfying the following conditions must be included in T' (a) $n \in RS(t, w, l)$ and (b) $m \in RS(t, w, l)$, where node m in CFG(P) corresponds to some statement in P that uses variable w.

P' can be obtained by making several other types of changes in P not discussed above. See Exercise 5.20 and work out how the relevant slice technique can be applied for modifications other than those discussed above.

5.6.7 Identifying Variables for Slicing

You might have noticed that we compute a relevant slice with respect to a variable at a location. In all examples so far, we used a variable that is part of an output statement. However, a dynamic slice can be constructed based on any program variable that is used at some location in P, the program that is being modified. For example, in Program P5.6 one may compute the dynamic slice with respect to variable z at line 9 or at line 11.

Some programs will have several locations and variables of interest at which to compute the dynamic slice. One might identify all such locations and variables, compute the slice of a variable at the corresponding location, and then take the union of all slices to create a combined dynamic slice (see Exercise 5.12). This approach is useful for regression testing of relatively small components.

In large programs, there might be many locations that potentially qualify to serve as program outputs. The identification of all such locations might itself be an enormous task. In such situations, a tester needs to identify critical locations that contain one or more variables of interest. Dynamic slices can then be built only on these variables. For example, in an access-control application found in secure systems, such a location might be immediately following the code for processing an activation request. The state variable might be the variable of interest.

5.6.8 Reduced Dynamic-dependence Graph

As described earlier, a DDG constructed from an execution trace has one node corresponding to each program statement in the trace. As the size of an execution trace is unbounded, so is that of the DDG. Here, we describe another technique to construct a reduced dynamic-dependence graph (RDDG). While an RDDG looses some information that exists in a DDG, the information loss does not impact the tests selected for regression testing (see Exercise 5.27). Furthermore, the technique for the construction of an RDDG does not require saving the complete trace in memory.

Construction of an RDDG G proceeds during the execution of P against a test t. For each executed statement s at location l, a new node n labeled l is added to G only when there does not already exist such a node. In case n is added to G, any of its control and data dependence

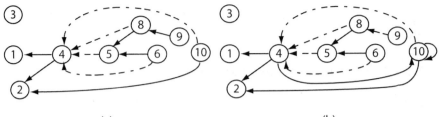

(a)   (b)

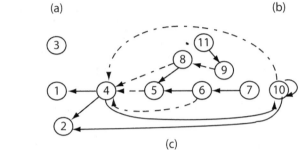

(c)

Fig. 5.12 RDDG for Program P5.6 obtained from *trace* $(t) = \{1, 2, 3, 4^1, 5,$ $6, 8, 9, 10|4^2, 5^2, 6^2, 8^2, 10^2|4^3, 5^3, 6^3, 7, 8^3, 10^3, |4^4, 11\}$. Intermediate status starting from (a) node 1 until node 10, (b) node 4^2 until node 10^2, and (c) complete RDDG for *trace*(t)

is also added. In case n is not added to G, the control and data dependence of n is updated. The number of nodes in the RDDG so constructed equals at most the number of distinct locations in P. In practice, however, most tests exercise only a portion of P thus leading to a much smaller RDDG.

Example 5.22: Suppose Program P5.6 is executed against t and *trace(t)* $= \{1, 2, 3, 4^1, 5, 6, 8, 9, 10, |4^2, 5^2, 6^2, 8^2, 10^2, |4^3,$ $5^3, 6^3, 7, 8^3, 10^3, 4^4, 11\}$. Construction of the RDDG G is shown in Figure 5.12. The vertical bars indicate the end of the first three iterations of the loop. Part (a) in the figure shows the partial RDDG at the end of the first iteration of the loop, part (b) at the end of the second iteration, and part (c) the complete RDDG at the end of program execution. We have ignored the declaration node in this example.

Notice that none of the statements in *trace(t)* corresponds to more than one node in G. Also, note how new nodes and new dependence edges are added. For example, in the second iteration, a data-dependence edge is added from node 4 to node 10, and from node 10 to itself. The RDDG contains only 10 nodes in contrast to a DDG, which would contain 22 nodes when constructed using the procedure described in Section 5.6.2.

The procedure for obtaining a dynamic slice from an RDDG remains the same as described in Section 5.6.2. To obtain the relevant slice one first discovers the potential dependences and then computes the relevant slice as illustrated in Section 5.6.5.

5.7 SCALABILITY OF TEST-SELECTION ALGORITHMS

The execution slice and dynamic-slicing techniques described above have several associated costs. First, there is the cost of doing a complete static analysis of program P that is modified to generate P'. While there exist several algorithms for static analysis to discover data and control dependence, they are not always precise especially for languages that offer pointers. Second, there is the run time overhead associated with the instrumentation required for the generation of an execution trace. While this overhead might be tolerable for OSs and nonembedded applications, it might not be for embedded applications.

In dynamic slicing, there is the additional cost of constructing and saving the DDG for every test. Whether this cost can be tolerated depends on the size of the test suite and the program. For programs that run into several hundred thousands of lines of code and are tested using a test suite containing hundreds or thousands of tests, the DDG (or the RDDG) at the level of data and control dependences at the statement level might not be cost-effective at the level of system, or even integration testing.

Thus, while both the execution trace- and DDG- or RDDG-based techniques are likely to be cost-effective when applied to regression testing of components of large systems, they might not be when testing the complete system. In such cases, one can use a coarse-level data- and control-dependence analysis to generate dependence graphs. One may also use coarse-level instrumentation for saving an execution trace. For example, instead of tracing each program statement, one could trace only the function calls. Also, dependence analysis could be done across functions and not across individual statements.

Example 5.23: Consider Program P5.1 in Example 5.5. In that example, we generate three execution traces using three tests. The traces are at the statement level.

Suppose that we want to collect the execution trace at the level of function calls. In this case, the program needs to be instrumented only at call points or only at the start of each function definition. Thus, the total number of probes added to the program to obtain a function-level execution trace is equal to the number of functions in the program, three in this case—main, g1, and g2. The function traces corresponding to the three tests are shown in the following table:

Test (t)	Execution trace ($trace(t)$)
t_1	main, g1, main
t_2	main, g2, main
t_3	main, g1, main

Note the savings in the number of entries in each execution trace. The function trace has a total of 9 entries for all 3 tests, whereas the statement level trace in Example 5.5 has 30. In general, the savings in storage requirements for a functional trace over statement trace will depend on the average size of the functions (see Exercise 5.37).

While tracing at a coarse level leads to reductions in the run time overhead, it also leads to a much smaller DDG. For example, rather than represent control and data dependencies across program variables, one can do the same across functions. In most practical applications, data and control dependence at a coarse level will lead to smaller DDGs relative to those constructed using dependencies at the level of program variables.

Consider two functions f_1 and f_2 in program P. Function f_2 has data dependency on f_1 if there is at least one variable defined in f_1 such that its definition reaches f_2. Similarly, f_2 is control dependent on f_1 when there are at least two paths from the start of P to the end that pass through f_1, but only one of these passes through f_2 after having passed through f_1 and the other path might be taken if a condition in f_1 evaluated differently. It is important to note that construction of the DDG (or the RDDG) requires static analysis of P to determine data and control dependences across various functions.

Example 5.24: Program P5.7 consists of main and three functions f1, f2, and f3. Consider the function trace consisting of the following calling sequence: main, f1, f3, f1, and main. The DDG corresponding to this trace appears in Figure 5.13.

Note the data and control dependences among various functions in the trace. main has data dependence on f1 because of its use of f1 to compute the value of z. Function f1 also has data dependence on main because of its use of x. f3 uses global variable y and hence has data dependence on main. Also, f3 is control dependent on f1 as it may be called upon entry to f1 (see Exercise 5.24).

Program P.5.7

```
1  main(){              1  int f1(int x){
2  int x, y, z;         2  int p;
3  input (x, y);        3  if(x>0)
4  z=f1(x);             4      p=f3(x, y);
5  if(z>0)              5  return(p);
6      z=f2(x);         6  }
7  output (z);
8  end
9  }
```

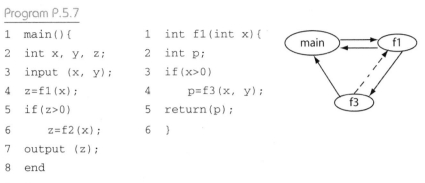

Fig. 5.13 Dynamic data dependence graph for P5.7 corresponding to the function trace: `main`, `f1`, `f3`, `f1`, and `main`.

Computing dynamic slices using a DDG based on function traces can be tricky. First, one needs to ask the proper question. In the program-variable-based slicing discussed earlier, we are able to specify a variable and its location for slicing. Against what should the slice be constructed when traces are based on functions? Second, the DDG exhibits dependencies at the function level and not at the level of program variables. Hence, how do we relate the slicing requirement to the DDG?

We can compute a dynamic slice based on a program variable at a specific location just as we did earlier. However, one needs to use static analysis to locate the function that contains the variable and its location. For example, if the slice is to be computed for z at line 7 in program P5.7, then we know that this variable and location is inside `main`. Once the containing function has been identified, the dynamic slice is constructed using the DDG as before (see Exercise 5.25).

5.8 TEST MINIMIZATION

Modification-traversing test selection finds a subset T' of T to use for regression testing. Now suppose that P contains n testable entities. Functions, basic blocks, conditions, and definition-use (def-use) pairs are all examples of testable entities. Suppose that tests in T' cover, that is test, $m < n$ of the testable entities. It is likely that there is an overlap among the entities covered by two tests in T'.

We therefore ask: Is it possible, and beneficial, to reduce T' to T'' such that $T'' \subseteq T'$ and each of the m entities covered by tests in T' is also covered by tests in T''? Such a test reduction process is commonly referred to in software testing as *test minimization*. Of course, we can also apply test minimization directly to T (see Exercise 5.30).

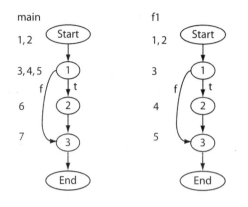

Fig. 5.14 CFG of Program P5.7.

Example 5.25: Consider Program P5.7 and test set $T = \{t_1, t_2, t_3\}$. Figure 5.14 shows the CFG of P 5.7. Let basic block be the entity of interest. The coverage of basic blocks for tests in T is as follows; note that we have excluded functions $f2$ and $f3$ from the coverage information assuming that these are library functions and that we do not have source code available to measure the corresponding block coverage.

$$t_1 \; main : 1, 2, 3 \; f1 : 1, 3$$
$$t_2 \; main : 1, 3 \quad f1 : 1, 3$$
$$t_3 \; main : 1, 3 \quad f1 : 1, 2, 3$$

Tests in T cover all six blocks, three in `main` and three in `f1`. However, it is easy to check that these six blocks can also be covered by t_1 and t_3. Hence rather than use T as a regression test one could also use $T' = \{t_1, t_3\}$, albeit with caution. Note that in this example the minimized test suite is unique.

One could obtain a significant reduction in the size of a test suite by applying coverage-based minimization as in the previous example. However, one might ask: *Will the minimized test suite has the same fault detection effectiveness as the corresponding nonminimized version?* The answer to this question depends on the modifications made to P to obtain P', the kind of faults in P', and the entity used for minimization (see Exercise 5.31).

5.8.1 THE SET-COVER PROBLEM

The test minimization problem can be formulated as the set-cover problem. Let E be a set of entities and TE a set of subsets of E. A set cover is a collection of sets $C \subseteq TE$ such that the union of all elements of C is TE.

The set-cover problem, more aptly the set-cover optimization problem, is to find a minimal C. Relating this to test minimization, set E could be, for example, a set of basic blocks and set TE a collection of sets of basic blocks covered by each test in T. The test minimization problem then is to find a minimal subset of TE that covers all elements of E.

Example 5.26: Let us formulate the test minimization problem as set-cover problem with reference to Example 5.25. We get the following sets:

$$E = \{main.1, main.2, main.3, f1.1, f1.2, f1.3\}$$
$$TE = \{\{main.1, main.2, main.3, f1.1, f1.3\},$$
$$\{main.1, main.3, f1.1, f1.3\},$$
$$\{main.1, main.3, f1.1, f1.2, f1.3\}\}$$

The solution to the test minimization problem is

$$C = \{main.1, main.2, main.3, f1.1, f1.3\},$$
$$\{main.1, main.3, f1.1, f1.2, f1.3\}$$

5.8.2 A Procedure for Test Minimization

There exist several procedures for solving the set-cover optimization problem. Given set TE, the naive algorithm computes the power set 2TE and selects from it the minimal covering subset. As the size of TE increases, the naive algorithm quickly becomes impractical (see Exercise 5.32).

The greedy algorithm is well known. Given a set of tests T and entities E, it begins by finding a test $t \in T$ that covers the maximum number of entities in E. t is selected, removed from T, and the entities it covers are removed from E. The procedure now continues with the updated T and E. The greedy algorithm terminates when all entities have been covered. While the greedy algorithm is faster than the naive set enumeration algorithm, it fails to find the minimal set cover in certain cases. Below, we present a slight variation of the greedy algorithm, named CMIMX.

```
Procedure to find minimal covering set
```

Input: An $n \times m$ matrix $C \cdot C(i, j)$ is 0 if test t_i covers entity j, else it is 1. Each column of C contains at least one nonzero entry. Each column corresponds to a distinct entity and each row to a distinct test.

Output: Minimal cover $minCov = \{i_1, i_2, \ldots, i_k\}$ such that for each column in C, there is at least one nonzero entry in at least one row with index in $minCov$.

Procedure: CMIMX

/* This procedure computes the minimal test cover for entities in C. */

Step 1 Set $minCov = \emptyset$. $yetToCover = m$.

Step 2 Unmark each of the n tests and m entities. An unmarked test is still under consideration, while a marked test is one already added to $minCov$. An unmarked entity is not covered by any test in $minCov$, whereas a marked entity is covered by at least one test in $minCov$.

Step 3 Repeat the following steps while $yetToCover > 0$:

3.1 Among the unmarked entities (columns) in C find those containing the least number of 1s. Let LC be the set of indices of all such columns. Note that LC will be nonempty as every column in C contains at least one nonzero entry.

3.2 Among all the unmarked tests (rows) in C that also cover entities in LC, find those that have the maximum number of nonzero entries. Let s be any one of these rows.

3.3 Mark test s and add it to $minCov$. Mark all entities covered by test s. Reduce $yetToCover$ by the number of entities covered by s.

End of Procedure CMIMX

Example 5.27: Suppose program P has been executed against the five tests in test suite T. A total of six entities are covered by the tests as shown in the following table; 0 (1) in a column indicates that the corresponding entity is not covered (covered). The entities could be basic blocks in the program, functions, def-uses, or any other testable element of interest. Further, a testable entity in P not covered by any of the five tests is not included in the table.

	1	2	3	4	5	6
t_1	1	1	1	0	0	0
t_2	1	0	0	1	0	0
t_3	0	1	0	0	1	0
t_4	0	0	1	0	0	1
t_5	0	0	0	0	1	0

Let us now follow procedure CMIMX to find the minimal cover set for the six entities. Input to the algorithm includes the 5×6 coverage matrix as shown in the above table.

Step 1: $minCov = \emptyset. yetToCover = 6.$

Step 2: All five tests and six entities are unmarked.

Step 3: As $yetToCover > 0$, we execute the loop body.

Step 3.1: Among the unmarked entities 4 and 6, each contain a single 1 and hence qualify as the highest priority entities. Thus, $LC = \{4, 6\}$.

Step 3.2: Among the unmarked tests, t_2 covers entities 1 and 4, and t_4 covers entities 3 and 6. Both tests have identical benefits of 2 each in terms of the number of entities they cover. We arbitrarily select test t_2. Thus $s = 2$.

Step 3.3: $minCov = \{2\}$. Test t_2 is marked. Entities 1 and 4 covered by test t_2 are also marked. $yetToCover = 6 - 2 = 4$.

Step 3.1: We continue with the second iteration of the loop as $yetToCover > 0$. Among the remaining unmarked entities, t_6 is the one with the least cost ($= 1$). Hence, $LC = \{6\}$.

Step 3.2: Only t_4 covers entity 6 and hence, $s = 4$.

Step 3.3: $minCov = \{2, 4\}$. Test t_4 and entities 3 and 6 are marked. $yetToCover = 4 - 2 = 2$.

Step 3.1: We continue with the third iteration of the loop as $yetToCover > 0$. The remaining entities, 2 and 5, have identical costs. Hence, $LC = \{2, 5\}$.

Step 3.2: Entities 2 and 5 are covered by unmarked tests t_1, t_3, and t_5. Of these tests, t_3 has the maximum benefit of 2. Hence $s = 3$.

Step 3.3: $minCov = \{2, 3, 4\}$. Test t_3 and entities 2 and 5 are marked. $yetToCover = 2 - 2 = 0$.

Step 3: The loop and the procedure terminate with $minCov = \{2, 3, 4\}$ as the output.

The difference between the greedy algorithm and CMIMX lies in Step 3.1 that is executed prior to applying the greedy test selection in Step 3.2. In this pre-greedy step, CMIMX prioritizes the entities for coverage. Entities covered by only one test get the highest priority, those covered by two tests get the next highest priority, and so on. One test that selects the highest priority entity is selected using the greedy algorithm. However, while the pre-greedy step allows CMIMX to find optimal solutions in cases where the greedy algorithm fails, it is not failproof (see Exercises 5.33 and 5.34).

5.9 TEST PRIORITIZATION

Given programs P and its modified version P', the various techniques for test selection discussed so far lead to a regression-test suite T' derived from T used for testing P. While T' is a subset of T, it might be overly large for testing P'. One might not have sufficient budget to execute P' against all tests in T'. While test minimization algorithms could be used to further reduce the size of T', this reduction is risky. Tests removed from T' might be important for finding faults in P'. Hence, one might not want to minimize T'. In such situations, one could apply techniques to prioritize tests in T' and then use only the top few high-priority tests. In this section, we introduce one technique for test prioritization.

Prioritization of tests requires a suitable cost criterion. Tests with lower costs are placed at the top of the list while those with higher cost at the bottom. The question obviously is: what cost criterion to use? Certainly, one could use multiple criteria to prioritize tests. It is important to keep in mind that tests being prioritized are the ones selected using some test selection technique. Thus, each test is expected to traverse at least some modified portion of P'. Of course, one could also prioritize all tests in T and then decide which ones to use when regression testing P'.

One cost criterion is derived directly from the notion of *residual coverage*. To understand residual coverage, suppose that E is a set of all executable entities in P. For example, E could be any of set of basic blocks, definition-uses, all functions, or all methods in P. Suppose E is the set of all functions in P. Let $E' \subseteq E$ be the set of functions actually called at least once during the execution of P against tests in T'. We say that a function is covered if it is called at least once during some execution of P. Let us also assume that the library functions are excluded from E and hence from E'.

Let $C(X)$ be the number of functions that remain to be covered after having executed P against tests in set $X \subseteq T'$; initially $C(\{\ \}) = |E'|$. $C(X)$ is the residual coverage of P with respect to X.

The cost of executing P' against a test t in T' is the number of functions that remain uncovered after the execution of P against t. Thus, $C(X)$ reduces, or remains unchanged, as tests are added to X. Hence, the cost of a test is inversely proportional to the number of remaining functions it covers. Procedure PrTest, following the next example, computes the residual coverage for all tests in T' and determines the next highest-priority test. This procedure is repeated until all tests in T' have been prioritized.

Example 5.28: Let $T' = \{t_1, t_2, t_3\}$ be the regression test for program P' derived from test set T for program P. Let E' be the set of functions covered when P is executed against tests in T' and $C(\{\ \}) = |E'| = 6$. Now suppose t_1 covers three of the six uncovered functions,

t_2 covers two, and t_3 covers four. Note that there might be some overlap between the functions covered by the different tests.

The costs of t_1, t_2, and t_3 are, respectively, 3, 4, and 2. Thus t_3 is the lowest cost test and has the highest-priority among the three tests. After having executed t_3, we get $C(\{t_3\}) = 2$. We now need to select from the two remaining tests. Suppose that t_1 covers none of the remaining functions and t_2 covers 2. Then the cost of t_1 is 2 and that of t_2 is 0. Hence, t_2 has higher priority than t_1. After executing t_2, we get $C(\{t_2, t_3\}) = 0$. The desired prioritized sequence of tests is $< t_3, t_2, t_1 >$. Note that execution of P against t_3 after having executed it against t_3 and t_1 will not reduce $C(X)$ any further.

Procedure for prioritizing regression tests

Input:
- T': Set of regression tests for the modified program P'.
- *entitiesCov:* Set of entities in P covered by tests in T'.
- *cov:* Coverage vector such that for each test $t \in T'$, $cov(t)$ is the set of entities covered by executing P against t.

Output: *PrT:* A sequence of tests such that (a) each test in PrT belongs to T', (b) each test in T' appears exactly once in PrT, and (c) tests in PrT are arranged in the ascending order of cost.

Procedure: PrTest

/*

PrT is initialized to test t with the least cost. The cost of each remaining test in T' is computed and the one with the least cost is appended to PrT and not considered any further. This procedure continues until all tests in T' have been considered.

*/

Step 1 $X' = T'$. Find $t \in X'$ such that $|cov(t)| \leq |cov(u)|$ for all $u \in X'$, $u \neq t$.

Step 2 Set $PrT =< t >$, $X' = X' \setminus \{t\}$. Update *entitiesCov* by removing from it all entities covered by t. Thus *entitiesCov* = *entitiesCov* $\setminus cov(t)$.

Step 3 Repeat the following steps while $X' \neq \emptyset$ and *entityCov* $\neq \emptyset$.

   3.1 Compute the residual coverage for each test $t \in T'$. $resCov(t) = |entitiesCov \setminus (cov(t) \cap entitiesCov)|$. $resCov(t)$ indicates the count of currently uncovered entities that will remain uncovered after having executed P against t.

3.2 Find test $t \in X'$ such that $resCov(t) \leq resCov(u)$, for all $u \in X', u \neq t$. If two or more such tests exist then randomly select one.

3.3 Update the prioritized sequence, set of tests remaining to be examined, and entities yet to be covered by tests in PrT. PrT $= append(PrT, t)$, $X' = X' \setminus \{t\}$, and $entitiesCov = entitiesCov \setminus cov(t)$.

Step 4 Append to PrT any remaining tests in X'. All remaining tests have the same residual coverage which equals $|entityCov|$. Hence these tests are tied. Random selection is one way to break the tie (also see Exercise 5.35).

End of Procedure PrTest

Example 5.29: Consider application P that consists of four classes $C_1, C_2, C_3,$ and C_4. Each of these four classes is composed of one or more methods as follows: $C_1 = \{m_1, m_{12}, m_{16}\}$, $C_2 = \{m_2, m_3, m_4\}$, $C_3 = \{m_5, m_6, m_{10}, m_{11}\}$, and $C_4 = \{m_7, m_8, m_9, m_{13}, m_{14}, m_{15}\}$. In the following, we refer to a method by an integer, for example m_4 by 4.

Suppose that regression-test set $T' = \{t_1, t_2, t_3, t_4, t_5\}$. The methods covered by each test in T' are listed in the following table. Note that method 9 has not been covered by any test in T' (see Exercise 5.28).

Test (t)	Methods covered ($cov(t)$)	$|cov(t)|$
t_1	1, 2, 3, 4, 5, 10, 11, 12, 13, 14, 16	11
t_2	1, 2, 4, 5, 12, 13, 15, 16	8
t_3	1, 2, 3, 4, 5, 12, 13, 14, 16	9
t_4	1, 2, 4, 5, 12, 13, 14, 16	8
t_5	1, 2, 4, 5, 6, 7, 8, 10, 11, 12, 13, 15, 16	13

Let us now follow procedure PrTest to obtain a prioritized list of tests using residual coverage as the cost criterion. The inputs to PrTest are: T', $entitiesCov$ = {1, 2, 3, 4, 5, 6, 7, 8, 10, 11, 12, 13, 14, 15, 16}, and the test coverage vectors for each test in T, as in the table above. Note that we have excluded method 9 from $entitiesCov$ as it is not covered by any test in T' and hence does not cause a difference in the relative residual coverage of each test.

Step 1: $X' = \{t_1, t_2, t_3, t_4, t_5\}$. t_5 covers the largest number of functions (13) in X' and hence has the least cost.

Step 2: $PrT =< t_5 > . X' = \{t_1, t_2, t_3, t_4\}$. $entitiesCov = \{3, 14\}$.

Step 3: We continue the process as X and $entitiesCov$ is not empty.

Step 3.1: Compute the residual coverage for each test in X'.

$resCov(t_1) = |\{3, 14\}\backslash(\{1, 2, 3, 4, 5, 10, 11, 12, 13, 14, 16\} \cap \{3, 14\})| = |\emptyset| = 0$
$resCov(t_2) = |\{3, 14\}\backslash(\{1, 2, 4, 5, 12, 13, 15, 16\} \cap \{3, 14\})| = |\{3, 14\}| = 2$
$resCov(t_3) = |\{3, 14\}\backslash(\{1, 2, 3, 4, 5, 12, 13, 14, 16\} \cap \{3, 14\})| = |\emptyset| = 0$
$resCov(t_4) = |\{3, 14\}\backslash(\{1, 2, 4, 5, 12, 13, 14, 16\} \cap \{3, 14\})| = |\{14\}| = 1.$

Step 3.2: t_1 and t_3 have the least cost. We arbitrarily select t_3. One may instead use some other criteria to break the tie (see Exercise 5.35).

Step 3.3: $PrT =< t_5, t_3 > . X' = \{t_1, t_2\}$, $entitiesCov = \emptyset$.

Step 3: There is no function remaining to be covered. Hence, we terminate the loop.

Step 4: t_1, t_2, and t_4 remain to be prioritized. As $entitiesCov$ is empty, the residual coverage criterion cannot be applied to differentiate amongst the priorities of these remaining tests. In this case, we break the tie arbitrarily. This leads to $PrT =< t_5, t_3, t_1, t_2, t_4 >$.

Prioritization of regression tests offers a tester an opportunity to decide how many and which tests to run under time constraints. Certainly, when all tests cannot be run, one needs to find some criteria to decide when to stop testing. This decision could depend on a variety of factors such as time constraint, test criticality, and customer requirements.

Note that the prioritization algorithm `PrTest` does not account for any sequencing requirements among tests in T'. As explained in Section 5.2.3, two or more tests in T' may be required to be executed in a sequence for P, and also for P'. Exercise 5.36 asks you to derive ways to modify `PrTest` to account for any test-sequencing requirements.

5.10 TOOLS FOR REGRESSION TESTING

Regression testing for almost any nontrivial application requires the availability of a tool. The mere execution of large number of regression tests can be daunting and humanly impossible under the given time and budget constraints. Execution of tests may require application and test setup, recording of the outcome of each test, performance analysis, test abortion, and several others.

A variety of commercial tools perform exactly the tasks mentioned above, and a few others. However, there exist few tools that offer facilities for test selection using static and dynamic analysis, test minimization, and test prioritization. While test execution is an essential and

Table 5.1 A summary of three tools to aid in regression testing

Attributes	ATAC/χ Suds	TestTube	Echelon
Developer	Telcordia Technologies	AT&T Bell Laboratories	Microsoft
Year reported	1992	1994	2002
Selective retesting	Yes	Yes	No
Selection basis	Control/data-flow coverage	Functions	Basic blocks
Test prioritization	Yes	No	Yes
Test minimization	Yes	No	No
Slicing	Yes	No	No
Differencing	Yes	Yes	Yes
Block coverage	Yes	No	Yes
Condition coverage	Yes	No	No
def–use coverage	Yes	No	No
p-use, c-use coverage	Yes	No	No
Language support	C	C	C and binary

time-consuming task in regression testing, test selection, minimization, and prioritization when used carefully could lead to a significant reduction in the cost of regression testing.

In the following paragraphs we briefly review three advanced tools for regression testing that feature one or more of the techniques discussed in this chapter. The tools we have selected have all been developed in commercial environments and tested on large programs. This is by no means a complete set of tools; there exist several others developed in research and commercial environments that are not reviewed here.

Table 5.1 summarizes the capability of the three tools across several attributes. Both ATAC/χ Suds and TestTube work on a given source program written in C. Echelon is different in that it does test prioritization based on binary-differencing technique. A key advantage of using binary differencing, in contrast to source code differencing, is that it avoids the complex static analyses required to determine the nature and impact of code changes such as variable renaming or macro definitions.

The strength of ATAC/χSuds lies in the assessment of test adequacy across a variety of criteria as well as a seamless integration of regression testing with test execution, slicing, differencing, code coverage computation, test minimization across a variety of coverage criteria, test prioritization, a combination of minimization and prioritization, and test management. The strength of TestTube lies in its use of a coarse coverage criterion for test selection, namely function coverage.

None of the tools described here has reported an application in the embedded domain. It is important to note that due to the hardware storage and application timing constraints, a regression-testing tool that is satisfactory in a nonembedded application might be unsuitable in an embedded environment.

SUMMARY

Regression testing is an essential step in almost all commercial software development environments. The need for regression testing arises as corrective and progressive changes occur frequently in a development environment. Regression testing improves confidence in that existing and unchanged code will continue to behave as expected after the changes have been incorporated.

While test execution and logging of the test results are important aspects of regression testing, we have focused in this chapter on techniques for test selection, minimization, and prioritization. These three areas of regression testing require sophisticated tools and techniques. We have described in detail the most advanced techniques for test selection using dynamic slicing. These techniques have evolved from research in program debugging and have found their way in regression testing.

While test selection using some form of program differencing is a safe technique for reducing the size of regression tests, test minimization is not. Despite research in the effect of test minimization on the fault-detection effectiveness of the minimized test sets, discarding tests based exclusively on coverage is certainly risky and not recommended while testing highly critical systems. This is where test prioritization becomes useful. It simply prioritizes tests using one or more criteria and leaves to the tester the decision on which tests to select. Of course, one might argue that minimization assists the tester in that it takes such decision away from the tester. ATAC/χSuds has a feature that allows a tester to combine minimization and prioritization.

BIBLIOGRAPHIC NOTES

Early research: Fischer *et al.* [147] proposed a formal method for selecting test cases for regression testing, known at that time as "retesting modified software." Their approach required both control flow and data-flow analyses to determine which tests should be selected. Their formulation is novel in that the test selection problem is formulated as a set of *m* linear conditions in *n* variables of the kind:

$$a_{i1}x_1 + a_{i2}x_2 + \ldots + a_{in}x_n \geq b_i$$

$$\text{for } 1 \leq i \leq m$$

Coefficient a_{ij} is 1 if test case t_j exercises one or more of the modified program segments i, such as a basic block, and 0 otherwise. Variable x_j is 1 if test t_j is a candidate for inclusion in the regression test. b_i represents a lower bound on the number of tests that must execute program segment i. An optimal solution is sought for x_js that minimizes the following cost function:

$$Z = c_1 x_1 + c_2 x_2 + \ldots + c_n x_n$$

where c_i is the cost associated with executing test t_i. An integer programming algorithm is used to find an optimal solution in terms of values of x_js, which then leads to the inclusion or exclusion of a test from the regression test suite for the modified program.

Hartmann and Robson extended the method of Fischer *et al.* and applied it to C programs [204, 205]. Their extensions allowed test selection to be performed at the unit and system levels. Yau and

Kishimoto [538] proposed a technique for test selection based on an original test suite generated using input domain partitioning.

Miller, while addressing the issues involved in the automation of software development processes, pointed out the need for the identification of program units where all changes can be localized [327]. Benedusi *et al.* [41] proposed a test selection technique based on path change analysis. They constructed a test table that, among others, associates each test case with paths. The test selection problem is to reduce the number of rows in the test table. This reduction is accomplished based on the coverage of input conditions and paths. Program paths are specified using algebraic expressions, and differencing between the expressions corresponding to the unmodified and modified versions of the program identifies the changed paths. Ostrand and Weyuker proposed a method for test selection using data-flow analysis [380].

Program-dependence graphs: PDGS have been in use for long in the context of parallelizing and optimizing compilers [67, 274], though their use in regression testing is relatively new. Ferrante *et al.* explain the use of PDG in program optimization [146]. Horwitz and Reps enumerated various uses of PDGs in software engineering. Horwitz *et al.* show that PDGs are an adequate representation of program behavior in the sense that isomorphism of two PDGs also implies strong equivalence of the corresponding programs [230].

Korel discussed the use of PDGs in program testing [266]. Bates and Horwitz used PDGs for incremental program testing [33]. Horwitz *et al.* showed how to compute slices using PDGs for entire programs consisting of several procedures [231, 232]. Binkley shows how to generate precise executable interpro cedural slices [48]. Binkley has proposed a technique based on calling context slice for test cost reduction during regression testing [49]. Agrawal and Horgan describe the construction of a dynamic PDG from an execution trace without having to save the trace [11]. Harrold *et al.* propose an efficient technique to construct PDGs during parsing [199].

Firewall testing: Leung and White have reported extensively on regression testing during integration and system-testing phases. In two classic publications [287, 518], they lay out the basic terminology related to regression testing, the regression, test process, and some techniques for test selection. In these publications, they also defined a program as *regression testable* "if most single statement modifications to the program entail rerunning a small proportion of test cases in the current test plan." White and Leung pioneered the *firewall* concept as an aid to decide which modules to retest [517]. The basic idea is to construct a narrow firewall around the set of modules to be retested. They explain how to calculate the firewall using the notions of code change, specification change, data and control flows, and call graphs.

More recently, White *et al.* have applied the firewall concept to the regression testing of GUIs [514]. White *et al.* have also applied the firewall concept to the regression testing of object-oriented programs [513, 516]. An industrial-strength case study applying the firewall concept to

regression study is reported where White and Robinson describe how to detect deadlocks in real-time systems [519].

Dynamic slicing: Slicing-based techniques for test selection have grown out of the basic idea of program slicing from Weiser [503, 504]. In early research, these techniques were applied to program debugging. The objective was to extract a *small* portion of the code that possibly contains the fault. Subsequently, the techniques were applied to RTS. Gupta et al. used the idea of static program slicing for selective regression testing [185].

Noting that static slicing may lead to an unduly large program slice, Korel and Laski proposed a method for obtaining dynamic slices from program executions [268]. Their method is able to extract executable and smaller slices and allow more precise handling of arrays and other structures. Agrawal in his doctoral work further refined the idea of a dynamic slice and proposed four algorithms for computing it from an execution trace [6]. Agrawal's work also includes techniques for (relevant) slicing in the presence of pointers and composite variables (see Chapter 4 of Agrawal's thesis also available as a technical report [7]).

In another publication, Agrawal and Horgan have described four dynamic-slicing algorithms [11]. Agrawal *et al.* have described dynamic slicing in the presence of unconstrained pointers [10]. Algorithm 4 described by Agrawal *et al.* does not require saving the execution trace and hence leads to significant space savings. Gyimóthy *et al.* [188] propose an efficient technique for relevant slicing used in program debugging. Zhang *et al.*

describe efficient algorithms for computing precise dynamic slices [543–545] using whole execution traces. The use of dynamic slicing in RTS has been reported by Agrawal *et al.* [12]. Hammer *et al.* combine dynamic path conditions and static-dependence graph to generate small dynamic slices [192]. The work of Hammer *et al.* was motivated by the need to identify all parts of a program that influence the security-relevant parts.

Modification-traversing tests: There are many ways to select tests for regression testing. Here, we focus on modification-traversing techniques that do not use slicing. In his doctoral work, Rothermel pioneered test selection using safe techniques [421]. The basic approach used was to identify tests in T that would traverse code segments modified in P to obtain P'. Details of the approach are found in Rothermel's thesis as well as in other publications with coauthors [44, 422–425]. Kim *et al.* have evaluated the effectiveness of tests selected using the proposed safe test selection technique [259].

Rothermel *et al.* have applied safe RTS to C++ programs [426]. Harrold *et al.* propose safe RTS for Java programs [196, 198]. Orso *et al.* have proposed ways to scale safe RTS to large systems and Java applications [377].

Often regression testing needs to be performed for component testing when source code is not available. Zheng *et al.* have found the RTS technique useful in such scenarios [546]. They use a mix of black-box and firewall approach for the identification of changes in components

and test selection. They report a reduction of up to 70% in the size of the resultant regression-test suite without any loss in the fault-detection effectiveness.

Program differencing: Most though not all RTS techniques use some form of source code differencing to identify testable code segments that might have changed during the modification process. Early work in differencing techniques includes that of Sankoff [430], Selkow [437], Miller and Meyers [331], and Horwitz [228]. Sankoff's work is in the context of matching molecular strings. Selkow's work is in the context of tree transformations. Horwitz proposed a semantic and textual-differencing technique for the identification of changes between two versions [229]. Horwitz's technique improves upon the differencing technique used in Douglas McIlroy's Unix utility `diff`. Suvanaphen and Roberts describe a technique for visualizing textual differences [463]. Their work is in the context of Web page search.

Program differencing can also be performed at a dynamic level. Reps *et al.* investigate the use of such techniques during maintenance [415]. They introduce the idea of *path spectrum* as the distribution of paths over a program execution. The idea was applied to the famous Year 2000 problem. A collection of path spectra can be treated as program spectra. Harrold *et al.* evaluate the effectiveness of program spectra as a failure-indicating metric [201]. Note that program spectra can be constructed as a sequence of coverage of a variety of testable items in a program including path, edge, basic block, and all-uses. The (definition–use) (def–use) chains presented in Chapter 6, this book, capture one type of path spectra. Boardman *et al.* propose a novel representation of program spectra as a sequence of musical notes played as portions of a program executed [51].

Rothermel and Harrold have proposed and used a technique for program differencing based on CFGs [425, 426]. The approach described in Section 5.5.2 is a slight variation of Rothermel and Harrold's approach in the use of syntax trees at each node of a CFG. Vokolos *et al.* propose a textual-differencing technique [493, 495]. Apiwattanapong *et al.* at Georgia Tech have developed a tool named JDiff for differencing object-oriented programs [24, 25]. Ball has performed a theoretical analysis of Rothermel and Harrold's RTS technique and proposed three new improved algorithms [30].

Test minimization: Harrold, *et al.* proposed a methodology to control the size of a regression-test suite [197]. Their methodology includes several criteria for test-suite reduction and is more general than techniques that minimize a testsuite based solely on code coverage. Test-suite reduction based on code coverage is one of the several criteria proposed by the authors for the reduction in the size of a test suite.

Wong *et al.* have reported several studies aimed at evaluating the fault-detection effectiveness of tests minimized while retaining one or more control-flow- and data-flow-based coverage metrics [522, 523]. They found little to no loss in the fault-detection effectiveness when tests that do not reduce overall block coverage are removed from a test suite. Graves *et al.* reported another study that,

among other techniques, evaluated the fault-detection effectivenes of test-suite minimization based on edge coverage [179]. They found that while there is a significant reduction due to minimization, this is also accompanied by a significant reduction in the fault-detection effectiveness of the minimized test suite. Section 5.4.4 offers an explanation for the discrepancy between the findings reported by Wong *et al.* and Graves *et al.*

The test minimization problem is a special case of the traditional set-cover problem [253]. While the set-cover optimization problem is NP-hard, several approximation algorithms exist for finding a minimal set cover [90, 248, 448]. ATAC uses an implicit enumeration algorithm to find a minimal covering set while maintaining one or more coverage metrics [225]. Tallam and Gupta [471] have proposed a delayed greedy minimization algorithm based on the idea of lattices and dominators [8, 184]. Black *et al.* have proposed a bi-criteria-based minimization technique that, while maintaining test coverage, maximizes error-detection rates.

Test prioritization: An early implementation of test prioritization was reported by Horgan and London [224, 225] in ATAC, an industrial-strength tool. ATAC, subsequently morphed into χSuds [475], allowed prioritization based on a variety of control-flow and data-flow-based coverage criteria. Wong *et al.* reported an experiment to investigate the fault-detection effectiveness of tests minimized and prioritized using each of block, decision, and the all-uses criteria [521]. Size reduction for minimization, precision, and recall for both minimization and prioritization were investigated. The precision of a test suite T is the fraction of tests in T that generate different outputs on P and its modified version P'. Recall is the fraction of tests selected from those that need to be reexecuted.

Several other test prioritization techniques have been reported, and implemented, since the development of ATAC. Srivastava and Thiagarajan [456] have reported Echelon, a tool to prioritize tests. Echelon is an industrial-strength tool developed and used at Microsoft. Kim and Porter [258] propose a history-based technique and discuss tradeoffs in the use of test selection using modification-traversing tests and test prioritization. In the case studies, they found that minimization requires the least effort and had the highest fault-detection effectiveness. They also report that the Least-Recently Used (LRU) method might be most cost-effective when the cost of failures is high, where the LRU technique prioritizes tests based on test execution history and selects a certain percentage of tests.

Elbaum et al. have reported several variants of test prioritization [138, 139]. Rummel et al. have exhibited renewed interest in test prioritization using data-flow information [428]. Do et al. performed a cost-benefits analysis of prioritizing JUnit test cases [131, 132].

Aggrawal et al. describe a coverage-based technique for test prioritization [5], where prioritization is based on the original test suite used for testing P and not the one used for testing the modified version P' or its descendants. Bryce and Colbourn propose a

prioritization technique based on "one-test-at-a-time" greedy approach [59]. Srikanth and Williams investigate the economic application of test prioritization [454]. They state "Coverage-based white-box prioritization techniques are most applicable for regression testing at the unit level and are harder to apply on complex systems." This statement needs to be considered against the work of Srivastava and Thiagarajan [456].

Once tests have been selected, minimized, and/or prioritized, one often needs to schedule them for execution. Xia et al. discuss a functional regression-test-scheduling strategy on a grid of machines [535]. The grid allows efficient testing of a product across different platforms. Their work is in the context of IBM's DB2 products.

Tools: ATAC/χSuds [225, 475] was an early set of tools that supported test minimization and prioritization. One of the many strengths of this toolset is that it computes a variety of control-flow and data-flow coverage metrics and offers a tester the option to select any one or more of these for test prioritization and/or minimization. Gittens et al. report a case study using ATAC to empirically evaluate the correlation between coverage and faults found during regression testing [171]. Their study involved code coverage measurement of a commercial application containing 221 modules totaling 201,629 lines of code.

Chen et al. report TestTube for selective regression testing [79]. TestTube analyzes C programs, and uses textual-differencing to identify functions and variables that differ between the original and the modified programs. Function coverage and differencing information is used for test selection. Vokolos and Frankl report a tool for regression testing that uses textual differencing [494]. They also report a case study, performed using Pythia, to investigate the reduction in the number of test cases [493, 495]. Srivastava and Thiagarajan report an industrial-strength tool for test prioritization [456]. This tool is used on large-scale software projects at Microsoft. Its novelty lies in the use of binary-to-binary code matching to identify differences in the original and the modified program.

Rothermel and Soffa's technique for finding differences between two programs is implemented in DeJavu [425]. Ren *et al.* have reported Chianti, a tool to perform change–impact analysis of Java programs [413]. The tool uses source code edits to identify atomic changes. The dynamic call graph is constructed and used to select tests that must be used in regression testing. The tool also identifies all changes in the modified program that might affect the behavior of a test case. Orso *et al.* report DeJavOO, a tool for RTS for large

programs [377] written in Java. DeJavOO uses syntactic differencing to partition to identify segments that might be affected by the changes. The changes are localized to classes and interfaces. The coverage information is then used for test selection. DeJavOO has been reportedly used successfully on Java programs as large as 500 KLOC.

There exist a number of commercially available tools for regression testing. Most of these tools automate tasks such as test execution, logging, and output viewing. An incomplete list of such tools follows: e-tester from Empirix for Web application testing, JUnit for Java, TestAdvantage from Infragistics for testing Windows Forms, HighTest Plus from Vermont Creative Software for stand-alone or browser-based applications, TestComplete from AutomatedQA, C++ Test from Parasoft, IBM/Rational Functional Tester, WinRunner from Mercury, χ Regress from Cleanscape (a part of the χSuds tools suite), and SQLUnit and DBUnit from SourceForge for database unit testing.

EXERCISES

5.1 In Example 5.2, we state "Under this assumption, when run as the first test, t_3 is likely to fail because the expected output will not match the output generated by SATM'." Under what conditions will this statement be false ?

5.2 Given program P and test t, explain the difference between an execution trace of P against t when recorded as (a) a sequence of nodes traversed and (b) a set of nodes traversed. Use storage space as a parameter in your explanation. Give one example where a sequence is needed and a set representation will not suffice.

5.3 Draw the syntax trees in Example 5.7 not shown in Figure 5.6.

5.4 Write an algorithm that takes two syntax trees T_r and T_r' as inputs and returns true if they are identical and false otherwise. Recall from Section 5.5 that a leaf node might be a function name, say foo. In this case, your algorithm must traverse the CFG of f, and the corresponding syntax trees, to determine equivalence.

5.5 In Example 5.9, there is only one function call at node 2 in main in Program P5.1. How will the application of SelectTests change if line 5 in main is replaced by: $\{p = g1(x, y) + g2(x, y)\}$?

5.6 Complete Example 5.9 to determine T' for the modified program.

5.7 Modify SelectTests such that (a) T' includes only tests that traverse modified nodes in the main program and any called functions and (b) it handles switch and case statements.

5.8 Consider the following two programs P and P'; the one on the right (P') is a modified version of P on the left. [This exercise is based on an observation by Hiralal Agrawal.]

```
1  main()}        1  main(){
2  if (P1) {      2  if (P1){
3    S1;           3    S1;S2;
4  }               4  } else {
5  S2;             5    S3;
6  end             6  }
7  }               7  end
                   8  }
```

(a) Show that SelectTests might select all or no tests to be re-executed depending on the order in which the true and false branches of an if-statement are traversed. (b) Modify

SelectTests so that only tests that execute P1.S2 are selected for re-execution.

5.9 (a) Procedure SelectTestsMainDecl in Section 5.5.4 ignores the addition of any new variable declaration and deletion of any existing variable declaration. Does this imply that SelectTests MainDecl is unsafe?

(b) Suppose that variables added or removed from declarations in *f* are added to *declChange_f*. In what ways will this change in the definition of *declChange* affect the behavior of SelectTests MainDecl?

5.10 (a) Modify the node equivalence check in SelectTests so it not only compares the syntax trees of two nodes for equality, but also checks if declarations of any variables used at that node have changed, and if so, consider the two nodes as not equivalent.

(b) Discuss the advantage of the above modification in terms of the number of tests selected for re-execution. [This exercise based on a suggestion by Hiralal Agrawal.]

5.11 List at least one advantage of RTS using the dynamic-slicing approach over the plain modification-traversing approach.

5.12 Suppose that the output statement at line 8 in Program P5.5 is replaced by:

$$output(x, w);$$

Compute the dynamic slice with respect to *x* at line 8. Find the union of the dynamic slices computed with respect to variables *x* and *w*.

5.13 Consider test case $t :< x = 1, \ y = 0 >$, Program P5.5, and its modification. Will *t* be selected by the SelectTests algorithm?

5.14 Consider the following test *t*, and the values of *f*1, *f*2, and *f*4, for program P5.5.

$$t :< x = 0, \ y = 3 >,$$

$$f1(0) = 0, \ f2(0) = 4, \ f4(0) = 5$$

Also assume that the output statement in Program P5.5 is as in Exercise 5.12. (a) Construct the DDG for Program P5.8 from its execution trace on *t*. (b) Compute the dynamic slices with respect to *x* and *w* at line 8. (c) Suppose *P'* is Program P5.8 obtained from *P* by adding two initialization statements for *w* and *z* and removing the `else` part from the `if` statement.

Program P5.8

```
1  input (x, y);
2  w=1;
3  z=1;
4  while(x<y){
5     (f1(x)==0)
6        z=f2(x);
7     x=f4(x);
8     w=f5(z);
   }
9  output(x, w);
   end
```

Will *t* be included in *T′* when using the dynamic-slicing approach for test selection? (d) What property must be satisfied by a test case for it not to be included in *T′* when using the dynamic-slicing approach? Construct one such test case, construct its DDG, and compute the dynamic slice with respect to *w* at line 9 in Program P5.8.

5.15 Consider *P* to be Program P5.9.

Program P5.9

```
1  input(x, y);
2  z=0;
3  w=0;
4  while (x < y){
5     if (f(x)<0){
6        if (g(y)<0)
7           z=g(x*y);
8        w=z*w;      }\\ End of first if
9     input (x,y);   } \\end of while.
10 output (w, z);
   end
```

Suppose now that *P* is executed against test *t* such that $trace(t) = (1, 2, 3, 4, 5, 6, 8, 9, 4, 10)$. (a) Construct the DDG for *P* from *trace(t)*. (b) Find the combined dynamic slice corresponding to variables *w* and *z* at line 10. (c) Compute the potential dependencies in the DDG. (d) Compute the combined relevant slice with respect to *w* and *z*.

5.16 Compute the relevant slice for Program P5.6 corresponding to the trace obtained while executing it against $t :< N = 2, \; x = 2, 4 >$. Assume that $f(2) = 0$ and $f(4) > 0$.

5.17 Let P and P' be the original and the modified programs, respectively. Let T be the tests for P. Suppose that P' is obtained by modifying an output statement s in P. Suppose also that s is the last executable statement in P. Which tests in T will not be selected when using the execution-slice approach and the dynamic-slicing approach?

5.18 Refer to Examples 5.17 and 5.20 and let P be Program P5.6. Let e denote some error in P that is corrected to create P'. Assume that correction of e requires a change to one of the existing statements, or the addition/deletion of a statement. You may also change the specification so that P becomes erroneous. Now suppose that P is executed against test t and e is not detected. Construct an e that will go undetected if (a) $DS(t, z, 11)$ and (b) $RS(t, z, 11)$ are used for test selection.

5.19 Consider the modification of Program P5.5, as indicated in Example 5.21. Suppose that $t :< x = 1, \; y = 0 >$ and $t \in T$. Will t be selected for inclusion in T' by steps given in Section 5.6.6?

5.20 (a) Suppose that Program P5.9 is modified by removing a predicate as shown in Program P5.10.

Program P5.10

```
1  input(x, y);
2  z=0;
3  w=0;
4  while(x< y){
5     if (f(x)<0){   ← Predicate g(y) < 0 immediately
                        following this line is removed.
6        z=g(x*y);
7        w=z*w;
      }" End of first if
8     input (x, y);
      }" end of while.
9  output(w, z);
   end
```

Should test t from Exercise 5.15 be included in the regression test for Program P5.10? (b) Now suppose that Program P5.10 is P and is modified to Program P5.9 by adding predicate $g(y) < 0$.

Consider test t such that $trace(t) = \{1, 2, 3, 4, 5, 6, 7, 8, 4, 9\}$. Should t be included in the regression test for Program P5.9 ? (c) Give a general condition that can be used to decide whether a test should be included in T' when a predicate is added.

5.21 Let P be a program tested against test set T. Under one maintenance scenario, P' is derived from P through a series of modifications. These modifications are a mix of statement addition and deletion, predicate addition and deletion, addition of and removal of output variables, and perhaps others. Propose a systematic way of applying the relevant slice-based test-selection technique that is scalable to large programs under the above maintenance scenario.

5.22 Dynamic slicing was originally proposed as a technique to aid in debugging programs. Subsequently it found an application in RTS. While the technique remains unchanged regardless of its application, the PDG used as a source for computing the dynamic or relevant slice can be simplified when used for regression testing. Explain why.

5.23 Explain how one could use dynamic slicing as an aid in (i) program understanding and (ii) locating code corresponding to a specific feature implemented in a program.

5.24 Consider Program P5.7 in Figure 5.13. Suppose the following function trace $trace(t)$ is obtained by executing the program against test t: main, f1, f2, main. (a) Draw the DDG from $trace(t)$. (b) Now suppose a change is made in function f3. Will t be included in the regression test? (c) Will t be included in the regression test if a change is made to f1?

5.25 Compute the dynamic slice from the DDG in Figure 5.13 with respect to variable z at line 7.

5.26 Explain how you would compute potential dependencies in a DDG constructed out of function traces.

5.27 Exactly one node for each statement in the execution trace of P appears in an RDDG constructed using the procedure described in Section 5.6.8. While such an RDDG is useful for RTS, it looses some information needed for constructing the dynamic slice with respect to a variable when debugging P. What information is lost and how does the loss might affect debugging of P?

5.28 In Example 5.29, method 9 is not covered by any test in the regression-test suite T'. Noting that $T' \subseteq T$, and T is the test set for application P what might be the possible explanations for the lack of coverage of method 9 by tests in T'?

5.29 In what ways does a call graph differ from the DDG based on function trace ?

5.30 Let T be a set of non-obsolete tests for P. Let P' be obtained by modifying P. Regression testing of P' is done using a subset T' of tests in T. What is the advantage of applying coverage-based test minimization procedure as in Section 5.8 to (a) T' and (b) T?

5.31 Let T be a test suite for testing P and T' a minimized test suite for testing the modified version P' of P. Give reasons why the fault-detection effectiveness of T' might be less than that of T. Construct an example to show that indeed there exist cases where a fault in P' is detected by a test case in T but by none in T'.

5.32 What is the time complexity of the naive algorithm for finding the minimal test set? Suppose that program P is tested against n tests and a total of m entities are covered. Estimate how long it will take to find the minimal covering set when $n = 100, m = 300$; make suitable assumptions about the time it takes to perform various operations, for example set enumeration, required by the naive algorithm.

5.33 Consider the following *tricky* set-cover problem. Let $E = \{1, 2, \ldots, p\}$, where $p = 2^{k+1} - 2$ for some $k > 0$. Let $TE = \{S_1, S_2, \ldots, S_k, X, Y\}$ be such that (a) S_i and S_j are disjoint for all $1 \leq (i, j) \leq k, i \neq j$, (b) S_i contains 2^i; elements, (c) $S_1 \cup S_2 \cup \ldots \cup S_k = E$, and (d) X contains half the elements from each S_i, and Y contains the remaining half. Thus, $X \cap Y = \emptyset$ and $X \cup Y = E$. The problem is to find the minimal set cover of E. For example, for $k = 2$, we have $E = \{1, 2, 3, 4, 5, 6\}$, $TE = \{S1, S2, X, Y\}, S1 = \{1, 2\}, S_2 = \{3, 4, 5, 6\}, X = \{1, 3, 4\}$, and $Y = \{2, 5, 6\}$. The minimal cover for this problem is $\{X, Y\}$. Show that both the greedy and the CMIMX algorithms fail to compute the minimal cover.

5.34 What is the importance of Step 3.1 in algorithm CMIMX in Section 5.8.

5.35 In Example 5.29, two tests in Step 1 may tie for the minimum cost. A tie could also occur in Step 4 in procedure PrTest. Suggest at least two quantitative criteria that could be used to break the tie instead of breaking it through random selection as mentioned in procedure PrTest.

5.36 Let T' be a regression test for program P'. Consider $X = \{< T'_1 >, < T'_2 > \ldots, < T'_k >\}, k > 0$ to be a set of sequences of tests such that each sequence T_i contains tests from T' and that each test in T' occurs in at least one sequence in X. Modify PrTest to account for the requirement that, if any $< T_i >$ is selected for execution, the given sequencing constraint is not violated. Note that the sequences in X might not be disjoint.

5.37 Given a program P composed of n functions and m tests, develop a formula to estimate the savings in storage requirements for function-level over statement-level execution traces. Make assumptions about the function size and coverage with respect to each test. How will your formula change for object-oriented programs where function-level execution trace is replaced by method-level execution trace?

EXERCISES

Part

Test Adequacy
ASSESSMENT AND
ENHANCEMENT

Techniques to answer "Is my testing adequate?" are introduced in the next two chapters. Chapter 6 presents the foundations of test completeness as defined by Goodnough and Gerhart. This is followed by definitions and illustrations of test-adequacy criteria based on the control-flow and data-flow structure of the program under test.

Chapter 7 is an in-depth presentation of some of the most powerful test-adequacy criteria based on program mutation. In each of the two chapters mentioned, we provide several examples to show how errors are detected, or not detected, while enhancing an inadequate test set with reference to an adequacy criterion.

6

Test-Adequacy Assessment Using Control Flow and Data Flow

This chapter introduces methods for the assessment of test adequacy and test enhancement. Measurements of test adequacy using criteria based on control flow and data flow are explained. These code-based coverage criteria allow a tester to determine how much of the code has been tested and what remains untested.

6.1 TEST ADEQUACY: BASICS

6.1.1 WHAT IS TEST ADEQUACY?

Consider a program P written to meet a set R of functional requirements. We notate such a P and R as (P, R). Let R contain n requirements labeled $R_1, R_2, \ldots, R_n$. Suppose now that a set T containing k tests has been constructed to test P to determine whether it meets all the requirements in R. Also, P has been executed against each test in T and has produced correct behavior. We now ask: *Is T good enough?* This question can be stated differently as: *Has P been tested thoroughly?* or as: *Is T adequate?* Regardless of how the question is stated, it assumes importance when one wants to test P thoroughly in the hope that all errors have been discovered and removed when testing is declared complete and the program P declared usable by the intended users.

In the context of software testing, the terms *thorough, good enough,* and *adequate,* used in the questions above, have the same meaning. We prefer the term adequate and the question *Is T adequate?* Adequacy is measured for a given test set designed to test P to determine whether P meets its requirements. This measurement is done against a given criterion C. A test set is considered adequate with respect to criterion C when it satisfies C. The determination of whether a test set T for program P satisfies criterion C depends on the criterion itself and is explained later in this chapter.

In this chapter, we focus only on *functional* requirements; testing techniques to validate nonfunctional requirements are dealt with elsewhere.

Example 6.1: Consider the problem of writing a program named `sumProduct` that meets the following requirements:

R_1 : Input two integers, say x and y, from the standard input device.

$R_{2.1}$: Find and print to the standard output device the sum of x and y if $x < y$.

$R_{2.2}$: Find and print to the standard output device the product of x and y if $x \geq y$.

Suppose now that the test adequacy criterion C is specified as follows:

C: *A test T for program (P, R) is considered adequate if for each requirement r in R there is at least one test case in T that tests the correctness of P with respect to r.*

It is obvious that $T = \{t :< x = 2, y = 3 >\}$ is inadequate with respect to C for program `sumProduct`. The lone test case t in T tests R_1 and $R_{2.1}$, but not $R_{2.2}$.

6.1.2 MEASUREMENT OF TEST ADEQUACY

Adequacy of a test set is measured against a finite set of elements. Depending on the adequacy criterion of interest, these elements are derived from the requirements or from the program under test. For each adequacy criterion C, we derive a finite set known as the *coverage domain* and denoted as C_e.

A criterion C is a *white-box* test adequacy criterion if the corresponding coverage domain C_e depends solely on program P under test. A criterion C is a *black-box* test adequacy criterion if the corresponding coverage domain C_e depends solely on requirements R for the program P under test. All other test adequacy criteria are of a mixed nature and not considered in this chapter. This chapter introduces several white-box test adequacy criteria that are based on the flow of control and the flow of data within the program under test.

Suppose that it is desired to measure the adequacy of T. Given that C_e has $n \geq 0$ elements, we say that T *covers* C_e if for each element e' in C_e there is at least one test case in T that tests e'. T is considered adequate with respect to C if it covers all elements in the coverage domain. T is considered inadequate with respect to C if it covers k elements of C_e, where $k < n$. The fraction k/n is a measure of the extent to which T is adequate with respect to C. This fraction is also known as the *coverage* of T with respect to C, P, and R.

The determination of when an element e is considered *tested* by T depends on e and P, and is explained below through examples.

> **Example 6.2:** Consider the program P, test T, and adequacy criterion C of Example 6.1. In this case, the finite set of elements C_e is the set $\{R_1, R_{2.1}, R_{2.2}\}$. T covers R_1 and $R_{2.1}$ but not $R_{2.2}$. Hence, T is not adequate with respect to C. The coverage of T with respect to C, P, and R is 0.66. Element $R_{2.2}$ is not tested by T, whereas the other elements of C_e are tested.

> **Example 6.3:** Next, let us consider a different test adequacy criterion that is referred to as the *path coverage* criterion.

> C: *A test T for program (P, R) is considered adequate if each path in P is traversed at least once.*

> Given the requirements in Example 6.1, let us assume that P has exactly two paths, one corresponding to condition $x < y$ and the other to $x \geq y$. Let us refer to these two paths as p_1 and p_2, respectively. For the given adequacy criterion C, we obtain the coverage domain C_e to be the set $\{p_1, p_2\}$.

> To measure the adequacy of T of Example 6.1 against C, we execute P against each test case in T. As T contains only one test for

which $x < y$, only the path p_1 is executed. Thus, the coverage of T with respect to C, P, and R is 0.5 and hence T is not adequate with respect to C. We also say that p_2 is not tested.

In Example 6.3, we assumed that P contains exactly two paths. This assumption is based on a knowledge of the requirements. However, when the coverage domain must contain elements from the code, these elements must be derived by program analysis and not by an examination of its requirements. Errors in the program and incomplete or incorrect requirements might cause the program, and hence the coverage domain, to be different from what one might expect.

Example 6.4: Consider the following program written to meet the requirements specified in Example 6.1; the program is obviously incorrect.

Program P6.1

```
1  begin
2     int x, y;
3     input (x, y);
4     sum = x + y;
5     output (sum);
6  end
```

The above program has exactly one path, which we denote as p_1. This path traverses all statements. Thus, to evaluate any test with respect to criterion C of Example 6.3, we obtain the coverage domain C_e to be $\{p_1\}$. It is easy to see that C_e is covered when P is executed against the sole test in T of Example 6.1. Thus, T is adequate with respect to P even though the program is incorrect.

Program P6.1 has an error that is often referred to as a *missing-path* or a *missing-condition* error. A correct program that meets the requirements of Example 6.1 is as follows:

Program P6.2

```
1  begin
2     int x, y;
3     input (x, y);
4     if (x<y)
5     then
6        output (x + y);
7     else
8        output (x*y);
9  end
```

This program has two paths, one of which is traversed when $x < y$ and the other when $x \geq y$. Denoting these two paths by p_1 and p_2, we obtain the coverage domain given in Example 6.3. As mentioned earlier, test T of Example 6.1 is not adequate with respect to the path-coverage criterion.

The above example illustrates that an adequate test set might not reveal even the most obvious error in a program. This does not diminish in any way the need for the measurement of test adequacy. The next section explains the use of adequacy measurement as a tool for test enhancement.

6.1.3 TEST ENHANCEMENT USING MEASUREMENTS OF ADEQUACY

While a test set adequate with respect to some criterion does not guarantee an error-free program, an inadequate test set is a cause for worry. Inadequacy with respect to any criterion often implies deficiency. Identification of this deficiency helps in the enhancement of the inadequate test set. Enhancement, in turn, is also likely to test the program in ways it has not been tested before such as testing untested portion or testing the features in a sequence different from the one used previously. Testing the program differently than before raises the possibility of discovering any uncovered errors.

Example 6.5: Let us reexamine test T for Program P6.2 in Example 6.4. To make T adequate with respect to the path coverage criterion, we need to add a test that covers p_2. One test that does so is $\{< x = 3, y = 1 >\}$. Adding this test to T and denoting the expanded test set by T', we get:

$$T' = \{< x = 3, y = 4 >, < x = 3, y = 1 >\}.$$

When Program P6.2 is executed against the two tests in T', both paths p_1 and p_2 are traversed. Thus, T' is adequate with respect to the path coverage criterion. Given a test set T for program P, test enhancement is a process that depends on the test process employed in the organization. For each new test added to T, P needs to be executed to determine its behavior. An erroneous behavior implies the existence of an error in P and is likely to lead to debugging of P and the eventual removal of the error. However, there are several procedures by which the enhancement could be carried out. One such procedure follows.

```
Procedure for test enhancement using measurements
of test adequacy
```

Step 1 Measure the adequacy of T with respect to the given criterion C. If T is adequate then go to Step 3, otherwise execute the next step. Note that during adequacy measurement, we will be able to determine the uncovered elements of C_e.

Step 2 For each uncovered element $e \in C_e$, do the following until e is covered or is determined to be infeasible.

    2.1 Construct a test t that covers e or is likely to cover e.

    2.2 Execute P against t.

        2.2.1 If P behaves incorrectly, then we have discovered the existence of an error in P. In this case, t is added to T, the error is removed from P, and this procedure repeated from the beginning.

        2.2.2 If P behaves correctly and e is covered, then t is added to T, otherwise it is the tester's option whether to ignore t or to add it to T.

Step 3 Test enhancement is complete.

End of Procedure

Figure 6.1 shows a sample test construction–enhancement cycle. The cycle begins with the construction of a nonempty set T of test cases. These tests cases are constructed from the requirements of program P under test. P is then executed against all test cases. P is corrected if

406

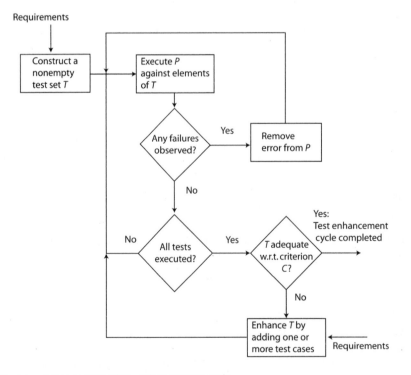

Fig. 6.1 A test construction–enhancement cycle.

it does not behave as per the requirements on any test case. The adequacy of T is measured with respect to a suitably selected adequacy criterion C after P is found to behave satisfactorily on all elements of T. This construction–enhancement cycle is considered complete if T is found adequate with respect to C. If not, then additional test cases are constructed in an attempt to remove the deficiency. The construction of these additional test cases once again makes use of the requirements that P must meet.

Example 6.6: Consider the following program intended to compute x^y, given integers x and y. For $y < 0$, the program skips the computation and outputs a suitable error message.

Program P6.3

```
 1  begin
 2     int x, y;
 3     int product, count;
 4     input (x, y);
 5     if (y≥0) {
 6        product=1; count=y;
 7        while(count>0){
 8           product=product*x;
 9           count=count-1;
10        }
11        output(product);
12     }
13     else
14        output ("Input does not match its specification.");
15  end
```

Next, consider the following test adequacy criterion:

C: *A test T is considered adequate if it tests Program P6.3 for at least one zero and one nonzero value of each of the two inputs x and y.*

The coverage domain for C can be determined using C alone and without any inspection of Program P6.3. For C, we get $C_e = \{x = 0, y = 0, x \neq 0, y \neq 0\}$. Again, one can derive an adequate test set for Program P6.3 by a simple examination of C_e. One such test set is

$$T = \{< x = 0, y = 1 >, < x = 1, y = 0 >\}.$$

In this case, we need not apply the enhancement procedure given above. Of course, Program P6.3 needs to be executed against each test case in T to determine its behavior. For both tests, it generates the correct output that is 0 for the first test case and 1 for the second. Note that T might well be generated without reference to any adequacy criterion.

Example 6.7: Criterion C of Example 6.6 is a *black-box* coverage criterion as it does not require an examination of the program under test for the measurement of adequacy. Let us consider the path coverage criterion defined in Example 6.3. An examination of Program P6.3 reveals that it has an indeterminate number of paths due to the presence of a while loop. The number of paths depends on the value of y and hence that of count. Given that y is any nonnegative integer, the number of paths can be arbitrarily large. This simple analysis of paths in Program P6.3 reveals that we cannot determine the coverage domain for the path coverage criterion.

The usual approach in such cases is to simplify C and reformulate it as follows:

C': *A test T is considered adequate if it tests all paths. In case the program contains a loop, then it is adequate to traverse the loop body zero times and once.*

The modified path coverage criterion leads to $C'_e = \{p_1, p_2, p_3\}$. The elements of C_e are enumerated below with respect to Figure 6.2.

p_1: $[1 \rightarrow 2 \rightarrow 3 \rightarrow 4 \rightarrow 5 \rightarrow 7 \rightarrow 9]$; corresponds to $y \geq 0$ and loop body traversed zero times.

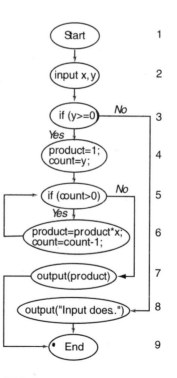

Fig. 6.2 CFG of Program P6.3.

p_2 : $[1 \rightarrow 2 \rightarrow 3 \rightarrow 4 \rightarrow 5 \rightarrow 6 \rightarrow 5 \rightarrow 7 \rightarrow 9]$; corresponds to $y \geq 0$ and loop body traversed once.

p_3 : $[1 \rightarrow 2 \rightarrow 3 \rightarrow 8 \rightarrow 9]$; corresponds to $y < 0$ and the control reaches the output statement without entering the body of the `while` loop.

The coverage domain for C' and Program P6.3 is $\{p_1, p_2, p_3\}$. Following the test enhancement procedure, we first measure the adequacy of T with respect to C'. This is done by executing P against each element of T and determining which elements in C'_e are covered and which ones are not. As T does not contain any test with $y < 0$, p_3 remains uncovered. Thus, the coverage of T with respect to C' is $2/3 = 0.66$.

Moving on to Step 2, we attempt to construct a test aimed at covering p_3. Any test case with $y < 0$ will cause p_3 to be traversed. Let us use the test case $t :< x = 5, y = -1 >$. When P is executed against t, indeed path p_3 is covered and P behaves correctly. We now add t to T. The loop in Step 2 is now terminated as we have covered all feasible elements of C'_e. The enhanced test set is

$$T = \{< x = 0, y = 1 >, < x = 1, y = 0 >, < x = 5, y = -1 >\}.$$

6.1.4 INFEASIBILITY AND TEST ADEQUACY

An element of the coverage domain is infeasible if it cannot be covered by any test in the input domain of the program under test. In general, it is not possible to write an algorithm that would analyze a given program and determine if a given element in the coverage domain is feasible or not. Thus, it is usually the tester who determines whether an element of the coverage domain is infeasible.

Feasibility can be demonstrated by executing the program under test against a test case and showing that indeed the element under consideration is covered. However, infeasibility cannot be demonstrated by program execution against a finite number of test cases. Nevertheless, as in Example 6.8, simple arguments can be constructed to show that a given element is infeasible. For more complex programs, the problem of determining infeasibility could be difficult. Thus, one might fail while attempting to cover e to enhance a test set by executing P against t.

The conditions that must hold for a test case t to cover an element e of the coverage domain depend on e and P. These conditions are derived later in this chapter when we examine various types of adequacy criteria.

Example 6.8: In this example, we illustrate how an infeasible path occurs in a program. The following program inputs two integers x and y and computes z.

Program P6.4

```
1   begin
2      int x,y;
3      int z;
4      input (x,y); z=0;
5      if (x<0 and y<0){
6         z=x*x;
7         if(y≥0) z=z+1;
8         }
9      else z=x*x*x;
10     output(z);
11     }
12  end
```

The path coverage criterion leads to $C_e = \{p_1, p_2, p_3\}$. The elements of C_e are enumerated below with respect to Figure 6.3.

p_1: $[1 \to 2 \to 3 \to 4 \to 5 \to 6 \to 8 \to 9]$; corresponds to conditions $x < 0$, and $y < 0$, and $y \geq 0$ evaluating to true.

p_2: $[1 \to 2 \to 3 \to 4 \to 5 \to 8 \to 9]$; corresponds to conditions $x < 0$ and $y < 0$ evaluating to true, and $y \geq 0$ to false.

p_2: $[1 \to 2 \to 3 \to 7 \to 8 \to 9]$; corresponds to $x < 0$ and $y < 0$ evaluating to false.

It is easy to check that path p_1 is infeasible and cannot be traversed by any test case. This is because when control reaches node 5, condition $y \geq 0$ is false and hence control can never reach node 6. Thus, any test adequate with respect to the path coverage criterion for Program P6.4 will only cover p_2 and p_3.

In the presence of one or more infeasible elements in the coverage domain, a test is considered adequate when all feasible elements in the domain have been covered. This also implies that in the presence of infeasible elements, adequacy is achieved when coverage is less than 1.

Infeasible elements arise for a variety of reasons discussed in the subsequent sections. While programmers might not be concerned with infeasible elements, testers attempting to obtain code coverage are concerned. Prior to test enhancement, a tester usually does not know which elements of a coverage domain are infeasible. It is only during an attempt to construct a test case to cover an element that one might realize the infeasibility of an element. For some elements, this realization might come after several failed attempts. This may lead to frustration on the

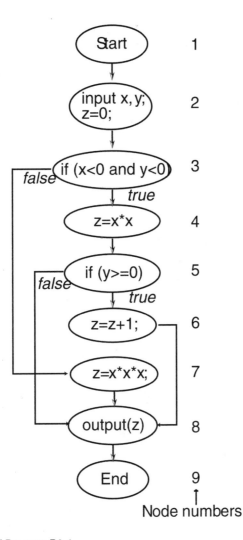

Fig. 6.3 CFG of Program P6.4.

part of the tester. The testing effort spent on attempting to cover an infeasible element might be considered wasteful. Unfortunately, there is no automatic way to identify all infeasible elements in a coverage domain derived from an arbitrary program. However, careful analysis of a program usually leads to a quick identification of infeasible elements. We return to the topic of dealing with infeasible elements later in this chapter.

6.1.5 ERROR DETECTION AND TEST ENHANCEMENT

The purpose of test enhancement is to determine test cases that test the untested parts of a program. Even the most carefully designed tests based exclusively on requirements can be enhanced. The more complex the set of requirements, the more likely it is that a test set designed using requirements is inadequate with respect to even the simplest of various test adequacy criteria.

During the enhancement process, one develops a new test case and executes the program against it. Assuming that this test case exercises the program in a way it has not been exercised before, there is a chance that an error present in the newly tested portion of the program is revealed. In general, one cannot determine how probable or improbable it is to reveal an error through test enhancement. However, a carefully designed and executed test enhancement process is often useful in locating program errors.

Example 6.9: A program to meet the following requirements is to be developed.

R_1: Upon start the program offers the following three options to the user:
- Compute x^y for integers $x \geq 0$ and $y \geq 0$.
- Compute the factorial of integer $x \geq 0$.
- Exit.

$R_{1.1}$: If the "Compute x^y" option is selected then the user is asked to supply the values of x and y, x^y is computed and displayed. The user may now select any of the three options once again.

$R_{1.2}$: If the "Compute factorial x" option is selected then the user is asked to supply the value of x, and factorial of x is computed and displayed. The user may now select any of the three options once again.

$R_{1.3}$: If the "Exit" option is selected, the program displays a goodbye message and exits.

Consider the following program written to meet the above requirements.

Program P6.5

```
1   begin
2     int x,y;
3     int product, request;
4     #define exp=1
5     #define fact=2
6     #define exit=3
7     get_request (request); // Get user request
      (one of three possibilities).
8     product=1; // Initialize product.
```

```
9    // Set up the loop to accept and execute requests.
10      while (request ≠ exit) {
11    // Process the "exponentiation" request.
12      if(request == exp){
13        input (x, y); count=y;
14        while (count > 0){
15          product=product * x; count=count-1;
16        }
17    } // End of processing the "exponentiation"
          request.
18    // Process "factorial" request.
19      else if(request == fact){
20        input (x); count=x;
21        while (count >0){
22          product=product * count; count=count-1;
23        }
24      } // End of processing the "factorial" request.
25    // Process "exit" request.
26      else if(request == exit){
27        output("Thanks for using this program. Bye!");
          break; // Exit the loop.
28      } // End of if.
29      output(product); // Output the value of
                          exponential or factorial.
30    get_request (request); // Get user request once
                              again and jump to loop begin.
31  }
32  end
```

Suppose now that the following set containing three tests have been developed to test whether Program P6.5 meets its requirements:

$$T = \{< request = 1, x = 2, y = 3 >, < request = 2, x = 4 >,$$
$$< request = 3 >\}$$

This program is executed against the three tests in the sequence they are listed above. The program is launched once for each input. For the first two of the three requests, the program correctly outputs 8 and 24, respectively. The program exits when executed against the last request. This program behavior is correct and hence one might conclude that the program is correct. It will not be difficult for you to believe that this conclusion is incorrect.

Let us evaluate T against the path coverage criterion described earlier in Example 6.9. Before you proceed further, you might want to find a few paths in Program P6.5 that are not covered by T.

The coverage domain consists of all paths that traverse each of the three loops zero times *and* once in the same or different executions of the program. We leave the enumeration of all such paths in Program P6.5 as an exercise. For this example, let us consider path p that begins execution at line 1, reaches the outermost `while` at line 10 , then the first `if` at line 12, followed by the statements that compute the factorial starting at line 20, and then the code to compute the exponential starting at line 13. For this example, we do not care what happens after the exponential has been computed and output has been generated.

Our tricky path is traversed when the program is launched and the first input request is to compute the factorial of a number followed by a request to compute the exponential. It is easy to verify that the sequence of requests in T does not exercise p. Therefore, T is inadequate with respect to the path coverage criterion.

To cover p, we construct the following test:

$$T' = \{< request = 2, x = 4 >, < request = 1, x = 2, y = 3 >,$$
$$< request = 3 >\}$$

When the values in T' are input to our example program in the sequence given, the program correctly outputs 24 as the factorial of 4 but incorrectly outputs 192 as the value of 2^3. This happens because T' traverses our tricky path that makes the computation of the exponentiation begin without initializing `product`. In fact, the code at line 14 begins with the value of `product` set to 24.

Note that in our effort to increase the path coverage, we constructed T'. Execution of the test program on T did cover a path that was not covered earlier and revealed an error in the program.

6.1.6 SINGLE AND MULTIPLE EXECUTIONS

In Example 6.9, we constructed two test sets T and T'. Note that both T and T' contain three tests one for each value of variable `request`. Should T be considered a single test or a set of three tests? The same question applies also to T'. The answer depends on how the values in T are input to the test program. In our example, we assumed that all three tests, one for each value of `request`, are input in a sequence during *a single execution of the test program*. Hence, we consider T as a test set containing one test case and write it as follows:

$$T = \left\{ \begin{array}{l} t_1: << request = 1, \ x = 2, \ y = 3 > \rightarrow \\ < request = 2, \ x = 4 > \qquad\qquad \rightarrow < request = 3 >> \end{array} \right\}$$

Note the use of the outermost angular brackets to group all values in a test. Also, the right arrow ($\rightarrow$) indicates that the values of variables are changing in the same execution. We can now rewrite T' also in a way similar to T. Combining T and T', we get a set T'' containing two test cases written as follows:

$$T'' = \begin{Bmatrix} t_1: << request = 1, \ x = 2, \ y = 3 > \to \\ \quad < request = 2, x = 4 > \qquad \to < request = 3 >> \\ t_2: << request = 2, x = 4 > \qquad \to \\ \quad < request = 1, x = 2, y = 3 > \qquad \to < request = 3 >> \end{Bmatrix}$$

Test set T'' contains two test cases, one that came from T and the other from T'. You might wonder why so much fuss regarding whether something is a test case or a test set. In practice, it does not matter. Thus, you may consider T as a set of three test cases or simply as a set of one test case. However, we do want to stress the point that distinct values of all program inputs may be input in separate runs or in the same run of a program. Hence, a set of test cases might be input in a single run or in separate runs.

In older programs that were not based on GUIs, it is likely that all test cases were executed in separate runs. For example, while testing a program to sort an array of numbers, a tester usually executed the sort program with different values of the array in each run. However, if the same sort program is *modernized* and a GUI added for ease of use and marketability, one may test the program with different arrays input in the same run.

In the next section, we introduce various criteria based on the flow of control for the assessment of test adequacy. These criteria are applicable to any program written in a procedural language such as C. The criteria can also be used to measure test adequacy for programs written in object-oriented languages such as Java and C++. Such criteria include plain method coverage as well as method coverage within context. The criteria presented in this chapter can also be applied to programs written in low-level languages such as an assembly language. We begin by introducing *control-flow-based* test-adequacy criteria.

6.2 ADEQUACY CRITERIA BASED ON CONTROL FLOW

6.2.1 STATEMENT AND BLOCK COVERAGE

Any program written in a procedural language consists of a sequence of statements. Some of these statements are declarative, such as the #define and int statements in C, while others are executable, such as the assignment, if and while statements in C and Java. Note that a statement such as

int count=10;

could be considered declarative because it declares the variable `count` to be an integer. This statement could also be considered as executable because it assigns 10 to the variable `count`. It is for this reason that in C, we consider all declarations as executable statements when defining test adequacy criteria based on the flow of control.

Recall from Chapter 1 that a *basic block* is a sequence of consecutive statements that has exactly one entry point and one exit point. For any procedural language, adequacy with respect to the statement coverage and block coverage criteria are defined as follows:

Statement coverage

The statement coverage of T with respect to (P, R) is computed as $|S_c|/(|S_e| - |S_i|)$, where S_c is the set of statements covered, S_i the set of unreachable statements, and S_e the set of statements in the program, that is the coverage domain. T is considered adequate with respect to the statement coverage criterion if the statement coverage of T with respect to (P, R) is 1.

Block coverage

The block coverage of T with respect to (P, R) is computed as $|B_c|/(|B_e| - |B_i|)$, where B_c is the set of blocks covered, B_i the set of unreachable blocks, and B_e the blocks in the program, that is the block coverage domain. T is considered adequate with respect to the block coverage criterion if the block coverage of T with respect to (P, R) is 1.

In the definitions above, the coverage domain for statement coverage is the set of all statements in the program under test. Similarly, the coverage domain for block coverage is the set of all basic blocks in the program under test. Note that we use the term *unreachable* to refer to statements and blocks that fall on an infeasible path.

The next two examples explain the use of the statement and block coverage criteria. In these examples, we use line numbers in a program to refer to a statement. For example, the number 3 in S_e for Program P6.2 refers to the statement on line 3 of this program, that is to the `input (x, y)` statement. We will refer to blocks by block numbers derived from the flow graph of the program under consideration.

Example 6.10: The coverage domain corresponding to statement coverage for Program P6.4 is given below:

$$S_e = \{2, 3, 4, 5, 6, 7, 7b, 9, 10\}$$

Here, we denote the statement $z = z + 1$ as 7b. Consider a test set T_1 that consists of two test cases against which Program P6.4 has been executed.

$$T_1 = \{t_1: < x = -1, y = -1 >, t_2: < x = 1, y = 1 >\}$$

Statements 2, 3, 4, 5, 6, 7, and 10 are covered upon the execution of P against t_1. Similarly, the execution against t_2 covers statements 2, 3, 4, 5, 9, and 10. Neither of the two tests covers statement 7b that is unreachable as we can conclude from Example 6.8. Thus, we obtain $|S_c| = 8, |S_i| = 1, |S_e| = 9$. The statement coverage for T is $8/(9 - 1) = 1$. Hence, we conclude that T is adequate for (P, R) with respect to the statement coverage criterion.

Example 6.11: The five blocks in Program P6.4 are shown in Figure 6.4. The coverage domain for the block coverage criterion $B_e = \{1, 2, 3, 4, 5\}$. Consider now a test set T_2 containing three tests against which Program P6.4 has been executed.

$$T_2 \begin{cases} t_1 < x = -1, \ y = -1 > \\ t_2 < x = -3, \ y = -1 > \\ t_3 < x = -1, \ y = -3 > \end{cases}$$

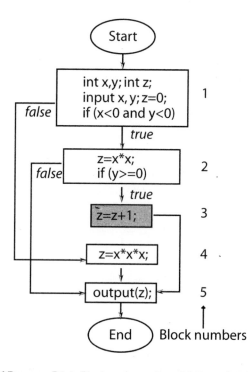

Fig. 6.4 CFG of Program P6.4. Blocks are numbered 1 through 5. The shaded block 3 is infeasible because the condition in block 2 will never be true.

Blocks 1, 2, and 5 are covered when the program is executed against test t_1. Tests t_2 and t_3 also execute exactly the same set of blocks. For T_2 and Program P6.4, we obtain $| B_e | = 5, | B_c | = 3,$ and $| B_i | = 1$. The block coverage can now be computed as $3/(5 - 1) = 0.75$. As the block coverage is less than 1, T_2 is not adequate with respect to the block coverage criterion.

It is easy to check that the test set of Example 6.10 is indeed adequate with respect to the block coverage criterion. Also, T_2 can be made adequate with respect to the block coverage criterion by the addition of test t_2 from T_1 in the previous example.

The formulas given in this chapter for computing various types of code coverage yield a coverage value between 0 and 1. However, while specifying a coverage value, one might instead use percentages. For example, a statement coverage of 0.65 is the same as 65% statement coverage.

6.2.2 CONDITIONS AND DECISIONS

To understand the remaining adequacy measures based on control flow, we need to know what exactly constitutes a condition and a decision. Any expression that evaluates to `true` or `false` constitutes a condition. Such an expression is also known as a *predicate*. Given that A, B, and D are Boolean variables, and x and y are integers, A, $x > y$, A or B, A and $(x < y)$, $(A$ and $B)$ or $(A$ and $D)$ and (D), $(A$ xor $B)$ and $(x \geq y)$ are all conditions. In these examples, and, or , xor, are known as Boolean, or logical, operators. Note that in programming language C, x and $x + y$ are valid conditions, and the constants 1 and 0 correspond to, respectively, `true` and `false`.

Simple and compound conditions: A condition could be *simple or compound*. A simple condition does not use any Boolean operators except for the ¬ operator. It is made up of variables and at most one relational operator from the set $\{<, <, >, \geq, ==, \neq\}$. A compound condition is made up of two or more simple conditions joined by one or more Boolean operators. In the above examples, A and $x > y$ are two simple conditions, while the others are compound. Simple conditions are also referred to as *atomic* or *elementary* because they cannot be parsed any further into two or more conditions. Often, the term *condition* refers to a compound condition. In this book, we will use *condition* to mean any simple or compound condition.

Conditions as decisions: Any condition can serve as a decision in an appropriate context within a program. As shown in Figure 6.5, most high-level languages provide `if`, `while`, and `switch` statements to serve as

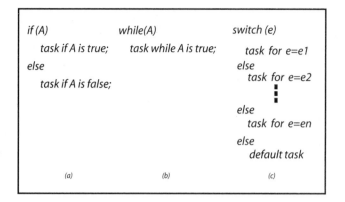

Fig. 6.5 Decisions arise in several contexts within a program. Three common contexts for decisions in a C or a Java program are (a) if, (b) while, and (c) switch statements. Note that the if and while statements force the flow of control to be diverted to one of two possible destinations, while the switch statement may lead the control to one or more destinations.

contexts for decisions. Whereas an `if` and a `while` contains exactly one decision, a `switch` may contain more.

A decision can have three possible outcomes—`true`, `false`, and `undefined`. When the condition corresponding to a decision evaluates to `true` or `false`, the decision to take one or the other path is taken. In the case of a `switch` statement, one of several possible paths gets selected and the control flow proceeds accordingly. However, in some cases the evaluation of a condition might fail in which the corresponding decision's outcome is undefined.

€xample 6.12: Consider the following sequence of statements:

Program P6.6

```
1  bool foo(int a_parameter){
2    while (true) { // An nfinite loop.
3      a_parameter=0;
4    }
5  } // End of function foo().
   ⋮
6  if(x< y and foo(y)){ // foo() does not terminate.
7    compute(x,y);
   ⋮
```

The condition inside the `if` statement on line 6 will remain undefined because the loop at lines 2–4 will never end. Thus, the decision on line 6 evaluates to undefined.

Coupled conditions: There is often the question of how many simple conditions are there in a compound condition. For example, $C' = (A$ and $B)$ or $(C$ and $A)$ is a compound condition. Does C' contain three or four simple conditions? Both answers are correct depending on one's point of view. Indeed, there are three distinct conditions A, B, and C. However, the answer is four when one is interested in the number of occurrences of simple conditions in a compound condition. In the example expression above, the first occurrence of A is said to be *coupled* to its second occurrence.

Conditions within assignments: Conditions may occur within an assignment statement as in the following examples:

1. $A = x < y$; // A simple condition assigned to a Boolean variable A.
2. $X = P$ or Q; // A compound condition assigned to a Boolean variable x.
3. $x = y + z * s$; if (x)... // Condition `true` if $x = 1$, `false` otherwise.
4. $A = x < y$; $x = A * B$; // A is used in a subsequent expression for x but not as a decision.

A programmer might want a condition to be evaluated before it is used as a decision in a selection or a loop statement, as in the previous examples 1–3. Strictly speaking, a condition becomes a decision only when it is used in the appropriate context such as within an `if` statement. Thus, in the example at line 4, $x < y$ does not constitute a decision and neither does $A * B$. However, as we shall see in the context of modified condition/decesion coverage (MC/DC) coverage, a decision is not synonymous with a branch point such as that created by an `if` or a `while` statement. Thus, in the context of the MC/DC coverage, the conditions at lines 1, 2, and the first one on line 4 are all decisions too!

6.2.3 DECISION COVERAGE

A decision coverage is also known as a *branch decision coverage*. A decision is considered *covered* if the flow of control has been diverted to all possible destinations that correspond to this decision, that is all outcomes of the decision have been taken. This implies that, for example, the expression in the `if` or `while` statement has been evaluated to `true` in some execution of the program under test and to `false` in the same or another execution.

A decision implied by the `switch` statement is considered covered if during one or more executions of the program under test the flow of control has been diverted to all possible destinations. Covering a decision within a program might reveal an error that is not revealed by covering all statements and all blocks. The next example illustrates this fact.

Example 6.13: To illustrate the need for decision coverage, consider Program P6.7. This program inputs an integer x and, if necessary, transforms it into a positive value before invoking function foo-1 to compute the output z. However, as indicated, this program has an error. As per its requirements, the program is supposed to compute z using foo-2 when $x \geq 0$. Now consider the following test set T for this program:

$$T = \{t_i :< x = -5 >\}$$

It is easy to verify that when Program P6.7 is executed against the sole test case in T, all statements and all blocks in this program are covered. Hence, T is adequate with respect to both the statement and the block coverage criteria. However, this execution does not force the condition inside the if to be evaluated to false thus avoiding the need to compute z using foo-2. Hence, T does not reveal the error in this program.

Program P6.7

```
1  begin
2    int x, z;
3    input (x);
4    if (x<0)
5        z=-x;
6        z=foo-1(x);
7        output(z);  ← There should have been an else
         clause before this statement.
8  end
```

Suppose that we add a test case to T to obtain an enhanced test set T'.

$$T' = \{t_1: < x = -5 > t_2: < x = 3 >\}$$

When Program P6.7 is executed against all tests in T, all statements and blocks in the program are covered. In addition, the sole decision in the program is also covered because condition $x < 0$ evaluates to true when the program is executed against t_1 and to false when executed against t_2. Of course, control is diverted to the statement at line 6 without executing line 5. This causes the value of z to be computed using foo-1 and not foo-2 as required. Now, if foo-1(3) $\neq$ foo-2(3), then the program will give an incorrect output when executed against test t_2.

The above example illustrates how decision coverage might help a tester discover an incorrect condition and a missing statement by forcing the coverage of a decision. As you may have guessed, covering a decision does not necessarily imply that an error in the corresponding condition will always be revealed. As indicated in the example above, certain other program-dependent conditions must also be true for the error to be revealed. We now formally define adequacy with respect to decision coverage.

Decision coverage

The decision coverage of T with respect to (P, R) is computed as $|D_c|/(|D_e| - |D_i|)$, where D_c is the set of decisions covered, D_i the set of infeasible decisions, and D_e the set of decisions in the program, that is the decision coverage domain. T is considered adequate with respect to the decision coverage criterion if the decision coverage of T with respect to (P, R) is 1.

The domain of the decision coverage consists of all decisions in the program under test. Note that each `if` and each `while` contribute to one decision, whereas a `switch` may contribute to more than one. For the program in Example 6.13, the decision coverage domain is $D_e = \{3\}$ and hence $|D_e| = 1$.

6.2.4 CONDITION COVERAGE

A decision can be composed of a simple condition such as $x < 0$, or of a more complex condition such as $((x < 0 \text{ and } y < 0) \text{ or } (p \geq q))$. Logical operators `and`, `or`, and `xor` connect two or more simple conditions to form a *compound* condition. In addition, ¬(pronounced as "not") is a unary logical operator that negates the outcome of a condition.

A simple condition is considered covered if it evaluates to `true` and `false` in one or more executions of the program in which it occurs. A compound condition is considered covered if each simple condition it is composed of is also covered. For example, $(x < 0 \text{ and } y < 0)$ is considered covered when both $x < 0$ and $y < 0$ have evaluated to true and false during one or more executions of the program in which they occur.

The decision coverage is concerned with the coverage of decisions regardless of whether a decision corresponds to a simple or a compound condition. Thus, in the statement

```
1    if (x < 0 and y < 0) {
2        z = foo (x, y);
```

there is only one decision that leads control to line 2 if the compound condition inside the `if` evaluates to `true`. However, a compound condition might evaluate to `true` or `false` in one of several ways. For example, the condition at line 1 above evaluates to `false` when $x > 0$ regardless of the value of y. Another condition such as $x < 0$ or $y < 0$ evaluates to true regardless of the value of y when $x < 0$. With this evaluation characteristic in view, compilers often generate code that uses *short-circuit* evaluation of compound conditions. For example, the `if` statement in the above code segment might get translated into the following sequence.

```
1  if (x < 0)
2      if (y < 0)  // Note that y < 0 is evaluated only if x < 0 is true.
3          z = foo(x,y);
```

In the code segment above, we see two decisions, one corresponding to each simple condition in the if statement. This leads us to the following definition of condition coverage.

Condition coverage

The condition coverage of T with respect to (P, R) is computed as $|C_c|/(|C_e| - |C_i|)$, where C_c is the set of simple conditions covered, C_i is the set of infeasible simple conditions, and C_e is the set of simple conditions in the program, that is the condition coverage domain. T is considered adequate with respect to the condition coverage criterion if the condition coverage of T with respect to (P, R) is 1.

Sometimes the following alternate formula is used to compute the condition coverage of a test:

$$\frac{|C_c|}{2 \times (|C_e| - |C_i|)}$$

where each simple condition contributes 2, 1, or 0 to C_c depending on whether it is completely covered, partially covered, or not covered, respectively. For example, when evaluating a test set T, if $x < y$ evaluates to `true` but never to `false`, then it is considered partially covered and contributes a 1 to C_c.

Example 6.14: Consider the following program that inputs values of x and y and computes the output z using functions `foo1` and `foo2`. Partial specifications for this program are given in Table 6.1. This table lists how z is computed for different combinations of x and y. A quick examination of Program P6.8 against Table 6.1 reveals that for $x \geq 0$ and $y \geq 0$ the program incorrectly computes z as `foo2(x,y)`.

Table 6.1 Truth table for the computation of z in Program P6.8

x < 0	y < 0	Output (z)
true	true	foo1(x, y)
true	false	foo2(x, y)
false	true	foo2(x, y)
false	false	foo1(x, y)

Program P6.8

```
1  begin
2    int x, y, z;
3    input (x, y);
4    if (x<0 and y<0)
5      z=foo1(x, y);
6    else
7      z=foo2(x, y);
8    output(z);
9  end
```

Consider T designed to test Program P6.8.

$$T = \{t_1: < x = -3, y = -2 > t_2: < x = -4, y = 2 >\}$$

T is adequate with respect to the statement coverage, block coverage, and the decision coverage criteria. You may verify that Program P6.8 behaves correctly on t_1 and t_2.

To compute the condition coverage of T, we note that $C_e = \{x < 0, y < 0\}$. Tests in T cover only the second of the two elements in C_e. As both conditions in C_e are feasible, $| C_i | = 0$. Plugging these values into the formula for condition coverage, we obtain the condition coverage for T to be $1/(2 - 0) = 0.5$.

We now add the test t_3: $< x = 3, y = 4 >$ to T. When executed against t_3, Program P6.8 incorrectly compute z as foo2(x, y). The output will be incorrect if foo1(3, 4) $\neq$ foo2(3, 4). The enhanced test set is adequate with respect to the condition coverage criterion and possibly reveals an error in the program.

6.2.5 CONDITION/DECISION COVERAGE

In the previous two sections, we learned that a test set is adequate with respect to decision coverage if it exercises all outcomes of each decision in the program during testing. However, when a decision is composed of a compound condition, the decision coverage does not imply that each simple condition within a compound condition has taken both values `true` and `false`.

Condition coverage ensures that each component simple condition within a condition has taken both values `true` and `false`. However, as illustrated in the next example, condition coverage does not require each decision to have taken both outcomes. The condition/decision coverage is also known as *branch condition coverage*.

Example 6.15: Consider a slightly different version of Program P6.8 obtained by replacing `and` by `or` in the `if` condition. For Program P6.9, we consider two test sets T_1 and T_2.

Program P6.9

```
1   begin
2     int x,y,z;
3     input (x,y);
4     if (x<0 or y<0)
5       z=foo-1(x,y);
6     else
7       z=foo-2(x,y);
8     output(z);
9   end
```

$$T_1 = \left\{ \begin{array}{l} t_1: < x = -3 \ y = 2 > \\ t_2: < x = 4 \quad y = 2 > \end{array} \right\}$$

$$T_2 = \left\{ \begin{array}{l} t_1: < x = -3, \ y = 2 > \\ t_2: < x = 4, \quad y = -2 > \end{array} \right\}$$

Test set T_1 is adequate with respect to the decision coverage criterion because test t_1 causes the `if` condition to be `true` and test t_2 causes it to be `false`. However, T_1 is not adequate with respect to the condition coverage criterion because condition $y < 0$ never evaluates to `true`. In contrast, T_2 is adequate with respect to the condition coverage criterion but not with respect to the decision coverage criterion.

The condition/decision coverage-based adequacy criterion is developed to overcome the limitations of using the condition coverage and decision coverage criteria independently. The definition is as follows:

Condition/decision coverage

The condition/decision coverage of T with respect to (P, R) is computed as $(| C_c | + | D_c |)/((| C_e | - | C_i |) + (| D_e | - | D_i |))$, *where*

C_c denotes the set of simple conditions covered, D_c the set of decisions covered, C_e and D_e the sets of simple conditions and decisions, respectively, and C_i and D_i the sets of infeasible simple conditions and decisions, respectively. T is considered adequate with respect to the multiple-condition-coverage criterion if the condition/decision coverage of T with respect to (P, R) is 1.

Example 6.16: For Program P6.8, a simple modification of T_1 from Example 6.15 gives us T that is adequate with respect to the condition/decision coverage criteria.

$$T = \left\{ \begin{array}{l} t_1: <x=-3,\ y=-2> \\ t_2: <x=4,\quad y=2> \end{array} \right\}$$

6.2.6 Multiple Condition Coverage

Multiple condition coverage is also known as *branch condition combination coverage*. To understand multiple condition coverage, consider a compound condition that contains two or more simple conditions. Using condition coverage on some compound condition C implies that each simple condition within C has been evaluated to true and false. However, it does not imply that all combinations of the values of the individual simple conditions in C have been exercised. The next example illustrates this point.

Example 6.17: Consider $D = (A < B)$ or $(A > C)$ composed of two simple conditions $A < B$ and $A > C$. The four possible combinations of the outcomes of these two simple conditions are enumerated in Table 6.2.

Now consider test set T containing two tests:

$$T = \left\{ \begin{array}{l} t_1: <A=2,\ B=3,\ C=1> \\ t_2: <A=2,\ B=1,\ C=3> \end{array} \right\}$$

The two simple conditions in D are covered when evaluated against tests in T. However, only two combinations in Table 6.2, those at lines

Table 6.2 Combinations in $D = (A < B)$ or $(A > C)$

	$A < B$	$A > C$	D
1	true	true	true
2	true	false	true
3	false	true	true
4	false	false	false

1 and 3, are covered. We need two more tests to cover the remaining two combinations at lines 2 and 4 in Table 6.2. We modify T to T' by adding two tests that cover all combinations of values of the simple conditions in D.

$$T' = \begin{cases} t_1: < A = 2,\ B = 3,\ C = 1 > \\ t_2: < A = 2,\ B = 1,\ C = 3 > \\ t_3: < A = 2,\ B = 3,\ C = 5 > \\ t_4: < A = 2,\ B = 1,\ C = 5 > \end{cases}$$

To define test adequacy with respect to the multiple-condition-coverage criterion, suppose that the program under test contains a total of n decisions. Assume also that each decision contains $k_1, k_2, \ldots, k_n$ simple conditions. Each decision has several combinations of values of its constituent simple conditions. For example, decision i will have a total of 2^{ki} combinations. Thus, the total number of combinations to be covered is ($\Sigma_{i=1}^{n} 2^{ki}$). With this background, we now define test adequacy with respect to multiple condition coverage.

Multiple Condition Coverage

The multiple condition coverage of T with respect to (P, R) is computed as $|\ C_c\ |/(|\ C_e\ | - |\ C_i\ |)$, where C_c denotes the set of combinations covered, C_i the set of infeasible simple combinations, and $|\ C_e\ | = \Sigma_{i=1}^{n} 2^{ki}$ the total number of combinations in the program. T is considered adequate with respect to the multiple-condition-coverage criterion if the condition coverage of T with respect to (P, R) is 1.

Example 6.18: It is required to write a program that inputs values of integers A, B, and C and computes an output S as specified in Table 6.3. Note from this table the use of functions $f1$ through $f4$ used to compute S for different combinations of the two conditions $A < B$ and $A > C$. Program P6.10 is written to meet the desired specifications. There is an obvious error in the program, computation

Table 6.3 Computing S for Program P6.10

	$A < B$	$A > C$	S
1	true	true	f1(P, Q, R)
2	true	false	f2(P, Q, R)
3	false	true	f3(P, Q, R)
4	false	false	f4(P, Q, R)

of *S* for one of the four combinations, line 3 in the table, has been left out.

Program P6.10

```
1  begin
2     int A,B,C,S=0;
3     input (A,B,C);
4     if(A<B and A>C) S=f1(A,B,C);
5     if(A<B and A≤C) S=f2(A,B,C);
6     if(A≥B and A≤C) S=f4(A,B,C);
7     output(S);
8  end
```

Consider test set *T* developed to test Program P6.10; this is the same test used in Example 6.17.

$$T = \left\{ \begin{array}{l} t_1: < A = 2, B = 3, C = 1 > \\ t_2: < A = 2, B = 1, C = 3 > \end{array} \right\}$$

Program P6.10 contains 3 decisions, 6 conditions, and a total of 12 combinations of simple conditions within the 3 decisions. Note that because all three decisions use the same set of variables, *A*, *B*, and *C*, the number of distinct combinations is only four. Table 6.4 lists all four combinations.

When Program P6.10 is executed against tests in *T*, all simple conditions are covered. Also, the decisions at lines 4 and 6 are covered. However, the decision at line 5 is not covered. Thus, *T* is adequate with respect to the condition coverage but not with respect to the decision coverage. To improve the decision coverage of *T*, we obtain *T'* by adding test t_3 from Example 6.17.

$$T' = \left\{ \begin{array}{l} t_1: < A = 2, B = 3, C = 1 > \\ t_2: < A = 2, B = 1, C = 3 > \\ t_3: < A = 2, B = 3, C = 5 > \end{array} \right\}$$

T' is adequate with respect to the decision coverage. However, none of the three tests in *T'* reveals the error in Program P6.10. Let us now evaluate whether *T'* is adequate with respect to the multiple-condition-coverage criteria.

Table 6.4 lists the 12 combinations of conditions in three decisions and the corresponding coverage with respect to tests in *T'*. From this table, we find that one combination of conditions in each of the three decisions remains uncovered. For example, at line 3 the (false, true) combination of the two conditions $A < B$ and $A > C$ remains uncov-

Table 6.4 Condition coverage for Program P6.10

	$A < B$	$A > C$	T	$A < B$	$A \leq C$	T	$A \geq B$	$A \leq C$	T
1	true	true	t_1	true	true	t_3	true	true	t_2
2	true	false	t_3	true	false	t_1	true	false	—
3	false	true	—	false	true	t_2	false	true	t_3
4	false	false	t_2	false	false	—	false	false	t_1

T, test.

ered. To cover this pair, we add t_4 to T' and get the following modified test set.

$$T' = \begin{cases} t_1: < A = 2, \; B = 3, \; C = 1 > \\ t_2: < A = 2, \; B = 1, \; C = 3 > \\ t_3: < A = 2, \; B = 3, \; C = 5 > \\ t_4: < A = 2, \; B = 1, \; C = 1 > \end{cases}$$

Test t_4 in T'' does cover all of the uncovered combinations in Table 6.4 and hence renders T'' adequate with respect to the multiple condition criterion.

You might have guessed that our analysis in Table 6.4 is redundant. As all three decisions in Program P6.10 use the same set of variables, A, B, and C, we need to analyze only one decision in order to obtain a test set that is adequate with respect to the multiple-condition-coverage criterion.

6.2.7 LINEAR CODE SEQUENCE AND JUMP (LCSAJ) COVERAGE

Execution of sequential programs that contain at least one condition proceeds in pairs where the first element of the pair is a sequence of statements (a block), executed one after the other, and terminated by a jump to the next such pair (another block). The first element of this pair is a sequence of statements that follow each other textually. The last such pair contains a jump to program exit, thereby terminating program execution. An execution path through a sequential program is composed of one or more of such pairs.

A *linear code sequence and jump* is a program unit composed of a textual code sequence that terminates in a jump to the beginning of another code sequence and jump. The textual code sequence may contain one or more statements. An LCSAJ is represented as a triple (X, Y, Z), where X and Y are, respectively, locations of the first and the last statements and

Z is the location to which the statement at Y jumps. The last statement in an LCSAJ is a jump and Z may be program exit.

When control arrives at statement X, follows through to statement Y, and then jumps to statement Z, we say that the LCSAJ (X, Y, Z) is *traversed*. Alternate terms for *traversed* are *covered* and *exercised*. The next three examples illustrate the derivation and traversal of LCSAJs in different program structures.

Example 6.19: Consider the following program composed of one decision. We are not concerned with the code for function g used in this program.

Program P6.11

```
1   begin
2       int x,y,p;
3       input (x, y);
4       if(x<0)
5           p=g(y);
6       else
7           p=g(y*y);
8   end
```

Listed below are three LCSAJs in Program P6.11. Note that each LCSAJ begins at a statement and ends in a jump to another LCSAJ. The jump at the end of an LCSAJ takes control to either another LCSAJ or to program exit.

LCSAJ	Start line	End line	Jump to
1	1	6	exit
2	1	4	7
3	7	8	exit

Now consider the following test set composed of two test cases:

$$T = \left\{ \begin{array}{l} t_1: < x = -5, \ y = 2 > \\ t_2: < x = 9, \quad y = 2 > \end{array} \right\}$$

When Program P6.11 is executed against t_1, the sequence of LCSAJs executed is (1,4,5) and (5, 8, exit). When Program P6.11 is executed against t_2, an LCSAJ (1, 6, exit) is executed. Thus, execution of Program P6.11

against both tests in T causes each of the three LCSAJs to be executed at least once.

Example 6.20: Consider the following program that contains a loop:

Program P6.12

```
1   begin
2   //Compute xʸ given non-negative integers x and y.
3       int x, y, p;
4       input (x, y);
5       p=1;
6       count=y;
7       while(count>0){
8           p=p*x;
9           count=count-1;
10      }
11      output(p);
12  end
```

The LCSAJs in Program P6.12 are enumerated below. As before, each LCSAJ begins at a statement and ends in a jump to another LCSAJ.

LCSAJ	Start line	End line	Jump to
1	1	10	7
2	7	10	7
3	7	7	11
4	1	7	11
5	11	12	exit

The following test set consisting of two test cases traverses each of the five LCSAJs listed above:

$$T = \left\{ \begin{array}{l} t_1: < x = 5, \ y = 0 > \\ t_2: < x = 5, \ y = 2 > \end{array} \right\}$$

Upon execution on t_1, Program P6.12 traverses LCSAJ (1, 7, 11) followed by LCSAJ (11, 12, exit). When Program P6.12 is executed against t_2, the LCSAJs are executed in the following sequence: $(1, 10, 7) \rightarrow (7, 10, 7) \rightarrow (7, 7, 11) \rightarrow (11, 12, \text{exit})$.

Example 6.21: Consider the following program that contains several conditions:

Program P6.13

```
1   begin
2      int x, y, p;
3      input (x, y);
4      p=g(x);
5      if(x<0)
6         p=g(y);
7      if(p<0)
8         q=g(x);
9      else
10        q=g(x*y);
11   end
```

Five LCSAJs for Program P6.13 follow.

LCSAJ	Start line	End line	Jump to
1	1	9	exit
2	1	5	7
3	7	10	exit
4	1	7	10
5	10	10	exit

The following test set consisting of two test cases traverses each of the five LCSAJs listed above:

$$T = \left\{ \begin{array}{l} t_1: < x = -5, \ y = 0 > \\ t_2: < x = 5, \quad y = 2 > \\ t_3: < x = -5, \ y = 2 > \end{array} \right\}$$

Assuming that $g(0) < 0$, LCSAJ 1 is traversed when Program P6.13 is executed against t_1. In this case, the decisions at lines 5 and 7 both evaluate to true. Assuming that $g(5) \geq 0$, the sequence of LCSAJs executed when Program P6.13 is executed against t_2, which is $(1, 5, 7) \rightarrow (7, 10,$ exit). Both decisions evaluate to false during this execution.

We note that the execution of Program P6.13 against t_1 and t_2 has covered both the decisions and hence T is adequate with respect to the decision coverage criterion even if test t_3 were not included. However, LCSAJs 4 and 10 have not been traversed yet. Assuming that $g(2) < 0$, the remaining two LCSAJs are traversed, LCSAJ 4 followed by LCSAJ 5, when Program P6.13 is executed against t_3.

Example 6.21 illustrates that a test adequate with respect to the decision coverage might not exercise all LCSAJs and more than one decision statement might be included in one LCSAJ, as for example is the case with LCSAJ 1. We now give a formal definition of test adequacy based on LCSAJ coverage.

LSCAJ coverage

The LCSAJ coverage of a test set T with respect to (P, R) is computed as

$$\frac{\text{Number of LCSAJs exercised}}{\text{Total number of feasible LCSAJs}}$$

T is considered adequate with respect to the LCSAJ coverage criterion if the LCSAJ coverage of T with respect to (P, R) is 1.

6.2.8 Modified Condition/decision Coverage

As we learned in the previous section, multiple condition coverage requires covering *all* combinations of simple conditions within a compound condition. Obtaining multiple condition coverage might become expensive when there are many embedded simple conditions.

When a compound condition C contains n simple conditions, the maximum number of tests required to cover C is 2^n. Table 6.5 exhibits the growth in the number of tests as n increases. The table also shows the time it will take to run all tests given that it takes 1 ms to set up and execute each test. It is evident from the numbers in this table that it would be impractical to obtain 100% multiple condition coverage for complex conditions. One might ask: "Would any programmer ever devise a complex condition that contains 32 simple conditions?" Indeed, though not frequently, some avionic systems do contain such complex conditions.

Table 6.5 Growth in the maximum number of tests required for multiple condition coverage for a condition with n simple conditions

n	Number of tests	Time to execute all tests
1	2	2 ms
4	16	16 ms
8	256	256 ms
16	65,536	65.5 s
32	4,294,967,296	49.5 days

A weaker adequacy criterion based on the notion of modified condition decision coverage, also known as an *MC/DC coverage*, allows a thorough yet practical test of all conditions and decisions. As is implied in its name, there are two parts to this criteria: the MC part and the DC part. The DC part corresponds to the decision coverage already discussed earlier.

The next example illustrates the meaning of the *MC* part in the MC/DC-coverage criteria. Be forewarned that this example is merely illustrative of the meaning of *MC* and is not to be treated as an illustration of how one could obtain an *MC/DC* coverage. A practical method for obtaining the *MC/DC* coverage is given later in this section.

> **Example 6.22:** To understand the MC portion of the MC/DC coverage, consider a compound condition $C = (C_1$ and $C_2)$ or C_3, where C_1, C_2, and C_3 are simple conditions. To obtain MC adequacy, we must generate tests to show that each simple condition affects the outcome of C *independently*. To construct such tests, we fix two of the three simple conditions in C and vary the third. For example, we fix C_1 and C_2 and vary C_3 as shown in the first eight rows of Table 6.6. There are three ways of varying one condition while holding the remaining two constant. Thus, we have a total of 24 rows in Table 6.6.
>
> Many of these 24 rows are identical as is indicated in the table. For each of the three simple conditions, we select one set of two tests that demonstrate the independent effect of that condition on C. Thus, we select tests (3, 4) for C_3, (11, 12) for C_2, and (19, 20) for C_1. These tests are shown in Table 6.7 that contains a total of only six tests. Note that we could have as well selected (5, 6) or (7, 8) for C_3.
>
> Table 6.7 also has some redundancy as tests (2, 4) and (3, 5) are identical. Compacting this table further by selecting only one among several identical tests, we obtain a minimal MC-adequate test set for C shown in Table 6.8.

The key idea in Example 6.22 is that every compound condition in a program must be tested by demonstrating that each simple condition within the compound condition has an independent effect on its outcome. The example also reveals that such demonstration leads to fewer tests than required by the multiple-condition-coverage criteria. For example, a total of at most eight tests are required to satisfy the multiple condition criteria when condition $C = (C_1$ and $C_2)$ or C_3 is tested. This is in contrast to only four tests required to satisfy the MC/DC creation.

6.2.9 MC/DC-Adequate Tests for Compound Conditions

It is easy to improve upon the brute-force method of Example 6.22 for generating MC/DC-adequate tests for a condition. First, we note that

Table 6.6 Test cases for $C = (C_1$ and $C_2)$ or C_3 to illustrate MC/DC coverage

Test	Inputs C_1	C_2	C_3	Output C
Fix C_1 and C_2 to true, vary C_3				
1(9, 5)	true	true	true	true
2(11, 7)	true	true	false	true
Fix C_1 to true, C_2 to false, vary C_3[a]				
3(10, 9)	true	false	true	true
4(12, 11)	true	false	false	false
Fix C_1 to false, C_2 to true, vary C_3[a]				
5(1, 6)	false	true	true	true
6(3, 8)	false	true	false	false
Fix C_1 and C_2 to false, vary C_3[a]				
7(2, 10)	false	false	true	true
8(4, 12)	false	false	false	false
Fix C_1 and C_3 to true, vary C_2				
9(1, 5)	true	true	true	true
10(3, 9)	true	false	true	true
Fix C_1 to true, C_3 to false, vary C_2[a]				
11(2, 7)	true	true	false	true
12(4, 11)	true	false	false	false
Fix C_1 to false, C_3 to true, vary C_2				
13(5, 6)	false	true	true	true
14(7, 10)	false	false	true	true
Fix C_1 and C_3 to false, vary C_2				
15(6, 8)	false	true	false	true
16(8, 12)	false	false	false	true

(*continued*)

Table 6.6 (*Continued*)

Test	Inputs C_1	C_2	C_3	Output C
Fix C_2 and C_3 to true, vary C_1				
17(1, 9)	true	true	true	true
18(5, 1)	false	true	true	true
Fix C_2 to true, C_3 to false, vary C_1[a]				
19(2, 11)	true	true	false	true
20(6, 3)	false	true	false	false
Fix C_2 to false, C_3 to true, vary C_1				
21(3, 10)	true	false	true	true
22(7, 2)	false	false	true	true
Fix C_2 to false, C_3 to false, vary C_1				
23(4, 12)	true	false	false	false
24(8, 4)	false	false	false	false

[a]Corresponding tests affect C and may be included in the MC-DC adequate test set.
Identical rows are listed in parentheses.

only two tests are required for a simple condition. For example, to cover a simple condition $x < y$, where x and y are integers, one needs only two tests, one that causes the condition to be true and another that causes it to be false.

Next, we determine the MC/DC-adequate tests for compound conditions that contain two simple conditions. Table 6.9 lists adequate tests for

Table 6.7 MC-adequate tests for $C = (C_1$ and $C_2)$ or C_3

Test	C_1	C_2	C_3	C	Effect demonstrated for
1[3]	true	false	true	true	
2[4]	true	false	false	false	C_3
3[11]	true	true	false	true	
4[12]	true	false	false	false	C_2
5[7]	true	true	false	true	
6[8]	false	true	false	false	C_1

[x], x is the corresponding test in Table 6.6.

Table 6.8 Minimal MC-adequate tests for $C = (C_1$ and $C_2)$ or C_3

Test	C_1	C_2	C_3	C	Comments
t_1	true	false	true	true	Tests t_1 and t_2 cover C_3
t_2	true	false	false	false	Tests t_2 and t_3 cover C_2
t_3	true	true	false	true	Tests t_3 and t_4 cover C_3
t_4	false	true	false	false	

such compound conditions. Note that three tests are required to cover each condition using the MC/DC requirement. This number would be four if multiple condition coverage is required. It is instructive to carefully go through each of the three conditions listed in Table 6.9 and verify that indeed the tests given are independent (also try Exercise 6.13).

We now build Table 6.10, which is analogous to Table 6.9, for compound conditions that contain three simple conditions. Notice that only four tests are required to cover each compound condition listed in Table 6.10. One can generate the entries in Table 6.10 from Table 6.9 by using

Table 6.9 MC/DC-adequate tests for compound conditions that contain two simple conditions

Test	C_1	C_2	C	Comments
Condition: $C_a = (C_1$ and $C_2)$				
t_1	true	true	true	Tests t_1 and t_2 cover C_2
t_2	true	false	false	
t_3	false	true	false	Tests t_1 and t_3 cover C_1
MC/DC-adequate test set for $C_a = \{t_1, t_2, t_3\}$				
Condition: $C_b = (C_1$ or $C_2)$				
t_4	false	true	true	Tests t_4 and t_5 cover C_2
t_5	false	false	false	
t_6	true	false	true	Tests t_5 and t_6 cover C_1
MC/DC-adequate test set for $C_b = \{t_4, t_5, t_6\}$				
Condition: $C_c = (C_1$ x or $C_2)$				
t_7	true	true	false	Tests t_7 and t_8 cover C_2
t_8	true	false	true	
t_9	false	false	false	Tests t_8 and t_9 cover C_1
MC/DC-adequate test set for $C_c = \{t_7, t_8, t_9\}$				

Table 6.10 MC/DC-adequate tests for compound conditions that contain three simple conditions

Test	C_1	C_2	C_3	C	Comments
Condition: $C_a = (C_1$ and C_2 and $C_3)$					
t_1	true	true	true	true	Tests t_1 and t_2 cover C_3.
t_2	true	true	false	false	
t_3	true	false	true	false	Tests t_1 and t_3 cover C_2.
t_4	false	true	true	false	Tests t_1 and t_4 cover C_1.
MC/DC-adequate test set for $C_a = \{t_1, t_2, t_3, t_4\}$					
Condition: $C_b = (C_1$ or C_2 or $C_3)$					
t_5	false	false	false	false	Tests t_5 and t_6 cover C_3.
t_6	false	false	true	true	
t_7	false	true	false	true	Tests t_5 and t_7 cover C_2.
t_8	true	false	false	true	Tests t_5 and t_8 cover C_1.
MC/DC-adequate test set for $C_b = \{t_5, t_6, t_7, t_8\}$					
Condition: $C_c = (C_1$ x or C_2 x or $C_3)$					
t_9	true	true	true	true	Tests t_9 and t_{10} cover C_3.
t_{10}	true	true	false	false	
t_{11}	true	false	true	false	Tests t_9 and t_{11} cover C_2.
t_{12}	false	true	true	false	Tests t_3 and t_{12} cover C_1.
MC/DC-adequate test set for $C_c = \{t_9, t_{10}, t_{11}, t_{12}\}$					

the following procedure that works for a compound condition C that is a conjunct of three simple conditions, that is $C = (C_1$ and C_2 and $C_3)$.

1. Create a table with four columns and four rows. Label the columns as Test C_1, C_2, C_3, and C from left to right. The column labeled Test contains rows labeled by test case numbers t_1 through t_4. The remaining entries are empty. The last column labeled Comments is optional.

Test	C_1	C_2	C_3	C	Comments
t_1					
t_2					
t_3					
t_4					

2. Copy all entries in columns C_1, C_2, and C from Table 6.9 into columns C_2, C_3, and C of the empty table.

Test	C_1	C_2	C_3	C	Comments
t_1		true	true	true	
t_2		true	false	false	
t_3		false	true	false	
t_4					

3. Fill the first three rows in the column marked C_1 with true and the last row with false.

Test	C_1	C_2	C_3	C	Comments
t_1	true	true	true	true	
t_2	true	true	false	false	
t_3	true	false	true	false	
t_4	false				

4. Fill entries in the last row under columns labeled C_2, C_3, and C with true, true, and false, respectively.

Test	C_1	C_2	C_3	C	Comments
t_1	true	true	true	true	Tests t_1 and t_2 cover C_3
t_2	true	true	false	false	
t_3	true	false	true	false	Tests t_1 and t_3 cover C_2
t_4	false	true	true	false	Tests t_1 and t_4 cover C_1

5. We now have a table containing the MC/DC-adequate tests for $C = (C_1$ and C_2 and $C_3)$ derived from tests for $C = (C_1$ and $C_2)$.

The procedure illustrated above can be extended to derive tests for any compound condition using tests for a simpler compound condition (see Exercises 6.14 and 6.15). The important point to note here is that for any compound condition, the size of an MC/DC-adequate test set grows *linearly* in the number of simple conditions. Table 6.5 is reproduced as Table 6.11 with columns added to compare the minimum number of tests required, and the time to execute them, for the multiple condition and the MC/DC-coverage criteria.

Table 6.11 MC/DC adequacy and the growth in the least number of tests required for a condition with n simple conditions

	Minimum tests		Time to execute all tests	
n	MC	MC/DC	MC	MC/DC
1	2	2	2 ms	2 ms
4	16	5	16 ms	5 ms
8	256	9	256 ms	9 ms
16	65,536	17	65.5 s	17 ms
32	4,294,967,296	33	49.5 days	33 ms

6.2.10 DEFINITION OF MC/DC COVERAGE

We now provide a complete definition of the MC/DC coverage. A test set T for program P written to meet requirements R is considered adequate with respect to the MC/DC-coverage criterion if upon execution of P on each test in T, the following requirements are met:

1. Each block in P has been covered.
2. Each simple condition in P has taken both `true` and `false` values.
3. Each decision in P has taken all possible outcomes.
4. Each simple condition within a compound condition C in P has been shown to independently effect the outcome of C. *This is the MC part of the coverage we discussed in detail earlier in this section.*

The first three requirements above correspond to block coverage, condition coverage, and the decision coverage, respectively, and have been discussed in earlier sections. The fourth requirement corresponds to the MC coverage discussed earlier in this section.

Thus, the MC/DC-coverage criterion is a mix of four coverage criteria based on the flow of control. With regard to the second requirement, it is to be noted that conditions that are not part of a decision such as the one in the following statement

$$A = (p < q) \ \text{or} \ (x > y)$$

are also included in the set of conditions to be covered. With regard to the fourth requirement, a condition such as (A and B) or (C and A) poses a problem. It is not possible to keep the first occurrence of A fixed while varying the value of its second occurrence. Here, the first occurrence of A is said to be coupled to its second occurrence. In such cases, an adequate test set need only demonstrate the independent effect of any one occurrence of the coupled condition.

A numerical value can also be associated with a test to determine the extent of its adequacy with respect to the MC/DC criterion. One way to do so is to treat separately each of the four requirements listed above for the MC/DC adequacy. Thus, four distinct coverage values can be associated with T namely the block coverage, the condition coverage, the decision coverage, and the MC coverage. The first three of these four have already been defined earlier. A definition of MC coverage is as follows:

Let $C_1, C_2, \ldots, C_N$ be the conditions in P; each condition could be simple or compound and may appear within the context of a decision. Let n_i denote the number of simple conditions in C_i , e_i the number of simple conditions shown to have independent effect on the outcome of C_i , and f_i the number of infeasible simple conditions in C_i . Note that a simple condition within a compound condition C is considered infeasible if it is impossible to show its independent effect on C while holding constant the remaining simple conditions in C. The MC coverage of T for program P subject to requirements R, denoted by MC_c, is computed as follows:

$$MC_c = \frac{\sum_{i=1}^{N} e_i}{\sum_{i=1}^{N}(e_i - f_i)}$$

Thus, test set T is considered adequate with respect to the MC coverage if MC of T is 1. Having now defined all components of the MC/DC coverage, we are ready for a complete definition of the adequacy criterion based on this coverage.

Modified condition/decision coverage

A test T written for program P subject to requirements R is considered adequate with respect to the MC/DC-coverage criterion if T is adequate with respect to block, decision, condition, and MC coverage.

The next example illustrates the process of generating MC/DC-adequate tests for a program that contains three decisions, one composed of a simple condition and the remaining two composed of compound conditions.

Example 6.23: Program P6.14 is written to meet the following requirements:

R$_1$: Given coordinate positions x, y, and z, and a direction value d, the program must invoke one of the three functions fire-1, fire-2, and fire-3 as per conditions below:

$R_{1.1}$: Invoke `fire-1` when $(x < y)$ and $(z*z > y)$ and (prev="East"), where *prev* and *current* denote, respectively, the previous and current values of *d*.

$R_{1.2}$: Invoke `fire-2` when $(x < y)$ and $(z*z \leq y)$ or (current = "South").

$R_{1.3}$: Invoke `fire-3` when none of the two conditions above is `true`.

R_2: The invocation described above must continue until an input Boolean variable becomes `true`.

Program P6.14

```
1   begin
2     float x,y,z;
3     direction d;
4     string prev, current;
5     bool done;
6     input (done);
7     current="North";
8     while (¬done) {← Condition C₁.
9        input (d);
10       prev=current; current=f(d); // Update
         prev and current
11       input (x,y,z);
12       if((x<y) and (z * z > y) and
          (prev=="East")) ← Condition C₂.
13         fire-1(x, y);
14       else if ((x<y and (z * z ≤  y) or
          (current=="South")) ← Condition C₃.
15         fire-2(x, y);
16       else
17         fire-3(x, y);
18     input (done);
19   }
20   output("Firing completed.");
21  end
```

First we generate tests to meet the given requirements. Three tests derived to test $R_{1.1}$, $R_{1.2}$, and $R_{1.3}$ are as follows note that these tests are to be executed in the sequence listed.

Test set T_1 for P6.14

Test	Requirement	done	d	x	y	z
t_1	$R_{1.2}$	false	East	10	15	3
t_2	$R_{1.1}$	false	South	10	15	4
t_3	$R_{1.3}$	false	North	10	15	5
t_4	R_2	true	—	—	—	—

Assuming that Program P6.14 has been executed against the tests given above, let us analyze which decisions have been covered and which ones have not been covered. To make this task easy, the values of all simple and compound conditions are listed below for each test case:

Test	C_1	Comment
t_1	true	
t_2	true	
t_3	true	Both C_2 and C_3 are false, hence fire-3 invoked
t_4	false	This terminates the loop, decision at line 8 is covered

$C_2 =(x<y)$ and $(z * z>y)$ and (**prev**=="**EasT**")

Test	$x<y$	$z*z>y$	**prev**=="**East**"	C_2	Comment
t_1	true	false	false	false	
t_2	true	true	true	true	fire-1 invoked, decision at line 12 is covered by t_1 and t_2 and also by t_2 and t_3
t_3	true	true	false	false	
t_4	—	—	—	—	Condition not evaluated, loop terminates

$C_3 =(x<y)$ and $(z * z \leq y)$ or (**current**=="**South**")

Test	$x<y$	$z*z\leq y$	**current**=="**South**"	C_3	Comment
t_1	true	true	false	true	fire-2 invoked
t_2	Condition not evaluated				
t_3	true	false	false	false	Decision at line 14 is covered by t_1 and t_3
t_4	—	—	—	—	Condition not evaluated, loop terminates

First, it is easy to verify that all statements in Program P6.14 are covered by test set T_1. This also implies that all blocks in this program are covered. Next, a quick examination of the tables above reveals that the three decisions at lines 8, 12, and 14 are also covered as both outcomes of each decision have been taken. Condition C_1 is covered by tests t_1 and t_4, by tests t_2 and t_4, and by t_3 and t_4. However, compound condition C_2 is not covered because $x < y$ is not covered. Also, C_3 is not covered because $(x < y)$ is not covered. This analysis leads to the conclusion that T_1 is adequate with respect to the statement coverage, block coverage, and the decision coverage criteria, but not with respect to the condition coverage criteria.

Next, we modify T_1 to make it adequate with respect to the condition coverage criteria. Recall that C_2 is not covered because $x < y$ is not covered. To cover $x < y$, we generate a new test t_5 and add it to T_1 to obtain T_2 given below. The value of x being greater than that of y makes $x < y$ false. Also, we looked ahead and set d to *South* to make sure that (current=="South") in C_3 evaluates to true. Note the placement of t_5 with respect to t_4 to ensure that the program under test is executed against t_5 *before* it is executed against t_4 or else the program will terminate without covering $x < y$.

Test set T_2 for Program P6.14

Test	Requirement	done	d	x	y	z
t_1	$R_{1.2}$	false	East	10	15	3
t_2	$R_{1.1}$	false	South	10	15	4
t_3	$R_{1.3}$	false	North	10	15	5
t_5	R_1 and $R_{1.2}$	false	South	10	5	5
t_4	R_2	true	—	—	—	—

The evaluations of C_2 and C_3 are reproduced below with a row added for the new test t_5. Note that test T_2, obtained by enhancing T_1, is adequate with respect to the condition coverage criterion. Obviously, it is not adequate with respect to the multiple condition coverage criteria. Such adequacy will imply a minimum of eight tests, and the development of these is left to Exercise 6.20.

Next, we check if T_2 is adequate with respect to the MC/DC criterion. From the table given above for C_2, we note that conditions $(x < y)$ and $(z * z > y)$ are kept constant in t_2 and t_3, while (prev=="East") is varied. These two tests demonstrate the independent effect of (prev=="East") on C_2. However, the independent effect of the remaining two conditions is not demonstrated by T_2. In the case of C_3, we note that in tests t_3 and t_4, conditions $(z * z \leq y)$ and $(current=="South")$ are held constant, while $(x < y)$ is varied. These two tests demonstrate the independent effect of $(x < y)$ on C_3. Tests t_1 and t_3 demonstrate the independent effect of $(z * z \leq y)$ on C_3. However, the independent effect of $(current=="South")$ on C_3 is not demonstrated by T_2. This analysis reveals that we need to add at least two tests to T_2 to obtain the MC/DC coverage.

$C_2 = (x < y)$ and $(z * z > y)$ and (**prev=="East"**)

Test	$x < y$	$z * z > y$	**prev=="East"**	C_2	Comment
t_1	true	false	false		false	
t_2	true	true	true		true	fire-1 invoked
t_3	true	true	false		false	
t_5	false	true	false		false	C_2 is covered because each of its component conditions is covered
t_4	—	—	—	—	Condition not evaluated, loop terminates

$C_3 = (x < y)$ and $(z * z \leq y)$ or (**current=="South"**)

Test	$x < y$	$z * z \leq y$	**current=="South"**	C_3	Comment
t_1	true	true	false		true	fire-2 invoked
t_2	Condition not evaluated					
t_3	true	false	false		false	
t_5	false	false	true		true	C_3 is covered because each of its component conditions is covered
t_4	—	—	—	—	Condition not evaluated, loop terminates

To obtain the MC/DC coverage for C_2, consider $(x < y)$. We need two tests that fix the two remaining conditions, vary $(x < y)$, and cause C_2 to be evaluated to `true` and `false`. We reuse t_2 as one of these two tests. The new test must hold $(z * z > y)$ and $(prev=="East")$ to `true` and make $(x < y)$ evaluate to `false`. One such test is t_6, which is to be executed right after t_1 but before t_2. Execution of the program against t_6 causes $(x < y)$ to evaluate to `false` and C_2 also to `false`. t_6 and t_2 together demonstrate the independent effect of $(x < y)$ on C_2. Using similar arguments, we add test t_7 to show the independent effect of $(z * z > y)$ on C_2. Adding t_6 and t_7 to T_2 gives us an enhanced test set T_3.

Test set T_3 for Program P6.14

Test	Requirement	done	d	x	y	z
t_1	$R_{1.2}$	false	East	10	15	3
t_6	R_1	false	East	10	5	2
t_7	R_1	false	East	10	15	3
t_2	$R_{1.1}$	false	South	10	15	4
t_3	$R_{1.3}$	false	North	10	15	5
t_5	$R_{1.1}$ and $R_{1.2}$	false	South	10	5	5
t_8	R_1	false	South	10	5	2
t_9	R_1	false	North	10	5	2
t_4	R_2	true	—	—	—	—

Upon evaluating C_3 against the newly added tests, we observe that the independent effects of $(x < y)$ and $(z * z \leq y)$ have been demonstrated. We add t_8 and t_9 to show the independent effect of $(current=="South")$ on C_3. The complete test set T_3 listed above, is the MC/DC adequate for Program P6.14. Once again, note the importance of test sequencing. t_1 and t_7 contain identical values of input variables but lead to different effects in the program due to their position in the sequence in which tests are executed. Also note that test t_2 is of no use for covering any portion of C_3 because C_3 is not evaluated when the program is executed against this test.

$C_2 = (x < y) \text{ and } (z * z > y) \text{ and } (\textbf{prev}==\textbf{"East"})$

Test	$x < y$	$z * z > y$	prev=="**East**"	C_2	Comment
t_1	true	false	false	false	
t_6	false	true	true	false	
t_7	true	false	true	false	t_7 and t_2 demonstrate the independent effect of $z * z > y$ on C_2
t_2	true	true	true	true	t_6 and t_2 demonstrate the independent effect of $x < y$ on C_2
t_3	true	true	false	false	t_2 and t_3 demonstrate the independent effect of (prev== "East") on C_2
t_5	false	true	false	false	
t_8	false	false	true	false	
t_9	false	false	true	false	
t_4	Condition not evaluated				

$C_3 = (x < y) \text{ and } (z * z \leq y) \text{ or } (\textbf{current}==\textbf{"South"})$

Test	$x < y$	$z * z \leq y$	current=="**South**"	C_3	Comment
t_1	true	true	false	true	
t_6	false	true	false	false	t_1 and t_6 demonstrate the independent effect of $x < y$ on C_3
t_7	true	true	false	true	
t_2	Condition not evaluated				
t_3	true	false	false	false	t_1 and t_3 demonstrate the independent effect of $z * z \leq y$ on C_3
t_5	false	true	true	true	
t_8	false	false	true	true	
t_9	false	false	false	false	t_8 and t_9 demonstrate the independent effect of current== "South" on C_3
t_4	Condition not evaluated				

6.2.11 Minimal MC/DC Tests

In Example 6.23, we did not make any effort to obtain the smallest test set adequate with respect to the MC/DC coverage. However, while generating tests for large programs involving several compound conditions, one might like to generate the smallest number of the MC/DC-adequate tests. This is because execution against each test case might take a significant chunk of test time, for example 24 h. Such execution times might be considered exorbitant in several development environments. In situations like this, one might consider using one of several techniques for the minimization of test sets. Such techniques are discussed in Chapter 5 of this book.

6.2.12 Error Detection and MC/DC Adequacy

In Example 6.14, we saw how obtaining condition coverage led to a test case that revealed a missing condition error. Let us now dwell on what types of errors might one find while enhancing tests using the MC/DC criterion. In this discussion, we assume that the test being enhanced is adequate with respect to the condition coverage but not the MC/DC coverage, and has not revealed an error. For this discussion, we consider the following three error types in a compound condition; errors in simple conditions have been discussed in Section 6.2.3.

1. Missing condition: One or more simple conditions are missing from a compound condition. For example, the correct condition should be $(x < y$ and done$)$ but the condition coded is (done).

2. Incorrect Boolean operator: One or more Boolean operators are incorrect. For example, the correct condition is $(x < y$ and done$)$ that has been coded as $(x < y$ or done$)$.

3. Mixed type: One or more simple conditions are missing and one or more Boolean operators is incorrect. For example, the correct condition should be $(x < y$ and $z * x > y$ and d="South"$)$ and has been coded as $(x < y$ or $z * x > y)$.

Note that we are considering errors in code. In this discussion, we assume that we are given a test set T for program P subject to requirements R. T is adequate with respect to the condition coverage criterion. The test team has decided to enhance T to make it adequate with respect to the MC/DC-coverage criterion. Obviously the enhancement process will lead to the addition of zero or more tests to T; no tests will be added if T is already MC/DC adequate.

We also assume that P contains a missing-condition error or an incorrect Boolean operator error. The question we ask is: "Will the enhanced T detect the error?" In the three examples that follow, we do not consider the entire program; instead we focus only on the erroneous condition (see Exercise 6.24).

Example 6.24: Suppose that condition $C = C1$ and C_2 and C_3 has been coded in a program as $C'' = C1$ and C_3. The first two tests below form a test set adequate with respect to condition coverage for C''. The remaining two tests, when combined with the first two, constitute an MC/DC-adequate test for C''. Note that the adequate test set is developed for the condition as coded in the program, and not the correct condition.

| Test | | C | C' | |
| | | C_1 and C_2 and C_3 | C_1 and C_3 | Error detected |
	C_1, C_2, C_3			
t_1	true, true, true	true	true	No
t_2	false, false, false	false	false	No
t_3	true, true, false	false	false	No
t_4	false, false, true	false	false	No

The first two tests do not reveal the error as both C and C'' evaluate to the same value for each test. The next two tests, added to obtain the MC/DC coverage, also do not detect the error. Thus, in this example, an MC/DC-adequate test is unable to detect a missing-condition error.

It should be noted in the above example that the first two tests are not adequate with respect to the condition coverage criterion if short-circuit evaluation is used for compound conditions. Of course, this observation does not change the conclusion we arrived at. This conclusion can be generalized for a conjunction of n simple conditions (see Exercise 6.23).

Example 6.25: Suppose that condition $C = C1$ and C_2 and C_3 has been coded as $C' = (C1$ or $C_2)$ and C_3. Six tests that form an MC/DC-adequate set are in the following table. Indeed, this set does reveal the error as t_4, and t_5 cause C and C' to evaluate differently. However, the first two tests do not reveal the error. Once again, we note that the first two tests below are not adequate with respect to the condition coverage criterion if short-circuit evaluation is used for compound conditions.

| Test | | C | C' | |
| | | C_1 and C_2 and C_3 | $(C_1$ or $C_2)$ and C_3 | Error detected |
	C_1, C_2, C_3			
t_1	true, true, true	true	true	No
t_2	false, false, false	false	false	No
t_3	true, true, false	false	false	No
t_4	true, false, true	false	true	Yes
t_5	false, true, true	false	true	Yes
t_6	false, false, true	false	false	No

Example 6.26: Suppose that condition $C = C_1$ or C_2 or C_3 has been coded as $C' = C_1$ and C_3. Four MC/DC-adequate tests are given below. All tests except t_1 reveal the error.

| Test | | C | C' | |
| | | $C = C_1$ or C_2 or C_3 | C_1 and C_3 | Error detected |
	C_1, C_2, C_3			
t_1	true, true, true	true	true	No
t_2	false, true, false	true	false	Yes
t_3	true, true, false	true	false	No
t_4	false, true, true	true	false	Yes

Not surprisingly, examples given above show that satisfying the MC/DC-adequacy criteria does not necessarily imply that errors made while coding conditions will be revealed. However, the examples do favor the MC/DC over condition coverage. The first two tests in each of the three examples above are also adequate with respect to the decision coverage. Hence, these examples also show that an MC/DC-adequate test is *likely* to reveal more errors than a decision coverage or condition coverage-adequate test. Note the emphasis on the word *likely*.

There is no guarantee that given that there are errors in the conditions as coded, an MC/DC-adequate test will reveal these errors when a decision coverage or condition coverage-adequate test set does not.

6.2.13 SHORT-CIRCUIT EVALUATION AND INFEASIBILITY

Short-circuit evaluation refers to the method of partially evaluating a compound condition whenever it is sufficient to do so. It is also known as *lazy evaluation*. C requires short-circuit evaluation and Java allows both. For example, consider the following decision composed of a conjunction of conditions: (C_1 and C_2).

The outcome of the above condition does not depend on C_2 when C_1 is false. When using short-circuit evaluation, condition C_2 is not evaluated if C_1 evaluates to false. Thus, the combination $C_1 =$ false and $C_2 =$ true, or the combination $C_1 =$ false and $C_2 =$ false, may be infeasible if the programming language allows *short-circuit* evaluation as in the programming language C.

Dependence of one decision on another might also lead to an infeasible combination. Consider the following sequence of statements:

```
1  int A, B, C
2  input (A, B, C);
3  if(A > 10 and B > 30) {
4      S₁ = f1(A, B, C)
5      if(A < 5 and B > 10){
6          S₂ = f2(A, B, C);
7  }
```

Clearly, the decision at line 5 is infeasible because the value of *A* cannot simultaneously be more than 10 and less than 5. However, suppose that line 3 is replaced by the following statement that has a side effect due to a call to the function foo().

```
3  if(A > 10 and foo ()) {
```

Given that the execution of foo() may lead to a modification of A, the condition at line 5 might be feasible.

Note that infeasibility is different from reachability. A decision might be reachable but not feasible, and vice versa. In the sequence above, both decisions are reachable, but the second decision is not feasible. Consider the following sequence:

```
1  int A, B, C
2  input (A, B, C);
3  if(A > A + 1){  ← Assume that overflow causes an
                      exception.
4      S₁ = f1(A, B, C)
5      if(A > 5 and B > 10){
6          S₂ = f2(A, B, C);
7  }
```

In this case, the second decision is not reachable due an error at line 3. It may, however, be feasible.

When enhancing a test set to satisfy a given coverage criterion, it is desirable to ask the following question: *What portions of the requirements are tested when the program under test is executed against the newly added test case?* The task of relating the new test case to the requirements is known as *test trace-back*.

Trace-back has at least the following advantages. First, it assists in determining whether the new test case is redundant. Second, it has the likelihood of revealing errors and ambiguities in the requirements. Third, it assists with the process of documenting tests against requirements. Such documentation is useful when requirements are modified. Modification of one or more requirements can simultaneously lead to a modification of the associated test cases, thereby avoiding the need for a detailed analysis of the modified requirements.

The next example illustrates how to associate a test, generated to satisfy a coverage criterion, to the requirements. The example also illustrates how a test generated to satisfy a coverage criterion might reveal an error in the requirements or in the program.

> Example 6.27: The original test set T_1 in Example 6.23 contains only four tests, t_1, t_2, t_3, and t_4. T_2 is obtained by enhancing T_1 through the addition of t_5. We ask, "Which requirement does t_5 correspond to?" Recall that we added t_5 to cover the simple condition $x < y$ in C_2 and C_3. Going back to the requirements for Program P6.14, we can associate t_5 with $R_{1.1}$ and $R_{1.2}$.

One might argue that there is nothing explicit in the requirements for Program P6.14 that suggests a need for t_5. If one were to assume that the given requirements are correct, then indeed this argument is valid and there is no need for t_5. However, in software development projects, requirements might be incorrect, incomplete, and ambiguous. It is, therefore, desirable to extract as much information from the requirements as one possibly can to generate new tests. Let us reexamine $R_{1.2}$ in Example 6.23 reproduced below for convenience.

$R_{1.2}$: Invoke `fire-2` when $(x<y)$ and $(z*z \leq y)$
or (current = "South").

Note that $R_{1.2}$ is not explicit about what action to take when (current="South") is `false`. Of course, as stated, the requirement does imply that `fire-2` is *not* to be invoked when (current="South") is `false`. Shall we go with this implication and not generate t_5? Or shall we assume that $R_{1.2}$ is ambiguous and hence we do need a test case to test explicitly that indeed the program functions correctly when (current="South") is `false`. It is often safer to make the latter assumption. Of course, selecting the former assumption is less expensive in terms of the number of tests, the time to execute all tests, and the effort required to generate, analyze, and maintain the additional tests.

Moving further, we ask, "What error in the program might be revealed by t_5 that will not be revealed by executing the program against all tests in T_1?" To answer this question, suppose that line 14 in Program P6.14 was incorrectly coded as given below while all other statements were coded as shown.

```
14     else if ((x<y) and (z*z≤y))
```

Clearly, now Program P6.14 is incorrect because the invocation of `fire-2` is independent of (current="South"). Execution of the incorrect program against tests in T_1 will not reveal the error because all tests lead to correct response independent of how (current="South") evaluates. However, execution of the incorrect Program P6.14 against t_5 causes the program to invoke `fire-2` instead of invoking `fire-3`; hence, the error is revealed. This line of argument stresses the need for t_5 generated to explicitly test (current="South").

An adamant tester might continue with the argument that t_5 was generated to satisfy the condition coverage criterion and was not based upon the requirements; it was through an examination of the code. If the code for Program P6.14 was incorrect due to the incorrect coding of C_3, then this test might not be generated. To counter this argument, suppose that $R_{1.2}$ as stated earlier is incorrect; its correct version is

$R_{1.2}$:Invoke `fire-2` when $(x<y)$ and $(z*z≤y)$.

Note that now the program is correct but the requirements are not. In this case, for all tests in T_1, Program P6.14 produces the correct response and hence the error in requirements is not revealed. However, as mentioned in Example 6.23, t_5 is generated with the intention of covering both $x < y$ and (current="South"). When Program P6.23 is executed against t_5, it invokes `fire-2` but the requirements imply the invocation of `fire-3`. This mismatch in the program response and the requirements is likely to lead to an analysis of the test results and discovery of the error in the requirements.

The above discussion justifies the association of tests t_5, t_6, t_7, t_8, and t_9 to requirement R_1. It also stresses the need for the trace-back of all tests to requirements.

6.3 DATA-FLOW CONCEPTS

So far, we have considered flow of control as the basis for deriving test-adequacy criteria. We examined various program constructs that establish flow of control and that are susceptible to mistakes by programmers. Ensuring that all such constructs have been tested thoroughly is a major objective of test-adequacy assessment based on flow of control. However, testing all conditions and blocks of statements is often inadequate as the test does not reveal all errors.

Another kind of adequacy criteria are based on the flow of *data* through the program. Such criteria focus on definitions of data and their subsequent use, and are useful in improving the tests adequate with respect to criteria based on the flow of control. The next example exposes an essential idea underlying data-flow-based adequacy asessment.

Example 6.28: The program given below inputs integer x and outputs z. The program contains two simple conditions. As shown, there is an error in this program at line 8. An MC/DC-adequate test follows the program.

Program P6.15

```
1   begin
2     int x, y; float z;
3     input (x, y);
4     z = 0;
5     if (x! = 0)
6        z = z+y;
7     else z = z - y;
8     if (y! = 0)   ← This condition should be
      (y! = 0 and  x! = 0)
9        z = z/x;
10    else z = z * x;
11    output(z);
12  end
```

Test	x	y	z
t_1	0	0	0.0
t_2	1	1	1.0

The two test cases above cover both conditions in Program P6.15. Note that the program initializes z at line 4 and then adjusts its value in subsequent statements depending on the values of x and y. Test t_1 follows a path that traverses updates of z at line 7 followed by another at line 10. Test t_2 follows a different path that traverses updates of z at lines 6 followed by another update on line 9. These two tests cause the value of z, set at line 4, to be used at lines 6 and 7 in the expression on the corresponding right-hand sides.

Just as z is defined at line 4, it is also defined subsequently at lines 6, 7, 9, and 10. However, the two MC/DC-adequate tests do not force the definition of z at line 7 to be used at line 9. A divide-by-zero exception would occur if the value of z were allowed to flow from line 7 to line 9. Though this exception is not caused by the value of z, forcing this path causes the program to fail.

An MC/DC-adequate test does not force the execution of this path and hence the error is not revealed. However, the error in this program would be revealed if the test is required to ensure that each *feasible* definition and use pair for z is executed. One such test is as follows:

Test	x	y	z	def–use pairs covered[a]
t_1	-0	0	0.0	(4, 7), (7, 10)
t_2	1	1	1.0	(4, 6), (6, 9)
t_3	0	1	0.0	(4, 7), (7, 9)
t_4	1	0	1.0	(4, 6), (6, 10)

[a]In the pair (l_1, l_2), z is defined at line l_1 and used at line l_2.

It is easy to see that an LCSAJ-adequate test set would have also revealed the error in Program P6.15, though an MC/DC-adequate test might not reveal. In the remainder of this section, we will offer examples where an LCSAJ-adequate test will also not guarantee that an error is revealed, but a test set derived based on data flow will reveal.

6.3.1 Definitions and Uses

A program written in a procedural language, such as C and Java, contains variables. Variables are defined by assigning values to them and are used in expressions. An assignment statement such as

$$x = y + z$$

defines the variable x. This statement also makes use of variables y and z. The following assignment statement

$$x = x + y$$

defines x and uses it in the right-hand side expression. Declarations are assumed to be definitions of variables. For example, the declaration

```
int x, y, A[10];
```

defines three variables x, y, A[10]. An input function, such as scanf in C also serves to define one or more variables. For example, the statement

$$\texttt{scanf(``\%d \%d'', \&x, \&y)}$$

defines variables x and y. Similarly, the C statement

$$\texttt{printf(``Output:\%d \ n'', x + y)}$$

uses, or *refers to*, variables x and y. A parameter x, passed as call-by-value to a function, is considered as a use of, or a reference to, x. A parameter x, passed as call-by-reference, serves as a definition and use of x. Consider the following sequence of statements that use pointers:

$$z = \&x;$$
$$y = z + 1;$$
$$*z = 25;$$
$$y = *z + 1;$$

The first of the above statements defines a pointer variable z, the second defines y and uses z, the third defines x through z, and the last defines y and uses x accessed through the pointer variable z. Arrays are also tricky. Consider the following declaration and two statements in C:

$$\texttt{int A[10];}$$
$$\texttt{A[i] = x+y;}$$

The first statement declares and defines variable A. The second statement defines A and uses i, x, and y. One might also consider the second statement as defining only A[i] and not the entire array A. The choice of whether to consider the entire array A as defined or the specific element depends upon how stringent is the requirement for coverage analysis (see Exercise 6.27).

6.3.2 C-USE AND P-USE

Uses of a variable that occurs within an expression as part of an assignment statement, in an output statement, as a parameter within a function call, and in subscript expressions, are classified as *c-use*, where the "c" in c-use stands for *computational*. There are five c-uses of x in the following statements:

$$z = x + 1;$$
$$A[x - 1] = B[2];$$
$$foo(x * x)$$
$$output(x);$$

An occurrence of a variable in an expression used as a condition in a branch statement, such as an `if` and a `while`, is considered a p-use. The "p" in p-use stands for *predicate*. There are two p-uses of z in the statements below:

```
if(z > 0){output(x)};
while(z>x){...};
```

It might be confusing to classify some uses. For example, in the statement:

```
if(A[x + 1] > 0){output (x)};
```

the use of A is clearly a p-use. However, is the use of x within the subscript expression also a p-use? Or, is it a c-use? The source of confusion is the position of x within the `if` statement. x is used in an expression that computes the index value for A; it does not directly occur inside the `if` condition such as in `if(x > 0){...}`. Hence, one can argue both ways: this occurrence of x is a c-use because it does not affect the condition directly or that this occurrence of x is a p-use because it occurs in the context of a decision.

6.3.3 GLOBAL AND LOCAL DEFINITIONS AND USES

A variable might be defined in a block, used, and redefined within the same block. Consider a block containing three statements:

```
p = y + z;
x = p + 1;
p = z * z;
```

This block defines p, uses it, and redefines it. The first definition of p is *local*. This definition is *killed*, or *masked*, by the second definition within the same block and hence its value does not survive beyond this block. The second definition of p is a *global* definition as its value survives the block within which it is defined and is available for use in a subsequently executed block. Similarly, the first use of p is a *local* use of a definition of p that precedes it within the same block.

The c-uses of variables y and z are *global* uses because the definitions of the corresponding variables do not appear in the same block preceding their use. Note that the definition of x is also global. In the remainder of this chapter, we will be concerned only with the global definitions and uses. Local definitions and uses are of no use in defining test adequacy based on data flows.

The terms *global* and *local* are used here in the context of a basic block within a program. This is in contrast to the traditional uses of these terms where a global variable is one declared outside, and a local variable within a function or a module.

6.3.4 DATA-FLOW GRAPH

A data-flow graph of a program, also known as def–use graph, captures the flow of definitions across basic blocks in a program. It is similar to a CFG of a program in that the nodes, edges, and all paths through the control flow graph are preserved in the data-flow graph.

A data-flow graph can be derived from its CFG. To understand how let $G = (N, E)$ be the CFG of program P, where N is the set of nodes and E the set of edges. Recall that each node in the CFG corresponds to a basic block in P. We denote these blocks by $b_1, b_2, \ldots, b_k$, assuming that P contains $k > 0$ basic blocks.

Let def_i denote the set of variables defined in block i. A variable declaration, an assignment statement, an input statement, and a call-by-reference parameter are all program constructs that define variables. Let $c\text{-use}_i$ denote the set of variables that have a c-use in block i, and $p\text{-use}_i$, the set of variables that occur as a p-use in block i. The definition of variable x at node i is denoted by $d_i(x)$. Similarly, the use of variable x at node i is denoted by $u_i(x)$. Recalling that we consider only the global definitions and uses, consider the following basic block b that contains two assignments and a function call:

```
p = y + z;
foo(p + q, number);//Parameters passed by value.
A[i] = x + 1;
if(x > y){. . . };
```

For this basic block, we obtain $def_b = \{p, A\}$, $c\text{-use}_b = \{y, z, p, q, x, number, i\}$, and $p\text{-use}_b = \{x, y\}$. We follow the procedure given below to construct a data-flow graph from program P and its a CFG.

Step 1 Compute def_i, $c\text{-use}_i$, and $p\text{-use}_i$ for each basic block i in P.

Step 2 Associate each node i in N with def_i, $c\text{-use}_i$, and $p\text{-use}_i$.

Step 3 For each node i that has a nonempty p-use set and ends in condition C, associate edges (i, j) and (i, k) with C and $!C$, respectively, given that edge (i, j) is taken when the condition is true and (i, k) is taken when the condition is false.

The next example applies the procedure given above to construct a data-flow graph in Figure 6.4.

Example 6.29: First we compute the definitions and uses for each block in Figure 6.4 and associate them with the corresponding nodes and edges of the CFG. The *def* and *use* sets for the five blocks in this program are given below. Note that the infeasible block 4 does not affect the computation of these sets.

Node (or Block)	def	c-use	p-use
1	$\{x, y, z\}$	$\{\}$	$\{x, y\}$
2	$\{z\}$	$\{x\}$	$\{y\}$
3	$\{z\}$	$\{z\}$	$\{\}$
4	$\{z\}$	$\{x\}$	$\{\}$
5	$\{\}$	$\{z\}$	$\{\}$

Using the def and use sets derived above, and the flow graph in Figure 6.4, we draw the data-flow graph of Program P6.4 in Figure 6.6. Comparing the data-flow graph with the CFG in Figure 6.4, we note that nodes are represented as circles with block numbers on the inside, each node is labeled with the corresponding def and use sets, and each edge is labeled with a condition. We have omitted the p-use set, such as for nodes 3, 4, and 5; when it is empty; p-uses are often associated with edges in a data-flow graph.

As shown in Figure 6.6, we associate p-uses with nodes that end in a condition such as in an if or a while statement. Each variable in this p-use set also occurs along the two edges out of its corresponding node. Thus, variables x and y belong to the p-use set for node 1 and also appear in the conditions attached to the outgoing edges of node 1.

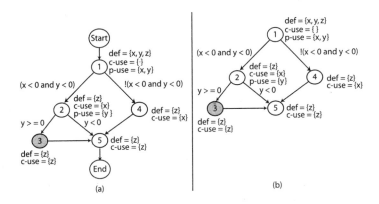

Fig. 6.6 Data-flow graph of Program P6.4 (a) Start and End nodes are shown explicitly. No def and use sets are associated with these nodes. (b) Nodes 1 and 5 serve as start and end nodes, respectively. Node 3 is shaded to emphasize that it is unreachable.

As shown in Figure 6.6(b), the Start node may be omitted from the data-flow graph if there is exactly one program block with no edge entering. Similarly, the End node may be omitted in Figure 6.6 and use nodes 1 and 5 as the start and end nodes, respectively.

6.3.5 Def–clear Paths

A data-flow graph can have many paths. One class of paths of particular interest is known as the *def–clear* path. Suppose that variable x is defined at node i and there is a use of x at node j. Consider path $p = (i, n_1, n_2, \ldots, n_k, j), k \geq 0$, that starts at node i, ends at node j, and nodes i and j do not occur along the subpath $n_1, n_2, \ldots, n_k$. p is a def–clear path for variable x defined at node i and used at node j if x is not defined along the subpath $n_1, n_2, \ldots, n_k$. In this case, we also say that the definition of x at node i, that is $d_i(x)$, is *live* at node j.

Note that several definitions of variable x may be live at some node j where x is used, but along different paths. Also, at most one definition could be live when control does arrive at node j where x is used.

Example 6.30: Consider the data-flow graph for Program P6.16 shown in Figure 6.7. Path $p = (1, 2, 5, 6)$ is def–clear with respect to $d_1(x)$ and $u_6(x)$. Thus, $d_1(x)$ is live at node 6. Path p is not def–clear with respect to $d_1(z)$ and $u_6(z)$ due to the existence of $d_5(z)$. Also, path p is def–clear with respect to $d_1(\text{count})$ and $u_6(\text{count})$.

Path $q = (6, 2, 5, 6)$ is def–clear with respect to $d_6(\text{count})$ and $u_6(\text{count})$ (see Exercise 6.28). Variables y and z are used at node 4.

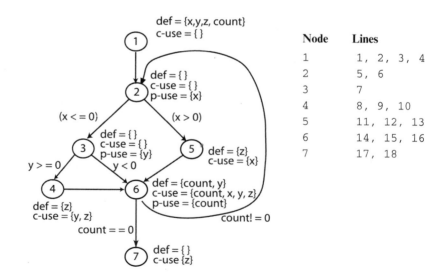

Node	Lines
1	1, 2, 3, 4
2	5, 6
3	7
4	8, 9, 10
5	11, 12, 13
6	14, 15, 16
7	17, 18

Fig. 6.7 Data-flow graph of Program P6.16.

It is easy to verify that definitions $d_1(y)$, $d_6(y)$, $d_1(z)$, and $d_5(z)$ are live at node 4.

Program P6.16

```
 1  begin
 2     float x, y, z=0.0;
 3     int count;
 4     input (x, y, count);
 5     do {
 6       if (x ≤ 0) {
 7          if (y ≥ 0) {
 8             z = y*z + 1;
 9          }
10       }
11       else{
12          z=1/x;
13       }
14       y=x*y+z
15       count=count-1
16     while (count>0)
17     output (z);
18  end
```

6.3.6 DEF–USE PAIRS

We saw earlier that a def–use pair captures a specific definition and its use for a variable. For example, in Program P6.4, the definition of x at line 4 and its use at line 9 together constitute a def–use pair. The data-flow graph of a program contains all def–use pairs for that program.

We are interested in two types of def–use pairs: those that correspond to a definition and its c-use, and those that correspond to a definition and its p-use. Such def–use pairs are captured in sets named **dcu** and **dpu**.

There is one **dcu** and one **dpu** set for each variable definition. For d_i (x), **dcu**(d_i (x)) is the set of all nodes j such that there exists u_j (x) and there is a def–clear path with respect to x from node i to node j. dcu(x, i) is an alternate notation for **dcu**(d_i (x)).

When u_k (x) occurs in a predicate, **dpu**(d_i (x)) is the set of edges (k, l) such that there is a def–clear path with respect to x from node i to edge (k, l). Note that the number of elements in a **dpu** set will be a multiple of two. **dpu**(x, i) is an alternate notation for **dpu**(d_i (x)).

Example 6.31: We compute the **dcu** and **dpu** sets for the data-flow graph in Figure 6.7. To begin, let us compute **dcu**(x, 1) that corresponds to the set of all c-uses associated with the definition of x at node 1. We note that there is a c-use of x at node 5 and a def–clear path (1, 2, 5) from node 1 to node 5. Hence, node 5 is included in **dcu**(x, 1). Similarly, node 6 is also included in this set. Thus, we get **dcu**(x, 1) = {5, 6}.

Next, we determine **dpu**(x, 1). There is a p-use of x at node 2 with outgoing edges (2, 3) and (2, 5). The existence of def–clear paths from node 1 to each of these two edges is easily seen in the figure. There is no other p-use of x and hence we get **dpu**(x, 1)={(2, 3), (2, 5)}. The remaining **dcu** and **dpu** sets are given below:

Variable (v)	Defined at node (n)	dcu (v, n)	dpu (v, n)
x	1	{5, 6}	{(2, 3), (2, 5)}
y	1	{4, 6}	{(3, 4), (3, 6)}
y	6	{4, 6}	{(3, 4), (3, 6)}
z	1	{4, 6, 7}	{ }
z	4	{4, 6, 7}	{ }
z	5	{4, 6, 7}	{ }
count	1	{6}	{(6, 2), (6, 7)}
count	6	{6 }	{(6, 2), (6, 7)}

6.3.7 DEF–USE CHAINS

A def–use pair consists of a definition of a variable in some block and its use in another block in the program. The notion of a def–use pair can be extended to a sequence of alternating definitions and uses of variables. Such an alternating sequence is known as a *def–use chain* or a *k–dr interaction*. The nodes along this alternating sequence are distinct. The *k* in *k–dr* interaction denotes the length of the chain and is measured in the number of nodes along the chain that is one more than the number of *def–use* pairs along the chain. The letters *d* and *r* refer to, respectively, *definition* and *reference*. Recall that we use the terms *reference* and *uses* synonymously.

Example 6.32: In Program P6.16, we note the existence of $d_1(z)$ and $u_4(z)$. Thus the *def–use* interaction for variable z at nodes 1 and 4 constitutes a *k–dr* chain for $k = 2$. This chain is denoted by the pair (1, 4).

A longer chain (1, 4, 6) is obtained by appending $d_4(z)$ and $u_6(z)$ to (1, 4). Note that there is no chain for $k > 3$ that corresponds to alternating def–uses for z. Thus, for example, path (1, 4, 4,

6) for $k = 4$, corresponding to the def–use sequence $(d_1(z), u_4(z),$ $d_4(z), u_4(z), d_4(z), u_6(z))$, is not a valid k–dr chain due to the repetition of node 4.

The chains in the above example correspond to the definition and use of the same variable z. k–dr chains could also be constructed from alternating definitions and uses of variables not necessarily distinct. In general, a k–dr chain for variables $X_1, X_2, \ldots, X_{k-1}$ is a path $(n_1, n_2, \ldots, n_k)$ such that there exist $d_{ni}(X_i)$ and $u_{ni+1}(X_i)$ for $1 \leq i < k$, and there is a def–clear path from n_i to n_{i+1}. This definition of a k–dr chain implies that variable X_{i+1} is defined at the same node as variable X_i. A chain may also include the use of a variable in a predicate.

Example 6.33: Once again, let us refer to Program P6.16 and consider variables y and z. The triple (5, 6, 4) is a k–dr chain of length 3. It corresponds to the alternating sequence $(d_5(z), u_6(z), d_6(y),$ $u_4(z))$. Another chain (1, 4, 6) corresponds to the alternating sequence $(d_1(y), u_4(y), d_4(z), u_6(z))$.

While constructing k–dr chains, it is assumed that each branch in the data-flow graph corresponds to a simple predicate. In the event a decision in the program is a compound predicate, such as $(x < y)$ and $(z < 0)$, it is split into two nodes for the purpose of k–dr analysis (see Exercise 6.35).

6.3.8 A LITTLE OPTIMIZATION

Often one can reduce the number of def–uses to be covered by a simple analysis of the flow graph. To illustrate what we mean, refer to the def–use graph in Figure 6.7. From this graph, we discovered that **dcu**(y, 1)={4, 6}. We also discovered that **dcu**(z, 1) = (4, 6, 7). We now ask: *Will the coverage of* **dcu**(z, 1) *imply the coverage of* **dcu**(y, 1) = {4, 6}? Path (1, 2, 3, 4) must be traversed to cover the c-use of z at node 4 corresponding to its definition at node 1. However, traversal of this path also implies the coverage of the c-use of y at node 4 corresponding to its definition at node 1.

Similarly, path (1, 2, 3, 6) must be traversed to cover the c-use of z at node 6 corresponding to its definition at node 1. Once again, the traversal of this path implies the coverage of the c-use of y at node 6 corresponding to its definition at node 1. This analysis implies that we need not consider **dcu**(y, 1) while generating tests to cover all c-uses; **dcu**(y, 1) will be covered automatically if we cover dcu(z, 1).

Arguments analogous to the ones above can be used to show that dcu(x, 1) can be removed from consideration when developing tests to cover all c-uses. This is because **dcu**(x, 1) will be covered when **dcu**(z, 5) is covered. Continuing in this manner, one can show that **dcu**(count, 1) can also be ignored. This leads us to a minimal set of c-uses to be covered as shown in the table below. Note that the total number of c-uses to consider has now been reduced from 17 to 12. The total number of p-uses to consider has been reduced from 10 to 4. Similar analysis for removing p-uses from consideration is left as an exercise (see Exercise 6.30).

Variable (v)	Defined at node (n)	dcu (v, n)	dpu (v, n)
y	6	{4, 6}	{(3, 4), (3, 6)}
z	1	{4, 6, 7}	{ }
z	4	{4, 6, 7 }	{ }
z	5	{4, 6, 7}	{ }
count	6	{6}	{(6, 2), (6, 7)}

In general it is difficult to carry out the type of analysis illustrated above for programs of nontrivial size. Usually test tools such as χSuds automatically do such analysis and minimize the number of c-uses and p-uses to consider while generating tests to cover all c-uses and p-uses. Note that this analysis does not remove any c-uses and p-uses from the program, it simply removes some of them from consideration because they are automatically covered by tests that cover some other c-uses and p-uses.

6.3.9 DATA CONTEXTS AND ORDERED DATA CONTEXTS

Let n be a node in a data-flow graph. Each variable used at n is known as an *input* variable of n. Similarly, each variable defined at n is known as an *output* variable of n. The set of all live definitions of all input variables of node n is known as the *data environment* of node n and is denoted by $DE(n)$.

Let $X(n) = \{x_1, x_2, \ldots, x_k\}$ be the set of input variables required for evaluation of any expression, arithmetic or otherwise, at node n in the data-flow graph F. Let $x_j^{i_j}$ denote the i_j^{th} definition of x_j in F. An *elementary data context* of node n, denoted as $EDC(n)$, is the set of definitions $\{x_1^{i_1}, x_2^{i_2}, \ldots, x_k^{i_k}\}$, $i_k \geq 1$, of all variables in $X(n)$ such that each definition is live when control arrives at node n. The *data context* of node n is the set of all its elementary data contexts and is denoted by $DC(n)$.

Given that the $i_j{}^{th}$ definition of x_j occurs at some node k, we shall refer to it as $d_k(\text{x})$.

Test-Adequacy Assessment Using Control Flow

Example 6.34: Let us examine node 4 in the data-flow graph of Figure 6.7. The set of input variables of node 4, denoted by $X(4)$, is $\{\text{y}, \text{z}\}$. The data environment for node 4, denoted by $DE(4)$, is the set $\{d_1(\text{y}), d_6(\text{y}), d_1(\text{z}), d_4(\text{z}), d_5(\text{z})\}$.

Recall that each definition in $DE(4)$ is live at node 4. For example, $d_4(\text{z})$ is live at node 4 because there exists a path from the start of the program to node 4, and a path from node 4 back to node 4 without a redefinition of z until it has been used at node 4. This path is (1, 2, 3, $\underline{4}$, 6, 2, 3, $\underline{4}$). The first-emphasized occurrence of node 4 is the one where z is defined and the second emphasized occurrence of node 4 is the one where this definition is live and used.

The data context $DC(4)$ for node 4, and all other nodes in the graph, is given in the following table. Note that the data context is defined only for nodes that contain at least one variable definition. Thus, while determining data contexts, we exclude nodes that contain only a predicate. Nodes 1, 2, and 3 are three such nodes in Figure 6.7. Also, we have omitted some infeasible data contexts for node 6 (see Exercise 6.40).

Node k	Data context DC(k)
1	None
2	None
3	None
4	$\{(d_1(\text{y}), d_1(\text{z})), (d_6(\text{y}), d_4(\text{z})), (d_6(\text{y}), d_5(\text{z}))\}$
5	$\{(d_1(\text{x}))\}$
6	$\{(d_1(\text{count}), d_1(\text{x}), d_1(\text{y}), d_1(\text{z})), (d_1(\text{count}), d_1(\text{x}),$ $d_1(\text{y}), d_5(\text{z})), (d_1(\text{count}), d_1(\text{x}), d_1(\text{y}), d_4(\text{z})),$ $(d_6(\text{count}), d_1(\text{x}), d_6(\text{y}), d_5(\text{z})), (d_6(\text{count}), d_1(\text{x}),$ $d_6(\text{y}), d_4(\text{z})), (d_6(\text{count}), d_1(\text{x}), d_6(\text{y}), d_1(\text{z}))\}$
7	$\{(d_4(\text{z})), (d_5(\text{z}))\}$

The definitions of variables in an elementary data context occur along a program path in an order. For example, consider the elementary data context $\{d_6(\text{y}), d_4(\text{z})\}$ for node 4 in Figure 6.7. In the second occurrence of node 4 along the path (1, 2, 3, 4, 6, 2, 3, $\underline{4}$, 6, 7), $d_4(\text{z})$ occurs first followed by $d_6(\text{y})$. The sequence $d_6(\text{y})$ followed by $d_4(\text{z})$ is not feasible when control arrives at node 4. Hence, only one sequence, that is $d_6(\text{y})$ followed by $d_4(\text{z})$, is possible for node 4.

Now consider the second occurrence of node 6 along the path (1, 2, 3, 6, 2, 5, 6, 7). The sequence of definitions of input variables of node 6 is $d_1(\texttt{x})$ followed by $d_6(\texttt{count})$, $d_6(\texttt{y})$, and finally $d_5(\texttt{z})$. Next, consider again the second occurrence of node 6, but now along the path (1, 2, 5, 6, 2, 3, 6). In this case, the sequence of definitions is $d_1(\texttt{x})$ followed by $d_6(\texttt{count})$, $d_5(\texttt{z})$, and finally $d_6(\texttt{y})$. These two sequences are different in that y and z are defined in a different sequence.

The above examples lead to the notion of an *ordered elementary data context* of node *n* abbreviated as *OEDC(n)*. An ordered elementary data context for node *n* in a data-flow graph consists of a set of ordered sequence of definitions of the input variables of *n*. An *ordered data context* for node *n* is the set of all ordered elementary data contexts of node *n* denoted by *ODC(n)*.

Example 6.35: Consider Program P6.17. The data-flow graph for this program appears in Figure 6.8. The set of input variables for node 6 is {x, y}. The data context *DC(6)* for node 6 consists of four elementary data contexts given below.

$$DC(6) = \{(d_1(\texttt{x}), d_1(\texttt{y})), (d_3(\texttt{x}), d_1(\texttt{y})), (d_1(\texttt{x}), d_4(\texttt{y})),$$

$$(d_3(\texttt{x}), d_4(\texttt{y}))\}$$

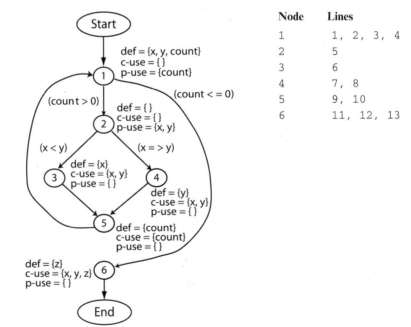

Node	Lines
1	1, 2, 3, 4
2	5
3	6
4	7, 8
5	9, 10
6	11, 12, 13

Fig. 6.8 Data-flow graph of Program P6.17 to illustrate ordered data context.

The ordered data context for the same node is given below:

$$ODC(6) = \{(d_1\,(\text{x})\,,d_1\,(\text{y})\,),(d_1\,(\text{y})\,,d_3\,(\text{x})\,),(d_1\,(\text{x})\,,d_4\,(\text{y})\,),$$

$$(d_3\,(\text{x})\,,d_4\,(\text{y})\,),(d_4\,(\text{y})\,,d_3\,(\text{x})\,)\}$$

Note that due to the inclusion of ordered elementary data contexts, $ODC(6)$ has all items from $DC(6)$ and one additional item that is not in $DC(6)$.

Program P6.17

```
1   begin
2      int x, y, z, count;
3      input (x, y, count);
4      while (count>0) {
5         if(x<y)
6            x=foo1(x-y);
7         else
8            y=foo1(x+y);
9         count=count-1;
10     }
11        z=foo2(x, y);
12     output (z);
13  end
```

6.4 ADEQUACY CRITERIA BASED ON DATA FLOW

To be able to construct test-adequacy criteria based on sets dpu and dcu, we first define some notions related to coverage. In the definitions below, we assume that the data-flow graph of P contains k nodes where nodes n_1 and n_k represent the start and end nodes, respectively. Some node s in the data-flow graph of program P is considered covered by test case t when the following complete path is traversed upon the execution of P against t:

$$(n_{i_1}, n_{i_2}, \ldots, n_{i_{m-1}}, n_{i_m})$$

and $s = n_{i_j}$ for some $1 \leq j \leq k$, that is node s lies on the path traversed. Similarly, an edge (r, s) in the data-flow graph of P is considered covered by t upon the execution of P against t, when the path listed above is traversed and $r = n_{i_j}$ and $s = n_{i_{j+1}}$ for $1 \leq j \leq (m - 1)$.

Let CU and PU denote, respectively, the total number of c-uses and p-uses for all variable definitions in P. Let $v = \{v_1, v_2, \ldots, v_n\}$ be the set of variables in P. d_i is the number of definitions of variable v_i for

$1 \leq i \leq n$. CU and PU are computed as follows:

$$CU = \Sigma_{i=1}^{n}\Sigma_{j=1}^{d}|\ \mathbf{dcu}(v_i, j)\ |$$

$$PU = \Sigma_{i=1}^{n}\Sigma_{j=1}^{d}|\ \mathbf{dpu}(v_i, j)\ |$$

Recall that $|\ S\ |$ denotes the number of elements in set S. For the program in Example 6.31, we get $CU = 17$ and $PU = 10$.

6.4.1 C-USE COVERAGE

Let z be a node in $\mathbf{dcu}(x, q)$, that is node z contains a c-use of variable x defined at node q [see Figure 6.9(a)]. Suppose that program P is executed against test case t and the (complete) path traversed is as follows:

$$p = (n_1, n_{i_1}, \ldots, n_{i_l}, n_{i_l+1}, \ldots, n_{i_m}, n_{i_m+1} \ldots n_k), \text{ where}$$

$$2 \leq i_j < k \text{ for } 1 \leq j \leq k.$$

This c-use of variable x is considered covered if $q = n_{i_l}$ and $s = n_{i_m}$, and $(n_{i_l}, n_{i_l+1}, \ldots, n_{i_m})$ is a def–clear path from node q to node z. All c-uses of variable x are considered covered if each node in $\mathbf{dcu}(x,q)$ is covered during one or more executions of P. All c-uses in the program are

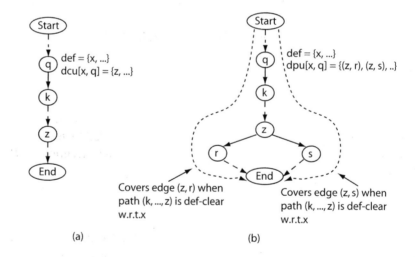

(a) (b)

Fig. 6.9 Paths for c-use and p-use coverage. Dotted arrows connecting two nodes indicate a path along which there might be additional nodes not shown. (a) Path (Start, ..., q, k, ..., z, ... End) covers the c-use at node z of x defined at node q given that (k, ..., z) is def–clear with respect to x. (b) The p-use of x at node z is covered when paths (Start, ..., q, k, ..., z, r, ... End) and (Start, ..., q, k, ..., z, s, ... End), shown by dotted lines, have been traversed, and (k...z) are def–clear with respect to x.

considered covered if all c-uses of all variables in P are covered. We now define test-adequacy criterion based on c-use coverage.

c-use coverage

The c-use coverage of T with respect to (P, R) is computed as

$$\frac{CU_c}{(CU - CU_f)},$$

where CU_c is the number of c-uses covered and CU_f the number of infeasible c-uses. T is considered adequate with respect to the c-use coverage criterion if its c-use coverage is 1.

Example 6.36: Suppose that Program P6.16 is under test. The dataflow graph of this program is shown in Figure 6.7. We want to devise a test t_c that covers node 6 in **dcu**(z, 5), that is, the desired test must cover the c-use of the definition of x at node 1. Consider the following test case:

$$t_c :< x = 5, y = -1, \text{count} = 1 >$$

The complete path traversed when Program P6.16 is executed against t_c is (1, 2, 5, 6, 7). Clearly, this path contains node 5 at which z is defined, node 6 where it has a c-use, and subpath (5, 6) is a def–clear path with respect to this definition of z. Hence, t_c covers node 6, an element of **dcu**(z, 6).

Note that t_c also covers node 7 but not node 4, which also contains a c-use of this definition of z. Considering that there are 12 c-uses in all, and t_c covers only 2 of them, the c-use coverage for T = $\{t_c\}$ is 2/12 = 0.167. Clearly, T is not adequate with respect to the c-use criterion for Program P6.16.

6.4.2 P-use Coverage

Let (z, r) and (z, s) be two edges in **dpu**(x, q), that is node z contains a p-use of variable x defined at node q [see Figure 6.9(b)]. Suppose that the following complete path is traversed when P is executed against some test case t_p:

$$(n_i, n_{i_2}, \ldots, n_{i_l}, n_{i_{l+1}}, \ldots, n_{i_m}, n_{i_{m+1}} \ldots n_k), \text{ where}$$
$$2 \le i_j < k \text{ for } 1 \le j \le k.$$

The following condition must hold for edge (z, r) for the p-use at node z of x defined at node q to be covered:

$q = n_{i_l}, z = n_{i_m}, r = n_{i_{m+1}}$ and $(n_{i_l}, n_{i_{l+1}}, \ldots, n_{i_m}, n_{i_{m+1}})$ is a def–clear path with respect to x.

Similarly, the following condition must hold for edge (z, s) :

$q = n_{i_l}, z = n_{i_m}, s = n_{i_m+1}$ and $(n_{i_l}, n_{i_l+1}, \ldots, n_{i_m}, n_{im+1})$ is a def–clear path with respect to x.

The p-use of x at node z is considered covered when the two conditions mentioned above are satisfied in the same or different executions of P. We can now define test-adequacy criterion based on p-use coverage.

p-use coverage

The p-use coverage of T with respect to (P, R) is computed as

$$\frac{PU_c}{(PU - PU_f)}$$

where PU_c is the number of p-uses covered and PU_f the number of infeasible p-uses. T is considered adequate with respect to the p-use coverage criterion if its p-use coverage is 1.

Example 6.37: Once again, suppose that Program P6.16 is under test. Consider the definition of y at node 6. Our objective now is to cover the p-use of this definition at node 3. This requires a test that must cause control to reach node 6 where y is defined. Without redefining y, the control must now arrive at node 3 where y is used in the if condition.

The edge labeled $y > 0$ is covered if taken, though the p-use is yet to be covered. Subsequently, control should take the edge labeled $y < 0$ during the same or in some other execution. Consider the following test case designed to achieve the coverage objective:

$$t_p: < x = -2, y = -1, \text{count} = 3 >$$

A careful examination of Program P6.16 and its data-flow graph reveals that the following path is traversed upon the execution of the program against t_p:

$$p = < 1, 2, 3, 6_1, 2, 3_1, 4_1, 6_2, 2, 3_2, 6_2, 7 >$$

The first two instances of subscripted node 6 correspond to the definitions of y in the first and the second iterations, respectively, of the loop. The remaining subscripted nodes indicate edges along which the values of y are propagated. An explanation follows.

Variable y is defined at node 6 when subpath $< 1, 2, 3, 6_1 >$ is traversed. This value of y is used in the decision at node 3 when $< 6_1, 2, 3_1, 4_1 >$ is traversed. Note that edge (3, 4) is now covered as there is a def–clear path $< 2, 3 >$ from node 6 to edge (3, 4).

Next, path $< 6_2, 2, 3_2, 6_2, 7 >$ is traversed where y is defined once again at node 6. This definition of y propagates to edge (3,6) via the def–clear path $< 2, 3_2, 6_2 >$. The control now moves to node 7 and the program execution terminates. Test t_p has successfully covered **dpu**(y, 6). In fact, all the p-uses in Program P6.16 are covered by the test set $T = \{t_c, t_p\}$. Thus, the p-use coverage of T is 1 and hence this test set is adequate with respect to the p-use coverage criterion (see Exercise 6.31).

6.4.3 ALL-USES COVERAGE

The all-uses-coverage criterion is obtained by combining the c-use and p-use criteria. The all-uses criterion is satisfied when all c-uses and p-uses have been covered. The definition can be stated as follows in terms of a coverage formula:

All-uses coverage

The all-uses coverage of T with respect to (P, R) is computed as

$$\frac{CU_c + PU_c}{((CU + PU) - (CU_f) + PU_f)}$$

471

where CU is the total c-uses, CU_c is the number of c-uses covered, PU_c is the number of p-uses covered, CU_f the number of infeasible c-uses, and PU_f the number of infeasible p-uses. T is considered adequate with respect to the all-uses-coverage criterion if its c-use coverage is 1.

Example 6.38: For Program P6.16 and the test cases taken from Examples 6.36 and 6.37, the test set $T = \{t_c, t_p\}$ is adequate with respect to the all-uses criterion.

6.4.4 K–DR CHAIN COVERAGE

Consider a k–dr chain $C = (n_1, n_2, \ldots, n_k)$ in program P such that d_{n_i} (X_i) and $u_{n_{i+1}}(X_i)$ for $1 \leq i < k$. We consider two cases depending on whether node n_k ends in a predicate. Given that node n_k does not end in a predicate, chain C is considered covered by test set T only if upon the execution of P against T, the following path is traversed:

$$(Start, \ldots, n_1.p_1, n_2, \ldots, p_{k-1}n_k, \ldots, End)$$

where each p_i for $1 \leq i < k$ is a def–clear subpath from node n_i to node n_{i+1} with respect to variable X_i. If node n_k ends in a predicate, then C is considered covered only if upon the execution of P against T, the following paths are traversed:

$$(Start, \ldots, n_1, p_1, n_2, \ldots, p_{k-1}n_k, r, \ldots, End)$$
$$(Start, \ldots, n_1, p'_1, n_2, \ldots, p'_{k-1}n_k, s, \ldots, End)$$

where $p_i s$ and $p'_i s$ are def–clear subpaths for variable X_i, and nodes r and s are immediate successors of node n_k. The above condition ensures that the decision containing the last use of a variable along the chain is covered, that is both branches out of the decision are taken. As shown in Example 6.40, it is possible to traverse both paths in one execution.

While determining k–dr chains, it is assumed that each branch in a data-flow graph corresponds to a simple predicate. In the event a decision in the program is a compound predicate, such as $(x < y)$ and $(z < 0)$, it is split into two simple predicates. Splitting ensures that each decision node in the corresponding data-flow graph will contain an atomic predicate (see Exercise 6.35).

When the first definition or the last reference of a variable is inside a loop, at least two iteration counts must be considered for the loop. We consider these two iteration counts to be 1 and 2, that is the loop is iterated once and exited, and in the same or a different execution, iterated twice and exited.

Example 6.39: Consider the 3-dr chain $C = (1, 5, 7)$ from Example 6.32 for Program P6.16. Chain C corresponds to the alternating def–use sequence $(d_1(x), u_5(x), d_5(z), d_7(z))$. The following test covers C:

$$T = \{t :< x = 3, y = 2, count = 1 >\}$$

Example 6.40: Consider the 3-dr chain $C = (1, 4, 6)$ from Example 6.32 for Program P6.16. We note that C ends at node 6 that ends in a predicate. Nodes 2 and 7 are immediate successors of node 6. Hence, to cover C, the following subpaths must be traversed:

$$\lambda_1 = (1, p1, 4, p_2, 6, 2)$$
$$\lambda_2 = (1, p'_1, 4, p'_2, 6.7)$$

where p_1, p_2, p'_1 and p'_2 are def-clear subpaths with respect to variable z. In addition, because the last reference of variable z is inside a loop, the loop must be iterated a minimum and a larger number of times. The following test set covers C :

$$T = \left\{ \begin{array}{l} t_1: < x = -5 \ y = 2 \ \text{count} = 1 > \\ t_2: < x = -5 \ y = 2 \ \text{count} = 2 > \end{array} \right\}$$

The following path is traversed when Program P6.16 is executed against t_1:

$$(1, 2, 3, 4, 6, 7)$$

Clearly, the above path is of the form λ_1, where $p_1 = (2, 3)$ and p_2 is empty. Here the loop containing $u_6(z)$ is traversed once, that is minimum number of times.

The loop containing the following (complete) path is traversed when Program P6.16 is executed against t_2:

$$(1, 2, 3, 4, 6, 2, 3, 6, 7)$$

This path can be written as

$$(1, p_1, 4, p_2, 6, 2, p_3)$$

and also as

$$(1, p_1', 4, p_2', 6, 7)$$

where $p_1 = (2, 3)$, $p_2 = (\ )$, $p_1' = (2, 3)$, and $p_2' = (6, 2, 3)$. Note that p_2 is an empty subpath. p_1, p_2, p_1', and p_2' are all def–clear with respect to z. Note also the condition that subpaths λ_1 and λ_2 be traversed is satisfied. Thus the test set t covers the k-dr chain C.

6.4.5 Using the k–dr Chain Coverage

To determine the adequacy of a test set T for program P subject to requirements R, k is set to a suitable value. The larger the value of k, the more difficult it is likely to cover all the k–dr interactions. Given k, the next step is to determine all l–dr interactions for $1 \leq l \leq k$. We denote this set of all l–dr interactions by k–$dr(k)$. The program is then executed against tests in T and the coverage determined. A formal definition of test adequacy with respect to k–dr coverage is as follows:

k–dr coverage

For a given $k \geq 2$, the k–$dr(k)$ coverage of T with respect to (P, R) is computed as

$$\frac{C_c^k}{(C^k - C_f^k)}$$

where C_c^k is the number of k–dr interactions covered, C^k is the number of elements in k–dr(k), and C_f the number of infeasible interactions in k–dr(k). T is considered adequate with respect to the k–dr(k) coverage criterion if its k–dr(k) coverage is 1.

6.4.6 Infeasible c-uses and p-uses

Coverage of a c-use or a p-use requires a path to be traversed through the program. However, if this path is infeasible, then some c-uses and p-uses that require this path to be traversed might also be infeasible. Infeasible uses are often difficult to determine without some hint from a test tool. The next example illustrates why one c-use in Program P6.16 is infeasible.

Example 6.41: Consider the c-use at node 4 of z defined at node 5. For this c-use to be covered, control must first arrive at node 5 and then move to node 4 via a path that is def–clear with respect to z.

Further analysis reveals that for the control to first arrive at node 5, $x > 0$. For the control to then move to node 4, it must pass through nodes 6, 2, and 3. However, this is not possible because edge (2, 3) can be taken only if $x \leq 0$.

Note that x is not defined anywhere in the program except at node 1. Hence, if $x > 0$ when control first arrives at node 2, then it cannot be $x \leq 0$ in any subsequent iteration of the loop. This implies that the condition required for the coverage of c-use at node 4 of z defined at node 5 can never be true and hence this c-use is infeasible.

Example 6.42: A `for` loop that iterates for a fixed number of times may lead to infeasible paths. Consider the following program that defines x prior to entering the loop and uses x inside the loop body and soon after loop exit. Thus, there is a c-use of x at lines 3 and 7. A def–use graph for this program is in Figure 6.10.

Program P6.18

```
1   begin
2     int x,z,i
3     input(x); z=0;
4     for(i=1; i<5, i++){
5     z=z+x*i;
6       }
7     output(x, z);
8   end
```

Path (`Start`, 1, 2, 4, End) must be traversed to cover the c-use of x at line 7. However, this path, and hence the c-use, is infeasible because

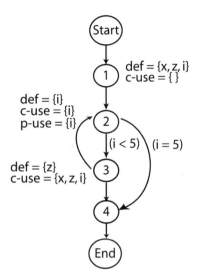

Fig. 6.10 Data-flow graph of Program P6.18.

the `for` loop body will be executed exactly five times and not zero times as required for this path to be traversed.

6.4.7 CONTEXT COVERAGE

Let P be the program under test, F its data-flow graph, t a test case against which P is executed, $X(k)$ the set of input variables for node k in F, and $EDC(k)$ and $OEDC(K)$ be, respectively, the elementary data and ordered elementary contexts for node k. $EDC(k)$ is considered covered by t if the following two conditions are satisfied during the execution of P:

1. Node k is along the path traversed during the execution of P against t.
2. When control arrives at n along this path, all definitions in $EDC(k)$ are live.

A data context $DC(k)$ for node k is considered covered when all elementary data contexts in $DC(k)$ are covered. Similarly, an ordered elementary data context $OEDC(k)$ is considered covered by t if the following conditions are satisfied during the execution of P:

1. Node k is along the path p traversed during the execution of P against t.
2. All definitions in $OEDC(k)$ are live when control arrives at n along p.
3. The sequence in which variables in $X[k]$ are defined is the same as that in $OEDC(k)$.

An ordered data context $ODC(k)$ for node n is considered covered when all elementary data contexts in $ODC(k)$ are covered.

Given a test set T for program P subject to requirements R, formal definitions of test adequacy with respect to data context and ordered data context coverage are as follow:

Elementary data context coverage

Given a program P subject to requirements R, and having a data-flow graph containing n nodes, the data context coverage of T with respect to (P, R) is computed as:

$$\frac{EDC_c}{(EDC - EDC_i)}$$

where EDC is the number of elementary data contexts in P, EDC_c is the number of elementary data contexts covered, and EDC_i is the number of infeasible elementary data contexts. T is considered adequate with respect to the data context coverage criterion if the data context coverage is 1.

Elementary ordered data context coverage

Given a program P subject to requirements R, and having a data-flow graph containing n nodes, the ordered data context coverage of T with respect to (P, R) is computed

$$\frac{OEDC_c}{OEDC - OEDC_i}$$

where OEDC is the number of ordered elementary data contexts in P, $OEDC_c$ is the number of ordered elementary data conexts covered, and $OEDC_i$ is the number of infeasible ordered elementary data contexts. T is considered adequate with respect to the ordered data context coverage criterion if the data context coverage is 1.

In the two definitions above, we have computed the coverage with respect to the elementary and ordered elementary data contexts, respectively. Another alternative is to compute the coverage with respect to data contexts and ordered data contexts (see Exercise 6.39). Such definitions would offer coarser coverage criteria than the ones above. For example, in such a coarse definition, a data context will be considered uncovered if any one of its constituent elementary data contexts is uncovered.

Example 6.43: Let us compute the adquacy of test T given below against the elementary data context coverage criteria.

$$T = \begin{cases} t_1: & <x = -2, & y = 2, & \text{count} = 1 > \\ t_2: & <x = -2, & y = -2, & \text{count} = 1 > \\ t_3: & <x = 2, & y = 2, & \text{count} = 1 > \\ t_4: & <x = 2, & y = 2, & \text{count} = 2 > \end{cases}$$

We assume that Program P6.16 is executed against the four test cases listed above. For each test case, the table below shows the path traversed, the elementary data context(s) covered, and the cumulative elementary data context (*EDC*) coverage. An asterisk against a node indicates that the corresponding elementary data context has already been covered and hence not counted in computed the cumulative *EDC*.

From Figure 6.7 and the table in Example 6.34, we obtain the total number of elementary data contexts as 11. Hence, the cumulative *EDC* for test case t_j, $1 \leq j \leq 4$ is computed as the ratio $EDC_c/11$, where EDC_c is the total number of elementary data contexts covered after executing the program against t_j. Note that we could also compute data context coverage using the four data contexts for nodes 4 through 7 in Example 6.34. In that case we will consider a data context as covered when all of its constituent elementary data contexts are covered.

Test case	Path traversed	Elementary context (Node: context)	Cumulative EDC
t_1	(1, 2, 3, 4, 6, 7)	4: $(d_1(y), d_1(z))$ 6: $(d_1(x), d_1(y), d_4(z),$ $d_1(\text{count}))$ 7: $(d_4(z))$	$\frac{3}{11} = 0.27$
t_2	(1, 2, 3, 6, 7)	6: $(d_1(x), d_1(y), d_1(z),$ $d_1(\text{count}))$ 7: $(d_1(z))$	$\frac{5}{11} = 0.45$
t_3	(1, 2, 5, 6)	5: $(d_1(x))$ 6: $(d_1(x), d_1(y), d_5(z),$ $d_1(\text{count}))$	$\frac{7}{11} = 0.64$
t_4	(1, 2, 5, 6, 2, 5, 6, 7)	5: $(d_1(x))$ 6*: $(d_1(x), d_1(y), d_5(z),$ $d_1(\text{count}))$ 6: $(d_1(x), d_6(y), d_5(z),$ $d_6(\text{count}))$	$\frac{9}{11} = 0.82$

It is clear from the rightmost column in the table above that T is not adequate with respect to the elementary data context coverage criterion. Recall that T is adequate with respect to the MC/DC-coverage criterion.

6.5 CONTROL FLOW VERSUS DATA FLOW

Adequacy criteria based on the flow of control aim at testing only a few of the many, sometimes infinitely large, paths through a program. For example, the block coverage criterion is satisfied when the paths traversed have touched each block in the program under test. Data-flow-based criteria has the same objective, that is these criteria assist in the selection of a few of the many paths through a program. For example, the c-use coverage criterion is satisfied when the paths traversed have covered all c-uses. However, sometimes data-flow-based criteria turn out to be more powerful than criteria based on the flow of control, including the MC/DC-based criteria. As evidence in support of the previous statement, let us reconsider Program P6.16. Consider the following test case devised based on the program's requirements (which we have not listed explicitly):

$$T = \{t_1 < x = -2, y = 2, \text{count} = 2 >,$$

$$t_2: < x = 2, y = 2, \text{count} = 1 >\}$$

Surprisingly, test set $T = \{t_1, t_2\}$ is adequate for Program P6.16 with respect to all the control-flow criteria described earlier except for the LC-SAJ criterion. In terms of coverage numbers, the block coverage, the condition coverage, the multiple condition coverage, and the MC/DC coverages are all 100%. However, the c-use coverage of T is only 58.3% and the p-use coverage is 75%. Translated in terms of error detection, the example illustrates that tests adequate with respect to data-flow coverage criteria are more likely to expose program errors than those adequate with respect to criteria based exclusively on the flow of control.

> **Example 6.44:** Suppose that line 14 in Program P6.16 has an error. The correct code at this line is
>
> 14 $y = x + y + z$
>
> The following test set is adequate with respect to the MC/DC criterion:

$$T = \begin{cases} t_1: & < x = -2, & y = 2, & \text{count} = 1 > \\ t_2: & < x = -2, & y = -2, & \text{count} = 1 > \\ t_3: & < x = 2, & y = 2, & \text{count} = 1 > \\ t_4: & < x = 2, & y = 2, & \text{count} = 2 > \end{cases}$$

Execution of Program P6.16 against T produces the following values of z:

$$P6.16(t_1) = 1.0$$

$$P6.16(t_2) = 0.0$$

$$P6.16(t_3) = 0.5$$

$$P6.16(t_4) = 0.5$$

It is easy to verify that the correct program also generates exactly the same values of z when executed against test cases in T. Thus, T does not reveal the simple error in Program P6.16. The c-use and p-use coverage of T is, respectively, 0.75 and 0.5 (these numbers include the infeasible c-use). One of the c-uses that is not covered by T is that of y at line 8 corresponding to its definition at line 14. To cover this c-use, we need a test that ensures the execution of the following event sequence:

1. Control must arrive at line 14; this will happen for any test case.
2. Control must then get to line 8. For this to happen, count > 1 so that the loop does not terminate and conditions x ≤ 0 and y ≥ 0 must be true.

The following test case satisfies the conditions enumerated above:

$$t_e: \quad < x = -2, \quad y = 2, \quad count = 2 >$$

$$T = \begin{cases} t_1: & < x = -2, & y = 2, & count = 1 > \\ t_2: & < x = -2, & y = -2, & count = 1 > \\ t_3: & < x = 2, & y = 2, & count = 1 > \\ t_4: & < x = 2, & y = 2, & count = 2 > \end{cases}$$

Execution of Program P6.16 against t_e causes the c-use at line 8 to be covered. However, the value of z is 1.0 while the correct version of this program outputs 2.0 when executed against t_e, thus revealing the error.

Though coverage of a c-use in the example above revealed the error, a key question one must ask is: "Will every test case that covers the c-use mentioned in Example 6.44 also reveal the error?" This question is the subject of Exercise 6.34. It is also important to note that even though T in the above example does not reveal the error, some other MC/DC-adequate test might reveal.

6.6 THE SUBSUMES RELATION

We have discussed a variety of control-flow- and data-flow-based criteria to assess the adequacy of tests. These criteria assist in the selection of tests from a large, potentially infinite set of inputs to the program under test. They also assist in the selection of a finite, and relatively small, number of paths through the program. All control-flow- and data-flow-based adequacy criteria are similar in that their objective is to assist a tester find a suitable subset of paths to be tested from the set of all paths in a given program. Given this similarity of objectives of the various adequacy criteria, the following questions are of interest:

Subsumes: Given a test set T that is adequate with respect to criterion C_1, what can we conclude about the adequacy of T with respect to another criterion C_2?

Effectiveness: Given a test set T that is adequate with respect to criterion C, what can we expect regarding its effectiveness in revealing errors?

In this chapter, we deal briefly with the first of the above two questions; an in-depth theoretical discussion of the subsumes relationship among various adequacy criteria is found in Volume II. Figure 6.11 exhibits the subsumes relationship among some adequacy criteria introduced in this chapter. The effectiveness question is also dealt with in Volume II. The next example illustrates the meaning of the subsumes relationship.

Example 6.45: Program P6.19 takes three inputs x, y, and z and computes p.

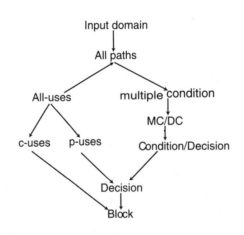

Fig. 6.11 The subsumes relationship among various control-flow-and data-flow-based test adequacy criteria. $X \rightarrow Y$ indicates that X subsumes Y. See the Bibliographic Notes section for citations to research that points to the assumptions that need to be satisfied for the relationship to hold.

Program P6.19

```
1   begin
2     int x, y, z, p;
3     input (x, y, z);
4     if (y≤0) {
5        p=y*z+1;
6     }
7     else{
8        x=y*z+1;
9     }
10    if (z≤0){
11       p=x*z+1;
12    }
13    else{
14       p=z*z+1;
15    }
16    output (p);
17  end
```

The following test set is adequate with respect to the p-use criterion for Program P6.19:

$$T = \begin{cases} t_1: & <x = 5, \quad y = -2, \quad z = 1 > \\ t_2: & <x = 5, \quad y = 2, \quad z = -1 > \end{cases}$$

However, T does not cover the c-use $(d_3(x), u_{11}(x))$. This example illustrates that a test set that is adequate with respect to the p-use criterion is not necessarily adequate with respect to the c-use criterion.

Note that for Program P6.19, a test that covers $(d_3(x), u_{11}(x))$ must cause the conditions at line 4 and 10 to evaluate to true. Such *coupling* of conditions is not required to obtain p-use adequacy (see Exercise 6.42). The next example illustrates that c-use adequacy does not imply p-use adequacy.

Example 6.46: Program P6.20 takes two inputs x and y and computes z.

Program P6.20

```
1  begin
2    int x, y, z,
3    input (x, y);
4    if (y≤0) {
5       z=y*x+1;
6    }
7    z=z*z+1;
8    output (z);
9  end
```

The following test is adequate with respect to the c-use criterion but not with respect to the p-use criterion:

$$T = \{t :< \text{x} = 5,\ \text{y} = -2 >\}$$

6.7 STRUCTURAL AND FUNCTIONAL TESTING

It is commonly believed that when testers measure code coverage, they perform *structural testing* also known as *white-box* or *glass-box* testing. In addition, it is also said that while structural testing compares test program behavior against the apparent intention of the programmer as expressed in the source code, functional testing compares test program behavior against a requirement specification. The difference between structural and functional testing is presented below in a different light.

As explained in Sections 6.1.2 and 6.1.3, measurement of code coverage is a way to assess the *goodness* or *completeness* of a test set T derived with the intention of checking whether the program P under test behaves in accordance with the requirements. Thus, when P is executed against a test case T that belongs to *t*, a tester indeed compares the behavior of T against its requirements as *t* itself is derived from the requirements.

Having successfully executed all tests in T, a tester might choose one of at least two options. One option is to assess the goodness of T using criteria not based on code coverage, while the other is to use code coverage. If the tester chooses the first option, we say that the tester is performing functional testing *without the aid of any code-based test-adequacy measurement*. Certainly, the tester could use non-code-based adequacy criteria, for example requirements coverage.

However, when the tester chooses the second option then some form of code coverage is measured and perhaps used to enhance T. If T is found adequate with respect to a code-based adequacy criteria, say C, then the tester may decide to either further evaluate T using a more powerful adequacy criteria or be satisfied with T.

When T is not adequate with respect to C, the tester must continue to test P against the newly derived tests in the same way as P was tested against tests in T. For example, suppose coverage measurement indicates that decision *d* at line 136 inside function myfunc has not been covered. We now expect the tester to determine, with respect to the requirements, why this decision was not covered. A few possible causes, using arbitrary labels for requirements, are given below:

- There was no test case in T to test for requirement $R_{39.3}$.
- Requirement R_4 was tested only with default parameters, testing it against any other value of an input parameter will cover *d*.

- Decision d can only be covered by a test that tests requirement $R_{2.3}$ followed by requirement $R_{1.7}$.

Once the cause for the lack of coverage is determined, the tester proceeds to construct a new test case t'. P is then executed against t' to ensure that it behaves correctly in accordance with the requirements.

There are several possible outcomes of executing P against t'. One outcome is that decision d remains uncovered implying improper construction of t'. Another possibility is that P behaves incorrectly on t'. In either case, testing is performed with respect to the requirements while the coverage measurement is used as a means to probe the inadequacy of T.

The discussion above leads us to conclude that structural testing is functional testing with the addition of code-based adequacy measurement. Thus, rather than treating functional and structural testing as two independent test methods, we treat one as supplementing the other. In this case, structural testing is supplementary to functional testing. One performs structural testing as part of functional testing by measuring code coverage and using this measure to enhance tests generated using functional testing.

6.8 SCALABILITY OF COVERAGE MEASUREMENT

One might argue that measurement of code coverage, and test enhancement based on such measurement, is practical only during unit testing. One implication of such an argument is that it is impractical to perform code coverage measurements for integration or system tests. In the remainder of this section, we discuss the practicality aspect of code coverage measurement. We offer suggestions on how testers could scale the coverage measurement and test enhancement process to large systems.

Suppose that testers have access to the source code of the application under test. While it is possible to measure code coverage on binaries, lack of such access makes coverage measurement a difficult, if not an impossible, task. Several tools such as JBlanket developed by Joy Augustin, and Quilt available as Apache Software License, measure certain forms of code coverage by instrumenting the object code (bytecode in Java). However, several other tools for coverage measurement often rely on instrumenting the source code and hence would fail to be of any use when the source is not available.

Open systems: First, let us consider open systems, applications that are not embedded in any specific hardware and can be executed in open desktop environments. Examples of such applications are abound and include products such as office tools, Web services, and database systems.

Access to the code of any such application offers testers an opportunity to evaluate the tests using code-based coverage criteria. However, the availability of a coverage measurement tool is almost a necessity when testing large systems. Tools for coverage measurement can be used to instrument the code. The coverage is monitored during execution and displayed after any number of executions. All coverage measurement tools display code coverage values in some form or another and can be used to determine test adequacy.

Incremental and selective coverage measurement: Coverage data for large applications can be overwhelming. For example, an application that contains 10,000 modules with a total of 45,000 conditions spread all over will lead to an enormous amount of coverage data. The display and storage of such data might create problems for the tester and the coverage measurement tool. For example, the test process might exhibit unacceptable slowdown, there might not be sufficient disk space to save all the coverage data, and the coverage measurement tool might breakdown as it might not have been tested to handle such large amounts of coverage data. Such problems can be overcome through incremental measurement and enhancement.

Incremental coverage measurement is performed in several ways. One way is to create a hierarchy of code elements. Elements in the hierarchy are then prioritized using criteria such as their frequency of use or their criticality to the application. Thus, in a large application with say 10,000 modules, one might create three sets of modules M_1, M_2, and M_3 with decreasing priority. The code measurement tool can then be asked to instrument and measure code coverage only in modules that belong to set M_1. Tests could then be enhanced based on the coverage data so obtained. The process could then be repeated for modules in M_2 and others.

Reducing the number of modules for which coverage measurements are taken will reduce the burden on the coverage measurement tool, as well as on the tester who must deal with the amount of coverage data and enhance the tests to improve coverage. However, such a reduction might not be sufficient. In that case, a tester could further subdivide elements of a module set, say M_1, into code elements and prioritize them. This further subdivision could be based on individual classes, or even methods. Such a subdivision further reduces the amount of code to be instrumented and the data to be analyzed by the tester for test enhancement.

In addition to constraining the portions of the code subject to coverage measurement, one could also constrain the coverage criteria. For example, one might begin with the measurement of method, or function, coverage in the selected modules. Once this coverage has been measured, tests enhanced, and adequate coverage obtained, one could move to the other portions of the code and repeat the process.

Embedded systems: Embedded systems pose a significant challenge in the measurement of code coverage. The challenge is primarily due to limited memory space and, in some cases, hard timing constraints. Instrumenting code while testing it in its embedded environment will certainly increase code size. The instrumented code might not fit in the available memory. Even when it fits, it might affect the real-time constraints and impact the application behavior.

Memory constraints can be overcome in at least two ways. One way is to use the incremental coverage idea discussed above. Thus, instrument only a limited portion of the code at a time and test. This would require the tests to be executed in several passes and hence increase the time to complete the coverage measurement.

Another approach to overcome memory constraints is hardware-based. One could use a tool that profiles program execution to obtain branch points in the machine code. Profiling is done in a nonintrusive manner by tapping the microprocessor-memory bus. These branch points are then mapped to the source program, and coverage measures such as block and branch coverage are computed and displayed.

Coverage measurement for object-oriented programs: Object-oriented (OO) programs allow a programmer to structure a program in terms of classes and methods. A class encapsulates one or more methods and serves as a template for the creation of objects. Thus, while all code coverage criteria discussed in this chapter apply to OO programs, some additional coverage measures can also be devised. These include method coverage, context coverage, object coverage, and others.

SUMMARY

This chapter covers the foundations of test assessment and enhancement using structural coverage criteria. We have divided these criteria as control-flow based and data-flow based. Each criterion is defined and illustrated with examples. Examples also show how faults are detected, or missed, when a criterion is satisfied. The simplest of all control-flow-based criteria such as the statement coverage and the decision coverage have found their way in a large number of commercially available testing tools.

We have introduced some of the several data-flow-based adequacy criteria, namely all-uses, p-uses, and c-uses. There are others not covered here and referred to in the Bibliographic Notes section. While adequacy with respect to data-flow-based criteria is stronger than that based on control-flow-based criteria, it has not found much use in commercial software development. However, the availability of good tools such as χSuds from Telcordia Technologies, and education, promises to change this state of affairs.

This chapter is certainly not a complete treatment of all the different control-flow- and data-flow-based adequacy criteria. There are many more, for example data context coverage and others. Some of the uncovered material is pointed to in the section on Bibliographic Notes.

BIBLIOGRAPHIC NOTES

Test adequacy: The notion of test adequacy, which we sometimes refer to as test completeness, is as ancient as software testing. While referring to the 1963 publication of Miller and Maloney [329], Page and Balkovich write, "The goal of this type of *testing is to* consider conditions such that every path will be traversed at least once." [383]. Obviously, Page and Balkovich were *recommending* a test completeness criterion, that of complete path coverage. Realizing the possibility of an infinite number of paths in the presence of loops, they further write, "Loops may be tested in two ways, depending on whether the number of repetitions of the loop is influenced by the input data or is fixed." They then suggest ways to test loops.

Howden defined the notion of boundary-interior test paths [233] and a method for selecting test data that exercise such paths when they are feasible. Howden defined the boundary-interior approach as one that tests all alternative paths through a program, through loops, and performs alternative boundary and interior tests of loops. A boundary test of a loop is conducted by ensuring that control arrives at the loop, but does not iterate it. An interior test of a loop exercises the loop body at least once. Thus, Howden's test completeness criteria is similar to that recommended by Page and Balkovich except in the ways Howden proposes to test loops (zero times, and one or more times). Chusho [89] proposed a method for the selection of paths for coverage using the concept of *essential branches*.

Zhu *et al.* offer a detailed survey of test coverage metrics and the measurement of test adequacy [54]. They define test data-adequacy criteria as stopping rules as well as measurements. Test-adequacy criteria are classified as specification based and program based. A large number of control-flow-and data-flow-based coverage criteria as well as mutation-based criteria are included in the survey.

Goodenough and Gerhart formally define properties of test completeness, or adequacy, criteria [174–176]. The notions of an ideal test, successful test, reliable criterion and valid criterion are formalized. Another significant contribution of the work of Goodenough and Gerhart the lies in their meticulous analysis of Naur's program [348] that was published and supposedly proven correct. Exposing errors in this program, Goodenough and Gerhart observed the fallibility of formal proofs and the complementary nature of software testing and formal proofs.

Yet another classic paper is by DeMillo *et al.* that introduced the powerful idea of program mutation and its use to assess the completeness of tests [122]. The idea of coupling effect, described in Chapter 7, is introduced and explained in this paper. The authors also showed, through examples, that test data derived with the intention of uncovering simple errors is superior to randomly selected data. The idea of multiple condition/decision coverage, not the MC/DC name, is embedded in the work of DeMillo *et al.* (see pages 35–36 in [122]). This paper for the first time exhibited how findings from error studies, such as those by Youngs

[54], can be used in deriving adequate test sets.

Woodward *et al.* defined the LCSAJ criteria for test generation [533] and used it in the testing of numerical programs [212]. They have reported an empirical study to assess the fault-detection effectiveness of the LCSAJ criterion.

Belli and Dreyer proposed the use of regular expressions to encode classes of paths corresponding to Howden's boundary-interior testing [40]. A regular expression R is used to represent the control-flow structure of a program. The notion of biexpansion is used to expand R into biclasses. A test set is considered adequate with respect to the set of biclasses when at least one path is covered from each biclass. Using the test criteria proposed, Belli and Dreyer studied its fault-detection effectiveness on five erroneous programs including the program by Naur[348], also studied earlier by Goodenough and Gerhart. They observed that the proposed criteria guaranteed the detection of all errors except in Naur's program; a more detailed analysis of the errors in Naur's program and their detection with the help of tests adequate with respect to various path-oriented adequacy criteria has been reported.

Pavlopoulou and Young have described an approach for the efficient monitoring of code coverage in a deployed environment [392]. Recent workshops have explored the techniques for remotely measuring quality of deployed software [376].

Marrè and Bertolino proposed the use of spanning sets to find a minimal set of entities sufficient to obtain full coverage of all entities in a given set E. The proposed algorithm can find minimal sets for E-containing elements required for adequacy with respect to various control-flow-and data-flow-based coverage criteria. An empirical study reveals that tests derived using spanning sets are effective at improving coverage and finding faults. Some results reported earlier by Wong *et al.* [522, 523] on the effectiveness of code coverage are confirmed by the study of Marrè and Bertolino.

Taylor *et al.* have proposed adequacy criteria for structural testing of concurrent programs [473]. Wong, *et al.* have described an approach for the generation of tests for concurrent programs using reachability graphs [524]. The tests so generated satisfy the all-nodes and all-edges criteria. Note that algorithm of Wong *et al.* generates tests for adequacy criteria different from that proposed by Taylor *et al.*.

While assessment of the adequacy of tests using different forms of code-based coverage criteria is nearly essential in improving the quality of delivered software, misuse of coverage data is possible. Marick exposes some undesirable interpretations of coverage data [308]. Weyuker offers four reasons why code coverage measurement is important despite the possibility that tests might fail to expose common faults even when they satisfy one or more code coverage criteria [509].

MC/DC coverage: The MC/DC coverage became popular after it was adopted as a standard requirement for airborne software [410, 411]. Hayhurst *et al.* have written an excellent tutorial on the MC/DC coverage [210]. Chilenski and Miller have described the applicability of the MC/DC coverage to software testing

[82]. Hayhurst and Holloway have published a brief article on guidelines for avionics software [209].

Leveson and Dupuy have evaluated the fault-detection effectiveness of the MC/DC-based test-adequacy criterion with reference to High Energy Transient Explorer 2 (HETE-2) satellite software [288]. Rayadurgam and Heimdahl have proposed a method for automatically generating MC/DC-adequate tests using model checking[409]. Kapoor and Bowen have reported variations in the fault-detection effectiveness of the decision coverage, full predicate coverage (FPC), and the MC/DC coverage [251]. They found that while the average effectiveness of DC and FPC criteria decreases with the increase in the number of conditions in the program under test, it remains constant for the MC/DC. Woodward and Hennel have compared the all *jump-to-jump* (JJ) paths with the MC/DC-coverage criteria [534]. They found that for programs written under specific conditions, all JJ paths subsume MC/DC.

Control-flow coverage-measurement tools: A large number of commercial and other tools are available to measure code coverage of various kinds. Only a few are covered here. ATAC and χSuds from Telcordia Technologies (sold by Cleanscape, www.cleanscape.net) measure block, decision, condition, and data-flow coverage for C programs [224, 225]. Magellan [455] is a set of tools used at Microsoft. One of the tools in this set collects block and edge coverage using instrumentation of binaries. Code coverage obtained at the binary level can be displayed graphically at the level of the source code. Code coverage data is collected both in the user and kernel modes.

Massol and Husted describe JUnit, a coverage measurement tool for Java classes [309]. JUnit measures block coverage and decision coverage. IBM's Rational PurifyPlus is a coverage analysis tool for use on Linux and Unix platforms for measuring block coverage of C, C++, and Java programs. Additionally, PurifyPlus is able to detect memory corruption and memory leaks. Agustin developed JBlanket that measures method coverage for Java programs [14]. JBlanket instruments the Java bytecode to measure method coverage. In addition to determining how many methods have been invoked, it also identifies untestable methods.

Several other tools are available for measuring adequacy of tests for Java programs. These include Clover from Cenqua (http://www.cenqua.com/clover/) Quilt, an open source tool (http://quilt.sourceforge.net/) and JCover from Codework (http://www.codework.com/). PureCoverage is available from IBM/Rational for Windows NT and Unix platforms and supports Java and Visual C++. BullseyeCoverage is a C++ coverage analyzer available from Bullseye Technology (http://www.bullseye.com/).

Cantata and Cantata++ are available from IPL (http://www.iplbath.com). These tools allow the measurement of coverage for OO programs. The notion of context coverage is used in Cantata++ to assist with the coverage measurement in the presence of polymorphism. Method coverage and their context, that is objects and classes that encapsulate them, are measured. Several other tools, for example Optimizeit from Borland (http://info.borland.com/techpubs/jbuilder/jbuilder2005/code_coverage/), provides user friendly ways to measure the coverage of methods and classes within an OO program.

Rocha has reported a tool named J-FuT for functional testing of Java programs using techniques such as equivalence partitioning and boundary-value analysis [419]. The novelty of J-FuT lies in its ability to assess the adequacy of functional tests using code-based coverage criteria. Thus, J-FuT, like several other coverage measurement tools, supports the test development–enhancement paradigm described in this chapter. Aspect-oriented programming is used in the implementation of J-FuT to enforce separation of concerns in testing-related program code.

Data-flow-based adequacy criteria:
Herman proposed the use of data-flow analysis in software testing in 1976. In the same year, Fosdick and Osterweil suggested the use of data-flow analysis for producing reliable software [149]. Beyond the 1970s, the theory and practice of data, flow-based test-adequacy criteria has been the focus of several researchers. In all cases, the goal has been to define adequacy criteria that allow selection of a subset of all paths through a program.

Korel and Laski [267], Laski [278], and Korel and Laski [280] proposed data-flow-oriented criteria for test selection. Independently, Rapps and Weyuker [407,408] also proposed various data-flow-based test-adequacy criteria. While the criteria proposed by Rapps

and Weyuker and by Laski and Korel are based on the concept of data flows in a program, the actual criteria are somewhat different. For example, the notion of ordered data context by Laski and Korel is different from any of the criteria defined by Rapps and Weyuker. Ntafos proposed the use of required k-tuple strategy as an extension of def–use pair strategy [352, 353]. Harrold and Rothermel have studied the application of data-flow testing to classes [200].

Using theoretical analysis, Clarke et al. have compared various control-flow-and data-flow-based adequacy criteria and developed hierarchical relationship among them [93, 94]. This work is a detailed and thorough study and defines precisely the *subsumes* relationship among different control-flow and data flow criteria. Ntafos has suggested changes to the hierarchy proposed by Clarke et al. [354]. The changes are based on Ntafos' interpretation of the definitions of data-flow strategies.

The early work in data-flow testing focused on data flows within a procedure or function. Harrold and Soffa studied interprocedural data-flow analysis and developed techniques for testing data flows across procedures [202]. Ostrand describes how to accurately determine data flows in a C program that uses pointers [378]. Liu, King, and Hsia have applied data flow testing to the testing of Web applications [296]. Tsai et al. have applied data-flow testing to the testing of classes in OO programs [478]. Liu has applied data-flow testing to testing Java server pages [295].

Effectiveness of data-flow testing:
Several theoretical and empirical studies

aimed at assessing the fault-detection effectiveness of various data-flow-oriented adequacy criteria have been reported. Hennel et al. used data flows in their study of numerical programs in ALGOL 68[214]. Howden used data-flow analysis in a study of errors in numerical programs and their validation [234, 237]. Through an example from an error in the IMSL library, Howden showed how an incorrect flow of data into a variable is the cause of the error. He termed this as a *data-flow-error*. Though this study was not aimed at assessing the effectiveness of data-flow-based adequacy criteria, it did show the importance of considering data flows in program testing.

An analytical study of the ability of data-flow testing to detect errors has been reported by Frankl and Weyuker [155]. They examined the relationship between the subsumes relation and the fault-detection effectiveness. Prior to this publication, Hamlet showed that given that criterion C_1 subsumes criterion C_2, a C_1-adequate test set for program P might not detect a fault in P whereas a C_2-adequate test set might detect. Weyuker has reported case studies to assess the cost and fault-detection effectiveness of data-flow testing [510, 511]. Mathur and Wong have reported an analytical comparison of the fault-detection abilities of data-flow- and mutation-based adequacy criteria [319].

Wong [520], Mathur and Wong [318], Frankl et al. [153], and Offutt et al. [367] have compared the fault-detection effectiveness of data-flow- and mutation-based test-adequacy criteria. The empirical studies mentioned here share a common conclusion, that the mutation-based criteria are more powerful in detecting faults in programs. However, in some studies the difference found was slight. Frankl and Weiss have compared the fault-detection effectiveness of branch testing and data-flow testing [152].

Data-flow-testing tools: Measurement of data-flow coverage is best done with the help of an automated tool. Frankl and Weyuker developed ASSET, a tool for measuring data-flow coverage for Pascal programs[154]. Laski reported an experimental tool named STAD to study data-flow patterns in a program [279].

Horgan's research group at Bellcore (now Telcordia) developed ATAC, a data-flow and control-flow coverage-measurement tool for C programs [224, 225]. A user-friendly graphical interface was later added to ATAC and the tool was extended further by adding additional tools useful to a tester. This led to the χSuds (visit http://xsuds.argreenhouse.com/) toolset.

Chaim developed POKE-TOOL, a data-flow-testing tool for C programs [73]. The novelty of POKE-TOOL lies in its implementation of the concept of potential uses described by Maldonado et al. [303]. Virgilio et al. have reported that the potential use-based coverage criteria has exhibited better fault-detection ability than the all-uses criterion [486].

Harrold and Soffa report a tool for interprocedural data-flow testing [202]. A number of empirical studies reported in the literature have been performed using ASSET, ATAC, and χSuds. χSuds continues to be used in several universities in courses on software testing and software engineering. Ostrand and Weyuker reported a tool named TACTIC for data-flow-adequacy measurement of tests for C programs [381]. The novelty of TACTIC lies in its thorough analysis of data flows in the presence of pointers.

Data-based coverage While this chapter has focused on adequacy criteria based on several code attributes, for example control flow and data flow, other criteria are also available based on attributes of test data. Netisopakul *et al.* [349] propose a data coverage strategy for test generation. The strategy generates inputs to test collections that are constrained by the size of the input. The idea is to generate test inputs that cover all sizes up to a critical size such that no errors are found when the collection is tested for inputs larger than the critical size. The strategy was empirically found superior to statement coverage in its ability to detect faults.

Nikolik [350] has proposed a novel approach to adequacy assessment based on a technique known as *oscillation diversity.* Oscillation diversity of a test suite is measured with respect to its ability to obtain dispersion in code and data-flow coverage. For example, amplitude is measured as differences in the counts of `true` and `false` outcomes of conditional branches executed. One could increase diversity of the test suite by adding tests so as to increase the amplitude along a given direction, for example along the `true` or the `false` direction. Another novelty of this work is that it defines notions such as resistance, inductance, and Terz (analogous to Herz) in the context of software testing.

Coverage of hardware designs:
Hardware designs are often expressed in special hardware description languages (HDLs) such as Verilog. The designs are

tested prior to being committed to silicon. Several researchers have proposed coverage criteria for assessing the adequacy of HDL tests. Tasiran and Keutzer define a set of coverage criteria for hardware designs [472]. They propose a different set of coverage criteria than that used for software applications. The concurrency of hardware designs motivates their criteria.

Katrowitz and Noack describe the use of coverage analysis in the testing of the design of the Alpha-based DECchip 21164 microprocessor [254]. They evaluated the adequacy of pseudorandom tests against various coverage measures. While the authors describe several coverage metrics, they also mention that a few errors did escape into the fabrication despite coverage analysis. They conclude that bypass coverage, where normal data flow is skipped, and multilevel event coverage are necessary for detecting the escaped errors.

Benjamin *et al.* have described a coverage-driven test generator, named GOTCHA, that generates tests to obtain state and transition coverage in a finite state model [42]. Wang and Tan discuss several coverage-based approaches for testing hardware designs in Verilog [501]. They claim that hardware designers can obtain useful feedback from coverage data despite incomplete coverage.

Shye *et al.* describe an approach and a prototype tool for using hardware performance-monitoring support to obtain measurements of code coverage [441]. Their experiments on the Itanium 2 processor revealed that more than 80% code coverage can be obtained with only 3% overhead when hardware performance monitoring is used.

Code coverage for large-scale systems:
Kim describes ways to obtain code coverage in large-scale industrial software systems [262]. The notion of coarse and detailed coverage analysis is presented. They propose the use of Pareto-like distribution of software defects [145], that is a small number of modules responsible for a large number of defects, to reduce the amount of code to be instrumented.

Kim applied the proposed coverage-assessment methodology to a system consisting of over 19.8 million lines of code written in a mix of languages such as C/C++, Java, and Perl. The ATAC tool was used to measure detailed code coverage, and an in-house tool to measure coarse coverage.

Gittens *et al.* conducted a detailed empirical study to determine the breadth of system and regression testing. They measured the breadth in terms of code coverage and defects discovered prior to, and after, product release. Block coverage was measured on a commercial system consisting of 201,629 lines of C/C++ code spread over 221 modules. Code coverage was measured using ATAC. One conclusion from their study is that an increase in defect detection correlates well until about 61%–70% coverage for regression testing and 51%–60% in system testing. This points to the existence of saturation effect in the rate of discovery of defects with increase in coverage. Similar conclusions were arrived at by Piwowarski *et al.* in their study of a large industrial system [399].

Code instrumentation: Measurement of code coverage requires instrumenting the code. Such instrumentation leads to intrusive coverage measurement in contrast to nonintrusive measurement that can be done using hardware monitoring described earlier. Code instrumentation adds monitoring code to the binary code and thus incurs run-time overhead. Thus, a reduction in the amount of instrumentation is worth the effort.

Early proposals for optimal placement of probes are by Ramammorthy *et al.* [404], Knuth and Stevenson [264], and Probert[401], where a probe is a piece of code that determines whether a block of instructions has been covered. Maheshwari showed that probe placement problems (he referred to probes as markers) are NP-complete [301].

Agrawal proposed the notion of dominators and super blocks as program entities useful for reducing the amount of instrumentation needed to obtain accurate code coverage [8]. Agrawal's techniques for the detection of dominators and super blocks are implemented in ATAC and χSuds.

Tikir and Hollingsworth describe efficient ways to perform code instrumentation [476]. Their approach is dynamic in that instrumentation can be added and removed during program execution. They used dominator trees, similar to those used by Agrawal [8], and obtained reduction in the number of blocks to be instrumented from 34% to 48.7%. Other efforts at reducing the memory and run-time overhead due to instrumentation have been reported, among others, by Ball and Larus[31], Larus [277], Pavlopoulou and Young [392].

EXERCISES

6.1 Consider the following often found statement in research publications: "Complete testing is not possible." What completeness criterion forms the basis of this statement? In light of the completeness criteria discussed in this chapter, is this statement correct?

6.2 Enumerate all paths in Program P6.5. Assume that each loop is required to be traversed zero times and once.

6.3 Why did we decide to input all tests in T during a single execution of Program P6.5? Will the error be revealed if we were to input each test in a separate execution ?

6.4 Draw the CFG for Program P6.5. Enumerate all paths through this program that traverse the loop zero times and once.

6.5 Let A, B, and C denote three Booleans. Let $Cond = (A$ and $B)$ or $(A$ and $C)$ or $(B$ and $C)$ be a condition. What is the minimum (maximum) number of tests required to (a) cover a decision based on $Cond$ and (b) cover all atomic conditions in $Cond$?

6.6 Construct a program in your favorite language that inputs three integers x, y, and z, and computes output O using the specification in Table 6.12. Assume that $f_1(x, y, z) = x + y + z$ and $f_2(x, y, z) = x \times y \times z$.
Introduce an error in your program. Now construct a test set T that is decision adequate, but not multiple condition adequate, and does not reveal the error you introduced. Enhance T so that it is multiple condition-adequate and does reveal the error. Will all tests that are multiple condition adequate for your program reveal the error?

Table 6.12 Computing O for the program in Exercise 6.6

	$x < y$	$x < z$	O
1	true	true	$f1(x, y, z)$
2	true	false	$f2(x, y, z)$
3	false	true	$f3(x, y, z)$
4	false	false	$f4(x, y, z)$

6.7 Suppose that test set T for a given program and the corresponding requirements are adequate with respect to the statement coverage criterion. Will T be always adequate with respect to the block coverage criterion?

6.8 (a) How many decisions are introduced by an `if` statement? (b) How many decisions are introduced by a `switch` statement? and (c) Does each decision in a program lead to a new path?

6.9 Consider the following claim: *If the number of simple conditions in a decision is n, then the number of tests required to cover all conditions is 2^n.* If possible, construct a program to show that in general this claim is not true.

6.10 Modify T in Example 6.15 to render it adequate with respect to the condition/decision criterion for Program P6.9.

6.11 Given simple conditions A, B, and C, derive minimal MC/DC-adequate tests for the following conditions: (a) A and B and C, (b) A or B or C, and (c) A xor B. Is the test set unique in each case?

6.12 While removing redundant tests from Table 6.6, we selected tests (3, 4) to cover condition C_3. What will be the minimal MC-adequate test set if, instead, tests (5, 6) or (7, 8) are selected?

6.13 Are the tests given for each of the three conditions in (a) Table 6.9 and (b) Table 6.10, unique?

6.14 In Section 6.2.9, we list a simple procedure to derive the MC/DC-adequate tests for condition $C = C_1$ and C_2 and C_3 from the MC/DC-adequate tests for condition $C = C_1$ and C_2. Using this procedure as a guide, construct another procedure to (a) derive the MC/DC-adequate tests for $C = C_1$ or C_2 or C_3, given the MC/DC-adequate tests for $C = C_1$ or C_2, and (b) derive the MC/DC-adequate tests for $C = C_1$ xor C_2 xor C_3, given MC/DC-adequate tests for $C = C_1$ xor C_2.

6.15 Extend the procedure in Section 6.2.9 to derive the MC/DC-adequate tests for $C = C_1$ and $C_2 \ldots$ and C_{n-1} and C_n, given the MC/DC-adequate tests for $C = C_1$ and $C_2 \ldots$ and C_{n-1}.

6.16 Use the procedures derived in Exercises 6.14 and 6.15 to construct an MC/DC-adequate test for (a) $(C_1$ and $C_2)$ or C_3, (b) $(C_1$ or $C_2)$ and C_3, and (c) $(C_1$ or $C_2)$ xor C_3.

6.17 Suppose that test set T is found adequate with respect to condition coverage for some program P. Is it also adequate with respect to the decision coverage? Is the opposite true?

6.18 Consider program P containing exactly one compound condition C and no other conditions of any kind. C is composed of n simple conditions. Let T be the test set adequate for P with respect to the MC/DC criterion. Show that T contains at least n and at most $2n$ test cases.

6.19 Consider a test set T adequate for program P with respect to some coverage criterion C. Now suppose that $T_1 \cup T_2 = T$ and that both T_1 and T_2 are adequate with respect to C. Let P' be a modified version of P. To test P', under what conditions would you execute P' against all of T, only T_1, and only T_2?

6.20 Is T_3 of Example 6.23 minimal with respect to the MC/DC coverage? If not then remove all redundant test cases from T_3 and generate a minimal test set.

6.21 (a) In Example 6.23, suppose that condition C_2 at line 12 is incorrectly coded as:

12   if((z * z > y) and (prev=="East"))

Will the execution of Program P6.14 against t_5 reveal the error?
(b) Now suppose that in Example 6.23, condition C_3 at line 14 is also incorrectly coded as:

14   else if ((z * z ≤ y) or (current=="South"))

Note that there are two erroneous statements in the program. Will the execution of the erroneous Program P6.14 against t_5 reveal the error?

(c) Construct a test case that will cause the erroneous Program P6.23 to produce an incorrect output, thereby revealing the error.

(d) What errors in the requirements are likely be revealed by each of the tests $t_5, t_6, \ldots t_9$ in Example 6.23?

6.22 Why does the MC/DC-adequate test set in Example 6.24 contain four tests when the MC/DC adequacy for a conjunction of two simple conditions can be achieved with only three tests?

6.23 (a) Given $C = C_1$ and C_2 and … and C_n, suppose that C has been coded as $C'' = C_1$ and C_2 and … and C_{i-1} and $C_{i+1} \ldots$ and C_n; note one missing simple condition in C''. Show that, in the general case, an MC/DC-adequate test set is not *likely* to detect the error in C''. (b) Can we say that an MC/DC-adequate test set will not detect this error? (c) Does the error-detection capability of the MC/DC criteria change as the number of missing simple conditions increases? (d) Answer parts (a) and (c) assuming that $C = C1$ or C_2 or ... or C_n and $C = C_1$ or C_2 or ... or Ci_1 or C_{i+1} ... or C_n.

6.24 (a) Suppose that Program P6.14 contains one error in the coding of condition C_2. The error is a missing simple condition. The incorrect condition is:

```
12    if((z * z > y)  and  (prev == "East"))
```

Develop an MC/DC-adequate test set for the incorrect version of Program P6.14. How many of the test cases derived reveal the error? Does the answer to this question remain unchanged for every minimal MC/DC-adequate test for this incorrect program? (b) Answer (a) for the following error in coding C_3:

```
14 else if  ((x<y or (z * z ≤ y) and (current=="South"))
```

6.25 Let A, B, and C denote Boolean expressions. Consider a compound condition C defined as follows:

$$C = (A \text{ and } B) \text{ or } (A \text{ and } C) \text{ or } (B \text{ and } C)$$

Assuming that C is used in a decision, construct a minimal set of tests for C that are adequate with respect to (a) the decision coverage, (b) the condition coverage, (c) the multiple condition coverage, and (d) the MC/DC coverage.

6.26 Show that a test set adequate with respect to the LSCAJ (MC/DC) criterion may not be adequate with respect to the LCSAJ (MC/DC) criterion.

6.27 There are at least two options to choose from when considering data-flow coverage of arrays. One option is to treat the entire array as a single variable. Thus, whenever this variable name appears in the context of an assignment, the entire array is considered defined; when it appears in the context of a use, the entire array is considered used. The other option is to treat each element of the array as a distinct variable.

Discuss the impact of the two options on (a) the cost of deriving data-flow-adequate tests and (b) the cost of keeping track of the coverage values in an automated data-flow coverage-measurement tool.

6.28 (a) In Example 6.30, (1, 2, 5, 6) is considered a def–clear path with respect to count defined at node 1 and used at node 5. Considering that count is defined at node 6, why is this redefinition of count not masking the definition of count at node 1? (b) Construct two complete paths through the data-flow graph in Figure 6.7 that are def–clear with respect to the definition of count at node 6 and its use in the same node.

6.29 Is test case t in Example 6.37 adequate with respect to c-use coverage and p-use coverage? Generate additional tests to obtain c-use and p-use coverage if t is inadequate with respect to these criteria.

6.30 In Section 6.3.8, we listed a minimal set of c-use and p-uses that when covered by a test set T ensure that all feasible c-use and p-uses are also covered by T. Show that the given set is minimal.

6.31 (a) Show that indeed set $T = \{t_c, t_p\}$, consisting of tests derived in Examples 6.36 and 6.37, is adequate with respect to the p-use criterion. (b) Enhance T to obtain T' adequate with respect to the c-use criterion. (c) Is T' minimal, that is, can you reduce T' and obtain complete c-use and p-use coverage from the reduced set?

6.32 Consider a path s through some program P. Variable v is defined along this path at some node n_d and used subsequently at some node n_u in an assignment, that is there is a c-use of v along s. Suppose now that path P is infeasible. (a) Does this imply that the c-use of v at node n_c is also infeasible? (b) Suppose now that there is a p-use of v at node n_p along path s. Given that s is infeasible, is this p-use also infeasible? Explain your answer.

6.33 Consider the following program due to Boyer, Elapas, and Levitt, and analyzed by Rapps and Weyuker in the context of data-flow testing in their seminal publication. The program finds the square root of input p, $0 < p < 1$, to accuracy e, $0 < e < 1$.

Program P6.21

```
1   begin
2      float x=0, p, e, d=1, c;
3      input (p, e);
4      c=2*p;
5      if (c≥2) {
6         output ("Error");
7      }
8      else{
9         while (d>e) {
```

```
10          d=d/2; t=c-(2*x+d);
11          if (t≥0) {
12             x=x+d;
13             c=2*(c-(2*x+d));
14          }
15          else{
16          c=2*c;  }
17          }
18       }
19    output ("Square root of p=", x);
20    }
21 end
```

For Program P6.21, (a) draw a data-flow graph, (b) develop an MC/DC-adequate test set T_{mcdc}, and (c) enhance T_{mcdc} to generate T that is adequate with respect to the all-uses criterion. (d) There is an error in Program P6.21. Lines 12 and 13 must be interchanged to remove this error. Does T reveal the error? (e) Does T_{mcdc} reveal the error? (f) Will every T, adequate with respect to the all-uses criterion, reveal the error?

6.34 (a) In Example 6.44, what condition must be satisfied by a test case for Program P6.21 to produce an incorrect output? Let us refer to the condition you derive as C_1. (b) Is C_1 the same as the condition, say C_2, required to cover the c-use of y at line 8 corresponding to its definition at line 14? (c) For Program P6.21, what would you conclude regarding the detection if C_1 does not imply C_2, or vice versa?

6.35 (a) In k–dr analysis, it is assumed that each node in the data-flow graph corresponds to a simple predicate. Modify the data-flow graph shown in Figure 6.6 such that each node in the modified graph corresponds to a simple predicate. (b) Does k–dr coverage for $k = 2$ imply the condition coverage, the multiple condition coverage, or the MC/DC coverage?

6.36 (a) Draw a data-flow graph F for Program P6.22. (b) Construct data context sets for all nodes in F. (c) Construct a test set adequate with respect to data context coverage. Assume that functions foo1(), foo2(), foo3(), foo4(), and P1() are defined elsewhere.

Program P6.22

```
1  begin
2     int x, y, z;
3     input (x, y);
4     y=foo1(x, y);
5     while (P1(x)){
6        z=foo2(x, y);
7        if(P2(x, y){
8           y=foo3(y);
```

```
 9        }
10        else{
11           x=foo4(x);
12        }
13    } // End of loop.
14    output(z);
15  end
```

6.37 (a) The table in Example 6.35 lists only the feasible elementary data contexts for various nodes for Program P6.16. Enumerate all elementary data contexts for nodes 4, 5, 6, and 7. Among these, identify the infeasible elementary data contexts. (b) How will the answer to (a) change if the initialization $z = 0$ is removed and the statement at line 4 is replaced by:

```
4    input(x, y, z, count);
```

6.38 Construct $ODC(n)$ for all nodes in the data-flow graph for Program P6.22. Is the test set constructed in Exercise 6.36 adequate with respect to the ordered data context coverage criterion? If not then enhance it to a set that is adequate with respect to the ordered data context coverage criterion.

6.39 (a) Define data context coverage and ordered data context coverage in a manner analogous to the definitions of elementary and ordered elementary data contexts, respectively. (b) Which of the two sets of definitions of context coverage would you recommend, and why, for the measurement of test adequacy and enhancement?

6.40 Find all infeasible elementary data contexts for node 6 in Figure 6.7.

6.41 For Program P6.23, construct a test set adequate with respect to the p-use criterion but not with respect to the c-use criterion.

Program P6.23

```
 1  begin
 2    int x, y, c, count;
 3    input(x, count);
 4    y=0;
 5    c=count;
 6    while(c>0){
 7       y=y*x;
 8       c=c-1;
 9    }
10    output(y);
11    }
12  end
```

6.42 Show that for programs containing only one conditional statement, and no loops, the p-use criterion subsumes the c-use criterion.

6.43 The statement "Structural testing compares test program behavior against the apparent intention of the source code." can also be restated as "Functional testing compares test program behavior against the apparent intention of the source code." Do you agree with these statements? Explain your answer.

6.44 Boundary-interior testing proposed by William Howden requires a loop to be iterated zero times and at least once. Construct a program with an error in the loop that can be revealed only if the loop is iterated at least twice. You may use nested loops. Note that it is easy to construct such an example by placing the construction of a function f inside the loop and executing f only in the second or subsequent iteration. Try constructing a more sophisticated program.

6.45 Suppose that a program contains two loops, one nested inside the other. What is the minimum number of boundary-interior tests required to satisfy Howden's boundary-interior adequacy criterion?

6.46 Critique the following statement obtained from a Web site: "White-Box tests suffer from the following shortcomings: (a) Creating a false sense of stability and quality. An application can often pass all unit tests and still appear unavailable to users due to a non-functioning component (a database, connection pool, etc.). This is a critical problem, since it makes the IT application team look incompetent, (b) Inability to validate use-case completeness because they use a different interface to the application."

EXERCISES

7

Test-Adequacy Assessment Using Program Mutation

CONTENT ▪▪

The purpose of this chapter is to introduce program mutation as a technique for the assessment of test adequacy and the enhancement of test sets. The chapter also focuses on the design and use of mutation operators for procedural and objected-oriented programming languages.

7.1 INTRODUCTION

Program mutation is a powerful technique for the assessment of the goodness of tests. It provides a set of strong criteria for test assessment and enhancement. If your tests are adequate with respect to some other adequacy criterion, such as the MC/DC-coverage criterion, then chances are that these are not adequate with respect to most criteria offered by program mutation.

Program mutation is a technique to assess and enhance your tests. Hereafter we will refer to *program mutation* as *mutation*. When testers use mutation to assess the adequacy of their tests, and possibly enhance them, we say that they are using *mutation testing*. Sometimes the act of assessing test adequacy using mutation is also referred to as *mutation analysis*.

Given that mutation requires access to all or portions of the source code, it is considered a white-box, or code-based, technique. Some refer to mutation testing as fault-injection testing. However, it must be noted that fault-injection testing is a separate area in its own right and must be distinguished from mutation testing as a technique for test adequacy and enhancement.

Mutation has also been used as a black-box technique. In this case, it is used to mutate specifications and, in the case of Web applications, messages that flow between a client and a server. This chapter focuses on the mutation of computer programs written in high-level languages such as Fortran, C, and Java.

While mutation of computer programs requires access to the source code of the application under test, some variants can do without it. Interface mutation requires access only to the interface of the application under test. Run-time fault injection, a technique similar to mutation, requires only the binary version of the application under test.

Mutation can be used to assess and enhance tests for program units such as C functions and Java classes. It can also be used to assess and enhance tests for an integrated set of components. Thus, as explained in the remainder of this chapter, mutation is a powerful technique for use during unit, integration, and system testing.

A cautionary note: Mutation is a significantly different way of assessing test adequacy than what we have discussed in the previous chapters. Thus, while reading this chapter, you are likely to have questions of the kind "Why this...?" or "Why that...?" With patience, you will find that most, if not all, of your questions are answered in this chapter.

7.2 MUTATION AND MUTANTS

Mutation is the act of changing a program, albeit only slightly. If P denotes the original program under test and M a program obtained by slightly changing P, then M is known as a *mutant* of P, and P the *parent* of M. Given that P is syntactically correct, and hence compiles, M must be syntactically correct. M might exhibit the behavior of P from which it is derived.

The term *to mutate* refers to the act of mutation. To *mutate* a program means to change it. Of course, for the purpose of test assessment, we mutate by introducing only *slight* changes.

€xample 7.1: Consider the following simple program:

Program P7.1

```
1  begin
2    int x,y;
3    input (x, y);
4    if (x < y)
5      output(x+y);
6    else
7      output(x*y);
8  end
```

A large variety of changes can be made to Program P7.1 such that the resultant program is syntactically correct. Below we list two mutants of Program P7.1. Mutant M_1 is obtained by replacing the "<" operator by the "≤" operator. Mutant M_2 is obtained by replacing the "∗" operator by the "/" operator.

Mutant M1 of Program P7.1

```
1  begin
2    int x, y;
3    input (x, y);
4    if(x≤y)   ← Mutated statement
5    then
6      output(x+y);
7    else
8      output(x*y);
9  end
```

Mutant M2 of Program P7.1

```
1  begin
2    int x, y;
3    input (x, y);
4    if(x<y)
5    then
6      output(x+y);
7    else
8      output(x/y);  ← Mutated statement
9  end
```

Notice that the changes made in the original program are simple. For example, we have not added any chunk of code to the original program to generate a mutant. Also, only one change has been made to the parent to obtain its mutant.

7.2.1 FIRST-ORDER AND HIGHER-ORDER MUTANTS

Mutants generated by introducing only a single change to a program under test are also known as *first-order* mutants. Second-order mutants are created by making two simple changes, third order by making three simple changes, and so on. One can generate a second-order mutant by creating a first-order mutant of another first-order mutant. Similarly, an nth-order mutant can be created by creating a first-order mutant of an $(n-1)$th-order mutant.

Example 7.2: Once again let us consider Program P7.1. We can obtain a second-order mutant of this program in a variety of ways. Here is a second-order mutant obtained by replacing variable y in the if statement by the expression $y + 1$, and replacing operator $+$ in the expression $x + y$ by the operator $/$.

Mutant M3 of Program P7.1

```
1  begin
2    int x,y;
3    input (x, y);
4    if (x < y+1)  ← Mutated statement
5    then
6      output(x/y);  ← Mutated statement
7    else
8      output(x*y);
9  end
```

Mutants other than first order are also known as *higher-order* mutants. First-order mutants are the ones generally used in practice. There are two reasons why first-order mutants are preferred to higher-order mutants. One reason is that there are many more higher-order mutants of a program than there are first-order mutants. For example, 528,906 second-order mutants are generated for program FIND that contains only 28 lines of Fortran code. Such a large number of mutants create a scalability problem during adequacy assessment. Another reason has to do with the coupling effect and is explained in Section 7.6.2.

Note that so far we have used the term *simple change* without explaining what we mean by *simple* and what is a *complex* change. An answer to this question appears in the following sections.

7.2.2 SYNTAX AND SEMANTICS OF MUTANTS

In the examples presented so far, we mutated a program by making simple syntactic changes. Can we mutate using semantic changes? Yes, we certainly can. However, note that syntax is the carrier of semantics in computer programs. Thus, given a program P written in a well-defined programming language, a *semantic change* in P is made by making one or more syntactic changes. A few illustrative examples are as follows.

Example 7.3: Let $f_{P7.1}(x, y)$ denote the function computed by Program P7.1. We can write $f(x, y)$ as follows:

$$f_{P7.1}(x, y) = \begin{cases} x + y \text{ if } x < y, \\ x * y \text{ otherwise.} \end{cases}$$

Let $f_{M_1}(x, y)$ and $f_{M_2}(x, y)$ denote the functions computed by Programs M_1 and M_2, respectively. We can write $f_{M_1}(x, y)$ and $f_{M_2}(x, y)$ as follows:

$$f_{M_1}(x, y) = \begin{cases} x + y \text{ if } x \leq y, \\ x * y \text{ otherwise.} \end{cases}$$

$$f_{M_2}(x, y) = \begin{cases} x + y \text{ if } x < y, \\ x/y \text{ otherwise.} \end{cases}$$

Notice that the three functions $f_{P7.1}(x, y)$, $f_{M_1}(x, y)$, and $f_{M_2}(x, y)$ are different. Thus, we have changed the semantics of Program P7.1 by changing its syntax.

The previous example illustrates the meaning of syntax as "syntax is the carrier of semantics." Mutation might, at first thought, seem to be just a simple syntactic change made to a program. In effect, such a simple syntactic change could have a drastic effect, or it might have no effect at all, on program semantics. The next two examples illustrate why.

Example 7.4: Nuclear reactors are increasingly relying on the use of software for control. Despite the intensive use of safety mechanisms, such as the use of 400,000 liters of cool heavy water moderator, the control software must continually monitor various reactor parameters and respond appropriately to conditions that could lead to a meltdown. For example, the Darlington Nuclear Generating Station located near Toronto, Canada, uses two independent computer-based shutdown systems. Though formal methods can be, and have been, used to convince the regulatory organizations that the software is reliable, a thorough testing of such systems is inevitable.

While the decision logic in a software-based emergency shutdown system would be quite complex, the highly simplified procedure below indicates that simple changes to a control program might lead to disastrous consequences. Assume that the *checkTemp* procedure is invoked by the reactor-monitoring system with three most recent sensory readings of the reactor temperature. The procedure returns a danger signal to the caller through variable `danger`.

Program P7.2

```
1   enum dangerLevel {none, moderate, high, veryHigh};
2   procedure checkTemp (currentTemp, maxTemp){
3     float currentTemp[3], maxTemp; int highCount=0;
4     enum dangerLevel danger;
5     danger=none;
6     if (currentTemp[0]>maxTemp)
7       highCount=1;
8     if (currentTemp[1]>maxTemp)
9       highCount=highCount+1;
10    if (currentTemp[2])>maxTemp)
11      highCount=highCount+1;
12    if (highCount==1) danger=moderate;
13    if (highCount==2) danger=high;
14    if (highCount==3) danger=veryHigh;
15    return(danger);
16  }
```

Procedure *checkTemp* compares each of the three temperature readings against the maximum allowed. A *none* signal is returned if none of the three readings is above the maximum allowed. Otherwise, a *moderate*, *high*, or *veryHigh* signal is returned depending on, respectively, whether one, two, or three readings are above the allowable maximum. Now consider the following mutant of Program P7.2 obtained by replacing the constant *veryHigh* with another constant *none* at line 14.

Mutant M1 of Program P7.2

```
1   enum dangerLevel {none, moderate, high, veryHigh};
2   procedure checkTemp (currentTemp, maxTemp) {
3     float currentTemp[3], maxTemp; int highCount=0;
4     enum dangerLevel danger;
5     danger=none;
6     if (currentTemp[0]>maxTemp)
7       highCount=1;
8     if (currentTemp[1]>maxTemp)
9       highCount=highCount+1;
10    if (currentTemp[2])>maxTemp)
11      highCount=highCount+1;
12    if (highCount==1) danger=moderate;
13    if (highCount==2) danger=high;
14    if (highCount==3) danger=none;   ← Mutated statement
15    return(danger);
16  }
```

Notice the difference in the behaviors of Programs P7.2 and M_1. While Program P7.2 returns *veryHigh* signal when all three temperature readings are higher than the maximum allowable, its mutant M_1 returns the *none* signal under the same circumstances.

While the syntactic change made to the program is trivial, the resultant change in its behavior could lead to an incorrect operation of the reactor shutdown software potentially causing a major environmental and human disaster. It is such changes in the behavior that we refer to as *drastic*. Indeed, the term *drastic* in the context of software testing often refers to the nature of the possible consequence of a program's, or its mutant's, behavior.

Example 7.5: While a simple change in a program might create a mutant whose behavior differs drastically from its parent, another mutant might behave exactly in the same way as the original program. Let us examine the following mutant obtained by replacing the == operator at line 12 in Program P7.2 by the ≥ operator.

```
1   enum dangerLevel {none, moderate, high, veryHigh}d;
2   procedure checkTemp (currentTemp, maxTemp){
3     float currentTemp[3], maxTemp; int highCount=0;
4     enum dangerLevel danger;
5     danger =none;
6     if (currentTemp[0]>maxTemp)
7       highCount=1;
8     if (currentTemp[1]>maxTemp)
9       highCount=highCount+1;
10    if (currentTemp[2])>maxTemp)
11      highCount=highCount+1;
12    if (highCount ≥1) danger=moderate;  ← Mutated statement
13    if (highCount==2) danger=high;
14    if (highCount==3) danger=veryHigh;
15    return(danger);
16  }
```

It is easy to check that for all triples of input temperature values and the maximum allowable temperature, Programs P7.2 and M_2 will return the same value of danger. Certainly, during execution, Program M_2 will exhibit a different behavior than that of Program P7.2. However, the values returned by both the program and its mutant will be identical.

As shown in the examples above, while a mutant might behave differently than its parent during execution, in mutation testing the behaviors of the two entities are considered identical if they exhibit identical behaviors at the specified points of observation. Thus, when comparing the behavior of a mutant with its parent, one must be clear about what are the points of observation. This leads us to strong and weak mutations.

7.2.3 STRONG AND WEAK MUTATIONS

We mentioned earlier that a mutant is considered distinguished from its parent when the two behave differently. A natural question to ask is "At what point during program execution should the behaviors be observed?" We deal with two kinds of observations, *external* and *internal*. Suppose we decide to observe the behavior of a procedure soon after its termination. In this case, we observe the return value and any side effects in terms of changes to values of global variables and data files. We shall refer to this mode of observation as *external*.

An *internal* observation refers to the observation of the state of a program and its mutant during their respective executions. Internal observations could be done in a variety of ways that differ in where the program state is observed. One could observe at each state change or at specific points in the program.

Strong mutation testing uses external observation. Thus, a mutant and its parent are allowed to run to completion at which point their respective outputs are compared. Weak mutation testing uses internal observation. It is possible that a mutant behaves similar to its parent under weak mutation but not under strong mutation.

Example 7.6: Suppose we decide to compare the behaviors of Program P7.2 and its mutant M_2 using external observation. As mentioned in the previous example, we will notice no difference in the behaviors of the two programs as both return the same value of variable `danger` for all inputs.

Instead, suppose we decide to use internal observation to compare the behaviors of Programs P7.2 and M_2. Further, the state of each program is observed at the end of the execution of each source line. The states of the two programs will differ when observed soon after line 12 for the following input t:

```
t: < maxTemp = 1200,currentTemp = [1250,1389,1127] >
```

For the inputs above, the states of Programs P7.2 and M_2 observed soon after the execution of the statement at line 12 are as follows:

	Danger	**HighCount**
P7.2	none	2
M2	moderate	2

Note that while the inputs are also a part of a program's state, we have excluded them from the table above as they do not change during the execution of the program and its mutant. The two states shown above are clearly different. However, in this example, the difference observed in the states of the program and its mutant does not effect their respective return values, which remain identical.

For all inputs, Program M_2 behaves identically to its parent Program P7.2 under external observation. Hence, Program M_2 is considered equivalent to Program P7.2 under strong mutation. However, as revealed in the table above, Program M_2 is distinguishable from Program P7.2 by test case t. Thus, the two are not equivalent under weak mutation.

7.2.4 WHY MUTATE?

It is natural to wonder why a program should be mutated. Before we answer this question, let us consider the following scenario likely to arise in practice.

Suppose you have developed a program, say, P. You have tested P. You found quite a few faults in P during testing. You have fixed all these faults and have retested P. You have even made sure that your test set is adequate with respect to the MC/DC-coverage criterion. After all this tremendous effort you have put into testing P, you are now justifiably confident that P is correct with respect to its requirements.

Happy and confident, you are about to release P to another group within your company. At this juncture in the project, someone takes a look at your program and, pointing to a line in your source code, asks "Should this expression be

```
boundary<corner, or
boundary<corner+1?"
```

Scenarios such as the one above arise during informal discussions with colleagues, and also during formal code reviews. A programmer is encouraged to show why an alternate solution to a problem is not correct, or better, than the one selected. The alternate solution could lead to a program significantly different from the current one. It could also be a simple mutant as in the scenario above.

There are several ways a programmer could argue in favor of the existing solution such as `boundary < corner` in the scenario above. One way is to give a performance-related argument that shows why the given solution is better than the alternate proposed in terms of the performance of the application.

Another way is to show that the current solution is correct and preferred, and the proposed alternate is incorrect or not preferred. If the proposed alternate is a mutant of the original solution, then the programmer needs to simply show that the mutant behaves differently than the current solution and is incorrect. This can be done by proposing a test case and showing that the current solution and the proposed solutions are different and the current solution is correct.

It is also possible that the proposed alternate is equivalent to the current solution. However, this needs to be shown for all possible inputs and requires a much stronger argument than the one used to show that the alternate solution is incorrect.

Mutation offers a systematic way of generating a number of scenarios similar to the one described above. It places the burden of proof on the tester, or the developer, that the program under test is correct while the mutant created is indeed incorrect. As we show in the remainder of this chapter, testing using mutation often leads to the discovery of subtle flaws in the program under test. This discovery usually takes place when a tester tries to show that the mutant is an incorrect solution to the problem at hand.

7.3 TEST ASSESSMENT USING MUTATION

Now that we know what mutation is, and what mutants look like, let us understand how mutation is used for assessing the adequacy of a test set. The problem of test assessment using mutation can be stated as follows:

> *Let P be a program under test, T a test set for P, and R the set of requirements that P must meet. Suppose that P has been tested against all tests in T and found to be correct with respect to R on each test case. We want to know "How good is T?"*

Mutation offers a way of answering the question stated above. As explained later in this section, given *P* and *T*, a quantitative assessment of the goodness of *T* is obtained by computing a *mutation score* of *T*. Mutation score is a number between 0 and 1. A score of 1 means that *T* is adequate with respect to mutation. A score lower than 1 means that *T* is inadequate with respect to mutation. An inadequate test set can be enhanced by the addition of test cases that increase the mutation score.

7.3.1 A Procedure for Test-adequacy Assessment

Let us now dive into a procedure for assessing the adequacy of a test set. One such procedure is illustrated in Figure 7.1. It is important to note that Figure 7.1 shows one possible sequence of 12 steps for assessing the adequacy of a given suite of tests using mutation; other sequencings are also possible and discussed later in this section.

Do not be concerned if Figure 7.1 looks confusing and rather jumbled. Also, some terms used in the figure have not been defined yet. Any confusion should be easily overcome by going through the step-by-step explanation that follows. All terms used in the figure are defined as we proceed with the explanation of the assessment process.

For the sake of simplicity, we use Program P7.1 throughout our explanation through a series of examples. Certainly, Program P7.1 does not represent the kind of programs for which mutation is likely to be used in commercial and research environments. However, it serves our instructional purpose in this section: that of explaining various steps in Figure 7.1. Also, and again for simplicity, we assume that Program P7.1 is correct as per its requirements. In Section 7.8, we will see how the assessment of adequacy using mutation helps in the detection of faults in the program under test.

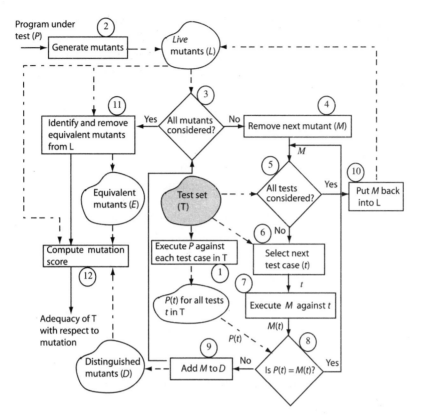

Fig. 7.1 A procedure used in the assessment of the adequacy of a test set using mutation. Solid lines point to the next process step. Dashed lines indicate data transfer between a data repository and a process step. L, D, and E denote, respectively, the set of live, distinguished, and equivalent mutants defined in the text. $P(t)$ and $M(t)$ indicate, respectively, the program and mutant behaviors observed upon their execution against test case t.

Step 1. Program execution

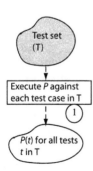

The first step in assessing the adequacy of a test set T with respect to program P and requirements R is to execute P against each test case in T. Let $P(t)$ denote the observed behavior of P when executed against t. Generally, the observed behavior is expressed as a set of values of output variables in P. However, it might also relate to the performance of P.

This step might not be necessary if P has already been executed against all elements in T, and $P(t)$ recorded in a database. In any case, the end result of executing Step 1 is a database of $P(t)$ for all $t \in T$.

At this point, we assume that $P(t)$ is correct with respect to R for all $t \in T$. If $P(t)$ is found to be incorrect, then P must be corrected and Step 1 executed again. The point to be noted here is that test-adequacy assessment using mutation begins when P has been found to be correct with respect to the test set T.

Example 7.7: Consider Program P7.1, which we shall refer to as P. P is supposed to compute the following function $f(x, y)$:

$$f(x, y) = \begin{cases} x + y & \text{if } x < y, \\ x * y & \text{otherwise.} \end{cases}$$

Suppose we have tested P against the following set of tests:

$$T_P = \begin{cases} t_1 : < x = 0, y = 0 >, \\ t_2 : < x = 0, y = 1 >, \\ t_3 : < x = 1, y = 0 >, \\ t_4 : < x = -1, y = -2 > \end{cases}$$

The database of $P(t)$ for all $t \in T_P$ is tabulated below:

Test case (t)	Expected output $f(x, y)$	Observed output $P(t)$
t_1	0	0
t_2	1	1
t_3	0	0
t_4	2	2

Note that $P(t)$ computes function $f(x, y)$ for all $t \in T_P$. Hence, the condition that $P(t)$ be correct on all inputs from T_P is satisfied. We can now proceed further with adequacy assessment.

Step 2: Mutant generation

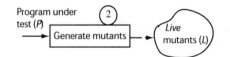

The next step in test-adequacy assessment is the generation of mutants. While we have shown what a mutant looks like and how it is generated, we have not given any systematic procedure to generate a set of mutants given in a program. We will do so in Section 7.4.

For now we assume that the following mutants have been generated from P by (a) altering the arithmetic operators such that any occurrence of the addition operator (+) is replaced by the subtraction operator (−) and that of the multiplication operator (*) by the divide operator (/), and (b) replacing each occurrence of an integer variable v by $v+1$.

Example 7.8: By mutating the program as mentioned above, we obtain a total of eight mutants, labeled M_1 through M_8, shown in the following table. Note that we have not listed the complete mutant programs for the sake of saving space. A typical mutant will look just like Program P7.1 with one of the statements replaced by the mutant in the table below:

Line	Original	Mutant ID	Mutant(s)
1	begin		None
2	int x, y		None
3	input (x, y)		None
4	if (x<y)	M_1	if (x+1<y)
		M_2	if (x<y+1)
5	then		None
6	output(x+y)	M_3	output(x+1+y)
		M_4	output(x+y+1)
		M_5	output(x−y)
7	else		None
8	output(x*y)	M_6	output((x+1)*y)
		M_7	output(x*(y+1))
		M_8	output(x/y)
9	end		None

In the table above, note that we have not mutated the declaration, input, then, and else statements. The reason for not mutating these statements is given later in Section 7.4. Of course, markers begin and end are not mutated.

At the end of Step 2, we have a set of eight mutants. We refer to these eight mutants as *live* mutants. These mutants are live because we have not yet *distinguished* them from the original program. We will make an attempt to do so in the next few steps. Thus, we obtain the set $L = \{M_1, M_2, M_3, M_4, M_5, M_6, M_7, M_8\}$. Note that *distinguishing* a mutant from its parent is sometimes referred to as *killing* a mutant.

Steps 3 and 4: Select next mutant

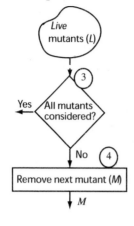

In Steps 3 and 4, we select the next mutant to be considered. This mutant must not have been selected earlier. Note that at this point we are starting a loop that will cycle through all mutants in L until each mutant has been selected. Obviously, we select the next mutant only if there is a mutant remaining in L. This check is made in Step 3. If there are live mutants in L, which have never been selected in any previous step, then a mutant is selected arbitrarily. The selected mutant is removed from L.

Example 7.9: In Step 3, we find that we do have eight mutants remaining in L and hence we move to Step 4 and select any one of these eight. The choice of which mutant to select is arbitrary. Let us select mutant M_1. After moving M_1 from L, we have $L = \{M_2, M_3, M_4, M_5, M_6, M_7, M_8\}$.

Steps 5 and 6: Select next test case

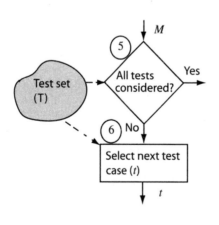

Having selected a mutant M, we now attempt to find whether at least one of the tests in T can distinguish it from its parent P. To do so, we need to execute M against tests in T. Thus, at this point we enter another loop that is executed for each selected mutant. The loop terminates when all tests are exhausted or M is distinguished by some test, whichever happens earlier.

Example 7.10: Now that we have selected M_1, we need to check if it can be distinguished by T from P. In Step 5, we select the next test. Again, any of the tests in T_P, against which M_1 has not been executed so far, can be selected. Let us select t_1: $< x = 0, y = 0 >$.

Steps 7, 8, and 9: Mutant execution and classification

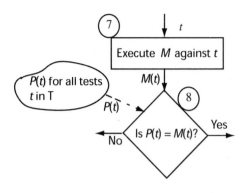

So far we have selected a mutant M for execution against test case t. In Step 7, we execute M against t. In Step 8, we check if the output generated by executing M against t is the same or different from that generated by executing P against t.

Example 7.11: So far we have selected mutant M_1 and test case t_1. In Step 7, we execute M_1 against t_1. Given the inputs $x = 0$ and $y = 0$, condition x + 1 < y is false leading to 0 as the output. Thus we see that $P(t_1) = M_1(t_1)$. This implies that test case t_1 is unable to distinguish M_1 from P. At Step 8, the condition $P(t) = M(t)$ is true for $t = t_1$. Hence, we return to Step 5.

In Steps 5 and 6, we select the next test case t_2 and execute M_1 against t_2. In Step 8, we notice that $P(t_2) \neq M(t_2)$ as $M(t_2) = 1$. This terminates the test-execution loop that started at Step 5, and we follow Step 9. Mutant M_1 is added to the set of distinguished (or killed) mutants.

Example 7.12: For the sake of completeness, let us go through the entire mutant-execution loop that started at Step 3. We have already considered mutant M_1. Next, we select mutant M_2 and execute it against tests in T until it is either distinguished or all tests are exhausted.

The results of executing Steps 3 through 9 are summarized in the following table. Column D indicates the contents of set D of distinguished mutants. As indicated, all mutants except M_2 are distinguished by T. Initially, all mutants are live.

As per Step 8 in Figure 7.1, execution of a mutant is interrupted soon after it has been distinguished. Entries marked NE in the table below indicate that the mutant in the corresponding row was not executed against the test case in the corresponding column. Note that mutant M_8 is distinguished by t_1 because its output is undefined (indicated by the entry marked "U") due to division by 0. This implies that $P(t_1) \neq M_8(t_1)$. The first test case distinguishing a mutant is marked with an asterisk (*).

Program	t_1	t_2	t_3	t_4	D
$P(t)$	0	1	0	2	$\{\}$

Mutant					
$M_1(t)$	0	0*	NE	NE	$\{M_1\}$
$M_2(t)$	0	1	0	2	$\{M_1\}$
$M_3(t)$	0	2*	NE	NE	$\{M_1, M_3\}$
$M_4(t)$	0	2*	NE	NE	$\{M_1, M_3, M_4\}$
$M_5(t)$	0	-1*	NE	NE	$\{M_1, M_3, M_4, M_5\}$
$M_6(t)$	0	1	0	0*	$\{M_1, M_3, M_4, M_5, M_6\}$
$M_7(t)$	0	1	1*	NE	$\{M_1, M_3, M_4, M_5, M_6, M_7\}$
$M_8(t)$	U*	NE	NE	NE	$\{M_1, M_3, M_4, M_5, M_6, M_7, M_8\}$

U, output undefined; NE, mutant not executed; (*), first test to distinguish the mutant in the corresponding row.

Step 10: Live mutants

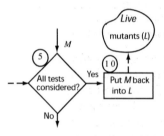

When none of the tests in T is able to distinguish mutant M from its parent P, M is placed back into the set of live mutants. Of course, any mutant that is returned to the set of live mutants is not selected in Step 4 as it has already been selected once.

Example 7.13: In our example, there is only one mutant, M_2, that could not be distinguished by T_P. M_2 is returned to the set of live mutants in Step 10. Notice, however, that M_2 will not be selected again for classification as it has been selected once.

Step 11: Equivalent mutants

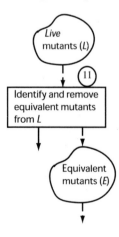

After having executed all mutants, one checks if any mutants remain live, that is set L is nonempty. Any remaining live mutants are tested for equivalence to their parent program. A mutant M is considered equivalent to its parent P if for each test input from the input domain of P, the observed behavior of M is identical to that of P. We discuss the issue of determining whether a mutant is equivalent, in Section 7.7. The following example illustrates the process with respect to Program P7.1.

Example 7.14: We note from Example 7.13 that no test in T_P is able to distinguish M_2 from P, and hence M_2 is live. We ask: *Is M_2 equivalent to P?* An answer to such questions requires careful analysis of the behavior of the two programs: the parent and its mutant. In this case, let $f_P(x, y)$ be the function computed by P, and $g_{M_2}(x, y)$ that computed by M_2. The two functions are as follows:

$$f_P(x, y) = \begin{cases} x + y & \text{if } x < y, \\ x * y & \text{otherwise.} \end{cases}$$

$$g_{M_2}P(x, y) = \begin{cases} x + y & \text{if } x < y + 1, \\ x * y & \text{otherwise.} \end{cases}$$

Rather than showing that M_2 is equivalent to P, let us first attempt to find $x = x_1$ and $y = y_1$ such that $f_P(x_1, y_1) \neq g_{M_2}(x_1, y_1)$. A simple examination of the two functions reveals that the following two conditions, denoted as C_1 and C_2, must hold for $f_P(x_1, y_1) \neq g_{M_2}(x_1, y_1)$.

$$C_1 : (x_1 < y_1) \neq (x_1 < y_1 + 1)$$
$$C_2 : x_1 * y_1 \neq x_1 + y_1$$

For the conjunct of C_1 and C_2 to hold, we must have $x_1 = y_1 \neq 0$. We note that while test case t_1 satisfies C_1, it fails to satisfy C_2. However, the following test case does satisfy both C_1 and C_2.

$$t :< x = 1, y = 1 > \tag{7.1}$$

A simple computation reveals that $P(t) = 2$ and $M_2(t) = 1$. Thus, we have shown that M_2 can be distinguished by at least one test case. Hence, M_2 is not equivalent to its parent P. As there is only one live mutant in L that we have already examined for equivalence, we are done with Step 11. Set E of equivalent mutants remains empty.

Step 12: Computation of mutation score

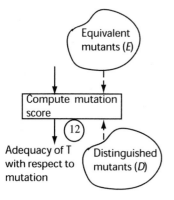

This is the final step in the assessment of test adequacy. Given sets L, D, and E, the mutation score denoted by MS_T of a test set T is computed as follows:

$$MS(T) = \frac{|D|}{|L| + |D|}.$$

It is important to note that set L contains only the live mutants, none of which is equivalent to the parent. As is evident from the formula above, a mutation score is always between 0 and 1.

Given that $|M|$ denotes the total number of mutants generated in Step 2, the following definition of mutation score is also used.

$$MS(T) = \frac{|D|}{|M| - |E|}.$$

If a test set T distinguishes all mutants, except those that are equivalent, then $L = 0$ and the mutation score is 1. If T does not distinguish any mutant, then $D = 0$ and the mutation score is 0.

An interesting case arises when a test set does not distinguish any mutant and all mutants generated are equivalent to the original program. In this case, $D = L = 0$ and the mutant score is undefined. Hence we ask, *Is the test set hopelessly inadequate*? The answer: *No it is not.* In this case, the set of mutants generated is insufficient to asses the adequacy of the test set. In practice, it is rare, if not impossible, to find a situation where $L = D = 0$ and all the generated mutants are equivalent to the parent. This fact will be evident when we discuss mutation operators in Section 7.4.

Note that a mutation score for a test set is computed with respect to a given set of mutants. Thus, there is no *golden* mutation score that remains fixed for a given test set. One is likely to obtain different mutation scores for a test set evaluated against a different set of mutants. Thus, while a test set T might be perfectly adequate, that is $MS(T) = 1$ with respect to a given set of mutants, it might be perfectly inadequate, that is $MS(T) = 0$ with respect to another.

> **Example 7.15:** Continuing with our illustrative example, it is easy to compute the mutation score for T as given in Example 7.7. We started out in Example 7.8 with eight mutants. At the end of Step 11, we are left with one live mutant, seven distinguished mutants, and no equivalent mutant. Thus, $|D| = 7$, $|L| = 1$, and $|E| = 0$. This gives us $MS(T_P) = 7/(7 + 1) = 0.875$.

We found a test case t in Example 7.14 that distinguishes the lone live mutant M_2 from its parent. Suppose we now add t to T_P such that the test set T_P' so modified now contains five test cases. What is the revised mutation score for T'? Obviously, $MS(T'_P) = 1$. However, by adding t, we have enhanced T_P.

7.3.2 Alternate Procedures for Test-Adequacy Assessment

Several variations of the procedure described in the previous section are possible, and often recommended. Let us start at Step 2. As indicated in

Figure 7.1, Step 2 implies that all mutants are generated before test execution. However, an incremental approach might be better suited given the large number of mutants that are likely to be created even for short programs or for short functions within an application.

Using an incremental approach for the assessment of test adequacy, one generates mutants from only a subset of the mutation operators. The given test set is evaluated against this subset of mutants and a mutation score computed. If the score is less than 1, additional tests are created to ensure a score close to 1. This cycle is repeated with additional subsets of mutant operators, and the test set further enhanced. The process may continue until all mutant operators have been considered.

The incremental approach allows an incremental enhancement of the test set at hand. This is in contrast to enhancing the test set at the end of the assessment process when a large number of mutants might remain live thereby overwhelming a tester.

It is also possible to use a multi-tester version of the process illustrated in Figure 7.1. Each tester can be assigned a subset of the mutation operators. The testers share a common test set. Each tester computes the adequacy with respect to the mutants generated by the operators assigned, and enhances the test set. New tests so created are made available to the other testers through a common test repository. While this method of concurrent assessment of test adequacy might reduce the time to develop an adequate test set, it might lead to redundant tests (see Exercise 7.11).

7.3.3 DISTINGUISHED VERSUS KILLED MUTANTS

As mentioned earlier, a mutant that behaves differently than its parent program on some test input is considered *killed*. However, for the sake of promoting a sense of calm and peace during mutation testing, we prefer to use the term *distinguished* in lieu of *killed*. A cautionary note: most literature on mutation testing uses the term *killed.* Some people prefer to say that "a mutant has been detected" implying that the mutant referred to is distinguished from its parent.

Of course, a *distinguished mutant* is not *distinguished* in the sense of a *distinguished professor* or a *distinguished lady.* It is considered "distinguished from its parent by a test case." Certainly, if a program mutant could feel and act like humans do, it probably will be happy to be considered *distinguished* like some of us do. Other possible terms for a distinguished mutant include *extinguished* and *terminated.*

7.3.4 CONDITIONS FOR DISTINGUISHING A MUTANT

A test case t that distinguishes a mutant M from its parent P must satisfy the following three conditions labeled as C_1, C_2, and C_3.

1. C_1: *Reachability*: Must force the execution of a path from the start statement of M to the point of the mutated statement.
2. C_2: *State infection*: Must cause the state of M and P to differ consequent to some execution of the mutated statement.
3. C_3: *State propagation*: Must ensure that the difference in the states of M and P, created due to the execution of the mutated statement, propagates until after the end of mutant execution.

Thus, a mutant is considered distinguished only when test t satisfies $C_1 \wedge C_2 \wedge C_3$. To be more precise, condition C_1 is necessary for C_2, which, in turn, is necessary for C_3. The following example illustrates the three conditions. Note that condition C_2 need not be true during the first execution of the mutated statement, though it must hold during some execution. Also, all program variables, and the location of program control, constitute program state at any instant during program execution.

A mutant is considered *equivalent* to the program under test if there is no test case in the input domain of P that satisfies each of the three conditions above. It is important to note that equivalence is based on identical behavior of the mutant and the program over the entire input domain and not just the test set whose adequacy is being assessed.

> **Example 7.16:** Consider mutant M_1 of Program P7.2. The reachability condition requires that control arrive at line 14. As this is a straight-line program, with a `return` at the end, every test case will satisfy the reachability condition.
>
> The state infection condition implies that after execution of the statement at line 14, the state of the mutant must differ from that of its parent. Let danger_P and danger_M denote, respectively, the values of variable `danger` soon after the execution of line 14. The state-infection condition is satisfied when $\text{danger}_P \neq \text{danger}_M$. Any test case for which `highcount` = 3 satisfies the state-infection condition.
>
> Finally, as line 14 is the last statement in the mutant that can affect the state, no more changes can occur to the value of `danger`. Hence, the state-propagation condition is satisfied trivially by any test case that satisfies the state-infection condition. Following is a test case that satisfies all three conditions.
>
> $t:$ < currentTemp = [20,34,29], maxTemp = 18 >

For test case t, we get $P(t) = \texttt{veryHigh}$ and $M(t) = \texttt{none}$, thereby distinguishing the mutant from its parent.

Example 7.17: Next, consider function findElement, in Program P7.3, that searches for a chemical element whose atomic weight is greater than w. The function is required to return the name of the first such element found among the first size elements, or return "None" if no such element is found. Arrays name and atWeight contain, respectively, the element names and the corresponding atomic weights. A global constant maxSize is the size of the two arrays.

Program P7.3

```
1   String findElement (name, atWeight, int size, float w){
2     String name[maxSize]; float atWeight[maxSize], w;
3     int index=0;
4     while (index<size){
5       if (atWeight[index]>w)
6         return(name[index]);
7       index=index+1;
8     }
9     return("None");
10  }
```

Consider a mutant of Program P7.3 obtained by replacing the loop condition by index≤ size.

The reachability condition to distinguish this mutant is satisfied by any test case that causes findElement to be invoked. Let C_P and C_M denote, respectively, the loop conditions in Program P7.3 and its mutant. The state-infection condition is satisfied by a test case for which the relation $C_P \neq C_M$ holds during some loop iteration.

The state-propagation condition is satisfied when the value returned by the mutant differs from the one returned by its parent. The following test satisfies all three conditions:

t_1 : < name = ["Hydrogen", "Nitrogen", "Oxygen"],
    atWeight = [1.0079,14.0067,15.9994],
    maxSize = 3, size = 2, w = 15.0 >

Upon execution against t_1, the loop in Program P7.3 terminates unsuccessfully and the program returns the string "None." On the contrary, when executing the mutant against t_1, the loop continues until index=size when it finds an element with atomic weight greater than w. While Program P7.3 returns the string "None", the mutant returns "Oxygen". Thus, t_1 satisfies all three conditions for distinguishing the mutant from its parent (also see Exercises 7.8 and 7.10).

7.4 MUTATION OPERATORS

In the previous sections, we gave examples of mutations obtained by making different kinds of changes to the program under test. Up until now, we have generated mutants in an ad hoc manner. However, there exists a systematic method, and a set of guidelines, for the generation of mutants, that can be automated. One such systematic method and a set of guidelines are described in this section. We begin our discussion by learning what is a mutation operator and how is it used.

A mutation operator is a generative device. Other names used for mutation operators include *mutagenic operator*, *mutant operator*, and simply *operator*. In the remainder of this chapter, the terms *mutation operator* and *operator* are used interchangeably when there is no confusion.

Each mutation operator is assigned a unique name for ease of reference. For example, ABS and ROR are two names of mutation operators whose functions are explained in Example 7.18.

As shown in Figure 7.2, when applied to a syntactically correct program P, a mutation operator generates a set of syntactically correct mutants of P. We apply one or more mutation operators to P to generate a variety of mutants. A mutation operator might generate no mutants or one or more mutants. This is illustrated in the next example.

Example 7.18: Consider an operator named CCR. When applied to a program, CCR generates mutants by replacing each occurrence of a constant c by some other constant d; both c and d must appear in P. When applied to Program P7.1, CCR will not generate any mutants as the program does not contain any constant.

Next, consider an operator named ABS. When applied, ABS generates mutants by replacing each occurrence of an arithmetic expression e by the expression abs(e). Here, it is assumed that *abs* denotes the *absolute value* function found in many programming languages. The following eight mutants are generated when ABS is applied to Program P7.1.

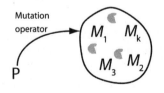

Fig. 7.2   A set of k mutants $M_1, M_2, \ldots, M_k$ of P generated by applying a mutation operator. The number of mutants generated, k, depends on p and the mutation operator; k could be 0.

Location	Statement	Mutant
Line 4	if(x < y)	if (abs(x) < y) if (x < abs(y))
Line 5	output(x + y)	output(abs(x) + y) output(x + abs(y)) output(abs(x + y))
Line 7	output(x * y)	output(abs(x) * y) output(x * abs(y)) output(abs(x * y))

Note that the input statement and declarations have not been mutated. Declarations are not mutated and are considered the source for variable names and types to be used for certain types of mutations discussed later in this section. The input statement has not been mutated as adding an *abs* operator to an input value will lead to a syntactically incorrect program.

7.4.1 OPERATOR TYPES

Mutation operators are designed to model simple programming mistakes that programmers make. Faults in programs could be much more complex than the simple mistakes modeled by a mutation operator. However, it has been found that, despite the simplicity of mutations, complex faults are discovered while trying to distinguish mutants from their parent. We return to this suspicious sounding statement in Section 7.6.2.

It is to be noted that some mutation tools provide mutation operators designed explicitly to enforce code and domain coverages. The STRP is one such operator for languages C and Fortran. When applied to a program, it creates one mutant for each statement by replacing the statement with a *trap* condition. Such a mutant is considered distinguished from its parent when control arrives at the replaced statement. A test set that distinguishes all STRP mutants is considered adequate with respect to the statement-coverage criterion.

The VDTR operator for C (see page 556) ensures that the given test set is adequate with respect to domain coverage for appropriate variables in the program under test. The domain is partitioned into a set of negative, zero, and positive values. Thus, for an integer variable, domain coverage is obtained, and the corresponding mutants distinguished, by ensuring that the variables take on any negative, zero, and any positive value during some execution of the program under test.

Table 7.1 A sample of generic categories of mutation operators and the common programming mistakes modeled

Category	Mistake modeled	Examples
Constant mutation	Incorrect constant	`x = x + 1;` `x = x + 3;` `y = y * 3;` → `y = y * 3;`
Operator mutations	Incorrect operator	if(x<y) → if(x ≤y) `x++` → `++x`
Statement mutation	Incorrectly placed statement	`z = x + 1;` → Delete `z = x + 1;` → `break;` break → `z = x + 1;`

Variable mutations	Incorrectly used variable	int `x, y, z`
		 `z = x + 1;`→`z = y + 1;`
		 `z = x + y;`→`z = abs(x) + y;`

While a set of mutation operators is specific to a programming language, it can nevertheless be partitioned into a small set of generic categories. One such categorization appears in Table 7.1. While reading the examples in the table, read the right arrow (→) as *mutates to*. Also, note that in the first entry, constant 1 has been changed to 3, as constant 3 appears in another statement (`y = y * 3`).

Only a set of four generic categories are shown in Table 7.1. As shown later in this section, in practice, there are many mutation operators under each category. The number and type of mutation operators under each category depends on the programming language for which the operators are designed.

The constant mutations category consists of operators that model mistakes made in the use of constants. Constants of different types, such as floats, integers, and booleans, are used in mutations. The domain of any mutation operator in this category is the set of constants appearing in the program that is mutated; a mutation operator does not invent constants. Thus, in the example that appears in Table 7.1, statement `x = x + 1` has been mutated to `x = x + 3` because constant 3 appears in another statement, that is in `y = y * 3`.

The operator mutations category contains mutation operators that model common mistakes made in relation to the use of operators. Mistakes modeled include incorrect use of arithmetic operators, relational operators, logical operators, and any other types of operators the language provides.

The statement mutations category consists of operators that model various mistakes made by programmers in the placement of statements in a program. These mistakes include incorrect placement of a statement, missing statement, incorrect loop termination, and incorrect loop formation.

The variable mutations category contains operators that model a common mistake programmers make when they incorrectly use a variable while formulating a logical or an arithmetic expression. Two incorrect uses are illustrated in Table 7.1. The first is the use of an incorrect variable x, a y should have been used instead. The second is an incorrect use of x, its absolute value should have been used. As with constant mutation operators, the domain of variable mutation operators includes all variables declared and used in the program being mutated. Mutation operators do no manufacture variables.

7.4.2 LANGUAGE DEPENDENCE OF MUTATION OPERATORS

While it is possible to categorize mutation operators into a few generic categories, as in the previous section, the operators themselves are dependent on the syntax of the programming language. For example, for a program written in ANSI C (hereafter referred to as C), one needs to use mutation operators for C. A Java program is mutated using mutation operators designed for the Java language.

There are at least three reasons for the dependence of mutation operators on language syntax. First, given that the program being mutated is syntactically correct, a mutation operator must produce a mutant that is also syntactically correct. To do so requires that a valid syntactic construct be mapped to another valid syntactic construct in the same language.

Second, the domain of a mutation operator is determined by the syntax rules of a programming language. For example, in Java, the domain of a mutation operator that replaces one relational operator by another is $\{<, <=, >, >=, !=, ==\}$.

Third, peculiarities of language syntax have an effect on the kind of mistakes that a programmer could make. Note that aspects of a language such as procedural versus object oriented are captured in the language syntax.

Example 7.19: The Access Modifier Change (AMC) operator in Java replaces one access modifier, for example `private`, by another for example `public`. This mutation models mistakes made by Java programmers in controlling the access of variables and methods.

While incorrect scoping is possible in C, the notion of access control is made explicit in Java through a variety of access modifiers and their combinations. Hence, the AMC operator is justified for mutating Java programs. There is no matching operator for mutating C programs due to the absence of explicit access control; access control in C is implied by the location of declarations and incorrect placement of declarations can often be checked by a compiler.

Example 7.20: Suppose x, y, and z are integer variables declared appropriately in a C program. The following is a valid C statement:

$$S: z = (x < y)?\ 0:1;$$

Suppose now that we wish to mutate the relational operator in S. The relational operator $<$ can be replaced by any one of the remaining five equality and relational operators in C, namely $==, != , >, <=,$ and $>=$. Such a replacement would produce a valid statement in C and in many other languages too, given that the statement to be mutated is valid in that language.

However, C also allows the presence of any arithmetic operator in place of the $<$ operator in the statement above. Hence, the $<$ can also be replaced by any addition and multiplication operator from the set $\{+, -, *, /, \%\}$. Thus, for example, while the replacement of $<$ in S by the operator $+$ will lead to a valid C statement, this would not be allowed in several other languages such as in Java and Fortran. This example illustrates that the domain of a mutation operator that mutates a relational operator is different in C than it is in Java.

This example also illustrates that the types of mistakes made by a programmer using C are different from those that a programmer might make, for instance, when using Java. It is perfectly legitimate to think that a C programmer has S as

$$S': z = (x + y)\ ?\ 0:1;$$

for whatever reasons, whereas the intention was to code it as S. While both S and S' are syntactically correct, they might lead to different program behavior, only one of them being correct. It is easy to construct a large number of such examples of mutations, and mistakes, that a programmer might be able to make in one programming language but not in another.

The example above suggests that the design of mutation operators is a language-dependent activity. Further, while it is possible to design mutation operators for a given programming language through guesses on what simple mistakes might a programmer make, a scientific approach is to base the design on empirical data. Such empirical data consolidates the common programming mistakes. In fact mutation operators for a variety of programming languages have been designed based on a mix of empirical evidence and collective programming experience of the design team.

7.5 DESIGN OF MUTATION OPERATORS

7.5.1 GOODNESS CRITERIA FOR MUTATION OPERATORS

Mutation is a tool to assess the goodness of a test set for a given program. It does so with the help of a set of mutation operators that mutate the program under test into an often large number of mutants. Suppose that a test set T_P for program P is adequate with respect to a set of mutation operators M. What does this adequacy imply regarding the correctness of P? This question leads us to the following definition:

Ideal set of mutation operators: Let P_L denote the set of all programs in some language L. Let M_L be a set of mutation operators for L. M_L is considered ideal if (a) for any $P \in P_L$, and any test set T_P against which P is correct with respect to its specification S, adequacy of T_P with respect to M_L implies correctness of P with respect to S and (b) there does not exist any M'_L smaller in size than M_L for which property (a) is satisfied.

Thus, an ideal set of mutant operators is minimal in size and ensures that adequacy with respect to this set implies correctness. While it is impossible to construct an ideal set of mutation operators for any but the most trivial of languages, it is possible to construct one that ensures correctness with relatively high probability. It is precisely such set of mutation operators that we desire. The implication of probabilistic correctness is best understood with respect to the *competent programmer hypothesis* and the *coupling effect* explained in Sections 7.6.1 and 7.6.2.

Properties (a) and (b), given in the definition of an ideal set of mutation operators, relate to the fault-detection effectiveness and the cost of mutation testing. We seek a set of mutation operators that would force a tester into designing test cases that reveal as many faults as possible. Thus, we desire high fault-detection effectiveness. However, in addition, we would like to obtain high fault-detection effectiveness at the lowest cost measured in terms of the number of mutants to be considered. The tasks of compiling, executing, and analyzing mutants are time consuming and must be minimized. The cost of mutation testing is generally lowered by a reduction in the the number of mutants generated.

7.5.2 GUIDELINES

The guidelines here serve two purposes. One, they provide a basis on which to decide whether something should be mutated. Second, they help in understanding and critiquing an existing set of mutation operators such as the ones described later in this chapter.

It is to be noted that the design of mutation operators is as much of an art as it is science. Extensive experimentation, and experience with other mutation systems, is necessary to determine the goodness of a set of mutation operators for some language. However, to gain such experience, one needs to develop a set of mutation operators.

Empirical data on common mistakes serves as a basis for the design of mutation operators. In the early days of mutation research, mutation operators were designed based on empirical data available from various error studies. The effectiveness of these operators has been studied extensively. The guidelines provided here are based on past error studies, experience with mutation systems, and empirical studies to assess how effective are mutation operators in detecting complex errors in programs.

1. *Syntactic correctness*: A mutation operator must generate a syntactically correct program.

2. *Representativeness*: A mutation operator must model a common fault that is simple. Note that real faults in programs are often not simple. For example, a programmer might need to change significant portions of the code in order to correct a mistake that led to a fault. However, mutation operators are designed to model only simple faults, many of them taken together make up a complex fault.

   We emphasize that simple faults, for example a < operator mistyped as a > operator, could creep in due to a variety of reasons. However, there is no way to guarantee that for all applications, a simple fault will not lead to a disastrous consequence, for example a multimillion dollar rocket failure. Thus, the term *simple fault* must not be equated with *simple, inconsequential,* or *low severity* failures.

3. *Minimality and effectiveness*: The set of mutation operators should be as small and effective as possible.

4. *Precise definition*: The domain and range of a mutation operator must be clearly specified; both depend on the programming language at hand. For example, a mutation operator to mutate a binary arithmetic operator, for example +, will have + in its domain and in the range. However, in some languages, for example in C,

replacement of a binary arithmetic operator by a logical operator, for example &&, will lead to a valid program. Thus, all such syntax-preserving replacements must be considered while defining the range.

7.6 FOUNDING PRINCIPLES OF MUTATION TESTING

Mutation testing is a powerful testing technique for achieving correct, or close to correct, programs. It rests on two fundamental principles. One principle is commonly known as the *competent programmer hypothesis* or *the competent programmer assumption*. The other is known as the *coupling effect*. We discuss these principles in Sections 7.6.1 and 7.6.2.

7.6.1 THE COMPETENT PROGRAMMER HYPOTHESIS

The competent programmer hypothesis (CPH) arises from a simple observation made of practicing programmers. The hypothesis states that given a problem statement, a programmer writes a program P that is in the general neighborhood of the set of correct programs.

An extreme interpretation of CPH is that when asked to write a program to find the account balance, given an account number, a programmer is unlikely to write a program that deposits money into an account. Of course, while such a situation is unlikely to arise, a devious programmer might certainly write such a program.

A more reasonable interpretation of the CPH is that the program written to satisfy a set of requirements will be a few mutants away from a correct program. Thus, while the first version of the program might be incorrect, it could be corrected by a series of simple mutations. One might argue against the CPH by claiming something like "What about a missing conditional as the fault? One would need to add the missing conditional in order to arrive at a correct program." Indeed, given a correct program P_c, one of its mutants is obtained by removing the condition from a conditional statement. Thus, a missing conditional does correspond to a simple mutant.

The CPH assumes that the programmer knows of an algorithm to solve the problem at hand, and if not, will find one prior to writing the program. It is thus safe to assume that when asked to write a program to sort a list of numbers, a competent programmer knows of, and makes use of, at least one sorting algorithm. Certainly, mistakes could be made while coding the algorithm. Such mistakes will lead to a program that can be corrected by applying one or more first-order mutations.

7.6.2 THE COUPLING EFFECT

While the CPH arises out of observations of programmer behavior, the coupling effect is observed empirically. The coupling effect has been paraphrased by DeMillo, Lipton, and Sayward as follows:

> *Test data that distinguishes all programs differing from a correct one by only simple errors is so sensitive that it also implicitly distinguishes more complex errors.*

Stated alternately, again in the words of DeMillo, Lipton and Sayward "...seemingly simple tests can be quite sensitive via the coupling effect." As explained earlier, a *seemingly simple* first-order mutant could be either equivalent to its parent or not. For some input, a nonequivalent mutant forces a slight perturbation in the state space of the program under test. This perturbation takes place at the point of mutation and has the potential of infecting the entire state of the program. It is during an analysis of the behavior of the mutant in relation to that of its parent that one discovers complex faults.

Extensive experimentation has revealed that a test set adequate with respect to a set of first-order mutants is very close to being adequate with respect to second-order mutants. Note that it may be easy to discover a fault that is a combination of many first-order mutations. Almost any test will likely discover such a fault. It is the subtle faults that are close to first-order mutations that are often difficult to detect. However, due to the coupling effect, a test set that distinguishes first-order mutants is likely to cause an erroneous program under test to fail. This error-detection aspect of mutation testing is explained in more detail in Section 7.8.

7.7 EQUIVALENT MUTANTS

Given a mutant M of program P, we say that M is equivalent to P if $P(t) = M(t)$ for all possible test inputs t. In other words, if M and P behave identically on all possible inputs, then the two are equivalent.

The meaning of *behave identically* should be considered carefully. In strong mutation, the behavior of a mutant is compared with that of its parent at the end of their respective executions. Thus, for example, an equivalent mutant might follow a path different from that of its parent, but the two might produce an identical output at termination.

A mutant that is equivalent under strong mutation might be distinguished from its parent under weak mutation. This is because in weak mutation, the behavior of a mutant and its parent are generally compared at some intermediate point of execution.

The general problem of determining whether a mutant is equivalent to its parent is undecidable and equivalent to the halting problem. Hence, in most practical situations, determination of equivalent mutants is done by the tester through careful analysis. Some methods for the automated detection of equivalent mutants are pointed to under Bibliographic Notes.

It should be noted that the problem of deciding the equivalence of a mutant in mutation testing is analogous to that of deciding whether a given path is infeasible in, say, MC/DC or data-flow testing. Hence, it is unwise to consider the problem of isolating equivalent mutants from nonequivalent ones as something that makes mutation testing less attractive than any other form of coverage-based assessment of test adequacy.

7.8 FAULT DETECTION USING MUTATION

Mutation offers a quantitative criterion to assess the adequacy of a test set. A test set T_P for program P, inadequate with respect to a set of mutants, offers an opportunity to construct new tests that will hopefully exercise P in ways different from those it has already been exercised. This, in turn, raises the possibility of detecting hidden faults that so far have remained undetected despite the execution of P against T_P. In this section, we show how mutants force the construction of new tests that reveal faults not necessarily modeled directly by the mutation operators.

We begin with an illustrative example that shows how a missing-condition fault is detected in an attempt to distinguish a mutant created using a mutation operator analogous to the VLSR operator in C.

Example 7.21: Consider a function named misCond. It takes zero or more sequence of integers in array data as input. It is required to sum all integers in the sequence starting from the first integer and terminating at the first 0. Thus, for example, if the input sequence is (6 5 0), then the program must output 11. For the sequence (6 5 0 4), misCond must also output 11.

```
1   int misCond(data, link, F){
2   int data[3], link [3], F;        ←Inputs.
3   int sum;        ← Output.
4   int L;        ← Local variable.
5   sum=0;
6   L=F;
7    if(L ≠ −1){        ←Part of the condition is missing.
```

```
8      while (L ≠−1){
9        if(data[L]≠0) sum=sum+data; ← Redundant condition.
10       L=link[L];
11       };
12     }
13     return(sum);
14     }
```

Array `link` specifies the starting location of each sequence in `data`. Array subscripts are assumed to begin at 0. An integer F points to the first element of a sequence in `data` to be summed. `link(F)` points to the second element of this sequence, `link(link(F))` to the third element, and so on. A −1 in a `link` entry implies the end of a sequence that begins at `data(F)`.

Sample input data is shown below. `data` contains the two sequences (6 5 0) and (6 5 0 4). F is 0 indicating that the function needs to sum the sequence starting at `data(F)`, which is (6 5 0). Setting F to 3 specifies the second of the two sequences in `data`.

Array index	→	0	1	2	3	4	5	6
data	=	6	5	0	6	5	0	4
link	=	1	2	−1	4	5	6	−1
F	=	0						

In the sample inputs shown above, the sequence is stored in contiguous locations in `data`. However, this is not necessary and `link` can be used to specify an arbitrary storage pattern.

Function `misCond` has a missing-condition error. The condition at line 7 should be

$$((L ≠ −1) \text{ and } (data[L] ≠ 0)).$$

Let us consider a mutant M of `misCond` created by mutating line 9 to the following:

$$\text{if } (data[F] ≠ 0) \text{ sum} = \text{sum} + \text{data};$$

We will show that M is an error-revealing mutant. Note that variable L has been replaced by F. This is a typical mutant generated by several mutation-testing tools when mutating with the variable replacement operator, for example the VLSR operator in C.

We will now determine a test case that distinguishes M from mis-Cond. Let C_P and C_M denote the two conditions $data(L) ≠ 0$ and data(F) $\neq$ 0, respectively. Let SUM$_P$ and sum$_M$ denote, respectively, the values of sum when control reaches the end of misCond and M. Any test case t that distinguishes M must satisfy the following conditions:

1. *Reachability:* There must be a path from the start of misCond to the mutated statement at line 9.
2. *State infection:* $C_P \neq C_M$ must hold at least once through the loop.
3. *State propagation:* SUM$_P \neq$ SUM$_M$.

We must have L = F $\neq$ -1 for the reachability condition to hold. During the first iteration of the loop, we have F = L due to the initialization statement right before the start of the loop. This initialization forces $C_1 = C_2$ during the first iteration. Therefore, the loop must be traversed at least twice, implying that link(F) $\neq$ -1. During any of the second and subsequent loop traversal, any one of the following two conditions could be true:

$$\text{if data(F)} \neq 0 \text{ then data(L)} = 0 \qquad (7.2)$$
$$\text{if data(F)} = 0 \text{ then data(L)} \neq 0 \qquad (7.3)$$

However, condition (7.1) will not guarantee the state-propagation condition because adding 0 to SUM will not alter its value from the previous iteration. Condition (7.2) will guarantee the state-propagation condition only if the sum of the second and any subsequent elements of the sequence being considered is nonzero.

In summary, a test case t must satisfy the following conditions for misCond$(t) \neq M(t)$:

$$\text{F} \neq -1$$
$$\text{link(F)} \neq -1$$
$$\text{data(F)} = 0$$
$$\sum_j \text{data}(j) \neq 0, \text{ where } j \text{ varies from link(F) to the index of the}$$
$$\text{last element in the sequence.}$$

Suppose P_c denotes the correct version of misCond. It is easy to check that for any t that satisfies the four conditions above, we get $P_c(t) = 0$, whereas the incorrect function misCond$(t) \neq 0$. Hence, test case t causes misCond to fail, thereby revealing the existence of a fault. A sample error-revealing test case is as follows:

Array index $\rightarrow$	0	1	2
data =	0	5	0

$$\text{link} = 1 \quad 2 \quad -1$$
$$\text{F} = 0$$

Exercises 7.19 and 7.20 provide additional examples of error-revealing mutants. Exercise 7.21 is designed to illustrate the strength of mutation with respect to path-oriented adequacy criteria.

In the above example, we have shown that an attempt to distinguish the variable replacement operator forces the construction of a test case that causes the program under test to fail. We now ask: Are there other mutations of misCond that might reveal the fault? In general, such questions are difficult, if not impossible, to answer without the aid of a tool that automates the mutant-generation process. Next, we formalize the notion of an error-revealing mutant such as the one we have seen in the previous example.

7.9 TYPES OF MUTANTS

We now provide a formalization of the error-detection process exemplified above. Let P denote the program under test that must conform to specification S. $\mathcal{D}$ denotes the input domain of P derived from S. Each mutant of P has the potential of revealing one or more possible errors in P. However, for one reason or the another it may not reveal any error. From a tester's point of view, we classify a mutant into one of the three types: error revealing, error hinting, and reliability indicating. Let P_c denote a correct version of P. Consider the following three types of mutants:

1. A mutant M is said to be of type *error revealing* ($\mathcal{E}$) for program P if and only if $\forall t \in \mathcal{D}$ such that $P(t) \neq M(t)$, $P(t) \neq P_c(t)$, and that there exists at least one such test case. t is considered to be an error-revealing test case.
2. A mutant M is said to be of type *error hinting* ($\mathcal{H}$) if and only if $P \equiv M$ and $P_c \not\equiv M$.
3. A mutant M is said to be of type *reliability indicating* ($\mathcal{R}$) if and only if $P(t) \neq M(t)$ for some $t \in \mathcal{D}$ and $P_c(t) = P(t)$.

Let S_x denote the set of all mutants of type x. From the definition of equivalence, we have $S_{\mathcal{E}} \cap S_{\mathcal{H}} = \emptyset$ and $S_{\mathcal{H}} \cap S_{\mathcal{R}} = \emptyset$. A test case that distinguishes a mutant either reveals the error in which case it belongs to $S_{\mathcal{E}}$ or else it does not reveal the error in which case it belongs to $S_{\mathcal{R}}$. Thus, $S_{\mathcal{E}} \cap S_{\mathcal{R}} = \emptyset$.

During testing, a tool such as MuJava or Proteum generates mutants of P and executes it against all tests in T. It is during this process that one determines the category to which a mutant belongs. There is no easy, or automated, way to find which of the generated mutants belongs to which of the three classes mentioned above. However, experiments have revealed that if there is an error in *P*, then with high probability at least one of the mutants is error revealing.

7.10 MUTATION OPERATORS FOR C

In this section, we take a detailed look at the mutation operators designed for the C programming language. As mentioned earlier, the entire set of 77 mutation operators is divided into four categories: constant mutations, operator mutations, statement mutations, and variable mutations. The contents of this section should be particularly useful to those undertaking the task of designing mutation operators and developing tools for mutation testing.

The set of mutation operators introduced in this section was designed at Purdue University by a group of researchers led by Richard A. Demillo. This set is perhaps the largest, most comprehensive, and the only set of mutation operators known for C. Josè Maldonado's research group at the University of Saõ Carlos at Saõ Carlos, Brazil, has implemented the complete set of C mutation operators in a tool named Proteum. In Section 7.12, we compare the set of mutation operators with those for some other languages. Section 7.13 points to some tools to assist a tester in mutation testing.

7.10.1 WHAT IS NOT MUTATED?

Every mutation operator has a possibly infinite domain on which it operates. The domain itself consists of instances of syntactic entities, which appear within the program under test, mutated by the operator. For example, the mutation operator that replaces a `while` statement by a `do-while` statement has all instances of the `while` statements in its domain. This example, however, illustrates a situation in which the domain is known.

Consider a C function having only one declaration statement `int x, y, z`. What kind of syntactic aberrations can one expect in this declaration? One aberration could be that though the programmer intended z to be a real variable, it was declared as an integer. Certainly, a mutation operator can be defined to model such an error. However, the list of such aberrations is possibly infinite and, if not impossible, difficult to enumerate. The primary source of this difficulty is the infinite set of type and identifier associations to select from. Thus, it becomes difficult to determine the domain for any mutant operator that might operate on a declaration.

The above reasoning leads us to treat declarations as *universe-defining* entities in a program. The universe defined by a declaration, such as the one mentioned above, is treated as a collection of facts. Declaration int *x*, *y*, *z* states three facts, one for each of the three identifiers. Once we regard declarations to be program entities that state facts, we cannot mutate them because we have assumed that there is no scope for any syntactic aberration. With this reasoning as the basis, declarations in a C program are not mutated. Errors in declarations are expected to manifest through one or more mutants.

Following is the complete list of entities that are not mutated:

- Declarations
- The address operator (&)
- Format strings in I/O functions
- Function declaration headers
- Control line
- Function name indicating a function call. Note that actual parameters in a call are mutated, but the function name is not. This implies that I/O function names such as scanf, printf, and open are not mutated.
- Preprocessor conditionals

7.10.2 LINEARIZATION

In C, the definition of a statement is recursive. For the purpose of understanding various mutation operators in the statement mutations category, we introduce the concept of *linearization* and *reduced linearized sequence*.

Let *S* denote a syntactic construct that can be parsed as a C *statement*. Note that *statement* is a syntactic category in C. For an iterative or selection statement denoted by *S*, $^c S$ denotes the condition controlling the execution of *S*. If *S* is a for statement, then $^e S$ denotes the expression executed immediately after one execution of the loop body and immediately before the next iteration of the loop body, if any, is about to begin. Again, if *S* is a for, then $^i S$ denotes the initialization expression executed exactly once for each execution of *S*. If the controlling condition is missing, then $^c S$ defaults to true.

Using the above notation, if *S* is an if statement, we shall refer to the execution of *S* in an execution sequence as $^c S$. If *S* denotes a for statement, then in an execution sequence we shall refer to the execution of *S* by one reference to $^i S$, one or more references to $^c S$, and zero or more references to $^e S$. If *S* is a compound statement, then referring to S in an execution sequence merely refers to any storage-allocation activity.

Example 7.22: Consider the following `for` statement:

$$\text{for (m=0, n=0; isdigit(s[i]); i++)}$$
$$\text{n =10* n +(s[i]) −'0');}$$

Denoting the above `for` statement by S, we get,

$$^iS : m = 0, n = 0$$
$$^cS : isdigit(s[i]), and$$
$$^eS : \text{i++.}$$

If S denotes the following `for` statement,

```
for(;  ){
    ⋮
}
```

then we have,

$$^iS :; \text{(the null expression-statement)},$$
$$^cS : \text{true}, and$$
$$^eS :; \text{(the null expression-statement)}.$$

Let T_f and T_S denote, respectively, the parse trees of function f and statement S. A node of T_S is said to be *identifiable* if it is labeled by any one of the following syntactic categories:

- Statement
- Labeled statement
- Expression statement
- Compound statement
- Selection statement
- Iteration statement
- Jump statement

A *linearization* of S is obtained by traversing T_S in preorder, and listing, in sequence, only the identifiable nodes of T_S.

For any X, let X_j^i, $1 \leq j \leq i$ denote the sequence $X_j X_{j+1} \ldots X_{i-1} X_i$. Let $S_L = S_1^l, : l \geq 0$ denote the linearization of S. If $S_i S_{i+1}$ is a pair of adjacent elements in S_L such that S_{i+1} is the direct descendant of S_i in T_S and there is no other direct descendant of S_i, then $S_i S_{i+1}$ is considered to be a *collapsible* pair with S_i being the *head* of the pair. A *reduced linearized sequence* of S, abbreviated as *RLS*, is obtained by recursively replacing all collapsible elements of S_L by their heads. The *RLS* of a function is obtained by considering the entire body of the function as S and finding the *RLS* of S. The *RLS*, obtained by the above method, will yield a statement sequence in which the indexes of the statements are not increasing in steps of 1. We shall always simplify the *RLS* by renumbering its elements so that for any two adjacent elements $S_i S_j$, we have $j = i + 1$.

We shall refer to the *RLS* of a function f and a statement S by *RLS(f)* and *RLS(S)*, respectively.

7.10.3 Execution Sequence

Though most mutation operators are designed to simulate simple faults, the expectation of mutation-based testing is that such operators will eventually reveal one or more errors in the program. In this section, we provide some basic definitions that are useful in understanding such operators and their dynamic effects on the program under test.

When f executes, the elements of *RLS(f)* will be executed in an order determined by the test case and any path conditions in *RLS(f)*. Let $E(f, t) = s_1^m, m \geq 1$ be the execution sequence of $RLS(f) = S_1^n R$ for test case t, where s_j, $1 \leq j \leq m - 1$ is any one of S_i, $1 \leq i \leq n$, and S_i is not a `return` statement. We assume that f terminates on t. Thus, $s_m = R'$, where R' is R or any other return statement in *RLS(f)*.

Any proper prefix s_1^k, $0 < k < m$ of $E(f, t)$, where $s_k = R'$, is a *prematurely terminating execution sequence* (subsequently referred to as *PTES* for brevity) and is denoted by $E^p(f, t) \cdot s_{k+1}^m$ is known as the *suffix* of $E(f, t)$ and is denoted by $E^s(f, t) \cdot E^l(f, t)$ denotes the last statement of the execution sequence of f. If f is terminating, $E^l(f, t) = $ `return`.

Let $E_1 = S_i^j$ and $E_2 = Q_k^l$ be two execution sequences. We say that E_1 and E_2 are *identical* if and only if $i = k$, $j = l$ and $S_q = Q_q$, $i \leq q \leq j$. As a simple example, if f and f' consist of one assignment each, namely, $a = b + c$ and $a = b - c$, respectively, then there is no t for which $E(f, t)$ and $E(f', t)$ are identical. It must be noted that the output generated by two execution sequences may be the same even though the sequences are not identical. In the above example, for any test case t that has $c = 0$, $P_f(t) = P_{f'}(t)$.

Example 7.23: Consider the function *trim* defined below. Note that this and several other illustrative examples in this chapter borrow program fragments for mutation from the well-known book by Brian Kernighan and Dennis Ritchie titled *The C programming Language*.

```
/* This function is from page 65 of the book by Kernighan and Ritchie. */
      int trim (char s [ ])
S₁  {
         int n;                                            F1
S₂  for (n = strlen(s)-1; n >= 0; n--)
S₃  if (s [n] !=   && s [n] != '\t' && s [n] != '\n')
S₄     break;
S₅  s [n+1] = '\0';
S₆  return n;
      }
```

We have $RLS(trim) = S_1\ S_2\ S_3\ S_4\ S_5\ S_6$. Let the test case t be such that the input parameter s evaluates to ab (a space character follows b), then the execution sequence $E(trim, t)$ is $S_1\ ^iS_2\ ^cS_2\ ^cS_3\ ^cS_2\ ^cS_3\ S_4\ S_5\ S_6$. $S_1\ ^iS_2$ is one prefix of $E(f, t)$ and $S_4\ S_5\ S_6$ is one suffix of $E(trim, t)$. Note that there are several other prefixes and suffixes of $E(trim, t)$. $S_1\ ^iS_2\ ^cS_2\ S_6$ is a proper prefix of $E(f, t)$.

541

Analogous to the execution sequence for $RLS(f)$, we define the execution sequence of $RLS(S)$ denoted by $E(S, t)$ with $E^p(S, t)$, $E^s(S, t)$, and $E^l(S, t)$ corresponding to the usual interpretation.

The composition of two execution sequences $E_1 = p_1^k$ and $E_2 = q_1^l$ is $p_1^k q_1^l$, and is written as $E_1 \circ E_2$. The conditional composition of E_1 and E_2 with respect to condition c is written as $E_1 \mid_c E_2$. It is defined as:

$$E_1 \mid_c E_2 = \begin{cases} E_1 & \text{if } c \text{ is false,} \\ E_1 \circ E_2 & \text{otherwise.} \end{cases}$$

In the above definition, condition c is assumed to be evaluated after the entire E_1 has been executed. Note that $\circ$ has the same effect as $\mid_{\text{true}}$. $\circ$ associates from left to right and $\mid_c$ associates from right to left. Thus, we have

$$E_1 \circ E_2 \circ E_3 = (E_1 \circ E_2) \circ E_3$$

$$E_1 \mid_{c1} E_2 \mid_{c2} E_3 = E_1 \mid_{c1} (E_2 \mid_{c2} E_3)$$

$E(f, *) (E(S, *))$ denotes the execution sequence of function f (statement S) on the *current* values of all the variables used by $f(S)$. We shall use this notation while defining execution sequences of C functions and statements.

Let $S, S_1,$ and S_2 denote a C statement other than `break`, `continue`, `goto`, and `switch`, unless specified otherwise. The following rules can be used to determine execution sequences for any C function:

R1 $E(\{ \},t)$ is the null sequence.

R2 $E(\{\}, t) \circ E(S, t) = E(S, t) = E(S, t) \circ E(\{\})$

R3 $E(\{\}, t) \mid_c E(S, t) = \mid_c E(S, t) = \begin{cases} \text{null sequence} & \text{if } c \text{ is false,} \\ E(S, t) & \text{otherwise.} \end{cases}$

R4 If S is an *assignment-expression*, then $E(S, t) = S$.

R5 For any statement S, $E(S,t) = RLS(S)$, if $RLS(S)$ contains no statements other than zero or more assignment-expressions. If $RLS(S)$ contains any statement other than the assignment-expression, the above equality is not guaranteed due to the possible presence of conditional and iterative statements.

R6 If $S = S_1; S_2;$ then $E(S, t) = E(S_1, t) \circ E(S_2, *)$.

R7 If $S = $ `while (c)` S_1', then

$E(S, t) = \mid_c (E(S_1', *) \circ E(S, *))$

If $RLS(S) = S_1^n, n > 1$, and $S_i = $ `continue`, $1 \leq i \leq n$, then

$E(S, t) = \mid_c E(S_1^i, *) \circ (\mid_{E^i(S_i^i \neq \text{continue})} E(S_{i+1}^n, *)) \circ E(S, *)$

If $RLS(S) = S_1^n, n > 1$, and $S_i = $ `break`, $1 \leq i \leq n$, then

$E(S, t) = \mid_c E(S_1^i, *) \circ (\mid_{E^i(S_i \neq \text{break})}(E(S_{i+1}^n \circ E(S, *))))$

R8 If $S = $ `do` S_1 `while(c);` then

$E(S, t) = E(S_1, t)\mid_c E(S, *)$

If $RLS(S)$ contains a `continue`, or a `break`, then its execution sequence can be derived using the method indicated for the `while` statement.

R9 If $S = $ `if (c)`S_1, then

$E(S, t) = \mid_c E(S1, *)$.

R10 If $S = $ `if (c)`S_1 `else:` S_2, then

$E(S, t) = \begin{cases} E(S_1, t) & \text{if } c \text{ is true,} \\ E(S_2, t) & \text{otherwise.} \end{cases}$

Example 7.24: Consider S_3, the `if` statement, in F1. We have $RLS(S_3) = S_3 \ S_4$. Assuming the test case of the example on page

541 and $n = 3$, we get $E(S_3, *) = {}^c S_3$. If $n = 2$, then $E(S_3, *) = {}^c S_3\, S_4$. Similarly, for S_2, which is a `for` statement, we get $E(S_2, *) = {}^i S_2\, {}^c S_2\, {}^c S_3\, {}^c S_2\, {}^c S_3\, S_4$. For the entire function body, we get $E(trim, t) = S_1\, E(S_2, *) \circ E(S_5, *) \circ E(S_6, *)$.

7.10.4 EFFECT OF AN EXECUTION SEQUENCE

As before, let P denote the program under test, f a function in P that is to be mutated, and t a test case. Assuming that P terminates, let $P_f(t)$ denote the output generated by executing P on t. The subscript f with P is to emphasize the fact that it is the function f that is being mutated.

We say that $E(f, *)$ has a distinguishable effect on the output of P if $P_f(t) \neq P_{f'}(t)$, where f' is a mutant of f. We consider $E(f, *)$ to be a *distinguishing execution sequence* (hereafter abbreviated as DES) of $P_f(t)$ with respect to f'.

Given f and its mutant f', for a test case t to kill f', it is necessary, but not sufficient, that $E(f, t)$ be different from $E(f', t)$. The sufficiency condition is that $P_f(t) \neq P_{f'}(t)$ implying that $E(f, t)$ is a DES for $P_f(t)$ with respect to f'.

While describing the mutant operators, we shall often use DES to indicate when a test case is sufficient to distinguish between a program and its mutant. Examining the execution sequences of a function, or a statement, can be useful in constructing a test case that distinguishes a mutant.

Example 7.25: To illustrate the notion of the effect of an execution sequence, consider the function *trim* defined in F1. Suppose that the output of interest is the string denoted by s. If the test case t is such that s consists of the three characters $a, b,$ and space, in that order, then $E(trim, t)$ generates the string ab as the output. As this is the intended output, we consider it to be correct.

Now suppose that we modify f by mutating S_4 in F1 to continue. Denoting the modified function by $trim'$, we get:

$$E(trim', t) = S_1\, {}^i S_2\, {}^c S_2\, {}^c S_3\, {}^e S_2\, {}^c S_3\, {}^e S_2\, {}^c S_3 S_4\, {}^e S_2\, {}^c S_3 S_4\, {}^e S_2 S_5 S_6 \quad (7.3)$$

The output generated due to $E(trim', t)$ is different from that generated due to $E(trim, t)$. Thus, $E(trim, t)$ is a DES for $P_{trim}(t)$ with respect to the function $trim'$.

DESs are essential to distinguish mutants. To obtain a DES for a given function, a suitable test case needs to be constructed such that $E(f, t)$ is a DES for $P_f(t)$ with respect to f'.

7.10.5 GLOBAL AND LOCAL IDENTIFIER SETS

For defining variable mutations in Section 7.10.10, we need the concept of global and local sets, defined in this section, and global and local reference sets, defined in the next section.

Let f denote a C function to be mutated. An identifier denoting a variable that can be used inside f, but is not declared in f, is considered global to f. Let G_f denote the set of all such global identifiers for f. Note that any *external* identifier is in G_f unless it is also declared in f. While computing G_f, it is assumed that all files specified in one or more # include control lines have been *included* by the C preprocessor. Thus, any global declaration within the files listed in a # include also contributes to G_f.

Let L_f denote the set of all identifiers declared either as parameters of f or at the head of its body. Identifiers denoting functions do not belong to G_f or L_f.

In C, it is possible for a function f to have nested compound statements such that an inner compound statement S has declarations at its head. In such a situation, the global and local sets for S can be computed using the scope rules in C.

We define GS_f, GP_f, GT_f, and GA_f as subsets of G_f, which consist of, respectively, identifiers declared as scalars, pointers to an entity, structures, and arrays. Note that these four subsets are pairwise disjoint. Similarly, we define LS_f, LP_f, LT_f, and LA_f as the pairwise disjoint subsets of L_f.

7.10.6 GLOBAL AND LOCAL REFERENCE SETS

Use of an identifier within an expression is considered a *reference*. In general, a reference can be *multilevel*, implying that it can be composed of one or more subreferences. Thus, for example, if *ps* is a pointer to a structure with components *a* and *b*, then in (*ps).a, *ps* is a reference and *ps* and (*ps).a are two subreferences. Further, **ps.a* is a three-level reference. At level 1 we have *ps,* at level 2 we have *(*ps),* and finally at level 3 we have *(*ps).a.* Note that in C, *(*ps).a* has the same meaning as $ps - > a.$

The global and local reference sets consist of references at level 2 or higher. Any references at level 1 are in the global and local sets defined earlier. We shall use GR_f and LR_f to denote, respectively, the global and local reference sets for function f.

Referencing a component of an array or a structure may yield a scalar quantity. Similarly, dereferencing a pointer may also yield a scalar quantity. All such references are known as *scalar* references. Let GRS_f

and LRS_f denote sets of all such global and local scalar references, respectively. If a reference is constructed from an element declared in the global scope of f, then it is a global reference, otherwise it is a local reference.

We now define GS'_f, and LS'_f, by augmenting GS_f and LS_f as follows:

$$GS'_f = GRS_f \cup GS_f$$
$$LS'_f = LRS_f \cup LS_f$$

GS'_f, and LS'_f, are termed as scalar global and local reference sets for function f, respectively.

Similarly, we define array, pointer, and structure reference sets denoted by, respectively, GRA_f, GRP_f, GRT_f, LRA_f, LRP_f, and LRT_f. Using these, we can construct the augmented global and local sets GA'_f, GP'_f, GT'_f, LA'_f, LP'_f, and LT'_f.

For example, if an array is a member of a structure, then a reference to this member is an array reference and hence belongs to the array reference set. Similarly, if a structure is an element of an array, then a reference to an element of this array is a structure reference and hence belongs to the structure reference set.

On an initial examination, our definition of global and local reference sets might appear to be ambiguous specially with respect to a pointer to an *entity*. An *entity* in the present context can be a scalar, an array, a structure, or a pointer. Function references are not mutated. However, if fp is a pointer to some entity, then fp is in set GRP_f or LRP_f depending on its place of declaration. On the other hand, if fp is an entity of pointer(s), then it is in any one of the sets GRX_f or LRX_f where X could be any one of the letters A, P, or T.

Example 7.26: To illustrate our definitions, consider the following external declarations for function f:

```
int i, j; char c, d; double r, s;
int *p, *q [3];
struct point {
  int x;
  int y;
};
struct rect {
  struct point p1;
  struct point p2; F2
};
struct rect screen;
struct key {
```

```
    char * word;
    int count;
} keytab [NKEYS];
```

The global sets corresponding to the above declarations are as follows:

$$G_f = \{i, j, c, d, r, s, p, q, screen, keytab\}$$

$$GS_f = \{i, j, c, d, r, s\}$$

$$GP_f = \{p\}$$

$$GT_f = \{screen\}$$

$$GA_f = \{q, keytab\}$$

Note that structure components x, fy, $word$, and $count$ do not belong to any global set. Type names, such as $rect$ and key above, are not in any global set. Further, type names do not participate in mutation due to reasons outlined in Section 7.10.1.

Now suppose that the following declarations are within function f:

```
int fi; double fx; int *fp, int (*fpa) (20)
struct rect fr; struct rect *fprct;
int fa [10 ]; char *fname [nchar]
```

Then, the local sets for f are as follows:

$$L_f = \{fi, fx, fp, fpa, fr, fprct, fa, fname\}$$

$$LA_f = \{fa, fname\}$$

$$LP_f = \{fp, fpa, fprct\}$$

$$LS_f = \{fi, fx\}$$

$$LT_f = \{fr\}$$

To illustrate reference sets, suppose that f contains the following references (the specific statement context in which these references are made is of no concern for the moment):

```
i*j + fi
r + s - fx + fa[i]
*p += 1
*q [j] = *p
```

```
screen.p1 = screen.p2
screen.p1.x = i
keytab [j].count = *p
p = q[i]
fr = screen
*fname[j] = keytab [i].word
fprct = &screen
```

The global and local reference sets corresponding to the above references are as follows:

$$GRA_f = \{\}$$

$$GRP_f = \{q[i], keytab[i].word, \& screen\}$$

$$GRS_f = \{keytab[j].count, *p, *q[j], screen.p1.x\}$$

$$GRT_f = \{keytab[i], keytab[j], screen.p1, screen.p2\}$$

$$LRA_f = \{\}$$

$$LRP_f = \{fname[j]\}$$

$$LRS_f = \{*fname[j], fa[i]\}$$

$$LRT_f = \{\}$$

The above sets can be used to augment the local sets.

Analogous to the global and local sets of variables, we define global and local sets of constants: GC_f and LC_f. GC_f is the set of all constants global to f. LC_f is the set of all constants local to f. Note that a constant can be used within a declaration or in an expression.

We define GCI_f, GCR_f, GCC_f, and GCP_f to be subsets of GC_f consisting of only integer, real, character, and pointer constants. GCP_f consists of only null. LCI_f, LCR_f, LCC_f, and LCP_f are defined similarly.

7.10.7 Mutating Program Constants

We begin our introduction to the mutation operators for C with operators that mutate constants. These operators model coincidental correctness and, in this sense, are similar to scalar variable replacement operators discussed later in Section 7.10.10. A complete list of such operators is available in Table 7.2.

Table 7.2 Mutation operators for the C programming language that mutate program constant

Mutop	Domain	Description
CGCR	Constants	Constant replacement using global constants
CLSR	Constants	Constant for scalar replacement using local constants
CGSR	Constants	Constant for scalar replacement using global constants
CRCR	Constants	Required constant replacement
CLCR	Constants	Constant replacement using local constants

7.10.7.1 Required Constant Replacement

Let I and R denote, respectively, the sets $\{0, 1, -1, u_i\}$ and $\{0.0, 1.0, -1.0, u_r\}$. u_i and u_r denote user-specified integer and real constants, respectively. Use of a variable where an element of I or R was the correct choice is the fault modeled by the **CRCR**.

Each scalar reference is replaced systematically by elements of I or R. If the scalar reference is integral, I is used. For references that are of type floating, R is used. Reference to an entity via a pointer is replaced by null. Left operands of assignment operators $++$ and $--$ are not mutated.

> **Example 7.27:** Consider the statement $k = j + *p$, where k and j are integers and p is a pointer to an integer. When applied on the above statement, the **CRCR** mutation operator generates the mutants given below:
>
> $$k = 0 + *p$$
> $$k = 1 + *p$$
> $$k = 1 + *p \qquad \text{M1}$$
> $$k = u_i + *p$$
> $$k = j + \text{null}$$

A **CRCR** mutant encourages a tester to design at least one test case that forces the variable replaced to take on values other than from the set I or R. Thus, such a mutant attempts to overcome coincidental correctness of P.

7.10.7.2 Constant for Constant Replacement

Just as a programmer may mistakenly use one identifier for another, a possibility exists that one may use a constant for another. The Mutation operators **CGCR** and **CLCR** model such faults. These two operators mutate constants in f using, respectively, the sets GC_f and LC_f.

> **Example 7.28:** Suppose that constant 5 appears in an expression, and $GC_f = \{0, 1.99, 'c'\}$, then 5 will be mutated to 0, 1.99, and $'c'$, thereby producing three mutants.

Pointer constant, `null`, is not mutated. Left operands of assignment and $++$ and $--$ operators are also not mutated.

7.10.7.3 Constant for Scalar Replacement

Use of a scalar variable, instead of a constant, is the fault modeled by the mutation operators **CGSR** and **CLSR**. The **CGSR** mutates all occurrences of scalar variables or scalar references by constants from the set GC_f. The **CLSR** is similar to the **CGSR** except that it uses LC_f for mutation. Left operands of assignment and $++$ and $--$ operators are not mutated.

7.10.8 MUTATING OPERATORS

Mutation operators in this category model common errors made while using various operators in C. Do not be confused with the overloaded use of the term *operator*. We use the term *mutation operator* to refer to a mutation operator as discussed earlier, and the term *operator* to refer to the operators in C such as the arithmetic operator $+$ or the relational operator $<$.

7.10.8.1 Binary Operator Mutations

The incorrect choice of a binary C-operator within an expression is the fault modeled by this mutation operator. The binary mutation operators fall into two categories: *comparable operator replacement* (**Ocor**) and *incomparable operator replacement* (**Oior**). Within each subcategory, the mutation operators correspond to either the *non-assignment* or to the *assignment* operators in C. Tables 7.3, 7.4, and 7.5 list all binary mutation operators in C.

Each binary mutation operator systematically *replaces* a C operator in its domain by operators in its range. The domain and range for all mutation operators in this category are specified in Tables 7.3, 7.4, and 7.5. In certain contexts, only a subset of arithmetic operators is used. For

Table 7.3 Domain and range of mutation operators in **Ocor**

Name	Domain	Range	Example
OAAA	Arithmetic assignment	Arithmetic assignment	$a+=b \rightarrow a-=b$
OAAN	Arithmetic	Arithmetic	$a+b \rightarrow a*b$
OBBA	Bitwise assignment	Bitwise assignment	$a\&=b \rightarrow a|/=b$
OBBN	Bitwise	Bitwise	$a\&b \rightarrow a|/b$
OLLN	Logical	Logical	$a\&\&b \rightarrow a||b$
ORRN	Relational	Relational	$a<b \rightarrow a<=b$
OSSA	Shift assignment	Shift assignment	$a\ll=b \rightarrow a\gg=b$
OSSN	Shift	Shift	$a\ll b \rightarrow a\gg b$

Read X $\rightarrow$ Y as "X gets mutated to Y".

example, it is illegal to add two pointers, though a pointer may be subtracted from another. All mutation operators that mutate C-operators are assumed to recognize such exceptional cases to retain the syntactic validity of the mutant.

7.10.8.2 Unary Operator Mutations

Mutations in this subcategory consist of mutation operators that model faults in the use of unary operators and conditions. Operators in this category fall into the five subcategories described in the following paragraphs:

Increment/Decrement: The ++ and −− operators are used frequently in C programs. The **OPPO** and **OMMO** mutation operators model the faults that arise from the incorrect use of these C operators. The incorrect uses modeled are: (a) ++ (or −−) used instead of −− (or ++) and (b) prefix increment (decrement) used instead of postfix increment (decrement).

The **OPPO** operator generates two mutants. An expression such as ++x is mutated to x++ and −−x. An expression such as x++, will be mutated to ++x and x−−. The **OMMO** operator behaves similarly. It mutates −−x to x−− and ++x. It also mutates x−− to −−x and x++. Both the operators will not mutate an expression if its value is not used. For example, an expression such as i++ in a `for` header will not be mutated, thereby avoiding the creation of an equivalent

Table 7.4 Domain and range of mutation operators in **Oior**: arithmetic and bitwise

Name	Domain	Range	Example
OABA	Arithmetic assignment	Bitwise assignment	$a+ = b \rightarrow a|/ = b$
OAEA	Arithmetic assignment	Plain assignment	$a+ = b \rightarrow a = b$
OABN	Arithmetic	Bitwise	$a + b \rightarrow a \& b$
OALN	Arithmetic	Logical	$a + b \rightarrow a \&\& b$
OARN	Arithmetic	Relational	$a + b \rightarrow a < b$
OASA	Arithmetic assignment	Shift assignment	$a + = b \rightarrow a \ll = b$
OASN	Arithmetic	Shift	$a + b \rightarrow a \ll b$
OBAA	Bitwise assignment	Arithmetic assignment	$a |/ = b \rightarrow a + = b$
OBAN	Bitwise	Arithmetic	$a \& b \rightarrow a + b$
OBEA	Bitwise assignment	Plain assignment	$a \& = b \rightarrow a = b$
OBLN	Bitwise	Logical	$a \& b \rightarrow a \&\& b$
OBRN	Bitwise	Relational	$a \& b \rightarrow a < b$
OBSA	Bitwise assignment	Shift assignment	$a \& = b \rightarrow a \ll = b$
OBSN	Bitwise	Shift	$a \& b \rightarrow a \ll b$

Read X → Y as "X gets mutated to Y".

mutant. An expression such as $*x++$ will be mutated to $*++x$ and $*x--$.

Logical negation: Often, the sense of the condition used in iterative and selective statements is reversed. The **OLNG** models this fault. Consider the expression *x op y*, where *op* can be any one of the two logical operators: && and ||. The **OLNG** will generate three mutants of such an expression as follows: *x op ! y*, *!x op y*, and *!(x op y)*.

Logical context negation: In selective and iterative statements, excluding the switch, often the sense of the controlling condition is reversed. The **OCNG** models this fault. The controlling condition in the iterative and selection statements is negated. The following examples illustrate how the **OCNG** mutates expressions in iterative and selective statements.

Table 7.5 Domain and Range of mutation operators in **Oior**: plain, logical, and relational

Name	Domain	Range	Example
OEAA	Plain assignment	Arithmetic assignment	$a = b \rightarrow a + = b$
OEBA	Plain assignment	Bitwise assignment	$a = b \rightarrow a \& = b$
OESA	Plain assignment	Shift assignment	$a = b \rightarrow a \ll = b$
OLAN	Logical	Arithmetic	$a \&\& b \rightarrow a + b$
OLBN	Logical	Bitwise	$a \&\& b \rightarrow a \& b$
OLRN	Logical	Relational	$a \&\& b \rightarrow a < b$
OLSN	Logical	Shift	$a \&\& b \rightarrow a \ll b$
ORAN	Relational	Arithmetic	$a < b \rightarrow a + b$
ORBN	Relational	Bitwise	$a < b \rightarrow a \& b$
ORLN	Relational	Logical	$a < b \rightarrow a \&\& b$
ORSN	Relational	Shift	$a < b \rightarrow a \ll b$
OSAA	Shift assignment	Arithmetic assignment	$a \ll = b \rightarrow a + = b$
OSAN	Shift	Arithmetic	$a \ll b \rightarrow a + b$
OSBA	Shift assignment	Bitwise assignment	$a \ll b \rightarrow a \;/= b$
OSBN	Shift	Bitwise	$a \ll b \rightarrow a \& b$
OSEA	Shift assignment	Plain assignment	$a \ll = b \rightarrow a = b$
OSLN	Shift	Logical	$a \ll b \rightarrow a \&\& b$
OSRN	Shift	Relational	$a \ll b \rightarrow a < b$

Read X → Y as "X gets mutated to Y".

```
if (expression) statement →
  if (!expression) statement

if (expression) statement else statement →
  if (!expression) statement else statement

while (expression) statement →
  while (!expression) statement

do statement while (expression) →
  do statement while (!expression)
```

```
for (expression; expression; expression) statement →
   for (expression; !expression, expression) statement

expression ? expression : conditional expression →
   !expression ? expression : conditional expression
```

The **OCNG** may generate mutants with infinite loops when applied on an iteration statement. Further, it may also generate mutants generated by the **OLNG**. Note that a condition such as (x < y) in an `if` statement will not be mutated by the **OLNG**. However, the condition ((x < y&&p > q) will be mutated by both the **OLNG** and the **OCNG** to (!(x < y)&&(p > q)).

Bitwise negation: The sense of the bitwise expressions may often be reversed. Thus, instead of using (or not using) the one's complement operator, the programmer may not use (or may use) the bitwise negation operator. The **OBNG** operator models this fault.

Consider an expression of the form *x op y*, where *op* is one of the bitwise operators | and &. The OBNG operator mutates this expression to *x op˜ y*, *x˜ op y*, and ˜ *(x op y)*. The **OBNG** does not consider the iterative and conditional operators as special cases. Thus, for example, a statement such as `if` (x && a | b) p = q will get mutated to the following statements by the OBNG:

$$\text{if } (x \text{ \&\&}a|{\char`\~}b)p = q$$
$$\text{if } (x \text{ \&\&}{\char`\~}a|b)p = q$$
$$\text{if } (x \text{ \&\&}{\char`\~}(a|b))p = q$$

Indirection operator precedence mutation: Expressions constructed using a combination of ++, −−, and the indirection operator (∗) can often contain precedence faults. For example, using ∗p++ when (∗p)++ was meant is one such fault. The **OIPM** operator models such faults.

The **OIPM** mutates a reference of the form ∗ *x op* to (∗*x*) *op* and *op* (∗*x*), where *op* can be ++ and −−. Recall that in C, ∗ *x op* implies ∗ (*x op*). If *op* is of the form [y], then only *(∗x) op* is generated. For example, a reference such as ∗*x*[*p*] will be mutated to (*x)[p].

The above definition is for the case when only one indirection operator has been used to form the reference. In general, there could be several indirection operators used in formulating a reference. For example, if *x* is declared as `int` ∗ ∗ ∗*x*, then ∗ ∗ ∗x++ is a valid reference in C. A more general definition of the **OIPM** takes care of this case.

Consider the following reference $\underbrace{* * \ldots *}_{n} x\ op$. The **OIPM** systematically mutates this reference to the following references:

$$\underbrace{* * \ldots *}_{n-1} \qquad (*x) \qquad op$$

$$\underbrace{* * \ldots *}_{n-1} \qquad op \qquad (*x)$$

$$\underbrace{* * \ldots *}_{n-2} \qquad (* * x) \qquad op$$

$$\underbrace{* * \ldots *}_{n-2} \qquad op \qquad (* * x)$$

$$\vdots \qquad\qquad \vdots \qquad\qquad \vdots$$

$$* \qquad (\underbrace{* * \ldots *}_{n-1} x) \qquad op$$

$$* \qquad op \qquad (\underbrace{* * \ldots *}_{n-1} x)$$

$$(\underbrace{* * \ldots *}_{n} x) \qquad op$$

$$op \qquad (\underbrace{* * \ldots *}_{n} x)$$

Multiple indirection operators are used infrequently. Hence, in most cases, we expect the **OIPM** to generate two mutants for each reference involving the indirection operator.

Cast operator replacement: A cast operator, referred to as *cast*, is used to explicitly indicate the type of an operand. Faults in such usage are modeled by the **OCOR**.

Every occurrence of a cast operator is mutated by the **OCOR**. Casts are mutated in accordance with the restrictions listed below. These restrictions are derived from the rules of C as specified in the ANSI C standard. While reading the cast mutations described below, $\leftrightarrow$ may be read as *gets mutated to*. All entities to the left of $\leftrightarrow$ get mutated to the entities on its right, and vice versa. The notation X* can be read as "X and all mutations of X excluding duplicates".

```
char ↔ signed char unsigned char
  int* float*

int ↔ signed int unsigned int
  short int long int
  signed long int signed long int
  float* char*
```

```
float ↔ double long double
  int* char*

double ↔ char* int*
  float*
```

Example 7.29: Consider the statement:

```
return (unsigned int)(next/65536) % 32768
```

Sample mutants generated when the **OCOR** is applied to the above statement and are shown below (only cast mutations are listed).

```
short int long int
  float double
```

Note that the cast operators, other than those described in this section, are not mutated. For example, the casts in the following statement are not mutated:

```
qsort((void**)lineptr, 0, nlines-1, (int(*) (void*, void*))
```
$$(\text{numeric ? numcmp :strcmp}))$$

The decision not to mutate certain casts was motivated by their infrequent use and the low probability of a fault that could be modeled by mutation. For example, a cast such as `void**` is used infrequently and when used, the chances of it being mistaken for, say, an `int` appear to be low.

7.10.9 MUTATING STATEMENTS

We now describe each one of the mutation operators that mutate entire statements or their key syntactic elements. A complete list of such operators is given in Table 7.6. For each mutation operator, its definition and the fault modeled are provided. The domain of a mutation operator is described in terms of the effected syntactic entity.

Recall that some statement mutation operators are included to ensure code coverage and do not model any specific fault. The **STRP** is one such operator.

The operator and variable mutations described in subsequent sections also affect statements. However, they are not intended to model faults in the explicit composition of the *selection, iteration,* and *jump* statements.

Table 7.6 List of mutation operators for statements in C

Mutop	Domain	Description
SBRC	`break`	`break` replacement by `continue`
SBRn	`break`	Break out to nth level
SCRB	`continue`	`continue` replacement by `break`
SDWD	`do-while`	`do-while` replacement by `while`
SGLR	`goto`	`goto` label replacement
SMVB	Statement	Move brace up and down
SRSR	`return`	`return` replacement
SSDL	Statement	Statement deletion
SSOM	Statement	Sequence Operator Mutation
STRI	`if` Statement	Trap on `if` condition
STRP	Statement	Trap on statement execution
SMTC	Iterative statements	n-trip continue
SSWM	`switch` statement	`switch` statement mutation
SMTT	Iterative statement	n-trip trap
SWDD	`while`	`while` replacement by `do-while`

7.10.9.1 Trap on Statement Execution

This operator is intended to reveal unreachable code in the program. Each statement is systematically replaced by trap_on_statement(). Mutant execution terminates when trap_on_statement is executed. The mutant is considered distinguished.

Example 7.30: Consider the following program fragment:

```
while (x != y)
  {
    if (x < y)                    F3
      y -= x;
    else
      x -= y;
  }
```

Application of the **STRP** to the above statement generates a total of four mutants shown in M2, M3, M4, and M5. Test cases that distinguish all these four mutants are sufficient to guarantee that all four statements in F3 have been executed at least once.

```
trap_on_statement();                              M2
while (x != y)
  {
      trap_on_statement();                        M3
  }
while (x != y)
  {
      if (x < y)                                  M4
        trap_on_statement();
      else
        x ˉ= y;
  }
while (x != y)
  {
      if (x < y)                                  M5
        y ˉ= x;
      else
        trap_on_statement();
  }
```

If the **STRP** is used with the entire program, the tester will be forced to design test cases that guarantee that all statements have been executed. Failure to design such a test set implies that there is some unreachable code in the program.

7.10.9.2 Trap on if Condition

The **STRI** mutation operator is designed to provide branch analysis for any if statements in P. When used in addition to the **STRP**, **SSWM**, and **SMTT** operators, complete branch analysis can be performed. The **STRI** generates two mutants for each if statement.

Example 7.31: The two mutants generated for statement if $(e)S$ are as follows:

```
v = e
if (trap_on_true (v)) S                           M6
v = e
if (trap_on_false (v)) S                           M7
```

Here, v is assumed to be a new scalar identifier not declared in P. The type of v is the same as that of e.

When trap_on_true (trap_on_false) is executed, the mutant is distinguished if the function argument value is true (false). If the argument value is not true (false), then the function returns false (true) and the mutant execution continues.

The **STRI** encourages the tester to generate test cases so that each branch specified by an if statement in P is exercised at least once.

For an implementor of a mutation-based tool, it is useful to note that the STRP provides partial branch analysis for the if statements. For example, consider a statement of the form: if(c) S_1 else S_2. The **STRP** operator will have this statement replaced by the following statements to generate two mutants:

- if (c) trap_on_statement() else S_2

- if (c) S_1 else trap_on_statement()

Distinguishing both these mutants implies that both the branches of the if-else statement have been traversed. However, when used with an if statement without an *else* clause, the **STRP** may fail to provide coverage of both the branches.

Test Adequacy Assessment

7.10.9.3 Statement Deletion

An **SSDL** is designed to show that each statement in P has an effect on the output. The **SSDL** encourages the tester to design a test set that causes all statements in the RAP to be executed and generates outputs that are different from the program under test. When applied on P, the SSDL systematically deletes each statement in $RLS(f)$.

Example 7.32: When SSDL is applied to F3, four mutants are generated as shown in M8, M9, M10, and M11.

```
;                                          M8
while (x != y)
   {                                       M9
   }
while (x != y)
   {
      if (x < y)                           M10
      ;
```

```
        else
            x ¯= y;
        }
    while (x != y)
        {
            if (x < y)                          M11
                y ¯= x;
            else
                ;
        }
```

To maintain the syntactic validity of the mutant, the **SSDL** ensures that the semicolons are retained when a statement is deleted. In accordance with the syntax of C, the semicolon appears only at the end of (i) *expression statement* and (ii) do-while *iteration statement.* Thus, while mutating an *expression statement,* the **SSDL** deletes the optional *expression* from the statement, retaining the semicolon. Similarly, while mutating a do-while *iteration statement,* the semicolon that terminates this statement is retained. In other cases, such as the *selection statement,* the semicolon automatically gets retained as it is not a part of the syntactic entity being mutated.

7.10.9.4 return Statement Replacement

When a function f executes on test case t, it is possible that due to some fault in the composition of f certain suffixes of $E(f, t)$ do not affect the output of P. In other words, a suffix may not be a DES of $P_f(t)$ with respect to f' obtained by replacing an element of $RLS(f)$ by a return. The **SRSR** operator models such faults.

If $E(f, t) = s_1^m R$, then there are $m + 1$ possible suffixes of $E(f, t)$. These are shown below:

$$s_1, s_2 \ldots s_{m-1}\ s_m\ R$$

$$s_2 \ldots s_{m-1}\ s_m\ R$$

$$s_{m-1}\ s_m\ R$$

$$\vdots$$

$$R$$

In case f consists of loops, m could be made arbitrarily large by manipulating the test cases. The **SRSR** operator creates mutants that generate a subset of all possible *PMESs* of $E(f, t)$.

Let $R_1, R_2, \ldots, R_k$ be the k return statements in f. If there is no such statement, a parameterless `return` is assumed to be placed at the end of the text of f. Thus, for our purpose, $k \geq 1$. The **SRSR** operator will systematically replace each statement in $RLS(f)$ by each one of the k return statements. The **SRSR** operator encourages the tester to generate at least one test case that ensures that $E^s(f, t)$ is a DES for the program under test.

Example 7.33: Consider the following function definition:

```
/* This is an example from page 69 of the book by Kernighan
and Ritichie.*/
int strindex (char s[ ], char t[ ])
{
  int i, j, k ;
  for (i = 0; s[i] != '\ 0'; i++){
    for (j = i; k = 0; t[k] != '\ 0' && s[j]==t[k];j++;k++)
      ;                                                          F4
    if (k > 0 && t[k] == '\ 0')
      return i;
  }
  return -1;
}
```

A total of six mutants are generated when the **SRSR** operator is applied to `strindex`, two of which are M12 and M13.

```
int strindex (char s[ ], char t[ ])
{
  int i, j, k ;
/* The outer for statement replaced by return i.
  return i; ← /* Mutated statement.*/                           M12
  return -1;
}
/* This mutant has been obtained by replacing
  the inner for by return -1.
int strindex (char s[ ], char t[ ])
{
  int i, j, k ;
```

```
for (i = 0; s[i] != '\ 0'; i++){
  return -1;  ← /* Mutated statement.*/          M13

    if (k>0 && t[k] == '\ 0')
    return i;
}
  return -1;
}
```

Note that both M12 and M13 generate the shortest possible *PMES* for f.

7.10.9.5 goto Label Replacement

In some function f, the destination of a goto may be incorrect. Altering this destination is expected to generate an execution sequence different from $E(f, t)$. Suppose that goto L and goto M are two goto statements in f. We say that these two goto statements are distinct if L and M are different labels. Let goto l_1, goto l_2,..., goto l_n be n distinct goto statements in f. The **SGLR** operator systematically mutates label l_i in goto l_i to $(n-1)$ labels $l_1, l_2, \ldots, l_{i-1}, l_{i+1}, \ldots, l_n$. If $n = 1$, no mutants are generated by the **SGLR**.

7.10.9.6 continue Replacement by break

A continue statement terminates the current iteration of the immediately surrounding loop and initiates the next iteration. Instead of the continue, the programmer might have intended a break that forces the loop to terminate. This is one fault modeled by the **SCRB**. Incorrect placement of the continue is another fault that the **SCRB** expects to reveal. The **SCRB** replaces the continue statement by break.

Given S that denotes the innermost loop that contains the continue statement, the **SCRB** operator encourages the tester to construct a test case t to show that $E(S, *)$ is a DES for $P_S(t)$ with respect to the mutated S.

7.10.9.7 break Replacement by continue

Using a break instead of a continue or misplacing a break are the two faults modeled by the **SBRC**. The break statement is replaced by the continue. If S denotes the innermost loop containing the break statement, then the **SBRC** encourages the tester to construct a test case t to show that $E(S, t)$ is a DES for $P_S(t)$ with respect to S', where S' is a mutant of S.

7.10.9.8 Break Out to *n*th Enclosing Level

Execution of a break inside a loop forces the loop to terminate. This causes the resumption of execution of the outer loop, if any. However, the condition that caused the execution of break might be intended to terminate the execution of the immediately enclosing loop, or in general, the *n*th enclosing loop. This is the fault modeled by **SBRn**.

Let a break (or a continue) statement be inside a loop nested *n*-levels deep. A statement with only one enclosing loop is considered to be nested one-level deep. The **SBRn** operator systematically replaces the break (or the continue) by the function break_out_to_level-*n*(j), for $2 \leq j \leq n$. When an **SBRn** mutant executes, the execution of the mutated statement causes the loop, inside which the mutated statement is nested, and the *j* enclosing loops to terminate.

Let S' denote the loop immediately enclosing a break or a continue statement and nested $n, n > 0$, levels inside the loop S in function f. The **SBRn** operator encourages the tester to construct a test case t to show that $E^*(S, t)$ is a DES of f with respect to $P_f(t)$ and the mutated S. The exact expression for $E(S, t)$ can be derived for f and its mutant from the execution sequence construction rules listed in Section 7.10.3.

The **SBRn** operator has no effect on the following constructs:

- The break or continue statements that are nested only one-level deep.
- A break intended to terminate the execution of a switch statement. Note that a break inside a loop nested in one of the cases of a switch is subject to mutation by the **SBRn** and **SBRC**.

7.10.9.9 Continue Out to *n*th Enclosing Level

This operator is similar to the **SBRn**. It replaces a nested break or a continue by the function continue_out_to_level_*n*(j), $2 \leq j \leq n$.

The **SCRn** operator has no effect on the following constructs:

- The break or continue statements that are nested only one-level deep.
- A continue statement intended to terminate the execution of a switch statement. Note that a continue inside a loop nested in one of the cases of a switch is subject to mutation by the **SCRn** and **SCRB**.

while Replacement by do-while

Though a rare occurrence, it is possible that a while is used instead of a do-while. The **SWDD** operator models this fault. The while statement is replaced by the do-while statement.

> **Example 7.34:** Consider the following loop:

> ```
> /* This loop is from page 69 of the book by Kernighan
> and Ritchie. */
>     while (−−lim>0 && (c=getchar()) != EOF && c !='\n')
>         [i++]=c;                                          F5
> ```

When the **SWDD** operator is applied, the above loop is mutated to the following.

```
do {
  s[i++]=c;                                          M14
}
  while (−−lim>0 && (c=getchar()) != EOF && c !='\n')
```

do-while Replacement by while

The do-while statement may have been used in a program when the while statement would have been the correct choice. The **SDWD** operator models this fault. A do-while statement is replaced by a while statement.

> **Example 7.35:** Consider the following do-while statement in P:

/* This loop is from page 64 of the book by Kernighan and Ritchie.*/

```
do {
  s[i++]=n% 10+'0';                                  F6
}
while (( n /= 10) > 0);
```

It is mutated by the SDWD operator to the following loop:

```
while (( n /= 10) > 0) {
  s[i++]=n% 10+'0';                                  M15
}
```

Note that the only test data that can distinguish the above mutant is one that sets n to 0 immediately prior to the loop execution. This test case ensures that $E(S, *)$, S being the original do-while statement, is a DES for $P_S(t)$ with respect to the mutated statement, that is the while statement.

7.10.9.10 Multiple Trip Trap

For every loop in P, we would like to ensure that the loop body satisfied the following two conditions:

- C1: the loop has been executed more than once.
- C2: the loop has an effect on the output of P.

The **STRP** operator replaces the loop body with the trap_on_statement. A test case that distinguishes such a mutant implies that the loop body has been executed at least once. However, this does not ensure two conditions mentioned above. The **SMTT** and **SMTC** operators are designed to ensure C1 and C2.

The **SMTT** operator introduces a guard in front of the loop body. The guard is a logical function named trap_after_$n$th_loop_iteration(n). When the guard is evaluated the nth time through the loop, it distinguishes the mutant. The value of n is decided by the tester.

Example 7.36: Consider the following `for` statement:

/* This loop is taken from page 87 of the book by Kernighan and Ritchie. */

```
for (i = left+1; i<= right; i++)
  if(v[i]<v[left])                                    F7
    swap (v, ++ last, i);
```

Assuming that $n = 2$, this will be mutated by the SMTT operator to the following.

```
for (i = left+1; i ≤ right; i++)
  if (trap_after_n^{th}_loop_iteration (2)){
    if(v[i]<v[left])                                  M16
      swap (v, ++last, i);
  }
```

For each loop in the program under test, the **SMTT** operator encourages the tester to construct a test case so that the loop is iterated at least twice.

7.10.9.11 Multiple Trip Continue

An **SMTT** mutant may be distinguished by a test case that forces the mutated loop to be executed twice. However, it does not ensure condition C2 mentioned earlier. The **SMTC** operator is designed to ensure C2.

The **SMTC** introduces a guard in front of the loop body. The guard is a logical function named false_after_$n$th_loop_iteration(n). During the first n iterations of the loop, false_after_$n$th_loop_iteration() evaluates to *true*, thus letting the loop body execute. During the $(n + 1)$th and subsequent iterations, if any, it evaluates to *false*. Thus, a loop mutated by the **SMTC** will iterate as many times as the loop condition demands. However, the loop body will *not* be executed during the second and any subsequent iterations.

Example 7.37: The loop in F7 is mutated by the **SMTC** operator to the loop in M17.

```
for (i = left+1; i ≤ right; i++)
  if (false_after_nth_loop_iteration()){
    if(v[i]<v[left])                          M17
      swap (v, ++last, i);
  }
```

The **SMTC** operator may generate mutants containing infinite loops. This is specially true when the execution of the loop body effects one or more variables used in the loop condition.

For a function f, and each loop S in RAP(f), the SMTC encourages the tester to construct a test case t that causes the loop to be executed more than once such that $E(f, t)$ is a DES of $P_f(t)$ with respect to the mutated loop. Note that the **SMTC** is stronger than the **SMTT**. This implies that a test case that distingushes an **SMTC** mutant for statement S will also distinguish an **SMTT** mutant of S.

7.10.9.12 Sequence Operator Mutation

Use of the *comma* operator results in the left to right evaluation of a sequence of expressions and forces the value of the rightmost expression to be the *result*. For example, in the statement f (a, (b=1, b+2), c), function f has three parameters. The second parameter has the value 3. The programmer may use an incorrect sequence of expressions, thereby forcing the incorrect value to be the result. The **SSOM** operator is designed to model this fault.

Let $e_1, e_2, \ldots, e_n$ denote an expression consisting of a sequence of n subexpressions. According to the syntax of C, each e_i can be an *assignment expression* separated by the *comma* operator. The **SSOM** operator generates $(n - 1)$ mutants of this expression by rotating left the sequence one subexpression at a time.

Example 7.38: Consider the following statement:

/* This loop is taken from page 63 of the book by Keringuan and Ritchie. */

```
for(i=0,j=strlen(s)-1;i<j;i++,j--)             F8
  c = s[i], s[i] = s[j], s[j] = c;
```

The following two mutants are generated when the **SSOM** operator is applied on the body of the above loop.

```
for (i=0, j=strlen(s)-1; i<j; i++, j--)
/* One left rotation generates this mutant.*/     M18
   s[i]=s[j], s[j]=c, c=s[i];
for (i=0, j=strlen(s)-1; i<j; i++, j--)
/* Another left rotation generates this mutant.*/ M19
   s[j]=c, c=s[i], s[i]=s[j];
```

When the **SSOM** is applied to the for statement in the above program, it generates two additional mutants, one by mutating the expression (i = 0, j = strlen(s)−1) to (j = strlen (s) −1 , i = 0), and the other by mutating the expression (i++, j−−) to (j−−, i++).

The **SSOM** operator is likely to generate several mutants equivalent to the parent. The mutants generated by mutating the expressions in the for statement in the above example are equivalent. In general, if the sub-expressions do not depend on each other, then the mutants generated will be equivalent to their parent.

7.10.9.13 Move Brace Up or Down

The closing brace (}) is used in C to indicate the end of a compound statement. It is possible for a programmer to incorrectly place the closing brace, thereby including, or excluding, some statements within a compound statement. The **SMVB** operator models this fault.

A statement immediately following the loop body is pushed inside the body. This corresponds to moving the closing brace *down* by one statement. The last statement inside the loop body is pushed out of the body. This corresponds to moving the closing brace *up* by one statement.

A compound statement that consists of only one statement may not have explicit braces surrounding it. However, the beginning of a compound statement is considered to have an implied opening brace, and the semicolon at its end is considered to be an implied closing brace. To be precise, the semicolon at the end of the statement inside the loop body is considered as a semicolon *followed by a closing brace*.

Example 7.39: Consider again the function *trim* from the book by Kernighan and Ritchie.

/* This function is from page 65 of the book by Kernighan and Ritchie. */

```
int trim (char s [ ] )
S₁  {
      intn;  F9
S₂    for (n = strlen(s)-1; n >= 0; n--)
S₃      if (s [n] != ' ' && s [n] != '\ t' && s [n] !=
'\ n')
S₄        break;
S₅      s[n+1 ] = '\0';
S₆      return n;
    }
```

The following two mutants are generated when *trim* is mutated using the **SMVB** operator:

/* This is a mutant generated by the **SMVB**. In this one, the `for` loop body extends to include the s [*n*+1] = '\0' statement. */

```
int trim (char s [ ] )
{
  int n;
  for(n=strlen(s)-1; n>=0;n--){                          M20
    if (s [n] != ' ' && s [n] != '\ t' && s [n] != '\ n')
      break;
  s [n+1 ] = '\ 0';
  }
  return n;
}
```

/* This is another mutant generated by the **SMVB**. In this one, the for loop body becomes empty. */

```
int trim (char s [] )
{
  int n;
  for(n = strlen(s)-1; n >= 0; n--);                    M21
  if (s[n] != ' ' && s[n] != '\t' && s[n] != '\n')
    break;
  s [n+1 ] = '\ 0';
  return n;
}
```

In certain cases, moving the brace may include, or exclude, a large piece of code. For example, suppose that a `while` loop with a substantial amount of code in its body follows the closing brace. Moving the brace down will cause the entire `while` loop to be moved into the loop body that is being mutated. A C programmer is not likely to make such an error. However, there is a good chance of such a mutant being distinguished quickly during mutant execution.

7.10.9.14 Switch Statement Mutation

Errors in the formulation of the cases in a `switch` statement are modeled by the **SSWM**. The expression e in the `switch` statement is replaced by the trap_on_case function. The input to this function is a condition formulated as $e = a$, where a is one of the case labels in the `switch` body. This generates a total of n mutants of a `switch` statement assuming that there are n case labels. In addition, one mutant is generated with the input condition for trap_on_case set to $e = d$, where d is computed as $d = e! = c_1 \&\& e != c_2 \&\& \ldots e! = c_n$. The next example exhibits some mutants generated by the **SSWM**.

Example 7.40: Consider the following program fragment:

/* This fragment is from a program on page 59 of the book by Kernighan and Ritchies.

```
switch(c) {
case '0': case '1': case '2': case '3':case '4':
case '5': case '6':case '7':case '8':case '9':
  ndigit[c-'0']++;
  break;
case ' ':
case '\ n':
case '\ t':                              F10
  nwhite++;
  break;
default:
  nother++;
  break;
}
```

The **SSWM** operator will generate a total of 14 mutants for F10. Two of them appear in M22 and M23.

```
switch(trap_on_case(c,'0')) {
case '0': case '1': case '2': case '3':case '4':
case '5': case '6':case '7':case '8':case '9':
  ndigit[c-'0']++;
  break;
case ' ':
case '\ n':
case '\ t':                              M22
  nwhite++;
  break;
default:
  nother++;
  break
}


c'=c; /* This is to ensure that side effects in c occur
once. */

d =c'!= '0'&& c'!= '1'&& c'!= '3'&& c'!= '4'&& c'!= '5'&&
  c'!= '6'&& c'!= 7'&& c'!= '8'&& c'!= '9'&& c'!= '\ n'&&
  c'!= '\ t';

switch(trap_on_case(c', d)){

  ⋮

/* switch body is the same as that in M22.*/    M23

  ⋮

}
```

A test set that distinguishes all mutants generated by the **SSWM** ensures that all cases, including the default case, have been covered. We refer to this coverage as a *case coverage*. Note that the **STRP** operator may not provide case coverage especially when there is fall-through code in the switch body. This also implies that some of the mutants generated when the **STRP** mutates the cases in a switch body may be equivalent to those generated by the **SSWM**.

Example 7.41: Consider the following program fragment:

```
/* This is an example of fall-through code. */
switch (c) {
case '\ n':
  if (n == 1) {
    n--;
    break;                                            F11
  }
  putc('\ n');
case '\ r':
  putc('\ r');
    break;
}
```

One of the mutants generated by the **STRP** when applied on F11 will have the putc('\ r') in the second case replaced by trap_on_statement(). A test case that forces the expression c to evaluate to '\ n' and n evaluate to any value not equal to 1 is sufficient to kill such a mutant. On the contrary, an **SSWM** mutant will encourage the tester to construct a test case that forces the value of c to be '\ r'.

It may, however, be noted that both the **STRP** and the **SSWM** serve different purposes when applied on the `switch` statement. The **SSWM** mutants are designed to provide case coverage, whereas mutants generated when the **STRP** is applied to a `switch` statement are designed to provide statement coverage *within* the `switch` body.

7.10.10 Mutating Program Variables

Incorrect use of identifiers can often induce program faults that remain unnoticed for quite long. Variable mutations are designed to model such faults. Table 7.7 lists all variable mutation operators for C.

7.10.10.1 Scalar Variable Reference Replacement

Use of an incorrect scalar variable is the fault modeled by the two mutant operators **VGSR** and **VLSR**. A **VGSR** mutates all scalar variable references by using GS_f' as the range. A **VLSR** mutates all scalar variable references by using LS_f' as the range of the mutation operator. Types are ignored during scalar variable replacement. For example, if i is an integer and x a real, i will be replaced by x and vice versa.

Table 7.7 List of mutation operators for variables in C

Mutop	Domain	Description
VASM	Array subscript	Array reference subscript mutation
VDTR	Scalar reference	Absolute-value mutation
VGAR	Array reference	Mutate array references using global array references
VGLA	Array reference	Mutate array references using both global and local array references
VGPR	Pointer reference	Mutate pointer references using global pointer references
VGSR	Scalar reference	Mutate scalar references using global scalar references
VGTR	Structure reference	Mutate structure references using global structure references
VLAR	Array reference	Mutate array references using local array references
VLPR	Pointer reference	Mutate pointer references using local pointer references
VLSR	Scalar reference	Mutate scalar references using local scalar references
VLTR	Structure reference	Mutate structure references using only local structure references
VSCR	Strcuture component	Structure component replacement
VTWD	Scalar expression	Twiddle mutations

Entire scalar references are mutated. For example, if *screen* is as declared on page 545, and *screen.p*1.*x* is a reference, then the entire reference, that is *screen.p*1.*x,* will be mutated. *p*1 or *x* will not be mutated separately by any one of these two operators. The individual components of a structure may be mutated by the **VSCR** operator. *screen* itself may be mutated by one of the strucuture reference-replacement operators. We often say that an entity *x* may be mutated by an operator. This implies that there may be no other entity *y* to which *x* can be mutated. Similarly, in a reference such as $*p$, for *p* as declared above, $*p$ will be mutated. p alone may be mutated by one of the pointer reference-replacement operators. As another example, the entire reference $q[i]$ will be mutated; q itself may be mutated by one of the array reference-replacement operators.

7.10.10.2 Array Reference Replacement

Incorrect use of an array variable is the fault modeled by two mutation operators **VGAR** and **VLAR**. These operators mutate an array reference in function f using, respectively, the sets GA'_f and LA'_f. Types are preserved while mutating array references. Here, name equivalence of types as defined in C is assumed. Thus, if a and b are, respectively, arrays of integers and pointers to integers, a will not be replaced by b and vice versa.

7.10.10.3 Structure Reference Replacement

Incorrect use of structure variables is modeled by two mutation operators VGTR and VLTR. These operators mutate a structure reference in function f using, respectively, the sets GT'_f and LT'_f. Types are preserved while mutating structures. For example, if s and t denote two structures of different types, then s will not be replaced by t and vice versa. Again, *name* equivalence is used for types as in C.

7.10.10.4 Pointer Reference Replacement

Incorrect use of a pointer variable is modeled by two mutation operators, **VGPR** and **VLPR**. These operators mutate a pointer reference in function f using, respectively, the sets GP'_f and LP'_f. Types are preserved while performing mutation. For example, if p and q are pointers to an integer and structure, respectively, then p will not be replaced by q and vice versa.

7.10.10.5 Structure Component Replacement

Often one may use the wrong component of a structure. A **VSCR** models such faults. Here, *structure* refers to data elements declared using the `struct` type specifier. Let s be a variable of some structure type. Let $s.c_1.c_2....c_n$ be a reference to one of its components declared at *level n* within the structure. $c_i, 1 \leq i \leq n$ denotes an identifier declared at level i within s. The **VSCR** systematically mutates each identifier at level i by all the other type-compatible identifiers at the same level.

Example 7.42: Consider the following structure declaration:

```
struct example {
int x;
```

```
int y;
char c;                    F12
int d[10];
}
struct example s, r;
```

Reference $s.x$ will be mutated to $s.y$ and $s.c$ by **VSCR**. Another reference $s.d[j]$ will be mutated to $s.x$, $s.y$, and $s.c$. Note that the reference to s itself will be mutated to r by one of the **VGSR** or the **VLSR** operators.

Next, suppose that we have a pointer to *example* declared as: `struct example *p`; a reference such as $p-> x$ will be mutated to $p-> y$ and $p-> c$. Now, consider the following recursive structure:

```
struct tnode {
  char *word;
  int count;
  struct tnode *left;
  struct tnode *right;              F13
}
struct tnode *q;
```

A reference such as $q-> left$ will be mutated to $q-> right$. Note that *left,* or any field of a structure, will *not* be mutated by the **VGSR** or the **VLSR** operators. This is because a field of a structure does not belong to any of the global or local sets, or reference sets, defined earlier. Also, a reference such as $q-> count$ will not be mutated by the **VSCR** because there is no other compatible field in F13.

7.10.10.6 Array Reference Subscript Mutation

While referencing an element of a multidimensional array, the order of the subscripts may be incorrectly specified. A **VASM** models this fault. Let a denote an n-dimensional array, $n > 1$. A reference such as $a[e_1][e_2]\dots[e_n]$ with e_i, $1 \le i \le n$, denoting a subscript expression will be mutated by rotating the subscript list. Thus, the above reference generates the following $(n-1)$ mutants when the **VASM** is applied:

$$a[e_n][e_1]\dots[e_{n-2}][e_{n-1}]$$
$$a[e_{n-1}][e_n]\dots[e_{n-3}][e_{n-2}]$$
$$\vdots$$
$$a[e_2][e_3]\dots[e_n][e_1]$$

Table 7.8 Functions* used by the **VDTR** operator

Function introduced	Description
trap_on_negative_x	Mutant distinguished if argument is negative, else return argument value.
trap_on_positive_x	Mutant distinguished if argument is positive, else return argument value.
trap_on_zero_x	Mutant distinguished if argument is zero, else return argument value.

*x can be integer, real, or double. It is integer if the argument type is int, short, signed, or char. It is real if the argument type is float. It is double if the argument is of type double or long.

7.10.10.7 Domain Traps

A **VDTR** operator provides domain coverage for scalar variables. The domain partition consists of three subdomains: one containing negative values, one containing a zero, and one containing only the positive values.

The **VDTR** mutates each scalar reference x of type t in an expression by $f(x)$, where f could be one of the several functions shown in Table 7.8. Note that all functions listed in Table 7.8 for a type t are applied on x. When any of these functions is executed, the mutant is distinguished. Thus, if i, j, and k are pointers to integers, then the statement $*i = *j + *k + +$ is mutated by the **VDTR** to the following statements:

$$*i = \text{trap\_on\_zero\_integer}(*j) + *k + +$$
$$*i = \text{trap\_on\_positive\_integer}(*j) + *k + +$$
$$*i = \text{trap\_on\_negative\_integer}(*j) + *k + +$$
$$*i = *j + \text{trap\_on\_zero\_integer}(*k + +)$$
$$*i = *j + \text{trap\_on\_positive\_integer}(*k + +)$$
$$*i = *j + \text{trap\_on\_negative\_integer}(*k + +)$$
$$*i = \text{trap\_on\_zero\_integer}(*j + *k + +)$$
$$*i = \text{trap\_on\_positive\_integer}(*j + *k + +)$$
$$*i = \text{trap\_on\_negative\_integer}(*j + *k + +)$$

In the above example, $*k + +$ is a reference to a scalar; therefore, the trap function has been applied to the entire reference. Instead, if the reference was $(*k) + +$, then the mutant would be $f(*k) + +$, f being any of the relevant functions.

7.10.10.8 Twiddle Mutations

Values of variables or expressions can often be off the desired value by ± 1. The twiddle mutations model such faults. Twiddle mutations are useful for checking boundary conditions for scalar variables.

Each scalar reference x is replaced by $pred(x)$ and $succ(x)$, where $pred$ and $succ$ return, respectively, the immediate predecessor and the immediate successor of the current value of the argument. When applied to a float argument, a small value is added (by $succ$) to, or subtracted (by $pred$) from, the argument. This value can be user defined, such as $\pm .01$, or may default to an implementation-defined value.

Example 7.43: Consider the assignment: $p = a + b$. Assuming that p, a, and b are integers, The **VTWD** will generate the following two mutants:

$$p = a + b + 1$$
$$p = a + b - 1$$

Pointer variables are not mutated. However, a scalar reference constructed using a pointer is mutated as defined above. For example, if p is a pointer to an integer, then $*p$ is mutated. Some mutants may cause overflow or underflow faults, implying that they are distinguished.

7.11 MUTATION OPERATORS FOR JAVA

Java, like many others, is an object-oriented programming language. Any such language provides syntactic constructs to encapsulate data and procedures into objects. Classes serve as templates for objects. Procedures within a class are commonly referred to as *methods*. A method is written using traditional programming constructs such as assignments, conditionals, and loops.

The existence of classes, and the inheritance mechanism in Java, offers a programmer ample opportunities to make mistakes that end up in program faults. Thus, the mutation operators for mutating Java programs are divided into two generic categories: traditional mutation operators and class mutation operators.

Mutation operators for Java have evolved over a period and are a result of research contributions of several people. The specific set of operators discussed here was proposed by Yu-Seung Ma, Tong-rae Kwon, and Jeff Offutt. We have decided to describe the operators proposed by this group as these operators have been implemented in the μJava (also known as muJava system) mutation system discussed briefly in Section 7.13. Sebastian Danicic from Goldsmiths College University of London has also implemented a set of mutation operators in a tool named Lava. Mutation operators in Lava belong to the *traditional mutation operators* category described in Section 7.11.1. Yet another tool named Jester, developed by Ivan Moore, has another set of operators that also fall into the *traditional mutation operators* category.

Though a large class of mutation operators developed for procedural languages such as Fortran and C are applicable to Java methods, a few of these have been selected and grouped into the *traditional* category. Mutation operators specific to the object-oriented paradigm and Java syntax are grouped into the *class mutation operators* category.

The five mutation operators in the *traditional* category are listed in Table 7.9. The class-related mutation operators are further subdivided into inheritance, polymorphism and dynamic binding, method overloading, OO, and Java-specific categories. Operators in these four categories are listed in Tables 7.9 through 7.13. We will now describe the operators in each class with examples. We use the notation

$$P \stackrel{Mutop}{\Longrightarrow} Q$$

to indicate that mutant operator Mutop when applied to program segment P creates mutant Q as one of the several possible mutants.

Table 7.9 Mutation operators for Java that model faults due to common programming mistakes made in procedural programming

Mutop	Domain	Description
ABS	Arithmetic expressions	Replaces an arithmetic expression *e* by *abs(e)*
AOR	Binary arithmetic operaerator	Replaces a binary arithmetic optor by another binary arithmetic operator valid in the context
LCR	Logical connectors	Replaces a logical connector by another
ROR	Relational operator	Replaces a relational operator by another
UOI	Arithmetic or logical expressions	Insert a unary operator such as the unary minus or the logical not

Table 7.10 Mutation operators for Java that model faults related to inheritance

Mutop	Domain	Description
IHD	Variables	Removes the declaration of variable x in subclass C if x is declared $parent(C)$
IHI	Subclasses	Adds a declaration for variable x to a subclass C if x is declared in the $parent(C)$
IOD	Methods	Removes declaration of method m from a subclass C if m is declared in $parent(C)$
IOP	Methods	Inside a subclass, move a call $super.M(..)$ inside method m to the beginning of m, end of m, one statement down in m, and one statement up in m
IOR	Methods	Given that method f_1 calls method f_2 in $parent(C)$, rename f_2 to f_2' if f_2 is overridden by subclass C
ISK	Access to parent class	Replace explicit reference to variable x in $parent(C)$ given that x is overridden in subclass C
IPC	super calls	Delete the super keyword from the constructor in a subclass C

7.11.1 TRADITIONAL MUTATION OPERATORS

Arithmetic expressions have the potential of producing values that are not expected by the code that follows. For example, an assignment $x = y + z$ might generate a negative value for x, which causes a portion of the following code to fail. The ABS operator generates mutants by replacing each component in an arithmetic expression by its absolute value. Mutants generated for $x = y + z$ are as follows:

$$x = abs(y) + z$$
$$x = y + abs(z)$$
$$x = abs(y + z)$$

The remaining traditional operators for Java have their correspondence with the mutation operators for C. The AOR operator is similar to OAAR, LCR to OBBN, ROR to ORRN, and UOI to OLNG and VTWD. Note that two similar operators, when applied to programs in different languages, are likely to generate a different number of mutants.

7.11.2 INHERITENCE

Subclassing can be used in Java to hide methods and variables. A subclass C can declare variable x, hiding its declaration, if any, in $parent(C)$. Similarly, C can declare a method m, hiding its declaration, if any, in $parent(C)$. The IHD, IHI, IOD, and IOP operators model faults that creep into a Java program due to mistakes in redeclaration of class variables and methods in a corresponding subclass.

> **Example 7.44:** As shown next, the IHD mutation operator removes the declaration of a variable that overrides its declaration in the parent class.

```
class planet{                                      class planet{
   double dist;                                       double dist;
   ⋮                                                   ⋮
}                                                  }
class farPlanet extends planet{    IHD     class farPlanet extends planet{
                                   ⟹
   double dist;                                      // declaration removed.
   ⋮                                                   ⋮
}                                                  }
```

Removal of the declaration for `dist` in the subclass exposes the instance of `dist` in the parent class. The IHI operator does the reverse of this process by adding a declaration as follows:

```
class planet{                                      class planet{
   String name;                                       String name;
   double dist;                                        double dist;
   ⋮                                                   ⋮
}                                                  }
class farPlant extends planet{     IHI     class farPlant extends planet{
                                   ⟹
   ⋮                                                  double dist
                                                      ⋮
}                                                  }
```

As illustrated next, the IOD exposes a method otherwise hidden in a subclass through overriding.

```
class planet{                          class planet{
    String name;                           String name;
    Orbit orbit (...);                     Orbit orbit (...);

        ⋮                                      ⋮

}                                      }
                            IOD
class farPlanet extends planet{ ⟹   class farPlanet extends planet{
    Orbit orbit(...);                      // Method orbit removed.

        ⋮                                      ⋮

}                                      }
```

As shown below, the IOP operator changes the position of any call to an overridden method made using the super keyword. Only one mutant is shown, whereas up to three additional mutants could be created by moving the call to the parent's version of orbit one statement up, one statement down, at the beginning and the end of the calling method (see Exercise 7.18).

```
class planet{                          class planet{
    String name;                           String name;
    Orbit orbit (...){                     Orbit orbit (...){
    oType=high;                            oType=high;

        ⋮                                      ⋮

    }                                      }

        ⋮                                      ⋮

}                                      }
                            IOP
class farPlant extends planet{ ⟹   class farPlant extends planet{
    Orbit orbit (...);                     Orbit orbit (...);

    oType=low; super.orbit( )               ⋮

        ⋮                                  super.orbit( ); oType=low;

}                                          ⋮

                                       }
```

As shown next, method `orbit` in class `planet` calls method `check`. The IOR operator renames this call to, say, `j_check`.

```
class planet{                           class planet{
   String name;                            String name;
   Orbit orbit (...)                       Orbit orbit (...)
   {...check();...};                       {...j_check();...};
   void check (. . .){. . .}               void check (. . .){. . .}
      .                     IOR               .
      .                     ⟹                 .
      .                                        .
}                                       }
class farPlanet extends planet{         class farPlanet extends planet{
   void check (. . .){. . .}               void check (. . .){. . .}
      .                                        .
      .                                        .
      .                                        .
}                                       }
```

Given an object X of type `farPlanet`, `X.orbit( )` will now invoke the subclass version of `check` and not that of the parent class. Distinguishing an IOR mutant requires a test case to show that `X.orbit( )` must invoke `check` of the parent class and not that of the subclass.

The ISK operator generates a mutant by deleting, one at a time, occurrences of the `super` keyword from a subclass. This forces the construction of a test case to show that indeed the parent's version of the hidden variable or method is intended in the subclass and not the version declared in the subclass.

```
class farPlanet extends planet{         class farPlanet extends planet{
   ...                                     ...
                           ISK
   p=super.name            ⟹              p=name

   ...                                     ...
}                                       }
```

Finally, the IPC operator in the inheritance fault-modeling category creates mutants by replacing any call to the default constructor of the parent class.

```
class farPlanet extends planet{         class farPlanet extends planet{
   ...                                     ...

   farPlanet (String p);                  farPlanet (String p);
                           IPC
   ...                     ⟹              ...

   super(p)                               // Call removed.
      .                                       .
      .                                       .
      .                                       .
}                                       }
```

This completes our illustration of all mutation operators that model faults related to the use of inheritance mechanism in Java. Exercise 7.17 asks you to develop conditions that a test case must satisfy to distinguish mutants created by each operator.

7.11.3 POLYMORPHISM AND DYNAMIC BINDING

Mutation operators related to polymorphism model faults related to Java's polymorphism features. The operators force the construction of test cases that ensure that the type bindings used in the program under test are correct and the other syntactically possible bindings are either incorrect or equivalent to the ones used.

Table 7.11 lists the four mutation operators that model faults due to incorrect bindings. The following example illustrates these operators.

Example 7.45: Let `planet` be the parent of class `farPlanet`. The PMC and PMD mutation operators model the incorrect use of a parent or its subclass as object types. The PPD operator models an incorrect parameter-type binding with respect to a parent

Table 7.11 Mutation operators for Java that model faults related to polymorphism and dynamic binding

Mutop	Domain	Description
PMC	Object instantiations	Replace type t_1 by t_2 in object instantiation via new; t_1 is the parent type and t_2 the type of its subclass
PMD	Object declarations	Replace type t_1 of object x by type t_2 of its parent
PPD	Parameters	For each parameter, replace type t_1 of parameter object x by type t_2 of its parent
PRV	Object references	Replace the object reference, e.g. O_1, on the right side of an assignment by a reference to a type-compatible object reference O_2, where both O_1 and O_2 are declared in the same context

and its subclass. Here are sample mutants generated by these two operators.

```
farPlanet p;              PMC   planet p;
   p=new farPlanet( )     ⟹       p=new farPlanet( )
```

```
planet p;                 PMD   planet p;
   p=new planet( )        ⟹       p=new farPlanet( )
```

```
void launchOrbit(farPlanet p){   PPD   void launchOrbit(planet p){
...                              ⟹    ...
};                                     };
```

The PRV operator models a fault in the use of an incorrect object, but of a compatible type. The next example illustrates a mutant generated by replacing an object reference on the right side of an assignment by another reference to an object that belongs to a subclass of the object on the left. Here, we assume that Element is the parent class of specialElement and gas.

```
Element anElement;                    Element anElement;
specialElement sElement;  PRV   specialElement sElement;
gas g;                    ⟹     gas g;
...                                   ...
anElement=sElement;                   anElement=g;
```

7.11.4 Method Overloading

Method overloading allows a programmer to define two or more methods within the same class, but with different signatures. The signatures allow a compiler to distinguish between the two methods. Thus, a call to an overloaded method *m* is translated to the appropriate method based on signature matching.

Overloading also offers a programmer an opportunity to make a mistake and use an incorrect method. A compiler will not be able to detect the fault due to such a mistake. The method-overloading operators, listed in Table 7.12, are designed to model such faults.

Example 7.46: A mutant generated by the OMR operator forces a tester to generate a test case that exhibits some difference in the behavior of two or more overloaded methods. This is accomplished

Table 7.12 Mutation operators for Java that model faults related to method overloading

Mutop	Domain	Description
OMR	Overloaded methods	Replace body of one overloaded method by that of another
OMD	Overloaded methods	Delete overloaded method
OAO	Methods	Change the order of method parameters
OAN	Methods	Delete arguments in overloaded methods

by replacing the body of each overloaded method with that of another. Here is a sample overloaded method and the two OMR mutants.

```
void init (int i){. . . };          void init (int i){ . . . };
void init (int i,          OMR  void init (int i, String s){
  String s){. . . };        ⟹      this.init (i); }
                                  }


void init (int i){ . . . };  OMR  void init (int i){
void init (int i,             ⟹      this.init (i);
  String s){ . . . };               }
                                  void init (int i,
                                    String s){. . . };
```

The OMD operator generates mutants by deleting overloaded methods one at a time. Test adequate with respect to the OMD mutants ensure complete coverage of all overloaded methods. Note that some of the OMD mutants might fail to compile (can you see why?). Here is a sample program and one of its two OMD mutants.

```
void init (int i){. . . };          void init (int i)
                            OMD       {...};
void init (int i,           ⟹// Second init deleted.}
  String s){. . . };
```

Two overloaded methods might have the same number of parameters, but possess a different signature. This raises the potential for a fault in the use of an overloaded method. The OAO operator models this fault and generates mutants by changing the parameter order, given that the mutant so created is syntactically valid.

$$\texttt{Orbit.getOrbit(p, 4);} \quad \overset{\text{OMR}}{\Longrightarrow} \quad \texttt{Orbit.getOrbit(4, p);}$$

Note that in case of three parameters, more than one OAO mutant might be generated. An overloaded method with fewer (or more) parameters might be used instead of a larger (or fewer) number of parameters. This fault is modeled by the OAN operator.

$$\texttt{Orbit.getOrbit(p, 4);} \quad \overset{\text{OMR}}{\Longrightarrow} \quad \texttt{Orbit.getOrbit(p);}$$

Again, note that the generated mutant must be syntactically valid. Furthermore, one could think of at least two mutants of the call to the `getOrbit` method, only one of which is shown here.

7.11.5 JAVA-SPECIFIC MUTATION OPERATORS

A few additional operators model Java language-specific faults and common programming mistakes. Eight such operators are listed in Table 7.13.

Table 7.13 Mutation operators for Java that model language-specific and common faults

Mutop	Domain	Description
JTD	this	Delete `this` keyword
JSC	Class variables	Change a class variable to an instance variable
JID	Member variables	Remove the initialization of a member variable
JDC	Constructors	Remove user-defined constructors
EOA	Object references	Replace reference to an object by its contents using *clone*( )
EOC	Comparison expressions	Replace == by *equals*
EAM	Calls to accessor methods	Replace call to an accessor method by a call to another compatible accessor method
EMM	Calls to modifier methods	Replace call to a modifier method by a call to another compatible modifier method

The JTD operator deletes `this` keyword. This forces a tester to show that indeed the variable or method referenced via `this` was intended. The JSC operator removes or adds the `static` keyword to model faults related to the use of instance versus class variables. The JID operator removes any initializations of class variables to model variable initialization faults. The JDC operator removes programmer-implemented constructors. This forces a tester to generate a test case that demonstrates the correctness of the programmer-supplied constructors.

Four operators model common programming mistakes. Using an object reference instead of the content of an object is a fault modeled by the EOA operator.

Example 7.47: The EOA operator models the mistake illustrated below.

```
Element hydrogen, hisotope;          Element hydrogen, hisotope;
                            EOA
hydrogen=new Element ();    ⟹        hydrogen=new Element ();
hisotope=hydrogen;                   hisotope=hydrogenclone();
```

There exists potential for a programmer to invoke an incorrect accessor or a modifier method. These faults are modeled by the EAM and EMM operators, respectively. The accessor (modifier) methods names are replaced by some other existing name of an accessor (modifier) method that matches its signature.

585

Example 7.48: The following two examples illustrate the EAM and EMM operators.

```
                       EAM
hydrogen.getSymbol();  ⟹     hydrogen.getAtNumber ( );

                       EMM
hydrogen.setSymbol();  ⟹     hydrogen.setAtNumber ( );
```

7.12 MUTATION OPERATORS FOR FORTRAN 77, C, AND JAVA: A COMPARISON

C has a total of 77 mutation operators compared to 22 for Fortran 77, hereafter referred to as Fortran, and 29 for Java. Note that the double appearance of the number 77 is purely coincidental. Table 7.14 lists all the Fortran mutation operators and the corresponding semantically nearest C and Java operators.

Fortran is one of the earliest languages for which mutation operators were designed by inventors of program mutation and their graduate

Table 7.14   A comparison of mutation operators proposed for Fortran, C, and Java

Fortran 77	Description	C	Java
AAR	Array reference for array reference	VLSR, VGSR	None
ABS	Absolute-value insertion	VDTR	ABS
ACR	Array reference for constant replacement	VGSR, VLSR	None
AOR	Arithmetic operator replacement	OAAN	AOR
ASR	Array reference for scalar variable replacement	VLSR, VGSR	None
CAR	Constant for array reference replacement	CGSR, CLSR	None
CNR	Comparable array name replacement	VLSR, VGSR	None
CRP	Constant replacement	CRCR	None
CSR	Constant for scalar replacement	CGSR, CLSR	None
DER	DO statement *END* replacement	OTT	None
DSA	DATA statement alterations	None	None
GLR	GOTO label replacement	SGLR	None
LCR	Logical connector replacement	OBBN	LCR
ROR	Relational operator replacement	ORRN	ROR
RSR	Return statement replacement	SRSR	None
SAN	Statement Analysis	STRP	None
SAR	Scalar variable for array reference replacement	VLSR, VGSR	None
SCR	Scalar for constant replacement	VLSR, VGSR	None
SDL	Statment deletion	SSDL	None
SRC	Source constant replacement	CRCR	None
SVR	Scalar variable replacement	VLSR, VGSR	None
UOI	Unary operator insertion	OLNG, VTWD	UOI

students. Hence, the set of 22 operators for Fortran is often referred to as *traditional mutation operators.*

Recall from Section 7.5.2 that there is no perfect, or optimal, set of mutation operators for any language. Design of mutation operators is an art as well as a science. Thus, one could always justifiably come up with a mutation operator not presented in this chapter. With this note of freedom, let us now take a comparative look at the sets of mutation operators designed and implemented for Fortran, C, and Java, and understand their similarities and differences.

1. Empirical studies have shown that often a small set of mutation operators is sufficient to obtain a strong test set capable of detecting a large number of program faults. For example, in one study, mutants generated by applying only the ABS and ROR operators to five programs were able to detect 87.67% of all faults.

   Similar data from several empirical studies has led to the belief that mutation testing can be performed efficiently and effectively using only a small set of operators. This belief is reflected in the small set of five traditional mutation operators for Java. While each one of the operators listed in Table 7.14 can be used to mutate Java programs, several have not been included in the set listed in Section 7.11.

2. C has many more primitive types than Fortran. Further, types in C can be mixed in a variety of combinations. This has resulted in a large number of mutation operators in C that model faults related to an incorrect use of an operator in a C program. Similar mistakes can also be made by a Java programmer, such as the replacement of the logical *and* operator (&&) by another version (&) that forces both operands to be evaluated. Hence, several mutation operators that mutate the operators in a C expression are also applicable to Java programs. The Lava mutation system does include an extensive set of operator mutations.

   Certainly, many of the C operators that could be used to mutate Java programs are not included in Java. The OEAA operator is one such example; others can be found by browsing through the mutation operators listed in Section 7.10.

3. The statement structure of C is recursive. Fortran has *single-line* statements. Though this has not resulted in more operators being defined for C, it has, however, made the definition of operators such as the **SSDL** and **SRSR** significantly different from the definition of the corresponding operators in Fortran. Java does not include such statement mutations.

4. Scalar references in C can be constructed nontrivially using functions, pointers, structures, and arrays. In Fortran, only functions and arrays can be used to construct scalar references. This has resulted in operators such as the **VSCR** and several others in the variable replacement category. Note that in Fortran, the **SVR** is one operator whereas in C, it is a set of several operators.

5. C has a *comma* operator not in Fortran. This has resulted in the **SSOM** operator. This operator is not applicable to Java.

6. All iterations, or the current iteration, of a loop can be terminated in C using, respectively, the `break` and `continue` statements. Fortran provides no such facility. This has resulted in additional mutant operators such as the **SBRC**, **SCRB**, and **SBRn**. Java also provides the `break` and `continue` statements, and hence these operators are valid for Java.

7. The interclass mutation operators for Java are designed to mutate programs written in object-oriented languages, and hence are not applicable to Fortran and C. Of course, some of these operators are Java specific.

7.13 TOOLS FOR MUTATION TESTING

Tool support is essential while assessing the adequacy of tests for even small programs, say 100 lines of C code. This aspect of mutation testing was known to its original developers. Consequently, research in program mutation was accompanied by the development of prototype or fully operational robust tools.

Table 7.15 is a partial list of mutation tools. Some of the tools listed here are now obsolete and replaced by newer versions, while others continue to be used or are available for use. Mothra, Proteum, Proteum/IM, μJava, and Lava belong to the latter category. Lava is novel in the sense that it allows the generation of second-order mutants; certainly Mothra has also been used in some scientific experiments to generate higher-order mutants.

Most mutation tools provide support for selecting a subset of the mutation operators to be applied and also the segment of the program under test. These two features allow a tester to perform incremental testing. Test sets could be evaluated against critical components of applications. For example, in a nuclear plant control software, components that relate to the emergency shutdown system could be mutated by a larger number of mutation operators for test assessment.

While mutation testing is preferably done incrementally, it should also be done after the test set to be evaluated has been evaluated against the control-flow and data-flow metrics. Empirical studies have

Table 7.15 A partial list of mutation tools developed and their availability

Language	Tool	Year	Availability
Fortran	PIMS	1976	Not available
	FMS	1978	Not available
	PMS	1978	Not available
	EXPER	1978	Not available
	Mothra	1988	http://www.isse.gmu.edu/ faculty/ofut/rsrch/mut.html
COBOL	CMS.1	1980	Not available
C	Proteum	1993	Available from Professor Josè Maldonado (jcmaldon@icmc.usp.br)
	PMothra	1989	Not available
	CMothra	1991	Not available
	Proteum/IM	2000	Not available
CSP	MsGAT	2001	http://www-users.cs.york.ac.uk/~jill/ Tool.htm
C#	Nester	2001	http://jester.sourceforge.net/
Java	Jester	2001	http://jester.sourceforge.net/
	μJava	2002	http://www.isse.gmu. edu/ofut/muJava/
	Lava	2004	http://igor.gold.ac. uk/~mas01sd/classes/mu-tations.tar.gz
Python	Pester	2001	http://jester.sourceforge.net/

shown that a test data that is adequate with respect to the traditional control-flow criteria, for example decision coverage, are not adequate with respect to mutation. Thus, there are at least two advantages of applying mutation after establishing control-flow adequacy. First, several mutants will likely be distinguished by control-flow adequate tests. Second, the mutants that remain live will likely help enhance the test set.

In practice, data-flow-based test-adequacy criteria turn out to be stronger than those based on control flow. Again, empirical studies have shown that test sets adequate with respect to the all-uses criterion are not adequate with respect to mutants generated by the ABS and ROR operators. Certainly, this is not true in some cases. However, this suggests that one could apply the ABS and ROR operators to evaluate the adequacy of a test set that is found to be adequate with respect to the all-uses criterion. By doing so, a tester is likely to gain the two advantages mentioned above.

7.14 MUTATION TESTING WITHIN BUDGET

The test-adequacy criteria provided by mutation has been found experimentally to be the most powerful of all the existing test-adequacy criteria. This strength of mutation implies that given a test set adequate with respect to mutation, it is very likely to be adequate with respect to any other adequacy criterion as well. It also implies that if a test set has been found adequate with respect to some other adequacy criterion, then it is not adequate with respect to some mutation-based adequacy criterion. Note that the adequacy criterion provided by mutation depends on the mutation operators used; the more the operators used, the stronger is the criterion assuming that the operators are chosen carefully.

The strength of mutation does not come for free. Let C_A be the cost of developing a test set adequate with respect to criterion A. One component of C_A is the time spent by testers in obtaining an A-adequate test set for the application under test. Another component of C_A is the time spent in the generation, compilation, and execution of mutants. C_{mut}, the cost of mutation, turns out to be much greater than C_A for almost any other path-oriented adequacy criterion A. We need strategies to contain C_{mut} to within our budget.

There are several strategies available to a tester to reduce C_{mut} and bring it down to an acceptable level within an organization. Some of these options are exercised by the tester, while others by the tool used for assessment. Here, we briefly review two strategies that have been employed by testers to reduce the cost of mutation testing. The strategy of combining mutants into one program to reduce compilation and executing the combined program in parallel to reduce the total execution time has been proposed, and is alluded to only in the Bibliography section.

7.14.1 PRIORITIZING FUNCTIONS TO BE MUTATED

Suppose that you are testing an application P that contains a large number of classes. It is recommended that you prioritize the classes such that classes that support the most critical features of the application receive higher priority than others. If your application is written in a procedure-oriented language such as C, then prioritize the functions in terms of their use in the implementation of critical features. Note that one or more

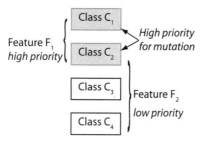

Fig. 7.3 Feature F_1 is accorded higher priority than feature F_2. Hence assign higher priority to classes C_1 and C_2 for mutation. Feature priority is based on criticality i.e. on the severity of damage in case the program fails when executing a feature.

classes, or one or more functions, might be involved in the implementation of a feature. Figure 7.3 illustrates class prioritization based on the criticality of features.

Now suppose that T_P is the test the adequacy of which is to be assessed. We assume that P behaves in accordance with its requirements when tested against T_P. Use the mutation tool to mutate only the highest priority classes. Now apply the assessment procedure shown in Figure 7.1. At the conclusion of this procedure you would have obtained the mutation score for T_P with respect to the mutated class. If T_P is found adequate, then you can either terminate the assessment procedure or repeat the procedure by mutating the classes with the next highest priority. If T_P is not adequate, then you need to construct T_P' by adding tests to T_P so that T_P' is adequate.

One can use the above strategy to contain the cost of mutation testing. At the end of the process, you would have developed an extremely reliable test set with respect to the critical features of the application. One major advantage of this strategy is that it allows a test manager to tailor the test process to a given budget. The higher the budget, the more classes you will be able to mutate. This strategy also suggests that mutation testing can be scaled to any sized application by a careful selection of portions of the code to be mutated. Of course, you might have guessed that a similar approach can also be used when measuring adequacy with respect to any code-coverage-based criterion.

7.14.2 SELECTING A SUBSET OF MUTATION OPERATORS

Most mutation tools offer a large palette of mutation operators to select from. In an extreme case, you can let the tool apply all operators to the application under test. This is likely to generate an overwhelmingly large set of mutants depending on the size of P. Instead, it is recommended that you select a small subset of mutation operators and mutate only

Table 7.16 A constrained set of mutation operators sufficient to achieve a mutation score close to 1

Study	Sufficient set of mutation operators
Offutt, Rothermel, and Zapf	ABS, ROR, LCR, UOI, AOR
Wong	ABS, ROR

the selected portions of *P* using these operators. An obvious question is: *What subset of mutation operators should one select?*

An answer to the question above is found in Table 7.16. The data in this table is based on two sets of independently conducted experiments. One experiment was reported by Jeff Offutt, Greg Rothermel and Christian Zapf in May 1993. The other experiment was reported by Eric Wong in his doctoral thesis published in December 1993. In both studies, it was found that a test set adequate with respect to a small set of mutation operators, listed in the table, is nearly adequate with respect to a much larger set of operators.

Offutt and colleagues found that by using the set of five mutation operators in the table, they could achieve an adequacy of greater than 0.99 on all 22 operators listed in Table 7.14. Wong found that using the ABS and ROR operators alone, one could achieve an adequacy of over 0.97 against all 22 operators in Table 7.14. The operators are listed in Table 7.16 in the order of their effectiveness in obtaining a high overall mutation score. Similar results have also been reported earlier and are cited in the Bibliography section.

The results of the two studies mentioned above suggest a simple strategy: assess the adequacy of your test set against only a small subset of all mutation operators. One might now ask: *Why do we need a larger set of operators?* as each mutation operator models a common error, it cannot be considered redundant. However, the two studies mentioned above suggest that some operators are *stronger* than the others in the sense that if a test set distinguishes all mutants generated by these, then it is likely to distinguish mutants generated by the *weaker* ones.

In practice, the mutation operators applied will depend on the budget. A lower-budget test process is likely to apply only a few operators than a higher-budget process. In a lower-budget situation, the operators in Table 7.16 turn out to be a useful set.

SUMMARY

This chapter offers a detailed introduction to mutation testing. While mutation offers a powerful technique for software testing, for some the technique might be difficult to understand, and hence the details. We have described in detail a test-adequacy assessment procedure using mutation. Once this procedure is understood, it should not be difficult for a tester to invent variants to suit the individual process needs.

A novice to mutation testing might go away believing that mutation testing is intended to detect simple mistakes made by programmers. While detection of simple mistakes is certainly an intention of mutation testing, it constitutes a small portion of the overall benefit one is likely to attain. Many independently conducted experiments over two decades have revealed that mutation testing is highly capable of detecting complex faults that creep into programs. One example and several exercises are designed to show you how mutants created by simple syntactic changes lead to the discovery of complex faults.

Mutation operators are an integral part of mutation testing. It is important for a tester to understand how such operators are designed and how they function. A basic understanding of mutation operators, and experience in using them, helps a tester understand the purpose and strength of each operator. Further, such understanding opens the door for the construction of a completely new class of operators should one need to test an application written in a language for which no mutation operators have ever been designed! It is for these reasons that we have spent a substantial portion of this chapter presenting a complete set of mutation operators for C and Java.

Several strategies have been proposed by researchers to reduce the cost of mutation testing. Some of these are implemented in mutation tools, while others serve as recommendations for testers. It is important to understand these strategies to avoid getting overwhelmed by mutation. Certainly, regardless of the strategy one employs, obtaining a high mutation score is often much more expensive than, for example, obtaining 100% decision coverage. However, the additional expense is highly likely to lead to improved reliability of the resulting product.

BIBLIOGRAPHIC NOTES

Research in mutation testing has been extensive. The earliest publications related to mutation appeared in 1978. Since then research publications and tools have continued to appear quite regularly. A summary of mutation research is as follows:

Early work: The idea of program mutation was proposed in 1971 by Richard Lipton while a graduate student at Carnegie Mellon University. Lipton's paper was titled *Fault Diagnosis of Computer Programs.* Early master's and doctoral dissertations under the advisement of DeMillo and Lipton were completed. St. Andrè wrote a master's thesis [22]. Acree [3] and Budd [61] completed doctoral theses on program mutation. The master's and doctoral theses led to the development of tools such as a Pilot Mutation System (PMS), and empirical studies to demonstrate the fault-detection effectiveness of mutation.

The status of mutation research was published in 1978 by Lipton and Sayward [293]. A landmark publication by DeMillo *et al.,* [122] that some prefer to refer to as the *hints paper,* appeared in 1978. This remains as one of the most often cited publications in the world of testing research. The competent programmer assumption and the coupling effect were first stated in the hints paper. Budd wrote an invited paper explaining mutation analysis [62]. (Exercise 7.23 is from the hints paper.) By the end of the 1970s, program mutation was established as a novel and powerful technique for test-adequacy assessment and test enhancement.

DeMillo [116] wrote the first comprehensive treatise on mutation, a masterpiece, showing how one can reason about program correctness with the aid of the CPH and the coupling effect. He constructed examples from Fortran, COBOL, and Lisp languages to show the fault-detection ability of mutation. DeMillo's report shows how to estimate the number of mutants generated for Fortran programs. He also introduced the notion of *mutant instability* as the average number of test cases needed to distinguish a mutant from its parent, and beautifully related it to the prevailing theory of software reliability.

The first automated test-case generator that generated test cases to distinguish mutants was developed by Offutt [357]. DeMillo and Offutt have reported the test-generation process and its empirical evaluation [126, 127]. A constraint-based test-generation technique was used and incorporated into the Mothra toolset [117, 118, 128]. The test-generation tool in Mothra is also known as Godzilla.

An idea analogous to program mutation was proposed independently by Hamlet [189, 190]. Hamlet used the term *substitution of simpler expressions* to indicate that his implementation tried out various versions of an expression to determine the adequacy of a test set. Hamlet's version of program mutation can be considered as weak mutation [189].

Voas proposed the propagation, infection, and execution (PIE) technique to estimate three probabilities [488]. The three probabilities are that of (a) reaching given program location L, (b) L infecting the program state, and (c) the infection propagating to the final state, or the output, of the program. Note that the conditions in (a), (b), and (c) correspond directly to the three conditions required to distinguish a mutant under the strong mutation criterion. Of course, items (b) and (c) are computed with respect to mutants of the line being considered. PIE is a run-time technique and works on binaries.

While program mutation is a test-adequacy assessment and enhancement technique, PIE is a technique to estimate the likelihood of faults hiding in a program despite extensive testing. PIE allows one to obtain an estimate of the *testability* of a program, where testability refers to a program's ability to hide faults while it is tested using tests sampled randomly from an input distribution [491].

There exist several tutorial and historical articles on mutation testing. These include a book by Demillo *et al.* [125], and articles by Budd [62], Mathur [313], Offutt [360], and Woodward [531].

Weak mutation: Howden observed that mutation testing may require the execution of a large number of mutants [235]. Using the example of mutants obtained by replacing variables in a program by other variables in the same program, Howden proposed a weaker criterion to distinguish a mutant from its parent. This weaker criterion required that, during some execution of the program under test, each occurrence of a variable take on a value different from all other variables.

Howden argued that the proposed weaker criterion would require only one execution of the program under test as opposed to a much larger number of mutants that might be generated by replacing program variables. Subsequently this weaker criterion was formalized by Howden into *weak mutation* [238].

As explained in Section 7.2.3, under the weak mutation hypothesis, a mutant is distinguished from its parent by a test case that satisfies the reachability and state-infection conditions. Given the relaxed nature of weak mutation, a natural question to ask is: "How strong is weak mutation?" Using theoretical arguments, Horgan and Mathur argued that weak mutation is probably the same as strong mutation [226]. Their argument implied that a test set adequate with respect to weak mutation is likely to be adequate with respect to strong mutation.

However, the simple proof given by Horgan and Mathur does not provide any idea of what is the *probability* of the two being the same. Girgis and Woodward [170], Woodward and Halewood [532], Marick [307], and Offutt and Lee [364, 365] have reported empirical studies of the fault-detection ability of weak mutation. The three studies reported lend support to the earlier theoretical result of Horgan and Mathur.

Offutt and Lee compared the strength of weak mutation relative to that of strong mutation [364, 365]. They used a total of 11 programs ranging in size from 11 to 29 lines of code. Based on this empirical study, Offutt and Lee observed that indeed when applied to basic blocks and statements, weak mutation is almost as powerful as strong mutation. However, they recommend using a combination of weak and strong mutation for critical applications requiring exceptionally high quality.

Marick studied the effectiveness of weak mutation in five widely used programs [307]. These programs ranged in size from 12,000 to 101,000 lines of code. Marick injected a total of 100 faults into these programs, thus creating 100 mutants. He was careful and discarded equivalent mutants, thus creating 100 nonequivalent mutants. Marick found that the weak mutation hypothesis holds for 60 faults. He further observed that if a weak sufficiency condition is added to the reachability and state-infection conditions, the hypothesis holds for 70 faults. Marick also experimented with a combination of traditional black-box test-generation techniques using program specification and weak mutation. He found that the two techniques, when used in combination, would certainly detect over 90% of the faults injected into the five programs.

Coupling effect: Offutt formulated the following question: "The coupling effect: Fact, or Fiction?" [358]. Lipton and Sayward have reported an experiment in which they found that tests that were adequate with respect to first-order mutants were also adequate for second-, third-, and fourth-order mutants [293]. The study by Lipton and Sayword was conducted on Hoare's program FIND used as a component of the famous Quicksort algorithm.

Offutt reported another empirical study aimed at answering the original question [358, 359]. He considered three programs, including Hoare's FIND, and generated first- and second- order mutants. A much larger number of mutants than those in the study by Lipton and Sayword were generated, for example 528,906 second order mutants of FIND generated in Offutt's study in contrast to 21,000 second, order mutants of the same program in the study by Lipton and Sayward. Offutt found that a test set adequate with respect to first-order mutants is almost adequate with respect to second-order mutants. The mutation scores with respect to second-order mutants were about 0.999.

Mutation operators: An early set of mutation operators were designed for Fortran. The operator set evolved with experience in the use of mutation. The doctoral theses by Budd [61], Acree [3], and Walsh [497], and a master's thesis by Hanks [193] contain an early set of mutation operators for Fortran and COBOL.

While at Purdue University, DeMillo directed the development of mutation operators for the C programming language [9]. Offutt, Payne, and Voas have reported mutation operators for the Ada programming language. Bieman *et al.* reported a set of mutation operators for mutating Java objects [45, 19].

A fault model for subtyping, inheritance, and polymorphism was proposed by Offutt *et al.* that formed a basis for the development of mutation operators for Java [361]. Ma *et al.* [299] proposed an extensive set of mutation operators for Java and implemented them in the μJava tool [300, 371]. The mutation operators for C and Java described in this chapter are taken from [9] and [298, 299], respectively.

Moore has reported a relatively small set of mutation operators for Java, Python, and C# [332]. Lava tool developed by Sebastian Danicic (s.danicic@gold.ac.uk) uses yet another, relatively small, set of mutation operators for Java. Budd and Lipton applied mutation to prove correctness of Lisp programs [66]. Bybro has proposed yet another tool for mutation testing of Java programs [71]. Kim *et al.* [260] have proposed mutation operators for Java using hazard and operability (HAZOP) studies. They also compare the Java mutation operators with those for Ada, C, Fortran, and C interface.

Ghosh has addressed the issue of testing concurrent Java programs [164]. He has proposed two approaches, one based on program conflict graphs to test for concurrency-related faults in Java programs. A mutation engine to automate parts of the test process is also described.

Use of a small set of mutation operators, also referred to as *constrained mutation* [311] or *selective mutation,* [369] and their fault-detection effectiveness, has been reported by Wong [520], Wong and Mathur [525], Maldonado *et al.* [304], Mathur and Wong [317], Offutt *et al.* [363, 369], and Mresa and Bottaci [334].

Interface mutation: Delamaro proposed an extension of mutation testing known as interface mutation [110]. The idea was to restrict the domain of applicability of mutation operators to the interfaces of components and statements directly involved in data and control transfer. In this case, the components were C functions. Further work on interface mutation is reported by Delamaro and Maldonado

[111] and Delamaro *et al.* [112, 113]. A total of 33 interface mutation operators have been defined. Proteum/IM supports interface mutation testing [114].

In his doctoral dissertation, Ghosh applied the idea of interface mutation to the testing of components [163]. The primary difference between the approaches proposed by Delamaro and Ghosh is in their domain of applicability. Whereas Delamaro's version mutates code inside a component requiring its availability, Ghosh's version mutates only the interface. Ghosh used interface mutation as a tool for testing distributed components such as those designed to CORBA standards [165–167, 314].

In response to a suggestion from Richard Lipton, Lee and Offutt extended the idea of interface mutation to the testing of peer-to-peer communication among Web clients [284]. The eXtensible Markup Language, popularly known as XML [195], is used to encapsulate data and requests prior to transmission to a Web client. The client checks the message for syntactic validity and responds to the requesting agent. Lee and Offutt propose mutating an XML message and comparing the client's response against the expected response. The mutated XML message is syntactically correct. Hence, if the response differs from that due to its parent message, the mutant is considered distinguished. If not, then the mutant is either equivalent to its parent or points to a possible problem with the client.

Lee and Offutt defined a small class of mutation operators for mutating the XML message. Offutt and Xu reported further development in the testing of

Web services [370]. In this work, they propose perturbing SOAP messages using data value and interaction perturbations. Using fault injection in a Web service, they were able to discover 14 of 18 faults. Another detailed set of the XML mutation operators and an empirical study has been reported by Li and Miller [289].

Dynamic mutation testing (DMT): Laski *et al.* have developed a variant of mutation testing to estimate the probability of correctness of a program that has passed all regression tests [281]. Given that program P' under test is obtained by modifying some program P, and P' has passed all regression tests, the DMT technique computes a statistical estimate of the probability of error propagation to verify the correctness hypothesis. DMT, analogous to PIE, mutates intermediate values of program variables and not its syntactic elements.

Fault-detection studies: An exceptionally large number of empirical studies have been devoted to assess the fault-detection effectiveness of program and specification mutation. In all cases, the results point to the extreme power of mutation in detecting faults that often could not be detected by tests generated using boundary-value analysis, equivalence partitioning, and path-oriented techniques.

A number of empirical studies appeared in the 1980s. Budd *et al.* published a theoretical and empirical study [63]. DeMillo made several presentations of mutation as a tool for obtaining highly reliable programs [115, 117]. All of the early doctoral and master's theses mentioned above report some empirical studies of the fault-detection effectiveness of mutation.

Effectiveness of selecting a small set of mutants by random sampling has been reported by Budd [61]. Girgis and Woodward have reported an empirical study aimed at assessing the error-exposition capability of mutation [170]. Woodward has compared some aspects of path-and mutation-based adequacy criteria [528].

DeMillo and Mathur [123] studied the errors of T_EX reported by Knuth [263]. They classified the errors using a code-based classification scheme and constructed examples to show the effectiveness of mutation in detecting complex errors [124]. Wong studied the effectiveness of mutation and data-flow-based adequacy criteria using a set of four Fortran programs translated into C [520].

Mathur and Wong reported theoretical comparison of mutation and data flow [318–320]. Richardson and Thompson have reported the RELAY model of fault detection for the analysis of test-data selection criteria [417].

Mathur [310] and Offut *et al.* [367] reported additional experimental comparisons of data-flow-and mutation-based adequacy criteria. Frankl *et al.* [153] reported yet another comparison of mutation-based and the all-uses adequacy criteria. They used a set of 10 programs ranging in size from 22 to 78 lines of code. While their results were mixed, they found that overall tests adequate with respect to mutation are more effective at finding faults than those adequate with respect to the all-uses criterion.

In Frankl *et al.* study, it is important to note that the reported difference is small and becomes apparent only at very high levels of mutation adequacy. That mutation is more effective than data flow does not imply that one should use one technique over the other. In fact, it is recommended that tests that are adequate with respect to data flow based or any other path-oriented code-coverage criteria must be evaluated against a mutation-based adequacy criteria for further enhancement.

Researchers have often used mutation as a means to study the fault-detection effectiveness of other test-adequacy criteria. Daran and Theévenod-Fosse [108] and Andrews *et al.* [23] have studied the representativeness of the results obtained from such studies.

Daran and Thèvenod-Fosse compared the nature of failures and errors in program states due to *real faults* with those of first-order mutations and the nature of failures due to such faults and mutations [108]. An error was defined as a variation from the correct program state that consists of variable–value pairs and the position in the program under test. The experiment was conducted on a "critical program from the civil nuclear field." The program has 12 known faults (referred to by the authors as *real faults*). In addition, they examined 24 mutants of a total of 2,419 generated using constant-value alteration, symbol replacement, and operator replacement. They concluded that 85% of the errors generated by mutations were also generated by real faults, thus giving credence to the hypothesis that the behavior of first-order mutants is similar to that of programs with errors made by competent programmers.

Andrews *et al.* [23] used a set of eight C programs in their study. One of these programs, Space [156, 160], has a known set of faults; faults were seeded in the remaining seven. Mutants were generated using a set of four operators: replace integer constants, replace operator, negate a decision, and delete a statement. Test suites of size 100 were constructed. For each test suite T, the number of mutants distinguished $Dm(T)$ and faults revealed $Df(T)$ was computed. The number of nonequivalent mutants Nm and nonequivalent faults Nf was also determined. The ratios $Am(T) = Dm(T)/Nm$ and $Af(T) = Df(T)/Nf$ were computed for each test suite. From a statistical analyses of the experimental data, the hypothesis "The mean of Am and Af is the same" was accepted for the Space program and rejected for the others. The authors concluded that mutation adequacy of a test set is a good indicator of its fault-detection ability.

Sung, Choi, and Lee have reported testing a hardware–software system using hardware fault injection and mutation [461, 462]. The goal of their study was to detect any faults due to the interactions between hardware and software of a Digital Plant Protection System (DPPS) of Korea Electric Power System. The DPPS is designed for the protection of advanced nuclear reactors. It receives analog/digital signals from four independent sets of sensors and generates a *trip signal* upon detection of any problem. Sung and Choi identified six types of hardware faults, for example power-surge fault, and modeled these as software faults to be injected in the DPPS software. The hardware fault is injected at the appropriate location in the software. Injection of the software versions of the hardware faults leads to mutants of the software in DPPS. Test data was then generated to ensure that all mutants are differentiated from the original program. A significantly high fault-detection rate was observed as compared to random test generation and the existing test-generation technique used in the DPPS project.

Mutation as an assessment tool for test techniques: The extreme fault-detection effectiveness of mutation has led researchers to use mutation as a means to evaluate the fault-detection effectiveness of new test-generation techniques. Such a task often requires the design of new mutation operators that suit the class of objects to be mutated. However, the basic idea of generating simple first-order mutants and generating tests to distinguish the nonequivalent mutants remains the same as explained in this chapter.

Duran and Ntafos reported an experiment to evaluate the effectiveness of random testing using mutation [135]. A comparison of random and mutation testing is also reported by Geist *et al.* [161] in the context of estimating and enhancing reliability of real-time software. Watanabe and Sakamura proposed a specification-based adaptive test-case generation method (SBATCG) for integration testing for the conformance of operating systems to open system standards [502]. They used mutation to evaluate the fault-detection effectiveness of

the SBATCG, a mix of black-box and path-oriented test-generation technique. It is interesting to note that while the SBATCG can attain high fault coverage as compared to black-box-only approach, the mutation score of tests generated using the SBATCG was 0.96 in one case and 1.0 in the other.

Burton proposed several heuristics to generate tests from statechart specifications [69]. One method uses a Z specification of aspects of the statechart and applies traditional black-box techniques to generate tests. Mutation operators are devised for mutating Z specifications. Test-generation heuristics are applied to the specification, and their mutants, to generate tests. In a case study, a correct Ada implementation from one specification in Z was the object under test used for the evaluation of the goodness of the proposed heuristics. Fourty-nine mutants of the implementation were generated. Tests generated from the Z specification were evaluated against the mutants. Overall, weak mutation scores for different heuristics ranged from 0.65 to 0.87.

Finding equivalent mutants: Finding equivalent mutants can often consume a good deal of tester time. The number of equivalent mutants depends on the nature of the program and the operators applied. In a meticulously conducted study of four programs, Wong found that the number of equivalent mutants varied from 12% to 17% [520]. Wong observed that most of these mutants could be identified easily without a thorough analysis of program behavior. However, he also found that about 0.5% of the equivalent mutants are hard to identify. In any case, to obtain an accurate mutation score, testers do need to examine mutants that their tests are unable to distinguish. Note that a similar task needs to be performed for the identification of infeasible paths when estimating code coverage using any path-oriented criteria.

Baldwin and Sayward provide heuristics for determining equivalent mutants [29]. Offutt and Pan have studied the problem of determining equivalence and its relation to infeasible paths [366]. Hierons *et al.* propose the use for program slicing to detect equivalent mutants [218]. Adamopoulos, Harman, and Hierons have proposed a coevolutionary approach to detect equivalent mutants when using selective mutation. A novel experiment to detect equivalent mutants with the aid of sound has been reported by Khandelwal [256].

Speeding-up mutation testing: Mutation testing could consume a substantial amount of tester and computer time if not done carefully and selectively. A significant amount of research has been devoted to reduce the cost of mutation testing using a variety of techniques. While testers could follow an incremental approach as described in Section 7.14, here we focus on techniques to reduce the time required to compile and execute mutants.

Based on a suggestion by DeMillo, a technique for combining a subset of mutants into one program, and executing it on a vector processor, has been proposed by Krauser and Mathur [315]. The technique of Krauser and Mathur is known as *program unification* [158]. This technique aims to exploit the architecture of a vector processor to speed up the execution of similar mutants.

Program unification has two advantages. First, a set of mutants is compiled in one compilation, thus saving on compilation time. Second, the similarity of mutants and their parent leads to improved vectorization of the compiled program, thus leading to faster execution, though not always. Program unification was further extended to work on SIMD architectures [272] such as that of the connection machine [220]. Mathur and Rego provide a formal analysis of the unification technique [316].

Krauser and Mathur also proposed a straightforward technique for scheduling mutants for execution on a massively parallel transputer-based system [271]. Choi, in her doctoral dissertation, further developed the idea of using massively parallel architectures for mutation testing [83]. Choi *et al.* have reported a tool named PMothra for scheduling mutants on a hypercube [87]. Experience with the use of PMothra on the Ncube machine and an analysis of the algorithms used are reported by Choi and Mathur [84–86]. Jackson and Woodward have reported a technique for the execution of Java mutants using concurrent threads [245].

Offutt *et al.* used an MIMD machine to execute mutants [368]. They ported Mothra's interpreter Rosetta to a 16-processor Intel iPSC/2 hypercube and reported speedup in mutant execution of up to 14. As expected, higher speedups were associated with larger programs.

Weiss and Fleyshgakkar developed novel serial algorithms for both strong and weak mutation [506]. Their algorithm uses a data structure, named MDS, to encode important information about the execution of the program against a test input. MDS is created during the execution of the program under test (see Step 1 on page 463). MDS is used subsequently during the execution of mutants to decide whether the mutant is distinguished. Both strong and weak mutation criteria are used. They show, analytically, that a speedup ranging from about 1.4 to 11.5 can be achieved by using their algorithm for mutation analysis. The speedup is obtained at the expense of increased space requirements resulting from the storage of MDS. Subsequently, the same authors described an improved algorithm, named *Lazy mutant analysis*, whose space complexity is approximately the same as that of Mothra, but has a much faster execution time [148]. Weiss and Fleyshgakkar have also proposed a new multiple-SIMD architecture suitable for fast mutation analysis [505]; a theoretical analysis of the architecture has also been reported.

Compiler-integrated program mutation is yet another idea to reduce the time to compile mutants. This idea has been explored by Krauser in his doctoral dissertation [270]. DeMillo *et al.* explain the technique and its advantages [119]. The idea requires modifications to the compiler for the language in which the program under test is written. A tester instructs the compiler to automatically generate compiled mutants of a given kind, for example variable replacement. Krauser modified the GNU C-compiler to illustrate

the idea, and performed experiments to assess the expected savings with this approach.

The idea of combining mutants to reduce compilation time has also been extended to single-processor machines. Mathur proposed the use of *mutant containers* to group a set of mutants into one compilable program unit [312]. In a C implementation, each container is a complete program under test with the mutants enclosed in a switch statement, each mutant followed by a break statement. A specific mutant is referenced by an integer value of the switch expression. This idea was used in the design of the ATAC-M tool, an extension of the ATAC tool [224, 225]. A sample mutant container obtained by applying the variable replacement operator to the statement *max = y* in Figure 7.4 is shown in Figure 7.5. Note the use of variable _mutant_num in the switch expression. The idea of mutant container has been used in the implementation of Proteum/IM [114].

```
1 main(){
2 int x, y, max;
3 scanf("%d%d", &x, &y);
4 if(x<y)
5 max=y;
6 else
7 max=x;
8 printf("%d\ n",max);
9 }
```

Fig. 4.4 Sample C program to be mutated.

Untch [480] and Untch *et al.* [481] independently proposed another method for combining mutants into one program. The mutant schema technique described by Untch *et al.* is more sophisticated in terms of its formalization compared to the simplistic mutant-container technique proposed by Mathur [312]. Their method creates a *meta-mutant*. A meta-mutant is a parameterized program that encompasses all mutants. Inside a meta-mutant, each mutation operator becomes a *meta-procedure*. Thus, each statement or expression to be mutated, is replaced by a meta-operator with arguments that reflect the entities, for example a variable, to be mutated. Each meta-operator is available as a library function and contains a switch statement to select the mutant to be executed. The creation of meta-operators is described by Untch *et al.* [481].

```
main(argc,argv)
  {
  int arg; charchar *argv[ ];
  int x, y, max;
  int_mutant_num;
_mutant_num =
get_mutant_num(argc,argv);
    scanf("%d%d", &x, &y);
  if (x<y)
   switch (_mutant_num)
     {
     case 1:
      max=x; break;
     case 2:
      max=max; break;
     case 3:
      x=y; break;
     case 4:
      y=y; break;
     };
   else
    max = x;
   printf("%d\ n",max);
  }
```

Fig. 7.5 A sample mutant container obtained from the source program in Figure 7.4.

Specification mutation: Decision tables are a simple low-level form of formal specifications. They specify decision rules that determine the behavior of some process. Budd and Lipton applied mutation testing to test decision-table specifications [65].

Budd and Gopal observed that most test-generation techniques (at the time the observation was made) rely on the program as the source of information to generate tests [64]. They argued that specifications are as important as the program, and hence specifications should also be used to generate tests. This led to the proposal for mutating specifications and generating tests that distinguish specification mutants from their parent. A specification mutant is considered distinguished from its parent by a test case if there is at least one input condition satisfied in the parent or the mutant, and for which an output condition is falsified. They proposed mutation operators, similar to the traditional operators, for mutating specifications using predicate calculus. Their method for test generation relies on the availability of a program supposed to satisfy the specification.

Jalote proposed evaluating the effectiveness of tests for algebraic specifications by deleting axioms from the original specification [246]. The goal in Jalote's study was to detect incompleteness of a set of axioms that form the formal specification. Test cases are generated automatically from the syntactic part of the algebraic specifications. While Jalote did not describe his approach to test generation in terms of mutation testing, the deletion of axioms to show the completeness of tests can be cast in mutation framework.

Woodward has proposed mutating algebraic specifications and generating mutation-adequate test expressions [527, 530]. The objective is to discover errors in algebraic specifications. Woodward has also developed a prototype tool named OBJTEST to automate portions of the proposed test process [529].

Murnane and Reed used a different approach to test generation using specification mutation. They considered the elements of a specification as terminal symbol sets of a language [336, 337]. Mutation operators then replace a terminal by another terminal, as for example in variable replacement. In one of the two case studies reported by Murnane and Reed, a mutation-adequate test set was able to discover errors that were not discovered by tests derived using boundary-value and equivalence-partitioning techniques.

Stocks [460] proposed the strategy of mutating specification written in Z notation to generate new tests. Fabbri et al. have proposed mutation for the validation of statecharts[144]. Ammann has proposed the automation of mutation analysis at the level of specifications [21]. Black et al. define mutation operators for formal specifications [50].

Abdurazik et al. [1] compared three specification-based coverage criteria, including specification mutation, using Mathur and Wong's PROBSUBSUMES relationship [318]. They concluded that techniques for specification mutation and predicate coverage are similar in their fault-revealing abilities. They also concluded that transition-pair coverage does not lead to high-specification mutation score or high predicate coverage, and vice versa, implying that transition coverage has something *different to offer* than the remaining two techniques.

Fabbri et al. developed a tool named Proteum/FSM to test specifications based on the FSMs [142, 143]. De Souza et al. have proposed mutation operators for testing Estelle specifications [130]. Simão and Maldonado have applied mutation testing to validate specifications based on Petri nets [445]. Proteum-RS/PN, a tool that incorporates Simão and Maldonado's techniques, has also been reported [446].

Srivatanakul [457] has applied mutation to the testing of specifications written in a subset of CSP, a process-centric notation for specifying concurrent systems developed by C. A. R. Hoare [221]. The mutant operators were designed using the hazard and operational study approach used in the analysis of safety critical systems. The mutation operators are classified into four distinct categories derived from the CSP subset. A tool named MsGAT, written in Java, has been developed to support mutation testing of CSP specifications. A unique feature of Srivatanakul's thesis is the detail in which the design and testing of MsGAT itself is described. Appendix A in his thesis describes a case study—a simple buffer—to illustrate the use of mutation to the testing of CSP specifications. Subsequently, Srivatanakul et al. have applied CSP-based specification mutation to the validation of security specifications for an electronic purse [458].

Aichernig has considered test design as a formal synthesis problem [18]. The abstraction proposed is used to relate to mutation testing and to contracts. Mutants of formal contracts are generated and test cases developed to distinguish such mutants. The notion of adequate tests is defined analogous to the one discussed in this chapter but with respect to formal contracts.

Okun has studied the use of mutation in test generation from specifications [374, 375]. Okun defines mutation operators to mutate Computation Tree Logic (CTL) specifications [91] input to the SMV[325] model checker developed at Carnegie Mellon University. Mutation operators are defined for mutating specifications input to SMV and their fault-detection effectiveness compared using case studies from automobile cruise control, aircraft collision avoidance, trusted operating system, and safety injection.

Zhan and Clark have proposed and evaluated a method for search-based mutation testing of Simulink models [542]. Simulink [321] is a tool for modeling and simulating designs of dynamic systems. A Simulink model is a collection of connected boxes with specified I/O functions. The original Simulink model is mutated using three types of mutation operators, namely Add, Multiply, and Assign that add, multiply, and assign to, respectively, signals carried by the input to a box. Using a case study, Zhan and Clark suggest mutation adequacy of tests for Simulink designs as an improvement over structural coverage-based adequacy.

EXERCISES

7.1 Given program P in programming language L and a nonempty set M of mutation operators, what is the smallest number of mutants generated when mutation operators in M are applied to P?

7.2 (a) Let D and R denote, respectively, the sets of elements in the domain of mutation operator M. Suppose that program P contains exactly one occurrence of each element of D and that $D = R$. How many mutants of P will be generated by applying M? (b) How might your answer to (a) change if $D \neq R$?

7.3 Create at least two mutants of Program P7.2 on page 509 that could lead to an incorrect signal sent to the caller of procedure checkTemp. Assume that you are allowed to create mutants by only changing constants, variables, arithmetic operators, and logical operators.

7.4 In Program P7.2, we have used three if statements to set danger to its appropriate value. Instead, suppose we use if-else structure as follows:

```
12 if (highCount==1) danger=moderate;
13 else if (highCount==2) danger=high;
14 else if (highCount==3) danger=veryHigh;
15 return(danger);
```

Consider mutant M_3 of the revised program obtained by replacing veryHigh by none. Would the behavior of mutant M_3 differ from that of M_1 and M_2 in Examples 7.4 and 7.5?

7.5 In Example 7.12, the tests are selected in the order t_1, t_2, t_3, t_4. Suppose the tests are selected in the order t_4, t_3, t_2, t_1. By how much will this revised order change the number of mutant executions as compared to the number of executions in Example 7.12?

7.6 Why is it considered impossible to construct an ideal set of mutation operators for nontrivial programming languages? Does there exist a language for which such a set can be constructed?

7.7 Consider the statement: "In mutation testing, an assumption is that programmers make small errors." Critique this statement in the light of the CPH and the coupling effect.

7.8 Consider Program P7.3 in Example 7.17 on page 472. Consider three mutants of Program P7.3 obtained as follows:

M_1: At line 4, replace index < size by index < size-1.

M_2: At line 5, replace atWeight > w by atWeight $\geq$ w.

M_3: At line 5, replace atWeight > w by atWeight> abs(w).

For each of the three mutants, derive a test case that distinguishes it from the parent or prove that it is an equivalent mutant.

7.9 Formulate a "malicious programmer hypothesis" analogous to the competant programmer hypothesis. In what domain of software testing do you think such a hypothesis might be useful?

7.10 Under weak mutation, a mutant is considered distinguished by a test case t if it satisfies conditions C_1 and C_2 on page 523. Derive a minimal sized test set T for Program P7.3 that is adequate with respect to weak mutation given the three mutants in Exercise 7.8. Is T adequate with respect to strong mutation?

7.11 As explained in Section 7.3.2, adequacy assessment and test enhancement could be done concurrently by two or more testers. While the testers share a common test database, it might be possible that two or more testers derive tests that are redundant in the sense that a test already derived by a tester might have distinguished a mutant that some other tester has not been able to distinguish.

Given that adequacy assessment is done by two testers, sketch a sequence of events that reveal the possibility of a redundant test case being generated. You could include events such as : tester 1 generates mutants, tester 2 executes mutants, tester 1 adds a new test case to the database, tester 2 removes a test case from the database, and so on. Assume that (a) tester TS is allowed to remove a test case from the database, but only if it was created by TS and (b) the adequacy assessment process is started all over when a fault is discovered and fixed.

7.12 Consider naming the statement-deletion operator for C as: *statement replacement by null statement*. Why would this be a poor naming choice?

7.13 Consider the following simple function:

```
1 function xRaisedToy(int x, y){
2  int power=1; count=y;
3  while(count>0){
4    power=power*x;
5    count=count-1;
6  }
7  return(power)
8 }
```

(a) How many *abs* mutants will be generated when `xRaisedToy` is mutated by the *abs* operator? (b) List at least two *abs* mutants generated? (c) Consider the following mutant of `xRaisedToy` obtained my mutating line 4:

power=power*abs(x);

Generate a test case that distinguishes this mutant, or show that it is equivalent to `xRaisedToy`.
(d) Generate at least one *abs* mutant equivalent to `xRaisedToy`.

7.14 Let T_D denote a decision-adequate test set for the function in Exercise 7.13. Show that there exists a T_D that fails to distinguish the *abs* mutant in part (c).

7.15 The AMC (access modifier change) operator was designed to model faults in Java programs related to the incorrect choice of the access modifiers such as `private` and `public`. However, this operator was not implemented in the μJava system. Offer arguments in support of, or against, the decision not to include AMC in μJava.

7.16 Let P_J denote a Java method corresponding to function `xRaisedToy` in Exercise 7.13. Which Java mutation operators will generate a nonzero number of mutants for P_J given that no other part of the program containing P_J is to be mutated?

7.17 Derive conditions a test case must satisfy to distinguish each mutant shown in Example 7.44.

7.18 Given the following class declarations, list all mutants generated by applying the IOP operator.

```
class planet{
    String name;
    Orbit orbit (...){
    oType=high;

        ⋮

    }

        ⋮

}
class farPlanet extends planet{
    float dist; Orbit orbit (...);

        ⋮

    float currentDistance(String pName){
        oType=low; super.orbit( );
        dist=computeDistance(pName);
        return dist;

    }   ⋮

}
```

7.19 Consider the following simple program *P* that contains an error at line 3. A mutant *M*, obtained by replacing this line as shown, is the correct program. The mutant operator used here replaces a variable by a constant from within the program. In C, this operator is named **CRCR**. Thus, the error in the program is modeled by a mutation operator.

```
1 input x, y
2   if x < y then
3     z=x*(y+x)           ←  z=x*(y+1)
4   else
5     z=x*(y-1)
```

(a) Construct a test case t_1 that causes P to fail and establishes the relation $P(t_1) \neq M(t_1)$. (b) Can you construct a test case t_2 on which P is successful but $P(t_2) \neq M(t_2)$ does not hold? (c) Construct a test set T that is adequate with respect to decision coverage, MC/DC coverage, and all-uses-coverage criteria, and that does not reveal the error. Does any test in T distinguish M from P?

7.20   As reported by Donald Knuth, missing assignments accounted for over 11% of all the faults found in T$_E$X. Considering a missing initialization as a special case of missing assignment, these faults account for over 15% of all faults found in T$_E$X. This exercise illustrates how a missing assignment is detected using mutation. In the program listed next, the position of a missing assignment is indicated. Let P_c denote the correct program.

```
1      int x, p, q
2         ← Default value assignment, x=0, is missing here.
3         if (q< 0) x = p * q
4         if (p ≥ 0 A q>0) x = p/q
5      y = x + 1
```

Show that each of the following mutants, obtained by mutating line 3, is error revealing.

```
if(q < 1) x = p * q
if((p ≥ 1) ∧ (q > 0)) x = p/q
  if ((p ≥ 1) ∧ (q > 0)) x = p/q
if((p ≥ 0) ∧ (q > −1)) x = p/q
  if ((p ≥ 0) ∧ (q > 1)) x = p/q
```

One might argue that the missing initialization above can be detected easily through static analysis. Assuming that the program fragment above is a small portion of a large program, can you argue that static analysis might fail to detect the missing initialization?

7.21   Example 7.21 illustrates how a simple mutation can reveal a missing-condition error. The example showed that the error must be revealed when mutation adequacy has been achieved. Develop test sets T_1, T_2, and T_3 adequate with respect to, respectively, decision coverage, MC/DC-coverage, and all-uses-coverage criteria such that none of the tests reveals the error in function misCond?

7.22 Some program faults might escape detection using mutation as well as any path-oriented testing strategy. Dick Hamlet provides a simple example of one such error. Hamlet's program is reproduced below:

```
1 real hamletFunction (x: real){
2 if (x<0) x = -x;
3 return(sqr(x)*2)   ← This should be return(sqrt(x) * 2)
4 }
```

The error is in the use of function *sqr,* read as *square,* instead of the function *sqrt,* read as *square root.* Note that there is a simple mutation that exists in this program, that of *sqrt* being mutated by the programmer to *sqr.* However, let us assume that there is no such mutation operator in the mutation tool that you are using. (Of course, in principle, there is nothing that prevents a mutation testing tool from providing such a mutation operator.) Hence, the call to *sqr* will not be mutated to *sqrt.*

Consider the test set $T = \{ <x = 0>, <x = -1>, <x = 1> \}$. It is easy to check that hamletFunction behaves correctly on T. Show that T is adequate with respect to (a) all path-oriented coverage criteria, such as all-uses coverage and MC/DC coverage, and (b) all mutants obtained by using the mutation operators in Table 7.14. It would be best to complete this exercise using a mutation tool. If necessary, translate hamletFunction into C if you have access to Proteum or Java if you have access to μJava.

7.23 Let M be a mutant of program P generated by applying some mutation operator. Suppose that M is equivalent to P. Despite the equivalence, M might be a useful program, and perform better (or worse) than P. Examine Hoare's FIND program and its mutant obtained by replacing the conditional I.GT.F, labeled 70, by FALSE. Is the mutant equivalent to its parent? Does it perform better or worse than the original program? (See the reference to FIND program on page 596.)

7.24 Let $MS(X)$ denote the mutation score of test set X with respect to some program and a set of mutation operators. Let T_A be a test set for application A and $U_A \subseteq T_A$. Develop an efficient minimization algorithm to construct $T'_A = T_A - U_A$ such that (a) $MS(T_A) = MS(T'_A)$ and (b) for any $T''_A \subset T_A, |T'_A| < |T''_A|$. (Note:

Such minimization algorithms are useful in the removal of tests that are redundant with respect to the mutation-adequacy criterion. One could construct similar algorithms for minimization of a test set with respect to any other quantitative-adequacy criterion.)

7.25 Suppose a class *C* contains an overloaded method with three versions. What is the minimum number of mutants generated when the OAN operator is applied to *C*?

7.26 The following are believed to be *myths of mutation*. Do you agree?

1. It is an error-seeding approach.
2. It is too expensive relative to other test-adequacy criteria.
3. It is *harder* than other coverage-based test methods in the sense that it requires a tester to think much more while developing a mutation-adequate test.
4. It discovers only simple errors.
4. It is applicable only to unit-level testing.
6. It is applicable only to numerical programs, for example a program that inverts a matrix.

7.27 Consider the following program originally due to Jeff Voas, Larry Morell, and Keith MIller:

```
1 bool noSolution=false;
2 int vmmFunction (a, b, c: int){
3  real x;
4  if (a ≠ 0){
5    d=b*b-5*a*c;   ← Constant 5 should be 4.
6    if (d < 0)
7      x=0;
8    else
9      x=(−b + trunc(sqrt(d)));
10   }
11   else
12     x= −c div b;
13   if(a * x * x + b * x + c == 0)
14     return(x);
15   else {
16     noSolution=true;
17     return(0);
18   }
19 }
```

Given inputs a, b, and c, vmmFunction is required to find an integral solution to the quadratic equation $a * x^2 + b * x + c = 0$. If an integral solution exists, the program returns with the solution, if not then it sets the global variable noSolution to true and returns a 0. Function vmmFunction has a fault at line 5—constant 5 should be a 4.

1. Consider the set M_W of mutants created by applying the mutation operators suggested by Wong, as in Table 7.16, to vmmFunction. Is any mutant in M_W error revealing?
2. Now consider the set M_O of mutants created by applying the mutation operators suggested by Offutt, as in Table 7.16, to vmmFunction. Is any mutant in M_O error revealing?
3. Next, suppose that we have fixed the fault at line 5 but line 6 now contains a fault, the faulty condition being d ≤ 0. Is there any error-revealing mutant of vmmFunction in M_W? M_O? (Note that M_W and M_O are now created by applying the mutation operators to vmmFunction with the fault in the condition at line 6.)

It might be best to do this exercise with the help of a tool such as Proteum or μJava. When using a tool, you will need to translate the pseudocode of vmmFuntion into C or Java as appropriate.

7.28 Program P7.4 shows a function named count that is required to read a character and an integer value. If the character input is "a" then the entry a[value] is incremented by one. If the character input is a "b" then entry b[value] is incremented by one. The input value is ignored for all other characters. The value input must satisfy the condition $0 \leq$ value $< N$.

The function count is supposed to read the input until it gets an end-of-file character, denoted by eof, when it terminates. Arrays a and b are global to the function. Note that as shown here, count does not check if the input value is in its intended range. Thus, an input integer value could force the function, and its containerprogram, to misbehave.

Program P7.4

```
1 #define N=10
2 int a[N], b[N];
3 void count(){
4 char code; int value;
5 for (i = 1; i ≤ N; i + +){
```

```
 6    a[i]=0;
 7    b[i]=0;
 8  }
 9  while (¬ eof){
10  input(code, value);
11  if (code=='a')a[value] = a[value] + 1;
12    elseif (code=='b') b[value] = b[value] + 1;
13  }
14 }
```

(a) Is it possible to develop a test set that is adequate with respect to the MC/DC-coverage criterion such that the input integer value is within its intended range in each test case?

(b) Is it possible to develop a test set that is adequate with respect to the all-uses-coverage criterion such that the input integer value is within its intended range in each test case?

(c) Is it possible to develop a test set that is adequate with respect to the mutation criterion such that the input integer value is within its intended range in each test case? Assume that all traditional mutation operators listed in Table 7.14 are used.

7.29 Some programming languages provide the set type. Java provides a SET interface. Specification language Z, functional language Miranda, and procedural language SETL are examples of languages that provide the set type. Consider a mutation operator named SM—abbreviation for set mutation. SM is applied to any object of type set in a specification. Thus, the application of SM to specification S_1 mutates it to another specification S_2 by changing the contents of an object defined as a set.

(a) Develop a suitable semantics for SM. Note that traditional mutation operators such as variable replacement will replace an object x of type set with another object y defined in the same program. However, SM is different in that it mutates the value of a set object in a specification.

(b) Think of applying SM to a program during execution by mutating the value of a set object when it is referenced. Why would such a mutation be useful?

REFERENCES

[1] Abdurazik, A., P. Ammann, W. Ding, and A. J. Offutt (September 2000). "Evaluation of three specification-based testing criteria." In *Proceedings of the Sixth International Conference on Engineering of Complex Computer Systems, 2000, ICECCS 2000,* pp. 179–187. Los Alamites, CA: IEEE Press.

[2] Abraham, J. A. and W. K. Fuchs (1986). "Fault and error models for VLSI." In *Proceedings of the IEEE,* Vol. 74, pp. 639–654. Piscataway, NJ.

[3] Acree, A. T. (1980). *On Mutation,* Ph.D. thesis. Atlanta, GA: Georgia Institute of Technology.

[4] Adrion, W. R., M. A. Branstad, and J. C. Cherniavsky (1982). "Validation, verification and testing of computer software," *ACM Computing Surveys,* **14**(2): 159–192.

[5] Aggrawal, K. K., Y. Singh, and A. Kaur (2004). "Code coverage based technique for prioritizing test cases for regression testing," *SIGSOFT Software Engineering Notes,* **29**(5): 1–4.

[6] Agrawal, H. (August 1991). *Towards Automatic Debugging of Computer Programs.* Ph.D. thesis. Indiana: Purdue University,

[7] Agrawal, H. "Towards automatic debugging of computer programs." Technical report SERC-TR-193-P, Purdue University, Indiana, August 1991.

[8] Agrawal, H. (1994). "Dominators, super blocks, and program coverage." In *Proceedings of POPL 94,* pp. 25–34. New York, NY: AMC Press.

[9] Agrawal, H., R. A. DeMillo, R. Hathaway, W. M. Hsu, W. Hsu, E. W.Krauser, R. J. Martin, A. P. Mathur, and E. H. Spafford. "Design of mutant operators for the C programming language." Technical report SERC-TR-41-P, Purdue University, West Lafayette, IN, 1989.

[10] Agrawal, H., R. A. DeMillo, and E. H. Spafford (1991). "Dynamic slicing in the presence of unconstrained pointers." In *TAV4: Proceedings of the Symposium on Testing, Analysis, and Verification,* pp. 60–73. New York, NY: ACM Press.

[11] Agrawal, H. and J. R. Horgan (1990). "Dynamic program slicing." In *PLDI '90: Proceedings of the ACM SIGPLAN 1990 Conference on Programming Language Design and Implementation,* pp. 246–256. New York, NY: ACM Press.

[12] Agrawal, H., J. R. Horgan, E. W. Krauser, and S. London (1993). "Incremental regression testing." In *ICSM '93: Proceedings of the Conference on Software Maintenance,* pp. 348–357. Washington, DC: IEEE Computer Society Press.

[13] Agrawal, V. D., S. C. Seth, and P. Agrawal (February 1982). "Fault coverage requirement in production testing of LSI circuit," *IEEE Journal of Solid-State Circuits*, **17**(1): 57–61.

[14] Agustin, J. M. (May 2003). *Improving Software Quality Through Extreme Coverage with JBlanket*. Master's thesis. Hawaii: University of Hawaii.

[15] Aho, A. V., A. T. Dahbura, D. Lee, and M. U. Uyar (1991). "An optimization technique for protocol conformance test generation based on UIO sequences and rural Chinese postman tours," *IEEE Transactions on Communications*, **39**(11): 1604–1615.

[16] Aho, A. V., R. Sethi, and J. D. Ullman (January 1986). *Compilers: Principles, Techniques, and Tools*. Addison-Wesley.

[17] Aho, A. V., R. Sethi, and J. D. Ullman (1986). *Compilers: Principles, Techniques, and Tools*. Boston, MA: Addison-Wesley Longman Publishing Co., Inc.

[18] Aichernig, B. K. (2002). "Contract-based mutation testing in the refinement calculus." In *REFINE02, Formal Aspects of Computing Refinement Workshop*. Atlanta, GA: Elsevier.

[19] Alexander, R. T., J. M. Bieman, S. Ghosh, and B. Ji (November 2002). "Mutation of Java objects." In *Proceedings of the 13th IEEE International Symposium on Software Reliability Engineering (ISSRE 2002)*. Los Alamitos, CA: IEEE Press.

[20] Amla, N. and P. Ammann (1992). "Using Z specifications in category partition testing." In *Proceeding of the Seventh Annual Conference on Computer Assurance*, June 1992, pp. 3–10.

[21] Ammann, P. (2000). System testing via mutation analysis of model checking specifications. SIGSOFT *Software Engineering Notes*, **25**(1): 33.

[22] Andre, D. M. S. (April 1979). "Pilot mutation system (PIMS) user's manual." Technical report GIT-ICS-79/04, Georgia Institute of Technology, Atlanta, GA.

[23] Andrews, J. H., L. C. Briand, and Y. Labiche. (2005) "Is mutation an appropriate tool for testing experiments?" In *ICSE '05: Proceedings of the 27th International Conference on Software Engineering*, pp. 402–411. New York, NY: ACM Press.

[24] Apiwattanapong, T., A. Orso, and M. J. Harrold (2004). A differencing algorithm for object-oriented programs." In *ASE '04: Proceedings of the 19th IEEE International Conference on Automated Software Engineering*, pp. 2–13, Washington, DC: IEEE Computer Society Press.

[25] Apiwattanapong, T., A. Orso, and M. J. Harrold (2007). "Jdiff: A differencing technique and tool for object-oriented programs," *Journal of Automated Software Engineering* (submitted for publication) **14**(1), pp. 3–36.

[26] Appel, A. W. (1998). *Modern Compiler Implementation in Java*. New York, NY: Cambridge University Press.

[27] Baker, A. L. and S. H. Zweben (November 1980). "A comparison of measures of control flow complexity," *IEEE Transactions on Software Engineering*, **SE-6**(6): 506–512.

[28] Balcer, M. J., W. Hasling, and T. J. Ostrand (1989). "Automatic generation of test scripts from formal test specifications." *In TAV3: Proceedings of the ACM*

SIGSOFT '89 Third Symposium on Software Testing, Analysis, and Verification, pp. 210–18. New York, NY: ACM Press.

[29] Baldwin, D. and F. G. Sayward (1979). "Heuristics for determining equivalence of program mutations." Technical research report no. 276, Department of Computer Science, Yale University, New Haven, CT.

[30] Ball, T. (1993). *The Use of Control-Flow and Control Dependence in Software Tools*. Ph.D. thesis, Madison, WI: University of Wisconsin—Madison.

[31] Ball, T. and J. R. Larus (1994). "Optimally profiling and tracing programs," *ACM Transactions on Programming Languages and Systems*, **16**(4): 1319–1360.

[32] Basili, V. R., L. C. Briand, and W. L. Melo (1996). "A validation of object-oriented design metrics as quality indicators," *IEEE Transactions Software Engineering*, **22**(10): 751–761.

[33] Bates, S. and S. Horwitz (1993). Incremental program testing using program dependence graphs. In *POPL '93: Proceedings of the 20th ACM SIGPLAN-SIGACT Symposium on Principles of Programming Languages*, pp. 384–396. New York, NY: ACM Press.

[34] Bazzichi, F. and I. Spadafora (July 1982). "An automatic generator for compiler testing," *IEEE Transactions on Software Engineering*, **SE-84**: 343–353.

[35] Beizer, B. (1990). *Software Testing Techniques*, 2nd edition. New York: Van Nostrand Reinhold.

[36] Belina, F. and D. Hogrefe (1989). "The CCIT-specification and description language SDL," *Computer Networks and ISDN Systems*, **16**(4): 311–341.

[37] Belina, F., D. Hogrefe, and A. Sarma (1991). *SDL with Applications from Protocol Specification*. Upper Saddle River, NJ: Prentice-Hall, Inc.

[38] Belli, F. (2001). "Finite state testing and analysis of graphical user interfaces." In *ISSRE 2001: Proceedings of the 12th International Symposium on Software Reliability Engineering*, pp. 34–43. Los Alamitos, CA: IEEE Computer Society Press.

[39] Belli, F., C. J. Budnik, and N. Nissanke (2004). "Finite-state modeling, analysis, and testing of system vulnerabilities." In *Proceedings of the 17th International Conference on Architecture of Computing Systems (ARCS), March 2004*, Vol. 2981, pp. 19–33. Springer-Verlag.

[40] Belli, F. and J. Dreyer (1997). "Program segmentation for controlling test coverage." In *Proceedings of the Eight International Symposium on Software Reliability Engineering (ISSRE 1997), Albuquerque, NM, November 1997*, pp. 72–83. Los Alamitos, CA: IEEE Press.

[41] Benedusi, P., A. Cmitili, and U. De Carlini (1988). "Post-maintenance testing based on path change analysis." In *Proceedings of the Conference on Software Maintenance, October 1988*, pp. 352–361.

[42] Benjamin, M., D. Geist, A. Hartman, G. Mas, R. Smeets, and Y.Wolfsthal (1999). "A study in coverage-driven test generation." In *DAC '99: Proceedings of the 36th ACM/IEEE Conference on Design Automation*, pp. 970–975. New York, NY: ACM Press.

[43] Bernhard, P. J. (1994). "A reduced test suite for protocol conformance testing," *ACM Transactions Software Engineering Methodology*, **3**(3): 201–220.

[44] Bible, J., G. Rothermel, and D. S. Rosenblum (2001). "A comparative study of coarse- and fine-grained safe regression test-selection techniques," *ACM Transactions on Software Engineering Methodology*, **10**(2): 149–183.

[45] Bieman, J. M., S. Ghosh, and R. T. Alexander (November 2001). "A technique for mutation of Java objects." In *Proceedings of the 16th IEEE International Conference on Automated Software Engineering (ASE 2001)*, pp. 337–340. Los Alamitos, CA: IEEE Press.

[46] Bieman, J. M. and H. Yin (1992). "Designing for software testability using automated oracles." In *Proceedings of International Test Conference, September 1992*, pp. 900–907. Los Alamitos, CA: IEEE Press.

[47] Biffl, S. (2003). "Evaluating defect estimation models with major defects," *Journal of System Software*, **65**(1): 13–29.

[48] Binkley, D. (March–December 1993). "Precise executable interprocedural slices," *ACM Letters on Programming Languages and Systems*, **2**(1–4): 31–45.

[49] Binkley, D. (1997). "Semantics guided regression test cost reduction," *IEEE Transactions on Software Engineering*, **23**(8): 498–516.

[50] Black, P. E., V. Okun, and Y. Yesha (2000). "Mutation operators for specifications." *In Automated Software Engineering*, pp. 81–88. Springer, Netherlands.

[51] Boardman, D. B., G. Greene, V. Khandelwal, and A. P. Mathur (1995). "Listen: A tool to investigate the use of sound for the analysis of program behavior." In *Proceedings of IEEE COMPSAC (Computer Software and Applications)*, pp. 184–191. Los Alamitos, CA: IEEE Press.

[52] Bochmann, G. v., R. Dssouli, and J. R. Zhao (November 1989). "Trace analysis for conformance and arbitration testing," *IEEE Transactions on Software Engineering*, **15**: 1347–1356.

[53] Boehm, B. W., J. R. Brown, and M. Lipow (1976). "Quantitative evaluation of software quality." In *ICSE '76: Proceedings of the Second International Conference on Software Engineering*, pp. 592–605. Los Alamitos, CA: IEEE Computer Society Press.

[54] Boehm, B. W., R. K. McClean, and D. B. Urfrig (March 1975). "Some experience with automated aids to the design of large-scale reliable software," *IEEE Transactions on Software Engineering*, **SE-1**(1): 125–133.

[55] Bose, R. C., I. M. Chakravarti, and D. E. Knuth (November 1960). "On methods of constructing sets of mutually orthogonal Latin squares using a computer. I," *Technometrics*, **2**(4): 507–516.

[56] Bose, R. C., I. M. Chakravarti, and D. E. Knuth (November 1961). On methods of constructing sets of mutually orthogonal Latin squares using a computer. II," *Technometrics*, **3**(4): 111–117.

[57] Bose, R. C., S. S. Shrikhande, and E. T. Parker (1960). "Further results on the construction of mutually orthogonal Latin squares and the falsity of Euler's conjecture," *Canadian Journal of Mathematics*, **12**: 189–203.

[58] Brownlie, R., P. James Prowse, and M. S. Phadke (1992). "Robust testing of AT&T PMX/StarMail using OATS," *AT&T Technical Journal*, **71**(3): 41–47.

[59] Bryce, R. C. and C. J. Colbourn (2005). "Test prioritization for pairwise interaction coverage." In *A-MOST '05: Proceedings of the First International Workshop on Advances in Model-Based Testing*, pp. 1–7. New York, NY: ACM Press.

[60] Buchsbaum, A. L., H. Kaplan, A. Rogers, and J. R. Westbrook (1998). "A new, simpler linear-time dominators algorithm," *ACM Transactions on Programming Languages and Systems*, **20**(6): 1265–1296.

[61] Budd, T. A (1980). *Mutation Analysis of Program Test Data*. Ph.D. thesis. New Haven, CT: Yale University.

[62] Budd, T. A. (July 1981). "Mutation analysis: Ideas, examples, problems and prospects." In *Computer Program Testing*, (B. Chandrasekaran and S. Radicchi, eds.), pp. 129–148. New York, NY: Elsevier Science.

[63] Budd, T. A., R. A. DeMillo, R. J. Lipton, and F. G. Sayward (1980). "Theoretical and empirical studies on using program mutation to test the functional correctness of programs." In *POPL '80: Proceedings of the Seventh ACM SIGPLAN-SIGACT Symposium on Principles of Programming Languages*, pp. 220–233. New York, NY: ACM Press.

[64] Budd, T. A., and A. S. Gopal (1985). "Program testing by specification mutation," *Computer Languages*, **10**(1): 63–73.

[65] Budd, T. A. and R. J. Lipton (1978). "Mutation analysis of decision table programs." In *Proceedings of the 1978 Conference on Informatlon Science and Systems*, pp. 346–349. Baltimore, MD: Johns Hopkins University.

[66] Budd, T. A. and R. J. Lipton (1978). "Proving LISP programs using test data." In *Digest for the Workshop on Software Testing and Test Documentation*, pp. 374–403. New York, NY: ACM Press.

[67] Burke, M. and R. Cytron (1986). "Interprocedural dependence analysis and parallelization." In *SIGPLAN '86: Proceedings of the 1986 SIGPLAN symposium on Compiler construction*, pp. 162–175. New York, NY: ACM Press.

[68] Burr, K. and W. Young (1998). "Combinatorial test techniques: Table-based automation, test generation, and test coverage." In *Proceedings of the International Conference on Software Testing*, Analysis, and Review, October 1998, pp. 503–513.

[69] Burton., S. (March 2002). *Automated Generation of High Integrity Test Suits from Graphical Specifications*. Ph.D. thesis. Department of Computer Science, University of York, York, UK.

[70] Bush, K. A. (1950). *Orthogonal Arrays*. Ph.D. thesis. Chapel Hill, North Carolina: University of North Carolina.

[71] Bybro, M. (August 2003). *A Mutation Testing Tool for Java Programs*. Master's thesis. Stockholm, Sweden: Department of Numerical Analysis and Computer Science, Royal Institute of Technology.

[72]   Celentano, A., S. C. Reghizzi, P. Della Vigna, C. Ghezzi, G. Granata, and F. Savoretti (1980). "Compiler testing using a sentence generator," *Software–Practice and Experience*, **10**: 897–918.

[73]   Chaim, M. L. (April 1991). Poke-tool–uma ferramenta para suporte ao teste estrutural de programas baseado em análise de fluxo de dados (in Portugese). Master's thesis. Campinas, Campinas, Brazil: DCA/FEEC/Unicamp.

[74]   Chan, W. Y. L., C. T. Vuong, and M. R. Otp (1989). "An improved protocol test generation procedure based on UIOS." In *Symposium Proceedings on Communications Architectures and Protocols*, pp. 283–294. ACM Press.

[75]   Chen, T. Y. and M. F. Lau (1997). "Two test data selection strategies towards testing of Boolean specifications." In *Proceedings of the 21st Annual International Computer Software and Applications Conference, 13–15 August 1997*, pp. 608–611. Los Alamitos, CA: IEEE Press.

[76]   Chen, T. Y., M. F. Lau, and Y. T. Yu (1999). "Mumcut: A fault-based strategy for testing Boolean specifications." In *APSEC '99: Proceedings of the Sixth Asia Pacific Software Engineering Conference*, p. 606. Washington, DC: IEEE Computer Society Press,

[77]   Chen, T. Y. and Y. T. Yu (December 1994). "On the relationship between partition and random testing," *IEEE Transactions on Software Engineering*, **20**(12): 977–980.

[78]   Chen, T. Y. and Y. T. Yu (February 1996). "A more general sufficient condition for partition testing to be better than random testing," *Information Processing Letters*, **57**(3): 145–149.

[79]   Chen, Y.-F., D. S. Rosenblum, and K.-P. Vo (1994). "Test Tube: a system for selective regression testing." In *ICSE '94: Proceedings of the 16th International Conference on Software Engineering*, pp. 211–220. IEEE Computer Society Press.

[80]   Chidamber, S. R., D. P. Darcy, and C. F. Kemerer (1998). "Managerial use of metrics for object-oriented software: An exploratory analysis," *IEEE Transactions Software Engineering*, **24**(8): 629–639.

[81]   Chidamber, S. R. and C. F. Kemerer (1994). "A metrics suite for object oriented design," *IEEE Transactions Software Engineering*, **20**(6): 476–493.

[82]   Chilenski, J. J. and S. P. Miller (September 1994). "Applicability of modified condition/decision coverage to software testing," *Software Engineering Journal*, **9**(5): 193–200.

[83]   Choi, B. (1990). *Software Testing Using High Performance Computers*. Ph.D. thesis. West Lafayette, IN: Purdue University. Advisor: Aditya P. Mathur.

[84]   Choi, B., and A. P. Mathur (1989). "Experience with PMothra: A tool for mutant based testing on a hypercube." In *Proceedings of Distributed and Multiprocessor Systems Workshop, October 1989*, pp. 237–254. Berkeley, CA: USENIX.

[85]   Choi, B. and A. P. Mathur. "Use of fifth generation computers for high performance reliable software testing (final report)." Technical report

SERCTR-72-P, Software Engineering Research Center, Purdue University, West Lafayette, IN, April 1990.

[86] Choi, B. and A. P. Mathur (February 1993). "High performance mutation testing," *Journal of Systems and Software*, **20**(2): 135–152.

[87] Choi, B., A. P. Mathur, and B. Pattison (1989). "PMothra: Scheduling mutants for execution on a hypercube." In *TAV3: Proceedings of the ACM SIGSOFT '89 third Symposium on Software Testing, Analysis, and Verification*, pp. 58–65. New York, NY: ACM Press.

[88] Chow, T. S. (May 1978). "Testing software design modelled by finite state machines," *IEEE Transactions on Software Engineering*, **SE-4**(3): 178–187.

[89] Chusho, T. (1987). "Test data selection and quality estimation based on the concept of essential branches for path testing," *IEEE Transactions on Software Engineering*, **13**(5): 509–517.

[90] Chvltal, V. (1979). "A greedy heuristic for the set-covering problem," *Mathematics of Operations Research*, **4**: 233–235.

[91] Clarke, E. M., E. A. Emerson, and A. P. Sistla (1986). "Automatic verification of finite-state concurrent systems using temporal logic specifications," *ACM Transactions on Programming Languages and Systems*, **8**(2): 244–263.

[92] Clarke, E. M., O. Grumberg, and D. A. Peled (2000). *Model Checking*. Cambridge, MA: The MIT Press.

[93] Clarke, L. A., A. Podgurski, D. J. Richardson, and S. J. Zeil (1985). "A comparison of data flow path selection criteria." In *ICSE '85: Proceedings of the Eighth International Conference on Software Engineering*, pp. 244–251. Los Alamitos, CA: IEEE Computer Society Press.

[94] Clarke, L. A., A. Podgurski, D. J. Richardson, and S. J. Zeil (1989). "A formal evaluation of data flow path selection criteria," *IEEE Transactions on Software Engineering*, **15**(11): 1318–1332.

[95] Cohen, D. M., S. R. Dalal, M. L. Fredman, and G. C. Patton (September 1996). "The combinatorial design approach to automatic test generation," *IEEE Software*, 13(5): 83–89.

[96] Cohen, D. M., S. R. Dalal, M. L. Fredman, and G. C. Patton (July 1997). "The AETG system: An approach to testing based on combinatorial design," *IEEE Transactions on Software Engineering*, **23**(7): 437–443.

[97] Cohen, D. M., S. R. Dalal, A. Kajla, and G. C. Patton (1994). "The automatic efficient tests generator." In *Procedings of the Fifth International Symposium on Software Reliability*, pp. 303–309. Los Alamitos, CA: IEEE Press.

[98] Cohen, D. M., S. R. Dalal, J. Parelius, and G. C. Patton (September 1996). "The combinatorial design approach to automatic test generation," *IEEE Software*, **13**(5): 83–89.

[99] Cohen, D. M. and M. L. Fredman. "New techniques for designing qualitatively independent systems." Technical report DCS-96-114, Rutgers University, New Jersey, November 1996.

[100] Cohen, M. B., C. J. Colbourn, and A. C. H. Ling (2003). "Augmenting simulated annealing to build interaction test suites." In *14th IEEE International*

Symposium on Software Reliability Engineering (ISSRE 2003), November 2003, pp. 394–405.

[101] Cohen, M. B., P. B. Gibbons, W. B. Mugridge, and C. J. Colbourn (2003). "Constructing test suites for interaction testing." In *Proceedings of the 25th International Conference on Software Engineering*, pp. 38–48. Los Alamitos, CA: IEEE Computer Society.

[102] Colbourn, C. J. and J. H. Dinitz (2001). "Mutually orthogonal Latin squares: A brief survey of constructions," *Journal of Statistical Planning and Inference*, **95**: 9–48.

[103] Colbourn, D. M. and J. H. Dinitz (eds.) (1996). *The CRC Handbook of Combinatorial Design*. CRC Press.

[104] Conte, S. D., H. E. Dunsmore, and V. Y. Shen (1986). *Software Engineering Metrics and Models*. San Francisco, CA: The Benjamin/Cummings Publishing Company, Inc.

[105] Dalal, S. R., A. Jain, N. Karunanithi, J. Leaton, and C. Lott (1998). "Model-based testing of a highly programmable system." In *Proceedings of the Ninth International Symposium on Software Reliability Engineering, November 1998* (Fevzi Belli, ed.), pp. 174–178.

[106] Dalal, S. R., A. Jain, and J. Poore (2005). "Workshop on advances in model-based software testing." In *Proceedings of the 27th International Conference on Software Engineering*, p. 860. St Louis: IEEE Press.

[107] Dalal, S. R. and C. L. Mallows (1998). "Factor-covering designs for testing software," Technometrics, **40**(3): 234–243.

[108] Daran, M. and P. Thèvenod-Fosse (1996). "Software error analysis: A real case study involving real faults and mutations."In *ISSTA '96: Proceedings of the 1996 ACM SIGSOFT International Symposium on Software Testing and Analysis,* pp. 158–171. New York, NY: ACM Press.

[109] Davis, E. "Software testing for evolutionary iterative rapid prototyping." Technical report, National Technical Information Service (NTIS). Naval Postgraduate School, Monterey, CA: 1990.

[110] Delamaro, M. E. (June 1997). *Mutação de interface: um critério de ade-quação interprocedemental para o teste de integração*. Ph.D. thesis. São Carlos: Physics Institute of São Carlos, University of São Paulo.

[111] Delamaro, M. E. and J. C. Maldonado (1999). "Interface mutation: Assessing testing quality at interprocedural level." In *Proceedings of SCCC '99 19th International Conference of the Chilean Computer Society*, pp. 78–86. Los Alamitos, CA: IEEE Press.

[112] Delamaro, M. E., J. C. Maldonado, and A. P. Mathur (1996). "Integration testing using interface mutation." In *Proceedings Seventh International Symposium on Software Reliability Engineering, October–November 1996,* pp. 112–121. Los Alamitos, CA: IEEE Computer Society.

[113] Delamaro, M. E., J. C. Maldonado, and A. P. Mathur (March 2001). "Interface mutation: An approach for integration testing," *IEEE Transactions on Software Engineering*, **27**(3): 228–247.

[114] Delamaro, M. E., J. C. Maldonado, and A. Vincenzi (October 2000). "Proteum/IM 2.0: An integrated mutation testing environment." In *Proceedings of Mutation 2000: Mutation Testing in the Twentieth Century*, Boston, MA: Kluwer Academic Publishers.

[115] DeMillo, R. A. (1980). "Mutation analysis as a tool for software quality assurance." In *Proceedings of COMPSAC'80*, October 1980. Los Alamitos, CA: IEEE Press.

[116] DeMillo, R. A. "Program mutation: An approach to software testing." Technical report, Georgia Institute of Technology, Atlanta, GA, 1983.

[117] DeMillo, R. A. (1991). " Progress toward automated software testing." In *ICSE '91: Proceedings of the 13th International Conference on Software Engineering*, pp. 180–183. Los Alamitos, CA: IEEE Computer Society Press.

[118] DeMillo, R. A., D. S. Guindi, K. N. King, W. M. McCracken, and A. J. Offutt. (July 1988). "An extended overview of the MOTHRA testing environment." In *Proceedings of the Second Workshop on Software Testing, Verification, and Analysis*, Banff, Canada.

[119] DeMillo, R. A., E. W. Krauser, and A. P. Mathur (1991). "Compiler integrated program mutation." In *Proceedings of COMPSAC'91*, pp. 351–356. Tokyo, Japan: IEEE Computer Society Press.

[120] DeMillo, R. A., R. J. Lipton, and A. J. Perlis (1977). "Social processes and proofs of theorems and programs." In *POPL '77: Proceedings of the Fourth ACM SIGACT-SIGPLAN Symposium on Principles of Programming Languages*, pp. 206–214. New York, NY: ACM Press.

[121] DeMillo, R. A., R. J. Lipton, and A. J. Perlis (1978). "Response from R. A. DeMillo and R. J. Lipton and A. J. Perlis," *SIGSOFT Software Engineering Notes*, **3**(2): 16–17.

[122] DeMillo, R. A., R. J. Lipton, and F. G. Sayward (April 1978). "Hints on test data selection," *IEEE Computer*, **11**(4): 34–41.

[123] DeMillo, R. A., and A. P. Mathur (February 1991). "On the use of software artifacts to evaluate the effectiveness of mutation analysis for detecting errors in production software." Technical report SERC-TR-92-P, Software Engineering Research Center, Purdue University, West Lafayette, IN.

[124] DeMillo, R. A. and A. P. Mathur (September 1995). "A grammar based fault classification scheme and its application to the classification of the errors of TEX." Technical report SERC-TR-165-P, Software Engineering Research Center, Purdue University, West Lafayette, IN.

[125] DeMillo, R. A., W. M. McCracken, R. J. Martin, and J. F. Passafiume (January 1987). *Software Testing and Evaluation*. Menlo Park, CA: The Benjamin/Cummings Publishing Company.

[126] DeMillo, R. A. and A. J. Offutt (1991). "Constraint based automatic test data generation." *IEEE Transactions on Software Engineering*, **17**(9): 900–910.

[127] DeMillo, R. A. and A. J. Offutt (April 1993). "Experimental results from an automatic test case generator," *ACM Transactions on Software Engineering Methodology*, 2(2):109–127.

[128] DeMillo, R. A. and A. J. Offutt (1993) "Experimental results from an automatic test case generator," *ACM Transactions Software Engineering Methodology*, **2**(2): 109–127.

[129] Dénes, J. and A. D. Keedwell (1974). *Latin Squares and Their Applications.* New York, Amsterdam: Academic Press.

[130] deSouza, D. S., J. C. Maldonado, S. C. P. F. Fabbri, and L. W. deSouza (2000). "Mutation testing applied to Estelle specifications." In *Proceedings of the 33rd Annual Hawaii International Conference on System Sciences, January 2000*, Vol. 1, pp. 1–10. Los Alamitos, CA: IEEE Press.

[131] Do, H., G. Rothermel, and A. Kinneer (2004). "Empirical studies of test case prioritization in a JUnit testing environment." In *Proceedings of International Symposium on Software Reliability Engineering*, pp. 113–124. Los Alamitos, CA: IEEE Press.

[132] Do, H., G. Rothermel, and A. Kinneer (March 2006). "Prioritizing JUnit test cases: An empirical assessment and cost-benefits analysis," *Empirical Software Engineering*, **11**(1): 33–70.

[133] Druseikis, A. and C. Frederick. "Syntax errors and their impact on recovery schemes and language design." Technical report, Computer Science Department, University of Arizona, Tucson, 1977.

[134] Duncan, A. G. and J. S. Hutchison (1981). "Using attributed grammars to test designs and implementations." In *ICSE '81: Proceedings of the Fifth International Conference on Software Engineering*, pp. 170–178. Piscataway, NJ: IEEE Press.

[135] Duran J. and S. C. Ntafos (July 1984). "An evaluation of random testing." *IEEE Transactions on Software Engineering*, **SE-10**(4): 438–444.

[136] Vranken, H. P. E., M. F. Witteman, and R. C. van Wuijtswinkel (1996). "Design for testability in hardware-software systems," *IEEE Design Test*, **13**(3): 79–87.

[137] El-Fakih, K., N. Yevtushenko, and G. v. Bochmann (2004). "FSM-based incremental conformance testing methods," *IEEE Transactionson Software Engineering*, **30**(7): 425–436.

[138] Elbaum, S., A. G. Malishevsky, and G. Rothermel (2000). "Prioritizing test cases for regression testing." In *ISSTA '00: Proceedings of the 2000 ACM SIG-SOFT International Symposium on Software Testing and Analysis*, pp. 102–112. New York, NY: ACM Press.

[139] Elbaum, S., G. Rothermel, S. Kanduri, and A. G. Malishevsky (2004). "Selecting a cost-effective test case prioritization technique," *Software Quality Control*, **12**(3): 185–210.

[140] Elmendorf, W. R. (October 1969). "Controlling the functional testing of an operating system," *IEEE Transactions on Systems, Science, and Cybernetics*, **SSC-5**(4): 284–289.

[141] Euler, L. (1782). "Recherches sur une nouvelle espèce de quarrés magiques. Verh. Zeeuwsch Gen. Wetensch," *Vlissingen*, **9**: 85–239.

[142] Fabbri, S. C. P. F., M. E. Delamaro, J. C. Maldonado, and P. C. Masiero (1994). "Mutation analysis testing for finite state machines." In *Proceedings of the*

Fifth International Symposium on Software Reliability Engineering, November 1994, pp. 220–229. Los Alamitos, CA: IEEE Press.

[143]   Fabbri, S. C. P. F., J. C. Maldonado, P. C. Masiero, and M. E. Delamaro (1999). "A tool to support finite state machine validation based on mutation testing." In *Proceedings of the 19th International Conference of the Chilean Computer Science Society, November 1999*, pp. 96–104. Los Alamitos, CA: IEEE Press.

[144]   Fabbri, S. C. P. F., J. C. Maldonado, T. Sugeta, and P. C. Masiero (1999). "Mutation testing applied to validate specifications based on statecharts." In *Proceedings of the 10th International Symposium on Software Reliability Engineering*, pp. 210–219. Los Alamitos, CA: IEEE Press.

[145]   Fenton, N. E. and N. Ohlsson (August 2000). "Quantitative analysis of faults and failures in a complex software system," *IEEE Transactions on Software Engineering*, **26**(8): 797–814.

[146]   Ferrante, J., K. J. Ottenstein, and J. D. Warren (1984). "The program dependence graph and its use in optimization." In *Proceedings of the 6th Colloquium on International Symposium on Programming*, pp. 125–132. London: Springer-Verlag.

[147]   Fischer, K., F. Raji, and A. Chruscicki (1981). "A methodology for retesting modified software." In *Proceedings of the National Telecommunications Conference*, Vol. B-6-3, pp. 1–6. Piscataway, NJ: IEEE Press.

[148]   Fleyshgakker, V. N. and S. N. Weiss (1994). "Efficient mutation analysis: A new approach." In *ISSTA '94: Proceedings of the 1994 ACM SIGSOFT International Symposium on Software Testing and Analysis*, pp. 185–195. New York, NY: ACM Press.

[149]   Fosdick, L. D. and L. Osterweil (September 1976). "Data flow analysis in software reliability," *Computing Surveys*, **8**(3): 305–330.

[150]   Foster, K. A. (May 1980). "Error sensitive test case analysis (ESTCA)," *IEEE Transactions on Software Engineering*, **SE-6**(3): 258–264.

[151]   Foster, K. A. (April 1984). "Sensitive test data for logic expressions," *ACM SIGSOFT Software Engineering Notes*, **9**(6): 120–126.

[152]   Frankl, P. G. and S. N. Weiss (1993). "An experimental comparison of the effectiveness of branch testing and and data flow testing," *IEEE Transactions on Software Engineering*, **19**(8): 774–787.

[153]   Frankl, P. G., S. N. Weiss, and C. Hu (1997). "All-uses vs mutation testing: An experimental comparison of effectiveness," *Journal of Systems and Software*, **38**(3): 235–253.

[154]   Frankl, P. G. and E. J.Weyuker (1985). "A data flow testing tool." In *Proceedings of the Second Conference on Software Development Tools, Techniques, and Alternatives*, pp. 46–53. Los Alamitos, CA: IEEE Computer Society Press.

[155]   Frankl, P. G. and E. J. Weyuker (1993). "An analytical comparison of the fault detecting ability of data flow testing techniques." In *ICSE '93: Proceedings of the 15th International Conference on Software Engineering*, pp. 415–424. Los Alamitos, CA: IEEE Computer Society Press.

[156]   Del Frate, F., P. Garg, A. P. Mathur, and A. Pasquini (1995). "On the correlation between code coverage and software reliability." In *Proceedings of the Sixth International Symposium on Software Reliability Engineering, October 1995*, pp. 124–132. Los Alamitos, CA: IEEE Press.

[157]   Fujiwara, S., G. v. Bochmann, F. Khendek, M. Amalou, and A. Ghedamsi (June 1991). "Test selection based on finite state models," *IEEE Transactions on Software Engineering*, **17**(6): 591–603.

[158]   Galiano, E. and A. P. Mathur (1988). "Inducing vectorization: A formal analysis." *In Proceedings of the Third International Conference on Supercomputing*, pp. 455–463. New York, NY: ACM Press.

[159]   Gang, L., G. v. Bochmann, and A. Petrenko (February 1994). "Test selection based on communicating nondeterministic finite-state machines using a generalized WP-method," *IEEE Transactions on Software Engineering*, **20**(2): 149–162.

[160]   Garg, P. (1995). *On Code Coverage and Software Reliability*. Master's thesis. West Lafayette, IN: Purdue University. Advisor: Aditya P. Mathur.

[161]   Geist, R., A. J. Offutt, and F. Harris (May 1992). "Estimation and enhancement of realtime software reliability through mutation analysis." *IEEE Transactions on Computers*. **41**(5): 550–558.

[162]   Van Ghent, R. (1978). "Letter on real software, regarding the commentary by Dijkstra and the reply by DeMillo, Lipton and Perlis," *SIGSOFT Software Engineering Notes*, **3**(3): 20–21.

[163]   Ghosh, S. (August 2000). *Testing Component-based Distributed Systems*. Ph.D.thesis. West Lafayette, IN: Department of Computer Science, Purdue University. Advisor: Aditya P. Mathur.

[164]   Ghosh, S. (2002). "Towards measurement of testability of concurrent object-oriented programs using fault insertion: a preliminary investigation." In *Proceedings of the Second IEEE International Workshop on Source Code Analysis and Manipulation*, pp. 17–25. Los Alamitos, CA: IEEE Press.

[165]   Ghosh, S. and A. P. Mathur (May 1999). "Issues in testing distributed component-based systems." In *Proceedings of the 1st ICSE Workshop on Testing Distributed Component-Based Systems*. Los Alamitos, CA: IEEE Press.

[166]   Ghosh, S. and A. P. Mathur (July–August 2000). "Interface mutation to assess the adequacy of tests for components." In *Proceedings of the 34th International Conference and Exhibition on Technology of Object-Oriented Languages and Systems (TOOLS USA 2000)*. Los Alamitos, CA: IEEE Press.

[167]   Ghosh, S. and A. P. Mathur (December 2001). "Interface mutation," Journal *of Testing, Verification and Reliability*, **11**(4): 227–247.

[168]   Gill, A. (1968). *Finite-State Models for Logical Machines*. New York: John Wiley & Sons, Inc.

[169]   Gill, S. (1951). "The diagnosis of mistakes in programmes on the EDSAC." In *Proceedings of the Royal Society*, Vol. A. 206, pp. 538–54.

[170]   Girgis, M. R. and M. R. Woodward (July 1986). "An experimental comparison of the error exposing ability of program testing criteria." In *Proceedings of the Workshop on Software Testing*, pp. 64–73. Los Alamitos, CA: IEEE Press.

[171] Gittens, M., H. Lutfiyya, M. Bauer, D. Godwin, Y. W. Kim, and P. Gupta (2002). "An empirical evaluation of system and regression testing." In CAS-CON '02: *Proceedings of the 2002 Conference of the Centre for Advanced Studies on Collaborative Research*, p. 3. IBM Press.

[172] Godskesen, J. C. (1999). "Models for embedded systems." In *Proceedings of CHARME'99, LNCS 1703, September 1999*, pp. 197–214. Berlin, Germany: Springer-Verlag.

[173] Gonenc, G. (June 1970). "A method for the design of fault detection experiments," *IEEE Transactions on Computers*, **C-19**: 551–558.

[174] Goodenough, J. B. and S. L. Gerhart (December 1975). "Correction to 'Toward a theory of test data selection,'" *IEEE Transactions on Software Engineering*, **SE-1**(4): 425.

[175] Goodenough, J. B. and S. L. Gerhart (June 1975). "Toward a theory of test data selection," *IEEE Transactions on Software Engineering*, **SE-1**(2): 156–173.

[176] Goodenough, J. B. and S. L. Gerhart (1975). "Toward a theory of test data selection." In *Proceedings of the International Conference on Reliable Software*, pp. 493–510. New York, NY: ACM Press.

[177] Gören, S. and F. J. Ferguson (1999). "Checking sequence generation for asynchronous sequential elements." In *Proceedings of the ITC International Test Conference*, pp. 406–413.

[178] Gören, S. and F. J. Ferguson (2002). "Testing Finite State Machines Based on a Structural Coverage Metric." In *Proceedings of the ITC International Test Conference*, pp. 773–780.

[179] Graves, T. L., M. J. Harrold, J. M. Kim, A. Porter, and G. Rothermel (2001). "An empirical study of regression test selection techniques," *ACM Transactions on Software Engineering Methodology*, **10**(2): 184–208.

[180] Grindal, M., B. Lindström, A. J. Offutt, and S. F. Andler. "An evaluation of combination test strategies for test case selection." Technical report HS-IDA-TR-03001, Department of Computer Science, University of Skövde, Sewden, October 2004.

[181] Grochtmann, M. (1994). "Test case design using classification trees." In *Proceedings of STAR'94, May 1994*, pp. 1–11. Washington, DC.

[182] Grochtmann, M. and K. Grimm (June 1993). "Classification trees for partition testing," *Software Testing, Verification, and Reliability*, **3**(2): 63–82.

[183] Grossman, F., J. Bergin, D. Leip, S. Merritt, and O. Gotel (2004). "One XP experience: introducing agile (XP) software development into a culture that is willing but not ready." In *CASCON '04: Proceedings of the 2004 Conference of the Centre for Advanced Studies on Collaborative Research*, pp. 242–254. IBM Press.

[184] Gupta, R. (1992). "Generalized dominators and post-dominators." In *POPL '92: Proceedings of the 19th ACM SIGPLAN-SIGACT Symposium on Principles of Programming Languages*, pp. 246–257. New York, NY: ACM Press.

[185] Gupta, R., M. J. Harrold, and M. L. Soffa (1992). "An approach to regression testing using slicing." In *Proceedings of the IEEE Conference on Software Maintenance, November 1992*, pp. 299–308.

[186] Gustafson, D. A. and B. Prasad (1992). "Properties of software measures." In *Proceedings of the BCS-FACS Workshop on Formal Aspects of Measurement*, pp. 179–193. London: Springer-Verlag.

[187] Gutjahr, W. J. (November 1999). "Partition testing vs. random testing: The influence of uncertainty," *IEEE Transactions on Software Engineering*, **25**(5): 661–674.

[188] Gyimóthy, T., A. Beszédes, and L. Forgács (1999). "An efficient relevant slicing method for debugging." In *ESEC/FSE-7: Proceedings of the 7th European Software Engineering Conference Held Jointly with the 7th ACM SIGSOFT International Symposium on Foundations of Software Engineering*, pp. 303–321. London: Springer-Verlag.

[189] Hamlet, R. G. (August 1977). "Programs with finite sets of data," *Computer Journal*, **20**: 232–237.

[190] Hamlet, R. G. (July 1977). "Testing programs with the aid of a compiler." IEEE Transactions on Software Engineering, **SE-3**(4): 279–290.

[191] Hamlet, R. G. and R. N. Taylor (December 1990). "Partition testing does not inspire confidence [program testing]," *IEEE Transactions on Software Engineering*, **16**(12): 1402–1411.

[192] Hammer, C., M. Grimme, and J. Krinke (2006). "Dynamic path conditions in dependence graphs." In *PEPM '06: Proceedings of the 2006 ACM SIG-PLAN Symposium on Partial Evaluation and Semantics-Based Program Manipulation*, pp. 58–67. New York, NY: ACM Press.

[193] Hanks, J. M. (1980). *Testing COBOL programs by mutation*. Master's thesis. Atlanta, GA: Georgia Institute of Technology.

[194] Brinch Hansen, P. (1973). "Testing a multiprogramming system," *Software–Practice and Experience*, **3**(2): 145–150.

[195] Harold, E. R. and W. S. Means (2004). *XML in a Nutshell*, 3rd edn. Cambridge, MA: O'Reilly.

[196] Harrold, M. J., J. A. Jones, T. Li, and D. Liang (2001). "Regression test selection for Java software." In *Proceedings of the ACM Conference on OO Programming, Systems, Languages, and Applications (OOPSLA '01)*.

[197] Harrold, M. J., R. Gupta, and M. L. Soffa (1993). "A methodology for controlling the size of a test suite," *ACM Transactions on Software Engineering Methodology*, **2**(3): 270–285.

[198] Harrold, M. J., J. A. Jones, T. Li, D. Liang, A. Orso, M. Pennings, S. Sinha, S. A. Spoon, and A. Gujarathi (2001). "Regression test selection for Java software." In *OOPSLA '01: Proceedings of the 16th ACM SIGPLAN conference on Object oriented programming, systems, languages, and applications*, pp. 312–326. New York, NY: ACM Press.

[199] Harrold, M. J., B. Malloy, and G. Rothermel (1993). "Efficient construction of program dependence graphs." In *ISSTA '93: Proceedings of the 1993 ACM*

SIGSOFT International Symposium on Software Testing and Analysis, pp. 160–170. New York, NY: ACM Press.

[200] Harrold, M. J. and G. Rothermel (1994). "Performing data flow testing on classes." In *Proceedings of the SIGSOFT'94 Symposium on Foundations of Software Engineering, New Orleans,* pp. 154–163. New York, NY: ACM Press.

[201] Harrold, M. J., G. Rothermel, R. Wu, and L. Yi (1998). "An empirical investigation of program spectra." In *PASTE '98: Proceedings of the 1998 ACM SIGPLAN-SIGSOFT Workshop on Program Analysis for Software Tools and Engineering,* pp. 83–90. New York, NY: ACM Press.

[202] Harrold, M. J. and M. Soffa (1989). "Interprocedual data flow testing." In *TAV3: Proceedings of the ACM SIGSOFT '89 Third Symposium on Software Testing, Analysis, and Verification,* pp. 158–167. New York, NY: ACM Press.

[203] Hartman, A. (2002). "Software and hardware testing using combinatorial covering suites." In *Haifa Workshop on Interdisciplinary Applications and Graph Theory, Combinatorics and Algorithms, June 2002.* Springer, US.

[204] Hartmann, J. and D. J. Robson (1990). "Retest—development of a selective revalidation prototype environment for use in software maintenance." In *Proceedings of the 23rd Hawaii International Conference on System Sciences,* pp. 92–101. Los Alamitos, CA: IEEE Press.

[205] Hartmann, J. and D. J. Robson (January 1990). "Techniques for selective revalidation," *IEEE Software,* **7**(1): 31–36.

[206] Hatton, L. (March 1997). "Re-examining the fault density-component size connection," *IEEE Software,* **14**(2): 89–97.

[207] Hatton, L. (April–June 1997)."The T experiments: Errors in scientific software," *IEEE Computational Science and Engineering,* **4**(2): 27–38.

[208] Hatton, L. and A. Roberts (October 1994). "How accurate is scientific software?" *IEEE Transactions on Software Engineering,* **20**(10): 785–797.

[209] Hayhurst, K. J. and C. M. Holloway (September/October 2002). "Aviation software guidelines," *IEEE Software,* **19**(5): 107.

[210] Hayhurst, K. J., D. S. Veerhusen, J. J. Chilenski, and L. K. Rierson. "A practical tutorial on modified condition/decision coverage." Technical report NASA/TM-2001-210876, NASA, NASA Center for Aerospace Information (CASI), Hanover, MD, May 2001.

[211] Hedayat, A. S., N. J. A. Sloane, and J. Stufken (1999). *Orthogonal Arrays.* New York: Springer.

[212] Hedley, D., M. A. Hennell, and M. R. Woodward (November 1980). "On the generation of test data for program validation." In *Production and Assessment of Numerical Software* (M. A. Hennel and L. M. Delves, eds.), pp. 128–135. Burlington, MA: Academic Press.

[213] Heller, E. (1995). "Using design of experiments structures to generate software tests." In *Proceedings of the 12th International Conference on Testing Computer Software,* pp. 33–41.

[214] Hennell, M. A., D. Hedley, and M. R. Woodward (1976). "Experience with an ALGOL 68 numerical algorithms testbed." In *Computer Software Engineering* (J. Fox, ed.), pp. 457–463. New York: Polytechnic Press.

[215] Hennie, F. C. (1962). *Introduction to the Theory of Finite State Machines*. New York: Mc-Graw Hill Book Company, Inc.

[216] Hetzel, W. C. (1973). *Program Test Methods*. Englewood Cliffs, NJ: Prentice Hall.

[217] Hierons, R. M. (2001). "Checking states and transitions of a set of communicating finite state machines," *Microprocessors and Microsystems* (special issue on testing and testing techniques for real-time embedded software systems), **24**(9): 443–452.

[218] Hierons, R. M., M. Harman, and S. Danicic (1999). "Using program slicing to assist in the detection of equivalent mutants," *Software Testing, Verification and Reliability*, **9**(4): 233–262.

[219] Hierons, R. M. and H. Ural (September 2002). "Reduced length checking sequences," *IEEE Transactionson Computers*, **51**(9): 1111–1117.

[220] Hillis, W. D. (1986). *The connection machine*. Cambridge, MA: MIT Press.

[221] Hoare, C. A. R. (1985). *Communicating Sequential Processes*. London, UK: Prentice Hall.

[222] Holzmann, G. J. (2003). *The SPIN Model Checker: Primer and Reference Manual*. Addison-Wesley Professional.

[223] Hopcroft, J. E. and J. D. Ullman (November 2000). *Introduction to Automata Theory, Languages, and Computation*. Reading, MA: Addison-Wesley.

[224] Horgan, J. R. and S. London (1991). "Data-flow coverage and the C language." In *Proceedings of the Fourth Symposium on Software Testing, Analysis, and Verification, October 1991*, pp. 87–97. Los Alamitos, CA: IEEE Press.

[225] Horgan, J. R. and S. London (1992). "ATAC: A data flow coverage testing tool for C." In *Proceedings of Symposium on Assessment of Quality Software Development Tools, May 1992*, pp. 2–10. Los Alamitos, CA: IEEE Press.

[226] Horgan, J. R. and A. P. Mathur (1990). "Weak mutation is probably strong mutation." Technical report SERC-TR-83-P, Software Engineering Research Center, Purdue University, West Lafayette, IN.

[227] Horgan, J. R. and A. P. Mathur (1996). "Software testing and reliability." In *Handbook of Software Reliability Engineering* (M. R. Lyu, ed.), pp. 531–566. New York, NY: McGraw-Hill.

[228] Horwitz, S. "Identifying the semantic and textual differences between two versions of a program." Technical report 895, Department of Computer Sciences, University of Wisconsin—Madison, Madison, WI, November 1989.

[229] Horwitz, S. (1990). "Identifying the semantic and textual differences between two versions of a program." In *PLDI '90: Proceedings of the ACM SIGPLAN 1990 conference on Programming Language Design and Implementation*, pp. 234–245. New York, NY: ACM Press.

[230] Horwitz, S., J. Prins, and T. Reps (1988). "On the adequacy of program dependence graphs for representing programs." In *POPL '88: Proceedings of*

the 15th ACM SIGPLAN-SIGACT Symposium on Principles of Programming Languages, pp. 146–157. New York, NY: ACM Press.

[231]   Horwitz, S., T. Reps, and D. Binkley (1988). "Interprocedural slicing using dependence graphs," *SIGPLAN Notices*, **39**(4): 229–243.

[232]   Horwitz, S., T. Reps, and D. Binkley (1990). "Interprocedural slicing using dependence graphs," *ACM Transactions on Programming Languages and Systems*, **12**(1): 26–60.

[233]   Howden, W. E. (May 1975). "Methodology for the generation of program test data," *IEEE Transactions on Computers*, **C-24**(5): 554–559.

[234]   Howden, W. E. (1980). "Applicability of software validation techniques to scientific programs," *ACM Transactions on Program ming Languages and Systems*, **2**(3): 307–320.

[235]   Howden, W. E. (1981). "Completeness criteria for testing elementary program functions." In *ICSE '81: Proceedings of the Fifth International Conference on Software Engineering*, pp. 235–243. Los Alamitos, CA: IEEE Press.

[236]   Howden, W. E. (1981). "A survey of dynamic analysis methods." In *Tutorial: Program Testing and Validation Techniques* (E. F. Miller and W. E. Howden, eds.). Washington, DC: IEEE Computer Society Press.

[237]   Howden, W. E. (1982). "Validation of scientific programs," *ACM Computing Surveys*, **14**(2): 193–227.

[238]   Howden, W. E. (1982). "Weak mutation testing and completeness of test sets," *IEEE Transactions on Software Engineering*, **8**(4): 371–379.

[239]   Howden, W. E. (1991). "Program testing versus proofs of correctness," *Software Testing, Verification, and Reliability*, **1**(1): 5–15.

[240]   J. C. Huang (September 1975). "An approach to program testing," *ACM Computing Surveys*, **7**: 113–128.

[241]   Huller, J. (2000). "Reducing time to market with combinatorial design method testing." In *Proceedings of the 2000 International Council on Systems Engineering (INCOSE) Conference, Englewood, CO, March 2000*.

[242]   ANSI/IEEE Std. 1008-1987 (1987). *IEEE Standard for Software Unit Testing*. Piscataway, NJ: IEEE Service Center.

[243]   ANSI/IEEE Std. 729-1983 (1983). *Glossary of Software Engineering Terminology. Piscataway,* NJ: IEEE Service Center.

[244]   IEEE Standard Computer Dictionary: A Compilation of IEEE Standard Computer Glossaries. New York, NY, 1990.

[245]   Jackson, D. and M. R. Woodward (2000). "Parallel firm mutation of Java programs." In *Proceedings of Mutation 2000, October 2000*, pp. 77–83. Boston, MA: Kluwer Academic Publishers.

[246]   Jalote, P. (May 1998). "Testing the completeness of specifications," *IEEE Transactions on Software Engineering*, **15**(5): 526–531.

[247]   Jeng, B. and E. J. Weyuker (1989). "Some observations on partition testing." In *Proceedings of the ACM SIGSOFT '89 Third Symposium on Software Testing, Analysis, and Verification*, pp. 38–47. ACM Press.

[248] Johnson, D. S. (1973). "Approximation algorithms for combinatorial prob-
       lems." In STOC '73: *Proceedings of the Fifth Annual ACM Symposium on
       Theory of Computing*, pp. 38–49. New York, NY: ACM Press.

[249] Juristo, N., A. M. Moreno, and S. Vegas (2004). "Reviewing 25 years of test-
       ing technique experiments," *Empirical Software Engineering*, **9**(1–2): 7–44.

[250] Kan, S. H., J. Parrish, and D. Manlove (2001). "In-process metrics for software
       testing," *IBM Systems Journal*, **40**(1): 220–241.

[251] Kapoor, K. and J. Bowen (2003). "Experimental evaluation of the variation in
       effectiveness for DC, FPC and MC/DC test criteria." In *Proceedings of 2003
       International Symposium on Empirical Software Engineering, October 2003*,
       pp. 185–194. Los Alamitos, CA: IEEE Press.

[252] Karoui, K., A. Ghedamsi, and R. Dssouli (1997). "A study of some influenc-
       ing factors in testability and diagnostics based on FSMs." Technical report TR
       P#1048, Dèpt. IRO, Universitè de Montrèal, Montrèal.

[253] Karp, R. M. (1960). "A note on the application of graph theory to digital
       computer programming," *Information and Control*, **3**(2): 179–190.

[254] Katrowitz, M. and L. M. Noack (1996). "I'm done simulating; now what?
       Verification coverage analysis and correctness checking of the DEC chip
       21164 Alpha microprocessor." In *DAC '96: Proceedings of the 33rd Annual
       Conference on Design Automation*, pp. 325–330. New York, NY: ACM
       Press.

[255] Kavi, K. M. and U. B. Jackson (1982). "Effect of declarations on software met-
       rics: An experiment in software science." In *SCORE '82: Selected Papers of
       the 1982 ACM SIGMETRICS Workshop on Software Metrics*, pp. 57–71, New
       York, NY: ACM Press.

[256] Khandelwal, V. (August 1995). *On Program Auralization*. Master's thesis. West
       Lafayette, IN: Department of Computer Science, Purdue University. Advisor:
       Aditya P. Mathur.

[257] Kilov, H. (1979). "Letter on Parnas' view of Dijkstra vs. DeMillo, Lipton and
       Perlis," *SIGSOFT Software Engineering Notes*, **4**(1): 19.

[258] Kim, J. and A. Porter (2002). "A history-based test prioritization technique for
       regression testing in resource constrained environments." In *ICSE '02:
       Proceedings of the 24th International Conference on Software Engineering*,
       pp. 119–129, New York, NY: ACM Press.

[259] Kim, J.-M., A. Porter, and G. Rothermel (2000). "An empirical study of regres-
       sion test application frequency." In *ICSE '00: Proceedings of the 22nd
       International Conference on Software Engineering*, pp. 126–135. New York,
       NY: ACM Press.

[260] Kim, S., J. Clark, and J. McDermid (December 1999). "The rigorous generation
       of Java mutation operators using HAZOP." In *Proceedings of the 12th
       International Conference on Software & Systems Engineering (ICSSEA'99)*.
       Paris, France: CNAM.

[261] Kim, T. H., I. S. Hwang, M. S. Jang, S. W. Kang, J. Y. Lee, and S. B Lee
       (1998). "Test case generation of a protocol by a fault coverage analysis." In

Proceedings of the 12th International Conference on Information Networking (ICOIN-12), January 1998, pp. 690–695. Los Alamitos, CA: IEEE Press.

[262]   Kim, Y. W. (2003). "Efficient use of code coverage in large-scale software development." In *CASCON '03: Proceedings of the 2003 Conference of the Centre for Advanced Studies on Collaborative Research*, pp. 145–155. Aramonk, NY: IBM Press.

[263]   Knuth, D. E. (1989). "The errors of TEX," *Software Practice and Experience*, **19**(7): 607–685.

[264]   Knuth, D. E. and F. R. Stevenson (1973). "Optimal measurement points for program frequency counts," *BIT*, **13**: 313–322.

[265]   Kohavi, Z. (1978). *Switching and Finite Automata Theory*, 2nd edn. Columbus, OH: McGraw-Hill.

[266]   Korel, B. (1987). "The program dependence graph in static program testing," *Information Processing Letters*, **24**(2): 103–108.

[267]   Korel, B. and J. W. Laski. "Data flow oriented program testing strategy." Technical report C/SJW11, School of Engineering, Oakland University, Rochester, MI, 1980.

[268]   Korel, B. and J. W. Laski (1988). "Dynamic program slicing," *Information Processing Letters*, **29**(3): 155–163.

[269]   Koufareva, I., A. Petrenko, and N. Yevtushenko (1999). "Test generation driven by user-defined fault models." In *Proceedings of the 12th International Workshop on Testing of Communicating Systems, Hungary*, pp. 215–233.

[270]   Krauser, E. W. (1991). *Compiler-integrated software testing*. Ph.D. thesis. West Lafayette, IN: Purdue University. Coadvisor: Aditya P. Mathur.

[271]   Krauser, E. W., and A. P. Mathur (1986). "Program testing on a massively parallel transputer based system." In *Proceedings of the ISMM International Symposium on Mini and Microcomputers and their Applications, November 1986*, pp. 67–71. Anaheim, CA: Acta Press.

[272]   Krauser, E. W., A. P. Mathur, and V. J. Rego (May 1991). "High performance software testing on SIMD machines," *IEEE Transactions on Software Engineering*, **17**(5): 403–423.

[273]   Krawczyk, H. and B. Wiszniewski. "Classification of software defects in parallel programs." Technical Report No. 2, pp. 80–111, Technical University of Gdansk, Poland, 1994.

[274]   Kuck, D. L. (1978). *Structure of Computers and Computations*. New York, NY: John Wiley & Sons, Inc.

[275]   Kuhn, D. R. and M. J. Reilly (2002). "An investigation of the applicability of design of experiments to software testing." In *SEW '02: Proceedings of the 27th Annual NASA Goddard Software Engineering Workshop (SEW-27'02)*, p. 91. Los Alamitos, CA: IEEE Press.

[276]   Kuhn, D. R., D. R. Wallace, and A. J. Gallo, Jr. (June 2004). "Software fault interactions and implications for software testing," *IEEE Transactions on Software Engineering*, **30**(6): 418–421.

[277]   Larus, J. R. (1990). "Abstract execution: A technique for efficiently tracing programs," *Software Practice and Experience*, **20**(12): 1241–1258.

[278]   Laski, J. W. (1982). "On data flow guided program testing," *SIGPLAN Notices*, **17**(9): 62–71.

[279]   Laski, J.W. (1990). "Data flow testing in STAD," *Journal of Systems and Software*, **12**(1): 3–14.

[280]   Laski, J. W. and B. Korel (May 1983). "A data flow oriented program testing strategy," *IEEE Transactions on Software Engineering*, **SE-9**(3): 347–354.

[281]   Laski, J. W., W. Szermer, and P. Luczycki (1993). "Dynamic mutation testing in integrated regression analysis." In *ICSE '93: Proceedings of the 15th International Conference on Software Engineering*, pp. 108–117. Los Alamitos, CA: IEEE Computer Society Press.

[282]   Lee, D., K. K. Sabnani, D. M. Kristol, and S. Paul (May 1996). "Conformance testing of protocols specified as communicating finite state machines—a guided random walk based approach," *IEEE Transactions on Communications*, **44**(5): 631–640.

[283]   Lee, D. and M. Yannakakis (1996). "Principles and methods of testing finite state machines: A survey." In *Proceedings of the IEEE*, Vol. 84, pp. 1090–1126.

[284]   Lee, S. C. and A. J. Offutt (2001). "Generating test cases for XML-based Web component interactions using mutation analysis." In *Proceedings of the 12th International Symposium on Software Reliability Engineering (ISSRE'01)*, pp. 200–209. Hong Kong: PRC.

[285]   Lei, Y. and K. C. Tai (1998). "In-parameter-order: A test generation strategy for pairwise testing." In HASE '98: *The Third IEEE International Symposium on High-Assurance Systems Engineering*, pp. 254–261. Washington, DC: IEEE Computer Society.

[286]   Lengauer, T. and R. E. Tarjan (1979). "A fast algorithm for finding dominators in a flowgraph," *ACM Transactions on Programming Languages and Systems*, **1**(1): 121–141.

[287]   Leung, H. K. N. and L. J. White (1989). "Insights into regression testing." In *Proceedings of the Conference on Software Maintenance*, pp. 60–69.

[288]   Leveson, N. G. and A. Dupuy (2000). "An empirical evaluation of the MC/DC coverage criterion on the HETE-2 satellite software." In *Proceedings of the Digital Aviation Systems Conference (DASC), Philadelphia, October 2000*. Los Alamitos, CA: IEEE Press.

[289]   Li, J. B. and J. Miller (July 2005). "Testing the semantics of W3C XML schema." In *Proceedings of the 29th Annual International Computer Software and Applications Conference*, pp. 443–448. Edinburgh, Scotland: IEEE Press.

[290]   Li, P. L., J. Herbsleb, M. Shaw, and B. Robinson (2006). "Experiences and results from initiating field defect prediction and product test prioritization efforts at ABB, Inc." In *ICSE '06: Proceeding of the 28th International Conference on Software Engineering*, pp. 413–422. New York, NY: ACM Press.

[291] Li, W. (December 1999). "Software product metrics," *IEEE Potentials*, **18**(5): 24–27.

[292] Li, W. and S. Henry (1993). "Object-oriented metrics which predict maintainability," *Journal of Systems and Software*, **2**: 111–122.

[293] Lipton, R. J. and F. G. Sayward (1978). "The status of research on program mutation." In *Digest for the Workshop on Software Testing and Test Documentation*, pp. 355–378. New York, NY: ACM Press.

[294] Litecky, C. R. and G. B. Davis (1976). "A study of errors, error-proneness, and error diagnosis in COBOL," *Communications of the ACM*, **19**(1): 33–37.

[295] Liu, C.-H. (2004). "Data flow analysis and testing of Java server pages." In *Proceedings of 28th Annual International Computer Software and Applications Conference (COMPSAC 2004)*, Vol. 2, pp. 114–119. Los Alamitos, CA: IEEE Press.

[296] Liu, C. H., D. C. Kung, and P. Hsia (2000). "Object-based data flow testing of web applications." In *Proceedings of First Asia-Pacific Conference on Quality Software, October 2000*, pp. 7–16.

[297] Luo, G., A. Das, and G. v. Bochmann (1994). "Software testing based on SDL specifications with Save," *IEEE Transactions on Software Engineering*, **20**(1): 72–87.

[298] Ma, Y. S. and Y. R. Kwon (September 2002). "A study on method and tool of mutation analysis for object-oriented programs," *Software Engineering Review*, **15**(3): 41–52.

[299] Ma, Y.-S., Y.-R. Kwon, and A. J. Offutt (November 2002). "Inter-class mutation operators for Java." In *Proceedings of the 13th International Symposium on Software Reliability Engineering*, pp. 352–363. Los Alamitos, CA: IEEE Press.

[300] Ma, Y.-S., A. J. Offutt, and Y.-R. Kwon (2005). "MuJava: An automated class mutation system," *Software Testing, Verification, and Reliability*, **15**(2): 97–133.

[301] Maheshwari, S. "Traversal marker placement problems are NP-complete." Technical report CU-CS-092-76, Department of Computer Science, University of Colorado, Colorado, 1976.

[302] Maity, S., A. Nayak, M. Zaman, N. Bansal, and A. Srivastava (2003). "An improved test generation algorithm for pair-wise testing." In *Proceedings of the 14th International Symposium on Software Reliability Engineering*, Fast Abstracts, pp. 1–2.

[303] Maldonado, J. C., M. L. Chaim, and M. Jino (1992). "Bridging the gap in the presence of infeasible paths: Potential uses testing criteria." In *Proceedings of the Fifth International Conference on Software Engineering and its Applications*, pp. 613–623. Los Alamitos, CA: IEEE Press.

[304] Maldonado, J. C., A. P. Mathur, and W. E. Wong (October 1994). "Constrained mutation in C programs." In *Proceedings of VIII Simposio Brasileiro De Enginharia De Software*, pp. 439–452. Los Alamitos, CA: IEEE Press.

[305] Mandl, R. (October 1985). "Orthogonal Latin squares," *Communications of the ACM*, 1054–1058. New York, NY: ACM Press.

[306]   Manhart, P. and K. Schneider (2004). "Breaking the ice for agile development of embedded software: An industry experience report." In *ICSE '04: Proceedings of the 26th International Conference on Software Engineering*, pp. 378–86. Washington, DC: IEEE Computer Society Press.

[307]   Marick, B. (1991). "The weak mutation hypothesis." In *TAV4: Proceedings of the Symposium on Testing, Analysis, and Verification*, pp. 190–199. New York, NY: ACM Press.

[308]   Marick, B. (1999). "How to misuse code coverage." Reliable Software Technologies. http://www.testing.com/writings/coverage.pdf

[309]   Massol, V. and T. Husted (2003). *JUnit in Action*. Greenwich, CT: Manning Publications Co.

[310]   Mathur, A. P. (1991). "On the relative strengths of data flow and mutation testing." In *Proceedings of the Ninth Annual Pacific Software Quality Conference*, pp. 165–181. http://www.pnsqc.org/proceedings/pnsqc99.pdf

[311]   Mathur, A. P. (1991). "Performance, effectiveness, and reliability issues in software testing." In *Proceedings of COMPSAC'91*, pp. 604–605. Los Alamitos, CA: IEEE Press.

[312]   Mathur, A. P. (August 1992). *CS 406 Software Engineering I: Course Project Handout*, available from Aditya P. Mathur at apm@purdue.edu

[313]   Mathur, A. P. (December 1994). *Mutation Testing. In Encyclopedia of Software Engineering* (J. J. Marciniak, ed.), pp. 707–713. New York, NY: John Wiley & Sons Inc.

[314]   Mathur, A. P., S. Ghosh, P. Govindarajan, and B. Sridharan (July 1999). "A framework for assessing test adequacy, architecture extraction, metering, monitoring and controlling distributed component-based systems." In *Proceedings of the First Symposium on Reusable Architecture and Components for Developing Distributed Information Systems*, pp. 657–660. New York, NY: ACM Press.

[315]   Mathur, A. P. and E. W. Krauser (1988). "Modeling mutation on a vector processor." In *Proceedings of the International Conference on Software Engineering, April 1988*, pp. 154–161. Los Alamitos, CA: IEEE Press.

[316]   Mathur, A. P., and V. J. Rego (1990). "Exploiting parallelism across program execution: a unification technique and its analysis," *IEEE Transactions on Parallel and Distributed Systems*, **1**(4): 399–414.

[317]   Mathur, A. P., and W. E. Wong (October 1993). "Evaluation of the cost of alternate mutation strategies." In *Proceedings of the Seventh Brazilian Symposium on Software Engineering*, pp. 320–335. Los Alamitos, CA: IEEE Press.

[318]   Mathur, A. P. and W. E. Wong (March 1994). "An empirical comparison of data flow and mutation-based test adequacy criteria." *Software Testing, Verification, and Reliability*, **4**(1): 9–31.

[319]   Mathur, A. P. and W. E. Wong (1994). "A theoretical comparison between mutation and data flow based test adequacy criteria." In *CSC '94: Proceedings of the 22nd Annual ACM Computer Science Conference on Scaling Up: Meeting the Challenge of Complexity in Real-World Computing Applications*, pp. 38–45. New York, NY: ACM Press.

[320] Mathur, A. P. and W. E. Wong (1995). "Fault detection effectiveness of mutation and data flow testing," *Software Quality Journal*, **4**: 69–83.

[321] MathWorks (2002). *Using Simulink-Model-Based and System Based Design. The MathWorks, Inc., Software Engineering*, **19**(6): 533–553.

[322] McCabe, T. J. (1976). "A complexity measure," *IEEE Transactions on Software Engineering*, **SE-2**(4): 308–320.

[323] McCall, J. A., P. K. Richards, and G. F. Walters. "Factors in software quality." Technical report AD/A-049-014/015/055, Rome Air Development Center, Hanscom AFB, MA; National Technical Information Service, Springfield, VA, 1977.

[324] McDonald, J., P. Strooper, and D. Hoffman (2003). "Tool support for generating passive C++ test oracles from Object-Z specifications." In *Proceedings of the 10th Asia-pacific Software Engineering Conference*, pp. 322–331.

[325] McMillan, K. L. (1993). *Symbolic model checking*. Boston, MA: Kluwer Academic Publishers.

[326] Memon, A. and X. Qing (2004). "Using transient/persistent errors to develop automated test oracles for event-driven software." In *Proceedings of the 19th International Conference on Automated Software Engineering*, pp. 184–195.

[327] Miller, E. F. (1998). "Advances in automating software testing." In *Proceedings of Software Engineering in 1990's Congress*, February 1998.

[328] Miller, E. F. and W. E. Howden (1978). *Software Testing and Validation Techniques*. Long Beach, CA: IEEE Computer Society Press.

[329] Miller, J. C. and C. J. Maloney (February 1963). "Systematic mistake analysis of digital computer programs," *Communications of the ACM*, **6**(2): 58–63.

[330] Miller, R. E. and S. Paul (1993). "On the generation of minimal-length conformance tests for communication protocols," *IEEE/ACM Transactions on Networking*, **1**(1): 116–129.

[331] Miller, W. and E. W. Myers (1985). "A file comparison program," *Software Practice and Experience*, **15(II)**: 1025–1040.

[332] Moore, I. (2001). Jester—a JUnit test tester. In *Proceedings of the Second International Conference on Extreme Programming and Flexible Processes in Software Engineering*, pp. 84–87. Los Alamitos, CA: IEEE Press.

[333] Moreira, A., J. Araùjo, and I. Brito (2002). "Crosscutting quality attributes for requirements engineering." In *SEKE '02: Proceedings of the 14th International Conference on Software Engineering and Knowledge Engineering,*" pp. 167–74. New York, NY: ACM Press.

[334] Mresa, E. S. and L. Bottaci (December 1999). "Efficiency of mutation operators and selective mutation strategies: an empirical study," *Software Testing, Verification, and Reliability*, **9**(4): 202–232.

[335] Müller, M. M. and F. Padberg (2003). "On the economic evaluation of XP projects." In *ESEC/FSE-11: Proceedings of the Ninth European Software Engineering Conference Held Jointly with Eleventh ACM SIGSOFT International Symposium on Foundations of Software Engineering*, pp. 168–77. New York, NY: ACM Press.

[336]   Murnane, T. (1999). *The Application of Mutation Techniques to Specification Testing*. Master's thesis. Melbourne, Australia: Department of Computer Science, La Trobe University.

[337]   Murnane, T. and K. Reed (2001). "On the effectiveness of mutation analysis as a black box testing technique." In *Proceedings Australian Software Engineering Conference*, pp. 12–20. Los Alamitos, CA: IEEE Press.

[338]   Myers, G. J. (1976). *Software Reliability: Principles and Practices*. Hoboken, NJ: John Wiley.

[339]   Myers, G. J. (1978). "A controlled experiment in program testing and code walkthroughs/inspections," *Communications of the ACM*, **21**(9): 760–768.

[340]   Myers, G. J. (1979). *The Art of Software Testing*. New York: John Wiley & Sons.

[341]]   Myers, G. J. (2004). *The Art of Software Testing*. New Jersey: John Wiley & Sons.

[342]   Nagappan, N., L. Williams, M. A. Vouk, and J. Osborne (2005). "Early estimation of software quality using in-process testing metrics: A controlled case study." In *3-WoSQ: Proceedings of the Third Workshop on Software Quality*, pp. 1–7. New York, NY: ACM Press.

[343]   Naik, K. (August 1997). "Efficient computation of unique input/output sequences in finite-state machines," *IEEE Transactions on Networking*, **5**(4): 585–599.

[344]   Nair, V. N., D. A. James, W. K. Ehrlich, and J. Zevallos (1998). "A statistical assessment of some software testing strategies and application of experimental design techniques," *Statistica Sinica*, **8**: 165–184.

[345]   Naito, S. and M. Tsunoyama (1981). "Fault detection for sequential machines by transition tours." In *Proceedings of IEE Fault Tolerant Computing Systems*, pp. 238–243. Los Alamitos, CA: IEEE Press.

[346]   Natwick, G. (2001). CMMIR technology conference and user group.

[347]   Naur, P. (1963). "The design of the Gier ALGOL compiler," *BIT*, **3**: 124–140; 145–166.

[348]   Naur, P. (1969). "Programming by action clusters," *BIT*, **9**(3): 250–258.

[349]   Netisopakul, P., L. J. White, and J. Morris (2002). "Data coverage testing." In *Ninth Asia-Pacific Software Engineering Conference (APSEC), December 2002*, p. 465–472. Los Alamitos, CA: IEEE Press.

[350]   Nikolik, B. (2006). "Test suite oscillations," *Information Procesing Letters*, **98**: 47–55.

[351]   "Testability of object-oriented systems." Technical report GCR 95-675, National Institute of Standards and Technology, June 1995.

[352]   Ntafos, S. C. (1981). "On testing with required elements." In *Proceedings of COMPSAC'81*, pp. 142–149. Los Alamitos, CA: IEEE Press.

[353]   Ntafos, S. C. (1984). "On required element testing," *IEEE Transactions on Software Engineering*, **SE-10**(6): 795–803.

[354]   Ntafos, S. C. (June 1988). "A comparison of some structural testing strategies," *IEEE Transactions on Software Engineering*, **14**(6): 868–874.

[355] Ntafos, S. C. (October 2001). "On comparisons of random, partition, and proportional partition testing," *IEEE Transactions on Software Engineering*, **27**(10): 949–960.

[356] Ockunzzi, K. A. and C. A. Papachristou (1998). "Testability enhancement for control-flow intensive behaviors," *Journal of Electronic Testing*, **13**(3): 239–257.

[357] Offutt, A. J. (1988). *Automatic Test Data Generation*. Ph.D. thesis. Atlanta, GA: Georgia Institute of Technology.

[358] Offutt, A. J. (1989). "The coupling effect: Fact or fiction." In *TAV3: Proceedings of the ACM SIGSOFT '89 Third Symposium on Software Testing, Analysis,and Verification*, pp. 131–140. New York, NY: ACM Press.

[359] Offutt, A. J. (1992). "Investigations of the software testing coupling effect," *ACM Transactions Software Engineering Methodology*, **1**(1): 5–20.

[360] Offutt, A. J. (June 1995). "Practical mutation testing." In *Proceedings of the 12th International Conference on Testing Computer Software*, pp. 99–109. Los Alamitos, CA: IEEE Press.

[361] Offutt, A. J., R. T. Alexander, Y. Wu, Q. Xiao, and C. Hutchinson (2001). "A fault model for subtype inheritance and polymorphism." In *12th International Symposium on Software Reliability Engineering, ISSRE November 2001*, pp. 84–93. Los Alamitos, CA: IEEE Press.

[362] Offutt, A. J. and A. Irvine (1995). "Testing object-oriented software using the category-partition method." In *Proceedings of the 17th International Conference on Technology of Object-Oriented Languages and Systems (TOOLS USA '95)*, pp. 293–304.

[363] Offutt, A. J., A. Lee, G. Rothermel, R. H. Untch, and C. Zapf (1996). "An experimental determination of sufficient mutant operators," *ACM Transactions on Software Engineering Methodology*, **5**(2): 99–118.

[364] Offutt, A. J. and S. D. Lee (1991). "How strong is weak mutation? In *TAV4: Proceedings of the Symposium on Testing, Analysis, and Verification*, pp. 200–213. New York, NY: ACM Press.

[365] Offutt, A. J. and S. D. Lee (1994). "An empirical evaluation of weak mutation," *IEEE Transactions on Software Engineering*, **20**(5): 337–344.

[366] Offutt, A. J. and J. Pan (September 1997). "Automatically detecting equivalent mutants and infeasible paths," *Software Testing, Verification, and Reliability*, **7**(3): 165–192.

[367] Offutt, A. J., J. Pan, K. Tewary, and T. Zhang (1996). "An experimental evaluation of data flow and mutation testing," *Software Practice and Experience*, **26**(2): 165–176.

[368] Offutt, A. J., R. P. Pargas, S. V. Fichter, and P. K. Khambekar (1992). Mutation testing of software using a MIMD computer. In *Proceedings of International Conference on Parallel Processing, August 1992*, pp. 257–266. Boca Raton, FL: CRC Press.

[369] Offutt, A. J., G. Rothermel, and C. Zapf (May 1993). "An experimental evaluation of selective mutation." In *Proceedings of the 15th International Conference on Software Engineering*, pp. 100–107. Los Alamitos, CA: IEEE Press.

[370] Offutt. A. J. and W. Xu (July 2004). "Generating test cases for web services using data perturbation," SIGSOFT Software Engineering Notes, **29**(5): 1–10.

[371] Offutt, J., Y.-S. Ma, and Y.-R. Kwon (2004). "An experimental mutation system for Java," *SIGSOFT Software Engineering Notes*, **29**(5): 1–4.

[372] Ohba, M. (1984). "Software reliability analysis models," *IBM Journal of Research and Development*, **28**(4): 428–443.

[373] Ohba, M. and X.-M. Chou (1989). "Does imperfect debugging affect software reliability growth?" In *ICSE '89: Proceedings of the 11th International Conference on Software Engineering*, pp. 237–44. New York, NY: ACM Press.

[374] Okun, V. (2004). *Specification Mutation for Test Generation and Analysis.* Ph.D. thesis. Baltimore County: University of Maryland.

[375] Okun, V., P. E. Black, and Y. Yesha (January 2003). "Testing with model checker: Insuring fault visibility," *WSEAS Transactions on Systems*, **2**(1): 77–82.

[376] Orso, A. and A. Porter (2003). "ICSE workshop on remote analysis and measurement of software systems (RAMSS)." In *ICSE '03: Proceedings of the 25th International Conference on Software Engineering*, pp. 791–792. Washington, DC: IEEE Computer Society Press.

[377] Orso, A., N. Shi, and M. J. Harrold (2004). "Scaling regression testing to large software systems." In *SIGSOFT '04/FSE-12: Proceedings of the 12th ACM SIGSOFT 12th International Symposium on Foundations of Software Engineering*, pp. 241–251. New York, NY: ACM Press.

[378] Ostrand, T. J. (1990). "Data-flow testing with pointers and function calls." In *Proceedings of the Pacific Northwest Software Quality Conference, October 1990*, pp. 218–227. Los Alamitos, CA: IEEE Press.

[379] Ostrand, T. J. and M. J. Balcer (1988). "The category-partition method for specifying and generating fuctional tests," *Communications of the ACM*, **31**(6): 676–686.

[380] Ostrand, T. J. and E. J. Weyuker (1988). "Using dataflow analysis for regression testing." In *Proceedings of the 6th Annual Pacific Northwest Software Quality Conference, September 1988*, pp. 233–247. Los Alamitos, CA: IEEE Press.

[381] Ostrand, T. J. and E. J. Weyuker (1991). "Data flow-based test adequacy analysis for languages with pointers." In *TAV4: Proceedings of the Symposium on Testing, Analysis, and Verification*, pp. 74–86. New York, NY: ACM Press.

[382] Padmanabhan, S. (2002). *Domain Testing: Divide and Conquer.* Master's thesis. Melbourne, Florida: Florida Institute of Technology.

[383] Paige, M. R. and E. E. Balkovich (1973). "On testing programs." In *Proceedings of the 1973 IEEE Symposium on Computer Software Reliability*, pp. 23–27. Los Alamitos, CA: IEEE Press.

[384] Paradkar, A. M. (1995). "A new solution to test generation for Boolean expressions." In *CASCON '95: Proceedings of the 1995 Conference of the Centre for Advanced Studies on Collaborative Research*, pp. 48. IBM Press.

[385] Paradkar, A. M. (1996). *Specification-Based Testing Using Cause-Effect Graphs.* Ph.D. thesis. North Carolina: North Carolina State University.

[386] Paradkar, A. M. (2000). "An integrated environment to automate generation of function tests for APIs." In *Proceedings of the International Symposium on Software Reliability, October 2000*, pp. 304–316. Los Alamitos, CA: IEEE Press.

[387] Paradkar, A. M. "Towards model-based generation of self-priming and self-checking conformance tests for interactive systems." Technical report RC22586, IBM Research, Yorktown Heights, NY, 2002.

[388] Paradkar, A. M. (2003). "Selecting small yet effective set of test data." In *Proceedings of 21st IASTED International Multi-Conference on Applied Informatics, February 2003*, Vol. 21, pp. 1013–1019.

[389] Paradkar, A. M. and K. C. Tai (1995). "Test generation for Boolean expressions." In *Proceedings of the Fifth International Symposium on Software Reliability Engineering, October 1995*, pp. 106–117. IEEE Computer Society Press.

[390] Paradkar, A. M., K. C. Tai, and M. A. Vouk (1997). "Automated test generation for predicates." In *Proceedings of the Seventh International Symposium on Software Reliability Engineering, November 1997*, pp. 66–75. Los Alamitos, CA: IEEE Press.

[391] Paradkar, A. M., K. C. Tai, and M A. Vouk (1997). "Specification-based testing using cause-effect graphs," *Annals of Software Engineering*, **4**: 133–157.

[392] Pavlopoulou, C. and M. Young (1999). "Residual test coverage monitoring." In *ICSE '99: Proceedings of the 21st International Conference on Software Engineering*, pp. 277–284. Los Alamitos, CA: IEEE Computer Society Press.

[393] Peters, D. K. and D. L. Parnas (1998). "Using test oracles generated from program documentation," *IEEE Transactions on Software Engineering*, **24**(3): 161–173.

[394] Petrenko, A., G. v. Bochmann, and M. Yao (1996). "On fault coverage of tests for finite state specifications," *Computer Networks and ISDN Systems*, **29**(1): 81–106.

[395] Petrenko, A. and N. Yevtushenko (2000). "On test derivation from partial specifications." In *Proceedings of the FIP TC6 WG6.1 Joint International Conference on Formal Description Techniques for Distributed Systems and Communication Protocols (FORTE XIII) and Protocol Specification, Testing and Verification (PSTV XX)*, pp. 85–102. Kluwer BV.

[396] Phadke, M. S. (1995). "Robust testing and robust design for software engineering (in Japanese)," *Journal of Quality Engineering Forum*, **3**(5): 21–27.

[397] Phadke, M. S. (October 1997). "Planning efficient software tests," *Crosstalk*, **10**: 11–15.

[398] Pimont, S. and J. C. Rault (1976). "A software reliability assessment based on a structural and behavioral analysis of programs." In *Proceedings of the Second International Conference on Software Engineering, October 1976*, pp. 486–491. Los Alamitos, CA: IEEE Press.

[399] Piwowarski, P., M. Ohba, and J. Caruso (1993). "Coverage measurement during function test." In *International Conference on Software Engineering, May 1993*, pp. 287–300. Los Alamitos, CA: IEEE Press.

[400] Pomeranz, I. and S. M. Reddy (July 1997). "Test generation for multiple state-table faults in finite-state machines," *IEEE Transactions on Computers*, **46**(7): 783–794.

[401] Probert, R. L. (1982). "Optimal insertion of software probes in well-delimited programs," *IEEE Transactions on Software Engineering*, **8**(1): 34–42.

[402] Purdom, P. (1972). "A sentence generator for testing parsers," *BIT*, **12**: 366–375.

[403] Raik, J., T. Nõmmeots, and R. Ubar (2005). "A new testability calculation method to guide RTL test generation," *Journal of Electronic Testing*, **21**(1): 71–82.

[404] Ramamoorthy, C. V., K. H. Kim, and W. T. Chen (December 1975). "Optimal placement of software monitors aiding systematic testing," *IEEE Transactions on Software Engineering*, **SE-1**(4): 403–411.

[405] Ramamoorthy, C. V., R. E. Meeker, and J. Turner (1973). "Design and construction of an automated software evaluation system." In *Proceedings of the 1973 IEEE Symposium on Computer Software Reliability*, pp. 28–37.

[406] Rao, C. R. (1946). "Hypercubes of strength d leading to confounded designs in factorial experiments," *Bulletin of Calcutta Mathematical Society*, **38**: 67–78.

[407] Rapps, S. and E. J. Weyuker. "Data flow analysis techniques for test data selection." Technical report 023, Department of Computer Science, Courant Institute of Mathematical Sciences, New York University, New York, August/December 1980/1981.

[408] Rapps, S. and E. J. Weyuker (1982). "Data flow analysis techniques for test data selection." In *ICSE '82: Proceedings of the Sixth International Conference on Software Engineering*, pp. 272–278, Los Alamitos, CA: IEEE Computer Society Press.

[409] Rayadurgam, S. and M. P. E. Heimdahl (2003). "Generating MC/DC adequate test sequences through model checking." In *Proceedings of the 28th Annual NASA Goddard Software Engineering Workshop*, December 2003, pp. 91–96. Goddard, MA: NASA.

[410] RCTA. "Final report for clarification of DO178B/ED12B: Software considerations in airborne systems and equipment certification." Technical report RTCA/DO-248B, EUROCAE/ED94B, RTCA, Inc., RCTA (formerly Radio Technical Commission for Aeronautics), December 1992. Washington, D.C.

[411] RTCA. "Software considerations in airborne systems and equipment certification." Technical report RTCA/DO-178B, EUROCAE/ED012B, RTCA, Inc., RCTA (formerly Radio Technical Commission for Aeronautics), December 1992. Washington D.C.

[412] Reid, S. C. (1997). "An empirical analysis of equivalence partitioning, boundary value analysis and random testing." In *Proceedings of the Fourth*

International Software Metrics Symposium, November 1997, pp. 64–73. Los Alamitos, CA: IEEE Press.

[413] Ren, X., F. Shah, F. Tip, B. G. Ryder, and O. Chesley (2004). "Chianti: A tool for change impact analysis of Java programs." In *Proceedings of the ACM Conference on Object-Oriented Programming Systems, Languages, and Applications (OOPSLA 2004), October 26–28*, 2004, pp. 432–448. New York, NY: ACM Press.

[414] Renè, C. B., C. J. Colbourn, and M. B. Cohen (2005). "A framework of greedy methods for constructing interaction test suites." In *ICSE '05: Proceedings of the 27th International Conference on Software Engineering*, pp. 146–155. New York, NY: ACM Press.

[415] Reps, T., T. Ball, M. Das, and J. Larus (1997). "The use of program profiling for software maintenance with applications to the year 2000 problem." In *ESEC '97/FSE-5: Proceedings of the 6th European Conference Held Jointly with the Fifth ACM SIGSOFT International Symposium on Foundations of Software Engineering*, pp. 432–449. New York, NY: Springer-Verlag New York, Inc.

[416] Richardson, D. J. and L. A. Clarke (1981). "A partition analysis method to increase program reliability." In *Proceedings of the Fifth International Conference on Software Engineering, March 1981*, pp. 244–253. Los Alamitos, CA: IEEE Press.

[417] Richardson, D. J. and M. C. Thompson (1993). "An analysis of test data selection criteria using the relay model of fault detection." *IEEE Transactions Software Engineering*, **19**(6): 533–553.

[418] Ripley, A. and G. David (1978). "A statistical analysis of syntax errors," *Journal of Computer Languages*, **3**(4): 227–240.

[419] Rocha, A. D. (January 2005). *Uma ferramenta baseada em aspectos para apoio ao teste funcional de programas Java.* Master's thesis. Saõ Carlos, Brazil: University of Saõ Paõ.

[420] Rosenberg, L. H., T. F. Hammer, and L. L. Huffman (1998). "Requirements, testing, & metrics." In *Proceedings of 16th Pacific Northwest Software Quality Conference, UTAH, October 1998*, pp. 1–12.

[421] Rothermel, G. (1996). *Efficient, Effective Regression Testing Using Safe Test Selection Techniques.* Ph.D. thesis. South Carolina: Clemson University.

[422] Rothermel, G. and M. J. Harrold (1993). "A safe, efficient algorithm for regression test selection." In *ICSM '93: Proceedings of the Conference on Software Maintenance*, pp. 358–367. Washington, DC: IEEE Computer Society Press.

[423] Rothermel, G. and M. J. Harrold (1994). "Selecting tests and identifying test coverage requirements for modified software." In *ISSTA '94: Proceedings of the 1994 ACM SIGSOFT International Symposium on Software Testing and Analysis*, pp. 169–184. New York, NY: ACM Press.

[424] Rothermel, G. and M. J. Harrold (1996). "Analyzing regression test selection techniques," *IEEE Transactions on Software Engineering*, **22**(8): 529–551.

[425] Rothermel, G. and M. J. Harrold (1997). "A safe, efficient regression test selection technique," *ACM Transactions on Software Engineering and Methodology*, **6**(2): 173–210.

[426] Rothermel, G., M. J. Harrold, and J. Dedhia (June 2000). "Regression test selection for C++ software," *Journal of Software Testing, Verification, and Reliability*, **10**(2): 77–109.

[427] Rubey, R. J., J. À. Dana, and P. W. Bichè (1975). "Quantitative aspects of software validation," *IEEE Transactions on Software Engineering*, **SE-1**(2): 150–155.

[428] Rummel, M. J., G. M. Kapfhammer, and A. Thall (2005). "Towards the prioritization of regression test suites with data flow information." In *SAC '05: Proceedings of the 2005 ACM Symposium on Applied Computing*, pp.1499–1504. New York, NY: ACM Press.

[429] Sabnani, K. K. and A. T. Dahbura (1988). "A protocol test generation procedure," *Computer Networks and ISDN Systems*, **15**: 285–297.

[430] Sankoff, D. (1972). "Matching sequences under deletion/insertion constraints." In *Proceedings of National Academy of Sciences, January 1972*, Vol. 69, pp. 4–6.

[431] Sarikaya, B. (1989). "Conformance testing: Architectures and test sequences," *Computer Networks and ISDN Systems*, **17**(5): 111–126.

[432] Sarikaya, B. and G. v. Bochmann (April 1984). "Synchronization and specification issues in protocol testing," *IEEE transactions on Communications*, **32**(4): 389–395.

[433] Sarikaya, B., G. v. Bochmann, and E. Cerny (May 1987). "A test design methodology for protocol testing," *IEEE transactions on Software Engineering*, **SE-13**(5): 518–531.

[434] Sauder, R. L. (1962). "A general test data generator for COBOL." In *Proceedings of the 1962 SJCC, May 1962*, pp. 317–323.

[435] Schick, G. J. and R. W. Wolverton (March 1978). "An analysis of competing software reliability models," *IEEE Transactions on Software Engineering*, **SE-4**(2): 104–120.

[436] Schneider, V. (1988). "Approximations for the Halstead software science software error rate and project effort estimators," *SIGPLAN Notices*, **23**(1): 40–47.

[437] Selkow, S. M. (December 1977). "The tree-to-tree editing problem," *Information Processing Letters*, **6**(6): 84–186.

[438] Shehady, R. K. and D. P. Siewiorek (1997). "A method to automate user interface testing using variable finite state machines." In *Twenty-Seventh Annual International Symposium on Fault-Tolerant Computing, FTCS-27. Digest of Papers*, pp. 80–88.

[439] Shen, Y. N., F. Lombardi, and A. T. Dahbura (1989). "Protocol conformance testing using multiple UIO sequences." In *Proceedings of the Ninth IFIP Symposium on Protocol Specification, Testing, and Verification, June 1989*. Amsterdam, The Netherlands: North-Holland Publishing Company.

[440] Sherwood, S. B. (May 1994). "Effective testing of factor combinations." In *Proceedings of the Third International Conference on Software Testing, Analysis, and Review*. Washington, DC.

[441] Shye, A., M. Iyer, V. J. Reddy, and D. A. Connors (2005). "Code coverage testing using hardware performance monitoring support." In *AADEBUG'05: Proceedings of the SixthInternational Symposium on Automated Analysis-Driven Debugging*, pp. 159–163. New York, NY: ACM Press.

[442] Sidhu, D. P. and C.-S. Chang (1989). "Probabilistic testing of protocols." In *Symposium Proceedings on Communications Architectures and Protocols*, pp. 295–302. ACM Press.

[443] Sidhu, D. P. and T. K. Leung (1988). "Experience with test generation for real protocols." In *Symposium Proceedings on Communications Architectures and Protocols*, pp. 257–261. New York, NY: ACM Press.

[444] Sidhu, D. P. and T. K. Leung (April 1989). "Formal methods for protocol testing: A detailed study," *IEEE Transactions on Software Engineering*, **15**(4): 413–426.

[445] Simão, A. S. and J. C. Maldonado (2000). "Mutation based test sequence generation for Petri nets." In *Proceedings of Third Workshop of Formal Methods*, pp. 68–79. New York, NY: ACM Press.

[446] Simão, A. S., J. C. Maldonado, and S. C. P. F. Fabbri (2000). "Proteum-RS/PN: A tool to support edition, simulation and validation of Petri nets based on mutation testing." In *Anais do XIV Simpósio Brasileiro de Engenharia de Software*, pp. 227–242. Springer, U.S.

[447] Singh, H., M. Conrad, and S. Sadeghipour (1997). "Test case design based on Z and the classification-tree method." In *Proceedings of First IEEE International Conference on Formal Engineering Methods*, pp. 81–90.

[448] Slavik, P. (1996). "A tight analysis of the greedy algorithm for set cover." In STOC '96: *Proceedings of the 28th Annual ACM Symposium on Theory of Computing*, pp. 435–441. New York, NY: ACM Press.

[449] Sloane, N. J. A. (1973). "Covering arrays and intersecting codes," *Journal of Combinatorial Designs*, **1**: 51–63.

[450] Smith, B., W. Millar, J. Dunphy, Y. W. Tung, P. Nayak, E. Gamble, and M. Clark (1999). "Validation and verification of the remote agent for spacecraft autonomy." In *Proceedings of the 1999 IEEE Aerospace Conference, March 1999*, Vol. 1, pp. 449–468. IEEE Press.

[451] Smith, G. (2000). "The Object-Z specification language," In *Advances in Formal Methods*. Kluwer Academic.

[452] ANSI/IEEE Std. 829-1983 (1983). *IEEE Standard for Software Test Documentation*. IEEE Computer Society Press.

[453] Rep. CST/HLNP-83-4 (January 1983). Specification of a transport protocol for computer communication, Vol. 4: Service specifications. Washington, DC: National Bureau of Standards.

[454] Srikanth, H. and L. Williams (2005). "On the economics of requirements-based test case prioritization." In *EDSER '05: Proceedings of the Seventh*

International Workshop on Economics-Driven Software Engineering Research, pp. 1–3. New York, NY: ACM Press.

[455] Srivastava, A., A. Edwards, and H. Vo (2001). "Vulcan: Binary Transformation in a Distributed Environment." Technical report MSR-TR-2001-50, Redmond, WA: Microsoft.

[456] Srivastava, A. and J. Thiagarajan (2002). "Effectively prioritizing tests in development environment." In *ISSTA '02: Proceedings of the 2002 ACM SIG-SOFT International Symposium on Software Testing and Analysis*, pp. 97–106, New York, NY: ACM Press.

[457] Srivatanakul, T. (September 2001). *Mutation testing for concurrency*. Master's thesis. York, UK: Department of Computer Science, University of York.

[458] Srivatanakul, T., J. A. Clark, S. Stepney, and F. Polack (2003). Challenging formal specifications by mutation: A CSP example. In *Proceedings of Tenth Asia Pacific Software Engineering Conference*, pp. 340–350. Los Alamitos, CA: IEEE Press.

[459] Stamelos, I. (April 2003). "Detecting associative shift faults in predicate testing," *Journal of Systems and Software*, **66**(1): 57–63.

[460] Stocks, P. A. (December 1993). *Applying Formal Methods to Software Testing*. Ph.D. thesis. Queensland: Department of Computer Science, The University of Queensland.

[461] Sung, A. and B. Choi (2003). "Interaction testing in an embedded system using hardware fault injection and program mutation." In *Proceedings of Workshop on Formal Approaches to Testing Software, October 2003*. pp. 18–25. Los Alamitos, CA: IEEE Press.

[462] Sung, A., B. Choi, and J. Lee (2003). "Interaction mutation testing." In *Fast Abstracts: Supplemental Proceedings of the 14th International Symposium on Software Reliability Engineering November 2003*, pp. 301–302. Los Alamitos, CA: IEEE Press.

[463] Suvanaphen, E. and J. C. Roberts (June 2004). "Textual difference visualization of multiple search results utilizing detail in context." In *Theory and Practice of Computer Graphics* (Paul G. Lever, ed.), pp. 2–8. Los Alamitos, CA: IEEE Press.

[464] Tai, K. C. (June 1989). "Condition testing for software quality assurance." In *Proceedings of the Fourth Annual Conference on Computer Assurance, COM-PASS'89*, June 1989, pp. 31–35.

[465] Tai, K. C. "Predicate-based test generation for computer programs." Technical report 92-23. Department of Computer Science, North Carolina State University, North Carolina, 1992.

[466] Tai, K. C. (1993). "Predicate-based test generation for computer programs." In *Proceedings of the 15th International Conference on Software Engineering*, pp. 267–76. Los Alamitos, CA: IEEE Computer Society Press.

[467] Tai, K. C. (1996). "Theory of fault-based predicate testing for computer programs," *IEEE Transactions on Software Engineering*, **22**(8): 552–562.

[468] Tai, K. C., A. M. Paradkar, H. K. Su, and M. A. Vouk (1993). "Fault-based test generation for cause-effect graphs". In *Proceedings of the 1993 Conference of*

the Centre for Advanced Studies on Collaborative Research, pp. 495–504. Armonk, NY: IBM Press.

[469]   Tai, K. C. and H. K. Su (1987). "Test generation for Boolean expressions." In *Proceedings of COMPSAC (Computer Software and Applications)*, pp. 278–283. Los Alamitos, CA.

[470]   Tai, K. C., M. A. Vouk, A. M. Paradkar, and P. Lu (September 1994). "Evaluation of a predicate-based software testing strategy," *IBM Systems Journal*, **33**: 445–457.

[471]   Tallam, S. and N. Gupta (2005). "A concept analysis inspired greedy algorithm for test suite minimization." In *PASTE '05: The Sixth ACM SIGPLAN-SIG-SOFT Workshop on Program Analysis for Software Tools and Engineering*, pp. 35–42. New York, NY: ACM Press.

[472]   Tasiran, S. and K. Keutzer (July–August 2001). "Coverage metrics for functional validation of hardware designs," *IEEE Design and Test of Computers*, **18**(4): 36–45.

[473]   Taylor, R. N., D. L. Levine, and C. D. Kelly (1992). "Structural testing of concurrent programs," *IEEE Transactions on Software Engineering*, **18**(3): 206–215.

[474]   Telcordia Technologies. AETG Web Home. http://aetgweb.argreenhouse.com/ (The AETG Web service is available via this site at the time of writing this book.)

[475]   Telcordia Software Visualization and Analysis Toolsuite. http://xsuds.argreenhouse.com/

[476]   Tikir, M. M. and J. K. Hollingsworth (2002). "Efficient instrumentation for code coverage testing." In *ISSTA '02: Proceedings of the 2002 ACM SIGSOFT International Symposium on Software Testing and Analysis*, pp. 86–96. New York, NY: ACM Press.

[477]   Trischler, E. (1984). "An integrated design for testability and automatic test pattern generation system: An overview." In *DAC '84: Proceedings of the 21st Conference on Design automation*, pp. 209–215. Piscataway, NJ: IEEE Press.

[478]   Tsai, B. Y., S. Stobart, and N. Parrington (2001). "Employing data flow testing on object-oriented classes." In *IEE Proceedings, April 2001 (see also Software Engineering, IEE Proceedings)*, Vol. 148, pp. 56–64. London, UK: The Institution of Engineering and Technology.

[479]   Tung, Y. W. and W. S. Aldiwan (2000). "Automating test case generation for the new generation mission software system." In *IEEE Aerospace Conference Proceedings, March 2000*, Vol. 11, pp. 431–437. Los Alamitos, CA: IEEE Press.

[480]   Untch, R. H. (1992). "Mutation-based software testing using program schemata." In *ACM-SE 30: Proceedings of the 30th Annual Southeast Regional Conference*, 1992, pp. 285–291. New York, NY: ACM Press.

[481]   Untch, R. H., A. J. Offutt, and M. J. Harrold (1993). "Mutation analysis using mutant schemata." In *ISSTA '93: Proceedings of the 1993 ACM SIGSOFT*

International Symposium on Software Testing and Analysis, pp. 139– 148. New York, NY: ACM Press.

[482] Ural, H., W. Xiaolin, and F. Zhang (1997). "On minimizing the lengths of checking sequences," *IEEE Transactions on Computers*, **46**(1): 93–99.

[483] Uyar, M. U. and A. T. Dahbura (1986). "Optimum test sequence generation for protocols: The Chinese Postman algorithm applied to Q.931." In *Proceedings of GLOBECOM'86*, pp. 3.1.1–3.1.5. Los Alamitos, CA: IEEE Press.

[484] Uyar, M. U. and A. Y. Duale (2000). "Test generation for EFSM models of complex army protocols with inconsistencies." In *MILCOM 2000: Proceedings of the 21st Century Military Communications Conference, October 2000*, Vol. 1, pp. 340–346. Los Alamitos, CA: IEEE Press.

[485] Vagoun, T. and A. Hevner (1997). "Feasible input domain partitioning in software testing: RCS case study," *Annals of Software Engineering, Special Issue on Software Testing and Quality Assurance*, **4**: 159–170.

[486] Virgilio, S. R., J. C. Maldonado, and M. Jino (1997). "Constraint based selection of test sets to satisfy structural software testing criteria." In *Proceedings of 27th International Conference of the Chilean Computer Science Society, November 1997*, pp. 256–263. Los Alamitos, CA: IEEE Press.

[487] Voas, J. M. "Dynamic testing complexity metric." Technical report, NASA Langley Technical Report Server, 1992.

[488] Voas, J. M. (August 1992). "PIE: A dynamic failure based technique," *IEEE Transactions on Software Engineering*, **18**(8): 717–727.

[489] Voas, J. M. and K. Miller (1992). "Improving the software development process using testability research." Technical report, NASA Langley Technical Report Server.

[490] Voas, J. M. and K. Miller (May 1995). "Software testability: The new verification," *IEEE Software*, **12**(3): 17–28.

[491] Voas, J. M, L. Morell, and K. Miller (March 1991). "Predicting where faults can hide from testing," *IEEE Software*, **8**: 41–48.

[492] Vokàç, M. (December 2004). "Defect frequency and design patterns: An empirical study of industrial code," *IEEE Transactions on Software Engineering*, **30**(12): 904–917.

[493] Vokolos, F. I. (January 1998). *A Regression Test Selection Technique Based on Textual Differencing*. Ph.D. thesis. Brooklyn, NY: Polytechnic University.

[494] Vokolos, F. I. and P. Frankl (1997). "Pythia: A regression test selection tool based on textual differencing." In *ENCRESS '97, Third International Conference on Reliability, Quality, and Safety of Software Intensive Systems, May 1997*.

[495] Vokolos, F. I. and P. G. Frankl (1998). "Empirical evaluation of the textual differencing regression testing technique." In *ICSM '98: Proceedings of the International Conference on Software Maintenance*, p. 44. Washington, DC: IEEE Computer Society Press.

[496] Vuong, C. T. and K. C. Ko (1990). "A novel approach to protocol test sequence generation." In *Global Telecommunications Conference, December 1990*, Vol. 3, pp. 1880–1884.

[497]   Walsh, P. J. (1985). *A Measure of Test Case Completeness*. Ph.D. thesis, Binghamton, NY: State University of New York.

[498]   Wang, B. and D. Hutchison (1987). "Protocol testing techniques," *Computer Communications*, **10**(2): 79–87.

[499]   Wang, C. J. and M. T. Liu (1993). Generating test cases for EFSM with given fault models. In *INFOCOM '93: Proceedings of the 12th Annual Joint Conference of the IEEE Computer and Communications Societies, April 1993*, Vol. 2, pp. 774–781. Los Alamitos, CA: IEEE Press.

[500]   Wang, L.-T., C.-W. Wu, and X. Wen (2006). *VLSI Test Principles and Architectures: Design for Testability*. San Francisco, CA: Morgan Kaufmann.

[501]   Wang, T.-H. and C. G. Tan (1995). "Practical code coverage for Verilog." In *Proceedings of International Verilog HDL Conference, March 1995*, pp. 99–104. Los Alamitos, CA: IEEE Press.

[502]   Watanabe, A. and K. Sakamura (1996). "A specification-based adaptive test case generation strategy for open operating system standards." In *ICSE '96: Proceedings of the 18th International Conference on Software Engineering*, pp. 81–89. Washington, DC: IEEE Computer Society.

[503]   Weiser, M. (1981). "Program slicing." In *Proceedings of the Fifth International Conference on Software Engineering*, pp. 439–449. Los Alamitos, CA: IEEE Press.

[504]   Weiser, M. (1984). "Program slicing," *IEEE Transactions on Software Engineering*, **SE-10**(4): 352–357.

[505]   Weiss S. N. and V. N. Fleyshgakker (1992). "Hitest: An architecture for highly parallel software testing." In *In Proceedings of the 1992 IEEE International Conference on Computer Systems and Software Engineering, May 1992*, pp. 347–352. Los Alamitos, CA: IEEE Computer Society.

[506]   Weiss, S. N. and V. N. Fleyshgakker (1993). "Improved serial algorithms for mutation analysis." In *ISSTA '93: Proceedings of the 1993 ACM SIGSOFT International Symposium on Software Testing and Analysis*, pp. 149–158. New York, NY: ACM Press.

[507]   West, C. H. (May 1992). "Protocol validation: Principles and applications," *Computer Networks ISDN Systems*, **24**(3): 219–242.

[508]   Weyuker, E. J. (1988). "Evaluating software complexity measures," *IEEE Transactions on Software Engineering*, **14**(9): 1357–1365.

[509]   Weyuker, E. J. (May 1989). "In defense of coverage criteria." In *11th International Conference on Software Engineering*, pp. 361 Los Alamitos, CA: IEEE Press.

[510]   Weyuker, E. J. (February 1990). "The cost of data flow testing: An empirical study," *IEEE Transactions on Software Engineering*, **16**(2): 121–128.

[511]   Weyuker, E. J. (September 1990). "More experience with data flow testing," *IEEE Transactions on Software Engineering*, **19**(9): 912–919.

[512]   Weyuker, E. J., T. Gordia, and A. Singh (1994). "Automatically generating test data from a Boolean specification," *IEEE Transactions on Software Engineering*, **20**(5): 353–363.

[513] White, L. J. and K. Abdullah (1997). "A firewall approach for regression testing of object-oriented software." In *Proceedings of 10th Annual Software Quality Week, May 1997*, pp. 1–27. San Francisco, CA: Software Research Inc.

[514] White, L. J., H. Almezen, and S. Sastry (2003). "Firewall regression testing of GUI sequences and their interactions." In *Proceedings of the International Conference on Software Maintenance, September 2003*, pp. 398–409. IEEE Computer Society Press.

[515] White, L. J. and E. I. Cohen (May 1980). "A domain strategy for computer program testing," *IEEE Transactions on Software Engineering*, **SE-6**: 247–257.

[516] White, L. J., K. Jaber, and B. Robinson (2005). "Utilization of extended firewall for object-oriented regression testing." In *Proceedings of the 21st IEEE International Conference on Software Maintenance, ICSM'05*, pp. 695–698. Los Alamitos, CA: IEEE Press.

[517] White, L. J. and H. K. N. Leung (1992). "A firewall concept for both control-flow and data-flow in regression integration testing." In *Proceedings of the Symposium on Software Maintenance, November 1992*, pp. 262–271.

[518] White, L. J. and H. K. N. Leung (1992). "On the edge: Regression testability," *IEEE Micro*, **12**(2): 81–84.

[519] White, L. J. and B. Robinson (2004). "Industrial real-time regression testing and analysis using firewalls." In *Proceedings of International Conference on Software Maintenance*, pp. 18–27. Los Alamitos, CA: IEEE Press.

[520] Wong, W. E. (1993). *On Mutation and Data Flow*. Ph.D. thesis. West Lafayette, IN: Purdue University. Advisor: Aditya P. Mathur.

[521] Wong, W. E., J. R. Horgan, S. London, and H. Agrawal (1997). "A study of effective regression testing in practice." In *ISSRE '97: Proceedings of the Eighth International Symposium on Software Reliability Engineering (IS-SRE '97)*, p. 264, Washington, DC: IEEE Computer Society Press.

[522] Wong, W. E., J. R. Horgan, S. London, and A. P. Mathur (1994). Effect of test set size and block coverage on the fault detection effectiveness." In *Proceedings of Fifth International Symposium on Software Reliability Engineering, November 1994*, pp. 230–238. Los Alamitos, CA: IEEE Press.

[523] Wong, W. E., J. R. Horgan, A. P. Mathur, and A. Pasquini (1997). "Test set size minimization and fault detection effectiveness: A case study in a space application." In *Proceedings of The 21st Annual International Computer Software and Applications Conference (COMPSAC '97), August 1997*, pp. 522–528. Los Alamitos, CA: IEEE Press.

[524] Wong, W. E., Y. Lei, and X. Ma (2005). "Effective generation of test sequences for structural testing of concurrent programs". In *Proceedings of the 10th IEEE International Conference on Engineering of Complex Computer Systems (ICECCS 2005), June 2005*, pp. 539–548. Los Alamitos, CA: IEEE Press.

[525] Wong, W. E. and A. P. Mathur (1995). "Reducing the cost of mutation testing: An empirical study," *Journal of Systems and Software*, **31**(3): 185–196.

[526] Wood, M., M. Roper, A. Brooks, and J. Miller (1997). "Comparing and combining software defect detection techniques: A replicated empirical study." In *ESEC '97/FSE-5: Proceedings of the Sixth European Conference Held Jointly with the Fifth ACM SIGSOFT International Symposium on Foundations of Software Engineering*, pp. 262–77. New York, NY: Springer-Verlag New York, Inc.

[527] Woodward, M. R. (1990). Mutation testing of algebraic specifications. In *Proceedings of the Software QualityWorkshop, June 1990*, pp. 169–178. Los Alamitos, CA: IEEE Press.

[528] Woodward, M. R. (1991). "Aspects of path testing and mutation testing." In *Software Quality and Reliability: Tools and Methods* (D. Ince, ed.), pp. 1–15. Norwell, MA: Chapman and Hall.

[529] Woodward, M. R. (June 1992). "OBJTEST: An experimental testing tool for algebraic specifications." In *IEE Colloquium Digest: Automating Formal Methods for Computer Assisted Prototyping*, pp. 2/1–2/2. London, UK.

[530] Woodward, M. R. (July 1993). "Errors in algebraic specifications and an experimental mutation testing tool," *Software Engineering Journal*, **8**(4): 211–224.

[531] Woodward, M. R. (March 1993) "Mutation testing: its origin and evolution," *Information and Software Technology*, **35**(3): 163–169.

[532] Woodward, M. R. and K. Halewood (July 1988). "From weak to strong, dead or alive." In *Proceedings of the Second Workshop on Software Testing, Verification and Analysis*, pp. 152–158. Banff, Canada: IEEE Computer Society Press.

[533] Woodward, M. R., D. Hedley, and M. A. Hennell (November 1976). "On program analysis," *Information Processing Letters*, **5**: 136–140.

[534] Woodward, M. R. and M. A. Hennell (July 2006). "On the relationship between two control-flow coverage criteria: All JJ-paths and MCDC," *Information and Software Technology*, **48**(7): 433–440.

[535] Xia, E., I. Jurisica, J. Waterhouse, and V. Sloan (2005). "Scheduling functional regression tests for IBM DB2 products." In *CASCON '05: Proceedings of the 2005 Conference of the Centre for Advanced Studies on Collaborative Research*, pp. 292–304. Armonk, NY: IBM Press.

[536] Xu, R., Y. Xue, P. Nie, Y. Zhang, and D. Li (2006). "Research on CMMI-based software process metrics." In *IMSCCS '06: Proceedings of First International Multi-Symposiums on Computer and Computational Sciences, April 2006*, Vol. 2, pp. 391–397. Los Alamitos, CA: IEEE Press.

[537] Yang, B. and H. Ural (1990). "Protocol conformance test generation using multiple UIO sequences with overlapping." In *Proceedings of the ACM symposium on Communications Architectures and Protocols*, pp. 118–125. New York, NY: ACM Press.

[538] Yau, S. S. and Z. Kishimoto (1987). "Revalidating modified programs in the maintenance phase." In *Proceedings of IEEE COMPSAC (Computer Software and Applications)*, pp. 272–277. Los Alamitos, CA: IEEE Press.

[539] Yevtushenko, N., A. R. Cavalli, and R. Anido (1999). "Test suite minimization for embedded nondeterministic finite state machines." In *Proceedings of the*

IFIP TC6 12th International Workshop on Testing Communicating Systems, pp. 237–250. Deventer, The Netherlands: Kluwer Press.

[540] Yin, H. and J. M. Bieman (1994). "Improving software testability with assertion insertion." In *Proceedings of International Test Conference, October 1994*, pp. 831–839. Los Alamitos, CA: IEEE Press.

[541] Youngs, E. A. (1970). *Error-Proneness in Programming*. Ph.D. thesis. North Carolina: North Carolina State University.

[542] Zhan, Y., and J. A. Clark (2005). "Search-based mutation testing for SIMULINK models." In *GECCO '05: Proceedings of the 2005 Conference on Genetic and Evolutionary Computation*, pp. 1061–1068. New York, NY: ACM Press.

[543] Zhang, X. and R. Gupta (2005). "Matching execution histories of program versions." In *ESEC/FSE-13: Proceedings of the 10th European Software Engineering Conference Held Jointly with 13th ACM SIGSOFT International Symposium on Foundations of Software Engineering*, pp. 197–206. New York, NY: ACM Press.

[544] Zhang, X. and R. Gupta (2005). "Whole execution traces and their applications," *ACM Transactions on Architecture and Code Optimization*, **2**(3).

[545] Zhang, X., R. Gupta, and Y. Zhang (2003). "Precise dynamic slicing algorithms." In *ICSE '03: Proceedings of the 25th International Conference on Software Engineering*, pp. 319–329. Washington, DC: IEEE Computer Society Press.

[546] Zheng, J., B. Robinson, L. Williams, and K. Smiley (2006). "Applying regression test selection for COTS-based applications." In *ICSE '06: Proceeding of the 28th International Conference on Software Engineering*, pp. 512–522. New York, NY: ACM Press.

[547] Zhu, H., P. A. V. Hall, and J. H. R. May (December 1997). "Software unit test coverage and adequacy." *ACM Computing Surveys*, **29**(4): 366–427.

[548] Zobrist, G. W. (1993). *VLSI Fault Modeling and Testing Techniques*. Greenwich, CT: Ablex Publishing.

[549] Zweben, S. H. and K. C. Fung (1979). "Exploring software science relations in COBOL and APL." In *Proceedings of COMPSAC, the IEEE Computer Society's Third International Computer Software and Application Conference, November 1979*, pp. 702–770. Los Alamitos, CA: IEEE Press.

Subject Index

Name Index